The Customs Valuation Agreement

Global Trade Law Series

VOLUME 58

Series Editors

Introduction and Contents/Subjects

The *Global Trade Law Series* addresses key issues in international trade law. It covers a broad range of topics, including WTO dispute settlement, free trade agreements, investment law and arbitration, export control, and compliance with international trade obligations.

Objective & Readership

The volumes published in this series are aimed at offering high-quality analytical information and practical solutions, for practitioners, policy makers and academics.

Frequency of Publication

2-3 new volumes published each year.

The titles published in this series are listed at the end of this volume.

The Customs Valuation Agreement

Origin, Standards and Interpretations

Mark K. Neville, Jr.

Wolters Kluwer

Published by:
Kluwer Law International B.V.
PO Box 316
2400 AH Alphen aan den Rijn
The Netherlands
E-mail: lrs-sales@wolterskluwer.com
Website: www.wolterskluwer.com/en/solutions/kluwerlawinternational

Sold and distributed by:
Wolters Kluwer Legal & Regulatory U.S.
920 Links Avenue
Landisville, PA 17538
United States of America
E-mail: customer.service@wolterskluwer.com

ISBN 978-94-035-3096-3

e-Book: ISBN 978-94-035-3146-5
web-PDF: ISBN 978-94-035-3156-4

This is for my father, who showed us the way

About the Author

Mark K. Neville, Jr., is a member of the bar of New York, with almost fifty years' experience. He is the Principal of International Trade Counsellors, and may be contacted at mkneville@itctradelaw.com.

Mr. Neville was educated in history and the law, with his ultimate degree being an LL.M. conferred by New York University. He began his career as a customs and international trade lawyer representing the Government of the United States in the trade courts. He has served on the adjunct faculty at several schools, including New York University and the University of California, Berkeley. One of Mr. Neville's proudest accomplishments has been his continuing role as a co-lead of the delegation of the International Chamber of Commerce in its official Observer status at the meetings of the Technical Committee on Customs Valuation of the World Customs Organization.

Table of Contents

Preface

Customs valuation is a key element in the corpus of international trade law. In many ways, this treatise is a chronicle of the past half-century's worth of critical events that have shaped that key element. We first retrace the development and promulgation of the Customs Valuation Agreement and then explore the various crisscrossing pathways that have marked the implementation and application of that Agreement. The twin facts that the Agreement remains unchanged in all material respects since its adoption in 1979 and that it has been adopted by virtually every trading nation on the planet have created what I have come to believe is a mistaken impression. Many will believe that after the syncretic exchanges of the Tokyo Round, we have been blessed with the legacy of a "fair, uniform and neutral" system for customs valuation that is universal in scope, well settled and "ticking over on all 8 cylinders."

We can hope that consensus may yet be achieved, but that impression does not withstand a close examination of the current state of play. True, that quoted phrase is the stated purpose for and the stated goal of the Agreement, but two readily discernible trends, one long-established and one still emerging, tell a different story. That is the story of an "ambition gap" between the ideal and the actual state of the customs valuation regime.[1]

The older—and enduring—trend is one of developing countries' continued push for the greater flexibility of the *ancien regime*, life under the Brussels Definition of Value (BDV). A fair reading of the negotiating history and the exceptional treatment afforded developing countries through Article 20 and Annex III of the Agreement reveal as much. You should recognize that the grant—and still more, the exercise—of discretionary authority is directly proportional to the lack of predictability which the Agreement was meant to remedy by means of its ordered constraints. That steady push for greater flexibility marks a departure from the equipoise that is the very essence of the Agreement. It is generally revealed only after close scrutiny today, but it is nonetheless real for that. The widespread misuse of customs valuation databases over

1. I have been reminded by Oscar Wilde that "If one doesn't talk about a thing it has never happened. It is expression that gives reality to things."

the past two decades proves that second point.[2] Any such misuse is especially pernicious, as each sanctioned misuse is a below-the-surface or silent nullification of the Agreement.

We must be mindful that many more developing countries have implemented the Agreement since its 1994 reinvigoration. To be sure, the challenges for developing countries remain at daunting levels. Many of them are faced with widespread fraud in the "informal sector," and they cannot rely on a well-trained, thoroughly modern administrative infrastructure to assert control. This is despite the decades' long sincere, well-intentioned and robust efforts at capacity building and technical assistance from international organizations and developed countries.[3]

The newer story is one of the perceptible fissures in the system, with diverging views on the nature of the central feature of the Agreement, the definition of the price actually paid or payable (the PAPP) which is a necessary, indeed the central, element in Transaction Value (TV). As is discussed at some length, there are actually two conflicts over the PAPP. First and foremost, a conflict has arisen over the status and role of paragraph 7 to Annex III of the Agreement in defining the PAPP as it relates to payments being "for the imported goods." We can hope that the conflict can be resolved in the near term. The second threat to stability is a growing trend by some customs authorities to reject declared customs values, even if the underlying prices were negotiated and are in fact *actually* being paid or payable to the seller because the underlying prices appear to be too low or are lower than reference prices.

Beyond those misguided animating principles, there is a rift in the interpretation of the Agreement as it relates to royalties and license fees (RLFs), with some jurisdictions taking the view that RLFs can be apportioned if there are objective and quantifiable data. The European Union (EU) is a prominent exponent of that view. The "condition of sale" criterion for RLFs is also a contested point, at least since the US Court of International Trade (CIT) issued an important decision in 2019. We can also point to the views on First Sale for Export (FSFE), with the US being the only customs territory where that doctrine is still permitted. It is interesting—and you should know—that the countries which have discontinued its use have relied on direct statutory changes, as reviewing courts have interpreted the implementing texts to respect the First Sale doctrine.

Apart from the definition of the PAPP, the criteria governing RLFs and the acceptability of First Sale, we can also point to differing views on such other questions as:

- The role of transport charges in valuing dutiable assists.
- The status of interest payments on deferred payments.
- The valuation of carrier media bearing software for data processing equipment.

2. It will be made clear that the misuse of customs valuation databases is not limited to developing countries.
3. A companion piece would be the special and differential treatment afforded to developing countries in the Trade Facilitation Agreement and the presence of the WTO Trade Facilitation Agreement Facility.

- The inclusion or exclusion of transport charges in the PAPP.
- The status of the World Trade Organization's (WTO's) moratorium on electronic transmissions.
- The status of payments of money for tools, etc., used in producing the imported goods.
- The status of International Instruments of Traffic (IITs).

Of significance is the relatively small number of instruments adopted in the past decade by the World Customs Organization's (WCO's) Technical Committee on Customs Valuation (TCCV), coupled with the much larger number of technical questions which, due to a failure to reach a consensus, were relegated to the limbo of Part III of the TCCV Conspectus. These, too, are indications that there is a lack of uniformity; i.e., there are fissures in the system which are preventing consensus on many contentious questions, despite best efforts to achieve consensus.

One of the trends that we may chronicle is the marked number of shifts by the EU in its interpretations of its legislation implementing the Agreement. These shifts are quite significant departures from long-standing EU practices in customs valuation.

Aside from the outsized role played by a small number of Member State customs authorities, one might speculate that the motivating force for the recent changes in position by EU Commission is a function of the key role played by customs duties in revenue collection for the EU. In 2020, the share of the EU's total revenues represented by the customs duties collected by the Member States was 11%.[4] The Member States forward all of the duties collected to the EU, so each of them shows a duty-derived 0.00% revenue input into their own municipal budgets.

In the US, duties play a minor role in revenue collection for the federal government. The World Bank records duties accounting for 3.62% of US federal revenues in 2019 and 3.28% in 2020—and those data reflect the spiking impact of the section 301 Tariffs levied on most Chinese products. The Republic of Korea, another developed country, shows duty collections as a revenue share at 2.6% (2019).

In comparison, data from the World Bank reveal that many developing countries show duty collections as a more significant percent of total revenues—e.g., Cameroon—13.47% (2018), Mali—11.91% (2019), Burkina Faso—13.0% (2019), Kenya—6.96% (2019), India—4.94% (2018).[5] These are all far greater than those of the US or Korea and place the revenue reliance on duties by the EU in an incongruous context.[6]

Taken altogether, there are different and competing interpretations espoused by the EU and certain other countries and those of some major trading partners, including the US and Canada. As for the likelihood of amendments to the Valuation Agreement

4. *See* https://ec.europa.eu/taxation_customs/customs-4/eu-customs-union-facts-and-figures/customs-duties-mean-revenue_en.
5. Available at https://data.worldbank.org/indicator/GC.TAX.IMPT.ZS.
6. As another part of the "own resources" funding, a portion of VAT revenues of the Member States are also shared. The reliance of the EU on VAT revenues, which contribute a further 10% of overall EU revenues, emphasizes this developing country level of dependence on duties and border taxes.

in order to reconcile these differences in position, or to address newly emerged challenges, the World Trade Organization (WTO) and the WCO, which together play principal roles in the development and administration of the customs valuation system, are both vastly different organizations from those which operated under the General Agreement on Tariffs and Trade (GATT). For one thing, there are many more Members of the WTO than there were Contracting Parties under the GATT at the time of the Tokyo or Uruguay Rounds. Given the consensus-based system, requiring a unanimous position among this expanded number of participants on customs valuation matters, the likelihood of attaining consensus for amendments to the Valuation Agreement could make for an Everest-like climb.

At the end of this day, at least, the Valuation Agreement sets forth the bases for the only extant international standard, whether fully honored in the observance or in the breach.[7] That is why the Valuation Agreement is worthy of our attention.

I have endeavored to present an in-depth analysis starting from the 1947 adoption of the GATT and then proceeding up thorough the negotiations and the promulgation of the Valuation Agreement in 1979 and its ensuing implementation by various customs authorities—principally the US, Canada and the EU. I am mindful that discussions with a focus only on local developments often miss developments in other jurisdictions which may eventually be adopted, or need to be distinguished, by that local jurisdiction. As a result, a purely domestic focus may lead to surprises in the treatment of exports into those other jurisdictions where those changes are taking place.

Since the Valuation Agreement sets a single authoritative standard, administrative rulings and court decisions are keenly followed from one jurisdiction to another. In a real sense, the Valuation Agreement is meant to present a uniform standard, quite beyond the normative level achieved under the Harmonized Tariff System which does not achieve uniformity of annotation beyond the six-digit level and which is marked by regular overhauls on five-year cycles. The role of the Agreement has led to an accompanying focus on developments at the WCO, where the "rubber meets the road" in the form of various instruments which guide customs authorities' administration of their domestic customs valuation statutes.

In my view—shaped by my role as an active customs lawyer—a book focused solely on developments at the WTO in Geneva is of sterile, academic interest only and offers little or nothing of practical benefit. That is because the customs valuation treatment of imported goods, whether in the case of any specific importation or as a general matter, is simply the application of the law and regulations in a given customs territory to specific importations. A study of only the Valuation Agreement and/or the case law under the WTO's Dispute Settlement Body (DSB) would be a review of the

7. This may remind us of Adam Smith's comment on the corn laws of Great Britain:

> this law seems to be inferior to the ancient system. With all its imperfection, however, we may perhaps say of it what was said of the laws of Solon, that, though not the best in itself, it is the best which the interests, prejudices, and temper of the times would admit of. It may perhaps in due time prepare the way for a better. Adam Smith, The Wealth of Nations (1789 ed.), Book IV, ch. V, at 510.

Agreement as an expression of public international law. That would be quite irrelevant to any "real world" customs valuation project except to the extent that an academic journal commentary on the Agreement or the DSB interpretation of a customs valuation precept admits of an application to a specific "live case." Of course, the fact that there have been precious few DSB cases and only a handful of WTO committee decisions would make for a very short discussion.

I have chosen to focus on the actual interpretations by the WCO and the reviewing courts and national customs authorities of the implementing statutes and regulations of the active provisions of the Agreement. As near-panoptical as this recitation may be, I have not devoted attention to certain of the provisions of the Agreement which generally have no direct applicability to the private sector but impose obligations on the WTO Members. For example, Part II of the Agreement, Articles 18-24, is not discussed. We might also point to Agreement obligations on national authorities which have direct relevance for importers. In this regard, we might cite Article 10 (treatment of confidential information), Article 11 (right of appeal) and Article 12 (publication of laws, regulations and administrative rulings). Having been noted here, there is no compelling reason to expound on these last three provisions, beyond the reflection that an aggrieved trader might seek to have his home country trade authority or foreign service take up these issues, along with a denial of the importer's right to have access to further detailed information where the customs authority has doubts about the declared value,[8] in consultations with the country of importation.

Another thought is in order here. The last-minute decision to drop the mandatory availability of binding rulings on customs valuation from the WTO's Trade Facilitation Agreement was especially lamentable. That should be obvious to anybody and everybody including the dogs on the street. Countries are merely "encouraged" to allow for such advance rulings.[9] I would go further and advocate for valuation rulings to be published and to be generally available. That is the standard practice in the US, where confidential treatment is provided to redact sensitive trade information, including the name of the importer and costing or other enterprise details. These rulings issued by US Customs and Border Protection (CBP) are available on its website through its readily accessible CROSS System.[10]

That system of publications has worked exceptionally well for decades, and I am unaware of any breach of confidential information after it has been sought and obtained. Such advance rulings ought to be of unlimited duration, being in force and effect while the material facts or the prevailing law or the customs authority position[11]

8. Agreement, Article 1, paragraphs 2(a).
9. Trade Facilitation Agreement, Article 3(9)(b)(i); available at https://docs.wto.org/dol2fe/Pages/SS/directdoc.aspx?filename=q:/WT/L/940.pdf&Open=True.
10. Customs Rulings Online Search System (CROSS) available at https://rulings.cbp.gov/home.
11. In the US practice, there is a specific protocol whereby CBP can revoke or modify previously published rulings. Section 1625 of Title 19 US Code, styled 19 USC § 1625. A key feature of that process is the public notice requirement, allowing for comments from the public and not simply from the party who had initially requested the ruling. *See* Neville, "Some Thoughts on Ruling Requests," 33 J. Int'l Tax'n (March 2022) at 27.

remains unchanged. I see no compelling reason for them to carry an expiration date of, say, three or five years.

Finally, I want to tip my hat to Messrs. Sherman and Glashoff whose 1988 work[12] has long been the standard reference book for customs valuation. I salute them and seek to build upon their many still-cogent comments and do not seek to replace their book or depose them. The passage of more than thirty years has resulted in many further developments which were beyond the scope of their book, but they and their work should not be forgotten. Rather, they should still be consulted on the topics covered here and on others besides—and honored for their insight and prescience.

12. Sherman and Glashoff, Customs Valuation Commentary on the GATT Customs Valuation Code (hereinafter Sherman and Glashoff).

Acknowledgments

I would like to express my sincere thanks for all of the encouragement and cogent insights from my friends and colleagues spanning the globe from Vilnius (Monika Bielskiene) through Paris (Jean-Marie Salva and Arnaud Fendler), Brussels (Paulette Vander Schueren), New York (Jerry Wiskin and John Peterson), Montreal (Peter Kirby), Ontario (John Bescec), Ottawa (Jean-Francois Bedard), Washington (Elif Eroglu and Ross Cunningham), Dallas (Bill Methenitis), Buenos Aires (Horacio Vicente) and on to Port Townsend (Jay Neville). No note could be complete without extending a heartfelt note of gratitude to my wife and the rest of my family for all of their unending patience, forbearance and support.

Part I Customs Valuation Writ Large

CHAPTER 1

Historical Antecedents

§1.01 INTRODUCTION TO CUSTOMS VALUATION

One sure place to start a discussion of customs valuation as it pertains to any jurisdiction is the domestic statute which imposes a responsibility to find the customs valuation for goods imported into the customs territory. In the US, we find that statutory mandate imposed on CBP:[1]

> The Customs Service shall, under rules and regulations prescribed by the Secretary—(a) fix the final appraisement of merchandise by ascertaining or estimating the value thereof, under section 1401a of this title, by all reasonable ways and means in his power, any statement of cost or costs of production in any invoice, affidavit, declaration, other document to the contrary notwithstanding.[2]

The general statutory authority of CBP to appraise merchandise is set forth in section 500 of the Tariff Act of 1930.[3] CBP Headquarters has made it quite clear that customs officials must follow the statutory scheme laid out by Congress, i.e., the strict hierarchy discussed below, noting that:

1. In the United States, the agency responsible for administering the customs laws, and for enforcement of the trade laws, is US Customs and Border Protection (CBP), formed in 2003 and placed within the Department of Homeland Security. From 1789 to that point, it had been housed within the US Treasury Department. That move signaled the importance of national security in the post-9/11 world. Parenthetically, the Canada Border Services Agency (CBSA) was established in 2003 for the same reason. As this excerpt shows, most of the US tariff and trade laws, and the customs regulations as well, continue to refer to the "US Customs Service." For the purpose of this book, indeed for all practical purposes, one should read "CBP" when encountering a reference to the US Customs Service in US source documents. For ease of reference, I refer to "CBP" whenever referring to the US customs authority, including the legacy Customs Service or earlier predecessor agencies.
2. 19 USC § 1500.
3. *Ibid.*

> Section 500 [19 USC § 1500] is the general authority for Customs to appraise merchandise. It is not a separate basis of valuation and cannot be used as such. Section 500 allows Customs to consider the best evidence available in appraising merchandise. ... Section 500 authorizes the appraising officer to weigh the nature of the evidence before him in appraising the imported merchandise. ... As broad as this grant of authority may be, it is clear, under authority of judicial decisions, that it does not give the appraising officer authority to do whatever he wants. He must and will appraise merchandise under the constraints of section 402 [19 USC § 1401a].[4]

For this purpose, CBP employs—and administers—the US customs valuation law[5] which implements the current GATT/WTO Valuation Agreement 1994 (Valuation Agreement or Agreement),[6] and the regulations promulgated under that domestic statute.[7] All 163 other current Members of the WTO are required to apply the Valuation Agreement as well,[8] and we might expect their implementing legislation should mirror that of the US—if they are being faithful to the Agreement.[9]

This mirroring of the domestic with the international standard will be reflected throughout this discussion with parallel citations to the Valuation Agreement and to the interpretations rendered by the customs authorities and reviewing courts of the domestic customs valuation law in the US, Canada and the EU.

As a result of this common implementation of a single standard, there is—or, at least, there should be—a higher degree of uniformity in the application of the customs valuation rules in force globally than is the case for the harmonization which marks the application of the tariff classification system. You may already know that the Harmonized Tariff System (HTS) is harmonized only through the six-digit subheading level.

---

4. Statement of Administrative Action, cited in ruling no. H019263 (November 8, 2010) (port officials admonished by Headquarters).
5. Trade Agreements Act, Act of July 26, 1979, Title II, § 201(a), 93 Stat. 1894, codified at 19 USC § 1401a.
6. Agreement on Implementation of Article VII of the General Agreement on Tariffs and Trade 1994. This customs valuation agreement was adopted as a part of the 1994 Uruguay Round Multilateral Agreements on Trade in Goods. In all relevant material respects, it is identical to the Agreement that had been adopted in 1979 at the conclusion of the Tokyo Round Multilateral Trade Negotiations conducted under the auspices of the GATT. Unless the context requires otherwise, "Valuation Agreement" hereinafter shall refer to the 1994 Agreement.
7. The US customs regulations are at Title 19, Code of Federal Regulations (CFR). The customs regulations on valuation are at 19 CFR §§ 152. 100-108.
8. The Marrakesh Agreement establishing the WTO (in Article II, paragraph 2) imposes such an obligation with respect to Agreements in Annexes 1 (such as the Valuation Agreement), 2 and 3 under a so-called Single Undertaking regime. To be sure, there are other agreements in Annex 4 thereto that remain in "plurilateral" status, for which participation is not obligatory. These latter include the Agreement on Trade in Civil Aircraft and the Agreement on Government Procurement.
9. For example, in the EU, the customs valuation regime is set forth in: (a) Articles 69-76 of the Union Customs Code ("UCC"), formally Commission Regulation (EU) No. 952/2013 of the European Parliament and of the Council of 9 October 2013 laying down the Union Customs Code (OJ L269, 10.10.2013 and (b)) Chapter 3 (Articles 127-146) of the UCC Implementing Act ("UCC IA"), formally Commission Implementing Regulation (EU) 2015/2447 of 24 November laying down detailed rules for implementing certain provisions of Regulation (EU) No. 952/2013 of the European Parliament and of the Council laying down the Union Customs Code. In Canada, the customs valuation regime is found in sections 44-57 of the Canada Customs Act 1985 (R.S.C., 1985, c. 1 (2nd Supp.)) (Customs Act).

After that, the system diverges to national practice choices, with varying statistical annotations up though eight-, ten- and even eleven-digit item numbers. And the applicable duty rates diverge wildly as well.[10] In fact, not unexpectedly, in the face of the jumbled state of affairs that prompted the Tokyo Round negotiations, the Preamble to the Valuation Agreement calls for a "fair, uniform and neutral system for the valuation of goods for customs purposes." The chaos that characterized the period from the adoption of the General Agreement on Tariffs and Trade (GATT) in 1947 until the adoption of the Valuation Agreement 1979 renders the present degree of uniformity all the more welcome.

Aside from the question of "fairness"—that is, valuation laws not applied selectively in a punitive or confiscatory fashion—this uniformity promotes predictability. An advisor based in one WTO participating country should be able to cite and apply the same standards in counseling an importer on the WTO customs valuation law practiced in another jurisdiction.

Relying on a common system also makes appropriate citation to foreign, e.g., EU, court decisions for a US or Canadian importer and vice versa. Consulting multilateral customs valuation precedents, i.e., WCO commentaries, case studies and advisory opinions, is also a good practice. Ordinarily, such citation to foreign authorities can be persuasive or instructive, but not dispositive, in dealings with the customs authority in the jurisdiction where a customs valuation question has arisen.

But predictability and certainty only go so far, for the logic that would run along the track from mirroring of the substantive standards through uniformity of implementation and administration by customs authorities and ending solidly with predictability comes off that track at the implementation/administration stage. This cautionary note should be committed to memory. Otherwise, an importer and his advisor may be frustrated in their dealings with customs authorities with different administrative agendas or political mandates or whose officials have little "real world" experience in the commercial realities which determine the ways in which international traders, or "economic operators" to borrow an EU term, organize and run their businesses. In short, there should be an interpretation of a valuation precept that is commonly accepted. If the interpretation differs from one jurisdiction to another, a commonly applied customs valuation result—uniformity—will be out of reach.

[A] Role of Commercial Practices

This common experience informing the interpretations of the customs authorities is grounded in the Valuation Agreement itself, with the General Introductory Commentary noting that:

> the customs value should be based on simple and equitable criteria consistent with commercial practices ... .

---

10. For example, the ad valorem duty rate for an imported passenger automobile is as low as 2.5% in the US and as high as 40% or more in other customs territories.

This guiding principle is the primary reason why the International Chamber of Commerce has been accredited with observer status to participate in meetings of the TCCV) of the WCO. The International Chamber of Commerce (ICC) provides valuable insight into both long-settled trade practices and emerging trends. As a general matter, the TCCV acknowledges the role of the ICC in ensuring that interpretations are based on commercial realities.

[B] TCCV

This takes us to the role of the TCCV, whose principal function for the purpose of this discussion is to promulgate agreed interpretations on specific technical questions.[11] Those interpretations are expressed in various instruments which, by accepted tradition, must be the result of a consensus[12] among the participating Members of the WCO in session.[13] That reliance upon a process depending upon unanimous support should ensure acceptance by the 183 WCO Members and much-needed guidance to customs authorities and private sector traders alike.

The TCCV is constantly engaged in the process at its twice-yearly sessions (typically held in May and October) in Brussels of discussing and ultimately issuing new commentaries and other instruments on technical questions arising under the Valuation Agreement. At a minimum, these provide guidance to customs authorities and the trade community, but some jurisdictions have conferred authoritative status. For those jurisdictions, these TCCV instruments have the force of law.

As has been made clear, the starting point for customs valuation today is the 1994 version of the Valuation Agreement. It is important to recognize the international authority of the Valuation Agreement, acceptance of which is a prerequisite for membership in the WTO, whose ranks now number 164 countries. As a result of the US and all of its trading partners using the same method of appraisement, as well as applying the same rules for tariff classification and for origin, as most of its trading partners, there is a higher degree of predictability in the trading system than at any time in the past.

In order to understand the inner dynamics of today's Agreement, we must first turn to its origins: the 1947 GATT Agreement and the ensuing thirty-year campaign to reach consensus on a methodology that culminated in the first Agreement in 1979. This effort may appear to be so much tracing of ley lines, but I am confident that it will deepen one's appreciation for the nuances in the Agreement that are revealed by careful study.

---

11. *See* Valuation Agreement, Annex II, paragraph 18.
12. There is no formal vote taken, but an expressed reservation will stop the process of adoption of any instrument under discussion and relegate the technical question to Part III of the TCCV's Conspectus—effectively tabled indefinitely in a limbo state.
13. To be sure, the private sector is represented in an accredited Observer status by a working group delegation from the International Chamber of Commerce Commission on Customs and Trade Facilitation (ICC). I have had the honor of serving on that ICC delegation for a number of years. The views expressed in this study are my own and should not be attributed to the ICC or to any other organization.

[C] GATT Valuation Agreement (1979)

The Valuation Agreement was one of the signal accomplishments of the Tokyo Round of Multilateral Tariff Negotiations because it introduced a single, fully self-contained system for the customs valuation of imported goods. Theretofore, there had been no single system at all, even among the signatories of the General Agreement on Tariffs and Trade 1947 (GATT 1947).

It is noteworthy that Article VII of the GATT 1947 had expressed only a basic principle of customs valuation based upon "actual value." That standard was defined (in paragraph 2 (b)) as "the price of the imported merchandise, or like merchandise, in sales in the ordinary course of trade under fully competitive conditions." You should note that it is the "like merchandise" reference which introduced a market value flavor into the valuation process even though "actual value" suggests a disdain for a value standard derived from market analysis or other external sources. You should also note the subjectivity inherent in the "fully competitive conditions" criterion.[14] Finally, in this early definition, we can discern the seed for what later flowered into the "price actually paid or payable for the merchandise," i.e., the current PAPP) standard, with its focus upon the actual price in the import transaction.

Other provisions of Article VII include a statement that currency exchange should not exert an influence on customs valuation (paragraph 4) and a recommendation (in paragraph 5) that the bases and methods for determining the value of goods subject to duties or other changes or restrictions by the signatories should be given sufficient publicity. Withal, Article VII stands as a brief hortatory statement of principle, leaving it to the Contracting Parties—each of the signatory countries—to devise their own "bases and methods" for fixing the customs value of imported merchandise.

You might be asking about the legal status of the Valuation Agreement vis-à-vis Article VII of the GATT. A side-by-side comparison reveals significant fundamental differences. Does it still make sense to discuss Article VII in any real sense? Or can a country defend its customs valuation practices as being aligned with Article VII even if they might conflict with the Valuation Agreement.

These are not idle musings, as India, for one, has gone on record at the WTO to explain and answer questions about certain amendments to its customs valuation statute in terms of Article VII.[15] The questions arose because India had used certain Article VII terms such as "actual value" and "fully competitive conditions." It was as though there was no Valuation Agreement.

What if there is a conflict between the two agreements? That is not an open question, as the Interpretative Note to Annex 1 A of the Marrakesh Agreement which established the WTO states:

14. The Annex I Notes to Article VII, in paragraphs 2 and 3, explain that this phrase will permit a customs authority to exclude any transaction wherein the buyer and seller are not independent of each other and price is not the sole consideration and from consideration prices that involve special discounts limited to exclusive agents. Note this 1947 concern for what we have come to refer to as "transfer pricing."

15. For a snapshot of this examination, *see* WTO, Committee on Customs Valuation, Minutes of Meeting of 8 March 2004, G/VAL/M/37 (30 April 2004), at 6-7.

> In the event of conflict between a provision of the General Agreement on Tariffs and Trade 1994 and a provision of another agreement in Annex 1A to the Agreement Establishing the World Trade Organization (referred to in the agreements in Annex 1A as the "WTO Agreement"), the provision of the other agreement shall prevail to the extent of the conflict.[16]

To be clear, the Valuation Agreement is "another agreement in Annex 1A to the WTO Agreement." In essence, Article VII is a dead letter in any conflict with the Valuation Agreement.

For its part, the ICC was alive to the risks and recognized the problems inherent in the spare GATT 1947 Article VII text as early as April 1947. The ICC called for the devising of a "satisfactory standard system of valuation after a full investigation of the requirements of both Customs and trader."[17] The ICC was not done, however, and it advanced an alternative solution with the draft text:

> The value for duty purposes of imported products shall be based on the actual price paid or payable by the importer or, where the goods are not purchased by the importer, the price paid by the purchase on the country of export, in each case as shown on the commercial or consular invoice, unless the Customs [Authority] have good reason to suspect that the invoice value is less than the real market value of the goods.[18]

An argument can be made that, despite the "real market value" referent, this is a very early progenitor of what we know today as the PAPP standard.

In the aftermath of the adoption of GATT 1947 and its failure to promulgate an actual methodology that went beyond the cited brief statement of principle,[19] countries took divergent paths to arrange for customs valuation. That led to much controversy and a desire at the WTO for an agreed customs valuation methodology.[20]

§1.02 WIDESPREAD DISSATISFACTION WITH PREVIOUS CUSTOMS VALUATION LAWS

The US first implemented the Valuation Agreement through enactment of the Trade Agreements Act of 1979 (TAA).[21]

---

16. Available online at https://www.wto.org/english/docs_e/legal_e/05-anx1a_e.htm.
17. GATT, E/PC/T.44 (14 April 1947) at 25.
18. *Ibid.*
19. Note that there had been later efforts to amend Article VII, but those efforts were unavailing. *See*, e.g., Italy's effort, GATT, W.9/62 (2 December 1954); Passages to Be Incorporated in the Draft Report of the Technical Group, GATT, Spec/22/55 (1 January 1955); Recommendations by Working Party II to Contracting Parties, GATT, W.9/191 (11 February 1955).
20. For further background beyond that offered here, *see* Streatfeild, Jeremy, A Brief Negotiating History of Customs Valuation in the Gatt and WTO (October 6, 2005). Available at SSRN https://ssrn.com/abstract=1483725 or http://dx.doi.org/10.2139/ssrn.1483725; Sherman and Glashoff; Rosenow and O'Shea, A Handbook on the WTO Customs Valuation Agreement (2010); Winham, International Trade and the Tokyo Round Negotiation (1986).
21. Trade Agreements Act of 1979, Title II, 19 USC § 1401a (1979). Act of July 26, 1979. The statute was amended in 1980, Pub. L. 96-490, § 2, Act of December 2, 1980, 94 Stat. 2556 (1980).

After that legislation revised the US customs valuation law in 1979, in the course of providing administrative guidance, the US acknowledged the controversies that had prompted the negotiations that bore fruit in the Valuation Agreement with the following summary:

> The [Valuation] Agreement was negotiated because of dissatisfaction in almost every country in the world with the customs valuation system of every other country. Every customs valuation system in use around the world has controversial and protective features that can act as nontariff barriers to international commerce. The Agreement lays down international rules for customs valuation that are designed to be fair, uniform, and neutral and that preclude the use of arbitrary and fictitious customs values.[22] It is important to note that the customs valuation methods that the US itself had employed attracted much spirited criticism.

[A] Anomalies of the Pre-1979 US Valuation System

The most controversial feature of the previous US customs valuation law was the special rule of the American Selling Price ("ASP") for certain imported footwear, chemicals and other specified products.[23] The ASP was a flashpoint even though it was applied to only 1% of US imports.[24]

The ASP, which disregarded the actual sales price negotiated between buyer and seller and applied prices set by a US competitor as the basis for fixing customs valuation, was intended to protect US producers from foreign competition.[25] The ASP had been especially objectionable to the European Community and other trading partners of the US. Those objections were well founded, as the ASP, true to its name, was a blatant violation of Article VII, paragraph 2(a), which prohibited basing customs value on the value of merchandise of national origin or on arbitrary or fictitious values. The US defended its reliance on ASP, however, on the grounds that its use had predated the adoption of the GATT and its validity was "grandfathered" in.

Those objections to the ASP were not at all limited to the trading partners of the US. The persons most directly affected by the ASP were the US customers of the sellers located in those foreign countries. Those US buyers who would import the foreign products were aggrieved by the levy of duty on the basis of the ASP method.[26] Parenthetically, the alignment of interests of importers and their customers, the

22. Statement of Administrative Action (1979), *reprinted in* Customs Valuation under the Trade Agreements Act of 1979, Customs Service Office of Commercial Operations 68 (1981).
23. Former 19 USC § 1401a(e). Because appraisement under "ASP" attached only to certain articles on a tariff classification-specific basis, such as rubber footwear, the importer would often have to fight a two-front war, disputing both the tariff classification and the valuation of the imported articles. *See*, e.g., *International Seaway Trading Corp. v. United States*, 464 F. Supp. 380, 81 Cust. Ct. 92 (1978) and related cases.
24. Customs Valuation, Report of the US Tariff Commission to the Committee on Finance and to the Subcommittee on International Trade, US Senate, ITC Pub 332-540 (March 14, 1973) (Tariff Commission Report), 19.
25. *See Albert F. Maurer Co. v. United States*, 51 CCPA 114, 119 C.A.D. 845 (1964).
26. For a then-contemporary discussion of the political controversy centered on Nike's imports, *see* Mark Asher, 3 Political Heavyweights Have Lined Up for the Great Sneaker snafu, Wash. Post

consumers in the country of import, with those of foreign suppliers and the tension with domestic suppliers in the country of import is an enduring characteristic of international trade.

Prior to 1980, the US customs valuation law,[27] dating to the Customs Simplification Act of 1956, itself an amendment to the Tariff Act of 1930,[28] was actually based on two separate hierarchies of valuation methodologies, both grounded in a marketplace price concept.

For a significant percentage of products designated by the Secretary of the Treasury,[29] the valuation law from the 1930 Tariff Act, which was referred to as the "old valuation law," continued to apply.[30] For these products, the higher of "foreign value" (the price for consumption in the foreign market) or "export value" (the price in the foreign market for export to the US) was to serve as the basis for appraisement.

For most imported products, however, the appraisement was accomplished under section 1402 of the Tariff Act of 1930,[31] with the preferred basis for appraisement being "export value," which was defined as:

> the price at the time of exportation to the United States at which such or similar merchandise is freely sold in the usual wholesale quantities and in the ordinary course of trade.[32]

As a result of the notion that there was a single qualifying price, discounted prices were rejected unless they were granted to all purchasers.[33] Even bargaining for a price was sufficient to disqualify such a price as the basis for an export value appraisement.[34] Sales to "selected purchasers" had to be justified as a price "which fairly reflects the market value of the merchandise."[35]

While some of the GATT documents and later commentators[36] regarded the US valuation approach as employing a "positive" system, based upon the actual price paid

---

July 8, 1979, available at https://www.washingtonpost.com/archive/business/1979/07/08/3-political-heavyweights-have-lined-up-for-the-great-sneaker-snafu/eb11bc68-8866-4045-bb8f-1181edfb2584/.

27. 19 USC § 1401a, amended (effectively repealed) by Trade Agreements Act of 1979 (TAA).
28. Customs Simplification Act, Act of August 2, 1956 Ch. 887, § 2(a), 70 Stat. 943.
29. These were the products specified in the "Final List," T.D. 54521 (1958), 93 Treas. Dec. 14. As was the case of ASP appraisements, tariff classification principles were often interjected in Final List valuation disputes. *See*, e.g., *B&K Instruments Inc. v. United States*, 82 Cust. Ct. 219, C.D. 4803 (1979) (issue: were instruments of a class or kind chiefly used for laboratory purposes). The Tariff Commission Report stated (at 18) that 20% of imports were classified on a Final List basis.
30. Former section renumbered in 1956 as § 1402a of the Tariff Act of 1930, codified at 19 USC § 1402. This hierarchy anticipated the application of the higher of foreign value, i.e., the internal price in the country of exportation, or export value, then to United States value and, finally, to Cost of Production.
31. Former 19 USC § 1401a.
32. Former 19 USC § 1401a(b).
33. *Castle & Cooke, Inc. and A.J. Fritz v. United States*, 64 Cust. Ct. 628, R.D. 11693 (1970).
34. *United States v. Mexican Products Co.*, 28 CCPA 80, C.A.D. 129 (1940).
35. Former 19 USC § 1401a(f)(1)(B). *See Ernest Lowenstein. Inc. v. United States*, 78 Cust. Ct. 169, R.D. 11779(1977), *aff'd* 80 Cust. Ct. 211, A.R.D. 325 (1978); *Cascade Corp. v. United States*, 81 Cust. Ct. 9, CD. 4757 (1978).
36. *See*, e.g., Rosenow and O'Shea, A Handbook on the WTO Customs Valuation Agreement, at 6-7.

for the imported goods, caution is advisable. In fact, a declared price might be acceptable only in the presence of certain specified conditions. The following observations were made at the GATT as early as 1973:

> A "positive" standard defines valuation in terms of the price at which goods are sold under, specified conditions. Because it bases value on actual specified conditions, it requires in ranking order, one or more additional standards to provide alternatives for valuation when the actual conditions of the primary standard are not met.
>
> A "notional" standard, on the other hand, defines customs valuation in terms of price at which goods would be sold under specified conditions. Because notional standards base valuation on the price at which goods would be sold under specified actual conditions, it permits any of the elements at variance to be adjusted, as required to meet the standard. Thus one notional standard may constitute the entire valuation system.[37]

The US definition of an acceptable "export value" was based on such a number of external conditions that it veered dangerously close to being a market value or "notional" concept, loosely defined as it was as the price at which the goods are freely offered for sale to all purchasers for export to the US.[38] In other words, the actual price would be acceptable only when gauged against external benchmarks. How is that not a notional standard in the same sense as the Brussels Definition of Value (BDV), which is discussed below?

As an element in its analysis of the customs valuation law amendments to implement the Valuation Agreement, the US Senate compared the 1956-era "export value" and the new TV standard, the two preferred bases for appraisement under the "old" and "new" laws, respectively, drawing a sharp distinction between the two standards:

> The use of transaction value as the primary basis for customs valuation will allow use of the price which the buyer and seller agreed to in their transaction as the basis for valuation, rather than having to resort to the more difficult concepts of "freely offered," "ordinary course of trade," "principal markets of the country of exportation," and "usual wholesale quantities" contained in existing U.S. law.[39]

That actual price paid in a specific transaction would be rejected under an export value analysis for being discordant from an external benchmark—here, the price that the goods would fetch in a sale to all (arguably, all other) purchasers—with the same finality that attended the rejection of a price in any notional system.

If an export value for the imported merchandise could not be ascertained, then the other valuation methodologies which might apply, in descending order of application, were US value, i.e., the internal price for domestic consumption in the US of such

37. For a 1973 omnibus listing of objectionable practices, *see* GATT, Committee on Trade and Development, Trade Barriers Arising in the Field of Customs Valuation, Note on Implications for Developing Countries of ad referendum Solutions, COM.TD/W/195, 1 (2 August 1973).
38. Former 19 USC § 1402(d).
39. S. Rep. No. 96-249, 96th Cong., 1st Sess. 119, *reprinted in* 1979 U.S. Code Cong. & Admin. News 381, 505.

or similar imported merchandise with allowances for commissions, profit, general expenses, transportation, duty and the like; constructed value, i.e., the cost of materials plus amounts for general expenses and profit and for packing; and finally, for certain products such as rubber footwear only ASP, i.e., the price at which US competitors were selling domestically produced competing ("like or similar") products.[40]

Concern about the validity of related party pricing, discussed at length in Part II, was as real an issue under the predecessor law as it is under the present law; e.g., the following:

> [It is a] fundamental fact that rigged prices in the export market may materially affect the importer's profits and general expenses in the United States.[41]

[B] BDV

Most countries relied on the BDV, which was based on a notional definition of "actual value," dating to 1950.[42] The BDV was formally introduced to the GATT in October 1952 by a representative of the European Customs Union Study Group, a forerunner of the WCO.[43] The BDV had been severely criticized by the ICC,[44] and that October presentation was in the nature of an apologia. In hindsight, that defense rings hollow.

It will appear that the ICC had been quite prescient. Even though it took another twenty-seven years, its position was ultimately adopted, forming the basis of the PAPP and TV, the heart of the Valuation Agreement.

In a filing made directly with the GATT,[45] the ICC had submitted proposals, and the Executive Secretary of the GATT responded,[46] noting:

> The ICC recommends that the Contracting Parties should consider the possibility of issuing a set of general recommendations and suggests that they might attempt, now or at some future date, to draw up a standard definition of valuation of goods for world-wide application.

---

40. Former 19 USC § 1401a(c)-(e).
41. *United States v. Geigv Chemical Corporation, et al.*, 73 Cust. Ct. 214, 221, A.R.D. 321 (1974).
42. Convention on the Valuation of Goods for Customs Purposes, signed in Brussels on December 15, 1950, entered into force on July 28, 1953, amended in 1967 (amendment coming into force in 1972).
43. Statement of Mr. F. Edmond-Smith, GATT, W.7/8 (7 October 1952).
44. Resolutions submitted by the International Chamber of Commerce on Valuation. Nationality of Manufactured Goods and Formalities Connected with Quantitative Restrictions (GATT/CP/1231) [so-called Lisbon Resolution], G/22 (29 August 1952). The Thirteenth Congress of the International Chamber of Commerce which was held in Lisbon in June 1951 passed a series of Resolutions relating to the reduction of barriers to trade. Among them were Resolutions dealing with Customs Treatment of Samples and Advertising Matter, Consular Formalities and Documentary Requirements. With regard to the Valuation of Goods for Customs Purposes, the ICC Congress suggested that the Contracting Parties should consider issuing a set of recommendations for action pursuant to Article VII of the GATT. These recommendations were filed with the GATT. *See* GATT/64 (30 October 1951).
45. Apparently, the ICC had sufficient standing at the GATT to submit position papers and recommendations. *See* also in this connection Communication from the International Chamber of Commerce, GATT/CP/98 (8 February 1951).
46. GATT, G/122 (29 August 1952).

The Executive Secretary summarized and commented upon the ICC recommendation (in paragraphs 7 and 8):

> 7. The "simple rule-of-thumb method" suggested by the International Chamber of Commerce would require governments to use the price shown on a commercial invoice[47] as the normal basis for valuation and to limit other methods to cases where there is a presumption of fraud or of undervaluation.
>
> 8. Similar proposals have been discussed before, but experience has shown that national customs administrations are not prepared to accept that system without further qualifications.

As for the adoption of a proper valuation standard, the GATT Executive Secretary threw cold water on the ICC proposal, which had echoed its 1947 comments. After first counseling delay (in paragraph 12), until such time that some experience with the BDV should have been gained, the GATT document noted:

> 13. The ICC further suggests that an attempt be made of drawing up a standard definition for world-wide application. It has been noted under paragraph 8 above that a number of European countries have ratified or intend ratifying in the near future the Convention prepared by the Brussels Study Group on valuation.
>
> 14. The ICC has drawn attention to what it considers as grave shortcomings in the Brussels Convention and has discussed with the Brussels Study Group a number of amendments. As the Convention has already been accepted by a number of governments, no change can be made at the present time but the matter will be considered in the near future by the Customs Cooperation Council to be set up in Brussels.
>
> 15. In those circumstances, it would seem that the most effective contribution that the Contracting Parties could make would be to examine how an early application of the principles embodied in Article VII of the GATT could be obtained. When this is achieved, they might consider whether further action along the lines suggested by the ICC with a view to reaching greater uniformity in national valuation systems is required.

As an aside: given the BDV's European origin, the irony is that the initial proposal for the core standard in the Valuation Agreement which we know as the PAPP, which is quite close to this 1952 proposal by the ICC, was made at the Tokyo Round by the European Communities in its draft customs valuation code.[48] To be sure, there were some notable differences between the ICC proposal and the final Valuation Agreement,[49] but the European Communities' proposal was a "game changer" for the Tokyo Round negotiations. Twenty-five years' experience with the BDV proved to be the sufficient experience for a new approach.

---

47. As cited in ruling no. H314296 (August 12, 2021), *Black's Law Dictionary* defines a "commercial invoice" as "A document needed for a customs agent to show the value of goods, duties, and taxes. It shows the buyer, seller, date, sale terms, amount, packaging, description, value, and insurance fees."
48. GATT, Multilateral Trade Negotiations Group, "Non-Tariff Measures," Sub-Group "Customs Matters," Customs Valuation, MTN/NTM/W/122 (8 November 1977).
49. For instance, the EC draft, in allowing for transaction values of identical or of similar merchandise, stated (Articles 2.2 and 3.2) that "If ... it is established that the goods are sold by the same seller to more than one other buyer, then the customs value of the imported goods shall be based on the average of the prices to such other buyers."

But by that time the BDV had enjoyed a long run. Having weathered the initial storms, with strong backing from the European countries, not surprising given its paternity, the BDV initiative gained acceptance in a widening circle of customs jurisdictions.[50] The Customs Cooperation Council (CCC) observed in 1973 that over a hundred countries were applying the BDV as a matter of law or practice.[51]

The BDV's version of "actual price" was based upon a Platonic-idealized model. Customs value was not to be based on the price actually paid by the buyer for the goods. Instead, the "normal price" was to be consulted. This was a resort to an external referent or benchmark—the price which they would fetch at the time when the duty becomes payable or on a sale in the open market between buyer and seller independent of each other.[52] Obviously, that standard begs the question—how does one find the normal price? Where does one look? For customs authorities, the answer was obvious—one can look to records of other imports of such or similar goods. That led to the question, how does one gauge whether the goods are comparable? So to speak, whether in an import of apples, those other reference point imported goods are apples, too? One tool at the customs authorities' disposal was to compile a list arranged on a tariff classification basis, what we would call a "database," to serve as the repository of these benchmark prices. The WTO has furnished the following brief commentary on the BDV practice:

> Factual deviations from this [normal] price were only fully taken into account where the declared value was higher than the listed value. Downward variations were only taken into account up to 10 per cent. This method caused widespread dissatisfaction among traders, as price changes and competitive advantages of firms were not reflected until the notional price was adjusted by the customs office after certain periods of time. New and rare products were often not captured in the lists, which made determination of the "normal price" difficult.[53]

We will revisit this issue of "valuation database" lists below—it remains a major source of distortion to this day. Some of these practices have the longevity of a red dwarf star or are zombie-like in their refusal to pass away.

Further clarifications showed that there was a concern that the relationship of the parties might influence the price ("the price is the sole consideration") and that the parties implicitly would not be independent of each other if they were "associated in business with one other." In fact, this association's focus was not primarily on parent/subsidiary or common ownership of buyers and sellers but on sole agents or

50. One boost in its status was its adoption by the European Economic Community (EEC) in 1968, superseding the six Member States' domestic customs valuation provisions. Regulation 803/68, OJ Special Edition 1968 (I), 170 adopted the BDV as the common customs valuation standard.
51. The US Tariff Commission reported in 1973 that the BDV was applied to 64% of trade in the free world in 1970. Tariff Commission Report, 42.
52. The US Tariff Commission traced the pedigree of this notional standard to a UK customs valuation standard first adopted in 1935. Tariff Commission Report, 39.
53. WTO, Customs Valuation: Technical Information, Technical Information on Customs Valuation, available at https://www.wto.org/english/tratop_e/cusval_e/cusval_info_e.htm.

sole concessionaires.[54] Today, we would refer to many of those traders as distributors or franchisees.

Three other BDV features are noteworthy. First, Article I, paragraph 2(b) and Annex II (in Addendum to Article I, Note 2) mandate that: (i) the seller will bear "all costs, charges and expenses" incidental to delivery in the port of importation and (ii) those "costs, charges and expenses" refer to international freight and insurance charges. In other words, the price for customs valuation purposes must be a Cost, Insurance and Freight (CIF) price.[55] This was unacceptable to the US, which effectively based customs valuation, *sub silentio*, on a Free-on-Board (FOB) basis.[56,57]

Another noteworthy aspect of the BDV, with ramifications for us today, is that the BDV defined a qualifying sale in the open market as one where "no part of the proceeds arising from any subsequent re-sale, use or disposal of the goods, will accrue either directly or indirectly to the seller or any natural or legal person associated in business with him." Note that this "associated in business" standard served to widen the disqualification that would follow from a sharing of subsequent proceeds.

In its treatment of royalties, the BDV embraced a standard that also has implications for us today. According to Article III of the BDV, the normal price of any good imported with a trademark or imported for sale under a foreign trademark will include the value of any "foreign trademark"—the normal price shall be determined on the assumption that it includes the right to use the patent, design or trademark in respect of the goods. In other words, the customs valuation would automatically include the value of any trademark. Payments for these intellectual property rights

54. The term "concessionaire" is not commonly used in the United States in this context. In the United States, the term normally has a limited meaning—a person or firm granted a contract to operate a concession in a state park or recreation area—as in "a concession stand." Another accepted usage would refer to a grant of mineral or other natural resource rights. The concessionaire is an independent contractor and not an employee or agent. The use in this customs context arises from a European understanding which is broader in scope; in that latter context, a concessionaire is a person who has been granted the right by another other property owner to operate a business in a particular location. This is very much like a sole agent or sole distributor; parties also granted exclusive rights.
55. The Incoterms (2020) are a set of predefined commercial terms published by the International Chamber of Commerce. The Incoterms are widely used by traders because they carry within each term the readily discernable bright lines that allow the parties to a transaction which is governed by a specific term to immediately calculate the extent of their respective costs and underlying responsibilities. The Incoterms assign risk of loss but do not assign transfer of title. Here, "CIF" refers to a Cost, Insurance and Freight sales term, which captures transport and insurance costs as an element of the price actually paid or payable for the imported goods.
56. The FOB Incoterm refers to a Free-on-Board sale, whereby the sale price does not include international freight and insurance charges. Purists will note that, in today's usage, FOB should be used only for breakbulk cargo to be loaded directly onto a vessel. Cargo being moved via container would normally be delivered to the shipping company's container yard and an FCA (Free Carrier) is more appropriate. Where the containers are not staged in a yard prior to loading, FAS (Free Alongside Ship) might be appropriate.
57. During the Tokyo Round negotiations, in a bid to win the support of the US and other countries which based customs valuation on an FOB basis, the CCC conceded some changes to the BDV on this point. GATT, Customs Matters: Communication from the Customs Co-operation Council, MTN/NTM/W/17 (26 August 1975) 10. Interestingly, when the US Tariff Commission issued its Report, there was a 4-2 split, with two Commissioners recommending that the US should adopt a CIF approach. Tariff Commission Report, 4.

(IPRs) were dutiable, as in "always and everywhere." There is no specific reference here to royalties or license fees, so presumably customs authorities were not limited to amounts paid as royalty or license fees. Further, Note 3(b) of the Addendum to Article III defines a foreign trademark as including a mark owned by any person associated in business with the seller. We have seen that an "association in business" was broadly defined. The fact that the royalty or license fee might be paid to a rights holder that was related to or a business associate of the seller made the trademark a "foreign" mark and thus dutiable.

Not unexpectedly, there were some vigorous criticisms of the BDV system and the degree of discretion afforded customs authorities, with a corresponding absence of predictability for traders, with the US harboring a determined resistance to any new system based on the BDV,[58] and there was an equally spirited defense of the BDV by the CCC.[59] It will be seen below that in the run-up to the Uruguay Round negotiations, after the 1979 Agreement had been in place, the CCC had become thoroughly converted, encouraging holdouts' switch over to the Agreement by pointing to the faults of the BDV.

[C] Canadian and Australian Practices

The customs valuation practices of Canada and Australia also came under criticism, *inter alia*, for practices which served to base customs values on the prices for home consumption in the country of export.[60]

One specific criticism was lodged against Canada's use of section 39(d) of the Customs Act, Revised Statutes of 1970 as an antidumping device. Another was the use of a minimum pricing mechanism in section 41.[61]

In the case of Australia, the US Tariff Commission summarized that country's approach:

58. *See*, e.g., GATT, Multilateral Trade Negotiations Group, "Non Tariff Measures," Sub-Group "Customs Matters," MTN/NTM/W/20 (29 September 1975), 5-10. Of note was this specific concern, "United States exporters have experienced problems with countries that use the Brussels Definition of Value in applying 'uplifts' whenever the importer and exporter are 'associated in business.' The customs official operating under the BDV fixes a percentage increase on merchandise between related parties or on entries by a buyer having exclusive purchasing rights. This may not always reflect the real costs involved in the transaction. The problem appears primarily related to the failure of customs officials to employ real costs in calculating uplifts and to explain how they arrived at the percentage of uplift." *Ibid.*, at 10.
59. For one such filing at the GATT early in the immediate run-up to the Tokyo Round, *see* GATT, Valuation, Comments by the Director of Valuation and External Relations of the Customs Co-operation Council on paragraph 17 of the Report of Working Group 2 on Non-Tariff Barriers Revision, Spec (70)133/Rev/.1 (21 April 1971).
60. For a 1973 sweeping omnibus of objectionable practices, *see* GATT, Committee on Trade and Development Trade Barriers Arising in the Field of Customs Valuation Note on Implications for Developing Countries of ad referendum Solutions, COM.TD/W/195 (2 August 1973). For a useful summary of the salient feature of the Canadian approach and its focus upon "fair market value" in the country of export, *see* Winham, 178-183.
61. An excerpt of the Canadian statute was contained in the Tariff Commission Report, A67-71.

> Australia bases dutiable value on the higher of (1) the actual f.o.b. transaction price adjusted to disallow any special discount, or (2) the value on the date of exportation of the same quantity of identical goods sold for domestic consumption in the country of export plus all charges necessary for placing the goods free on board at the port of export. The alternate to actual transaction value, the current domestic value, is similar to the foreign value standard used by the United States under section 402a. Most Australian imports are valued on the basis of current domestic value.[62]

The Tariff Commission also reported that Australia made use of selected "support prices":

> The Customs Tariff provides "support values" for certain specified products made in Australia. If the landed, duty-paid cost of an imported product is less than the support value established for that product, the importer must pay, in addition to the regular import duty, an additional duty equal to 90 percent of the difference between the landed, duty paid cost and the support value. Support values have been fixed for a number of chemical products, including synthetic resins, synthetic rubber, ethylene glycol, and triethanolarnine. Products covered by support values account for only a small proportion of all Australian imports.

[D] Continued Pursuit of a Remedy (1950s-1970s)

Despite the early rebuff to the ICC proposal, the need for a comprehensive, agreed customs valuation methodology could not be gainsaid entirely. There was a split among the Contracting Parties—some felt that an amendment to Article VII would suffice, while others saw the need for a comprehensive, generally accepted comprehensive system. The GATT pursued both objectives simultaneously. The GATT was also intent on conforming customs valuation practices to Article VII.[63] Even while the discussions to amend Article VII of the GATT continued, the GATT Secretariat proceeded to poll the Contracting Parties in 1954-1955 through questionnaires to get a sense of existing practices, with a view to formulating that comprehensive methodology.[64] In that effort, a table of valuation practices was compiled and shared by the Secretariat in January 1955.[65]

The mid-1950s proved to be a busy time. Rosenow & O'Shea report a Scandinavian proposal in 1954[66] that work on a new customs valuation instrument might be a fit project for the proposed Organization for Trade Co-operation (OTC), a body which would have supplanted the GATT Secretariat. The US delegation formally proposed the

62. Tariff Commission Report, 88-89.
63. GATT, Multilateral Trade Negotiations Group, "Non-Tariff Measures," Customs Matters Background Note by the Secretariat, L/81/Add. 1 (7 August 1953) [a report prepared by the Secretariat based upon submissions by various countries].
64. *See*, e.g., GATT, L/1228 (29 September 1954) and the subsequently filed "Add." Addenda; GATT, W.9/34 (24 November 1954), GATT, MGT/4/55 (1 January 1955).
65. GATT, Tables for Valuation of Products, MGT/1/55 (1 January 1955).
66. GATT, Contracting Parties Ninth Session Review Working Party II on Tariffs, Schedules and Customs Administration, Proposals Affecting Customs Administration, W.9/46 (29 November 1954).

formation of the OTC[67] some two days later, but not enough countries became signatories to the OTC Agreement and it never entered into force.[68] The world would have to wait another forty years before the WTO was founded to fill the institutional role anticipated in the stillborn OTC and the even earlier (1947) International Trade Organization.

Customs valuation process improvements continued to demand attention. The Kennedy Round (1964-1967) achieved some success when the US agreed to drop the much-resented ASP after negotiation with the European Economic Community (EEC) on an agreement to lower chemical tariffs.[69] Unfortunately, this was for naught, as was the case with the Antidumping Agreement as well, the US having reneged after domestic political pressures, and the arrangement never took effect.

The stage was truly set for the Tokyo Round negotiations when Working Group 2 of the Committee on Trade in Industrial Goods reported in 1971 on the result of their efforts undertaken in 1970.[70] That report serves as a useful summary of the myriad issues swirling about. The starting point for future discussions might be taken to be the GATT *ad referendum* statement of principles that had been compiled by Working Group 2 and which made its appearance in that February 1971 GATT Report.[71] Those principles served consistently as a touchstone throughout the discussions,[72] and many found their way into the Preamble of the Valuation Agreement.

It was clear that, as late as March 1975, there was no consensus on whether to adopt a new, comprehensive approach or not. That was the same state of play as had been the case fully two decades before. The question was starkly posed:

> What is the most appropriate way to deal with problems arising in the field of customs valuation: an overall solution through the elaboration of general rules or a case-by-case approach or a combination of both?[73]

---

67. GATT, Review of the Agreement, Proposal by the United States Delegation, Agreement Establishing the Organization for Trade Co-operation, L/292 (1 December 1954). *See also* GATT, Contracting Parties Ninth Session Review Working Party IV on Organizational and Functional Questions Subgroup A on Organizational Questions Joint Report on the Establishment of an Organization and on the transfer of the Contracting Parties' powers to that Organization, Submitted by the representatives of France, Norway and the United States as Rapporteurs, W.9/93 (14 December 1954).
68. This was despite an extension of the closing date for countries to sign. GATT, Contracting Parties Thirteenth Session Entry into Force of the Amendment Protocols and the Establishment of the Organization for Trade Cooperation Resolution of 22 November 1958, L/942 (26 November 1958).
69. For a useful background discussion, *see* Streatfeild, 145-146.
70. GATT, Committee on Trade in Industrial Products, Report to Council, L/3496 (10 February 1971), 32-40.
71. A set of Interpretative Notes was later appended to the *ad referendum* principles. For a copy of both, *see* GATT, Committee on Trade in Industrial Products, Group 2 on Valuation, Report by the Chairman, COM.IND/W/64 (5 November 1971).
72. For an insight into the role of the principles and their accompanying interpretative notes, *see* GATT, Committee on Trade and Development, Trade Barriers Arising in the Field of Customs Valuation, Note on Implications for Developing Countries of ad referendum Solutions, COM.TD/W/195 (2 August 1973), Appendix 1.
73. GATT, Multilateral Trade Negotiations Group, "Non-Tariff Measures," Customs Matters Background Note by the Secretariat, MTN/NTM/W/7 (29 April 1975), 3.

What was not in dispute was the notion that something had to be done. Nor was there any dispute that customs valuation standards and practices could operate as a nontariff barrier. In fact, the GATT itself had recognized this danger from inception. We learn that Article II Schedules of Concessions warned (in paragraph 3):

> No contracting party shall alter its method of determining dutiable value or of converting currencies so as to impair the value of any of the concessions provided for in the appropriate Schedule annexed to this Agreement.

The easiest and perhaps most surefire way to nullify a tariff concession would be to honor the negotiated rate of duty assessed at import but to undermine a proper customs valuation by resorting to practices so as to increase the customs value of the imported article. After all, with an ad valorem tariff rate, the customs value serves as the taxable base against which the duty rate would be applied. Surely, it was precisely that experience which had added to the clamor to make sweeping changes so that the rules might be made more uniform and tariff concessions not nullified or impaired.

§1.03 TOKYO ROUND (1973-1979)

A close study of the GATT/WTO archives reveals that there are large gaps in the official record, with much of our present understanding of how and why the Valuation was finally formed based on anecdotal evidence only. For a customs professional sometimes tasked with a project in which the accessibility of what is termed "legislative history" would be a benefit, this empty space is frustrating. For example, take the case of a question whether certain services not now specifically named in Article 8.1 might be analogous to and actually might be considered to be a dutiable assist under one of the provisions of Article 8.1 of the Valuation Agreement. In such a case, it would be helpful if we could ascertain if the potential for that category of services to be a dutiable assist had been weighed but rejected outright or otherwise disposed of.

Conceivably there could be explicit evidence that the parties considered that a separate listing was not necessary because the service was so obviously subsumed in another already-listed category. That would serve to buttress an argument that the specifically named category of service in the Valuation Agreement should be interpreted as including the service under consideration. To be sure, if a category of services was proposed but subsequently deleted, that would be strong evidence that the category had been considered but rejected, with the result that it should not be resurrected now.

Let the following two explicit examples illustrate how access to the drafts can be rewarding. Dating to November 1978, in this working draft of the "code,"[74] the status accorded the Valuation Agreement at the time, the fluidity of the adjustments to the PAPP was very much unsettled at that late date. Among other suggestions, the following nonproduction services were floated as dutiable assists:

---

74. GATT, Multilateral Trade Negotiations Group, "Non-Tariff Measures," Sub-Group "Customs Matters," Customs Valuation Revision, W/175/Rev. 1 (6 November 1978).

(v) technical assistance, such as the services of a manager, attorney, or cost accountant relating to the imported goods;
and
(vi) other services for which the seller would otherwise have to pay directly or indirectly, such as ADP services or accounting services relating to the imported goods.

Should there be any question about these categories today, by citing the subsequent exclusion which may be viewed as a rejection, the customs authority or the importer can easily dispel any doubts that Article 8 does not embrace an open-ended interpretation. To the contrary, these nonproduction services should be nondutiable. There is a growing trend to look closely at all payments made by an importer/buyer, and not simply those made by the buyer to the seller, and to ask whether the payment is dutiable either as an integral part of the PAPP or as an adjustment under Article 8.1. In such an event, a walk through the echoing vaults of the GATT/WTO archives might be helpful. With this background, it would be immensely beneficial if care were taken to ensure accessibility to a full archival record of any future action to amend or replace the Agreement.

One major factor in shaping the course of the Tokyo Round was the striving to convince developing countries to participate in the process and to adopt the Valuation Agreement and the various other trade agreements that were the negotiating goal. It is no little coincidence that the early to mid-1970s marked the peak of the North-South Dialogue, one signal accomplishment of which was the wildly popular Generalized System of Preferences (GSP), the unilateral tariff preference scheme for lesser developed countries (LDCs) promulgated by the US and such other developed international trade jurisdictions as Canada, Japan and the EEC.[75] Early evidence of the solicitude shown by the GATT Secretariat was the compilation, at the request of developing countries, of trade barriers posed by valuation systems.[76] The Secretariat included the following complaints raised by developing countries in a recitation of nontariff barriers:

> Developing countries have pointed out that the existence of such valuation procedures posed special problems for their trade. In particular it has been stated that the system prevalent in some countries of levying customs duty on the basis of f.o.b. value or current domestic value, whichever was higher, made it difficult for exporters to know in advance the amount of duty payable: resulting uncertainty had adverse effects on exports. It has been further stated that these systems acted particularly to the disadvantage of developing countries as in a large number of cases, because of structural imbalances, supply scarcities and such other factors, the domestic prices in these countries ruled at artificially high levels. In

75. In the US, the GSP was originally enacted under the Trade Act of 1974, Act of January 3, 1975, Title V, §§ 501 et seq., 88 Stat. 2066 and codified at 19 USC §§ 2461-2467. The tariff preferences are provided for certain "beneficiary developing countries"; note that eligibility for a number of bases for ineligibility are set forth and that not all countries that might qualify as LDCs nor certain specified products will qualify for BDC status.
76. GATT, Committee on Trade and Development Trade Barriers. Arising in the Field of Customs Valuation Note on Implications for Developing Countries of ad referendum Solutions, COM.TD/W/195 (2 August 1973).

> addition, in some cases, goods which were produced by specially established export-oriented industries were not sold in the domestic market, which created special difficulties in ascertaining comparable current domestic value.[77]

For their part, the developing countries had acknowledged their use of minimum prices, "official values" and other special arrangements which would make adoption of a positive valuation basis challenging:

> In regard to "official values," while some of these countries fix such values for the entire range or a significantly large number of imported products, a few others determine such values for a limited number of products only. The developing countries maintaining "official indicative values" for a limited number of products have stated that they have found it necessary to adopt such a system to curb "under-invoicing" of goods or similar unfair practices. It has been stated that apart from such cases, fixing official values on the basis of "average prices of imports" may be necessary for commodities which are subject to wide fluctuations in prices ... *In regard to "minimum values," developing countries fixing such values have explained that they were being determined for a limited number of products, in order,* inter alia, *to protect their nascent industries from competition from well-established industries in other countries*[78] (emphasis added).

This last is a rather overt admission of using customs valuation as a nontariff barrier (NTB). The developing countries signaled as early as this December, 1974 document that they would probably need dispensation to make needed changes to conform to any new valuation system on a relaxed timetable.[79]

The practice appears to be that the "developing countries" were never identified in the proceedings when that phrase was used in the Tokyo Round GATT documents. We do know, however, that such individual countries as India, Brazil and Mexico took active roles.

A tour of the archives reveals an evolving effort centered on the attempt to convince the US and the other holdouts (Canada, Australia, New Zealand) to accede to the BDV. We have already referred to the 1974 amendment by the CCC which would accommodate countries based on an FOB system. Given the numbers of BDV advocates, the expectation was high that the holdouts would come on board and that the BDV, perhaps with suitable amendments, would be designated as the basis for the international valuation system.

As we know now, that was not to be. The lead role in the Tokyo Round was played by the EEC, and it would be fair to say that in the earlier stages of those talks that the negotiations took on a bilateral US/EEC character.

The November 1977 *volte face* by the EEC in abandoning the BDV and in proposing a positive approach was seen as a betrayal by the developing countries. And that sense lingers yet, as shown in this example from a website of the Federal Board of Revenue in Pakistan:

---

77. GATT, Multilateral Trade Negotiations, Non-Tariff Measures Affecting Trade of Developing Countries Note by the Secretariat, MTN/3B/23 (31 December 1974), paragraph 53.
78. *Ibid.*, in paragraph 58.
79. *Ibid.*, in paragraph 59.

> It was expected that the resulting precise criteria would induce the four major countries namely USA, Canada, Australia and New Zealand to change their systems and join the BDV.
>
> The elaboration of these texts did not have however, any perceptible influence on their negotiating approach and stand.
>
> In November 1977, however, the European Union (EU) [sic] suddenly and unexpectedly announced dramatic change in its position. It declared that the Community countries had agreed to make a fundamental change in the valuation system by opting out for a positive approach and that the proposals it was making were based on what it "believed to be good features of the United States Valuation System." The draft Agreement which it presented, provided that in almost all cases customs should determine dutiable value on the basis of "price paid or payable" for imported goods in the particular transaction. The customs [sic] could reject transaction value only in a limited number of exceptional cases. In all such cases however, the customs were expected to determine it by using the five prescribed methods by applying them in the hierarchical order in which they were listed.
>
> In the international negotiations, countries often change their position by redefining their objectives. But in this case, the decision of the European Union almost amounted to agreeing with the adversary, in the mid-term of the negotiations, that the position that the adversary was taking was right and its own stand was worng [sic].
>
> The reactions of developing countries to the EU proposal were of complete surprise and disbelief. Many of them were only recently persuaded by CCC to join BDV or to apply on de facto basis. The CCC, while was working towards BDV, a global system considered itself badly let down by the EU on whose support they had relied till then.
>
> One of the major concerns of developing countries was that the system proposed by EU, which required customs to accept transaction value declared by the importers, would not enable them to deal with the practice resorted by traders of under valuation of goods and with other customs related malpractices. They therefore wanted a certain degree of flexibility in the rules to enable their customs authorities to reject transaction value when they has [sic] reasons to doubt its truth or accuracy.
>
> This EU and USA refused to concede once they were able to secure support to the basic ideas in the proposal from the other developed countries. In the Tokyo Round the only concession which developing countries were able to achieve, despite the arduous efforts made by them was the acceptance that a developing country acceding to the Agreement could delay its implementation by five years.

A comparison of the EEC proposal and the final version of what we know as the main text of the Valuation Agreement 1979[80] reveals that there is a natural progression, but the basic contours of the final version were already present in November 1978. What has been overlooked in commentaries to this point is that the US had made a proposal of its own in 1973. It has been noted that the US Tariff Commission had recommended to the Senate that the US should adopt an international customs valuation system.[81] The obvious effect would be to create momentum for adoption of such a system. What has been missing, however, is that the Tariff Commission had

80. GATT, Multilateral Trade Negotiations Group, "Non-Tariff Measures," Sub-Group "Customs Matters," Customs Valuation Agreement on Implementation of Article VII of the General Agreement on Tariffs and Trade, MTN/NTM/W/229/ Rev.1 (9 April 1979).
81. Winham, 109.

actually advanced a draft of its own.[82] A comparison of that 1973 draft shows that there is no daylight between its abbreviated outline expression of the methodology hierarchy and the later, more fully developed expressions of the Valuation Agreement.

[A] Developing Countries Push the Protocol

We come next to a juncture where the lack of record evidence is especially frustrating. We have seen that the developing countries were disappointed in their effort to have the BDV accepted as the basis for the new valuation system. They were surely frustrated in influencing the direction of the project as it progressed in another direction. We find that in the closing days—literally—of the negotiations in 1979, the developing countries seem to have accepted that there would be a draft put forward by the developed countries. In fact, that was promulgated by the Secretariat on March 26.[83] The very next day, March 27, the developing countries' suggestions—amendments and insertions into the basic draft and not a separate, new draft—were published by the Secretariat.[84] While we have no evidence of the discussions, no transcripts or background notes, their motivation was manifest:

> This document is circulated at the request of several developing countries which feel that there would be serious prejudice to the interests of such countries unless the Agreement on Customs Valuation that may be finally adopted contains special provisions to meet the trade, financial and development needs of such countries.

The proposal contained a number of provisions, and were sufficiently unique that there was no meeting of the minds, no possibility of reconciling these suggestions with the extant draft in the time left available. In releasing the various negotiated agreements for review and signatures, the GATT Secretariat included both the separate drafts in a Proces-Verbal,[85] evidently with the hope that both of them might be submitted to the authorities in the home countries of all of the delegates. One may surmise that the hope was that developing countries might yet be persuaded to adhere to the draft if enough of their goals were met.

In the event, some of those suggested changes were agreed to,[86] but not in a form that worked organic changes to the Valuation Agreement itself. Instead, the agreed

82. Tariff Commission Report, 4-16.
83. This was GATT, MTN/NTM/W/229 (26 March 1979).
84. GATT, Multilateral Trade Negotiations Group, "Non-Tariff Measures," Sub-Group "Customs Matters," MTN/NTM/W/222/Rev.1 (27 March 1979). The proposals had been originally introduced in another format in GATT, Multilateral Trade Negotiations Group, "Non-Tariff Measures," Sub-Group "Customs Matters," Customs Valuation (28 February 1979).
85. GATT, Multilateral Trade Negotiations Trade Negotiations Committee Proces-Verbal, MTN/28 (11 April 1979). The Sub-Group had met on April 3 and the notes reveal the impasse. *See* Trade Negotiations Committee—Proceedings of the Session-Held in the International Labour Office, Geneva, 11 and 12 April 1979, GATT, MTN/P/5 (9 July 1979), 13-15.
86. The developing countries had wanted the declared price to be tested by comparison to test values, as provided for in Article 1, paragraphs 2(b) and (c), in all instances and not restricted to related party transactions. Obviously that cuckoo maneuver would have effectively reestablished a notional value system. The developing countries also wanted a ten-year transition period.

changes were embodied in a separate "Protocol" in the nature of an addendum, really, which was formally promulgated by the GATT in October 1979.[87] The Secretariat introduced the[88] Protocol:

> This document is circulated at the request of a number of delegations.
>
> * * *
>
> Consultations have recently been held between delegations from developed countries and developing countries in order to arrive at a single text of an Agreement on Implementation of Article VII of the General Agreement on Tariffs and Trade. As a result of these consultations the attached Protocol has been drawn up. It is the intention of these delegations to seek the approval of their respective authorities to sign this Protocol so as to ensure that the Agreement is applied together with the Protocol.

Here we are left puzzled and wishing for some traces of those consultations between the developed and developing countries which must have marked the seven months since the developing countries' proposal had been submitted. That is because the Protocol contains eight paragraphs—many fewer than had been in their work product—five of which called for a relaxation of the burden on developing countries in having the Valuation Agreement come into force. Those would have been expected. The other three were of general application. The Protocol in paragraph 1 deleted the provision of Article 1.2 (b) (iv)[89] which provided another acceptable "test value" proof for otherwise identical goods produced in another country—that may or may not have been at the instance of the developing countries. Paragraph 7 supplied what is clearly a gloss on Article 17, which addresses the customs authority's empowerment to satisfy itself as to the truth or accuracy of the statements or documents before them. That, too, may have been at the urging of the developing countries, as it is consistent with earlier statements of concern and of a desire for just such cooperation.[90] Paragraph 8 of the Protocol was of general application, too, and it discusses the PAPP. Much more on that paragraph follows below.

In fact, the Protocol was introduced several months after the Valuation Agreement had been implemented and passed into law in the US. As it came to pass, the US

87. The idea of a separate protocol with flexible standards for accession by developing countries was first proposed by Brazil in July 1978. GATT, Multilateral Trade Negotiations Group, "Non-Tariff Measures," Sub-Group "Customs Matters," Customs Valuation, MTN/NTM/W/167 (7 July 1978).
88. GATT, Multilateral Trade Negotiations Group, "Non-Tariff Measures," Sub-Group "Customs Matters," Customs Valuation Agreement on Implementation of Article VII of the General Agreement on Tariffs and Trade Addendum, MTN/NTM/W/229 Rev.1/Add. 1 (22 October 1979).
89. That text had stated: "(iv) the transaction value in sales to unrelated buyers for export to the same country of importation of goods which would be identical to the imported goods except for having a different country of production provided that the sellers in any two transactions being compared are not related."
90. The March 27 alternative proposal had included a specific provision calling for such assistance: "Developed countries party to this Agreement (referred to in this Agreement as 'developed parties') shall furnish, on mutually agreed terms, technical assistance to developing parties that so request ... ."

later acceded to the Protocol, but only some months later.[91] That December 1980 implementation did delete the subsection that was contained in Article 1.2 (b) (iv),[92] but it did not otherwise work any change to its implementation of the Valuation Agreement in any way. In other words, it did not incorporate either paragraph 7 or 8 of the Protocol. Unlike many of its major trading partners, that 1980 statutory deletion marks the last time that the US amended its customs valuation law. A survey of the US customs regulations on customs valuation,[93] which was promulgated in 1981, after the accession to the Protocol, reveals no text that can be traced to paragraph 7 or 8.

One interesting feature of the US accession to the Protocol was the time of the effective date for the amendment. The latest of the following dates was to serve as the effective date: date on which the amendment was made by statute (December 2, 1980); date on which the Protocol was accepted by the President for the US (December 30, 1980); in line with the bilateral discussion that characterizes much of the Tokyo Round, the date on which the Protocol was implemented by the EEC. The EEC had implemented the Valuation Agreement in May 1980,[94] but that effort had not extended to the Protocol.

Canada had a delayed implementation of the Valuation Agreement. It was not until 1985 that the Customs Act entered into force.

The reason why this line of inquiry into the Protocol is of importance to us today is that the Protocol appears, after the removal of paragraph 1, as not necessary due to the text of Article 1.2(b)(iv) being deleted from the Valuation Agreement 1994, identical in every respect to Annex III to the Valuation Agreement 1994. With its status as an Annex, per Article 14 of the Valuation Agreement 1994, its renumbered text, paragraphs 1-7, the Protocol survives as an integral element of the Valuation Agreement 1994. Paragraph 7 of Annex III finally made an appearance in the EU UCC Implementing Act in Article 129.1.

What would be interesting is to survey how many other Members of the WTO have directly embedded the text of the Annex III, paragraph 7 provision in their national legislation.

We shall *see* below how Annex III, paragraph 7—paragraph 8 of the original Protocol—raises important questions today. Those questions must be addressed without the benefit of any record evidence of discussion among the Tokyo Round parties about the October 1979 text and to that earlier March 1979 developing countries' proposal. It is small comfort that there may be private correspondence or notes of the individual negotiators, most of whom have long retired or are deceased after the passage of nearly fifty years. Then, too, there may be documentation tucked away in the drafty passages of national archives. If there is, it has not yet surfaced. A

91. Act of December 2, 1980, Pub. L. 96-490, § 2, 94 Stat. 2556.
92. This had been codified at 19 USC § 1401a(b)(2)(B)(iii). Note: the US statute combines the references to the test values for deductive and computed values.
93. 19 CFR §§ 152.100-108, T.D. 81-7, 46 Fed. Reg. 2600 (January 12, 1981). The customs regulations are based upon and faithful to the various Interpretative Notes that comprise Annex I of the Valuation Agreement.
94. Council Regulation (EEC) No. 1224/80 of 28 May 1980 on the valuation of goods for customs purposes, OJ L 134, 31.5.1980.

review of the literature will show that no earlier commentaries have focused on the profound implications of paragraph 8 of the Protocol. That is a shame because those commentaries would have been decades closer to the events, and a pursuit of information might have been fruitful since the documentary or anecdotal evidence may have been more accessible.

Flushed with the success represented by the adoption of the Valuation Agreement, the stage was set for further developments in the Uruguay Round.

§1.04 URUGUAY ROUND (1986-1994)

The Uruguay Round did not effect many significant changes to the 1979 Valuation Agreement, with one exception. With the advent of a separate Dispute Settlement Agreement, there was no longer any need for the ad hoc panels to be established by the WTO's Committee on Customs Valuation Committee (CCV) within the dispute settlement apparatus that had been prescribed by Annex III of the earlier agreement. Accordingly, that Annex was eliminated.

[A] Developing Countries' Challenges

The negotiating history of the Uruguay Round is quickly told, and in one respect, it proved to be a sequel to the Tokyo Round. The GATT Secretariat was still eager to increase participation among the developing countries. The "single undertaking" and its required accession to the Valuation Agreement was one way to accomplish that.

The CCC did its part, criticizing the BDV in a pamphlet, in the hope of convincing those countries which continued to follow the BDV to adopt the Agreement. That critique was summarized:

- the BDV is too simplistic and leaves too much to the discretion of the administration—leading to arbitrariness and uncertainty;
- the BDV is imprecise, creating a lack of uniformity—particularly evident in related party transactions;
- the BDV was drawn up in 1950 on the basis of a much-changed trade environment, with many more related person transactions now;
- the BDV has not achieved the objective of worldwide uniformity;
- the procedure for amending the BDV is too inflexible;
- the system for making adjustments is vague and is dealt with in the Explanatory Notes which have no binding effect;
- the system is artificial, based on a purely theoretical level, isolated from commercial reality.[95]

For those developing countries that did adopt the Agreement, many of them pushed for retaining—or imparting—the same or a similar degree of BDV's "flexibility"

95. Customs Co-Operation Council, a Single International Valuation System (1992).

in customs valuation under the Agreement. Another way of expressing this point is that developing countries advocated for the authority to disregard the declared PAPP and go, instead, to an external source. As justification, the developing countries once again called attention to their special circumstances. The Valuation Agreement in Article 1 paragraph 2 (a) (in the case of related party transactions) and generally in Article 17 and paragraph 7 of the Protocol recognized the authority of the customs authority to satisfy itself that the entry documentation was truthful and accurate. An Advisory Opinion adopted by the TCCV was relevant to that issue.[96]

The burden of proof in a potential fraud case was a pressing issue, and one raised by India in 1987.[97] At the CCV meeting in May 1988, India returned to the task, taking the position that amendments to Article 17 and paragraph 7 of the Protocol:

> did not provide an adequate basis for customs authorities to satisfy themselves as to the truth or accuracy of any statement, document or declaration in the specific circumstances cited in the proposal. If the burden of proof were shifted from customs administrations to importers, under specific circumstances, the importer would be responsible for establishing that the declared value represented bona fide transactions.[98]

The EC, the US, New Zealand and Japan rejoined that there was no need for any amendment. The US even noted that Article 17 was included in the Valuation Agreement at India's suggestion. In my view, I am hard pressed to imagine that the burden would never be on the importer to establish the bona fides of the declared customs value. If there is national legislation to the contrary, we would be dealing with a customs valuation regime which creates a rebuttable presumption that the importer's declared value is correct.

The burden of proof issue came to be addressed in CCV Decision 6.1.[99] Two other nagging issues for developing countries were: (i) minimum values and (ii) the valuation of importations into their countries by sole agents, sole distributors and sole concessionaires, which were the twin subjects of the future CCV Decision 7.1. These were first raised as suitable topics for a CCV Decision at the same time—October

96. TCCV, AO 19.1, Application of Article 17 of the Agreement and paragraph 6 of Annex III [originally, paragraph 7 of the Protocol] (March 1988).
97. For an interim report of those discussions, *see* GATT, Group of Negotiations on Goods, Negotiating Group on MTN Agreements and Arrangements Agreement on Implementation of Article VII of the General Agreement on Tariffs and Trade (Customs Valuation Code) Aspects of the Code Proposed for Negotiation Note by the Secretariat, GATT, MTN.GNG/NG8/W/19 (2 December 1987).
98. GATT, Committee on Customs Valuation Minutes of the Meeting of 3 May 1988, VAL/M/22 (28 July 1988), 9-11, 10.
99. Dec. 6.1, Decision Regarding Cases Where Customs Administrations Have Reasons To Doubt The Truth Or Accuracy of the Declared Value, was first proposed in October 1990. GATT, Group of Negotiations on Goods (GATT) Negotiating Group on MTN Agreements and Arrangements Agreement on Implementation of Article VII (Customs Valuation Code), MTN.GNG/NG8/W/8 3/Add.4/Rev.1 (23 October 1990). It is maintained in the TCCV compendium as Committee on Customs Valuation Decisions, Dec. 6.1. This decision was formally adopted as a Marrakesh Ministerial Decision, WTO, Committee on Customs Valuation, G/VAL/1 (27 April 1995).

1990.[100] We will dilate on this topic below when we evaluate the terms of the Valuation Agreement, but it is useful to touch lightly on the approach sought by developing countries.

For that second subject, you will have noted that parties within one of these business relationships would be "persons who are associated in business" which we have seen is a concept in the BDV. Article 15.5 not only specifically refers to them but also cautions that these persons who are associated in business who are sole agents, sole distributors and sole concessionaires are not related persons, as defined in Article 15.4, "unless they fall within the criteria of paragraph 4 [i.e., Article 15.4]." India had sought to delete the just-quoted proviso[101] The effect of that change would have made sole agents, sole distributors and sole concessionaires *ipso facto* related persons.

The subcategory of Article 15.4 that would most often be relevant for an inquiry involving these sole or exclusive business relationships would be subsection (e), which speaks of "control." Importantly, Note to Article 15 paragraph 4 (e) places a limiting interpretation: "... one person shall be deemed to control another when the former is legally or operationally in a position to exercise or direction over the latter." More precise guidance was offered by the TCCV in 1985 when it adopted an instrument that held that control that was cognizable under Article 15.4 (e) was that which was marked by a person being in "... a position to exercise restraint or direction in respect of essential aspects relating to the management activities of the other person."[102]

With CCV Dec. 7.1, which took effect in April 1995, the CCV recommended that the TCCV should formulate and conduct studies on the issue. This led to the issuance of TCCV's Case Study 9.1 in record time.[103]

Note that, very early in its tenure, the Tokyo Round TCCV had issued two instruments that were also relevant to this general issue of fraud.[104] As an Annex to its Report to the CCV of its 10th Session (October 1985), the TCCV issued a Report on the effects of false invoicing on customs valuation.[105] Clearly, taken altogether, the CCV and the TCCV were not at all dismissive; on the contrary, those bodies were—and later developments show that they continue to be—attentive to the developing countries' needs.

Those needs arose from the circumstance that these countries were more reliant on the collection of duty and border taxes than the developed countries for their

100. *Ibid.* It is maintained in the TCCV compendium as Committee on Customs Valuation Decisions, Dec. 7.1. This decision was formally adopted as a Marrakesh Ministerial Decision, WTO, Committee on Customs Valuation, G/VAL/1 (27 April 1995).
101. GATT, Multilateral Trade Negotiations Group, "Non-Tariff Measures," Sub-Group "Customs Matters," Customs Valuation, Comments by Delegation of India, MTN/NTM/W/218 (9 February 1979).
102. TCCV, EN 4.1, Consideration of Relationship Under Article 15.5, Read in Conjunction with Article 15.4 (October 1985).
103. TCCV, CS 9.1, Sole Agents, Sole Distributors and Sole Concessionaires (October 1995).
104. These are Advisory Opinions 2.1 Acceptability of a Price Below Prevailing Market Prices (October 1981) and 10.1 Treatment of Fraudulent Documents (September 1983).
105. *See* GATT, Report by the Technical Committee on Customs Valuation Concerning the Effects of False Invoicing on Customs Valuation, VAL/W/32 (7 November 1985).

revenues, and they were plagued by under-invoicing.[106] The international trade community responded, with the WTO's CCV commissioning a TCCV study in 1985.[107] Parenthetically, in very recent presentations at the TCCV, some developing countries, especially in Africa, point to astonishing levels of "informal trade" of 70% and more.[108] It is impossible not to be sympathetic to their plight.

One of the enduring challenges facing developing countries has been a lack of technical expertise, with obvious repercussions for the drafting of informed policy prescriptions and for staffing. Having attended dozens of TCCV sessions over the years, I can personally attest to the pleas of some delegations for greater assistance from developed countries. You will find specific commitments to provide such assistance in Article 20 of the Valuation Agreement. One often-repeated request by developing countries has been access to developed country databases of their exports, such as the EU's Eurostat database of prices declared at export. This would allow the developing country to compare the prices declared at import. National security is another motivation for the sharing of information between the country of export and the country of import. In these latter cases it is normally the developed country which is seeking the information.

The dedication to providing technical assistance and capacity building by the WCO and some of its more active members such as the US, Canada, Japan and the EU is apparent from reports from the CCV and the TCCV. One development that bears special notice is the Revenue Package, fashioned by the WCO to assist developing countries in coping with the effects of falling revenues stemming from the global financial crisis in 2008-2009 and the lowering of duty rates pursuant to the WTO MTNs.[109] The late Ian Cremer, sorely missed by all of his many friends in the WCO community, played a key role in the WCO Secretariat's development of the Revenue

106. To be clear, some countries were harmed by over-invoicing, usually associated with efforts to avoid exchange control or capital flow restrictions. This was a particular concern of Brazil, which had raised the issue as early as 1978, when it sought the inclusion of a provision in the Preamble of the EC draft then under consideration: "Recognizing that valuation procedures should protect parties to this Code against illicit transfer of currency arising from the over-declaration of the value of imported goods." GATT, Multilateral Trade Negotiations Group, "Non-Tariff Measures," Sub-Group "Customs Matters," Customs Valuation Brazil, MTN/NTM/W/167 (7 July 1978).

107. *See*, e.g., GATT, Committee on Customs Valuation Report by the Technical Committee on Customs Valuation Concerning the Effects of False Invoicing on Customs Valuation, VAL/W/32 (7 November 1985).

108. Informal trade has been defined in many ways, including the term "shadow economy," but it is largely synonymous with what I would term a "smuggling rich" environment. For an informative WCO Study, *see* WCO Research Paper No. 22, Informal Trade Practices (May 2012) available at http://www.wcoomd.org/-/media/wco/public/global/pdf/topics/research/research-paper-series/cantens_informal_trade_en.pdf?la=en.

For a 2018 WCO Study, published as part of its Revenue Package offering, *see* Developing Policies with respect to Informal Trade, available at https://www.wcoesarocb.org/wp-content/uploads/2018/07/Developing-policies-with-respect-to-informal-trade-FINAL-EN.pdf.

109. For more information, consult the WCO website http://www.wcoomd.org/en/topics/key-issues/revenue-package.aspx.

Package as well as in the WCO's formidable technical assistance efforts more generally. RIP Ian.

Another solution for developing countries in the period after the closing of Tokyo Round, and before the Uruguay Round came to a close, was the reliance on private sector companies to conduct pre-shipment inspections (PSIs) by many developing countries which lacked an internal capacity.[110] The US had shared its criticism of the abuses that arose from the use of PSI programs.[111] Leaving aside a role in phytosanitary, safety, quantity and quality enforcement, we might see the program as an interim or stopgap measure, really, one that might suffice until the local customs authority developed sufficient expertise and "band width" to discharge its mission responsibilities for customs valuation. In fact, many developing countries' customs officials came to resent the use of PSI companies, one reason being that the contracting fostered corruption. There was a time in the 2012-2017 time period where PSIs came up for criticism at every session of the TCCV, but there have been no interventions raised since then. Even then, one had the sense that the use or popularity of PSIs had been steadily declining.

Still another development has seen developing countries turning to the ASYVAL customs valuation module, a 2011 outgrowth of the United Nations Conference on Trade and Development (UNCTAD) Automated Systems for Customs Data (ASYCUDA) program. This is touted as an alternative to the reliance on PSIs,[112] but I see it as simply a reliance on just another PSI enterprise under another name.

This reliance speaks to a lack of internal capability and a resort to an outsourcing of this important function. I count myself among those who question the benefits of this exercise amid worries about the misuse of customs valuation databases, discussed at some length below.

Just before the lights went out, at its last meeting on October 24, 1995, the WTO's CCV adopted the decision to terminate the Tokyo Round Agreement on Customs Valuation with effect from January 1, 1996.[113]

---

110. Indeed, one of the 1994 Uruguay Round agreements was a separate Agreement on Preshipment Inspection. In addition to quantity and quality inspections, paragraph 20 specifically provided for price verifications to prevent over- and under-invoicing and fraud.
111. GATT, Committee on Customs Valuation, Experiences with Preshipment Inspection, Communication from the United States, VAL/W/43 (11 May 1987). *See also*, e.g., GATT, Committee on Customs Valuation Minutes of the Meeting Held on 30 April 1986, VAL/M/17 (19 June 1986), 8-9 and GATT, Committee on Customs Valuation Private Companies Engaged in Customs Valuation "Conclusions and proposals" submitted to the ECE Working Party on Facilitation of International Trade Procedures, VAL/M/41 (12 January 1987).
112. UNCTAD reported that the WCO and the WTO Agreement on Trade Facilitation advise against the use of PSI as it increases burden and costs in international trade and can be counterproductive for the country of importation and for its traders. UNCTAD, Compendium 2019 Case Studies ASYCUDA, at 54.
113. GATT, Tokyo Round Committee on Customs Valuation Minutes of the Meeting of 24 October 1995, VAL/M/36 (31 December 1995).

CHAPTER 2
Overview of Valuation Agreement 1994

§2.01 VALUATION AGREEMENT 1994

[A] Summary Outline

A brief annotated index of the major load-bearing elements of the Valuation Agreement from 30,000 feet, or 10,000 meters if you will, may help keep things in perspective.

General Introductory Commentary—a short summary of the Agreement and an important interpretative tool.[1] I draw your attention to the confusing text referring to the PAPP, TV and Article 8. We will discuss this later in connection with Article 8:

> Article 1 is to be read together with Article 8 which provides, inter alia, for adjustments to the Price actually paid or payable in cases where certain specific elements which are considered to form a part of the value for customs purposes are incurred by the buyer but are not included in the price actually paid or payable for the imported goods. Article 8 *also* provides for the inclusion in the transaction value of certain considerations which may pass from the buyer to the seller in the form of specified goods or services rather than in the form of money (emphasis added).

Preamble—statement of guiding principles, consistent with the *ad referendum* principles which were a guiding constellation for the Tokyo Round negotiators. The first principles are uniformity and certainty; fair, uniform and neutral system; prohibition on arbitrary or fictitious customs values; simple and equitable criteria consistent with commercial practices; valuation should not be used to combat dumping.

Articles 1-8—the heart of the Agreement. The valuation methods are arranged in the strict hierarchical order which importers and customs authorities must follow.

1. E.g., the TCCV made repeated citations to this Commentary in its Com. 22.1, Meaning of the Expression "Sold for Export to the Country of Importation" In a Series of Sales (April 2007). The Commentary also appeared in Com. 14.1, Application of Article 1, paragraph 2 (November 1989).

Article 1 TV—based on the PAPP, should be the basis for appraisement unless it is disqualified on specified bases, including: (i) restrictions on the buyer's disposition or use of the imported goods, or (ii) there are conditions or consideration for which a value cannot be determined, (iii) there are proceeds from the subsequent sale or use that cannot be valued, and (iv) the price in a related party transaction has been influenced by the relationship.

Article 2 TV of identical merchandise.

Article 3 TV of similar merchandise.

Article 4 If necessary to proceed past this point, the importer can opt to apply Article 6 first (note that Annex III, paragraph 3 allows developing countries to make a reservation against this order reversal).

Article 5 Deductive Value based on deducting certain elements (profit or commission, expenses) from the first arm's-length price of a resale within ninety days of importation.

Article 6 Computed Value based on the sum of costs of input materials, production and amounts for usual profit and general expenses and, in CIF countries, international transport and insurance costs.

Article 7 Value when other values cannot be determined using any of the previous methods (often referred to as the "fallback method")—a flexible or modified application of one of the previous Articles; certain methods are prohibited (e.g., price is sales for export to third countries, minimum values, arbitrary or fictitious value).

Article 8 Additions to the PAPP for missing elements of consideration. Article 8.1 lists container and packing costs, dutiable assists, RLFs, value of any proceeds of subsequent resale, disposal or use accruing to the benefit of the seller. Article 8.2 notes that countries can decide whether to include or not the costs of international transportation and insurance in determining customs value. Article 8.3 notes that these additions and no others can be added to the PAPP.

Article 15 Definitions of key terms (except for the PAPP; *see* Article 1, Interpretative Notes, Annex III, paragraph 7).

Annex I—Interpretative Notes.

Annex II—TCCV function, formation, rules of governance.

Annex III—Special rules for developing countries (paragraphs 1-5), clarifying or "amplifying" commentaries on Article 17 inquiries by customs authorities and on the PAPP (paragraphs 6 and 7, respectively).

[B] Strict Hierarchy

As noted in the Outline, the Valuation Agreement ordains that the importer and the customs authority must follow its strict hierarchy of appraisement methodologies. This is set forth in the rubric for each of the methods following Article 1. The text for several of the later methods begins, "If the customs value of the imported goods cannot be determined under the provisions of [the immediately preceding] Article ... ." The sequential ordering is made explicit in the Interpretative Note, General Note, paragraphs 1 and 2.[2]

The importer and the customs authority alike must rigorously follow this sequential ordering and may not proceed to a later basis of appraisement unless an earlier listed method is unavailable.[3]

You may consider the case of an importer into the US who sought to have the entry appraised on the basis of deductive value. The importer was rebuffed because there was no showing that transaction value was not available.[4]

For an example of a CBP ruling that illustrates the hierarchy at work, we have a 2013 ruling that does very nicely for us. Goods imported under four different scenarios were to be appraised through four different methodologies: purchased goods under transaction value; consignment and reimported goods resold within ninety days under deductive value; goods resold more than ninety days under a fallback method comprised of a modified deductive value and goods not resold appraised under a fallback method represented by insurance value.[5]

In the US, the general statutory authority of CBP to appraise merchandise is set forth in section 500 of the Tariff Act of 1930.[6] CBP Headquarters has made it quite clear that customs officials must follow the statutory scheme laid out by Congress, i.e., the strict hierarchy, noting that:

> Section 500 [19 U.S.C. § 1500] is the general authority for Customs to appraise merchandise. It is not a separate basis of valuation and cannot be used as such. Section 500 allows Customs to consider the best evidence available in appraising merchandise. ... Section 500 authorizes the appraising officer to weigh the nature of the evidence before him in appraising the imported merchandise. ... As broad as this grant of authority may be, it is clear, under authority of judicial decisions, that it does not give the appraising officer authority to do whatever he wants. He must and will appraise merchandise under the constraints of section 402 [19 USC § 1401a].[7]

2. In the US, this is laid out in 19 USC § 1401a(a)(2), 19 CFR § 152.101(b). In the US, the convention is to refer to the non-TV methods as "alternative methods." In Canada, the operative text is in subsections 47(1) and 47(2) [with the later methods designated as "subsidiary methods"]. In the UCC, the EU provides for this ordering in Article 74 [you will note that the EU labels these later methods as "secondary methods"].
3. 19 USC § 1401a(a); E.g., *VWP of America, Inc. v. United States*, 175 F.3d 1327, 1331 (Fed. Cir. 1999). *See also* ruling nos. 547978 (December 1, 2001), 44409 (November 20, 1989) and 543581 (September 3, 1985).
4. *Macclenny Products v. United States*, 963 F. Supp 2d 1348 (CIT 2014). *See also Midwest-CBK, LLC v. United States*, Slip Op. 22- (CIT 2022), discussed below in the sale for export context.
5. Ruling no. H233019 (November 14, 2013).
6. 19 USC § 1500.
7. Statement of Administrative Action, cited in ruling no. H019263 (November 8, 2010) (port officials admonished by Headquarters).

CHAPTER 3

Transaction Value as the Preferred Method: Questions Raised and Answered

§3.01 TRANSACTION VALUE

The preferred methodology under the customs valuation statutes is TV. As defined by the statute, TV is:

> the price actually paid or payable for the imported merchandise when sold for exportation to the country of importation.[1]

As should be clear by now, the customs valuation standard first ushered in by the Valuation Agreement in 1979 was a radical departure from the previous rules which could be frustrating in the extreme. The frustration with the previous statutory regime in the US is evident in the following excerpt from an opinion of the reviewing trial court in a 1971 decision, a frustration that would have been shared by all who had been forced to toil in the vineyard of the pre-1980 law, and would not have been limited to a US Value appraisement:

> The proceedings and record reflect the difficulty that attends the valuation of a newly developed product when it is offered for sale to all purchasers and sold at various prices, in a relatively new and commercially untested market, on United States value basis. ...[2]

In comparison with, or in outright contrast to, the BDV, the current valuation approach which is grounded in TV might be seen as a "positive system" because it is

1. *Mutatis mutandis*, US—19 USC § 1401a(b); Canada Customs Act—subsection 48(1) ("... the transaction value of the goods if the goods are sold for export to Canada to a purchaser in Canada"), *see also* Canada Memorandum D13-1-3, *Customs Valuation—Purchaser in Canada*, July 4, 2014; EU, UCC, Article 70.1.
2. *Clayton Chemical & Packaging Company v. United States*, 331 F. Supp. 312, 67 Cust. Ct. 557, 558 A.R.D. (Cust. Ct. 1971).

based on the PAPP. But, as was the case with the prior US export value method, that characterization remains correct only in relative terms. TV is not defined as being based solely upon the PAPP. Instead, that PAPP will itself be acceptable only under certain specific conditions. That is, only if the conditions of Article 1.1 are met, meaning there are no disqualifying circumstances. Further, to ascertain TV one must always take into account the possibility of adjustments made under Article 8, which would work additions to the PAPP for missing elements of consideration to make transaction value.[3]

Still, as a general statement, with the Valuation Agreement, customs valuation looks to the PAPP, the actual price paid for the imported merchandise, no matter how derived and whether discounted or otherwise, and not to a fair market value. That is a departure from the BDV's notional standard of a "normal price."

The strength of that commitment may be measured by the TCCV instrument on a PAPP that is actually below the cost of production. Case Study 12.1[4] holds that if there are no other grounds on which to invalidate the PAPP, then the fact that the PAPP is below the cost of production should not disqualify a transaction value appraisement. In a similar fashion, a price that is below prevailing market prices may be acceptable.[5]

Still, the importer is not given carte blanche to make entry with a declared value and not face the possibility that the customs authority will ask for proof because there are doubts as to the truth or accuracy of that declared value. That is the authority's prerogative under Article 17 of the Agreement.[6]

Moreover, the operating scheme still requires all related party transactions[7] to be justified on the strength of objective criteria. Put another way, the Valuation Agreement and the implementing legislation presume that the price paid by an unrelated buyer reflects market value, but that market value must still be proven in related party transactions. The benchmark standard for a related party price is that the price was not influenced by the relationship.

As a practical matter, TV must account for something on the order of 95% or more of importations. This is a very good thing for both importers and the customs authorities alike because, as will be seen, the alternative valuation methodologies can require a great degree of detailed calculation. In almost every instance, that will trigger a far more involved practical exercise than simply looking to an underlying commercial invoice issued by a seller to a buyer and, where necessary, adjusting the price thereon, pursuant to the Article 8 "statutory additions." In short, in the absence of an acceptable sale for export, life becomes immediately more complicated for all parties

3. *See* below for a discussion of "consideration."
4. TCCV, CS 12.1, Application of Article 1 of the Valuation Agreement for Goods Sold for Export at Prices Below Their Cost of Production (November 2000).
5. TCCV, AO 2.1, Acceptability of a Price Below Prevailing Market Prices for Identical Goods (October 1981). This was one of the very first TCCV instruments adopted.
6. *See* also Annex III, paragraph 6 and CVC Decision 6.1, Cases Where Customs Administrations Have Reasons to Doubt the Truth or Accuracy of Declared Value (April 1995) and TCCV, CS 13.1, Application of Decision 6.1 of the Committee on Customs Valuation (October 2001) and CS 13.2, Application of Decision 16.1 of the Committee on Customs Valuation (April 2008).
7. Or at least all those related party transactions where there are doubts about acceptability. Article 1.2(a) and accompanying Interpretative Note to Article 1.2(a).

concerned—the importer, the customs authority, the customhouse broker and other service providers.

With its emphasis upon the sale price as negotiated by the parties, the PAPP will generally equate to the invoice price for the imported goods, restated if necessary to either an FOB or CIF basis depending upon the jurisdiction.[8] As will be demonstrated below, there may be a question over the qualifying "sale for exportation" if there have been several competing sales which might serve as the basis for appraisement.[9]

The elements of the PAPP for a valid transaction value appraisement include the following:

- A bona fide sale.
- For export to the country of importation.
- Price actually paid or payable.
- To or for the benefit of the seller.
- Condition of sale.
- Adjustments (actually, additions) under Article 8 for missing consideration.

[A] A Bona Fide Sale

[1] Broad Interpretation of "Sale"

First and foremost, the Valuation Agreement does not define "sale" for export. In one of its earliest instruments, the TCCV set out the following prescription:

> in conformity with the basis intention of the Agreement that the transaction value of imported goods should be used to the greatest extent possible for Customs valuation purposes, uniformity of interpretation and application can be achieved by taking the term "sale" in the widest sense, to be determined only under the provisions of Articles 1 and 8 read together.[10]

After the TCCV made that hortative statement about using "sale" in the widest sense, Advisory Opinion 1.1 did call out certain types of transactions which are not sales. These include barter,[11] lease and consignment arrangements. In those non-sale

8. The US customs law requires that accurate invoices and supporting documentation be presented to CBP at entry. 19 USC §§ 1481(a)(5), 1484(a)(1)(A) and (B). CBP regulations and practice impose an obligation on importers to fully and accurately disclose all relevant information with the commercial invoice that forms part of the customs entry. 19 CFR §§ 141.81-92, TD 86-56 (February 20, 1986) (inconsistencies between commercial invoices and visaed invoices must be explained or reconciled or entry will not be accepted). Note that TD 86-56 has been broadly applied to refer to other faulty or inconsistent documents. *See* ruling no. 547697 (December 27, 2001). The reference "TD" applies to CBP Treasury Decisions.
9. *See* discussions below on foreign middleman sales in §3.01[D][1] (First Sale) and §3.01[I][2] (Agency).
10. TCCV, AO 1.1, The Concept of "Sale" in the Agreement (October 1981, additional example inserted March 1982). Canada explicitly follows this approach in one of its D Memos. Customs Memorandum D13-4-2, *Customs Valuation: Goods Sold for Export to Canada*, November 21, 2013, paragraph 3.
11. One of the earliest TCCV instruments was on barter. TCCV, AO 6.1, Treatment of Barter or Compensation Deals Under the Agreement (March 1982). You should note that this instrument

cases, an alternative method must be found. At least in the US, many of these importation scenarios give rise to an Article 7 "fallback" customs valuation, 19 USC § 1401a(f), depending on the availability of information.[12]

An expansive definition of a "sale for export" was plainly the rationale in a 2012 CBP ruling, which was modified by CBP shortly after publication, concerning previously imported consumer products being reimported into the US by the original seller after their foreign internet or catalogue purchasers had returned them to the seller. The seller was unable to claim duty-free entry because the returned goods, which had originally entered the US on a duty-free basis under the US/Colombia Free Trade Agreement, were not eligible for the duty-free benefits of item no. 9801.00.26, Harmonized Tariff Schedule of the United States (HTSUS).[13] CBP took the view that the product returns from the customers to the company constituted sales, insofar as they fall within the risk assumption, title passage and valuable consideration analyses.[14] In the original ruling, CBP looked to an intermediate California appellate court's decision which interpreted that state's version of the Uniform Commercial Code (UCC)—a comprehensive set of laws governing commercial transactions in the US, uniformly adopted by the fifty individual states and not to be confused with the Union Customs Code—on the issue whether a catalogue sale was a "sale on approval" as a means of discrediting an earlier CBP ruling dating to 1999 which had relied on UCC analysis.[15] In

notes that pure barter deals are rare, most transactions being based on value being expressed in monetary terms, such as a price expressed on the basis of current world market prices, although a financial settlement may not be made. Only if there is no ability to assign a meaningful value that may be expressed in the currency required for customs clearance should transaction value be excluded. This would mean that a sale transaction with consideration in the form of a certain number of publicly traded shares, a given quantity of metals or other tangible articles traded on a public exchange, or a payment in units of cryptocurrency should support a transaction value appraisement. All of those situations will allow for those nonmonetary quantities to be assigned a value in US dollars or other reserve currency, which value can then be translated to the local currency of the country of importation, if needed.

12. *See*, e.g., ruling nos. H230778 (September 23, 2021) (the merchandise [leased machinery] should be appraised under the fallback method using a modified transaction value based on the option to purchase in the rental agreement) and H303695 (September 12, 2019) (it is acceptable to use the AMS [marketing service] pricing data as the basis of appraisement for the imported consigned fresh tomatoes. If the AMS [published price list] prices are used to appraise the imported fresh tomatoes, then no deductions will be permitted from the reported AMS prices. However, if information on an actual sale at the first commercial level after importation is available, then the fresh tomatoes should be appraised using deductive value); H307779 (March 24, 2020) (computed value method).
13. This is one of the "US Goods Returned" provisions which are provided for in Chapter 98, HTSUS. *See* discussion below in §3.01[A][2].
14. Ruling no. H231895 (September. 4, 2012) (a product return of a good that was originally entered into the US on a duty-free basis was treated as a sale back to the US seller) modifying ruling no. H218759 (July 9, 2012) (both catalogue and internet sales).
15. Ruling no. 546941 (August 11, 1999). Aside from the fact that the UCC, which has limited or tangential applicability to international sales, may not have controlled either the initial sale or the return in the case of the ruling, there was no showing that the state whose governing law controlled the transactions has ever adopted the ruling by this California appellate court, which might indeed be limited to its own particular facts. There was certainly no discussion of any of these points by CBP. Another point that is worth exploring in any extensive analysis is whether these internet or catalogue sales were of another type of conditional sale altogether—a "sale or return" [a "sale or return" is a type of contract under which a buyer purchases the goods but has

the later modifying ruling, CBP backed away and sidestepped the UCC question by stating opaquely that "... information has been provided with regard to the transfer of title, recognition of revenue, and the burden of shipping costs. It is therefore not necessary to resort [to] the U.C.C. to determine when title passes, and the transactions at issue are not 'sales on approval'."

We would have welcomed a more robust discussion on the merits. Instead, at least until this issue is more properly briefed and perhaps finds its way to judicial review by the CIT, the import community is left with a CBP rule that advances the notion that in some circumstances, products purchased over the internet or in response to catalogue offers and being returned by consumers for exchange or credit are being sold by those individual customers back to the company.[16]

Another excellent example of this broad interpretation is found in the US and EU regimes for assembled or processed merchandise.

[2] Assembled or Outward Processed Merchandise

The US customs regulations explicitly recognize that a TV analysis may apply to imported goods which had been assembled abroad.[17] In such a case, the definition of the PAPP can represent an amount paid for the assembly of goods even if the "seller" has no interest other than as an assembler (a "toll manufacturer," a term familiar to international tax advisers).[18]

In practice, the customs valuation for assembled merchandise is extended well beyond assembly only. Other business practices that will be familiar to apparel importers are the "cut make and trim" (CMT) or "cut make and sew" (CMS) operations in which a party is engaged to perform those enumerated functions, usually with the fabric, accessories and findings supplied to that party or, where the processor purchases some or all of those materials, from an approved list of suppliers.[19] In those latter cases, the order will be for the producer to use the materials and to be reimbursed for those purchases, with the assembly or production charge to be separately billed.

---

a conditional right to return the goods within a specified time period. Depending on the jurisdiction, this may not be limited to sales intended for resale]—and not a "sale on approval" at all. This point, too, was not discussed in the ruling. Beyond that, while CBP took a bit of time to explain why it was departing from the 1999 ruling, the ruling did not explain why a 2003 ruling (ruling no. 548211, July 2, 2003) that held that product returns were not eligible for transaction value appraisement was not applicable. I am mindful that there might be a legal distinction under sales law principles between product returns shipped for exchange or credit viz. returns for repair or replacement, but again these distinctions were not parsed.

16. Perhaps the central feature of ruling no. H231895 is the following, "... upon receipt of the returned goods, the company credits the full purchase price to the customer's credit card. This is a transfer of title for consideration, and thus a sale."
17. 19 CFR § 152.103(a)(3).
18. A "toll manufacturer" is distinguished from a "contract manufacturer" by reason of the former having been supplied with the raw materials or parts by its customer.
19. *See*, e.g., ruling no. 545550 (September 13, 1995). For an example of CMT in a First Sale for Export context, *see* ruling no. H086776 (October 25, 2011).

Still another variant seen in the US, with special application to assembly undertaken in Mexico, is the "shelter operation" by which assembly work is performed in Mexico on behalf of US companies.[20]

The "price" in all of these cases will represent the aggregate of the value of any raw materials or parts provided for free, which are dutiable assists as defined below, and an amount representing the assembly or production charges.[21] This protocol was demonstrated in the US in a 1986 ruling, in which a US importer had purchased oil well tubing from a Japanese company and sent it to Canada for a plastic coating process.[22] The transaction value applied to the importation was represented by the processing charges paid to the Canadian company plus the value of the tubing which had been furnished without charge to the Canadian processor. The latter costs were in the nature of a dutiable assist.

In the case of the EU, we find a similar result accorded to "processed" merchandise. Buried in a Commentary from the 2022 Compendium on licence fees and outward processing relief,[23] we find that the parties had engaged in a production contract whereby the buyer/importer had supplied the foreign processor with the materials to make the finished product. In US parlance, this is "toll packing." The EU Commission cited the 2013 European Court of Justice (ECJ) decision in *Christodoulou*[24] for the proposition that:

> The term "sale" for the purposes of the usage of this method should be interpreted broadly. The Court ruled that it applies to "the determination of the customs value of goods imported on the basis of a contract which, although described as a contract of sale, in fact proves to be a working or processing contract."

The Commission advised that this treatment is irrespective of the use or not of the outward processing procedure to export goods and import products processed from those goods. As a result, we may conclude that the same results might be expected for imports of articles as a result of what the Commission termed as a "processing" or "production" contract as imports into the US under its broad term, an "assembly" contract.

The TCCV was called to action in an early instrument which dealt with such questions as the treatment of imported goods that had been exported for repair.[25] The TCCV observed that in the latter case, at first glance, it would appear that what was being contracted for was a supply of services. TCCV opined that, as far as possible:

20. *See* ruling no. 547729 (September 20, 2002).
21. If the foreign operation is too extensive, however, CBP will deny assembled merchandise treatment. *See* ruling no. W548697 (June 13, 2006).
22. Ruling no. 543737 (July 21, 1986), modifying ruling no. 542516 (October 7, 1981) (TAA 39).
23. EU, Commission, Compendium of Customs Valuation Texts (2022 ed.) ("EU Commission Compendium 2022"), Commentary No. 16: Licence fees and royalties - outward processing procedure, 90.
24. Case C-116/12, *Ioannis Christodoulou and Others v. Elliniko Dimosio*, 12.12.2013, ECLI: EU:C:2013:825, paragraphs 43-51.
25. TCCV, Com. 5.1, Goods Returned After Temporary Exportation for Manufacturing, Processing or Repair (March 1983).

- all reimported goods should be treated in the same way for valuation purposes;
- primacy is to be given to transaction value; and
- "sale" should be broadly defined.

In fact, the TCCV concluded that such goods imported after repair should be treated in the same way as those resulting from manufacture or processing. Otherwise, the result would be a fallback appraisal under a flexible interpretation of Article 1 and Article 8 anyway.

Sherman and Glashoff cogently observe that this broad application of Article 1 appraisement might be interpreted as an exception or as a qualification to the requirement of a sale.[26]

After establishing that TV will most likely apply, another question that is sure to arise when discussing these outward processing or "returned goods" tariff provisions is the full or partial duty exemptions to be granted at the time of entry. The TCCV merely noted that such exemptions could be granted under national legislation. In the US, there are a number of quite specific tariff provisions.[27] For example, we find that duty is applied on imported goods that have been assembled abroad with some or all US-fabricated components on the full value of the imported articles less the value of the US components.[28] The policy behind this "assembly abroad" provision,[29] which has its origins in the 1956 tariff legislation, is to encourage the use of US parts. Other provisions allow for the duty-free import of goods that had been exported for temporary use abroad,[30] the duty-free import of goods being imported on a temporary basis for repairs and then to be reexported,[31]or for goods being imported into the US after foreign repairs, alterations, processing or other change in condition, with duty assessed only on the value of those foreign activities.[32] In the case of this stream of imports,[33] it may be of interest that the US Congress has sanctioned the use of a reasonable estimate where the reimported goods had been repaired or processed on a no-cost basis.[34]

You should know that the standards for each of these US programs are quite precise, eligibility is strictly scrutinized by CBP and eligibility for duty relief is easily lost.

---

26. Sherman and Glashoff, no. 92, 73.
27. These are to be found in Subchapters I and II of Chapter 98, HTSUS. Some of these provisions require US origin, while others will extend to previously imported goods.
28. Unlike the cost of non-US goods which may be dutiable assists, the value of the US components does not include the cost of transport to the foreign assembler.
29. Tariff item 9802.00.80, HTSUS.
30. Tariff item 9801.00.10, HTSUS.
31. Tariff item 9801.10.12, HTSUS.
32. Tariff item 9802.00.40, HTSUS.
33. Actually, tariff items 9802.00.40-9802.00.60, HTSUS.
34. US Note 3(a)(ii), Subchapter II, Chapter 98, HTSUS (the value of repairs, alterations, processing or other change in condition outside the US shall be the cost or value as set out in the invoice and entry papers; except that, if the appraiser concludes that the amount so set out does not represent a reasonable cost or value, then the value of the change shall be determined in accordance with section 402 of the Tariff Act of 1930, as amended), 19 CFR § 10.8(d); *see* ruling no. 558860 (February 16, 1995).

While—or because—the Valuation Agreement does not define sale, customs authorities must turn to the definitions in use in their own countries.

[3] Legal Definition of Sale

[a] Common Law

In the US, and we assume in the United Kingdom (UK), Canada, and other countries with a common law tradition, unless the term "sale" is defined in an internal national code,[35] the customs authority may decide whether there has been a "qualifying sale for exportation" on the basis of the classic common law definition of a sale: is there a transfer of property from one party to another for a consideration? In the US, this is the enduring legacy of the decision in *J. L. Wood v. United States*.[36,37]

While *JL Wood* was decided under the prior appraisement statute, CBP adheres to this definition under the 1979 legislation implementing the Valuation Agreement. The primary factors that normally come to mind in determining whether there has been a transfer of property or ownership are whether the alleged buyer has assumed the risk of loss, and whether the buyer has acquired title to the imported merchandise.

Passage of title and assumption of risk of loss should be self-explanatory, but "consideration" may not be readily apparent. It is a term derived from, and at the center of, the law of contracts, at least in the common law tradition. Where the seller is the person who promises to sell or transfer ownership of an article, consideration refers to something of value given by the promisee, who in this case is the buyer, to the promisor in exchange for the promise (to transfer ownership).[38] It is the consideration which makes the promise to transfer ownership enforceable rather than being an unenforceable gratuitous promise.

When there are mutual promises—as when a seller promises to deliver a product in turn for the buyer's promise to pay at the time of delivery—a bilateral contract is

---

35. Of course, the sales agreement may contain a choice of law clause which will govern the operative terms of the agreement. Moreover, the sale of goods may be a matter of state or local law and not of the national law. That is the case in the US, where the individual states have enacted their own law of sales of goods, which are closely patterned on the Uniform Commercial Code (UCC). There is no federal version of the UCC. Because CBP, in finding customs valuation, is exercising a function controlled by federal law, CBP applies the common law standard. That does not rule out a role for UCC analysis on such sale for export issues as passage of title especially in the context of a post-importation sale or if delivery to the US customer is relevant. *See*, e.g., ruling nos. H314296 (August 12, 2021), H273866 (April 5, 2017) and H235553 (December 23, 2014).
36. 62 CCPA 26, 33, C.A.D. 1139, 505 F.2d 25 (1974). *See also VWP of Am., Inc. v. United States*, 175 F.3d 1327, 1337-1338 (Fed. Cir. 1999) (following *JL Wood*).
37. In Canada, the administrative guidance of the relevant D Memo instructs. The term "sale" will be taken to mean the transfer of ownership of the goods for a monetary consideration. Customs Memorandum D13-4-1, *Transaction Value Method of Valuation*, August 22, 2013.
38. We must note that in its classic form at common law consideration could take the form of a detriment to the promisee (the buyer for our purposes). That buyer's detriment might meet the formation requirements for an enforceable contract of sale but would be inimical to the design of the Valuation Agreement with its definition based upon a payment made or to be made to the seller.

formed. A promise made to pay accompanied by a delivery of the product, without a reciprocating promise in return, would be termed a unilateral contract, as there is a promise for an anticipated performance. For our purposes, classification as a bilateral contract (seller promises to deliver or make available the product, buyer agrees to pay) or unilateral contract (buyer promises to pay, seller delivers or makes available the product) is a distinction without a difference. The key is that the buyer in either case agrees to pay consideration—it could be money or something else of value.

As Professor Farnsworth, a leading legal scholar in the US, commented:

> Virtually anything that anyone would bargain for in exchange for a promise can be consideration for that promise.[39]

On this very point, we have already seen that the General Introductory Commentary uses the term "considerations" in connection with certain Article 8 additions to the PAPP. We will revisit the usage of "consideration" in our analysis of the PAPP, as it appeared in the developing countries' March 1979 proposal, and it is actually the essence of the Interpretative Note to Article 1 and Annex III, paragraph 7.

Why is this important? The lack of consideration would mean that there is no valid sale. With no sale, there can be no TV.

Under the *J.L. Wood* rubric, it is clear that passage of title and risk of loss are more important than the means of payment used by parties. But the method of payment will not be ignored, especially when the payment cannot be linked to a specific transaction. In the US, the mere general transfer of money from one corporate entity to another which cannot be linked to a specific import transaction has been held sufficient to meet the *J.L. Wood* requirement of a payment of consideration.[40] Evidence to establish that consideration has passed includes payment by check, bank transfer, or payment by any other commercially acceptable means.[41] *See*, e.g., ruling no. 545705 (Jan 27, 1995).

In Canada, a seminal 1999 decision of the Canadian International Trade Tribunal (the "Tribunal") in *Brunswick*[42] established the principle that a sale has been determined to be established if three distinct criteria are present:

(1) there must be two parties, standing in relation of buyer and seller to one another;
(2) both parties must agree to the same proposition; and
(3) there must be passage of title and consideration.[43]

39. E. Allen Farnsworth, Contracts (1982), 42-43, 46.
40. C.S.D. 82-137, ruling no. 542673 (June 10, 1982). There, a Canadian company operated a wholly owned US subsidiary. The subsidiary remitted lump-sum payments. CBP held that there was not a bona fide sale on which appraisement could be based. *See also* ruling nos. 543698 (June 11, 1986), 543511 (May 29, 1986) and 543446 (April 2, 1986).
41. *See*, e.g., ruling no. 545705 (January 27, 1995).
42. *Brunswick International (Canada) Limited v. The Deputy Minister of National Revenue* (December 14, 1999), AP-98-100 (CITT) (*Brunswick*).
43. *Brunswick* at 8, citing an Ontario court decision on the definition of sale which, in turn, was derived from *Black's Law Dictionary*.

The *Brunswick* decision opined further on the notion of separate entities:

> In order for there to be two parties, standing in relation of buyer and seller to one another, there must be two separate legal entities involved in the transaction. It is a cornerstone of Canadian corporate law that corporations, even where one is a wholly owned subsidiary of the other or where they are both wholly owned subsidiaries of the same parent corporation, are distinct legal entities. Thus, generally, there can be a sale between a corporation and its parent, subsidiary or sister corporation. However, the presumption of separate legal identity can be rebutted in exceptional circumstances. Where the corporate structure was established as a sham, where one corporation is completely dependent on the other or is its puppet, or where a subsidiary is "bound hand and foot to the parent company and must do just what the parent company says," Canadian courts have "pierced the corporate veil" and found that the two corporations are but one entity. Citations omitted.

We might properly view this 1997 decision in *Brunswick* as the Canadian *JL Wood*.

A 2010 decision in another Canadian case, *Cherry Stix*,[44] furnishes us with another important lesson. Here, the focus was on a qualifying sale for export, and a principal feature of the Canadian standard was whether the buyer in a putative sale held to the goods at the time of importation.[45] After looking to the contractual terms and the conduct of the parties, the Tribunal relied on the relevant domestic law of sales, the Ontario Sale of Goods Act.[46] The Ontario term employed was "property in the goods," and title to the goods took place at the time intended by the parties.[47] In the facts underlying the *Cherry Stix* case, the parties called for property to pass only after Cherry Stix fulfilled individual purchase orders ("POs"). Fulfillment equated with delivery of the goods to the customer, Walmart, and delivery took place at the customer's various distribution centers in Canada. Thus, although there had been a blanket order for Cherry Stix to sell to Walmart, that blanket order was only an intention to sell. The actual sale took place only after importation, which invalidated a transaction value appraisement. The citation to the TCCV's AO 1.1 and its "widest sense" of sale could not prevail in a direct conflict with the commercial law of the jurisdiction which defines a sale. To be sure, the narrow focus was on passage of title.

---

44. *Cherry Stix Ltd. v. President of the Canada Border Services Agency* (May 10, 2010), AP-2008-028 (CITT).
45. This topic is explored at length below in the context of a sale for export.
46. In much the same manner that CBP looks to the controlling Incoterms under the *JL Wood* principles to ascertain when title to the goods was passed to the buyer.
47. The Ontario Sale of Goods Act, Sale of Goods Act, R.S.O. 1990, C. S. 1(December 9, 1994) (OSGA) provides, in subsections 18(1) and (2):

    (1) Where there is a contract for the sale of specific or ascertained goods, the property in them is transferred to the buyer at such time as the parties to the contract intend it to be transferred.

    (2) For the purpose of ascertaining the intention of the parties, regard shall be had to the terms of the contract, the conduct of the parties and the circumstances of the case.

Notwithstanding this court decision that an agreement to sell is not itself a qualifying sale, CBSA maintained its view that a sale for export may be a contemplated sale. In that view, the goods presented to the CBSA have been "sold" when the vendor has transferred, or has agreed to transfer, title for a price to the purchaser of the subject goods).[48] In view of recent court decisions by the Canadian International Trade Tribunal, discussed below, CBSA is taking the issues of sale for export and Purchase in Canada under advisement. As a result, legislative amendment to the customs valuation statute and to the accompanying regulations[49] may be proposed.

It may be useful to consider the question of "sale" from a civil law perspective.

[b] Civil Law

As an example, we can cite the law in Colombia.

[i] Colombia

The Colombian Civil Code (*Código Civil de Colombia*) regulates contracts for the sale of goods. A sale of goods contract is defined as a contract under which one of the parties is obliged to give one thing and the other must pay for it in money (*Article 1849, Civil Code*).

Title II of the Colombian Code of Commerce (*Código de Comercio de Colombia*) regulates commercial sale of goods contracts. It also contains rules on prohibited sales, object of the contract, price, and the parties' obligations. A commercial sale is a contract that falls within the definition of an act of commerce under Article 20 of the Code of Commerce. For example, an acquisition of goods to dispose of them for consideration will qualify as a commercial sale.

Código de Comercio

Artículo 905. Definición de compraventa:

> La compraventa es un contrato en que una de las partes se obliga a trasmitir la propiedad de una cosa y la otra a pagarla en dinero. El dinero que el comprador da por la cosa vendida se llama precio.
>
> Cuando el precio consista parte en dinero y parte en otra cosa, se entenderá permuta si la cosa vale más que el dinero, y venta en el caso contrario.
>
> Para los efectos de este artículo se equipararán a dinero los títulos valores de contenido crediticio y los créditos comunes representativos de dinero.

48. Customs Memorandum D13-4-2, *Customs Valuation: Goods Sold for Export to Canada*, November 21, 2013, paragraph 2.
49. Valuation for Duty Regulations, SOR 86-792 (*Regulations*).

Code of Commerce

Article 905. Definition of Sale:

> The sale is a contract in which one of the parties undertakes to transfer the ownership of one thing and the other [party] to pay it in money. The money that the buyer gives for the thing sold is called the price.
>
> When the price consists partly of money and partly of something else, it will be understood as a barter if the thing is worth more than the money, and sale in the opposite case
>
> For the purposes of this article, securities of credit content and common credits representing money shall be equated with money.

[ii] France

In the case of France, we find analogous treatment. The concept of sale is defined in Article 1582 of the French Civil Code (Code Civile):

> Article 1582
>
> La vente est une convention par laquelle l'un s'oblige à livrer une chose, et l'autre à la payer.
>
> Article 1582
>
> A sale is as an agreement whereby one party commits to deliver one thing and the other party [to the agreement] commits to pay [for that thing].

[c] What Is Not a Sale

The EU Commission has taken pains to distinguish a PO from a qualifying sale. In its 2022 edition of its Compendium, we find that:

> a purchase order cannot serve as the basis for the determination of the customs value for the imported goods. A purchase order is an official offer submitted by a potential buyer to a potential seller, expressing the will of the first entity to conclude a sale agreement. Unlike a sales agreement, a purchase order in itself is not a binding contractual arrangement. Only when the future seller confirms (accepts) the purchase order a sale agreement is deemed to be concluded between the buyer and the seller. This applies to transactions in general, as offers may also be submitted by a potential seller (offeror/promisor) to a potential buyer (offeree/promisee).[50]

This is compatible with the Canadian view that an agreement to sell or an agreement to purchase is not itself a sales agreement.[51] In strictly legal terms, a PO is an offer, not an agreement.

---

50. EU Commission Compendium 2022, Commentary No. 13: Guidance on Articles 128 and 136 UCC IA, 54, paragraph 10.
51. *See* the Canadian International Trade Tribunal in *Cherry Stix Ltd. v. President of the Canada Border Services Agency*, Appeal No. AP-2008-028 (May 10, 2010).

It is also important to recognize that dealings with a branch that does not have a separate legal entity status, such as an inventory transfer, cannot be a sale. As the EU Commission cogently notes:[52]

> As a sale necessarily implies a transaction between two distinct persons, the delivery to [a branch in Europe that does not have a legal personality distinct from that of the parent company] only constitutes a transfer of goods between two sections of the same legal entity.
>
> as the goods imported by [the EU branch] for stock are not the subject of a sale, Article 70 is not applicable and the customs value is to be determined under the other methods of valuation in due order, in accordance with Article 74 of the Code.

The US takes the same view on transfers to a branch.[53]

[d] Law of Sales Conflicts with Valuation Agreement

For those readers who might wish to explore this topic even further, the International Institute for the Unification of Private Law (UNIDROIT) Principles of International Commercial Contracts 2016[54] are in direct conflict with the Valuation Agreement or, at the least, the underlying principles of the two cannot be reconciled. Article 3.1.2 of the UNIDROIT dispenses altogether with the need for consideration: A contract is concluded, modified or terminated by the mere agreement of the parties, without any further requirement.

For our purposes, the Valuation Agreement would disregard the validity of a transaction based on mere agreement and no consideration. Indeed, the Valuation Agreement seeks to ensure that the TV includes all elements of consideration,[55] as well as the related concept that the PAPP includes all payments whether in the form of a money payment or otherwise. We shall explore this in greater depth when we address the PAPP below.

While we are on the subject, and at the risk of a digression, the United Convention on Contracts for the International Sale of Goods 1980 (CISG)[56] also establishes a conflict with the Valuation Agreement, at least in the sense that some

52. EU Commission Compendium 2022, Conclusion No. 5, Imports by branches, 111.
53. *See*, e.g., ruling no. 548698 (October 4, 2005) (no sale exists when a transfer of merchandise merely involves the movement of goods from one portion to another of the same corporate entity [i.e., a branch office]. *See Mitsui & Co., Ltd. v. United States*, 68 Cust. Ct. 266, 270 (1972), rev'd on other grounds, 70 Cust. Ct. 301, 306, 359 F. Supp., 1398, 1402 (1973). The absence of a sale precludes the use of transaction value as an appraisement method in this particular case).
54. Promulgated by the International Institute for the Unification of Private Law, available at https://www.unidroit.org/english/principles/contracts/principles2016/principles2016-e.pdf.
55. In the Spanish text of the Valuation Agreement, this is rendered "prestacion del comprador en favor del vendedor." In the French text, consideration is translated as "prestation de l'acheteur en faveur du vendeur."
56. Available at https://uncitral.un.org/sites/uncitral.un.org/files/media-documents/uncitral/en/19-09951_e_ebook.pdf.

enforceable contracts under the CISG would not be recognized as giving rise to a valid sale for export for our customs valuation purposes. After directing (in Article 54) that the buyer has an obligation to "pay the price," the CISG employs a "gap filler" to validate some contracts. We find in Article 55 that a missing price can nonetheless be supplied:

> Art. 55
>
> Where a contract has been validly concluded but does not expressly or implicitly fix or make provision for determining the price, the parties are considered, in the absence of any indication to the contrary, to have impliedly made reference to the price generally charged at the time of the conclusion of the contract for such goods sold under comparable circumstances in the trade concerned.

At this point, you should have sensed that this resort to "the price generally charged" is unacceptable under the Valuation Agreement. Further, specific cause for invalidity in the case of a sale in which there is no agreed price is set forth as one of the disqualifying factors discussed below.

Several additional observations must be considered.

[B] Disqualifying Circumstances

What if there were a sale for export but with conditions attaching to the sale? The Valuation Agreement demands that there be no significant "strings" attached to the sale. The PAPP is acceptable if there are no concerns arising from the following considerations:

> Article 1.1
>
> (a) that there are no restrictions on the disposition or use of the goods by the buyer other than restrictions which—
>   (i) are imposed or required by law or by the public authorities in the country of importation,
>   (ii) limit the geographical area in which the goods may be resold, or
>   (iii) do not substantially affect the value of the goods;
>
> (b) that the sale or price is not subject to some condition or consideration for which a value cannot be determined with respect to the goods being valued
>
> (c) that no part of the proceeds of any subsequent resale, disposal, or use of the goods by the buyer will accrue directly or indirectly to the seller, unless an appropriate adjustment can be made in accordance with the provisions of Article 8; and
>
> (d) that the buyer and seller are not related, or the buyer and seller are related, that the transaction value is acceptable for purposes of this subsection, under the provisions of paragraph 2.[57]

57. Valuation Agreement, Article 1.1; US—19 USC § 1401a(b)(2)(A) (i)-(iv); Canada Customs Act, paragraphs 48(1)(a)-(d); EU—UCC, Article 70.3.

[1] Restrictions

As for restrictions, lest it be thought that this is a wide-ranging prohibition against restrictions, the Interpretative Notes make it clear that restrictions which do not affect substantially the value of imported goods will not prevent a TV appraisement. The example given is where a seller requires a buyer of automobiles not to sell or exhibit them before a fixed date which represents the beginning of the model year.[58]

At the international level, the US customs regulations track the Interpretative Notes to the Valuation Agreement on this point.[59] Furthermore, the WCO published a Commentary on the meaning of "restrictions" which is worthy of notice:

> [A] number of factors may have to be taken into consideration to determine whether the restriction has substantially affected the value or not. These factors include the nature of the restriction, the nature of the imported goods, the nature of the industry and its commercial practices, and whether the effect on the value is commercially significant. Since these factors may vary from case to case, it would not be proper to apply a fixed criterion in this respect. For example, a small effect on the value in a case involving one type of goods may be treated as substantial while a much greater change in the value of goods of another type may not be treated as substantial. ...[60]

Continuing, the TCCV implicitly recognized the important role played by commercial practices, noting that:

> a restriction which could have a substantial effect on the value of the imported goods is one that is not usual in the trade concerned. An example of such a restriction would be the case where a machine is sold at a nominal price on condition that the buyer uses it only for charitable purposes.

With the underlying emphasis on applying an Article 1 transaction value to an entry whenever possible,[61] it is important to understand that moving away from transaction value per Article 1.1(a)(iii) [in the US context, 19 USC § 1401a(b)(2)(A)(iii)] should be undertaken only after careful consideration. That is why a CBP ruling applying an Article 1.1 (a) (iii) rationale to eliminate a transaction value appraisement is worthy of extended comment.

Ruling no. H038381

In ruling no. H038381 (November 17, 2014), CBP considered the customs valuation status of various payments by an importer. This was a related party transaction, in which the price was set under a "target-based" scheme as a percentage of the retail price in a post-importation sale. There was a Distribution Agreement which posed

58. Interpretative Note to Article 1, paragraph 1(a)(iii); US—19 CFR § 152.103(k).
59. This is not a surprise because the US customs regulations on customs valuation are derived directly from the Interpretative Notes.
60. TCCV, Com. 12.1, Meaning of the Term "Restrictions" in Article 1.1(a)(iii) (October 1985).
61. *See*, e.g., TCCV, AO 1.1, The Concept of "Sale" in the Agreement (October 1981, additional situation added March 1982); Com. 12.1, Meaning of the Term "Restrictions" in Article 1.1 (a) (iii) (October 1985); CS 3.1, Restrictions and Conditions in Article 1 (March 1985).

problems for the importer, as well as two Service Agreements under which the importer paid certain fees for services received.[62]

CBP made a leap to assert that certain restrictions in the Distribution Agreement affected the value and thus disqualified the transaction from transaction value. The written agreement between the parties bestowed the right upon the seller to withdraw and stop sales of certain merchandise, i.e., obsolete or shop-worn goods. In CBP's view, such a right constituted a restriction upon the disposition or use of the imported merchandise which may be exercised at any time.

But a restriction on sale or disposition of imported goods is cognizable under the customs valuation law only if it substantially affects the value of the goods. The primary lesson of the TCCV's Commentary 12.1 is that a number of factors need to be taken into consideration when examining a question arising under this provision. Factors to be considered include the nature of the restriction, the nature of the goods, the nature of the industry and its commercial practices, and whether the effect on value is commercially significant.

Here, CBP only presumed that this restriction substantially affected the value of the goods. There was no discussion, let alone a proof, of any of these factors at all beyond CBP's conclusory *ipse dixit* assertion that there was an effect on value. In fact, the ruling tellingly stated (at 12) that:

> CBP *believes* this restriction by the Seller substantially affects the value of the imported merchandise, enhancing its value, due to the control exerted by the Seller over distribution in stores of its products. The image created by the Seller for its trademarked goods is enhanced by its ability to control the distribution of its goods (emphasis added).

This is susceptible to an attack on three fronts: (1) as already noted, there has been no showing of any effect on value; (2) if there were any impact on value, it would go in the opposite direction and lower the value as the restrictions would seem to reduce the importer's full rights over the imported goods; and (3) these brand protection elements are quite common commercial measures and, quite apart from the trademark royalty issues that would be raised in a license context, this CBP rationale would serve to take all such cases where there is a trademark license with these brand protection features out of a transaction value appraisement.

Under the Service Agreement with the seller, CBP observed (at 13) that "transaction value is also not applicable because some of the services for which the [i]mporter pays a fee to the [s]eller intrinsically relate to the imported merchandise, while others do not."

There are several points to be made here.

First and foremost, it is not enough for a payment to relate to the imported merchandise, "intrinsically" or otherwise, or that the payment is a condition of sale for

62. There were two such agreements, one with the seller regarding the retail operations and one with the parent company, governing various back-office functions. The latter is not relevant for this discussion.

the payment to come within the PAPP. No, the payment must be "for the merchandise,"[63] a principle that we discuss extensively throughout this book. In that context, it will be seen that the payment must relate to the imported goods for inclusion within the PAPP in the sense that it can only be equated with the payment being for the imported goods.

In this connection, we should look to a 2013 ruling from CBP for guidance and for strong authority for nondutiable status. In ruling no. H239671 (June. 7, 2013), discussed in depth below, the payment was to the seller and was for a software unlocking fee. While clearly related in a broad sense to the imported merchandise, that fact was not sufficient to make the payment dutiable as a part of the PAPP. That is because the payment was not for the imported merchandise but for optional application software. It is apropos to observe that if the payments do not form part of the PAPP, then they are dutiable only if they fall within one of the five statutory additions (packing, assists, etc.) discussed below in §3.01[I].

Second, the inability to ascertain the status and make an allocation of some of the service fees should not disqualify a transaction value appraisement. I am mindful of the statutory language at play here, but I suggest that the approach taken by CBP in dutiable assist inquiries might apply here. If the importer cannot segregate payments or costs which are clearly dutiable from those which are clearly nondutiable, then all of the payments might be deemed dutiable.[64] Another way to go about it would be to segregate payments for those services which are clearly not dutiable and to only assess duty on the portions of payments which are clearly dutiable and/or which cannot be determined one way or another. The importer should be afforded the opportunity to make that allocation.

But all of this is begging the question because we only have CBP's view that some of the payments are dutiable while others are not. CBP specifically discusses trademark protection and advertising and marketing activities.

The status of the trademark protection element is difficult to gauge since the cited 2009 ruling (no. 548419) is not accessible. I find it hard to see how a separate payment for TM protection is transmuted into an integrated element of the PAPP, and I would want to see their analysis in that 2009 ruling. My sense is that TM protection fees are neither a part of PAPP nor are they classed as a dutiable adjustment to the PAPP. We could look to a 2014 ruling on an extended warranty, which held that the separate payment was not dutiable.[65]

On the status of advertising and promotion expenses, CBP is especially vulnerable. Their logic fails because the payment is not for the merchandise but for these services, as noted (at 16):

63. 19 USC § 1401a(b)(1).
64. Ruling no. 545341 (August 3, 1994).
65. Ruling no. H253493 (September 4, 2014). Such a separate payment is to be distinguished from those cases in which the price for the goods includes an element for warranty, for which there may be no authority to deduct an amount for the warranty. *See*, e.g., ruling no. 545153 (December 21, 1993). This is discussed below.

> Despite the claim that the [i]mporter may choose to not use services offered by the [s]eller, based on the language of the agreements between the parties, the [i]mporter does not have an option regarding advertising and marketing. The [i]mporter must "use any publicity tools that may be provided to it by the Company" as the [s]eller directs. Therefore, the portion of the service fee related to advertising and marketing, prorated to account for only the imported merchandise, would be considered part of the price actually paid or payable.

Again, just because the payments are "in the neighborhood" or are "related to the imported goods" does not transform them into a requisite payment "for the merchandise."

Further, CBP was wrong in denying the importer the benefit of the exemption conferred by the regulations for payments made for activities undertaken by the importer "on his own account."[66] Just because the payments are required by the seller does not mean that they are not for the buyer's "own account." In any event, the buyer and seller have agreed to the payments. Further, in accepted usage in the US and other English-speaking countries, that "own account" phrase does NOT mean that it must be "at buyer's initiative" but rather that the buyer/importer is financially responsible for the payments or, stated otherwise, that the payments are not being incurred for or being paid on behalf of someone else. To be sure, this conflation of the terms "on one's own account" and "on one's own initiative" can and does arise, especially in those countries where English is not the native tongue.[67]

Finally, it appears that the importer's counsel may have committed two strategic errors. In the first place, as we note in Part II, as even a hasty review will show, probably a full 80% or more of importers' attempts to validate the price in a related party transaction by meeting the Circumstances of Sale (COS) test by the "all costs plus a profit" exemplar will fail. It was a mistake to try and meet the COS test under that exemplar. Further, the importer argued that the service fees only covered actual costs. This was also a major mistake because once the importer raised the question, the importer then had to prove that there was no profit element. The importer failed to meet his own self-imposed test.

A quick point should be made here. If there had been a profit on the services provided, then that still does not mean that the fees should become dutiable. The seller earning a profit on the services that it provided does not transmute that profit into a profit on the sale of the goods. In short, the payment was still for the service and not

66. 19 CFR § 152.103(a)(2) states, in discussing indirect payments to the seller: "Activities such as advertising, undertaken by the buyer on his own account, other than those for which an adjustment is provided in § 152.103(b) [referring to additions to the price actually paid or payable, which includes the proceeds of any subsequent resale, disposal, or use of the imported merchandise that accrue, directly or indirectly, to the seller], will not be considered an indirect payment to the seller though they may benefit the seller."

67. At the international level, this "on buyer's own account" note is found in Interpretative Note to Article 1(b), note 2. That Note also includes a further observation—the payment on buyer's own account may be made "even though by agreement with the seller." It is unfortunate that this text is missing from the US regulation, as it clarifies the issue and reinforces this limitation of the exception to the buyer acting sua sponte and not pursuant to an agreement with the seller.

"for the merchandise." We will explore this "for the merchandise [or goods]" criterion when examining the definition of the PAPP.

We are also left to wonder if the level of the service fee payments had been reviewed by the US Internal Revenue Service (IRS) for validity under the transfer pricing regime. Surely if the level of such payments had been vetted and approved by the IRS, then that might have revealed valuable information about the level of services provided and whether there had been any profit earned, although as noted, a profit need not be a disqualifying factor here.

[2] Condition or Consideration

One might hazard a guess that the offer, "I shall sell to you this product for 100 currency units if you employ my brother-in-law," implicates Article 1.1(b).

The present formulation of Article 1.1(b), with its reference to a "condition or consideration" that is not capable of being determined, is baffling.[68] We will explore the PAPP generally and this provision specifically in that context, but we raise this issue here as transaction value may be disallowed following an application of this provision.

One can readily understand that the PAPP should be comprised of all "consideration" paid to the seller for the goods. What makes no sense at all, however, is the very notion that a condition can ever carry a value, in the sense that a thing of value which is being proffered, presumably to the seller, is defined as a consideration—not a condition.

The consequence of that value on the condition being indeterminable is that the goods cannot be valued under Article 1. I find the drafting here imprecise and confusing, and the lack of clear definitions of "condition" and "consideration" here or anywhere else in the Valuation Agreement is at the heart of the confusion. What is notable is that the relevant Interpretative Note adds to the confusion, or at least does nothing to dispel it. First, it does not delineate whether any of the exemplars given are meant to illustrate a condition or a consideration and second, it fails to provide any exemplar of conditions or consideration that are capable of being valued.[69]

[3] Unquantified Proceeds of Subsequent Sale, Disposal or Use

We will be exploring in our review of Article 8.1(d), which is triggered when the buyer agrees to remit proceeds of subsequent sale, disposal or use of the imported goods to the seller. The explicit inclusion of this inability to fix the value of such remitted proceeds as a factor disqualifying the declared PAPP, and the consequential loss of a

68. The original draft text dating to June 1978 may have been clearer. The disqualifying criterion was drawn as "the sale or price does not include or is not conditioned on some factor or consideration not subject to valuation." GATT, Multilateral Trade Negotiations Group, "Non-Tariff Measures," Sub-Group "Customs Matters," Customs valuation, MTN/NTM/W/162 (21 June 1978).

69. Interpretative Note Article 1, Paragraph 1(b).

transaction value appraisement underscores the overarching principle that the PAPP includes the value of *all* consideration. From a purist's view of the drafting, this provision is superfluous because the inability to fix with certainty any of the adjustments mandated by Article 8, including Article 8. 1(d), will prohibit transaction value:

> Where objective and quantifiable data do not exist with regard to the additions to be made under the provisions of Article 8, the transaction value cannot be determined under Article 1.***[70]

[4] Related Party Transactions

As was noted at the very outset of this book, Part II is devoted entirely to the subject of related party transaction AKA transfer pricing. In this specific context of a disqualifying circumstance, it suffices to observe that a related party transaction where it cannot be shown that the relationship has not influenced the PAPP will not be eligible for TV.

[5] Package Deals and Tie-In Sales

Although they are not mentioned in the Valuation Agreement, two types of sale which may require a close analysis to avoid disqualification from TV are what the TCCV has separately classed as "package deals" and "tie-in" sales ("ventes interdépendantes" in French). At the TCCV, there were separate instruments issued, as discussed below. We shall see that the US classes them together as "tie-in" sales.[71]

Regardless of the category into which they have been placed, the challenge is to determine whether the customs authority has been presented with a condition or consideration for which a value cannot be determined.

[a] "Package Deals"

With Commentary 8.1,[72] the TCCV presents three types of package deal transactions:

(A) Different goods are sold and invoiced at a single overall price.
(B) Goods of different quality sold and invoiced at a single overall price are only partially declared for home use in the country of importation.
(C) Different goods, included in the same transaction, are invoiced at individual prices established solely for tariff or other reasons.

The first point to make is that the TCCV signals that the single overall price for goods classified in different tariff headings need not lead to a rejection of transaction value.

70. Interpretative Note Article 8, paragraph 3.
71. Canada also provides administrative guidance on tie-in sales in the broader context of package deals. Customs Memorandum D13-3-9, *Package Deals*, April 29, 2014.
72. TCCV, Com. 8.1, Treatment of Package Deals (March 1984).

As for the "home use" factor in (B), that phrase appears irrelevant. This early reference may be a vestigial remainder of the "home consumption" feature of the BDV. The explanation in the Commentary for (B) which appears to focus on "home use" is floating and imprecise as a result. Beyond that, when properly parsed, the derivation of the individual pricing ("established solely for tariff or other reasons") in (C) is entirely open-ended. The example given is a clear instance of a transaction value-disqualifying lumping together to gain an artificial and impermissible advantage on duty liability—a "tariff reason." The result represents a condition or consideration for which the value cannot be determined. There is no example given of any "other reasons." Rather than being so entirely open-ended as to lose any instructive value, would it not have been more valuable to refer to "solely for tariff or other artificial (non-commercial) reasons"?

[b] Countertrade and Tie-In Sales

Transaction value has been generally denied to "tie-in" sales which are crossing sales between buyer and seller because it is not possible to fix a price for each of the individual articles.

The TCCV has explored tie-in sales in some depth, pointing to two subcategories: the condition or consideration relates to the: (i) price of the goods and (ii) sale of the goods.[73] The latter includes countertrade, with a number of subcategories such as barter and counterpurchase.[74] First, the TCCV remark that countertrade "is becoming a large factor in world trade" may no longer appear correct almost forty years later.

The TCCV takes an open position on the status of countertrade under the Valuation Agreement, with a case-by-case review considered necessary.[75]

By contrast, in the US, CBP came to define tie-in sales as those in which the sale of or price for the imported merchandise is conditioned on the sale of or consideration of other merchandise. In fact, CBP took the position that a use of transaction value where there is a tie-in sale was a failure to use reasonable care and a violation of the customs law.[76] Earlier, CBP had observed a true tie-in sale is one in which the price of certain goods is conditioned on the purchase of other goods, whether or not both are contained in the same shipment. For example, in a situation where a manufacturer agrees to sell a quantity of item A at a particular price if the purchaser buys or agrees to buy a quantity of Item B at a particular price, transaction value would be precluded as a basis of appraisement since there is present a condition (i.e., the agreement to

73. TCCV, Com. 11.1, Treatment of Tie-in Sales (March 1985).
74. For a still-useful International Trade Commission (successor to the US Tariff Commission) study, *see* Assessment of the Effects of Barter and Countertrade Transactions on U.S. Industries, Report on Investigation No. 332-185 Under section 332 of the Tariff Act of 1930, Pub. No. 1766 (October 1985).
75. *Ibid.*, in paragraphs 8-11.
76. Notice, Tie-in Sale Transactions, 30 Cust. Bull. & Dec. No. 23 (June 5, 1996) (Tie-In Sales Notice).

purchase item B at a particular price if item A is offered at a particular price) for which a value cannot be ascertained.[77]

An example of a tie-in sale as a condition which cannot be valued and that will eliminate a transaction value appraisement is the practice of "off setting," i.e., setting of a higher than contract price on one article offset by a lower than contract price on another article.[78]

In 1996, CBP notified the trade community that tie-in sales will preclude TV appraisements.[79] CBP's reminder was barbed, insofar as the advice contained the note that to enter goods in a tie-in sale under transaction value would be a failure to exercise reasonable care by the importer.[80] Such a failure would justify a civil penalty under 19 USC § 1592. One might surmise that the reason for the disqualification of transaction value is that the payment would not be only for the goods but for something else as well.

[C] There May Be a Different Sale for Export

In the aftermath of *J.L Wood* and its progeny, some key questions posed by CBP in a bona fide sale inquiry include the following:—

- will the US importer pass orders to the foreign entity for acceptance?
- will the importer maintain inventory and will the importer take care of returned or defective goods?
- do the payments remitted to the foreign company correspond to specific invoices?
- does the foreign company have direct contact with the US customers?[81]

[1] Substance over Form: Is There a Different *Sale?*

Related party transactions in sale for export cases have been controversial. We will be addressing most of the issues later. We pause to discuss one sale for export question that arises in some related party cases.

If the sale to the related party importer is to be negated by CBP, the importer will generally argue as a fallback that, if that sale were to be rejected, there is no sale for

77. Ruling no. 543611 (September 6, 1985); TD 86-56. That tie-in sales have posed an issue for customs appraisement for quite some time is demonstrated by the discussion in *Superior Merchandise Co. v. United States*, 54 Cust. Ct. 781, A.R.D. 185 (1965) *cited in* ruling no. 541145 (September 28, 1977). *See also* ruling no. 543881 (December 3, 1987).
78. Ruling no. 542747 (June 3, 1982).
79. Tie-In Sales Notice. Ironically, the US established an interagency group on countertrade. *See* 15 USC § 4712. This was a measure aimed at export enhancement of US exports to developing countries.
80. This superseded 1991 advice that importers involved in countertrade should consider obtaining an advance ruling from CBP. Notice, Countertrade Transactions, 25 Cust. Bull. & Dec. No. 6 (February 6, 1991).
81. *See* ruling nos. 543708 (April 21, 1988) and 543511 (May 29, 1986).

exportation to the US. This would defeat TV and mandate an alternative basis of appraisement. If deductive value is the alternative basis, then the importer will be able to make a deduction for the importer's profits and general expenses to arrive at dutiable value.

But we often encounter a situation where the consequence of the negation of the seller-to-importer sale does not automatically lead to an alternate basis of appraisement. Instead, the customs authority may seek to negate the importer's argument that the resale from the purported buyer/importer to the customer is a wholly domestic, post-importation transaction. The customs authority will look to a constructive or "virtual" sale for export transaction, going directly from the foreign seller to the local customer in the country of importation. In that view, this putative sale will form the basis for transaction value, after backing out various nondutiable charges, but after leaving in any markup by the related party buyer/importer, who is a domestically based middleman. CBP and other customs authorities will consider this markup a dutiable selling commission because that middleman is a sales agent. Obviously, revenue is enhanced because duty is thereby assessed on an amount that includes the domestic entity's markup.

An early case in which the US CIT reviewed the issue of the qualifying "sale for exportation" in such a context is *Orbisphere Corp. v. United States.*[82] Despite CBP's vigorous efforts, the court concluded that the only sales there were post-importation, domestic transactions and that there was no sale for exportation to the US. Accordingly, TV was eliminated, and deductive value was the appropriate method of appraisement.

In response to the decision in *Orbisphere*, CBP published a "Limiting Treasury Decision" that it would "continue to regard transactions in which a selling agent participates as a sale from the agent's principal, the seller, to the ultimate purchaser ... ."[83] Of course, this begs the question whether the importer is a true buyer or merely a selling agent.

Following *Orbisphere*, CBP followed through with its pledge, and other court challenges arose, as CBP sought to collect duty on the basis of TV which was grounded in the price paid by the customer in the US to the importer. In a 1998 CIT decision, the trial court found that the relationship had influenced the price paid to the importer, and a qualifying sale status was denied to that transaction. Instead, the court validated CBP's levy of duty established on a TV basis arising from supposed sales from the foreign seller to the US customers of the importer.[84]

I had formerly believed that this line of cases and CBP rulings following this rationale is always unsound and a detour from the correct interpretation in *Orbisphere*. I have revised my thinking.

---

82. 13 CIT 866, 726 F. Supp. 1344 (1989).
83. 26 Cust. Bull No. 8 at 13 (February 19, 1992).
84. *La Perla Fashions, Inc. v. United States,* 22 CIT 393 (1998), aff'd 185 F.3d 885 (1999). *See Victor Woollen Products, Inc. v. United States,* 21 CIT 1109 (1997) and its subsequent history culminating in 259 F. Supp. 1289 (CIT 2003) (appraisal based on fallback method arising from sales from importer to US customers). *See also* ruling nos. H263559 (July 1, 2016), H249150 (January 28, 2014) and H023094 (July 22, 2010).

Close observers will have seen that the absence of a bona fide sale for export should have disqualified any transaction value appraisement based on that transaction because there was no qualifying sale from the foreign seller to the importer. Some will still argue, as had I, that proceeding to an alternative basis of appraisement in the statutory hierarchy should be the next step rather than appraising on a transaction value that would be based on an entirely notional sale, which is prohibited under the statute.[85] In truth, the validity of that analysis rests on a showing that the sale in question to the US customer was indeed only notional.

The prudent way to approach this contested question is whether the reality is that the foreign seller was indeed dealing with the customer in the country of importation, i.e., whether the real buyer was that customer and there was a sale from the foreign seller to that customer. In such a scenario, the purported buyer/importer remains in the picture, but its role is merely that of a selling agent, facilitating that sale to the customer in the country of importation.

Another way to frame the question is to ask whether the buyer/importer has all of the substance and displays all of the attributes of ownership that would be expected of a stand-alone buyer and reseller. This issue most often comes up in the case of a foreign seller setting up a related party entity in the country of importation to act as a buyer/reseller. Often, that new entity has little or no in-house capability in the so-called backoffice functions (administration, finance, accounting, payroll, etc.) or even some of the "line" corporate functions such as management, sales and logistics. That forces the foreign seller to provide those services. Even the "charge back" billing by the foreign parent for those services may not suffice if there is a failure to show the attributes of ownership.

Perhaps the outer limit was reached by CBP in a 2021 ruling which merits some discussion.[86] In ruling no. H314296, there was a multitier series of transactions with all parties except the US customer with related party status. The Swiss manufacturer sold the goods to the German parent company acting as middleman, who sold to the US importer (X) who was acting as the distributor and, in turn, that company sold to the US customer (R). The ruling engaged in an informative but in the circumstances essentially gratuitous discussion of related party pricing rules.[87]

The key features presented by the facts refer to the laws of sales and the passing of title. Under the controlling German law, the manufacturer—the seller in the original transaction—retained title until it had been paid in full by the middleman. In the case of the last sale, from the US importer to the US customer, under the applicable law of the state of Connecticut, title was passed upon delivery of the goods to US customer R.

CBP reasoned (at 13, 16) that:

85. The Valuation Agreement includes arbitrary and fictitious values in its proscriptions of Article 7, paragraph 2; *see* US, 19 USC § 1401a(f)(2)(F), 19 CFR § 152.108 (Unacceptable bases of appraisement); Canada, Customs Memorandum D13-9-1, *Residual Basis of Appraisal Method*, November 19, 2013, paragraph 7; EU, UCC IA, Article 144.2(g).

86. Ruling no. H314296 (August 12, 2021).

87. To be sure, it is helpful and a good reference source for exploring the contemporary US position on transfer pricing.

> In the instant matter, title passed directly from the Swiss manufacturer to Company R when the U.S. importer [X] delivered the goods to Company R on October 15, 2015. After the transfer of title, the importer [X] retained no security interest in the goods under the UCC because Company R paid in full for the merchandise on October 14, 2015.
>
> The roles of the parties and the circumstances of the transactions between the related manufacturer, middleman and U.S. importer indicate that the parties are not functioning as a buyer and seller. A sale involves a transfer of title from one party to another for consideration. ... No sales occurred between the manufacturer and the middleman and between the middleman and the importer because the middleman had no title to the merchandise when it was shipped to the importer and delivered to Company R. The title transferred directly from the Swiss manufacturer to Company R in Alabama.
>
> * * *
>
> We conclude that the imported merchandise may be appraised using transaction value based on the price paid or payable by the final U.S. customer Company R to the U.S. importer. Company R is unrelated to the Swiss manufacturer and the U.S. importer. The manufacturer is functioning as a *bona fide* seller and Company R is functioning as a *bona fide* buyer. The submitted documentation as described above reveals that title to the goods transferred directly from the manufacturer to Company R who paid consideration for the merchandise. The middleman and the U.S. importer did not have title to the goods during the transactions. Company R held title to the goods when they were delivered to it in Alabama. As Company R is unrelated to the [X] Group, the sale to Company R is presumed to be at "arm's length." The laser machine is "clearly destined" for the U.S. when sold to Company R because it was made per order and the only possible destination for the imported merchandise was the US (internal citation omitted).

That marks quite a leap—the qualifying sale for export is a sale to final US customer R. This marks a radical shift from the standard analysis centering on the question of the substance of the importer. Here, there was nothing to suggest anything but that US importer X was a fully functioning, full-service distributor.

A close reading of the text reveals that, despite the discussion of title retention and title passing, it does not directly identify the seller in the qualifying sale for export to Company R. The sentence, "The manufacturer is functioning as a bona fide seller and Company R is functioning as a bona fide buyer," does not resolve the matter either. It is not enough to state that the manufacturer has the role of *a* seller or that US customer R is in the role of *a* buyer. The facts reveal three parties in the role of either seller or buyer. What is required is to answer the question and to show directly who is *the* seller and who is *the* buyer in *the* relevant sale for export transaction? After arguing that there had been a sale for export, the ruling refers to the price paid by R to US importer X as forming the basis of the PAPP which supports a transaction value. Surely that would suggest that there was a presumed sale from importer X to US customer R, but that would conflict with the emphasized role of the manufacturer as a seller and with the twin points that the manufacturer has retained title and that company X did not have title. This remains an open question.

As a final point, the ruling does not address the conflict of laws arising from the application of German law which suggests that title remained in the Swiss manufacturer until it was paid. Under German law, the timing of delivery of the imported good, which was central to Connecticut law, was irrelevant. According to the analysis here, based upon application of Connecticut law,[88] even if importer X did not have title to the goods, title was passed directly from the Swiss manufacturer to company R upon delivery. I would venture that in the event of a conflict, perhaps arising from a failure of the middleman to make full payment to the manufacturer—admittedly unlikely in these related party circumstances—there would be a challenge to R's title or ownership to the imported goods. The question of which law of sales should control would be a central issue in any such dispute.

To return to the more usual focus, the US and Canada customs authorities have had decades of mirror image experience in monitoring their bilateral trade, with a focus upon the substance or lack thereof of the purported buyer/importers.

While Canada employs a "Purchaser in Canada" criterion as a matter of statute, and the First Sale doctrine is inapposite there since that doctrine has been disallowed,[89] the US employs an implied "Purchaser in America" approach as a matter of practice when examining whether there has been a qualifying sale.

[2] Buyer's Substance: The "Purchaser in ..." Requirement[90]

Under one customs planning approach, the foreign vendor sells to a related entity buyer, perhaps newly set up for this purpose, with either the affiliated purchaser or the foreign vendor itself acting as Importer of Record (IOR).[91]

You may come to see why this approach has been seen as a species of "first sale." In fact, I am confident that many advisors who have been pushing a "First Sale" strategy are, in fact, looking to what I have termed a "Purchaser in ..." strategy.

The affiliated buyer/importer would then resell to its customer on a post-clearance, i.e., domestic sale, basis. The bulk of the vendor parties' markup would be earned on the domestic sale in the country of importation which, in the case of most imports into the US from China, would shield the markup from the additional 7.5% or 25% section 301 tariffs[92] but would expose the local affiliate's markup to US income tax. You will recognize this as the mirror image of the First Sale for Export (FSFE) strategy, where the bulk of the markup is earned on the foreign First Sale.

---

88. The ruling applied Connecticut laws as the sale from importer X to US customer R involved the retaining of a security interest in the goods by X under the Connecticut law of sales. Ruling no. H314296 at 12-13.
89. Discussed below in §3.01[D].
90. The following discussion is based upon an analysis which first appeared in Neville, "Sale for Export from China: Customs Valuation Plays," 30 J. Int'l Tax'n (November 2019) at 32. While the focus there was on strategies to minimize the impact of the section 301 tariffs, its rationale is of general application.
91. Depending on the circumstances, including the practical effect of the Incoterm employed, a foreign vendor can act as a nonresident importer of record in the US and in Canada. For more on IOR status in the US generally, *see* Neville, "The Right to Import Goods," 25 J. Int'l Tax'n (October 2014) at 14.
92. *See* Neville, "China Trade Sanction: What to Do?," 29 J. Int'l Tax'n (September 2018) at 26 and Neville, "Sales for Export from China: Customs Valuation Plays," 30 J. Int'l Tax'n (September 2019) at 32.

We should note that this strategy of a sale from the foreign vendor to an affiliated entity has been pursued for many years along the US Northern Border, by many companies in the US and in Canada looking to export to the other country.

While there are some differences between the two, on balance, Canadian and US customs authorities will display a near-identical level of interest in and take remarkably similar approaches to their analyses of these "Purchaser in ..." strategies.

[a] Canadian Experience

In contrast to the US customs valuation statute, Canada has an explicit "Purchaser in Canada" requirement.[93] As a result, sale for export and Purchaser in Canada analyses are normally interrelated.

The Valuation for Duty Regulations set forth the qualifications of a Purchaser in Canada. The party may be:

(1) a resident of Canada, or
(2) a nonresident but one who maintains a permanent establishment (P/E) in Canada, or
(3) one who is neither a resident nor maintains a P/E but either (1) imports the goods for consumption or use but not for sale or (2) imports for sale and has not already agreed to sell the goods to a resident in Canada before the party has itself purchased the goods.[94]

In turn, a P/E is defined as a fixed place of business through which the person carries on business. You should recognize the P/E standard as a means of ensuring a measure of sufficient substance in the purchaser. In this connection, one limitation employed by Canada restricts the ability of a foreign company to act as a nonresident importer of record. In the Regulations,[95] a nonresident company without a P/E in Canada can qualify as a purchaser in Canada only if the company has not yet agreed to sell the goods to a resident in Canada. In other words, the nonresident company can only be importing in order to stage inventory in Canada.

As has been noted, Canada does not recognize First Sale. In order to minimize the customs duty impact, many US companies elected to set up Canadian entities and to sell to that entity as a sort of "poor man's first sale." In that way, the duties are assessed on the lower price paid by the importing entity, which is the putative Purchaser in Canada. The Canadian entity then resells at a profit to Canadian customers.

CBSA can be counted on to scrutinize this arrangement to determine if the Canadian entity has enough substance to qualify as a buyer/reseller. The Tribunal, the

93. Customs Act, subsection 48(1); Regulation, section 2. *See* Customs Memorandum D13-1-3, *Customs Valuation—Purchaser in Canada*, July 4, 2014.
94. Valuation for Duty Regulations, SOR 86-792 (*Regulations*), section 2.1, available at https://laws-lois.justice.gc.ca/eng/regulations/SOR-86-792/page-1.html#h-898037.
95. *Regulations*, section 2.

Canadian body tasked with the review of CBSA determinations of the first instance,[96] has made it clear that there is a two-step process that must be undertaken. We see this clearly in the *Delta Galil* decision,[97] the first of a series of consequential Tribunal decisions in 2021-2022. There must first be a showing that there is a sale for export and then the buyer in that sale must be seen to be a Purchaser in Canada.[98]

In *Delta Galil*, the Tribunal first found that the importer was a buyer in the qualifying sale for export and then found that the company had a permanent establishment in Canada, allowing it to be treated as a Purchaser in Canada.

Turning to the first task, ascertaining if there was a sale for export, a 2010 decision in another Canadian case, *Cherry Stix*,[99] furnishes us with another important lesson. Here, the focus was on a qualifying sale for export, and a principal feature of the Canadian standard was whether the buyer in a putative sale held to the goods at the time of importation.[100] The Tribunal was applying the limiting precept set forth in the 2001 Supreme Court decision in *Mattel*:

> For the purposes of valuation under s. 48 of the Customs Act, *the relevant sale for export is the sale by which title to the goods passes to the importer. The importer is the party who has title to the goods at the time the goods are transported into Canada.* The importer may be the intermediary or the ultimate purchaser, depending on which party actually imports the goods into the country. For the purposes of determining whether a sale is for export, the residency of the purchaser or of the party transporting the goods is not material[101] (emphasis added).

To put it plainly, following the precedent of the *Mattel* decision, the buyer in a qualifying sale for export is that party who held title at the time the goods were imported. Thus, the timing of passage of title is a key element in sale for export analyses.

After looking into the contractual terms and the conduct of the parties, the Tribunal in *Cherry Stix* relied on the relevant domestic law of sales, the Ontario Sale of Goods Act,[102] for guidance on the title passage issue.

The Ontario term employed was "property in the goods," and title to the goods took place at the time intended by the parties.[103] In the facts underlying the *Cherry Stix*

---

96. The Canadian International Trade Tribunal (CITT or Tribunal) is a quasi-judicial body.
97. *Delta Galil USA Inc. v. President of the Canada Border Services Agency* (March 5, 2021), AP-2020-002.
98. *Ibid.*, in paragraphs 29-31.
99. *Cherry Stix Ltd. v. President of the Canada Border Services Agency* (May 10, 2010), AP-2008-028 (CITT).
100. This topic is explored at length below.
101. *Canada (Deputy Minister of National Revenue) v. Mattel Canada Inc.* 2001 SCC 36, [2001] 2 SCR 100 (*Mattel*), in paragraph 45. To be clear, the *Mattel* principle is routinely cited in all of these customs valuation decisions.
102. *OSGA*. In much the same manner that CBP looks to the controlling Incoterms under the *JL Wood* principles to discern when title to the goods was passed to the buyer.
103. The OSGA provides, in subsections 18(1) and (2):

> 1. Where there is a contract for the sale of specific or ascertained goods, the property in them is transferred to the buyer at such time as the parties to the contract intend it to be transferred.

case, the parties called for property to pass only after Cherry Stix fulfilled individual POs. Fulfillment equated with delivery of the goods to the customer, Walmart, and delivery took place at the customer's various distribution centers in Canada. Thus, although there had been a blanket order for Cherry Stix to sell to Walmart, that blanket order was only an intention to sell. The actual sale took place only after importation, which invalidated a transaction value appraisement. The citation to the TCCV's AO 1.1 and its "widest sense" of sale could not prevail in a direct conflict with the commercial law of the jurisdiction which defines a sale. To be sure, the narrow focus was on passage of title.

Notwithstanding the *Cherry Stix* decision that an agreement to sell is not itself a qualifying sale for export, CBSA maintained its view that a sale for export may be a contemplated sale. In that view, the goods presented to the CBSA have been "sold" when the vendor has transferred, or has agreed to transfer, title for a price to the purchaser of the subject goods.[104] In view of recent court decisions by the Tribunal, however, CBSA is taking the issues of sale for export and Purchaser in Canada under advisement. As a result, legislative amendment to the customs valuation statute and to the accompanying regulations may be proposed.

This two-step inquiry ((1) was there a sale for export? and (2) does the buyer qualify as a Purchaser in Canada?) was applied by the Tribunal in its *Spyder* decision[105] where the Tribunal was dealing with a case in which CBSA had determined at the administrative level that there was a sale from Spyder USA to the Canadian customers, disregarding the participation of Spyder Canada. While the importer and CBSA disputed which transaction was the qualifying sale for export and the status of Spyder Canada (buyer/reseller or sales agent?), the Tribunal held that they were both wrong. The Tribunal took the view that there was no qualifying sale for export. In its telling, Spyder Canada was indeed an agent, with the outsized role and continuing contacts by Spyder USA leading to a diminution of Spyder Canada's role as a putative buyer and reseller. If there is a principal/agency transaction, there cannot be a sale (paragraphs 44, 49, 78).[106] But the Tribunal assigned prime importance to the timing of the title transfer. The Tribunal found that there was no sale for export from Spyder USA to the Canadian customers because the latter only took title after importation.

---

2. For the purpose of ascertaining the intention of the parties, regard shall be had to the terms of the contract, the conduct of the parties and the circumstances of the case.

104. Customs Memorandum D13-4-2, *Customs Valuation: Goods Sold for Export to Canada*, November 21, 2013, paragraph 2. *See OSGA*, in sections 3 and 4, which distinguish between a sale and an agreement to sell: "(3) Where under a contract of sale the property in goods is transferred from the seller to the buyer, the contract is called a sale, but, where the transfer of the property in the good is to take place at a future time or subject to some condition thereafter to be fulfilled, the contract is called an agreement to sell. (4) An agreement to sell becomes a sale when the time elapses or the conditions are fulfilled subject to which the property in the goods is to be transferred."
105. *GBG Spyder Canada Holding ULC v. President of the Canada Border Services Agency* (August 2, 2022), AP-2019-033 (CITT), paragraphs 34-35.
106. Citing *Brunswick* for the proposition that a sale requires a "transaction between two parties standing in relation of buyer and seller to one another."

The *Spyder* decision was followed by the Tribunal's decision in *G-III Apparel*,[107] another case presenting sale for export and Purchaser in Canada questions. There (in paragraph 69), the Tribunal referred to the already-cited *Mattel* criterion of title to the goods at the time of importation.

The Tribunal in *G-III Apparel* went on to deny that the Canadian entity was acting as an agent (paragraphs 137-143) and also rejected the principal CBSA argument that there was a sale from the US parent to the Canadian retail customers. The Tribunal ruled that, regardless of the roles of the US parent company or the Canadian entity, there was no chance that the Canadian retail customers could ever qualify as purchasers in qualifying sales for export to Canada because they did not hold title at the time of importation (paragraphs 144-150).

You should note that, in the US, there could be a different result on this passage of title question. The contemplated passage of title after importation would not necessarily disqualify the transaction from a bona fide sale for export status.[108] In fact, if we consider a sale on DDP Incoterms—Delivered Duty Paid—risk of loss will always, and almost invariably title passage as well, occur after importation. Would a DDP sale not qualify as a sale for export? And if not, why not?

The *G-III* decision was followed in quick succession by another Tribunal decision with significant customs valuation repercussions. This was the decision in *Scentsy*[109] in which determining the sale for export again turned on the issue: (1) whether there was a qualifying sale for export from a foreign parent company to the local Canadian affiliate, with the accompanying Purchaser in Canada requirement also having been met or (2) whether the sale for export was a sale from the foreign parent company to the customers of the Canadian affiliate. A second question arose: whether, in the event that there was a valid sale for export to the importer/buyer, the PAPP, comprised of certain payments to the foreign parent company, should be adjusted by adding separate amounts paid by the importer/buyer. The acceptability of the price in the related party situation was yet another issue.

The Tribunal in *Scentsy* held that the local affiliate in Canada was not a sales agent despite the lack of much internal functional capability by the local affiliate (paragraphs 45-63) and, the *Brunswick* criteria having been met, that there had been a sale for export to the local affiliate (paragraphs 64-72), which also qualified as a Purchaser in Canada (paragraphs 73-108). The Tribunal saw no reason not to accept the importer's position that there was no basis for not accepting that the various separate payments should not be added to the PAPP as a portion of subsequent proceeds or for any other reason. The payments were made pursuant to various

---

107. *G-III Apparel Canada ULC v. President of the Canada Border Services Agency* (August 22, 2022), AP-2020-028 (CITT) (Canadian subsidiary was purchaser in a sale for export from foreign vendors and qualified as a purchaser in Canada).

108. *See*, e.g., ruling nos. H065028 (January 8, 2014), H092448 (May 4, 2010) and H012659 (November 14, 2007). *But see* ruling no. 545622 (April 28, 1994) (application of Uniform Commercial Code (UCC) which requires title passage with final delivery—this may be an outlier as it presumes application of the UCC to international transactions).

109. *Scentsy Canada Enterprises LLC v. President of the Canada Border Services Agency* (October 4, 2022), AP-2019-021 (CITT) *(Scentsy)*.

intercompany agreements for various services, and the documentation that had been prepared for income tax purposes did not raise concerns about its probative value (paragraphs 121-125). It may be a challenge to reconcile the *Scentsy* and *Brunswick* decisions in light of the already quoted admonition of the latter authority to disregard sham transactions or those in which one party was a mere "puppet" or was "bound hand and foot."

[b] US Experience

In the case of the US, too, there has been a long-standing practice of over thirty years' duration, with CBP closely examining whether there is sufficient substance in the related party importer for it to qualify as a buyer in a sale for exportation to the US. While this arose especially in the context of imports from Canada it has been applied more generally. Most recently, we saw a flurry of activity in setting up related party buyer/importers, prompted by a concern over the additional section 301 China Tariffs, most of which were set at 25% ad valorem.

[i] Effect of China Tariff

In the context of the special China tariff regime, one way to lessen the impact of 301 tariffs is to lower the dutiable value of the goods by inserting an intermediate party into the sales transactions and creating a multitiered transaction. With a Purchaser in America strategy, we will see a US affiliate of the China vendor as the putative buyer/importer.

CBP will want to determine whether the US entity would qualify as: (i) a true buyer/reseller or, instead (ii) where there is insufficient substance and functionality, it is merely a selling agent for its parent company.

In that latter case, CBP would look to a transaction value appraisement based on a sale for export from China to the US customer, disregarding or "leap frogging" over the transaction with the US importer. The customs duty, including the additional China tariffs, would be assessed against that final US customer's price, albeit after backing out any nondutiable charges (NDCs). There would be no concern about including the importer's markup since it would be a deemed selling agent, whose markup is dutiable. 19 USC § 1401a(b)(1)(B).

This would be the very same approach that has been well honed after years of application to imports from Canada.[110]

The general rule is succinctly set forth in a 2012 ruling:

110. As discussed, if there were not a bona fide sale for export to the importer to support a valid transaction value appraisement, then an alternative method of valuation would be needed. *Orbisphere Corp. v. United States*, 13 CIT 866 (1989). But CBP will first want to satisfy itself that there is not another qualifying sale for export to another party, i.e., the US customer of the importer.

> To determine whether a transaction between two parties is a bona fide sale, CBP must consider the circumstances of the transaction, including: passage of title, assumption of the risk of loss, payment of consideration, ability of the buyer to instruct the seller, ability of the buyer to resell the merchandise at any price to any customer, and the ability of the buyer to order merchandise for the buyer's own account, i.e., the overall relationship of the parties and whether it demonstrates that they act as buyer and seller.[111]

There are a number of different criteria which CBP will apply in its review of the question of whether the importer is a true buyer of the imported goods. The first and foremost question, of course, is whether the buyer owns the imported goods, i.e., takes title and assumes risk of loss. Then, there is an inquiry into whether the buyer shows ownership attributes including, *inter alia*, whether the importer:

(1) freely negotiates and sets its own pricing with customers;
(2) earns a profit that varies on its resales and not a stated percentage markup, which would more closely resemble a sales commission;
(3) needs authorization or approval from its vendor for sales or for pricing;
(4) has orders placed to it by customer;
(5) issues invoices to its customers;
(6) receives payments by customers into its own bank account;
(7) is responsible for issues of quality, delivery, etc.

The inquiry into the role of the entity in the country of importation as a "buyer" versus a selling agent will arise also in the context of income taxation. There, the International Financial Reporting Standard (IFRS 15) on the status of limited risk distributor versus sales agent may play a role.[112] In both the customs and the direct taxation inquiries, the challenge may be to prove that the related party importer is a stand-alone entity acting in its individual capacity as buyer/importer and reseller.[113]

[c] Limited Risk Distributor (LRD) as Buyer Versus Sales Agent

One oft-encountered issue in some jurisdictions is ascertaining whether there has been a sale for export to a limited risk distributor or whether the importer is not a buyer at all but is only an agent acting on behalf of the seller. The customs valuation law

111. Ruling no. H008101 (October 9, 2012), citing ruling nos. H092448 (May 4, 2010), 547197 (August 22, 2000) and 546602 (January 29, 1997).
112. International Financial Reporting Standard (IFRS) 15, *Revenue from Contracts with Customers*, defines the accounting protocol for distribution models. The following discussion owes a debt to Neville, "International Accounting Standard on Distribution, Principal vs. Agent," 29 J. Int'l Tax'n (November 2018) at 29.
113. Even assuming that hurdle has been overcome, the additional burden that accompanies all related party transactions will take effect. The importer will need to prove that the relationship did not influence the price paid to its related party seller. In other words, the local entity will need to justify the low profit earned by the foreign seller and/or the high profit earned on its own resales to the customers in the country of importation. *See* discussion below.

consequences are profound since a TV appraisement requires a sale for export. Moreover, a sales agent's commission is dutiable.[114]

In this connection, an internationally agreed accounting protocol that took effect from January 1, 2018, may be helpful. The new standard serves to lay out those characteristics which are associated with a sale versus an agency function.

Other readers, and specifically those who ply their trade in international tax, will also know that it is important to ascertain whether a given transaction qualifies as a sale. One reason for this is that the revenue recognition rules under accounting standards will distinguish between revenue arising from a sale and revenue earned in compensation for a rendered service.

And to get straight to the point, both direct tax authorities and private sector professionals and their counterparts in the customs field need to discern whether there has been a sale for export or whether, instead, the putative buyer/importer is not a buyer at all but a selling agent, or to use the European term a "commissionaire,"[115] representing the interests of a foreign principal.

The classic dilemma faced by an importer/taxpayer is how "limited" the LRD's role should be. The risk is that if the importer's role is whittled or "skinnied" down too far, meaning the attributes of ownership are discarded, then the fact of an underlying sale is denied and the importer's status as a buyer/reseller is lost.

This analysis can be traced back in the US at least as far back to the CBP's unsuccessful efforts in the *Orbisphere* case, which was followed by the Limiting TD discussed above.[116]

With the post-BEPS[117] migration to LRD structures, customs and income tax authorities are sure to confront many more instances in which the buyer/agent issue must be decided.

Customs authorities can look to customs law jurisprudence in that effort. In the US, for example, we have already cited a body of case law and to some of the many binding rulings issued by CBP and available on CROSS.[118] At the international level,

---

114. This is discussed in §3.01[I][2] below.
115. Some have defined "sales agent" in the narrow sense to refer only to those persons who solicit orders on behalf of a principal and refer the sales prospects to that principal. When used in this discussion, however, the term "sales agent" refers broadly to those persons who not only fall under that narrow descriptor but also to those who actually sell products in their own name but on behalf of another, i.e., in the same sense as "commissionaire." In the US, we use the single term "sales agent" or "selling agent" to refer to both of these connotations, the term "commissionaire" not being generally used.
116. *Orbisphere Corp. v. United States*, 13 CIT 866, 726 F. Supp 1344 (1989).
117. The acronym "BEPS" refers to the practice of Base Erosion and Profit Shifting. The BEPS project has been organized under the auspices of the OECD to redress what it saw as abuses or gaps arising from corporate tax planning strategies used by multinational enterprises to "shift" profits from higher-tax jurisdictions to lower-tax jurisdictions or no-tax locations (so-called tax havens) where there is little or no economic activity, thus "eroding" the "tax-base" of the higher-tax jurisdictions using deductible payments such as interest or royalties. We will see that developments in the BEPS project are relevant to buyer versus selling agent status, which we discuss here, and to transfer pricing which we discuss in Part II.
118. *See* n. 10 above.

TCCV Case Study 9.1 (dating from 1995)[119] is also helpful, with the importer's status as an independent legal entity, taking title and assuming risk of loss and assuming financial risk of nonpayment by the customer all supporting a finding of a sale for export. The fact that the distributor has an exclusive right to import—it is styled a "sole distributor"—has no effect on its status as a buyer/reseller, and it was not effectively controlled for the purposes of Article 15.4 (e). The Agreement is clear that the mere fact there is a business association in the nature of a sole agent, sole distributor or sole concessionaire is not enough to create a related party status. Instead, there must be a showing that one or more of the Article 15.4 criteria have been met.[120]

[i] Customs Valuation Law Impact

The customs law effect of the importer being an agent and not a buyer would expose the compensation of the importer/agent to customs duty, as selling agents' commissions are dutiable.[121] This is discussed below.

[ii] Income Tax Effects

For income tax purposes, the foreign principal might be exposed to income tax liability in the country of importation because the foreign party would have a "Permanent Establishment" (PE) in the person of the agent that was entering into local contracts that bound the principal.

Actions taken in the BEPS project undertaken at the Organisation for Economic Co-operation and Development (OECD) spoke to this issue directly. Action 7 of the BEPS project was designed to forestall artificial avoidance of PE status through commissionaire strategies and similar arrangements. Action 7 explained this succinctly:

> A commissionaire arrangement may be loosely defined as an arrangement through which a person sells products in a State in its own name but on behalf of a foreign enterprise that is the owner of these products. Through such an arrangement, a foreign enterprise is able to sell its products in a State without technically having a permanent establishment to which such sales may be attributed for tax purposes and without, therefore, being taxable in that State on the profits derived from such

119. TCCV, CS 9.1, Sole Agents, Sole Distributors and Sole Concessionaires (October 1995). The title is misleading, as it does not discuss agents or concessionaires.
120. During the negotiations, India had argued for the deletion of the Article 15.4 proviso, which would have meant that any of those exclusive party dealings would have created a related party status. GATT, Multilateral Trade Negotiations, Group "Non-Tariff Measures," Sub-Group "Customs Matters," Customs Valuation, Agreement on Implementation of Article VII of the General Agreement on Tariffs and Trade, MTN/NTM/W/206 (14 December 1978). That proposal was not adopted.
121. Valuation Agreement, Article 8.1 (a) (i). US— 19 USC § 1401a(b)(1)(B); Canada, Customs Act, subparagraph 48(5)(a)(i); EU Regulation (EU) No. 952/2013 of 9 October 2013—the Union Customs Code ("UCC"), Article 71.1(a)(i).

> sales. Since the person that concludes the sales does not own the products that it sells, that person cannot be taxed on the profits derived from such sales and may only be taxed on the remuneration that it receives for its services (usually a commission).[122]

The approach taken in Action 7 is to amend certain provisions of Article 5 of the OECD Model Tax Convention. As a result of such changes, a foreign enterprise is deemed to have a PE in a country if it has a person acting there on behalf of the enterprise and, in doing so, that person habitually concludes contracts or habitually plays the principal role leading to the conclusion of relevant contracts that are routinely concluded without material modifications by the enterprise (paragraph 5) and drawing a sharp distinction between an "independent agent" and a "dependent agent," i.e., a person that "acts exclusively or almost exclusively on behalf of one or more enterprises to which it is closely related" (paragraph 6).

Moreover, the specific exemptions created by Article 5 (4), such as the maintenance of inventory stocks, were limited to instances in which they are preparatory or auxiliary activities only.

[iii] Post-BEPS Experience

When faced with the possibility that a tax authority will find a PE for the foreign entity through application of Action 7 standards, one reaction to the BEPS has been the migration from the sales agent model to a buy/resell model for related party transactions.

The binary choice—buyer/reseller versus sales agent—is frequently isolated in the context of a distribution agreement. This is because a distributor can be set up so that the importer can act in either capacity.

If the issue of PE is skirted by moving to a buy/resell model, there is a further great and obvious international tax planning advantage to be gained if the related party distributor is a limited risk, buy/resell distributor (LRD). Consider if the country of importation is a "high tax" jurisdiction, and the country where the seller is located is a low tax jurisdiction. By assigning functions, assets and risks that are limited in scope, the income tax liability of the LRD in the country of importation is managed in a "tax efficient" manner, and it is at the same time appropriate to recognize a larger share of the revenue by the foreign seller in the low tax jurisdiction.

As an example, the LRD, like its full-risk distributor brethren, will also take title, but its other risks are limited—another party (the exporter or another related party) may assume some responsibility for fulfilling such other aspects of the customer contract as after-sales service.

Inventory and credit risks may be limited, as well, and some brand-building and advertising may be undertaken by the exporter or brand owner.

---

122. OECD, BEPS Project, Action 7, Preventing the Artificial Avoidance of Permanent Establishment Status, at 9 (2015).

We must note that the LRD strategy has been applied for many years but that it has gained much greater momentum post-BEPS.

Tax authorities may be guided by the principles set forth in the BEPS instruments, and they may also turn to the International Accounting Standards Board (IASB) issuance of a new revenue standard: International Financial Reporting Standard (IFRS) 15, Revenue from Contracts with Customers and Accounting Standards Codification (ASC) 606. The effect of IFRS 15 is to differentiate between the two models.

A buy-resell model requires recognition of gross revenue by the distributor with a deduction for cost of goods.

A sales agent model requires recognition only of the net revenue (the commission) earned by the sales agent.

The IFRS 15 Standard is entirely consistent with the principles underlying both income tax and customs law analysis; viz., it is the substance not the form which controls the analysis. Further, that Standard draws the same distinction between principal (in this case, meaning a buyer/reseller that is acting on its own behalf) and agent that any customs authority needs to draw in analyzing an import transaction, on the basis of performance obligation (defined as a promise to transfer to the customer a good or service (or a bundle of goods or services) that is "distinct"):

- A "principal" has a performance obligation directly with [or owed directly to] a customer.
- An "agent" arranges for another party (the principal) to have the performance obligation.

You will recognize here the alignment with BEPS Action 7.

IFRS 15 paragraph B35 (Principal versus agent considerations) states: "An entity is not necessarily acting as a principal if the entity obtains legal title only momentarily before legal title is transferred to a customer." This is a reference to "flash title," a device very much in vogue for international tax planners seeking to restrict a taxpayer's functions and financial undertakings but disfavored and often disregarded by customs authorities unless the importer can prove there was an otherwise valid sale.[123] As for the standards to be applied to "agent" status, IFRS 15 sets forth several indicators (in paragraph 37) of agent status, all of which I submit which are entirely consistent with both BEPS Action 7 and customs valuation law principles:

- Another party is primarily responsible for fulfilling the contract.
- The entity does not have inventory risk before or after the goods have been ordered by a customer, during shipping, or on return.
- The entity does not have discretion in establishing prices.
- The entity's consideration is in the form of a commission.
- The entity does not have a credit risk for the customer receivables.

123. For US authorities, *see*, e.g., ruling nos. H281340 (December 12, 2017) and H266540 (September 8, 2016).

Can it be argued that this standard is not relevant to a customs valuation inquiry into a sale for export? No. It is beyond cavil that the standard is entirely consistent with the customs valuation law principles and the interpretations of those principles expressed in the extant customs law jurisprudence with which I am familiar.

Examples 45 and 46 are quite relevant illustrations of this Principal/Agent dichotomy.

To those customs practitioners in the private sector and to those responsible officials in customs authorities, be certain that I am not suggesting that the BEPS 15 and/or the IFRS 15 Standard take precedence over, or supersede, the pertinent customs valuation law statutes or the WCO and the country-by-country interpretations promulgated in administrative rulings. Likewise, I am not counseling that they should be ignored altogether. That would be a dreadful mistake, and one that flies in the face of these realities.

Instead, as with a general discussion of most transfer pricing analysis and documentation, the document or other external standard should be evaluated on a case-by-case basis and on its merits and dispassionately and, where the external sources are then found to be relevant and helpful, they might be/should be consulted.[124]

In this buyer versus agent connection, we have seen that the customs valuation authorities have wrestled with these issues for more than three decades. I submit that these tax and accounting standards are both relevant and helpful, especially so in the context of the "totality of facts and circumstances" standard of review that characterizes, or should characterize, most customs authority reviews.

As an illustration, I would submit that the BEPS distinction between "dependent" and "independent" agents, while helpful in eliminating harmful profit shifting for income tax purposes, is also helpful for customs valuation purposes. Recall, a sole or exclusive distributor, one that might be classed a "dependent agency" for tax purposes, is not regarded as a related party unless it is subject to management control.[125] A review of the Action 7 discussion on this Article 5(6) issue reveals a focus on what may be characterized as "dependent" status," one that might be paraphrased "management control" and thus would be consistent with and relevant to a customs valuation law review under Valuation Agreement, Articles 15.4 and 15.5, albeit with a different end result in mind. *See* Article 5 Commentary, paragraph 38.2 of BEPS.

It is not sufficient to establish that all of the foregoing criteria have been met and there has been a sale. The qualifying event for a transaction value is a sale "for export" to the country of importation.

124. *See*, e.g., TCCV Com. 23.1, Examination of the Expression "Circumstances of Sale" Under Article 1.2 (A) in Relation to the Use of Transaction Value (October 2010). *See also* discussion on CCV Dec. 7.1, n. 100 in Ch. 1.

125. Valuation Agreement, Articles 15.4 and 15.5. *See* TCCV Explanatory Note 4.1, Consideration of Relationship Under Article 15.5, Read in Conjunction with Article 15.4 (October 1985).

[D] Sale for Export

The customs authority and the importer will have an easy time of it if the Incoterm governing the sale is a "destination" term[126] calling for a delivery to the country of importation. Failing that, if delivery to the buyer is to take place in the country of export, say EXW (ex-works) or FCA (Free Carrier), if the international transportation calls for a direct shipment to the country of importation, then this requirement should be easily met. Thus, a Bill of Lading (B/L) or an Air Way Bill that calls for that direct shipment will be an important element of proof.

In the US, the standard is that the goods are "irrevocably destined for the US" or that the goods are "clearly destined for the US."[127]

That standard was challenged when an importer argued that a qualifying sale for export must be an international sale, and when the buyer and seller were both located in the US, that sale was a domestic sale and could not be seen as a qualifying sale for export.[128] In *Midwest-CBK*, the CIT rejected that notion. The underlying facts showed that the subject goods were sold on an "FOB Buffalo" basis, but they had been stored in Canada, having been previously imported into Canada from foreign countries. Upon orders from US customers being accepted in the US by the plaintiff's representatives, the goods were packaged and shipped directly to the US customers. The court rejected an argument based upon a 1933 case[129] that a sale where the buyer and seller had both been located in the US could not qualify as a sale for export. That 1933 decision interpreted a predecessor valuation statute, and had been cited in *Orbisphere*, which we have already discussed. The court limited the *Orbisphere* decision and also held that the "FOB Buffalo" sales term did not establish that the sales were intended to be a domestic sale.[130] Finally, the court's assertion that domestic sales might qualify as a sale for export raises a concern. The court referred to a 1999 Federal Circuit decision[131] which held that if sales by a Canadian company (VWPC) to its US affiliate (VWPA) cannot serve as the basis for transaction value, then transaction value must be based upon sales by the US affiliate to its US customers. I find that troubling because, as we have seen in the "Purchaser in ..." discussion, the customs authority's normal recourse after rejecting that initial sale is to characterize the importer as a sales agent in a putative sale from the foreign company to the local customer, rather than characterizing the sale from the US affiliate to the local customer as a qualifying sale for export. I question the validity of the court's analysis. Query, if the sale to the US affiliate has been disqualified as a sale for export, meaning that the US affiliate has not taken title to the goods, how can the US affiliate then sell—pass title—to the US customers? Only

126. These "D Incoterms" include DAP, DPU and DDP.
127. *E.C. McAfee Co. v. United States*, 842 F.2d 314, 319 (Fed. Cir. 1988).
128. *Midwest-CBK, LLC v. United States*, Slip Op. 22-51 (CIT 2022).
129. *United States v. Massce & Company*, 21 CCPA 54 (1933).
130. The discussion about the sales term is confusing. Because the court had already disposed of the domestic versus international nature of a qualifying sales, the issue was rendered moot. As a further aside, the use of "FOB Buffalo" on these facts makes no sense under the Incoterms. Instead, "DDP" would have been more appropriate.
131. *VWP of America, Inc. v. United States*, 175 F.3d 1327, 1334 (Fed. Cir. 1999).

in the singular case where the US affiliate had bought the goods first and intended to keep them in Canada would the US affiliate have acquired title in a sale that did not qualify as a valid sale for export to the US. Of course, that would be an entirely different fact pattern than was presented to the *VWP* court and that court's sweeping pronouncement would need to be severely retrenched. To their credit, the government attorneys in the 1999 decision had argued for the sales agent status of the US affiliate and for there being a qualifying sale for export from the Canadian company to the US customers.

A "sale for export" inquiry typically arises when there is a shipment to an intermediate country. The presumption is that merchandise shipped to a foreign location is not sold for export to the US.[132] The importer must be able to overcome that presumption and prove to the satisfaction of the customs authority that the transaction nevertheless is a qualifying sale for export.

In the case of goods purchased and shipped to an intermediate country, and then later shipped to the US by the owner, who retains ownership until the goods are sold in a post-import transaction, CBP may say that the importation into the US in the second movement of the goods was not pursuant to a sale. True, there had been a sale—that was the occasion of the movement of the goods into the intermediate country. The later movement was an inventory shift or "stock transfer" by the owner. There would be no basis for a TV on the importation into the US.[133]

In several instances, CBP has determined that use of an imported product in an intermediate country for an extended period of time will disqualify a sale for export finding.[134]

Nevertheless, some importers have been successful. The presumption that merchandise shipped to an intermediate country is not sold for export to the US may be rebutted by sufficient evidence to show that the merchandise is clearly destined for the US at the time of the sale by the foreign producer.[135] It helps if the goods remain in customs custody, such as in a bonded warehouse or free trade zone, in the intermediate country or if they are imported on a qualified, export-mandatory basis in that intermediate country or if they remain in an "in transit" status in the intermediate country.[136] You should know that, at least in the US, the "clearly destined" issue is most often encountered in First Sale importations, discussed below, as well as in those instances where the goods are shipped to an intermediate country first rather than directly to the US.

132. *See* ruling no. 563420 (April 14, 2006).
133. This was the outcome in ruling no. H229701 (September 19, 2012).
134. Ruling nos. 542310 (May 22, 1981) (no sale for exportation to the United States when drill bits manufactured in Italy were stored in France for an indefinite period); 542962 (December 29, 1982) (no sale for exportation when motorcycle purchased in Japan for the purpose of being used for an extended period overseas before being imported); 547197 (August 22, 2010) (no sale for exportation when vehicles were used in Europe for up to twelve months after the sale from the manufacturer).
135. *See especially* ruling no. 563420 (April 14, 2006).
136. Canada anticipates the importation of such goods that had been "in transit." Customs Act, section 54.

This standard might be compared to the "imported directly" requirement of the GSP regime in the US, the standard being defined in the customs regulations, in pertinent part:[137]

> (d) If the shipment is from any beneficiary developing country to the US through the territory of any other country and the invoices and other documents do not show the US as the final destination, the articles in the shipment upon arrival in the US are imported directly only if they:
> (1) remained under the control of the customs authority of the intermediate country;
> (2) did not enter into the commerce of the intermediate country except for the purpose of sale other than at retail, and the Center director is satisfied that the importation results from the original commercial transaction between the importer and the producer or the latter's sales agent; and
> (3) were not subjected to operations other than loading and unloading, and other activities necessary to preserve the articles in good condition.

Parenthetically, a "direct shipment" criterion prohibiting transshipment via intermediate countries is a standard feature of Free Trade Agreements (FTAs).[138]

In one line of rulings, CBP has applied an interpretation that I believe is misguided. CBP has looked to a "contingency of diversion" where the product may be shipped for inspection or testing in an intermediate country and, on that basis, there is no qualifying sale for export for any of the products that, in fact, had been actually imported.

Cheese made in Lithuania but routed to Holland for testing before being sent to the US was deemed to not meet a strict application of the "clearly destined" test.[139] CBP stressed that the terms of the contract provided that: (i) the cheese could be rejected (in CBP's view, this meant that the goods were not destined for US) if of inferior quality and (ii) none of the commercial documents pertaining to the first sale referenced the US as the ultimate destination of the cheese. Several subsequent rulings quoted the rationale of this ruling, the grandfather of the "contingency of diversion" rulings, in failing to find Sale for Export.

This CBP interpretation—the rejection of some of the goods, causing that portion not to be shipped to the US, will disqualify the remainder of the goods that are, in fact, actually shipped—is suspect. It has never been subjected to judicial scrutiny.

This "contingency of diversion" line notably aside, these interpretations appear sound. There is no reason to believe that other customs authorities would or should take a different view on the "sale for export" criterion.

---

137. 19 CFR § 10.175(d).
138. For example, Article 4.11 of the US-Chile FTA: "Each Party shall provide that a good shall not be considered an originating good if the good undergoes subsequent production or any other operation outside the territories of the Parties, other than unloading, reloading, or any other process necessary to preserve the good in good condition or to transport the good to the territory of a Party."
139. Ruling no. 546069 (August 1, 1996). *See also* ruling nos. 546427 (June 18, 2014), 547825 (July 16, 2001) and 547349 (May 5, 2000).

Moving away from the issue of an intervening importation into an intermediate country, the next question that arises will be that of two competing, back-to-back sales for export to the country of importation. If there are two or more such sales, which sale should be used by the customs authority to make a transaction value appraisement?

We come now to the controversial doctrine.[140]

[1] First Sale for Export

We should start this discussion with the acknowledgement that a flow chart depicting the movement of imported goods from the point of manufacture to the point of entry into the customs territory will actually represent two movements, not one. The flow chart will trace the physical goods' movements—perhaps beginning with the factory, extending to the point at which the goods are loaded onto a conveyance and ultimately to the point of customs clearance and perhaps to the delivery to the buyer after customs clearance in the country of importation. There will be B/Ls and other documents such as cargo receipts which will evidence those physical movements. Typically, the goods will begin their journey at the manufacturer's factory or warehouse.

But the flow chart might also trace the sales of the products, and that might introduce some complexity. There could be a "drop shipping" of the goods, in the sense that the goods purchased by the buyer might be delivered to the buyer's customer. The buyer and his customer might be in different countries.

The flow chart might also reveal more than one sale on the chart between the production of the goods and their purchase by the buyer. In the simplest scenario, one which would have been the norm in bygone days, the imported goods would be manufactured and then sold by the same company. There would be one sale of the goods. To be sure, there would always have been trading companies which would have bought goods produced by others and resold them to customers.

In a trend that developed with business reorganization efficiencies and income tax planning goals in mind, we started to see in the 1980s more and more companies split off either the manufacturing functions or the sales and marketing functions, or both, to newly created related party entities. Or the decision was taken to outsource those functions altogether to third parties. In either event, the commercial trend was to introduce a new level of complexity, in the sense that the buyer in a foreign country would be entering into a sales agreement with a company that did not manufacture the goods. Instead, that seller, whom we might call the "vendor," had to arrange for the goods to be manufactured for him by another party, whom we might call the "factory." That party might or not be related to the vendor. Thus, there would be two sales—the sale by the factory to the vendor and then the sale by the vendor to the buyer/importer. This is a "series of sales" or "chain of sales" of the same goods.

---

140. This is not to be confused with a quite separate US legal doctrine. That other "first-sale" doctrine (also sometimes referred to as the "right of first sale" or the "first sale rule") is an American legal concept that limits the rights of an intellectual property owner to control resale of products embodying its intellectual property.

While many sales are still patterned on a one-sale basis—the same party makes the goods and sells them to the buyer—this series of sales model raises the question: if there are these seriatim sales of the goods, which one of them should serve as the basis for a transaction value appraisement? Stated more directly, can the earlier or "first" sale in the series fit the statutory definition of the qualifying sale for export?

This is the quandary of the First Sale for Export, often shortened to FSFE or First Sale. It has been an up again, down again issue ever since the Valuation Agreement was concluded. At the present time, only the US recognizes the FSFE doctrine; i.e., the earlier or "first" sale can function as the qualifying sale for export. In the past, Canada recognized the FSFE approach.[141] Likewise, the prelapsarian EU position was a recognition of FSFE from the inception of its implementation of the Valuation Agreement,[142] but the EU Commission spearheaded its scrapping with the adoption of the Union Customs Code (UCC) which took full effect in May 2016.[143] Reports are that dropping First Sale was a hotly contested, divisive issue among the Member States. New Zealand had also applied First Sale until its statute was amended in 2018. It is worthwhile to note that the three jurisdictions to have dropped the First Sale rule did so by way of legislative amendments, presumably at the bidding of the customs authorities. No reviewing court in those jurisdictions held that the First Sale rule was unsound.

The operative provision of the UCC IA is Article 128, which establishes that:

> 1. The transaction value of the goods sold for export to the customs territory of the Union shall be determined at the time of acceptance of the customs declaration on the basis of the sale occurring immediately before the goods were brought into that customs territory.

At the international level, the TCCV adopted Commentary 22.1[144] which counseled for a "last sale" customs valuation based upon the concept that the buyer for these customs valuation purposes should be construed as being in the country of

141. After the Canadian customs authorities lost in court [*Harbour Sales (Windsor) Ltd v. D/MNR* [1994] 4647 ETC], they succeeded in getting the valuation law changed to require transaction value based on a sale to a purchaser in Canada.
142. The CCC IR, Article 147.1, third sentence, allowed the declarant to ask the customs authority to accept the price of a sale prior to the last sale, provided that the declarant can demonstrate that there are specific and relevant circumstances, which led to an export of the goods to the customs territory of the Community.
143. UCC IA, Article 347 provided a transitional period for elimination of First Sale where it could be shown that there had been a contract in place prior to 18 January 2016. The grace period lasted until 31 December 2017.
144. TCCV, Com. 22.1, Meaning of the Expression "Sold for Export to the Country of Importation" in a Series of Sales (April 2007). This followed an aborted attempt at revising Advisory Opinion 14.1 with the same title, that attempt being shelved in October 2001. AO 14.1 was first adopted by the TCCV in March 1985, and later examples were twice provided in the 1986 Sessions. The discussions in AO 14.1 did not address the FSFE question directly, with the validity only of the later sale being examined where there were series of sales. Also note that the facts in Examples 5 and 6 do not make for a valid FSFE claim, and an attempt to seek FSFE for an importation into the US on those facts would fail.

importation.[145] A close review of the analysis employed by TCCV there and a point-by-point refutation is beyond the scope of this discussion, but it does bear notice that its observations do not withstand close scrutiny.

For instance, the remark that the buyer was "normally" expected to be located in the country of importation runs counter to, and would have us actually ignore, the long-standing commercial practice of goods being "drop shipped" for importation by a buyer located outside the country of importation. The qualifying term "normally" here is unfounded and brings no appreciable value to the discussion. If anything, its presence indicates that there are sales—indeed, perhaps many sales—where the buyer is not located in the country of importation. And, of course, there are many importations where there have been a series of sales. Finally, the notion that First Sale presented undue burdens on the customs authority is belied entirely by the experience in the US, where the burden has been squarely imposed on the importer to present a complete "paper trail," or in the EU, where the Commission had proceeded on the same assumption that the burden was that of the declarant.[146]

The actual text of the Valuation Agreement, let us be reminded, looks to a sale *for* export. The text does not require an actual sale *into* the country of importation. Note the not-so-subtle difference. An early GATT draft had proposed:

> The value for customs purposes of imported merchandise is the "actual value," which is understood to be *the price at which,* at a time and place determined by the legislation of the country of importation, the *merchandise imported or like merchandise is sold or would be sold to that country in the ordinary course of trade* under fully competitive conditions (emphasis added).[147]

Of course, that text was not adopted. Instead, the Valuation Agreement looks to the price derived when "goods are sold *for export* to the country of importation ..." (emphasis added). The "for export" criterion here must mean goods that are intended to be exported. This was the very meaning of the draft interpretative note, styled as a "Rule," suggested by the EC in 1975.[148] Let us see how they phrased that Rule:

> *The value for customs purposes is the price at which the goods are sold or would be sold with a view to importation into the country of importation* in the ordinary course of trade under fully competitive conditions between a buyer and a seller independent of each other, where that price is the sole consideration (emphasis added).

145. Because the TCCV rules require a consensus, its adoption signifies that the US and the EU delegations both took positions which contravened the legal status of FSFE in their jurisdictions. In fact, we know from the CCV Minutes reporting on the TCCV meetings that it was the EU delegation which had introduced the question.
146. *See* European Community Customs Code Committee (Customs Valuation Section), Commentary No. 7 on the Application of Article 147 of Commission Regulation (EEC) No. 2454/93 of 2 July 1993, in Compendium of Customs Valuation texts of the Customs Code Committee, TAXUD/800/2002-EN, September 2008 ("EU Commission Compendium 2008"), 39.
147. GATT, Group 2 on Valuation, Draft Interpretative Notes, Spec (71)128 (28 October 1971).
148. GATT, Multilateral Trade Negotiations Group, "Non-Tariff Measures," Sub-Group "Customs Matters," Customs Valuation, Addendum, MTN/NTM/W/20/Add.1 (29 September 1975).

You should have grasped the implications. Whether the phrase is focused upon an intended, or perhaps anticipated, export to the country of importation or an intended, or anticipated, importation into that country, it is equally clear that a first sale from factory to vendor would qualify. The standards employed by the US in continuing to apply an FSFE approach are clear, and they are faithful to this interpretation.

While the EC had advanced this "intention to export" criterion in 1975—you may note that it was supported on the formal record by Korea and the Nordic countries as well—in November 1977, the EC unveiled the draft proposal which we showed had generated such a strong negative reaction in some quarters, especially developing countries.[149] I raise it again here because in that first draft we see that the EC had explicitly proposed a "buyer is established in the country of importation" condition on Article 1. That condition was rejected and was never adopted.[150] Thus, in the face of the negotiation history of the Valuation Agreement, to argue as though that rejected explicit condition should in some manner be later teased out of the text in some implied fashion and to have been reanimated should be unacceptable.[151]

Two other points from the Commentary deserve responses, drawn from long and hard-won experience with the US practice. As the US practice makes clear, additions under Article 8, especially dutiable assists, must be added to a First Sale price. Second, the burden is placed entirely on the importer to prove its case. Many a US importer has seen its FSFE application founder as a result of failing to meet that heavy burden. This protocol imposes no undue or even additional "practical" burden on the customs authority in the US. There is no expectation that an application of the same rigorous standards would not yield the same result on FSFE entries elsewhere. And we might add a final underscoring of the need to harmonize the customs valuation rules on the basis of actual commercial practices. It needs hardly to be mentioned that "middleman sales" or "series of sales" has a long-standing history as a business model, especially within certain industry sectors.[152]

What is the upshot? In the absence of a formal, fully binding Decision of the CCV or of an amendment to the Valuation Agreement itself, I believe that with FSFE we are dealing with an interpretation on a customs valuation matter that is optional for the WTO Members. It appears that its current continued viability in the US reflects an unspoken choice between alternative interpretations, in much the same category as the

149. GATT, Multilateral Trade Negotiations Group, "Non-Tariff Measures," Sub-Group "Customs Matters," Customs Valuation, MTN/NTM/W/122 (8 November 1977), 5.
150. We need not refer to the final, agreed text of the Valuation Agreement. As early as the very next relevant document in the negotiation history at the GATT/WTO repository we see the now-familiar "sale for export" formulation. GATT, Multilateral Trade Negotiations Group, "Non-Tariff Measures," "Sub-Group" "Customs Matters," Customs Valuation, MTN/NTM/W/162 (21 June 1978).
151. It is ironic in the extreme that the EU would then have reverted to its original 1975 position. Its early application of and long-term adherence to FSFE signaled it had unequivocally accepted the viability of that doctrine.
152. It may surprise you to learn that the *McAfee* case, AKA the Hong Kong Tailors' Case, can trace its origins to the earliest days of the US practice under the Valuation Agreement legislation. An Internal Advice request filed by the CBP port was filed on January 16, 1980—suggesting that the issue had arisen in 1979. Ruling no. 065056 (October 17, 1980 (TAA 10)).

discretionary treatment of interest charges under Decision 3.1 or the customs value of computer software in Decision 4.1 in the same Article 1 context.[153] There is hardly a "uniform" rule at present.

At this juncture, we should turn to the US practice, for this is the one jurisdiction where FSFE is still available. As alluded in the discussion immediately above, a body of US case law and rulings on FSFE has arisen over the course of the past four decades which has been in equal measures controversial and beneficial. These FSFE determinations were formerly better known in the US as "Nissho Iwai" cases, after the leading US court case, which was a victory on appeal for the importer.[154]

This reversal in favor of the importer was based upon the importer's ability to establish that there was a sale in Japan from the foreign manufacturer/seller, Kawasaki, to Nissho Iwai, a foreign "middleman," who was a related Japanese trading company. The trading company imported the merchandise, subway cars, which were sold to the US purchaser, the Metropolitan Transit Authority ("MTA") in New York.

CBP had successfully argued at trial that of the two foreign sales which could qualify as the basis for transaction value: (i) the sale from Kawasaki to the trading company or (ii) the sale from the trading company to the MTA, the qualifying sale for the purposes of the valuation law was the later sale to the MTA. This had the obvious effect of capturing all of the trading company's markup as part of dutiable value.

The Government's position, which came to be expressly overruled in *Nissho Iwai*, had been that if there were two qualifying sales, then that sale which "most directly caused the exportation" must be employed.[155] In effect, this was a "but for" test. The argument was that, but for the order from the US customer, the goods would not have been ordered by the middleman and, therefore, CBP was justified in going to the later sale.

This "but for" test had been based on an analysis which had been rejected on appellate review in an earlier court loss by CBP. That was the so-called Hong Kong Tailors case.[156] There, the appellate court overturned a trial court holding that made-to-measure clothing (men's suits) should be valued on the basis of the price paid by the US customers rather than the price paid by the distributors to the Hong Kong tailors. In the face of its loss in *McAfee*, CBP had published a Limiting Treasury Decision (a "Limiting TD"), which announced that CBP would follow that decision

153. We must be mindful that Dec. 3.1 is focused upon the PAPP and with FSFE we are dealing with an Article 1 "sale for export" question.
154. *Nissho Iwai American Corp. v. United States.*, 982 F.2d 505 (Fed. Cir. 1992), rev'g 16 CIT 86 (1992). For further reading, *see*, e.g., Neville, "First Sale for Export via Canada," 31 J. Int'l Tax'n (August 2020) at 31, Neville, "Further Thoughts on First Sale for Export," 27 J. Int'l Tax'n (January 2016) at 31, Neville, "First Sale for Export under Attack Again," 19 J. Int'l Tax'n 17 (April 2008) at 17 and "First Sale for Export Customs Valuation Rule: The Second Time Around," 16 J. Int'l Tax'n (August 2005) at 24.
155. This was the standard enunciated in *Brosterhous, Coleman & Co. v. United States*, 14 CIT 307 (1990). The appellate court in *Nissho Iwai* expressly overruled this CIT decision, whose authority was already questionable in light of *E. C. McAfee Co. v. United States*, 6 Fed. Cir. 92, 842 F.2d 314 (Fed Cir. 1988) (McAfee), rev'g *American Air Parcel Forwarding Co. v. United States*, 664 F. Supp. 1434 (CIT 1987).
156. *McAfee.*

only for made-to-measure clothing, i.e., only on other Hong Kong Tailor cases![157] and would continue to appraise all other merchandise on the basis of the later of two alternative PAPPs.[158]

In a third "middleman" case decided shortly after *Nissho Iwai*, the Court of International Trade provided even more guidance to importers. In *Synergy Sport International v. United States*,[159] Judge Restani locked the door which *Nissho Iwai* had earlier closed. The CBP test of selecting the later sale if there were two sales competing for "sale for exportation" status was declared to be contrary to the valuation statute's prohibition against appraising merchandise on the basis of the higher of two alternative values.[160]

As developed by the US courts, the FSFE strategy looks to the transaction between the foreign seller and the middlemen *if* the sale and the price meet the statutory criteria. Those criteria require that the prospective FSFE: (i) qualifies as a sale[161]which (ii) is negotiated at arm's length free from any nonmarket influences and (iii) involves goods "clearly destined for export to the United States."

With its multiple losses in the courts, CBP grudgingly applied the FSFE principle, but not without keeping the bar high. As set forth in a 1996 Treasury Decision TD, CBP has required complete details of all relevant transactions.[162] Moreover, CBP practice diverged on some key points from the decisions, such as adopting the view in some rulings that if the foreign goods were going to be inspected after they left the factory and before they were imported into the US, then there was a possibility that some of the goods would be rejected and would not be shipped to the US. As we have already seen, in CBP's eyes, because some could be "diverted," none of the goods would then be able to meet the "clearly destined" test.[163] This CBP view was at odds with the facts in *McAfee*, where the men's suits were, in actual fact, inspected in Hong Kong after they left the factory; the fact that some were, in fact, rejected was not fatal to the "clearly destined" requirement being met there.

In some instances, the importers' bids for FSFE treatment were rejected when the purchased and subsequently imported goods were not unique to the US market, which supposedly created risks of diversion to other countries.[164] In many other instances, FSFE was rejected for insufficient information because the importer was unable to

157. 22 Cust. Bull. & Dec. No. 18 (May 4, 1988).
158. 19 USC § 1401a(f)(2)(B).
159. 17 CIT 18 (CIT 1993).
160. 19 USC § 1401a(f)(2)(B). This is identical to the Valuation Agreement, Article 7.2(b).
161. Importers must take particular care to avoid "flash title" scenarios, where the first and second sales have identical sales terms, such as "FOB port." CBP normally will take the view that there is no valid first sale because the middleman never assumed risk nor took title except possibly for an instant. Ruling no. 547712 (August 1, 2002). *But see* ruling no. 546316 (May 29, 1996) (additional documentation presented which establishes that a bona fide sale occurs between the foreign seller and the US supplier and that the sale constitutes a sale for exportation upon which transaction value may be based).
162. General Notice—Determining Transaction Value in Multi-Tiered Transactions, TD 96-87, 30/31 Cust. Bull. & Dec. 52/1 (January 2, 1997) (TD 96-87). *See also* ruling no. 547607 (February 1, 2002).
163. E.g., ruling no. 546427 (December 19, 1997).
164. *See*, e.g., ruling nos. 545985 (December 19, 1996) and 546901 (January 3, 1996).

provide the strict audit trail of documents.[165] Finally, it is important to understand that third criterion, proving that the FSFE must be shown to be "freed of non-market influences." Where the factory and the middleman are not related, the importer has an easy case. Such a third-party sale is presumptively valid. Only relatively few FSFE applications have been accepted where the factory and the middleman were related, and in those the importer was able to use transfer pricing principles to validate the first sale.[166] Make no mistake—this is ordinarily a foreign seller-to-a foreign buyer fact pattern for the transfer pricing analysis.[167] The recent trend has been for CBP to be asked to issue advance rulings on such facts, but more typically the issues have arisen at the port or the Center of Excellence and been forwarded to CBP Headquarters.[168]

After the *Synergy* decision and the 1996 TD, the FSFE practice was well settled. But in early 2008,[169] CBP proposed to scrap FSFE because, *inter alia*, it was claimed to be in contravention of the US obligations to the multinational consensus as expressed at the WCO in Commentary 22.1. An easy observation to make in this regard is that the then 28-member EU[170] and New Zealand were likewise still applying the FSFE rule at the time. Surely, this would negate any view that the US was either isolated or wrong in its application of the First Sale. Nevertheless, we await developments which may impact the acceptance of First Sale in other jurisdictions. At this writing, the effect of the "BREXIT" vote in the UK on trade and customs matters has yet to be fully measured. We know that the UK had been a strong supporter of First Sale. It could be that a UK which is extra-EU and charting its own course on customs and trade matters again will bring back First Sale but that would be a long way off.

In response to CBP's proposal, an ad hoc alliance of trade associations representing the trade community was able to mount a response, and the result was that a "sense of the Congress" message was inserted into the "2008 Farm Bill,"[171] literally at the last minute. This provision called for an ITC investigation and for CBP to engage in consultation before proceeding further with any action on FSFE, which was recommended to be delayed until 2011. Accordingly, the ITC conducted its study,[172] but CBP took no further action on its proposal—perhaps because the ITC reported that only

---

165. *See*, e.g., ruling no. 547155 (March 22, 2001).
166. Ruling no. 546429 (February 5, 1998); cf. ruling no. 546518 (February 9, 1998). For a longer discussion on this topic, *see* Neville, "When First Sale Meets Transfer Pricing," 31 J. Int'l Tax' (January 2020) at 18.
167. To be sure, CBP has accepted a sale price between a factory and a middleman as being freed of nonmarket influences even where the factory makes no profit, but CBP will want an explanation of the circumstances. Ruling no. H097035 (November 15, 2011) and rulings cited therein; affirmed on reconsideration by ruling no. H215658 (June 11, 2012). Such a sale may still be a bona fide sale.
168. *See*, e.g., ruling nos. W563542 (July 24, 2009), H029330 (January 2. 2009) and H016585 (December 20, 2008).
169. 73 Fed. Reg. 4254 (January 24, 2008).
170. Although some will recall that there had been some discussion within the EU in the mid-1990s about scrapping FSFE.
171. Food, Conservation, and Energy Act of 2008, Pub. L. 110-234, Title XV, § 15422, May 22, 2008, 122 Stat. 1548-49.
172. ITC, Use of the "First Sale Rule" for Customs Valuation of U.S. Imports, Pub. No. 4121, Inv. 332-505 (December 2009), available at https://www.usitc.gov/publications/industry_econ_

2.4% of imports were made on an FSFE basis. CBP had previously required importers to identify that they were claiming FSFE in their customs entry papers. There do not appear to have been any further developments. At this point, it is doubtful whether the US Congress would countenance a change in the customs valuation law or permit the agency's raising of a highly regressive indirect tax, in the form of customs duties, which is what a statutory or administrative repeal of FSFE actually would bring about.

The well-settled rubric applied by CBP and acknowledged by the trade community in First Sale cases was almost undone with the 2021 decision in *Meyer*.

[a] Meyer Corp. US v. United States

The understanding had long been settled that a successful "First Sale" application must be based on a showing of a bona fide sale for export to the US, meaning at arm's length, and that the goods must be clearly destined for the US. A 2021 decision of the CIT[173] introduced, from out-of-the-blue, the additional notion that if the imported goods or the inputs of those goods were from a nonmarket economy (NME) country, then the importer must be able to prove that the sales price was not influenced by that NME status. This "NME" concept is one that is a function of antidumping and countervailing duty law, and has hitherto played no role in customs valuation matters.[174] Having reviewed the available records of the entire negotiating history of the Valuation Agreement, I can assure you that NME status never made an appearance in the discussions. The other interesting backdrop—and this may be news to some—is that while there was no NME analysis in the *Nissho Iwai* or *McAfee* cases, Chinatex, the seller in the first sale in *Synergy Sport International Ltd. v. United States*, was based in a designated NME, China. It is also relevant to note that the subject importations in *Synergy* were made in February 1991, also long after China had been designated as an NME. The *Meyer* court analysis of FSFE grounded in NME status was thus all the more strained.

---

analysis_332/2009/use_%E2%80%9Cfirst_sale_rule%E2%80%9D_customs_valuation_us_imports.htm.

173. *Meyer Corporation, US v. United States*, No. 13-00154, 2021 WL 777788 (CIT March 1, 2021), Slip Op. 21-26 (CIT 2021) (*Meyer II*). For a comprehensive review, *see* Neville, "Customs Valuation Infused with Antidumping Concept: Confusion at the Court," 32 J. Int'l Tax'n (May 2021) at 38. Note that there had been a previous decision in the same court case, *Meyer Corporation, U.S. v. United States*, 255 F. Supp 3d 1348 (CIT 2017) (*Meyer I*). Of interest in this context that *Meyer I* decision held that CBP was justified in seeking financial information from the parent company of the seller to determine whether the price from the seller to the related buyer had been influenced by that relationship under the All Costs Plus a Profit test. *See* discussion at §10.03[D][6] below.

174. In this regard, recall that the General Introductory Commentary of the Valuation Agreement cordons off customs valuation from antidumping measures. Further marking the delineation between the two disciplines, the US statute notes that the list of prohibited valuation methods shall not apply to antidumping cases. 19 USC § 1401a(f)(2). The US trade enforcement regime may treat a lease as the equivalent of a sale, 19 USC § 1677(19), and sales and offers for sale are treated interchangeably. *See* 19 USC § 1677b(a)(1)(B). As a further aside, do not confuse NME status with Normal Trade Relations (NTR) status, which is the term in use by the US to connote Most Favored Nations (MFN) status.

Most commentators missed the fact that there would be no way to limit the application of this precept to First Sale entries, and it would be applied to any and all TV entries from countries with NME status. The *Meyer II* decision was appealed, and a well-deserved reversal was issued by the appellate court in 2022.[175] The opinion repudiated the trial court's interpretation:

> The trial court misinterpreted our decision in Nissho Iwai to require any party to show the absence of all "distortive nonmarket influences." There is no basis in the statute for Customs or the court to consider the effects of a non-market economy on the transaction value. The statute requires only that "the relationship between [the] buyer and seller did not influence the price actually paid or payable." 19 USC § 1401a(b)(2)(B). This provision concerns effects of the relationship between the buyer and seller, not effects of government intervention, and especially not with government intervention that affects the industry as a whole. Neither Nissho Iwai nor the government's briefing identifies other statutes or regulations that could require Customs or the Court of International Trade to consider whether the goods were sold in a nonmarket economy or were otherwise affected by a nonmarket economy.[176]

The appellate court rebuke in *Meyer III* signaled a return to the settled jurisprudence on First Sale. This is defined by the earlier court decisions and the playbook established by CBP in TD 96-87. The decision then promulgated by the trial court after remand invalidated the first sale price on the grounds that the importer had failed to provide financial data for the parent company of the seller and thus had prevented CBP from conducting a review under the All Costs Plus a Profit test. That later *Meyer IV* decision will likely be appealed, presumably on the basis, *inter alia*, that the All Costs Plus a Profit test should be focused solely on examining the experience of the seller itself and not its parent company. A review of the court filings reveals that this discrete question, in contrast to the NME issue, has not heretofore been extensively briefed, let alone resolved by the courts.

CBP's ruling no. 548526 (Jan. 5, 2005) will provide further useful insight. This ruling set forth a nice summary of the documents exchanged between middleman and foreign factory that comprise a "paper trail" that will satisfy the "clearly destined" test. CBP will check to ensure a linkage of POs, pro forma invoices, invoices and payment documents that confirm that the merchandise imported by the middleman was "clearly destined" for the US when it was ordered from the manufacturer. This summary recitation appeared in the ruling—noting that the "clearly destined" test was satisfied:

> Customs and Border Protection notes that the merchandise was shipped directly to the importer by the manufacturer. The invoice from the manufacturer to the middleman confirms direct shipment to the United States from the country of manufacture. This fact, in conjunction with the fact that the manufacturer's

175. *Meyer Corporation, US v. United States*, 43 F. 4th 1325 (Fed. Cir. 2022) (*Meyer III*). After remand, the judge at the CIT issued *Meyer Corporation, US v. United States*, Slip Op. 23-13 (CIT 2023) (*Meyer IV*).
176. *Meyer III*, 43 F. 4th at 1332-33.

invoices note the importer's purchase order numbers, garment style numbers and the middleman's pro forma invoice numbers, indicate that the merchandise was clearly destined for export to the United States when it is ordered by the middleman from the manufacturer.

CBP will closely examine the sales terms and all other aspects of the sales for export, such as the dates of the related POs and invoices.[177] Importers must take particular care to avoid "flash title" scenarios, where the first and second sales have identical sales terms, such as "FOB port." Normally CBP will take the view that there is no valid first sale because the middleman never assumed risk or took title, except possibly for an instant.[178]

The importer will want to avoid a scenario where the parent company aggregates orders from distributors in the US and from other markets and then places that aggregated order on the factory. Example: US affiliate orders 100 units, and Canadian affiliate orders 100 units from the parent company. The parent company places an order for 200 units on the factory, and the factory sells the 200 units to the parent company. Such a scheme will NOT qualify for First Sale, even if each of the two lots of 100 units will be separately drop shipped to the US and to Canada. From CBP's perspective, at the time of the first sale from the factory to the parent company, not all of the 200 units in that aggregated order that were being sold to the parent company were clearly destined for the US.

On a final note on First Sale, especially for international tax aficionados, although this topic is included in the later transfer pricing discussion in Part II, the presence of section 1059A of the US income tax law must be acknowledged. Section 1059A of the US Internal Revenue Code posits that the customs entered value for imported goods sets the ceiling for the cost basis for the imported goods for federal income tax purposes. In 1993, the IRS, with the issuance of a Private Letter Ruling,[179] determined that section 1059A will not pose an obstacle to an importer/taxpayer claiming a lower customs value under FSFE but claiming the higher sale price it has paid for the merchandise in computing its Cost of Goods Sold (COGS) in determining its income tax liability.

For all of those other jurisdictions that do not recognize the First Sale doctrine, it is the Last Sale which forms the basis as the qualifying sale for export.

[2] Last Sale for Export

We have already seen the Canadian Purchaser in Canada requirement. This is clearly a "last sale" provision. In the case of the EU, the relevant authorities are as follows.

177. *See*, e.g., ruling nos. H221835 (August 13, 2012) and H137455 (February 6, 2012) (sham transactions will be disregarded and a First Sale claim will fall).
178. *See*, e.g., ruling nos. H097616 (November 21, 2011) (bank's trust receipt also muddled any conclusion that the middleman assumed risk or took title) and 547712 (August 1, 2002). *But see* ruling no. 546316 (May 29, 1996).
179. PLR 9406026 (November 15, 1993). *See also* PLR 9515011 (January 10, 1995).

Article 70.1 UCC

The primary basis for the customs value of goods shall be the transaction value, that is the price actually paid or payable for the goods when sold for export to the customs territory of the Union, adjusted, where necessary.

Article 128 UCC IA

The transaction value of the goods sold for export to the customs territory of the Union shall be determined at the time of acceptance of the customs declaration on the basis of the sale occurring immediately before the goods were brought into that customs territory.

That may appear to be straightforward and we can assume that an importation into the EU customs territory in a no-sale basis would eliminate transaction value.[180] But the reference to the sale occurring before entering the customs territory introduces a complicating factor. The Commission has taken the view that a sale that takes place while the goods are in a customs warehouse which is physically located within the territory of the EU is not a domestic sale (a sale concluded between two parties residing in the EU) but, instead, is the qualifying last sale that takes place before the goods are brought into the customs territory.[181]

Article 128.2 UCC IA

Where the goods are sold for export to the customs territory of the Union not before they were brought into that customs territory but while in temporary storage or while placed under a special procedure other than internal transit, end-use or outward processing, the transaction value will be determined on the basis of that sale.

Examples 6 and 7 provided by the Commission illustrate that after the goods have been transported on a non-sale basis by the owner of the goods into a customs warehouse located in the EU, the sale by the owner to a buyer for the goods still in the warehouse will qualify as a sale for export under Article 128.2. This will be the case even if that first buyer were to subsequently sell the goods to another buyer while the goods remained in the customs warehouse.[182] This perspective of the first sale within the customs warehouse as a qualifying sale for export appears to be incongruous.

---

180. Likewise, for any goods imported into the US on a no-sale basis and later placed in a warehouse, transaction value would be eliminated. The same result would apply in Canada. *See* Memorandum D13-4-2, Customs Valuation: Goods Sold for Export to Canada, November 21, 2013, APPENDIX, Examples of Import Transaction Situations, Situation J.
181. EU Commission Compendium 2022, Commentary No. 13: Guidance on Articles 128 and 136 UCC IA, 52-68.
182. In the US, for goods admitted into a foreign trade zone on a no-sale basis, the customs value of those goods later transferred from the foreign trade zone on a consumption entry basis will be the value in the transaction which caused the withdrawal from the zone. 19 CFR § 146.62(b)(1). Thus, if there had been two sales of the goods within the zone, the customs value upon the consumption entry would be derived from the second sale. Imported goods may also be placed into a customs bonded warehouse (CBW) on a warehouse entry basis, per 19 USC § 1557 and 19 CFR § 144.0 et seq., in the absence of a sale. There would not be a sale for export to the US for the imported goods withdrawn from either type of bonded facility. As a practical matter, however, transaction value would be available upon the withdrawal of the imported

[E] Price Actually Paid or Payable (PAPP)

Once it has been established that there is a bona fide sale for export, we progress to the all-important matter of price on the road to a TV appraisement.

In the US, most of the Interpretative Notes are not embodied in the statute but are found in the customs regulations. There is an exception for the definition of the PAPP, which is defined in identical terms in both authorities, which includes text from Interpretative Note 1.1:

> The total payment (whether direct or indirect, and exclusive of any costs, charges, or expenses incurred for transportation, insurance, and related services incident to the international shipment of the merchandise from the country of exportation to the place of importation in the United States) made, or to be made, for imported merchandise by the buyer to, or for the benefit of, the seller.[183]

In Canada, we see a consistent definition of the PAPP:

> The transaction value of goods shall be determined by ascertaining the price paid or payable for the goods when the goods are sold for export to Canada and adjusting the price paid or payable in accordance with subsection (5) [the adjustments contemplated by Art. 8 of the Valuation Agreement].[184]

In the case of the EU, Article 70 of the UCC directs:

> 1. The primary basis for the customs value of goods shall be the transaction value, that is the price actually paid or payable for the goods when sold for export to the customs territory of the Union, adjusted, where necessary.
> 2. The price actually paid or payable shall be the total payment made or to be made by the buyer to the seller or by the buyer to a third party for the benefit of the seller for the imported goods and include all payments made or to be made as a condition of sale of the imported goods.

[1] PAPP Defined

I believe that the Valuation Agreement's positive focus on the PAPP created a coherent and self-contained system. A central focus within that system is the price paid or payable for the imported goods, usually but not always shown in a single invoice price.

The definition of the PAPP is both broad and narrow at the same time. The PAPP is broad if we consider the allowable adjustments, which accept that consideration for the imported goods may take the form of goods and services and not money and if we are mindful that the PAPP is defined to include the total of all such payments. Any

goods from the FTZ, while the goods withdrawn from the CBW would need to be appraised under an alternative method. Any sale occurring within the CBW would be disregarded as a domestic sale.

183. 19 USC § 1401a(b)(4)(A); 19 CFR § 152.102(f). Note that, apart from the TV context, in the US, with its position on international transport and insurance charges, a deductive value appraisement will also call for the deduction of actual, as opposed to estimated, costs of international freight and insurance. 19 USC § 1401a(d)(3)(B)(ii); ruling no. 544236 (October 31, 1998).

184. Canada Customs Act, subsection 48(4).

payment that is inextricably tied to the imported goods' production or sale, without any other independent basis, may be viewed as a part of the PAPP itself. But it will be seen that the PAPP definition is also narrow and delimited, as it is restricted to payments for the imported goods.

The essence of Article 1 is that the declared value should be respected even if it appears to be very low. The TCCV has issued several instruments that direct that result.[185]

Fair enough. But the designers of the system wisely recognized that some elements might have a separate commercial status of their own. That is especially the case for RLFs. Then, too, there is the opportunity for trading parties to "game the system."

The special rules focused upon related party pricing are the best-known example of two key characteristics of the Valuation Agreement: (1) it reflects a knowing assessment by the drafters that the relationship of the parties might influence the price and (2) it provides the means of redressing any such distortion.

I would submit that the broad reach of the PAPP's definition might be seen in the same light. It is a knowing response by the drafters to include all forms of the payment for the imported goods.

The next point in this discussion is the realization that, broad as the reach might be, only some of the payments made by a buyer should be dutiable under Article 1. That is the narrowing or limiting effect of the two limiting requirements for inclusion within the "price actually paid or payable": (a) the payment must be for the imported goods and (b) the payment must be to or for the benefit of the seller.

The "price actually paid or payable" is not defined in Article 1 itself but is defined first in the Valuation Agreement by the Interpretative Notes to Article 1, PAPP, paragraphs 1, 2, 3 and 4, with special emphasis on paragraphs 1 and 4. Second, additional clarity is found in the text of Annex III, paragraph 7 which is in actuality another Interpretative Note in all but name, which is how I treat it.[186]

I submit that only the timing of its introduction to the GATT, October 22, 1979, coming six months after the close of negotiations and the promulgation of the main body of the Agreement and Annex I, prevented its inclusion (as well as that of the paragraph 6 text) as an Interpretative Note. Along with paragraph 6, their elaborating,[187]

---

185. TCCV, AO 2.1, Acceptability of a Price Below Prevailing Market Prices for Identical Goods (October 1981), Com. 3.1, Goods Sold at Dumping Prices (March 1982); CS 12.1, Application of Article 1 of the Valuation Agreement for Goods Sold for Export at Prices Below Their Cost of Production (November 2000); TCCV, AO 23.1, Valuation of Imported Goods Purchased in "Flash Sales" (May 2019). For an EU treatment of a related "penny auction" conducted over the internet, *see* EU Commission Compendium 2022, Conclusion No. 35: Goods purchased in internet auctions (penny auctions), 162.

186. We introduced Annex III, paragraph 7 earlier in the background of the Valuation Agreement. We are forced to pay close attention to the Annex III, paragraph 7 language, as it has come to be employed as the basis for some overly broad interpretations of the PAPP.

187. TCCV, AO 19.1 Application of Article 17 of the Agreement and paragraph 6 of Annex III, paragraph 2 (October 1994).

clarifying[188] and amplifying[189] roles are those of nothing other than an Interpretative Note.[190]

We must apply all of these Notes taken altogether, rather than any single one of them in isolation or in an abbreviated combination. We are forced to pay particularly close attention to the Annex III, paragraph 7 language, as it has come to be employed as the basis for some overly broad interpretations of the PAPP.

These especially relevant Interpretative Notes are:

- Paragraph 1 of the Interpretative Note to Article 1: "The price actually paid or payable is the total payment made or to be made by the buyer to or for the benefit of the seller for the imported goods. The payment may not necessarily take the form of a payment of money."
- Paragraph 4 of the Interpretative Note to Article 1: "The price actually paid or payable refers to the price for the imported goods. Thus the flow of dividends or other payments from the buyer to the seller that do not relate to the imported goods are not part of the customs value."
- Paragraph 7 of Annex III: "The price actually paid or payable includes all payments actually made or to be made as a condition of sale of the imported goods, by the buyer to the seller, or by the buyer to a third party to satisfy an obligation of the seller."

Paragraphs 1 and 4 of the Notes posit the notion of the PAPP as embracing all forms of consideration for the imported goods. At a high level, that is consistent with the General Introductory Commentary which also makes the point that transaction value can include "considerations" which take the form of goods and services rather than money.[191]

Paragraph 2 of the Notes cautions that payments for certain activities will be not dutiable. This refers to activities undertaken by the buyer for the buyer's own account, even though they might benefit the seller. The Note proceeds to declare that the costs of such activities shall not be added to the PAPP in determining the customs value. To

188. TCCV, EN 5.1, Confirming Commissions, paragraph 9 (March 1992).
189. TCCV, CS 6.1, Insurance Premiums for Warranty, paragraph 5 (October 1990), TCCV, Com. 20.1, Warranty Charges (October 1998).
190. The text of Annex III, paragraph 6, reflects the oft-stated concerns of developing countries, so there is a rational basis for its inclusion in the Annex, unlike the paragraph 7 text, for which there is no showing of developing countries' concerns.
191. A close reading of the General Introductory Commentary text on Article 8 shows it to be redundant and less than clear. Adjustments to the PAPP take the form of adjustments in the form of specified goods or services rather than in the form of money (Articles 8.1(a)-(c)) and the use of "*inter alia*" merely hints at the money payment that is presumed by Article 8.1(d). The total payment concept for the PAPP which is set forth in the relevant Interpretative Notes and in the Annex III, paragraph 7 text is absent.

this point, the TCCV has issued only one instrument on the meaning of the phrase "on the buyer's own account."[192] A further discussion of this question will be of benefit.[193]

Additionally, Annex III paragraph 7 also plays a role. We introduced the topic of this last text earlier in the background of the Valuation Agreement. It first appeared only in October 1979, more than six months after the Agreement had already been put into its final form in April 1979. We will be forced to pay close attention to the Annex III, paragraph 7 language, as it has come to be employed as the basis for some overly broad interpretations of the PAPP.

[2] *The Role of the Interpretative Notes, Including Annex III, Paragraph 7, in Defining the PAPP*

From my perspective, the trade community has wrestled with a recurring question, what is the intersection of: (i) Article 1 and the Interpretative Notes thereto and (ii) Annex III, paragraph 7 on the meaning of the PAPP? We recognize that this definition goes to the very beating heart of the Valuation Agreement since transaction value is the basis for appraisement of imported merchandise for over 90% of imports.

This question has arisen in discussions at the TCCV. Some suggestions have been made to analyze specific technical questions from the perspective of Annex III, paragraph 7 only, as though that were an independent authority and Article 1 need not be satisfied, or that we should look upon these two sources as setting up an option, such that, alternatively, either Article 1 or Annex III, paragraph 7, might be satisfied in finding the PAPP. Other comments have focused on the "condition of sale" requirement of that Annex III, paragraph 7, to the exclusion of the underlying "payment for the imported goods" criterion of Article 1.[194]

As discussed earlier, extensive research reveals that there is scant information in the GATT archives for Annex III, paragraphs 6 and 7. The source documents reveal that the Protocol was presented in October 1979 as an addendum to the draft of the Valuation Agreement in the hope of inducing more developing countries to adopt the

192. Note that TCCV, Com. 9.1, Treatment of Costs of Activities Taking Place in the Country of Importation (October 1984) is not relevant and TCCV, Com. 16.1, Activities Undertaken By the Buyer on His Own Account After Purchase of the Goods But Before Importation (October 1990) is of limited benefit.
193. It may be helpful to note that the phrase "on one's own account" would normally be understood in commercial activities to refer to a payment for which the ultimate financial responsibility is that of the person in question. Such a payment is not being made by a person on behalf of another or with any expectation of reimbursement; rather, it is a payment made to settle one's own obligation or to obtain a benefit for oneself. In a way, it would be consistent with the notion of one acting on one's own behalf or in "one's own stead" and not as an agent or deputy of another.
194. A focus on the payment being "to or for the benefit of the seller" has not arisen in public discussions on Annex III, paragraph 7 but we might return to the hypothetical case: the offer, "I shall sell to you this product for 100 currency units if you employ my brother-in-law." This raises the fact that the buyer's employment of the seller's brother-in-law is a form of consideration—a benefit—to the seller but it is not a "payment to the seller." As a result, Annex III, paragraph 7 may not be relevant. In fact, TV may be disallowed per Article 1.1(b) because a value cannot be attached to the employment.

Valuation Agreement. The Protocol was itself based upon a list of proposed amendments for developing countries' special treatment which they had introduced only days before the negotiations ended in April 1979. A great many of those sought-after concessions were rejected and never adopted in the Protocol.

There is no record of any debate nor any record of how present Annex III, paragraph 6[195] came to be appended to the Protocol, as it was not included within that April draft.

As for the text we now know as Annex III, paragraph 7, to be sure, there had been a proposal by the developing countries to take into account "additional consideration," but that differed in substantive ways. This was the March 1979 developing countries' draft of the only text that even remotely has a connection with today's paragraph 7:

> Developing parties, in framing their national legislation, may provide for the inclusion in the customs value, in whole or in part, of the value of any additional consideration not specified in paragraph 1 of Article 8, which the buyer is obliged to discharge himself or to require others to discharge as a condition of sale.

First, this text, which was proposed to be a new Article 26, was a special breakout—it was to apply as an option only for developing countries and second, there was discretion in fixing the amount to be added to make customs value. Third, the suggested text was for the "inclusion in the customs value, in whole or in part, of the value of any additional consideration not specified in paragraph 1 of Article 8, which the buyer is obliged to discharge himself or to require others to discharge as a condition of the sale." This proposed text is reminiscent of the Article 1 focus on customs value, the reference to "customs value" calling to mind Article 8.1(b) and (d), as well as the Article 8.1(c) reliance on "condition of sale" and the "whole or in part" discretion afforded by Article 8.2. What the developing countries were seeking was, in effect, a new Article 8.1(e) for developing countries' use. Their effort was rejected. The Annex III, paragraph 7 text, which is tethered to the PAPP, bears only the remotest connection to that April 1979 proposal.

Annex III, paragraph 7 is not a lineal descendant of those efforts of the developing countries. It must be said that, unlike the case of its neighbor, paragraph 6, a traceable genealogy cannot be discerned—or has not yet been discerned at this point. One final observation—the close linkage between Article 1 and Article 8 is borne by the fact that, as evident in the Interpretative Notes, the final agreed text placed the additional, missing consideration in Article 1 rather than Article 8, even though an argument might be made—indeed that argument was made in the March 1979 draft—that an additional broad "basket provision" insertion could be made in Article 8.[196]

There could be, and in fact there have been, situations where a separate payment is being made for goods or services that have such a close connection to the imported

195. Paragraph 6 concerns the conduct of customs authority inquiries undertaken under Article 17. It, too, has all of the hallmarks of an Interpretative Note.

196. As previously noted, the General Introductory Comment is problematic. Beyond its lack of precision, it introduces a question on this Article 1 versus Article 8 addition.

goods that they should be properly dutiable. They should be considered a part of the total consideration paid or payable for the goods.

A good example would be a seller charging a price for the goods and also separately invoicing for certain production costs. An overly literalistic approach would lead to the production charge being nondutiable, as it is not a part of the stated price for the goods, nor would it fall under Article 8. But a separately invoiced charge for production costs should be dutiable as a missing portion of the PAPP. It has no independent rationale outside the PAPP and thus should be treated as a part of the PAPP. Similarly, a separate payment by the buyer for the manufacturer to pay for tooling cannot be a dutiable assist under Article 8.1(b) because the tooling itself is not being provided for free or at a reduced cost. Nevertheless, it should be included within the PAPP. In both of these examples, the subject payments should be seen to be indirect payments for the imported goods, and the payments would form part of the PAPP.[197]

As the paragraph 1 Note text reminds us, the PAPP is comprised of the total payment for the imported goods,[198] and the payments may be made in forms other than money. All of these payments in their entirety are to comprise the PAPP.

We submit that in those examples and in myriad others as well, the authority for adding those separated charges in order to find the PAPP lies in Article 1 and its Notes, read in conjunction with Annex III, paragraph 7. We conclude that Annex III. Paragraph 7 should have no independent status in this or any other customs valuation analysis; rather, yoked as it is to Article 1 and that Article's Interpretative Notes,[199] its role is to take into account and to provide the authority to deal with these artificially bifurcated payments, which are indirect payments for the imported goods.

In contrast, if the payment is for "something else," as established, the payment may not become a part of the PAPP. We could conjure up innumerable examples of requirements placed on the buyer/importer as express conditions in a sales agreement which should not be dutiable unless the payments are "for the goods."

Taking one example, a buyer of frozen foods is specifically required in the sales contract to store the imported goods after importation in an identified warehouse and to pay the warehouse charges for the required space. Presumably, the seller is concerned with maintaining the product in controlled conditions and is worried about the damage to its commercial reputation if they were to spoil ("go bad" or "go off" in the vernacular"). The buyer enters into a storage agreement and pays for that right. The buyer has been required to make that payment. The payment is not for the goods—it is for the storage space—even though it might be argued that it is an amount that is a condition of sale. Finally, it should make no difference if the owner of the warehouse paid by the buyer/importer is a company related to the seller or is the seller itself.

---

197. This is certainly the case in the US, where such costs are seen as indirect payments and a part of the PAPP. *See*, e.g., ruling no. H301764 (June 10, 2019) (testing fees discussion) and the *Chrysler* decision (tooling charges formed part of the PAPP).
198. For our purposes, perhaps a better phraseology here would have been "the total of all payments."
199. Nor should we neglect the role of the General Introductory Commentary, paragraph 1, and its crucial role in guiding us to focus on the notion of consideration passing from the buyer to the seller.

What is the effect of the payment not being for the imported goods but for the right to store the goods in the warehouse? A separate payment by the buyer for a truly separate right is a condition of that buyer's acquisition of that right and is not a condition of sale of the imported goods. Simply put, such a payment remains separate and apart from and is not a payment for the imported goods and is therefore not to be included in the PAPP.

We might add that the mere fact that the invoicing for any charges at issue—whether optional or not—may be on a per-unit-of-imported-product basis is NOT enough to make the payment one for the imported goods under an Article 1 and Annex III, paragraph 7 study. A foreign seller's explicit requirement that the importer/buyer store imported goods in facilities located in the country of importation, whether the facility is owned by, and the payment is made to, the seller, a party related to the seller or a third party, with a separate payment for that storage being imposed on a per-unit charge, is but one of the countless examples of a nondutiable payment.

It bears emphasis that there may be a prominent role in this discussion for the goods being or not being related to the goods. Annex III, paragraph 7 does not itself refer to payments being related to the goods. After a reference to the price for the imported goods, the Interpretative Note to Article 1, in paragraph 4 establishes that payments that are not related to the goods are not part of the customs value. Interpretative Note to Article 1, paragraph 4 instructs us in the first sentence that the PAPP refers to the price for the imported goods. In the second sentence, the Note tells us that "... the flow of dividends or other payments from the buyer to the seller that do not relate to the imported goods are not part of the customs value."

I submit that the proper interpretation for this "related to the goods criterion" is that it was an effort to avoid a tautology in the drafting. The text opens up the distinct possibility that there will be dividends and other payments which are not for the imported goods and thus are not part of the PAPP.

The definition of the PAPP articulated in Article 1 and its Notes were "amplified" by Annex III, paragraph 7 (to use the phrase employed in Commentary 20.1, in paragraph 8 and in Case Study 6.1, in paragraph 5). Article 1 was NOT replaced by the Annex III, paragraph 7 text. Article 14 instructs that, along with the Interpretative Notes, the two sources are on equal footing. This means that to fall within the PAPP the payment must still be shown to have been *for the imported goods*, and the payment was made to the seller or to a third party to satisfy an obligation of the seller.

The only circumstance in which there is a tension between the other Interpretative Notes and the Annex III, paragraph 7 text will be if there is a truncated reading of the latter. The condition of sale there is fully defined by the qualification that it must be a "condition of sale *of the imported goods*" which is consistent with the "for the imported goods" term identified in the other Interpretative Notes.

Correctly applying the Interpretative Notes, we find that the "price actually paid or payable" refers to the "price for the imported goods" (Note, paragraph 4 of Article 1 "Price actually paid or payable"). We might state that the two terms are equated with one another. The price for the imported goods is the total payment for the imported goods and the payment may take the form of something other than money (note, paragraph 1 of Article 1 "Price actually paid or payable"). This is clearly aligned with the statement that the PAPP means "all payments actually made or to be made as condition of sale of the imported goods" (Annex III, paragraph 7).

When we proceed to examine these Interpretative Notes side-by-side, we discover that the "condition of sale" in Annex III, paragraph 7 requirement refers to the payment for the imported goods in the same sense as the paragraph 4 text, the essential element being that the condition, or requirement, is imposed on the sale of the imported goods. This is a crucial finding. Only those payments imposed on the buyer as a condition of sale *of the imported goods* are to be included within the PAPP. Stated otherwise: (i) as the Note, paragraph 1 text would have it, a price paid not for the imported goods but for something else or, in another expression of the same principle; (ii) as the Annex III, paragraph 7 text would have it, a payment made as a condition of sale not for the imported goods but for a sale of something else or for some other purpose is not a part of the PAPP.

This understanding takes us to the next point to be acknowledged, and that is that the use of the terms "for the imported goods" in the first sentence of Note, paragraph 4 PAPP text and the term "relate to the imported goods" in the second sentence carry the same meaning. The term "relate to the imported goods" cannot widen the meaning of the PAPP beyond the "for the imported goods" as used in paragraph 1 and the first sentence of paragraph 4 of those Interpretative Notes without an impermissible inconsistency.[200]

The Annex III, paragraph 7 reference to "all payments," which is entirely consistent with the Note in paragraph 1 "total payment" phrasing, tells us that we may be dealing with more than one payment.[201] A bifurcated or separate payment which falls within the PAPP is one that has such a relationship to the production or sale of the goods that it should have been "included in" the PAPP in the first instance. Such an artificially split payment will not avoid dutiable status. Instead, Annex III, paragraph 7 serves to reinforce the relevant text from the General Introductory Commentary and to clarify the central point of the Interpretative Note to Article 1, in paragraph 1, that the PAPP is the "total payment" for the goods.

Whether there is such an innate connection between the separate payments and the PAPP as to ordain dutiable status might be gauged by accepted industry or trade practice or convention, standardized accounting rules or by reference to such governing trade rules as the Incoterms. The Incoterms describe which ancillary costs (such as consular or export license fees) will be borne by the seller or by the buyer depending on the specific sales term governing the sales transaction. A separate charge by the

---

200. It is a maxim of treaty interpretation that all provisions should be read harmoniously and *in pari materia* (given equal weight), such that the provisions are internally consistent and none are rendered superfluous. That stricture apples to the Agreement including its Interpretative Notes.

201. You may infer that we are in an Article 8-type situation, where there is most likely an invoice price but there are other payments being made. We may say "like Art. 8" because these payments do not and cannot fall within an Article 8 definition. If they did, then they would be covered by Article 8 and the Interpretative Notes to Article would be superfluous, irrelevant or redundant.

seller for such costs might be added to the invoice price for the goods and made a part of customs value.

The constraints of logic being what they are, it follows that if a payment is not for the imported goods but for something else, it is not dutiable. This is the teaching of paragraph 4 of the Interpretative Note to Article 1 PAPP and of Annex III, paragraph 7. In the specific context of the latter, not all payments that are a condition imposed by the seller or imposed on the buyer are dutiable under Article 1. That dutiable treatment will follow only if a payment is a condition of sale of the imported goods.

The second sentence of paragraph 4 of the Interpretative Note to Article 1 PAPP refers to dividends as an example of "payments unrelated to the imported goods" which could be seen in trade practices. That is an exemplar only. There are countless types of payments that might fall outside the "for the imported goods" limitation and would thus not form a part of the PAPP.

The decisive point for determining whether a payment forms part of the PAPP lies in determining whether it constitutes a payment to the seller or to a third party for the benefit of the seller for the imported goods or for something else. If one seeks to express the test in terms of the Annex III, paragraph, 7 text, the test will be in determining whether the subject payment has been imposed as a condition of sale of the imported goods by the seller and is for the imported goods and whether it is a payment made by the buyer to the seller or to a third party for the benefit of the seller. In turn, determining whether the payment is for something else will depend on whether the buyer has acquired something that is independent of or apart from the acquisition of the imported good. Payments that are: (1) for something else (inferred from the Article 1 Notes) or (2) that are imposed as a condition of the sale of something else or for some other purpose (per Annex III, paragraph 7) are not to be included within the PAPP.

If we were to evaluate the hypothetical case of a payment for the post-importation storage facility applying the principles grounded in paragraph 4, Note 1 and Annex III, paragraph 7 we would find that it is not dutiable because, despite being a condition of sale of the imported goods ("I will not sell you this frozen merchandise unless you pay me for storage in this designated refrigerated warehouse"), the payment is for something else, the storage rights in that climate-controlled environment, and not for the subject imported frozen merchandise. For those who might question why the seller might insist on this, perhaps the seller wants to be sure that the goods do not spoil and cause damage to the company's reputation.

We might remember that logic tells us that "all dogs are animals, but not all animals are dogs." In the same way, it might be said that "all payments for the imported goods are imposed as a condition of sale of those goods, but not all payments imposed as a condition of sale of the imported goods are payments for those goods."

To sum up, if any payment to the seller is for the imported goods and not for something else, it will be included as a part of the PAPP under Article 1. Only if any other payment, i.e., a payment arguably for something else, falls within the strict confines of Article 8, will such other payment, or more precisely, the payment for something else, become a part of transaction value by being added to the PAPP.

Why are we dilating on this topic of the PAPP? There is an alarming trend in some jurisdictions to broaden the definition of the PAPP beyond the price "for imported merchandise" (US phrase) or "for the imported goods" (Valuation Agreement term) to include a payment for seemingly anything so long as it is perceived to be[202] a condition of sale. As an example, some have suggested that the key questions in determining whether a payment forms part of the PAPP may be presented thusly: "is it a condition of sale by the seller and is it a payment to the seller or to a third party for the benefit of the seller?"

That plasticizing move is rooted in the differing expressions of the Notes to Article 1 and the text of Annex III, paragraph 7, of the Valuation Agreement. To follow this approach is to move away from Article 1 and to apply Annex III, paragraph 7 in isolation, as an alternative or as a separate, superseding legal standard, the "for the imported goods" standard being cast aside. But the reality is that the text of Annex III, paragraph 7, is compatible in every way with the other Interpretative Notes. These provisions elaborate upon or add greater clarity to the definition of "the price actually paid or payable" from different perspectives. In short, not surprisingly, given their role as Interpretative Notes, they collectively clarify, explain and amplify the meaning of the term "price actually paid or payable." Their observations mutually complement or reinforce each other.

[3] Determinations on the PAPP: US, EU, Canada and the TCCV

To be clear, at one time, the dispensation from the need to show expressly that to be a part of the PAPP the payment is "for the imported goods" was reflected in the US jurisprudence. That was the state of the law for a scant three years.

In the US, it bears repeated emphasis that all payments made to the seller are presumed dutiable as elements of the PAPP, but that presumption may be rebutted. The leading case is an appellate court decision in which the payment to the seller included an amount made not for the goods but for quota charges.[203] The overbroad reach of *Generra,* which failed to recognize that the payment was not for the imported goods but for a separate right to export, was limited in effect by the 1993 *Chrysler* decision at the CIT. The government elected not to file an appeal.[204]

202. In this, perception, which is an inherently subjective process, is often valued more dearly than reality.
203. *Generra Sportswear Co. v. United States,* 905 F.2d 377 (Fed. Cir. 1990) (quota charges paid to seller by buying agent were dutiable).
204. *Chrysler Corporation v. United States,* 17 CIT 1049 (1993). Note that the usual CBP reference to a payment needing to be "completely" unrelated [*see,* e.g., ruling no. H088115 (April 19, 2010)] is a CBP invention. The court's opinion does not use that qualifying term. Further, the term "related" does not itself appear in the US statute or regulations in connection with a definition of the PAPP, and the court's usage here appears to follow the importer's argument that the payment was unrelated to the purchase. You will recall that the Interpretative Note 1, paragraph 4 usage of related is itself defined restrictively to mean "for the goods." As a further observation it bears noting that *Generra* was an appellate court decision, while *Chrysler* was a decision of the CIT, the trial court. The Government can decide not to take up the case on appeal, and one can surmise that one reason is because the Government may have guessed that

Parenthetically, the EU approach to payments for quota for export, even if made to the seller, is contrary to *Generra* and thus is aligned with *Chrysler*. This was first made clear in two ECJ decisions from the 1980s.[205] This position is currently presented in the 2022 version of the Compendium:

> The quotas, being transferable, have in themselves a value independent of the value of the textiles to which they relate; and, in the present case, [EU buyer] bears the additional cost incurred in acquiring the quota entitlement, either by purchasing himself or by reimbursing [foreign seller] X for doing so. In these circumstances such additional duly proven costs cannot be regarded as forming part of the price actually paid or payable for the goods concerned. The type (own or third party quota) and the amount of related payments need to be demonstrated on request.[206]

Under the *Chrysler* standard, this presumption of dutiability attaching to payment to the seller may be overcome if the importer can prove that the payments are unrelated to the imported merchandise. Stated otherwise, the redeeming virtue of the *Chrysler* decision is that it established that the US definition of the PAPP imposes a "for [the] imported merchandise" criterion.[207] Thus, an amount paid, even if to the seller, will not comprise a part of the PAPP unless it is for the goods. If the payment is for something else, then it is not for the goods and, it follows, that it cannot fall within the PAPP.

The 1994 ECJ decision in *Malt*[208] illustrates this approach in practice. There, the payments in question were for certificates of authenticity under a tariff rate quota regime[209] on imports of beef. The decision concluded that the fees paid did not enjoy a separate status:

> 14 Under the system of importation applicable to beef of high quality the certificate of authenticity and the goods are, on the other hand, inseparably connected. The function of the certificate is to certify that the goods comply with the specifications laid down in Article 1 of Regulation No 263/81. Since

it would lose on appeal and it wanted to avoid the even greater authority of a Federal Circuit decision. This was likewise the case in another 1993 decision, *Synergy International*, discussed in the FSFE context. A later example, discussed below, is the CIT decision on royalties and license fees in *Trimil*.

205. Case C-7/83, *Ospig Gesellschaft KG v. Hauptzollamt Bremen-Ost*, 9.2.1984, ECLI:EU:C:1984:51 (quota charges relating to the acquisition of export quotas do not form an integral part of the value for customs purposes of goods imported into the Community) and Case C-29/93, *KG in Firma OSPIG Textil-Gesellschaft W. Ahlers GmbH & Co. v. Hauptzollamt Bremen-Freihafen*, 19.5.1994, ECLI:EU:C:1994:207 (immaterial that third-party quotas cannot be the subject of lawful trade in the country of export).
206. EU Commission Compendium 2022, Conclusion No. 11: Purchase of export quotas—textile products, 117.
207. Title 19 USC § 1401a(b)(4)(A). An important feature of *Chrysler* was that it relied on the importer's accounting treatment, which showed that the subject fees were accounted for separately from the cost of the goods, including, by necessity, the price paid for the goods.
208. Case C-219/88, *Malt GmbH v. Hauptzollamt Düsseldorf*, 28.3.1990, ECLI:EU:C:1990:146. To the same effect, *see* EU Commission Compendium 2022, Conclusion No. 15: Quota charges claimed in respect of certificates of authenticity, 122.
209. Under a tariff rate quota regime, imports of a given article up to a predetermined volume of imports will enjoy a lower duty rate on entry. After that ceiling level has been reached, additional imports will attract a higher duty rate.

> those specifications concern the state of the beef cattle the certificate cannot be issued without examination of the cattle by the slaughterhouse which issues the certificate. Contrary to what happens under the system for quotas applicable to textiles, certificates of authenticity cannot lawfully be traded separate from the goods to which they relate. Even in the case of an indirect transfer of quotas between slaughterhouses, the certificate of authenticity and the information contained in it relate to very specific goods.
>
> 15 It follows that the costs of the acquisition of certificates of authenticity must be regarded as an integral part of the "price paid or payable for the goods" and therefore of the customs value.[210]

The ECJ revisited the issue of quota charges in *Thierschmidt*, a 1994 decision[211] in which a further nuance was raised. This question focused on the difference between a third-party quota and an "own quota." A third-party quota has a distinct commercial value, and the ECJ held that charges to obtain such quotas were not dutiable. An "own quota" was defined as a quota that had been assigned at no charge to the exporter. As a result, the *Thierschmidt* court concluded (in paragraph 19) that:

> Although quotas allocated free of charge may have a commercial value for the seller, they entail no charges for him. Thus amounts invoiced in respect of those quotas relate, as the Commission rightly points out, to notional quota charges, which in reality constitute a disguised element of the price of the goods. If such notional amounts fell to be deducted from the price invoiced for the goods, the customs value would be artificially reduced...

This appears to be the correct result. The amount charged for the quota—in reality a recouping by the seller of his cost—is dutiable as a missing element of the PAPP.

While we are on the subject of payments for quota, Canada does not make the *Ospig* versus *Thierschmidt* distinction between purchased and allotted quota. All quota payments billed by the vendor to the buyer will be dutiable as a part of the PAPP.[212]

Occasionally, CBP will stray far from this *Chrysler* "for-the-goods?" analysis. We cite a 2004 ruling. This is ruling no. W548464 (5/25/04), which dealt with the valuation law status of a payment in the nature of a 2% Technical Consulting and Retail Services Fee. CBP concluded that:

> One of the significant facts for the Office of Regulations and Rulings in rendering this decision is the fact that no information has been brought forward nor has any been identified that would have enabled this office to conclusively establish that the sums paid by Zegna in the U.S. only inure to the benefit of Zenga [sic] Group sales in the United States. If the technical services and consulting fees even partially inure to the benefit of other Zegna Group entities or franchisees, the fees must be considered as being for imported merchandise.

---

210. *Ibid.*, paragraphs 14-15.
211. Case C-340/93, *Klaus Thierschmidt GmbH v. Hauptzollamt Essen*, 9.8.1994, ECLI: EU:C:1994:313.
212. Memorandum D13-3-14, *Quota Payments*, August 22, 2013, paragraphs 3-7 and Appendix.

This text suggests that if any portion of the fee gets to the seller, it is deemed "for the imported merchandise" and is thus, irrevocably, dutiable. But this is exactly wrong. The *Generra* decision does not extend that far. Instead, *Generra* and *Chrysler*, taken together, stand for the proposition that payments to the seller are subject to review. Fair enough. If the importer can show that the payments are for something separate from the goods, then—despite the fact that they are being made even directly to the seller—they are not dutiable.

This analysis was employed, and the same conclusion was reached by the ECJ in the line of quota cases cited above. In the *Ospig* decisions, it could be argued that the quota payments were: (i) related to the imported goods and further argued (ii) that the payments were a condition of the sale if we were to apply the broad prescription that, presumably, the sale would not have been made if the quotas had not been made. Thus, the Annex III, paragraph 7 test would be met. In the event, the court never addressed Annex III, paragraph 7. I submit that even if the gloss imparted by the latter authority had been employed to play its subsidiary role in the court's review, the court would have correctly applied the definitive Article 1 test, finding that the payments were for something of commercial value, a property right that was other than for the imported goods. The court in the later *Malt* decision reached the correct result, which happened to be contrary to *Ospig*. That is because the payment was not "for something else" other than the imported goods. As a result, the quota payment to the seller was dutiable as a missing element of the PAPP because it could only have been "for the imported goods."

The lesson in all of this is that a further inquiry by the customs authority may be needed. This 2004 ruling simply shuts down that further inquiry. Its implied but inescapable prescription that payments to the seller are invariably deemed for the imported goods is inconsistent with the *Generra* and *Chrysler* jurisprudence and with the CBP position expressed in its ruling no. H242894 on exclusive distributorship fees,[213] as well as the ECJ jurisprudence. In short, the close and extensive analysis that we saw in ruling no. H242894 should always be applied.

Moreover, this 2004 ruling suggests a possibly flawed argument put forward by the importer's counsel. Apparently, the importer argued that there was no profit element represented by the 2% fee ("the fee is adequate to cover the costs of the services provided and nothing more").[214] Even if the recipient of the services were the seller and even if the payment included an element of profit, those facts would still not convert the payment into a payment for the goods.

More tax accounting support could have been adduced to demonstrate that any profits generated from the services would remain in that separate category and would not automatically be transferred over to—or altered to become—an enhanced seller's profit on the sales of goods.

Since these were related parties, one can surmise (or hope) that if the issue were to arise anew—some years after the issue addressed in that 2004 ruling first

213. Ruling no. H242894 (December 4, 2013), discussed below.
214. You will recognize that the same argument was put forth by importer's counsel in ruling no. H (November 17, 2014), discussed above.

surfaced—then perhaps there would be more robust transfer pricing documentation and accounting support, justifying not only the sale price (the ruling stated that there was no sales agreement available for review) but also the level of the fees paid by the importer.

A 2013 CBP ruling may be quite instructive on the question of a payment for the imported goods versus a payment for something else. After its usual close scrutiny of the operative facts, CBP held that a license "key" fee was not a part of the PAPP nor was it in the nature of a royalty or license fee.[215] There, CBP was asked about the customs valuation status of fees paid for software upgrades and rebates from the seller:

> The FOB price of the software alterable machine will correspond to the price currently charged for a conventional machine with the capabilities that have been programmed into the software alterable machine at the time it is sold for exportation to the United States. As imported into the United States, the software alterable machines will be fully functional. The software alterable machines consist of both hardware components and software components (or firmware that controls all the functions of the software alterable machines). However, the firmware on these machines can be reprogrammed so as to either expand or limit the capabilities of the machines. This reprogramming requires a license key from the Manufacturer and the download of a new program. Therefore, after the sale for export to the United States of the software alterable machines, Company A [the buyer] may purchase a license key from Manufacturer [the seller] and download the software necessary to expand the capabilities of the imported machines, from the Manufacturer's website. At the time of download, Company A will be invoiced by Manufacturer for the cost of the software embodying the intellectual property. Additionally, if Company A's customer requires an upgrade in its software, Company A may download a license key, and if the software is downloaded, Company A may receive a post-importation rebate from Manufacturer to account for a difference between the price of the firmware installed on the machine that was originally purchased and the new firmware.

The first question was whether the fee for a license key, with payment made by Company A to the manufacturer of the imported software-alterable machines, is part of the PAPP. CBP declared:

> the fees for a license key and a program as well as the rebates that could be received by Company A from Manufacturer for reprogramming of machines after the importation, are not part of the price actually paid or payable. The software alterable machines are fully functional when sold for export to the United States, and Company A has no obligation to purchase the license key or a program in order to import the machines. The license fee is not paid for the imported merchandise, but is a post-importation payment made for additional software. In other words, this fee is paid for the license key and the instructions that are being downloaded from the Manufacturer's website upon completion of the sale of additional software from Manufacturer to Company A.

215. Ruling no. H239671 (June 7, 2013). The EU Commission reached a similar conclusion in its review of a hypothetical case. EU Commission Compendium 2022, Conclusion No. 37: Treatment of payment for activating an additional software function of goods after release for free circulation, 168. Perhaps, the TCCV will revisit this interesting question again after having failed to reach a consensus after some considerable ventilation of the question.

In other words, the payment was not for the imported goods but for something else. Its assigned nondutiable status is correct.[216] You should also have inferred that because the rebate in the cost differential for the software was not part of the PAPP, the importer would not be able to seek a refund of duty. When a second payment is *not* for a separately identified good, service, or intangible asset, then it would follow that that the second payment is actually further consideration for the imported good. In such a case, the buyer is implicitly required to make the payment as a condition of sale of the imported good to the buyer. A detailed analysis is relevant when the separate payment is not readily identified as being either "for the imported goods" or for "something else."

In the same vein, the Annex III, paragraph 7 criterion of condition of sale may also be seen as being implicit in a payment related to the goods that would comprise a part of the total payment for the goods. But a payment with only an attenuated connection to or relationship with the production or sale of the imported goods would fall outside the ambit of this discussion. We will be revisiting this question in the discussion on RLFs below. We will learn that we can apply the teaching of Advisory Opinion 4.17[217]—the "franchise" fees there were not related to the production or sale of the imported goods and were not dutiable.

After we have closely examined the role of the Interpretative Notes, we are also able to reexamine some of the older TCCV instruments dealing with the PAPP in a fresh light.

Explanatory Note 5.1[218] deals with confirming commissions, payments made to financial institutions to manage and insure the risk of nonpayment by the buyer or the buyer's bank. A "confirmed letter of credit" would be issued by a second bank guaranteeing payment in the face of a default or a failure to honor the L/C. Typically, there would be a charge by the second bank for that guarantee of payment.[219]

That background discussion takes us to a financing or payment mechanics concern. The TCCV did not see it that way, as it raised and then dismissed status as a commission or as an insurance-related charge. If they had stepped back, however, what may have come into view was its status as a financing mechanism, embedded in the mechanics of payment. In essence, it is a bank charge.[220]

216. *See also* ruling no. W563562 (November 20, 2008). The question of the license key fee as an RLF was also raised—we discuss that question below.
217. TCCV, AO 4.17, Royalties and Licence Fees Under Article 8.1(c) (May 2017).
218. TCCV, EN 5.1, Confirming Commissions (March 1992). *See also* Customs Memorandum D13-4-11, *Confirming Commissions and Credit Insurance*, August 8, 2013.
219. A confirmed letter of credit is a guarantee a borrower gets from a second bank in addition to the first letter of credit. The confirmed letter decreases the risk of default for the seller. By issuing the confirmed letter, the second bank promises to pay the seller even if the first bank declines to do so. In fact, the confirming bank undertakes to pay the seller in the first instance and then seek reimbursement from the first issuing bank.
220. A possible topic for a TCCV instrument would be the payment of bank fees for wire transfers or for other services. As an example, unless the parties have arranged for a "gross up," if the buyer's bank sends a wire transfer for the invoiced amount, the bank typically withholds an amount for a "wire fee." This results in the seller receiving the invoiced amount less the amount of the fees. Is the dutiable amount the full invoice fee paid by the buyer or the net amount received by the seller?.

They might have endeavored to examine it as grounded in financing and as something akin to an interest charge. This would have taken them to Decision 3.1[221] on interest charges where an analogy might have been discerned.[222]

What the TCCV actually did in 1992 was to bank on support from Annex III, paragraph 7 in applying a novel standard. In pertinent part:

> if a confirmation of the instrument of payment for the imported goods is considered to be for the benefit of the seller because it insured the seller against the risk of non-payment by the buyer's bank, and if the confirming commissions are paid by the buyer to the seller or to a third party as a condition of sale of the imported goods, the price actually paid or payable would include any confirming commissions.

Gather a search party because what is missing is any reference to the price being for the imported goods. Instead, we have a new two-prong standard—the payment needs only to be "a condition of sale" and "for the benefit of the seller."

The elision of the "for the imported goods" criterion is remarkable. This supernumerary standard in EN 5.1 is either no standard at all or it is a usurper of the Article 1 standard.[223]

An argument could be fashioned that any payment to anyone no matter how remote the connection to the sale would be "related to" or "in respect of" the goods and be "of benefit" to or for the seller. The "for the benefit of the seller" test was broadly interpreted (in paragraph 9) to embrace the notion that the confirmation of the letter of credit payment was for the seller's benefit because it ensured the seller against the risk of nonpayment. If such a broad interpretation is to be employed, virtually any payment to any third party would be likely to be so characterized as the payment would be presumed to play a role in the sales transaction. In the US, the court in *Trimil*[224] rejected such a broad interpretation and specifically noted that the "for the benefit of the seller" language should be narrowly interpreted.

An argument for dutiability on these grounds is directly at odds with the rationale of the CCV's Decision 3.1, where the CCV had specifically held that interest charges were nondutiable regardless whether the financing is provided by the seller, a bank or another natural or legal person. If the other criteria were met, arguably, those interest charges would be related to the imported goods and would be a condition of sale and might be paid to the seller or presumably to a party related to the seller and, on the attenuated plane in which the phrase is often examined, the interest charge payment

221. CCV, Decision 3.1, Treatment of Interest Charges in the Customs Value of Imported Goods (April 1984).
222. We discuss Dec. 3.1 and interest charges more generally below in §3.01[K][4].
223. Sherman and Glashoff are in full accord. They regard confirming commissions as financing charges and they see them as "not payments for the goods but costs of securing payment or credit." Nos. 224-226 at 110. So, too, may we assume that they would view exchange rate protection fees as nondutiable banking charges; again, because such charges would not be for the goods but for something else of value.
224. *Trimil S.A. v. United States*, 419 F. Supp. 3d 1307 (CIT 2019) (pointing to US regulations which added the notion of a credit on a current importation to the settlement of a debt example given in Interpretative Note to Article 1).

would be of benefit to the seller (in that rarified analysis, by allowing for payment over time, albeit with interest charges the buyer might be more willing to make the purchase and, you guessed it, the making of the sale will be of benefit to the seller). Nevertheless, according to the CCV, none of these payments would be nondutiable. I submit that the CCV held that they lie outside the zone for inclusion within the PAPP for the simple reason that the charges were not for the imported goods.

The TCCV's Explanatory Note 5.1 has never been tested, but it is a likely candidate for removal by the TCCV itself or by a scrupulous CCV or rebuke by a court of competent jurisdiction. It might be that the bank charges at play here might be a candidate for its own CCV Decision. If so, its status might be within the same opt-in category as Decisions 3.1 and 4.1, which would further establish a split and not a uniformity of interpretation.

Parenthetically, Canada has followed the TCCV lead on confirming commissions in its D Memo series. Note the progression from D Memo 13-4-11:

> 3. To determine whether ... payments by a purchaser are to be included in the value for duty, it is necessary to know whether the payment:
>   (a) is in respect of the goods which have been sold for export to Canada; and
>   (b) is made either directly or indirectly to the vendor of the goods or to a third party for the benefit of the vendor.
> 4. If the payment is either not in respect of the goods, as in paragraph 3*(a)*, or is not to or for the benefit of the vendor, as in paragraph 3*(b)*, it does not form part of the price paid or payable for the goods and is not dutiable.
> 5. A confirming commission [a payment made to a financial institution, usually in a country other than Canada, in consideration of that institution guaranteeing payment to the vendor in the event that the letter of credit issued by the purchaser's bank is not paid] will be paid by the purchaser at the request of the vendor and for his benefit. It is therefore part of the price paid or payable for the imported goods and included in the value for duty. However, fees paid by a purchaser to a financial institution for the initial issuance of a letter of credit in favour of the vendor are not dutiable as they are considered usual expenses in establishing the purchaser's ability to pay for the goods.[225]

The logic here appears to be based on the judgment that the confirming commission might have been paid directly by the vendor in the first instance, and in that case it would have been/should have been subsumed within the PAPP itself as the seller would have recouped the additional cost it had incurred.

A more recent TCCV instrument addressed another bank charge or treasury function question. In Advisory Opinion 25.1, the TCCV was presented with three

225. Customs Memorandum D13-4-11, *Confirming Commissions and Credit Risk Insurance*, August 8, 2013. A similar logic was applied to a discussion of credit risk insurance charges in paragraph 6. Note the standard at work here is not "for the goods"—which is the term used in the statute in section 48(4)—but "in respect of the goods," which is the term used in the definition of transaction value in section 45(1). We may safely assume that the terms as used here are interchangeable.

separate charges paid by the buyer.[226] The first two were seen as nondutiable because they were not for the imported goods nor covered in any of the provisions of Article 8.

The first category of payments was for "savings program charges." The seller would provide free units of the imported goods to the importer subject to the condition that the importer purchases a minimum predetermined quantity of goods from the seller in a given period of time. This was a voluntary program. If the importer opts to join, a fixed additional amount per unit of the imported goods becomes payable. This amount is not refunded whether or not the purchasing target is not met.

The second category was described as "club charges." Under this program, hotel packages and gifts are offered to importers, depending on the buyer meeting purchasing targets that have been fixed by the seller for a given period of time. If the importer opts to join this program, the importer pays an additional amount per unit of the imported goods. This amount paid to the seller is not refunded whether or not the purchasing target is met.

The third category was a mandatory "currency surcharge" whereby the seller was enabled to maintain the price of the product with regard to any change that might occur in the foreign exchange market. The text specifically noted that the payment was not shown to be a payment for something other than for the other goods. As a result, the payment was seen as a payment for the imported goods and was a condition of sale of the imported goods. It was considered to form part of the PAPP. Still, it might be that the foreign exchange protection was an independent benefit for the buyer and that an argument might be made that it was, therefore, not for the imported goods. A similar argument might apply even if it had been a benefit for the seller.

We should also look to Case Study 7.1.[227] This instrument has a checkered history. It was finally adopted in October 1993, but that was only after the version which had been adopted by the TCCV in May 1993 had been sent back to the TCCV by the CCV at the specific request of the US.[228]

This exercise was an attempt to employ the Interpretative Notes and Annex III, paragraph 7 in setting forth an instructive case study to illustrate the proper manner to assess whether a separate payment might form part of the PAPP. It was a failed effort.

The case deals with the purchase of a machine for 10,000 currency units and the separate purchase and billing of an instructional course for 500 units.

In the first of three scenarios, the course was optional and the machine could be purchased without paying for the course. The payment for the course was considered not part of the customs value because it was not a condition of the sale.

226. TCCV, AO 25.1, Valuation Treatment of Ancillary Charges in Relation to Article 1 of the Agreement (October 2022).
227. TCCV, CS 7.1, Application of the Price Actually Paid or Payable (October 1993).
228. This history emerges from the CCV documents: GATT, Committee on Customs Valuation, Minutes of the Meeting of 12 October 1993, VAL/M/32 (4 February 1994), 4-5; Committee on Customs Valuation, Meeting of 5 May 1993 (Agreement to send back a case to the Technical Committee for further consideration), VAL/48 (7 June 1993); Minutes of the Meeting of 5 May 1993, VAL/M/31 (28 July 1993), 4-5. These publicly available documents show that the US was very much pushing its *Generra* approach—still, the *Chrysler* decision, which repudiated that interpretation, was issued three weeks before the final adoption of CS 7.1—with US support—at the TCCV.

In scenario 2, the payment is an explicit requirement in the contract of sale and must be made even if the buyer does not attend. In scenario 3, the contract of sale obliges the buyer to both attend and pay for the course (this third scenario differs from scenario 2 in that the attendance is mandatory). The payments for the separately billed course were held dutiable in scenarios 2 and 3 "because they were made as a condition of the sale."

For the same reasons discussed above in regard to Annex III, paragraph 7 generally and to its contemporary TCCV instrument, EN 5.1, these instructional course payments should be nondutiable in all three scenarios. In all of the cases concerned with the PAPP, the nature of the payment must be examined. The question must be, "What is this payment for?" That is because, as has been established, not all payments made to the seller are payments for the imported goods.

True, the course here was paid for and that payment was a condition of a sale—but it was a condition of the sale of the course and not of the sale of the imported machine. To more plainly state the case, unlike the AO 25.1 analysis, the rationale of the Case Study interpretation ducked the central question, "Could the payment have been for something else?"

That ignoring of the distinctions in accounting treatment of payments for the imported goods versus payments for other goods or services with a separate and independent identity is certainly not in accord with standard accounting or commercial practice—supposedly guiding stars for the Valuation Agreement and its interpretations. The reference to the Generally Accepted Accounting Principles (GAAP) in the General Interpretative Note is and should remain especially relevant when examining a sales price not only for customs valuation purposes but also because the correct sale price will have direct repercussions for Value Added Taxes (VAT) and the income tax laws. Such an aberrant treatment would also disregard the Interpretative Notes on Article 1, as discussed above.

In fact, in 1979, toward the end of negotiations, India had proposed changes to the Interpretative Note to the PAPP which would have had the same effect of broadening the reach of the PAPP. The proposals were not adopted. The rationale was boldly stated:

> All charges, expenses and costs in respect of all activities which are undertaken on behalf of the seller and the benefit of which accrues directly or indirectly to the seller, must to the extent to which they are on behalf of him and the benefits accrue to him, be regarded as the cost of the goods and should be included in the customs value.[229]

That principle was not acceptable then, and it should not be acceptable today—it was rejected then and it should be rejected today.

229. GATT, Multilateral Trade Negotiations, Group "Non-Tariff Measures," Sub-Group "Customs Matters," Customs Valuation, Comments by Delegation of India, MTN/NTM/W/218 (9 February 1979).

There is hope that the TCCV—or perhaps the WTO—will issue more definitive guidance on this all-important feature of Article 1 and, by extension, the Valuation Agreement itself.

Further discussion of the PAPP in the context of other common categories of payment streams from the buyer/importer is found below in §3.01[I][5].

[4] *The PAPP is the Gross Amount Paid by the Buyer*

The Agreement is silent on the question whether the amount paid to the seller should be the gross amount paid by the buyer to or on behalf of the seller or only the net amount received by the seller after bank charges or taxes imposed in the country of importation have been deducted. The issue of bank charges has not been addressed, but the TCCV promulgated an instrument in 2015 on the status of an income tax withholding paid by the buyer on behalf of the seller in the context of a royalty.[230] The full amount received by the buyer—1,000 currency units for the imported good plus 75 currency units as a royalty payment—plus the 25 currency units paid to the tax authorities on behalf of the seller were dutiable. In other words, the dutiable royalty (100 currency units) included the amount paid as withholding tax.

This was followed by another Advisory Opinion in 2021,[231] with the same result. The dutiable royalty amount was the total gross payment of royalty inclusive of withholding tax.

These questions arose in a royalty or license fee context, but their rationale should apply equally to PAPP questions in which a tax payment is being made by the buyer on behalf of the seller. Indeed, charges paid by the buyer on behalf of the seller for banking and/or other services should be treated likewise.

At this point, we are ready to address the next criterion—the price must be paid to the seller.

[F] To or for the Benefit of the Seller

The text of the Valuation Agreement is remarkably consistent. To play a role in the PAPP, the payment must be made to the seller or it must be shown as being made to a third party for the benefit of the seller. The payment may be direct or indirect. Viewed through this prism, we find a broad perspective which is in very much the same sense that we have just seen: a payment might be separately paid but it would still qualify as a part of the PAPP. But there is a ring fence around that broad view which is in very much the same sense: not all payments to a seller will be part of the PAPP. Instead, as we have just seen, the payment must be for the goods. Here, the ring fence is that the payment is made to the seller, directly or indirectly, or to someone else for the benefit of the seller.

---

230. TCCV, AO 4.16, Royalties and Licence Fees Under Article 8.1(c) of the Agreement (May 2015).
231. TCCV, AO 4.18, Royalties and License Fees Under Article 8.1(c) of the Agreement (May 2021).

As an example of an indirect payment to the seller, we might consider a credit being given on a current importation to allow for a discrepancy on an earlier shipment. While a 1982 TCCV instrument does not expressly state that the credit must be included within the PAPP on the current import transaction because it is an indirect payment to the seller, that is undoubtedly the legal basis for the inclusion of the credit in the PAPP for the second importation.[232]

At no point in the Valuation Agreement is there text which provides direct support, nor any such that would justify an inference, for the proposition that a payment being made to a party related to the seller is to be invariably treated as an indirect payment to the seller. That bears repetition: there is no support for the notion that a payment—any payment—being made to a party related to the seller is to be treated in all circumstances as a payment to the seller.

Put otherwise, there is no language in the Valuation Agreement which equates a payment made to a party related to the seller as an indirect payment to the seller. True enough, the Interpretative Note to Article 1 in paragraph 1 speaks of payments that may be made indirectly. The example given is of a payment to a third party in satisfaction of a debt of the seller. We will also see other instances of payments deemed to be indirect payments, e.g., certain allowances for defective or missing goods.

The Valuation Agreement marked a departure from the BDV, which had specified in one narrow context, that a subsequent proceed accruing to an associate in business would be a disqualification under the normal value standard. In the BDV, it was necessary to specifically provide for that exceptional treatment. But even that specific text in the BDV would not have supported the view that a payment to a related party was necessarily to be seen as an indirect payment to the seller.

That meaningful absence from the Valuation Agreement, and from many if not most implementing statutes, has not prevented customs authorities from routinely advancing the view as a matter of practice that a payment to a related party must be treated as a payment to the seller. In the US, we can find evidence from the outset of CBP's administration of the new customs valuation law from 1979 onward. For instance, in a very early ruling dealing with the status of quota payments,[233] CBP took pains to observe that there was no relationship:

> We agree with your conclusions where the quota payments are made to an unrelated third party and where they are made by the buyer to the quota holder, who is unrelated to either the buyer or the seller ... .

The implication being that a payment to a related party would carry a different result. For another in what would be a long line of examples, we find a 2010 CBP ruling instructive. Financing fees paid by a buyer/importer (A) to a related party lender (B)

232. TCCV, AO 8.1, Treatment Under the Agreement of Credits in Respect of Earlier Transactions (March 1982). We revert to this AO below in the context of allowances/credits for defective goods.
233. Ruling no. 542169 (September 18, 1980) (TAA No. 6). *See also*, e.g., ruling nos. 544971 (October 20, 1993) and 544640 (April 26, 1990).

were under review. CBP found it important to note that neither A nor B was related to the seller:

> Even though Company A and Company B are related, the companies do not have a relationship of buyer and seller. Pursuant to the Financing Agreement between these parties, the finance fees will not inure, directly or indirectly, to the benefit of the unrelated sellers/manufacturers. The manufacturers are not parties to the Financing Agreement. Additionally, neither Company A nor Company B are related to any of the manufacturers/sellers.

The fact that the financing company was not related to the seller is—and should be—entirely irrelevant. It is important to note that this interpretation of CBP on payments made to a related party has never been tested, let alone approved by a reviewing court.

While this CBP theory is untested, we can anticipate that one justification would be that a payment to a party related to the seller would be an indirect payment to the seller, in the vein of an assumed debt. Of course, to argue that any such payment will be deemed a payment to the seller in any and all circumstances would make a folly of the bedrock principle that the separate legal status of entities should be respected. For these purposes, the logical inference of that precept, i.e., that payments to one such entity, without more, should not, indeed must not, be considered as a payment to any other entity, would be discarded. If that rule were honored, the result would be that payments to a third party will not automatically be subsumed within the PAPP. Thus, to cite US rulings as examples, the following will not be included within the PAPP: financing fees paid to a third party,[234] inspection fees paid to an independent company[235] and testing fees.[236]

To pay this attention to whether the payment is made to a party related to the seller will be justified only if there is an arrangement between buyer, seller and the related payee whereby the related payee will remit all or a portion of that payment to the seller. That, indeed, would be an indirect payment scheme.

Such a fee-split arrangement may be present, but it is not the province of related parties alone. In the same sense, it must be stated that all of these various related parties are separate legal entities and many related corporate parties are fiercely independent, operating as separate profit centers. They will resist pressure to take action they perceive as being inimical to their individual interests even if supposedly it would be "for the good of the group." I learned that as a young lawyer only after I left Government service when I started to work with corporate clients.

In plain terms, the rule should be that a payment to a party related to a seller that would be nondutiable if paid to a third party is not transmuted into a dutiable, indirect payment to the seller solely by virtue of the relationship of the payee to the seller. At the same time, it must be recognized that an inquiry into the question "will there be a sharing of payments such that there is or will be an indirect payment to the seller?" may

234. Ruling no. H099255 (May 24, 2010).
235. Ruling no. W563469 (March 21, 2006) and rulings cited therein.
236. Ruling no. W563480 (June 9, 2006).

be appropriate, regardless whether or not there is any relationship between the payee and the seller.

In this connection, the EU's Implementing Regulation for the UCC[237] bears special notice. It holds (at UCC IA, Article 129.1) that payments to a third party related to the seller comprise a part of the PAPP:

> The price actually paid or payable within the meaning of Article 70(1) and (2) of the Code shall include all payments made or to be made as a condition of sale of the imported goods by the buyer to any of the following persons:
>
> (a) the seller;
> (b) a third party for the benefit of the seller;
> (c) a third party related to the seller;
> (d) a third party where the payment to that party is made in order to satisfy an obligation of the seller.

This approach, without any grounding in the "for the goods" criterion of Article 1 and its Notes, appears to do two things: (1) apply an abbreviated form of the Annex III, paragraph 7 text as an independent, self-contained, alternative legal standard and (2) equate payment to a party related to the seller in subsection (c) as automatically dutiable, omitting the additional qualifications of subsections (b) and (d). This first point may or may not be a unique statutory formulation but, based on statements of positions of other countries, we have learned that other countries apply the same Annex III, paragraph 7 text as a matter of practice. As for point (2) (payments to related parties), the US and others have adopted the same approach.

While we have already disposed of the issue of condition of sale we should list it as a separate criterion.

[G] Condition of Sale

This criterion makes an appearance in the context of a PAPP discussion only through the intervention of Annex III, paragraph 7. That text and its role, in showing that the payment being a condition of sale of the imported goods is simply another means of stating that the payment is a payment for the imported goods, have been thoroughly discussed above.

The only other references to "condition" are not relevant. These are in Article 1.1 (b), discussed above, and Article 8.1(c), on RLFs, which is discussed below.

This definition of the PAPP is the start of determining what costs should be within or outside of a TV appraisal. But it is only the start, as there may be the need to add one or more of the further elements that are listed in Article 8.

237. Commission Implementing Regulation (EU) No. 2015/2447 of 24 November 2015 (the UCC Implementing Act, hereinafter "UCC IA").

If the general rule is that TV is based on the invoice price for the imported merchandise, then it is possible that the parties might resort to off-invoice payments to lower the dutiable value. The valuation law implicitly recognizes that certain categories of costs might be missing from the invoiced price for the goods. These five cost categories, which are sometimes referred to collectively in the US as the "statutory additions," must be added to the declared price to make dutiable value.

Before turning to the issue of the adjustments to the PAPP, we should first address the status under TV of certain elements that can affect the price paid for the goods.

[H] Inclusion/Exclusion of Various Costs in the PAPP

[1] Indirect Taxes in Country of Export

The dutiable status of VAT or similar indirect taxes in the country of export has been an issue for some importers. In the US, the case of Caterpillar Inc. raised the question in the specific case of British truck components which were purchased on a VAT-inclusive basis. The purchases were sometimes stored for up to five months before exportation to the US. The invoice broke out the underlying price for the goods and the VAT. The VAT was refunded in full, as befits the destination tax principle for indirect taxes in which such taxes are refunded or remitted in full upon exportation. Upon judicial review, the CIT held that the refunded VAT should not form part of the PAPP.[238]

In a recent ruling,[239] the importer had paid internal Indian taxes/levies for the purchase of apparel. These taxes/levies were separately identified in the shipping bill for export but were not included in the commercial invoice. The shipping bill for export indicated a notation that the importer intended to claim a refund of the paid tax/levies from the Indian authorities and included a bank account number for the deposit of the refund. CBP applied *Caterpillar* and determined that the refunded taxes played no role in the PAPP.

[2] Discounts

A hallmark of TV is its grounding in the PAPP, even if the PAPP represents a discount from a price list or other established standard. In the US, certainly one of the principal differences between export value under the prior customs valuation law and transaction value is the treatment of discounts. Under the US customs regulations, discounts

238. *Caterpillar Inc. v. United States*, 20 CIT 1169, 941 F. Supp. 1241 (1996).
239. Ruling no. H304236 (June 4, 2020). *See also* two rulings which held that refunded, separately identified Canadian indirect taxes on automobiles purchased there and imported into the US were not dutiable: nos. 548161 (August 21, 2002) and 548128 (July 15, 2002).

are anticipated[240]—and validated if they meet CBP's criteria. CBP has fixed three criteria for valid discounts, the importer being required to show:

- the discount of price adjustment must be agreed on prior to the importation of the merchandise;
- sufficient documentary evidence to support existence of the discount and establish that it was agreed prior to the time of entry;
- discount or price adjustment must be unconditional, or if conditional, all of the conditions must be met prior to importation.[241]

In the EU, the Implementing Act provides that discounts will be recognized if, at the time of acceptance of the customs declaration, the sales contract provides for their application and their amount.[242] For clarity, the regulations go on to state that post-import discounts will be disregarded.[243]

The TCCV issued an early Advisory Opinion on discounts with the same result: quantity discounts that are established prior to the importation of the goods will be honored and given effect, but those that are established after importation will be disregarded.[244]

The reference to discounts invokes the more general notion of price adjustments.

[3] Price Adjustments

The US statute dictates that post-importation price decreases must be ignored by CBP.[245] As the customs regulations also make clear:

> the price actually paid or payable will be considered without regard to its method of derivation. It may be the result of discounts, increases, or negotiations, or may be arrived at by the application of a formula, such as the price in effect on the date of export in the London Commodity Market.[246]

---

240. Cash, or prompt pay, discounts are specifically authorized in 19 CFR § 152.103 (a) (1): Example 5. A seller offers merchandise at USD 100, less a 2% discount for cash. A buyer remits USD 98 cash, taking advantage of the cash discount. The transaction value is USD 98, the price actually paid or payable.
241. *See Allied International v. United States*, 16 CIT 545, 795 F. Supp. 449 (CIT 1992) (importer required to affirmatively show that there was a pre-importation agreement for the claimed discount) and ruling nos. H137455 (February 6, 2012), H133044 (March 9, 2011) (useful summary of requirements), H003356 (February 2, 2007) and W563462 (October 11, 2006) and authorities cited therein.
242. UCC IA, Article 130.1.
243. UCC IA, Article 130.3 (discounts arising from amendments to the contract subsequent to the time of acceptance of the customs declaration shall not be taken into account). This practice of disregarding price reductions that were only agreed post-importation is aligned with the US customs regulations, 19 CFR § 152.103(a)(4), and the Canadian practice as well.
244. TCCV, AO 15.1, Treatment of Quantity Discounts (March 1986).
245. 19 USC § 1401a(b)(4)(B).
246. 19 CFR § 152.103(a)(4). *See* ruling nos. 547178 (January 13, 1999) and 545532 (September 14, 1994).

To the contrary, price increases must be reported to CBP, or the importer runs the risk of civil or criminal penalties for an undervaluation of merchandise. To avoid this pitfall, importers will point to an adjustment made pursuant to a pricing agreement with two conditions: it was in place prior to the time of importation and the parties have no control over the controlling standard.[247]

In this same connection, a TCCV Commentary anticipates the use of pricing formulas to fix the PAPP.[248]

CBP has issued several rulings discussing the application of pricing formulas, including formulas with an escalator clause tied to indices such as the US Bureau of Labor Statistics.[249] One 1994 CBP ruling explains the rules in a succinct manner.[250] We can infer from the following excerpt that the PAPP was related to the resale price of the imported goods:

> All monies paid to the foreign seller are generally part of the "price actually paid or payable" for the imported merchandise. Where the "price actually paid or payable" is not certain at the time of importation, appraisement under transaction value is still appropriate so long as a fixed formula or methodology exists for later determining the price, which formula must be determined prior to importation of the merchandise and which also must be based on a future event over which neither the seller nor the buyer has any control. ...
>
> [] However, where the merchandise is not resold or leased after importation the "price actually paid or payable" under transaction value is not ascertainable under this formula. The uncertainty regarding payment under these circumstances precludes appraisement of the merchandise under transaction value.

Transaction value has been rejected when CBP perceives that the alleged formula used in determining the PAPP allows for adjustments that can be renegotiated or depends on events which are within the control of the parties.[251]

Canadian practice follows the same approach, with CBSA observing that:

> CBSA will only accept a reduction in the price paid or payable that occurs after importation if:
>
> a) the purchaser takes advantage of cash discount terms offered by the vendor prior to importation; or
> b) an agreement in writing to later reduce the price paid or payable was in effect at the time of importation, and the reduction results from the agreement.
>
> * * *
>
> In accordance with [the provision for transaction value], any rebate or decrease in the price paid or payable effected after importation of goods must be disregarded. Consequently, this applies when a purchaser and a vendor enter into

247. Ruling no. 546736 (March 31, 1998).
248. TCCV, Com. 4.1, Price Review Clauses (March 1982). *See also* 19 CFR § 152.103(a)(1).
249. Ruling nos. 543352 (March 30, 1984) and 542671 (March 15, 1982).
250. Ruling no. 545622 (April 28, 1994).
251. Ruling nos. 545618 (August 23, 1996), 544840 (September 28, 1994). Cf. ruling no. 546736 (March 31, 1998).

> an agreement to reduce the price paid or payable of goods after those goods have been imported to Canada.[252]

The practice of declaring a lower price on a current entry as a means of accounting for the impact of a defect in a prior shipment is another example of an interrelationship between specific sales transactions.

[4] Allowances/Credit for Defective Goods

In this connection, we may expect to be concerned with problems arising with the imported goods. Beyond damaged or defective goods, these problems may take the form of quantity differences—over-or under-shipments—shrinkages, late deliveries, etc. Typically, the seller will issue credit notes to "make the customer whole." That raises the question, what is the impact on customs valuation for the importer who has contracted for first quality goods, paid for first quality goods and declared and paid duty on the invoiced price for the first quality goods?

[a] TCCV Guidance

In March 1982, the TCCV issued two instruments which provide guidance for customs authorities and for the private sector. In Advisory Opinion 8.1,[253] the TCCV resolved the question of how to treat an importation of merchandise whose price reflects a credit that had been granted in respect of earlier transactions. The instrument pointed out that the credit should be seen to form part of the total payment for the goods and thus is an element of the PAPP. The Advisory Opinion noted that the treatment of the earlier transaction would be a matter for national legislation.

In Explanatory Note 3.1,[254] the TCCV dilated on the varied ways in which goods might be not in conformity with the order: wholly or partially damaged goods, goods that we would call "out of spec," i.e., the goods do not conform to ordered specifications and the importation of replacement goods—and the importation of replacement goods. The issue of credits for defects in previous imports was not raised in this second instrument, but the status of goods sent as replacements in a subsequent shipment was discussed. If the replacement goods are invoiced at the original price, there is no issue. If the goods are invoiced free of charge, then the TCCV vaguely counsels that:

> they should be regarded as goods imported in fulfillment of the original transaction; in these circumstances it would be therefore appropriate to accept the price in that transaction for determination of the Customs value under Article 2, the treatment of the first shipment being a matter for separate consideration.

---

252. Customs Memorandum D13-4-10, *Price reductions*, February 6, 2018, paragraphs 6 and 9. *See also* paragraphs 4 and 12.
253. TCCV, AO 8.1, Treatment Under the Agreement of Credits in Respect of Earlier Transactions (March 1982).
254. TCCV, EN 3.1, Goods Not in Accordance with Contract (March 1982).

This text instructs that we should use the price from the previous transaction as the PAPP, but it leaves open whether customs duty should be collected on that price in the subsequent shipment. Presumably that was the intended result, with the treatment of the duty paid on the original transaction being left to national practice.

The practice in the US on the treatment of credits in the present transaction is in accord, and we might profit from a discussion of the US views on dealing with the effect of defects and the process whereby refunds of duties are to be handled.

[b] US Practice

While price offsets may be contemplated by parties to settle disputes arising from short shipments or defective goods, CBP has ruled that an importer who receives a credit on future shipments of merchandise in settlement of a claim for previous shipments receives an indirect payment of a portion of the PAPP. An example would be the seller who says, in essence, "I owe you 10 currency units (cus) for each unit that you received, so I can simply "cut the price"—I shall reduce the same 10 cu from the unit price on your next shipment." In the US, CBP will levy a duty on the full, un-discounted price, so importers should avoid this as a means of settling claims for defective merchandise.[255] In fact, the CIT has held that an importer who had taken undocumented credits on its entries for allegedly defective prior shipments was properly liable for civil penalties for undervaluation of merchandise.[256]

Instead, importers into the US should deal with the issue of damaged goods or shortages by filing a timely pre-liquidation[257] Post Summary Correction (PSC)[258] or a protest after liquidation.[259] Until a statutory revision in 2004, a US importer could also file a petition under section 1520(c) of the Tariff Act of 1930,[260] on the theory that it was a mistake of fact to have declared the goods at full value as "first quality goods" when they were, in fact, damaged or if there were some missing from the shipment.[261]

---

255. Ruling nos. 543772 (July 22, 1986) and 543830 (November 7, 1986).
256. The civil penalties were issued under section 592 of the Tariff Act of 1930, 19 USC § 1592. *United States v. Menard*, 16 CIT 410 (1992) (purpose of section 1592(d) is to make the government whole for revenue lost as a result of submission of false statements to Customs).
257. Liquidation is the point in the administrative process at which the final computation or ascertainment of duties accrues on an entry. 19 CFR § 159.1. Customs duties will have been tendered on an estimated basis at entry—the final customs duty exposure is fixed at liquidation. Practically speaking, it marks finality for the entry process.
258. This process was established in 2011. More information is available on the CBP website at https://www.cbp.gov/trade/programs-administration/entry-summary/post-summary-correction.
259. Under the authority of section 514, 19 USC § 1514. *See* 19 CFR Part 174.
260. Under former section 1520(c) of the Tariff Act of 1930, 19 USC § 1520(c), repealed by Act of December 3, 2004, Pub. L. No. 108-429, Title II, § 2105, provided relief for clerical errors or mistakes of fact.
261. *See* ruling no. 544879 (April 3, 1992) (importer filing a section 1520 (c) petition must present supporting evidence for claimed defective merchandise).

[i] Post-entry Claim

The importer may be in the position of seeking a refund of some of those duties to factor in their defective condition. The US customs regulations expressly provide for such an allowance:

> (a) Allowance in value. Merchandise which is subject to an ad valorem or compound duties and found by the district director to be partially damaged at the time of importation shall be appraised in its condition as imported, with an allowance made in the value to the extent of the damage. ...[262]

This provision is noteworthy because it marks an exception to the general stricture that rebates or price discounts effected after importation are to be disregarded.[263]

But this scheme requires close attention to detail and a tightly organized application. For one thing, the importer has the burden of showing by clear, concise and convincing evidence that the goods were defective at the time of importation.[264] If there is insufficient evidence available to substantiate the importer's claim that the imported merchandise was defective when imported, or to indicate that the merchandise was of a lesser quality than that which was ordered, an allowance will not be made. CBP is expecting to see evidence of communications between the importer and the supplier or between the importer and its customers.[265]

Sometimes CBP will not accept the importer's allowance for a claimed defect without a verification. After all, there is a strong incentive for an importer to make such a claim, with allowances for defective merchandise about the only exception to the rule against post-importation rebates. CBP has sent samples to its own laboratories to verify the presence of a defect, and if the lab analysis does not substantiate the claim, the allowance will be denied.[266]

[ii] Entry-Specific, Product-Specific Proofs

The importer must be able to quite specifically describe the nature of the defects. In a series of decisions from the 1990s involving imports by Samsung Electronics America,

262. 19 CFR § 158.12(a). Be advised that the allowance may be curtailed by statute, with the cited paragraph in the regulation giving as an example the fact that no allowance is available for rusting of imported steel. There are also specific allowance provisions in the regulations for moisture and impurities, for both petroleum and petroleum products as well as other nonspecified products.
263. 19 USC § 1401a(b)(4)(B) and 19 CFR § 152.103(a)(4) posit the rule:

> Any rebate of, or other decrease in, the price actually paid or payable made or otherwise effected between the buyer and seller after the date of importation of the merchandise will be disregarded in determining the transaction value ... .

264. Ruling no. 543106 (June 29, 1983).
265. Ruling no. 546311 (September 19, 1996).
266. *See* ruling no. 546354 (7/19/96) (imported yarn not found to have been contaminated with polypropylene or vegetable matter).

the customs courts enunciated the general rule that an importer must be able to tie specific defects to specific merchandise contained in specific entries.[267] Several rulings stand for the proposition that the port will not award a defective merchandise allowance that is not tied to specific entries and where the importer cannot demonstrate a link in the diminution in value due to defects in specific merchandise in those entries.[268] But the appellate court soon departed from this strict line and its burden imposed on the importer with a 2001 decision in *Fabil Mfg. Co. v. United States*.[269]

In *Fabil*, the court noted that the importer had alleged that all of the imported goods were defective. This marked a real distinction from the *Samsung* cases, wherein only some of the imported goods were alleged to be defective. The *Fabil* court found that the importer was not required to tie defects to particular entries and was not required to meet a "clear and convincing evidence" standard in proving its case but only the lesser evidentiary standard of a "preponderance of the evidence." The result is that an importer of goods which are defective in their entirety will have, or at least should have, a considerably easier time in dealing with CBP on its refund claims than a counterpart with only partial losses due to defects. In reality, the clear and convincing standard has crept back into the picture within the "preponderance" context.[270]

With the *Saab*[271]and *Volkswagen*[272] line of cases, the courts went back on the road with a particularly onerous, specificity-driven requirement that the importer establishes through independent, corroborative evidence that specifically identifiable defects to specific imported articles existed at the time of importation. In this harsh glare, even VIN-specific identifications with accompanying records of damage codes, repair cost proofs will often not suffice. In the case of automobiles, an exception has been created for so-called port repairs, those typically undertaken on imported motor vehicles at a "port processor's" facility which is usually located at or near a seaport and almost immediately after importation. When a repair is made at any time afterward, the courts require that a claimant must provide more specific evidence proving that the defects existed at the time of importation. Even if the importer is able to show that the repairs were made before the goods were sold (before their "in-service date"), the

267. *Samsung Electronics America, Inc. v. United States*, 904 F. Supp. 1403 (CIT 1995), *rev'd and remanded, Id. v. Id.*, 106 F.3d 376 (Fed. Cir. 1997*), Id. v. Id.*, 35 F. Supp. 2d 942 (CIT), *aff'd*, 195 F.3d 1367 (Fed. Cir. 1999).

268. *See*, e.g., ruling nos. 548093 (April 26, 2002) and 548184 (November 5, 2002). These rulings followed the reasoning of *Fabil Mfg. Co. v. United States*, 237 F.3d 1335 (Fed. Cir. 2001), *rev'g* 56 F. Supp.2d 1183 (CIT 1999).

269. 237 F.3d 1335 (Fed. Cir. 2001), *rev'g* 56 F. Supp.2d 1183 (CIT 1999).

270. *Volkswagen of America, Inc. v. United States*, 484 F. Supp.2d 1314, n. 8 at 1320 (CIT 2007):

> [T]he language in the *Samsung* cases regarding sufficiency of evidence for § 158.12 claims has been adopted in later cases applying the preponderance of the evidence standard. The requirement of independent verification must be met in order to meet the preponderance of the evidence standard.

Perhaps this development should be directly challenged.

271. *Saab Cars USA, Inc. v. United States*, 434 F.3d 1359 (Fed Cir. 2006), *Id. v. Id.*, 306 F. Supp.2d 1279 (2004) and *Id. v. Id.*, 27 CIT 979, 276 F. Supp.2d 1322 (2003).

272. *Volkswagen of America, Inc. v. United States*, 484 F. Supp.2d 1314 (CIT 2007*), Id. v. Id.*, 27 CIT 1201, 277 F. Supp.2d 1364 (2003).

courts have been unwilling to infer that the defects could not have been caused by intervening misuse or mishandling. Thus, the lesser standard for "port repairs" is narrowly applied to those repairs made at the time of importation at the port processor facility.

There is an obvious practical near-impossibility of discovering latent defects within this frame. Even if arguably existing at the time of importation, a reviewing court will not exercise jurisdiction if the defects had not been included within a timely filed protest. This saddles the US importer with the clearly unenviable, entirely disagreeable, and in many instances practically impossible, task of satisfying the strict time limitations frequently associated with customs procedures. Here, an importer has 180 days after liquidation of the entry to file its protest.[273] Because liquidation normally occurs 314 days after importation, the importer effectively has a bit less than one and one-half years to do it all—find the defects, ascertain the cost impact and, importantly, file a valid, which is to say a densely specific, claim.

The practical problem is thus exposed—how does the importer identify a latent defect so as to make a justiciable claim for an adjustment within the strictly controlled time period allowing for refund claims? Maybe the only way to satisfy the administrative time demands and to meet the evidentiary burden is to meet the problem head-on and to establish a rigorous, up-front protocol, one with a full inspection of the imported goods. The importer might then be prepared to show all aspects, in detail, of the post-importation movements of the imported articles—under what circumstances they are moved or otherwise used, how and where inspections are done and to undertake all of this within the regulatory framework.

The question of a pervasive defect comes to mind as a final point here. Query, if there is evidence of a widespread design defect, such as faulty brakes or an errant accelerator, such that a product recall is warranted, or even required under vehicle safety laws, would CBP and the courts deny that this design defect existed at the time of importation? What sort of independent verification would be demanded in that situation?

An earlier ruling presents an interesting planning vehicle for dealing with defective goods which CBP has approved. The importer negotiated a current price which included a factor for defective goods. An importer of ceiling fans presented invoices to CBP which showed original as well as adjusted prices. The adjusted prices were based on "defective allowances" which ranged from 1% to 7% of the original price. These allowances depended on the vendor and its prior two-year history of product defects. The price adjustments were to the current importations. CBP initially

273. It used to be a tighter schedule. Prior to the statutory revisions of 2004, the protest period was a mere ninety days after liquidation. Tariff Act of 1930, section 514, 19 USC § 1514(c)(3) *as amended by* Act of December 3, 2004, Pub. L. No. 108-429, Title II, § 2103 (2) (A). You should know that importers who identify defects or who seek to correct an entry can seek to rectify errors or otherwise revise the entry prior to liquidation by filing an amended entry or a Post Summary Amendment (PSA) up to twenty days before the scheduled liquidation date for the entry.

ruled that amounts for the "defective allowances" were not dutiable.[274] As CBP later itself observed:

> Another way of handling the problem of defective merchandise was examined in HRL 544762, dated January 17, 1992. There, a set percentage, labeled as "defective allowance," was deducted from each original price to arrive at the adjusted price ... The importer paid the foreign vendor a price which had been discounted for defective merchandise. Consequently, the price actually paid for the imported merchandise was the discounted or adjusted price.[275]

This ruling suggests that the importer would be wiser to employ historical data on defects to negotiate an up-front lower price—recall, the role of the PAPP, no matter how derived—than to file a post-importation claim for an allowance based on the actual experience to the subject entry. If the importer were to periodically update and review the historical data before they became too stale, then the defective allowance could be recalibrated and the price could be correspondingly renegotiated in close proximity and in response to the actual experience.

Beyond the issue of "attached strings" or other restrictions on a sale transaction, what are the consequences for customs purposes if there is no sale transaction?

[c] Canadian and EU Regimes

Not surprisingly, both of these jurisdictions allow for relief when the imported goods are discovered to be defective. Canada explains that the different results may occur depending on such circumstances as whether the goods are retained by the importer, and the purchaser subsequently receives a refund or credit for a portion of the original price or whether the goods are exported.[276]

In the EU, the status of defective goods is provided for in the UCC package.[277] In the Implementing Act, the importer is assured that an adjustment made by the seller will be honored if the goods were defective at the time of acceptance of the customs declaration for release for free circulation and the seller's adjustment was made to fulfill a contractual or statutory obligation.[278] There is an early ECJ decision on defective goods which is aligned with this approach.[279]

---

274. Ruling no. 544672 (January 17, 1992). *See also* ruling no. 544841 (January 17, 1992).
275. Ruling no. 544680 (June 26, 1992).
276. *See* Memorandum D13-2-4, *Valuation of Goods Imported Into Canada that are not in Accordance with Contract*, August 8, 2013 and Memorandum D6-2-3, *Refund of Duties*, September 10, 2018.
277. UCC, Article 118.
278. UCC IA, Article 132.
279. Case C-183/85, *Hauptzollamt Itzehoe v. H. J. Repenning GmbH*, 12.6.1986, ECLI:EU:C:1986:247 (where goods bought free of defects are damaged before being released for free circulation, the price actually paid or payable, on which the transaction value is based, must be reduced in proportion to the damage suffered). This is distinguishable from the decision in Case C-11/89, *Unifert Handels GmbH v. Hauptzollamt Münster*, 6.6.1990, ECLI:EU:C:1990:237 (*Unifert Handels*) (where the contract provides for a weight discrepancy allowance, the PAPP should not be reduced proportionately where the quantity discrepancy falls within the agreed weight discrepancy and does not give rise to a reduction in the purchase price).

[5] *Used Merchandise*

The proper customs value of used merchandise, especially used motor vehicles in the case of many developing countries, has been a nagging problem. At the WCO, the issue was so significant that a study was one of the first instruments adopted by the TCCV in 1982.[280] Canada has published very helpful guidance for the customs valuation of used goods[281] and for used automobiles.[282]

[I] Article 8: Statutory Additions to the PAPP

Arguably, the various goods and services falling under the sway of that Article 8 have some claim to an independent status. In fact, when one analyzes Article 8, one sees a common underlying theme. Each of these is an off-invoice or separately invoiced charge that could be/should be or normally would be included in the price for the imported goods. The Valuation Agreement, Article 1.1 in combination with Article 8.4, holds that these "unbundled" costs which do not fall within the PAPP itself—and only these costs—must be added to what is in fact an artificially lowered PAPP so as to arrive at the proper customs value of imported goods.

We might start with the de facto preface to the Agreement, the General Introductory Commentary:

> The primary basis for customs value under this Agreement is "transaction value" as defined in Article 1. Article 1 is to be read together with Article 8 which provides, *inter alia,* for adjustments to the price actually paid or payable in cases where certain specific elements which are considered to form a part of the value for customs purposes but are not included in the price actually paid or payable for the imported goods. Article 8 *also* provides for the inclusion in the transaction value of certain considerations which may pass from the buyer to the seller in the form of *specified* goods or services rather than in the form of money (emphasis added).

The instruction to read Articles 1 and 8 together is both clear and sound. This tallies with the observation that Article 8 provides for adjustments—additions, actually—to the PAPP so as to account for certain missing elements that, by their nature, might have been considered to be a natural part of the PAPP in every instance.

But there is that insertion of the "*inter alia*" in the second sentence. Since that Latin phrase means "among other things," we are being told that Article 8 provides for other things as well as adjustments for certain missing specific elements to the PAPP. What other things? With Articles 8.3 and 8.4 both dealing generally with the additions

280. Study 1.1, Treatment of Used Motor Vehicles (September 1982), Supplement added March 1995. Parenthetically, the challenges of finding customs values for imported used vehicles will arise in contemporary TCCV session discussions.
281. Customs Memorandum D13-10-1, *Used Goods*, November 19, 2013.
282. Customs Memorandum D13-10-2, *Used automobiles, motor vehicles, boats, and other vessels*, July 19, 2021.

to the PAPP, the only possible substantive inclusion in the transaction value is to be found in Articles 8.1(c), covering RLFs, 8.1(d), which deals with payments for the proceeds of subsequent resale or use, and 8.2, which deals with the inclusion or exclusion in customs value of all or part of international transport and insurance charges, which we have just discussed.

I conclude that the *inter alia* usage here can only have been set up to make a distinction of these payments in money from the "non-monetary" additions contemplated by the following sentence. This brings us to the third sentence, which tells us that Article 8 *also* provides for the inclusion in transaction value of nonmonetary consideration in the form of specified goods or services. That will refer to the various specific goods and services provided for in Articles 8.1(a) and (b).

To cite the terms of Article 8, certain elements of value, if they are not already subsumed within the PAPP, must be added to that price. Importantly, Article 8.4 explicitly allows the price to be increased by these "and no others." These additional, or to use the EU term "supplemental," dutiable costs may be summarized as follows (following the US ordering):

- packing costs, whether for labor or materials;
- commissions and brokerage, except buying commissions;
- value of any assist;
- any royalty or license fee [RLF] related to the imported merchandise that the buyer is required to pay as a condition of the sale of the imported merchandise for exportation to the country of importation;
- the proceeds of any subsequent resale, disposal or use of the imported merchandise that accrue, directly or indirectly, to the seller.[283]

The underlying rationale for these "statutory additions," to apply the US parlance, goes back to the simple fact that TV is based on the price paid for the goods, and is normally both evidenced by and equated with the invoice price. It would be very easy for a buyer and seller to arrange for a separate, off-invoice payment or to furnish materials and services on a *gratis* basis. For example, instead of paying USD 100 for the goods, in a bid to lower the dutiable value, the buyer might offer to pay USD 95 for the goods and separately pay USD 5 for packing.

The statutory additions share these attributes—they are all intimately involved in the manufacture or sale of the imported goods; they all confer a benefit to the seller in the sense that, in the absence of Article 8, they might be construed to be indirect payment for the goods; they are all easily segregated and their exclusion from dutiable value would artificially lower the true value of the goods.

While the implementation of some of these Article 8.1 categories is relatively well settled (i.e., commissions, assists), others (i.e., RLFs, proceeds of subsequent resale) have been contentious.

283. Valuation Agreement, Articles 8.1(a)-(d); 19 USC § 1401a(b)(1)(A)-(E); Canada Customs Act, subsection 48(5); UCC, Article 71.1.

Beyond these, per Article 8.2, we must consider the addition to customs value—not to the PAPP—amounts for certain transport and insurance, loading, unloading and handling and insurance. We will discuss the treatment of those charges later.

Let us begin by looking at packing costs.

[1] Packing Costs

At first glance, packing costs present a straightforward case. But the element of timing plays a role in the US administration. The term "packing costs" is defined in the statute and the customs regulations to mean the cost of all containers (exclusive of instruments of international traffic) and coverings of whatever nature and of packing, whether for labor or materials, used in placing merchandise in condition, packed ready for shipment to the US.[284]

In ruling no. 542834,[285] CBP noted that the phrase "packed ready for shipment to the United States" was analogous to the merchandise being "in seaworthy condition." Therefore, in that case the costs of services performed, which were incident to placing the merchandise in condition packed, ready for shipment to the US, were held to be dutiable as "packing costs." The costs incurred *subsequent* to the merchandise attaining that status, however, were held to be not dutiable. The same nondutiable treatment was accorded certain expenses incurred for vacuum packing in ruling no. 543026 (Mar. 17, 1983) (held to be not part of the dutiable value of the imported merchandise because such took place subsequent to the merchandise being placed in condition, packed ready for shipment to the US).

In Canada, there is a similar narrow definition, with the packing costs falling with the statute explained to be "the packing costs and charges incurred by the purchaser in respect of the goods, including the cost of cartons, cases and other containers and coverings that are treated for customs purposes as being part of the imported goods and all expenses of packing incident to placing the goods in the condition in which they are shipped to Canada."[286] This treatment is consistent with the US and Canadian exclusions of international transport charges from customs valuation consideration.

We also note that the EU does not employ a similarly time-defined view, referring simply to "the cost of packing, whether for labour or materials."[287] This might lead to the view that such packing or repacking costs incurred after the goods have been placed ready for their international movement might be deemed to be dutiable. Arguably, this open-ended reference would be consistent with the EU stance on international transport charges under Article 8.2, and it would be of academic interest only whether the inclusion of such charges would be a function of the charges as a

284. 19 USC § 1401a(h)(3) and 19 CFR § 152.102(e).
285. July 20, 1982 (TAA #49). *See also* ruling nos. 546690 (June 18, 1997), 546479 (October 29, 1996) 543985 (February 1, 1988) and 542384 (July 20, 1982).
286. Canada Customs Act, subparagraph 48(5)(a)(ii).
287. UCC, Article 71(a)(iii).

dutiable packing cost under Article 8.1 or as a dutiable "handling charge" subsumed under international transport costs under Article 8.2.

We note that the Valuation Agreement does not define packing costs. In that vacuum, this potential difference in treatment is one among a growing number of questions where there may be a difference between the standards applied by the US and the EU.

This question whether packing materials and packing containers should be treated as separate imported articles for import purposes—assigned a separate tariff classification with a separately declared customs value—arises at the point of intersection with tariff classification. The general rule as expressed in the General Rules of Interpretation (GRIs) of the Harmonized System is that packing materials and containers presented with the goods shall be classified with the goods if they are of a kind normally used for packing such goods.[288] That means that, as a general rule, the packing materials and packing containers are subsumed within the imported goods and their value included within the value of the imported goods. There is the matter of the status of reusable containers, with reusability creating an exception to the general rule. That just-cited general rule "... is not binding when such packing materials or packing containers are clearly suited for repetitive use."[289] Consistent with the GRI, the EU sets a separate rule for such containers,[290] which are treated as being one for customs purposes with the goods in question.[291]

As can be expected, the issue of reusability or capability of repetitive use may be in dispute.[292] CBP has cautioned that:

> the applicable standard for "clearly suitable for repetitive use" is not that the containers could possibly be reused. The second sentence of GRI 5(b) provides that to be classified separately, containers must be clearly suitable for repetitive use.[293]

The treatment of camera cases, musical instrument cases, gun cases and the like marks an exception to the exception. Under GRI 5(a), they will be classified with such

288. Formally, the Harmonized Commodity Description and Coding System, General Rule of Interpretation (GRI) 5(b).
289. *Ibid.*
290. Curiously packing materials are not mentioned.
291. UCC, Article 71(a)(ii).
292. In the US, *see* ruling nos. H048276 (March 27, 2009) (reusable security tags at issue in this case are not dutiable as packing costs, as an addition to the price actually paid or payable of the imported garments, but are separately classifiable and dutiable) and 085915 (February 21, 1990) (metal box imported with scotch whisky bottle separately classified—it is not the normal container under GRI 5(b) nor does it fall within GRI 5(a) as it is a promotional item, offered to attract purchasers and it is not specially shaped or fitted to contain a specific article or set of articles nor is it suitable for long-term use).
293. Ruling no. 088170 (February 20, 1991) (one type of container that is clearly suitable for repetitive use, as provided by the Explanatory Notes to GRI 5(b), p. 7, is a container of iron or steel for compressed or liquefied gas).

articles.[294] Perhaps, it is better to perceive that suitability for "long-term" use is distinguished from repetitive use.[295]

In the US, another category of container, instruments of international traffic (IITs), is entitled to be separately classified upon import. There is a specific tariff item number providing for duty-free treatment.[296] One caveat is that the IITs must be reexported, that obligation being backed up by a surety bond. If they enter the stream of commerce in the US, they will be dutiable under the tariff provision and at the duty rate that applies to their status as containers.

A line of CBP rulings dating to 2003 on beer containers relied on excellent analyses.[297] In the 2003 ruling, CBP noted that the commercial invoices reflect the value of the imported beer and separately identify the returnable deposit. In addition, each invoice bore a statement explaining that a deposit is paid to the supplier to guarantee return of the reusable barrels and pallets and that the deposit is credited to Heineken USA when the items are returned. This statement appeared on each invoice whether or not reusable items are involved. Moreover, each invoice also included a handwritten statement specifically stating either: (1) that the shipment contains reusable items, and the number of reusable items; or (2) that the shipment does not contain any reusable items. CBP concluded that the reusable beer containers were not garden-variety packing or containers but IITs and should be treated as such.

A contrary result on remarkably similar facts had been obtained in an older ECJ decision, the 1988 judgment *Albert Schmid*.[298]

In *Schmid*, the court found that the expression "packing" includes beer barrels, beer bottles and plastic crates for beer bottles even where those articles are to be returned to the seller of the beer in another country. The facts were that the importer purchased beer from Czechoslovakia in barrels or in bottles in crates for resale in Germany. According to the sales contract, the price of the beer did not include the cost of the containers or rental fees or the like, but the importer was required to return the empty containers to the Czech sellers at its own expense on an "as soon as possible" basis. If the containers were not returned, the loss of containers had to be made good

294. The ENs note that cases, boxes and the like that are covered by GRI 5(a) will be governed by that rule and not the more general rule of GRI 5(b). For a thorough analysis applying GRI 5(a), *see* ruling no. H317327 (May 26, 2021) (tent carrying case). IITs are to be distinguished from the substantial containers or holders which are the subject of 19 CFR § 10.7 and entitled to duty-free treatment.

295. CBP declares that "repeated use" means "more than twice." *See*, e.g., ruling no. 108658 (November 21, 1986).

296. 19 USC § 1322(a); item no. 9803.00.50, HTSUS; 19 CFR § 10.41a. *See* CBP Informed Compliance Publication (ICP), What Every Member of the Trade Community Should Know About Instruments of International Traffic, August 2012, available at https://www.cbp.gov/sites/default/files/assets/documents/2020-Feb/InstrumentsofInternationalTraffic%20ICP.pdf.

297. Ruling nos. 548257 (March 19, 2003) (reusable pallets and barrels are IIT, separately classifiable under subheading 9803.00.50, HTSUSA, the value of the pallets and barrels is not included in the appraised value of the imported beer; payments of refundable deposits were not dutiable), H309674 (August 10, 2020) (stainless steel beer kegs are IITs) and H303749 (June 13, 2019).

298. Case C-357/87, *Firma Albert Schmid v. Hauptzollamt Stuttgart-West*, 5.10.1988, ECLI: EU:C:1988:478.

either in kind or by way of financial compensation fixed at the rate of 75% of the new value of barrels and 100% of the new value of bottles and crates. Between 1981 and March 31, 1984, the plaintiff returned on average 96% of the containers and made compensatory payments in respect of the remainder. The question raised was whether, under the 1980 customs valuation regime,[299] the containers should be seen as "packings." If so, because packings are chargeable at the same rate of customs duty as the goods contained therein, then the follow-up question was, is duty on packings, which are themselves dutiable, paid with the duty on the goods in such a way that the duty on the goods also discharges the duty on the packings, or are the packings chargeable on the basis of their own customs value but at the rate applicable to the goods?

The court concluded that the expression "packing" includes beer barrels, beer bottles and plastic crates for beer bottles even where those articles are to be returned to the seller of the beer in another country. In doing so, there was no discussion of the limitation on dutiable status (as an addition to the PAPP) being restricted to containers that are treated as one with the goods for customs purposes. As we have seen, that should have prompted a proper tariff classification analysis and an analysis under GRI 5(a) and (b). The AG Opinion and the Judgment were silent on that point.

The court then determined that duty is payable on packings at the rate applicable to the goods contained therein. However, where the [costs of the] packings are not included in the PAPP and, in fact, the containers are to be returned to the seller in another country, with the buyer being required to pay the seller financial compensation only in respect of packings that are not returned (here, that was 4% of the containers), only such compensation constitutes a dutiable cost under Article 8.1(a).

The ECJ logic appears to be that the separate identity of the containers whose value is not embedded in the PAPP is proven only after importation. When those containers are returned via a reexport to the seller, their separate identity is confirmed and no duty is assessed on them. For those containers not returned to the seller, however, their separate identity is not established, and duty should be assessed at the rate that applies to the finished goods, in this case, the beer. One wonders how that protocol would work in practice.

Under the CBP approach, by contrast, with the IIT protocol, the reusable and returnable containers are treated as separately classifiable imported articles at entry, eligible for duty-free entry if they are reexported. Only if the containers have not been reexported and, instead, enter the stream of commerce by virtue of remaining in the customs territory, will they become dutiable, and treated as the separate articles that they are and not tied in any way to the imported goods. Tariff classification will be assigned to the containers qua containers with the duty rate for the containers assigned.

299. Council Reg (EEC) 1224/80 of 28 May 1980. The operative provision, Article 8.1(a), is identical in all material respects to UCC, Article 71.1(a).

In this connection, we must be mindful of three conventions on IITs: (1) the 1956 Customs Convention on Containers,[300] (2) the IMO Convention on Safe Containers (1972)[301] and (3) the Economic Commission for Europe's Convention on Customs Treatment of Pool Containers Used in International Transport (1994).[302] It appears the US is a signatory to the first two but not the third. Vice versa for the EU, although a number of the Member States are signatories.[303]

As I see it, we should be clear about the customs treatment of two types of containers:

(1) containers capable of repeated use (e.g., stainless steel kegs, bottles, etc.);
(2) freight containers (normally 20' or 40') for loading onto vessels or into aircraft.

At the same time, we must be clear about the exceptional status of various conveyances, such as airplanes, trucks and trailers, ships, locomotives and other rolling stock (rail cars), which should not be subject to treatment as imported articles of commerce themselves—entry declaration, payment of duty and other taxes, etc.—if they are not intended to remain permanently. There are international conventions on such conveyances as well.

As any additional charges for IITs may increase dutiable value, they have been the subject of spirited debate between customs authorities and the import community. Rulings and current administrative practice present planning opportunities to those willing to follow where there are bright lines.

As one additional consideration, if qualifying domestic-origin packaging materials are used, under a form of outward processing relief or, to use the US terminology, American (or US) Goods Returned, then their value may *not* be added to make dutiable value for the imported article itself.[304]

[2] Selling Versus Buying Commissions, Brokerage

The first remark to make is that there is a difference in the statutory implementations. The US statute refers to "any selling commission incurred by the buyer."[305] It makes no reference to brokerage nor to buying commissions, only stating that selling commissions are dutiable. Both Canada and the EU include brokerage in their statutory

300. Available at 20 UST 30; TIAS 6634 and at the UN Treaty Collection https://treaties.un.org/Pages/ViewDetails.aspx?chapter = 11&clang = _en&mtdsg_no = XI-A-9&src = TREATY.
301. Discussed at https://www.imo.org/en/OurWork/Safety/Pages/Containers-Default.aspx.
302. Available at https://unece.org/DAM/trans/conventn/poolcon.pdf.
303. *See* UCC IA, Article 322.1.
304. This is the case in the US *see* ruling nos. 547352 (July 8, 1999) (separately classified items must be separately appraised) and 546827 (April 25, 1996).
305. 19 USC § 1401a(b)(1). Selling agent commissions are dutiable even if the services are to be performed in the United States. Ruling no. H137455 (February 16, 2012). US Goods Returned provisions are set forth in Chapter 98, HTSUS and in 19 CFR Part 10.

frame.[306] In the case of the EU, buying commissions, which are defined as the "fee paid by an importer to an agent for representing him or her in the purchase of goods being valued,"[307] are exempted.

The rationale for making selling commissions dutiable is easy to discern. After all, a seller could easily settle for a USD 95 payment for the goods with a separate USD 5 payment to a designated "selling agent." Especially if the selling agent were related to the seller and it could be shown that the payment would be funneled to the seller, if allowed to stand, such a "two pocket" arrangement would lower the dutiable value, but the seller would effectively be paid in full measure. Where the selling agent is not related, one may suppose that the rationale for dutiable status is that the selling function costs have been artificially excluded from the seller's costs by resort to an outside agent and such costs must be "clawed back" to make a full customs value.

The WCO Technical Committee Explanatory Note 2.1[308] (paragraphs 7 and 8) is a useful resource for understanding some of the dynamics of this area:

> 7. A selling agent is a person who accounts for the account of a seller; he seeks customers and collects orders, and in some cases he may arrange for storage and delivery of the goods. The remuneration he receives for services rendered in the conclusion of a contract is usually termed "selling commission." Goods sold through the seller's agent cannot usually be purchased without payment of the selling agent's commission. These payments can be made in the ways set out below.
> 8. Foreign suppliers who deliver their goods in pursuance of orders placed through a selling agent usually pay for the latter's services themselves, and quote inclusive prices to their customers. In such cases, there is no need for the invoice price to be adjusted to take account of these services. If the terms of the sale require the buyer to pay, usually direct to the intermediary, a commission that is additional to the price invoiced for the goods, this commission must be added to the price when determining the transaction value under Article 1 of the Agreement.

There is an important point to be made here. As we have discussed, quite often an importer may be set up as a "stripped down" distributor or a "*commissionaire*" to use a European term, i.e., an importer with minimal commercial risk, such as little or no risks associated with carrying inventory, assuming little financing and few credit risks, and correspondingly modest compensation, often expressed to be a "commission." This might make sense from a tax planning perspective, exposing a lower level of income to tax in a jurisdiction with a relatively high rate of income tax, e.g., the US.

But these same facts and circumstances could lead CBP or another customs authority to apply its "sale for export" analysis, discussed above, and conclude that there is no sale to the importer.[309] This would render the importer, whose principal role within its narrowed horizon is to solicit orders from local in the country of importation

306. Respectively, Canada Customs Act, subparagraph 48(5)(a)(i), UCC, Article 71.1(b)(i).
307. UCC, Article 5(41).
308. TCCV, EN 2.1, Commissions and Brokerage in the Context of Article 8 of the Agreement (March 1992).
309. The Tribunal decision in *Scentsy* notwithstanding.

customers, a mere selling agent for its related party foreign seller. The effect of such an analysis and its conclusion would be to disqualify a TV appraisement in the context of the purported sale to the importer, and expose the importer's markup to dutiable status as a selling agent's commission.[310] As CBP has observed in a 2002 ruling, in speaking of a multinational corporation (MNC):

> In this case a foreign subsidiary of the MNC produced the subject merchandise. The US company did not function as an independent buyer of the imported merchandise, but rather as a selling agent on behalf of the MNC. Therefore, the commissions received by the U.S. company constitute dutiable selling commissions. In the absence of a bona fide sale between the foreign subsidiary of the MNC and the U.S. company, the price paid by the U.S. purchasers, which already includes the selling commission, is the appropriate transaction value to be used for customs valuation.[311]

To take another case: with the silence of the statute in the US, amounts paid as bona fide commissions to buying agents are nondutiable.[312] Certainly, there are many companies which are organized to play a vital role in the sourcing of goods from overseas vendors, acting as buying agents and doing all of the functions associated with that sourcing function, e.g., finding qualified factories, performing quality control (QC) inspections, ensuring adherence to delivery schedules, arranging for the furnishing of components and raw materials and so forth. One reason is that more companies find that they are relying heavily on (read "more vulnerable to") their supply chain, which is a consequence of their heavier flow of foreign-sourced goods. In turn, that shift is a consequence of adopting the business model in which many companies have reduced themselves to a customer-facing, design-heavy, brand franchise-owning status, outsourcing production to others.[313]

These import-dependent companies are often motivated by a desire to more closely monitor and control the sourcing function. These companies know that mastery of the supply chain has been the secret of success for a number of companies, e.g., the "fast fashion" model pioneered by MAST Industries in the US. Thus prompted, the companies turn to an existing offshore entity, or set up their own entity, to perform that dual sourcing/monitoring role. Many of these agents have been located in Hong Kong or Singapore to be closer to Asian suppliers.[314]

---

310. Ruling nos. 545958 (April 12, 1996), 544949 (March 17, 1993), 543774 (June 4, 1987), 544116 (April 19, 1988).
311. Ruling no. 548173 (December 6, 2002).
312. For a fuller discussion, *see* Neville, "Offshore Buying Agents: Some Customs and Tax Considerations," 19 J. Int'l Tax'n (July 2008) at 12 and Neville, "Buying Agency (Part 1)," 29 J. Int'l Tax'n (December 2018) at 26 and "Buying Agency (Part 2)," 30 J. Int'l Tax'n (January 2019) at 41. The latter two articles discuss the plethora of functions assumed by latter-day buying agents and also the task of allocating a buying agent commission when it is based upon an admixture of dutiable and nondutiable tasks. This last point was raised with great prescience by Sherman and Glashoff in no. 223 at 110.
313. Heightened exposure to adjustments to be made for dutiable assists is another consequence, as the foreign vendors may be provided with various goods or services in order to facilitate the production process.
314. Due to the political turmoil in Hong Kong, there is a growing trend to relocate these operations to Singapore.

This insertion of an intermediary company as an agent in the sourcing flow will lead to a payment to that agent for services, and that payment will usually be claimed as a nondutiable buying commission. Such a claim will lead to three possible results. From the importer's perspective, two are negative. In the first place, CBP or another customs authority can decide that the putative agent was acting for its own account, and was not an agent. Its profit is dutiable.[315] This would be the case if the agreement between the two established that the foreign middleman was an independent contractor.[316] Second, the agent could be acting as an agent, but its principal could be the foreign producer.[317] The agent's commission would be a selling agent's commission and thus dutiable. Finally, the agent might be acting for the buyer and earning a nondutiable buying commission.

Depending on the status of a foreign vendor (producer of the goods or reseller) and the relationship of an importer with its vendor, and the markup of the vendor, it is possible that an intermediate party could be convinced to transform itself into a buying agent. This would normally be the case where the importer and the selling party are related.

Assume, for example, that an importer purchases the merchandise from a foreign company which is not itself the producer, but only acts as an intermediate buy/resell entity. Presumably, the foreign intermediate company earns a markup on the goods which it purchases from the foreign manufacturer and resells to the importer. That markup of the trading company is included in the price actually paid by the importer, with the result that the markup is dutiable. Instead of this approach, if all three parties can come to terms, the trading company might act as an agent for the importer in sourcing goods for the importer. The importer would buy directly from the factory, and pay duty on the price it paid to the foreign producer. This reworking and reinvention exercise will work if the middleman buyer/reseller profit is within the range of what would be an acceptable commission as an agent. It should be noted that if the importer/buyer and the middleman are related parties, then the level of profit or commission, as the case may be, will be subject to transfer pricing scrutiny by the income tax authorities.

CBP, and presumably all other customs authorities, will closely scrutinize all claimed buying commission structures, examining all relevant factors.[318] In this connection, the failure to reduce the relationship to a written agreement which delineates the rights and responsibilities of the purported principal and agent is a major negative factor.[319] That having been said, CBP and, again, other customs authorities

315. *See*, e.g., ruling nos. 546539 (October 30, 1996) 543305 (December 27, 1984).
316. *See* ruling no. 546543 (August 6, 1997).
317. *See*, e.g., ruling nos. 547623 (February 21, 2002), 54550 (September 13, 1995).
318. *J. C. Pennev Purchasing Corp. v. United States*, 80 Cust. Ct. 84, 94, 451 F. Supp. 973, 982, CD 4741 (1978). In Canada, which follows an "all facts and circumstances" approach, *see Browns Shoe Shops Inc. v. Commissioner CCRA* (February 11, 2004), AP-2002-096 (CITT).
319. *See* TCCV, Com. 17.1, Buying Commissions (October 1990) in paragraph 6. *See also* CBP ICP, "What Every Member of the Trade Community Should Know About: Buying and Selling Commissions" (October 2006).

will want to ensure that the parties in fact do act in accord with the agreement, i.e., that the agreement is not a "dead letter."[320]

The fact that the buyer and seller are related is not fatal, but the agent must be considered sufficiently independent of the related seller and act as an agent at the direction and under the control of the importer/principal.[321] While a relationship between the buying agent and the seller does not preclude the existence of a buying agency, the circumstances surrounding such related party transactions are subject to closer scrutiny in determining whether a commission is a bona fide buying commission.[322] There is no legal impediment to a parent corporation acting as an agent for its subsidiary corporation.[323]

Sherman and Glashoff introduce the possibility of a branch office filling the role of a buying agent.[324] They speculate that any payment would be an "intercompany" payment and that the "agent" is "really just a part of the principal." They conclude that any such payments would be in the nature of "purchasing costs." I have no quarrel with most of their analysis but would venture that the payment of any "commission" would be an "intracompany" payment since, as we have already seen, the branch purporting to act as a buying agent is not a separate legal entity but just a part of the principal (the buyer). I would also press for a direct statement that any such payment would be nondutiable.

Another point fraught with the potential for controversy is the notion of a buying agent as an invoicing party. There may be some who would conclude that it would be an anomaly, that it is impossible for an intermediate party to issue an invoice for the imported goods and to maintain its status as a buying agent. But the TCCV has spoken to this:

> In certain transactions, the agent concludes the contract, reinvoices the importer distinguishing the price of his goods and his fee. The mere act of invoicing does not make him the seller of the goods.[325]

The US,[326] Canada[327] and the EU[328] are in accord. But a cautionary note: all of these jurisdictions take the view that a failure to separately identify ("break out") the buying agent commission from the invoice price for the goods will be fatal.[329]

320. *See*, e.g., ruling no. 545421 (August 3, 1994).
321. *Jav-Arr Slimwear Inc. v. United States*, 12 CIT 133 (1988); ruling no. 545988 (May 18, 1995).
322. Ruling no. 544512 (December 20, 1992).
323. Ruling no. 542912 (June 28, 1983).
324. Sherman and Glashoff, no. 222 at 110.
325. TCCV, Com. 17.1, Buying Commissions (October 1990) in paragraph 13.
326. *See* ruling no. 544669 (August 15, 1991) and its progeny.
327. Memorandum D13-4-12, *Commissions and Brokerage*, November 24, 2014, paragraph 1 (if they are invoiced or identified separately from the goods, they do not need to be added to the price paid or payable for the goods).
328. EU Commission Compendium 2022, Conclusion No. 14, Imports through contract agents, 120.
329. In the US, *see* ruling nos. 548258 (October 9, 2003), 547087 (July 30, 1998) and 545296 (August 16, 1993). In the EU, *compare* Case C-379/00, *Overland Footwear Ltd v. Commissioners of Customs & Excise*, 5.12.2002, ECLI:EU:C:2002:723 *with* Case C-468/03, *Overland Footwear Ltd v. Commissioners of Customs & Excise*, 20.10.2005, ECLI:EU:C:2005:624.

The leading US court cases remain the venerable decisions in *Rosenthal-Netter, Inc. v. United States,*[330] *J. C. Penney*, and *Pier 1 Imports v. United States.*[331]

The *Rosenthal-Netter* decision is especially helpful for its recitation of the duties typically borne by an agent. But there are limits to the agent's responsibilities, which are typically enunciated in the agency agreement. For instance, the agent cannot be ultimately responsible for the quality of the goods or for other incidents of the transaction outside the scope of its agency. As the court stated:

> It is uncharacteristic of an agency relationship to allow the intermediary to bear the risk for damaged, lost or defective merchandise.[332]

There is authority that a bona fide buying agent of a particular importer may act as a selling agent for the seller in another separate transaction without losing the buying agent relationship altogether.[333] Note, payment must be made directly by the importer to the agent. An importer cannot pay a gross amount to the seller, with instructions to the seller to disburse funds to the buyer's agent, without having the agent's commission swept up in dutiable value with duties assessed thereon.[334] It bears repeated emphasis that in the US all payments made to the seller are presumed dutiable.[335] As stated elsewhere, this presumption may be overcome if the importer can prove that the payments are unrelated to the imported merchandise.[336] Helpfully, CBP rulings on buying agency commission issues abound, meaning that there is a plethora of administrative guidance for the US importer's planning purposes.[337]

We are not without helpful EU advice. In the 1990 judgment of the ECJ in *Unifert Handels*, we find the familiar refrain, all payments to the seller are presumed dutiable,

---

330. 12 CIT 77, *aff'd* 861 F.2d 261 (Fed. Cir. 1988).
331. 13 CIT 161 (1989).
332. *Rosenthal-Netter, Inc. v. United States, Id.* at 83, *citing New Trends, Inc. v. United States,* 10 CIT 637, 641 (1986).
333. Ruling no. 543053 (July 11, 1983).
334. *Moss Manufacturing Co., Inc. v. United States,* 13 CIT 420, 714 F. Supp. 1223 (1989), *aff'd* 8 Fed. Cir. 40 (1990).
335. *Generra Sportswear Co. v. United States,* 905 F.2d 377 (Fed. Cir. 1990) (quota charges paid to seller by buying agent were dutiable).
336. *Chrysler Corporation v. United States,* 17 CIT 1049 (1993). An argument might be fashioned to the effect that a separately stated portion of the payment to the seller which was to be remitted to the buying agent was indeed a payment for something other than for the goods.
337. For its part, CBSA has issued a D Memo, Customs Memorandum D13-4-12, *Commissions and Brokerage,* November 24, 2014. Interestingly, the D Memo makes the point that a bona fide buying agent has a fiduciary responsibility to its principal, although its discussion at point 9 is confusing (if the agent makes a complete disclosure to the purchaser, and the purchaser contracts to engage the agent, then the agent's fiduciary responsibility has been satisfied, and the agent is deemed to be acting in the best interest of the purchaser. An agency agreement alone is not sufficient evidence that a principal-agent relationship exists in which an agent has met its fiduciary responsibility to a purchaser). On this point, CBP has not pointed to a fiduciary relationship but it has made the point that a written agreement is not dispositive of a valid buying agency relationship. The conduct of the parties will be examined.

in play. There, the seller had issued an invoice with a separate amount that purported to be a "buying commission" for services performed by the seller. Obviously, allocating a separate payment as a selling commission would not have helped, as that would have been fully dutiable. The solution: set up a separate payment to the seller as a buying commission.

The ECJ wrote that simply applying a name to something does not make it so:

> the [PAPP] is the total payment made or to be made by the buyer to or for the benefit of the seller for the imported goods. It follows that all sums paid by the buyer to the seller as consideration for the sales transaction are included in the [PAPP] and, therefore, in the transaction value.
>
> the term "buying commission" means a fee paid by an importer to his agent for the service of representing him in the purchase of the goods being valued. It does not include, therefore, an amount paid by the buyer to the seller if the amount is calculated in such a way as to permit the seller to cover his administrative costs and other general costs not directly related to the sale in question.[338]

Arising from our earlier discussion on the definition of the PAPP, we might also add that there was no possibility of ascribing the payment, separately noted on the invoice though it may have been, to anything other than as a dutiable payment for the imported goods.

As for brokerage fees, the status completely omitted from the US statute, we have some guidance from the TCCV. In EN 2.1, we are instructed that in some countries the term is rarely used and that brokers have a limited role as an intermediary in putting the buyer and seller together. Because they might be paid by either the buyer or seller or both, the TCCV advised that they should be treated as: (i) selling agents if the seller paid their fees, and their fees would be dutiable or as (ii) buying agents if and to the extent that the buyer paid their fees. In that latter case, the brokerage fee would not be dutiable.

There was one 2003 ruling issued by CBP on brokerage fees.[339] The long-standing approach taken by CBP is that if the amount in question is included with the PAPP, there is no authority to separate it and treat is as nondutiable. That was the unfortunate case for an importer where the relevant documents indicated that the fees at issue were already included in the seller's price. The buyer and seller determined that this is how they wanted to structure their transaction. Once these payments were included in the contract price, however, they became a part of the total payment for the goods. Moreover, the brokerage firm described its mission in terms that suggested that the broker was in fact one who works on behalf of grain producers (sellers) and not grain purchasers (buyers). Different facts might support a stronger case for nondutiable status.

338. *Unifert Handels*, paragraphs 23-24.
339. Ruling no. 548258 (October 9, 2003).

[3] Dutiable Assists

The customs authority can be expected to apply the local customs valuation law, which tracks the Valuation Agreement,[340] to increase the dutiable value if the buyer of imported merchandise supplies, directly or indirectly, either free or at a reduced cost, the foreign manufacturer or seller with any of the following four types of goods or services:

(i) materials, components, parts, and similar items incorporated in the imported goods;
(ii) tools, dies, molds, and similar items used in the production of the imported goods;
(iii) materials[341] consumed in the production of the imported goods;
(iv) engineering, development, artwork, design work, and plans and sketches that are undertaken elsewhere than in the country of importation and are necessary for the production of the imported goods.

The policy behind the dutiability of assists springs from the premise that if the manufacturer had been forced to develop the assist itself, or had purchased it at arm's length, its cost would have been passed along to the buyer in the form of a higher selling price. Thus, its omission is an artificial lowering of the true value of the imported merchandise. You may have recognized the resort to a notional aspect of customs valuation at play here.[342]

Before we proceed further, we should draw attention to the fact that the various categories that comprise the different categories of assists are based upon goods or services being provided free or at reduced cost. They do *not* embrace payments of money. Thus, the CIT has held that sums of money provided to a seller for tooling charges are not dutiable assists. They are dutiable as missing elements of the PAPP.[343] In much the same way, a seller who separately invoices the buyer for some or all of the production charges faces the prospect of an addition to the PAPP. You will recall that the ECJ directed the payment for a certificate of authenticity to be added to the PAPP in the *Malt* decision, discussed above. For its part, the EU Commission in Conclusion No 15 of the 2022 Compendium followed suit.

---

340. Valuation Agreement, Article 8. 1(b); 19 USC §§ 1401a(b)(1)(C) and (h)(1)(A); Canada Customs Act, subparagraph 48(5)(a)(iii); UCC, Article 71.1.(b), EU Commission Compendium 2022, Commentary No. 1, Application of Article 71(1)(b) of the UCC on the valuation of goods for customs purposes, 23.
341. In the US statute, "merchandise."
342. As a matter of historical interest, the pre-Agreement US statute precluded an export value appraisement in the presence of assists. *See* ruling no. 541652 (January 23, 1979 (CSD 79-275)).
343. *Chrysler*, 17 CIT at 1058 (payments for tooling). *See also* ruling nos. 544381 (November 25, 1991), 544516 (January 9, 1991), 543951 (September 23, 1987), 543882 (March 13, 1987), 543595 (April 17, 1986) and 542812 (July 19, 1982) (CSD 83-3). The distinction between status as an adjustment-required "assist" and as "part of the price paid or payable" is generally of academic interest only, except in one major respect. Unlike goods or services in the nature of assists, tooling charges may not be apportioned unless the contract under which the payments were made provides a basis for an apportionment. Ruling nos. 544525 and 544484 (January 31, 1991).

The Commission missed the mark in Conclusion 13 of the Compendium,[344] however, when it characterized a payment for a separately invoiced charge to fabricate tooling as an assist that had been supplied indirectly. It is of equal importance that we assign the proper rationale for dutiable or nondutiable status. The fact that the payment in question relates back to tooling charges is of no consequence. Applying the US perspective, the payment of money to the seller does not fall within Article 71.1(b)(ii) of the UCC. To be clear, the consistently held CBP view is that such a payment may be dutiable, but as an element of the PAPP under Article 1. The notion that a payment of money might serve as an indirectly provided assist was explicitly rejected by CBP as early as 1982.[345] This marks a US versus EU difference of opinion.

In the US, CBP has paid special attention to assists in the context of related party transactions, often opening its inquiry with a formal CF 28 Request for Information, roughly the equivalent of an Information Document Request (IDR) by the IRS. Importers are encouraged to take these information requests seriously.[346] CBP also takes extra care in reviewing the subject in the course of regulatory audits. You can be confident, too, that whenever an importer has relied on a contract manufacturing arrangement with a foreign supplier, a dutiable assist inquiry is sure to follow.

The issue of goods and services being furnished to offshore affiliates is also of interest to the IRS, and they have developed their own rules to determine whether such costs should be borne by the foreign seller or the importing US taxpayer. The customs administrative practice is to draw the line on the dutiability of personnel charges and plant, equipment and machinery costs by reference to whether the persons are engaged, or the objects used, in the production of the imported merchandise.[347] Thus, CBP has held to be nondutiable such nonproduction functions as management services furnished to the seller,[348] salaries of persons providing administrative services, including management, accounting, legal and other services.[349]

The US Court of International Trade has upheld this administrative practice as it relates to the dutiability of the value of equipment.[350] There is no reason to doubt that the practice as it relates to personnel charges would not be similarly approved by the CIT.

There is one major exception to the dutiable assist status of the foregoing listed goods and services. Category (b)(iv) of dutiable assists is comprised of engineering,

344. EU Commission Compendium 2022, Conclusion No. 13: Tool Costs, 122.
345. *See* ruling no. 542812 (July 19, 1982) (CSD 83-3).
346. Parenthetically, it is a serious mistake for importers to assign lower-level clerical staff to respond to such official requests. As is the case with inquiries by the income tax authorities, management should review all such requests, preferably with the assistance of the importer's customs advisor. Inquiries by CBP into the relationship of the parties and the manner in which the prices for the imported merchandise were settled are often made in the context of the CF-28. The importer will be bound by its responses, with CBP relying upon them to ascertain the proper tariff classification and the valuation of imported goods.
347. CSD 81-186, 15 Cust. Bull. 1099 (1981).
348. Ruling no. 543877 (March 17, 1987).
349. Ruling no. 544353 (October 24, 1989).
350. *Texas Apparel Co. v. United States*, 12 CIT 1002, 1007 (1988) (CBP's interpretation of the statute is reasonable and consistent with congressional intent).

development, artwork, design work, and plans and sketches that are undertaken elsewhere than in the country of importation and are necessary for the production of the imported merchandise.[351] That subsection already states that the named activities or products must be undertaken or produced outside the country of importation to fall within the customs valuation provision for dutiable assists. To be sure that domestically produced services or work is accorded nondutiable status, however, the US Congress separately provided in 19 USC § 1401a(h)(1)(B) that no such service or work undertaken within the US shall be treated as an assist.

CBP's ruling no. 547487 (June 23, 2000) established that the "Tech Packs" or "Tech Packages" were dutiable assists.[352] These consisted of patterns (alleged typically not to be used by manufacturers); detailed technical drawings; drawings showing colors of parts; part maps; specifications for particular parts; and itemized parts lists specifying materials, suppliers, quality codes and colors), which were provided to the factories by the parent company.

The importer had argued that the Tech Packs were not needed for the production of the imported goods and thus could not be classified as dutiable assists.[353] In framing its ruling determination, CBP stated in its ruling that some of the Tech Packs did represent dutiable assists while other Tech Packs did not fit within the statutory definition of an assist:

> design work carried out by [the importer] in the U.S. is not treated as an assist. The only matter for inquiry here is extent to which the cost of design work performed by [the importer's] foreign parent is added as an assist to the price actually paid or payable by [the importer] to foreign manufacturers of shoes which it imports.

In that 2000 ruling, CBP drew a distinction on the basis of the location where the design and development work that constituted the Tech Packs were performed. In doing so, CBP was following the statutory split in treatment based on the geography where the services or materials embodying those services were being created.

Note that "research" as in "research and development" (R&D) is not named. If there is "pure" or "blue skies" research, as opposed to "applied research" and not tied to the development of a product, the argument might be made that the costs should be nondutiable. The problem is that such costs might not be tracked in sufficient detail to separate what is a development cost versus a pure research cost. In the case of the EU, the Commission sought to address this in the Implementing Act.[354] In the absence of

351. Valuation Agreement, Article 8.1(b)(iv); 19 USC § 1401a(h)(1)(A)(iv); Canada Customs Act, subparagraph 48(5)(a)(iii)(D); EU, UCC, Article 71.1(b)(iv).
352. Not surprisingly, CBP has issued other rulings holding that US-based design and development work is not a dutiable assist. *See*, e.g., ruling nos. 547643 (February 13, 2002) (Product Development Program fees not dutiable) and 548532 (July 13, 2004) (foreign "knitdowns" were used to create US-origin designs which were not dutiable assists).
353. Only activities necessary for the production of imported merchandise will be considered assists. *See* ruling no. 544621 (April 22, 1991) (artist's renditions of various tone and color combinations necessary for the production of imported merchandise and therefore an assist).
354. UCC IA, Article 135.5 ("For the purposes of Article 71(1)(b)(iv) of the Code, the costs of research and preliminary design sketches shall not be included in the customs value").

such a strict accounting, the entire R&D expenditure will be treated as a potential dutiable assist.

Another point to be made here is that "dead end" R&D and other activities identified in subsection (b)(iv) are liable to be treated as a part of the dutiable assist activity. In the EU, this is made explicit:

> The value of the services referred to in Article 71(1)(b) of the Code, shall include the costs of unsuccessful development activities insofar as those were incurred in respect of projects or orders relating to the imported goods.[355]

Regarding design work, sketches, and the like, CBP has promulgated a three-factor test for dutiable status of design work as an assist:

(1) Was the design work undertaken elsewhere than in the US?
(2) Was the design work provided free or at reduced cost for use in connection with the production of the imported merchandise?
(3) Was the design work necessary for production?

In one ruling, CBP determined that sketches, written explanations, and paper patterns, as well as discussions with the licensor's chief designer, conveyed general styling information to the maker of the goods and the buyer/importer. CBP held that the design activities were used in designing the apparel for the imported ready-to-wear apparel line. Thus, CBP concluded that the technical information was "used in the production of the imported merchandise" and constituted an assist.[356] A contrary result will follow if the sketches or designs are only "conceptual in nature," as would be true if they were to be altered prior to the production stage and after being made available to the factory.[357]

The third question—whether the design was necessary for production of the imported good—is often overlooked by importers, who might be missing an opportunity to achieve nondutiable status in the face of negative answers to the first two questions. Indeed, CBP has issued rulings that have posited this precise question as an essential factor for dutiable status as an assist—the necessity of design work in the production of imported merchandise.[358]

355. UCC IA, Article 135.4.
356. Ruling no. 546782 (December 2, 1999).
357. Ruling no. 543417 (February 11, 1985). *See also* ruling no. 563669 (January 11, 2006). In the latter case, CBP held that a roughly drawn sketch by a foreign designer was merely "inspirational" and, therefore, not a dutiable assist. CBP considered whether the sketch was essential to the manufacturing process and whether the manufacturer could have produced the goods with a narrative alone. CBP found that the sketches merely facilitated the oral and narrative descriptions of the design and that the rough sketches were not unique. *See also* ruling no. H206976 (August 17, 2012) (US designer creates a sketch that is used to create a storyboard in a foreign country, and the storyboard is later changed in the United States to create a final design. Foreign storyboard is not a dutiable assist). But *see* ruling no. 544609 (August 12, 1991), in which even initial drawings that were subsequently replaced by more detailed drawings were found to be the basis for an assist.
358. It is interesting to note that the pre-Agreement statutory scheme in the US provided for a "constructed value" appraisement. Further, within that construct, the question "was the

CBP has issued rulings that turned on the answer to that third question. One 2005 ruling was no gift to the importer, as CBP held that payments for design consultation in the production of Armani apparel were dutiable as assists. The lump-sum payment to Armani for the design services could not be allocated in such a way so as to exclude from the value of the assist the value of those designs not used in connection with the imported merchandise.[359] The full amount was owed whether usable or non-usable. As a result, CBP observed that the business must charge a sufficient sales price to recover the full amount paid to Armani in order to adequately recover costs.

The design services were conducted outside the US (in Italy) and were necessary for the production of the imported apparel. The activities included: research, selection, or approval of component materials, creation or design of styles and designs of the imported products, review and approval of any changes to be made to the products, and review and approval of samples. Where the licensor reviews and approvals are extensive, they might be seen as "offering significant assistance to the overall production of the garment," to use the language of the ruling.

The CBP view was that given the statutory definition of "Engineering, development, artwork, design work ... are necessary for the production of the imported merchandise," the total payment is necessary for the production of the imported merchandise, rather than only the payment amount after allocation between usable and non-usable designs. The collective development of the designs was necessary for the production of the imported merchandise. The payment for the designs was for all of the designs, not just for those used in the manufacture of the imported merchandise. Accordingly, the total design royalty payment was the value of the assist.

The CBP expanded view of what might be "necessary for production" even extended to include the payment for a separately imported—and duty paid—prototype as a dutiable assist to be reckoned in the dutiable value of later produced and imported engines.[360]

A planning opportunity for all importers arises from the policy underlying the valuation law to foster local research and development (R&D) and design work. If the work is performed in the country of importation, it is exempt from assist status.[361] The policy is sketched against an even broader canvas in the US: even if the work were done in a foreign country, it would still be exempt if it were done by US domiciliaries who are temporarily abroad and is incidental to such work being undertaken in the US.[362] These bright lines create opportunities for those companies that have flexibility as to where and by whom such R&D and related services are performed.

---

drawing necessary for production" applies with equal relevance to today's inquires under the post-implementation program. *See*, e.g., ruling no. 055194 (October 18, 1978) (CSD 79-279) (implicitly asking, "were the photomasks necessary for production—essential production expenses—or were they merely nondutiable 'antecedent' expenses?"). In fact, this history may explain both the derivation and significance of this third "necessary for production" factor in Article 8.

359. Ruling no. W548626 (April 18, 2005).
360. Ruling no. 545907 (October 11, 1996).
361. 19 USC § 1401a(h)(1)(A)(iv). As expected, the genesis of this rule is in the Valuation Agreement. Article 8.1(b)(iv).
362. 19 USC § 1401a(h)(1)(B).

In one of its rulings, CBP held that while later drawings provided the blueprints actually used in the production, the engineering that produced the initial layout was certainly necessary for the production of the imported article.[363] The ruling recited that "the fact that the initial drawings were refined by the manufacturing department does not make the engineering required for the project any less necessary a step in producing the ultimate article." But there was a contrary result when foreign designs underwent extensive revision in the US. Because the designs that were furnished to the vendor were consequently of US origin, the revised designs fell within the exemption.[364] Special care must be taken if some design work is performed in the US and some in a foreign country. The inability to account for the breakdown between the two sources may lead to all of the design costs being dutiable.[365] Of course, another outcome could be that transaction value could be discarded.[366]

CBP has also determined that design fees paid to the German affiliate of Esprit, for developing styles for a global collection, were dutiable.[367] The German affiliate furnished an Esprit affiliate located in Macau, which provided distribution services to the Esprit companies, with all materials, information, patterns, and styles which CBP deemed necessary for production by unrelated factories. The design fee constituted the basis for valuing a dutiable assist.

In a ruling for Tahari, Ltd., CBP also dealt with the issue of dutiable assists, as represented by garment patterns.[368] The ruling is helpful because it focused on the criterion of a good or service being "necessary for the production of the imported merchandise." What emerged in the course of the Tahari ruling's discussion was the issue whether the producer itself possessed the technical expertise to produce the article, such that the sample or pattern was not necessary for the production. In an earlier cited ruling, samples were treated as a narrative specification.[369] The key is whether a sample conveyed information without which the article cannot be made. If the manufacturer is capable of producing the goods on its own, any drawings, samples, prototypes, etc., would not be necessary and would therefore be nondutiable.[370]

---

363. Ruling no. 544609 (August 12, 1991).
364. Ruling no. 548532 (July 13, 2004) (foreign "knitdowns" used to create US-origin designs). *See also* ruling no. 547578 (January 18, 2000). But in ruling no. H225296 (July 27, 2012), CBP made it clear that while the cost of exempt US-origin designs could not be counted toward the value of an assist, if those designs were placed onto "sublimation papers" that were consumed in apparel manufacture, the value of those dutiable assists would consist of the cost of producing the papers, i.e., the cost of: (1) acquisition of the sublimation paper from a US vendor plus the cost of applying the heart-shaped design on the acquired paper and (2) transportation costs to the place of production of the finished garment.
365. Ruling no. 545341 (August 3, 1994).
366. Although the text of Article 1.1(c) of the Valuation Agreement only refers to an inability to quantify the subsequent proceeds as justifying a move away from transaction value, the Interpretative Note to Article 8, Paragraph 3 more broadly supports the notion that a lack of objective and quantifiable data in connection with Article 8 adjustments will support the ouster of the transaction value method.
367. Ruling no. 548420 (January 13, 2004).
368. Ruling no. 548566 (October 19, 2004).
369. Ruling no. 542591 (September 18, 1991).
370. That was the lesson of ruling no. 542830 (July 28, 1982).

But the Tahari ruling makes it clear that these situations must be examined closely, case by case. Where a pattern or design is unique, and the manufacturer cannot produce the merchandise without it, dutiable status will result. While the Tahari ruling quoted extensively from ruling no. 542591, it adopted the regimen of ruling no. 548230. The following two-prong test was enunciated:

(1) Is the pattern or design new or unique or simply a minor modification of an existing style?
(2) Is there evidence that the manufacturer has the ability to make the imported articles without having to rely on the input of the furnished pattern or design?

The record in the Tahari ruling did not contain sufficient information to establish that the imported garments could be made without the patterns of the prototypes, and CBP thus concluded that the patterns were necessary for production.[371] Accordingly, the patterns of the prototypes were dutiable assists.

As a final point, note that the exception to subsection (b)(iv) for country of importation-derived services is narrow. If the engineering or design work has been followed by the step of producing a tangible article, even if that article is also produced in the country of importation, then the exception will not apply to the tangible article which has been subsequently provided to the manufacturer. What is being provided to the foreign producer is not, say, engineering or design work but a physical product. If given at free or reduced cost, that would be an assist. But these inquiries may lead to "close calls." For example, in a 1995 ruling,[372] CBP held that the software provided for free "represented engineering and design work undertaken in the United States" which is excluded from the definition of dutiable assists. Therefore, CBP ruled that the US-origin design work should be excluded from the transaction value of the imported merchandise at issue.

But we saw a contrary result in an early CBP ruling where an integrated circuit (chip) which is supplied by the buyer at a reduced cost to the seller is deemed to be a component that is included in the imported merchandise and is, therefore, an assist.[373] The value of the assist was the full cost of acquisition, including any research and development costs incurred in New York in producing the chip, whether the chip itself is fabricated in the US or elsewhere. In a similar fashion, as was reported in a 2004 ruling,[374] CBP had held in a 1989 ruling that in instances where a mold is produced by the importer or person related to him, in the US or in another country, the value of the mold (assist) will be the cost of producing the mold as mandated by the valuation statute. Included in the cost of production of the mold were the design and development costs incurred when the work to produce the design and development is either within or outside the US. In other words, the fact that the design and the development

371. *But see* ruling no. 543064 (June 1, 1983) (factory did not need pattern to make the garment and thus the pattern was not a dutiable assist).
372. Ruling no. 545987 (August 28, 1995).
373. Ruling no. 542948 (November 29, 1982) (TAA No. 55).
374. Ruling no. W548568 (October 19, 2004), citing ruling no. 544192 (June 16, 1989).

were done in the US was disregarded—the exclusion treatment enjoyed by the design and development was lost when the mold was produced.[375]

The lesson here is that the exceptional treatment for subsection (b)(iv) services is limited to that subsection. If the putative assist would fall under another subsection, such as (b)(i) or (b)(iii), there is no exceptional treatment. Fair enough, but that should mean that the exclusionary effect should be respected where it does apply.

The EU was not well pleased with that result, so it has come up with a bit of sleight of hand to narrow the exclusion even more. We refer to a recent ECJ decision on the notion of "intangible assets" under a dutiable assist inquiry.[376] The EU Commission advanced a too-clever-by-half view that engineering work done in the EU, and thus nondutiable per UCC, Article 71.1(b)(iv), was not really engineering work at all. No, it was actually an "intangible asset" and thus to be examined under another subsection, UCC, Article 71.1(b)(i) as materials, components, parts and similar items incorporated into the imported goods. Given the fact that the ECJ has adopted the Commission view in its *BMW* decision, we can only hope that this notorious Commission initiative will be tested properly at the WTO.[377]

The EU Commission followed up with a hypothetical case[378] addressing the status as an assist under (b)(ii), which it terms a "production assist" versus (b)(iv), the latter termed "intellectual assists." The hypothetical concerned outputs of Computer-aided Design (CAD) programs used in the textile industry and supplied free of charge by the buyer of the imported goods to the manufacturer for use in connection with the production and sale of the imported goods should be taken into account in the customs value of the goods. In the cases in question, CAD programs are used to produce cutting-position images in the EU, which are then sent by email to manufacturers in third countries.

375. *See also* ruling no. 544147 (July 5, 1988) (the value of the assist is the cost of production which includes the engineering and development costs incurred in the United States by the importer in producing the photomask).

376. Case C-509/19, *BMW Bayersiche Motorenwerke AG*, 10.9.2020, ECLI:EU:C:2020:694 (*BMW*).

377. To show how much the EU has strayed from its earlier views, you might want to review the EU comments on a 2000 proposal by India to scrap subsection (b)(iv). The EC saw that as changing the rules—"... the proposal was asking that something that had been part of the Agreement since its inception be changed. Such a change would have a hard, economic effect because commerce and industry had assumed specific rights and had built their businesses around the valuation treatment presently in the Agreement." WTO, Compilation of Discussions in Various WTO Bodies on Implementation-Related Issues Concerning Customs Valuation, 26 Mar, 2002, G/VAL/W/97, Discussions in the Committee on Customs Valuation, Minutes of the Meeting of 7, 13, 24, and 29 November 2000 (G/VAL/M/17 - ITEM 2) in paragraphs 2.49, 40-41. At the CVC meeting on 21 May 2002, in defending the broad exemption, the EEC delegate noted, "There seemed to be a different reading of Article 8.1(b)(iv) because one Member seemed to consider that the carrying out of engineering, design or similar work in the country of importation by a buyer would under the existing rules, be an economic activity which would have to be taken into account in establishing the customs value. His delegation did not believe that this interpretation was a valid one. The only reasonable interpretation of Article 8.1(b)(iv) was that the carrying out of engineering design and development work by anybody in the country of import was covered." WTO, Committee on Customs Valuation, Minutes of the Meeting of 27 March 2002, G/VAL/M/26, paragraph 1.130 (21 May 2002).

378. EU Commission Compendium 2022, Conclusion No. 28: Production Inputs under points (ii) and (iv) of Article 71(1)(b) of the Union Customs Code, 137.

The Commission reported that the inputs in question: (1) are essential to the production of the goods, (2) determine the size and shape of the finished goods, (3) determine the design of the finished goods, (4) are integrated into the production process, and (5) are used to determine the physical properties of the finished goods. On that basis, they concluded that they should fall within (b)(ii)—which would not carry the exemption that would follow under (b)(iv) from the EU origin of the designs.

I see the reasoning here as contrived. Each one of these factors applies with equal vigor to design work, etc., that fall within (b)(iv). In fact, for a service to fit within (b)(iv), it must be necessary for the production of the imported goods. Thus, the relationship of the CAD programs to the production effort is not unique to (b)(ii) status. Especially since the CAD programs are sent via internet and are not imported in a physical form, I do not see them as being "similar items" to such specifically named tangible articles as tools, dies and molds. To borrow a statutory construction tool in wide use in tariff classification, there is no *ejusdem generis* linkage.

Then there is the matter of consistency. The advice provided in Conclusion 26 is directly opposite to the advice given in Conclusion 28, where software that was seen as necessary for production was to be placed in (b)(iv):

> There are intangible assists (e.g. also software/technologies), which are made available by the buyer for purposes of the production of the imported goods. In other words, they are a necessary part of the production process of the goods. Examples include the know-how of production (patented or not patented) or design.
>
> Such intangible assists fall under Article 71(1)(b)(iv) UCC.[379]

The EU Commission was not yet done with the proper disposition of intangibles. Another aspect of Conclusion No 26 is the following EU Commission distinction:

> The opinion of the Advocate General in the Compaq case C-306-04 is useful to consider in this context. The Advocate General made a distinction between:
>
> 1. "Intangible components" installed in the imported goods which are not strictly necessary for the production of the goods but are a constituent part of the end product, enhance its capabilities, or even add a new functionality and thereby contributes significantly to the value of the imported goods (Article 71(1)(b)(i) UCC), and
> 2. "Intellectual assists" (patents, designs, models etc.) which are necessary for the production process of the goods (Article 71(1)(b)(iv) UCC).[380]

---

379. EU Commission Compendium 2022, Conclusion No. 26: Software and related technology: treatment under Article 71 (1)(b) Union Customs Code (UCC), 133, Conclusion 2.

380. The Compaq decision is Case C-306/04, *Compaq Computer International Corporation v. Inspecteur der Belastingdienst Douanedistrict Arnhem*, 16.11.2006, ECLI:EU:C:2006:716 (*Compaq*). It should be noted that this distinction between (b)(i) and (b)(iv) was not reached in the court's judgment in *Compaq* (paragraphs 34-35) although the court observed (in paragraph 31) that the ECJ had previously held that software is intangible property, the cost of acquiring which, when such property is incorporated in an item of goods, must be regarded as an integral part of the price paid or payable for the goods, and hence of the transaction value. In fact, the court left open (in paragraph 36) whether the operating software on the subject laptop computers might be subject to an adjustment under (b) as an assist or (c) as a royalty or license fee.

To be clear, the treatment by the Commission of this first category for software that has been preloaded or "embedded" into the imported article is entirely consistent with the tariff classification treatment of such software. Such software is not separately classified, and it should be subsumed within the imported article, with its value being included within the customs value of the imported article.[381] Exceptional treatment should be available for optional, preloaded software accessed after importation by the end user.

Even where (b)(iv) status was settled, the EU has also pointed to another interesting dilemma, whether such (b)(iv) development work done within the importing country—actually, a Member State—and provided to a foreign producer of the imported goods, should be examined as an assist under Article 71(b) or as a royalty under Article 71(c). This question arose because the foreign producer was charged a royalty for the know-how.[382]

I agree with the stated conclusions: (i) a royalty or license fee may be a suitable means of payment for an assist and (ii) the means of payment—here, a royalty—does not transmute what is obviously a dutiable assist inquiry into an RLF question.[383] What is unclear is the underlying question whether there was the possibility of a dutiable assist because there was no statement to the effect that the 2.5% royalty was set at a reduced cost. Perhaps, it was sufficient to conclude that the payment should be examined as a potential assist, and the "reduced charge" criterion would be then questioned in the course of that examination.

One further comment is in order. Assuming there is a potential assist under (b)(iv), and some of the work was done in the country of importation and some of the work was done in another country, the RLF may be apportioned to account for the exempt status of the country of importation work, such apportionment being provided for in Article 8.1(b) of the Valuation Agreement. If the RLF is being reviewed in the context of Article 8.1(c), however, no apportionment is sanctioned by the Valuation Agreement. This prohibition is examined in depth below.

In the US, there is a distinct three-phase approach in dealing with dutiable assists. The CBP position is that, after first determining whether the statutory elements required for status as an assist or as a part of the PAPP have been met, there are two

381. In the US, *see*, e.g., ruling nos. N189638 (November 15, 2011), R02602 (October 19, 2005), 967759 (August 11, 2005), 965272 and 965276 (January 23, 2002).

382. EU Commission Compendium 2022, Conclusion No. 30, Application of Articles 71(1)(b) and 71(1)(c) of the Union Customs Code, 143.

383. This fact pattern was at the center of two 1994 instruments. In TCCV, CS 8.1, Application of Article 8.1 (October 1994), a license fee of 10% of the resale price of imported dresses was paid for rights to use paper patterns. The importer provided the patterns on a no-charge basis to a foreign producer to make dresses. The license fee served as the value for the dutiable assist. In TCCV, CS 8.2, Application of Article 8.1 (March 1994), a 5% license fee paid for the right to use a master tape, which was provided on a no-charge basis to the foreign producer, was the value of that dutiable assist. Because dutiable assist status under Article 8.1(b) was found, the TCCV considered it unnecessary to consider Article 8.1(c) implications in both of these Case Studies.

other separate phases that must be accomplished, first, valuation and then, apportionment of the assist.[384] As articulated in a 2014 ruling:

> Based on the statutory and regulatory language ..., it remains CBP's position that in regard to material or components which may constitute assists, a three-part analysis must be employed. *First, the material or components must fit the definition of an assist; second, it must appropriately be valued as an assist; and third, the value of the assist must be apportioned to the imported merchandise*[385] (emphasis added).

The general rule for establishing a value for a dutiable assist is that if the assist was acquired by a buyer from an unrelated seller, its value is the cost of acquisition. If the assist had been produced by the buyer or a person related to the buyer, the value of the assist is the cost of its production. In the US, in either case, the value must also include the transportation costs incurred in moving the assist to the place of production.[386]

The EU has introduced a novel third means of assist valuation. Where the value of the assist cannot be established under a straightforward acquisition or production cost inquiry, then it shall be determined on the basis of other, unspecified data that are "objective and quantifiable."[387] Given that "objective and quantifiable data" is an across-the-board standard applying to all additions under Article 8, per Article 8.3, this appears to sanction an entirely open-ended exercise, as though the data being objective and quantifiable were itself an independent and sufficient basis for an assist valuation.

The treatment of the costs associated with transporting a dutiable assist to the foreign producer presents another divergence in the interpretation of the Valuation Agreement. In the case of the US and Canada, the value of assists must include the cost of transporting the assist to the place of production.[388] In the EU, transport costs are not included with the value of an assist except to the extent that they are embedded within the cost of acquisition itself.[389] There is no apparent role for transport charges in the case of self-produced assists.

384. This is consistent with the Valuation Agreement, Interpretative Note, Article 8 paragraph 1.(b)(ii).
385. Ruling no. H235895 (August 22, 2014). For an earlier expression of this three-phase analysis of charges that are potentially design assists, *see* ruling no. 548626 (April 18, 2005), which applied the rationale of the General Notice regarding the Modification and Revocation of Customs Ruling Letters Relating to Assists, published in Customs Bulletin, Vol. 2, No. 51 on December 20, 1995 (dealing with scrap materials). We see this scheme of a valuation phase followed by apportionment in the Interpretative Note to Article 8, paragraph 1 (b) (ii) in paragraph 1 of the Customs Valuation Agreement, formally the Agreement on Implementation of Article VII of the General Agreement on Tariffs and Trade 1994.
386. 19 CFR § 152.103(d)(1). Cf. Canada, Valuation for Duty Regulations, paragraph 4(1)(a); UCC, Article 135.1.
387. UCC IA, Article 135.2.
388. Respectively, 19 CFR § 152.103 (d) and Valuation for Duty Regulations, paragraph 4 (1) (b), Customs Memorandum D13-3-12, Treatment of Assists in the Determination of the Value for Duty, August 16, 2013 ("Customs Memorandum D13-3-12"), note in paragraph 6.
389. The EU legislation is silent. This administrative position is expressed in EU Commission Compendium 2022, Commentary No. 1: Application of Article 71(1)(b) of the UCC on the valuation of goods for customs purposes, 23, paragraphs 5-6.

In the case of tooling, molds, or other goods that have been used, should the original acquisition or purchase costs be used to set the value of the assist, or is depreciation permitted? We find that the role of standards established by GAAP to account for a dutiable assist should apply when an assist has been depreciated. This is the case because, at the international level, the Interpretative Note to Article 8, paragraph 1(b)(ii), which is accorded the full authority of the Valuation Agreement, is clear on this point:

> If the element had been previously used by the importer, regardless of whether it had been acquired or produced by such importer, the original cost of acquisition or production would have to be adjusted downward to reflect its use in order to arrive at the value of the element.[390]

We might imagine that the extent of this text might not be as limited as its precise phrasing, i.e., if the element comprising the assist had been previously used only by the importer, not the least reason being that Article 8 speaks of the "buyer" and not the "importer" supplying the assist.

The CBP practice is to allow depreciation if it is in line with GAAP standards. In fact, CBP has allowed importers to take advantage of a full depreciation, accepting the value of a mold to consist only of the associated transportation costs where the mold has been depreciated to zero.[391]

Another issue that might arise in the context of a dutiable assist inquiry is the value to be assigned to an article that is available in the public domain. Consider the case of some engineering drawings, for example, or perhaps some "know-how" available on the Internet. If the importer can point to that public provenance, the value of the assist is limited to the cost of obtaining a copy of the assist.[392] To take the opposite case, if there is a separate charge, such as a royalty or license fee that is associated with the cost of producing or acquiring an assist, in the US, the cost of that royalty or license fee must be added to the value of the assist.[393] This is also the teaching of a TCCV instrument which looked to include all costs incurred by the importer in respect of acquiring the assist.[394]

When it comes to apportionment of the assist to individual entries, both CBP and US importers alike are guided by the customs regulations which state, in pertinent part:

390. In the US customs regulations, this provision is at 19 CFR § 152.103(d)(2); in Canada, the analogous provision for used goods is at Valuation for Duty Regulations (SOR/86-792) at 4.1 (c).
391. Ruling no. 543233 (August 9, 1984) (if a mold that is supplied free of charge to the foreign manufacturer is depreciated to zero on the books of the importer in a manner consistent with generally accepted accounting principles, then the value of the assist will be limited to the cost incurred in transporting the assist to the place of production) cited in ruling nos. 544256 (November 15, 1988) and 544243 (October 24, 1988).
392. 19 USC § 1401a(h)(1)(C)(i); 19 CFR § 152.102(a)(3).
393. Ruling nos. 548568 (October 19, 2004), 544459 (May 30, 1991) and 542152 (December 4, 1980) (TAA No. 13). In the case of Canada, this issue of licensing as an element of production or acquisition costs is not directly discussed. *See* Customs Memorandum D13-3-12.
394. TCCV, Com. 24.1, Determination of the Value of an Assist Under Article 8.1(b) of the Agreement (October 2011).

> 19 CFR § 152.102(a)(1).
> * * * (e) Apportionment. (1) The apportionment of the value of assists to imported merchandise will be made in a reasonable manner appropriate to the circumstances and in accordance with generally accepted accounting principles.

Further, the Valuation Agreement[395] and implementation by some individual customs authorities[396] set forth three specific apportionment methods. These include the value of the assist being apportioned to the first shipment if the importer wishes to account for the entire value of the assist at one time. The importer may apportion the value over the number of units produced up to the time of the first shipment. The value may also be apportioned over the entire anticipated production if a firm contract exists for the total production.[397]

CBP has shown itself to be receptive to apportionment methods beyond those three. Citing the regulations, CBP has set GAAP-approval as a measure of its flexibility:

> The importer may also request another method of apportionment as long as the apportionment is in accordance with GAAP.[398]
> Also note that CBP is worried about the apportionment method overstating the value of the dutiable assist:
> It is the understanding of Customs and Border Protection from a review of the agreement and from counsel's submission that a link exists between the method of apportionment proposed and the merchandise imported ... . Should it become evident in the actual implementation of the proposed method that a portion of the assist's value would not be subject to duty, the proposed method would then be found to be unreasonable and not in accordance with Customs regulations. Internal citation omitted.[399]

In other words, for CBP, an overstated amount for dutiable assists is as problematic as an understated amount.

The amortization of tooling or molds on a prorated basis over the full anticipated production run is a GAAP-accepted apportionment methodology.[400] If an agreement is in place, then the amortization charge (full value of assist/transport allocated

395. Valuation Agreement, Interpretative Note, Article 8, paragraph 1(b)(ii), points 3 and 4.
396. In the US, 19 CFR § 152.103(e)(1) and (2); in Canada, Customs Memorandum D13-3-12, paragraphs 7 and 8 (for tools, dies, molds and goods consumed in production). In contrast, the EU merely states, "The value of the goods and services supplied, as established in accordance with paragraphs 1 to 5 shall be apportioned pro rata over the imported goods." UCC IA, Article 135.6.
397. To be clear, note that CBP has confirmed that "the full production run" is based on the total number of units expected to be produced and not only those units that are destined for importation into the US. This yields a per-unit assist factor that is then applied on a per-unit basis to the goods actually imported into the US. *See* ruling no. 548316 (7/16/03) (the "per garment design charge" is added to the price actually paid or payable at the time of each entry), modified in other respects, ruling no. W548547 (March 7, 2006).
398. Ruling no. H312455 (October 28, 2020).
399. Ruling no. W548547 (March 7, 2006) confirming ruling no. 548316 (July 16, 2003).
400. This can be traced to a 1981 ruling, no. 542324 (June 22, 1981) (TAA No. 33). The ruling sanctioned the methodology dating to a 1971 decision by the Customs Court [the predecessor of the CIT], *United States v. Border Brokerage Company, Inc.*, 66 Cust. Ct. 639, ARD 288 (1971), applying the pre-Agreement statute.

to/divided by expected production run) should cease once the expected run total has been achieved.[401] This approach was also applied by the court in *Chrysler*.[402]

Amortization is a method of apportionment that is fully acceptable under the customs valuation law. When the amortized amount of the assist is built into the PAPP of each shoe, there is no valuation issue, as the fully loaded PAPP serves as the basis for a transaction value appraisement of each article. The customs value issues potentially arise in the context of so-called under-amortization and over-amortization.

The term "under-amortization" refers to the result when production of a given product is halted before the entire anticipated production run has been reached. In that case, when the original target has not been met, the factory may separately bill the importer for the remaining cost—i.e., the cost of the tooling or mold that has not been recouped by the seller.

The question that arises is whether such an additional payment is dutiable, in the sense that it should be added to the PAPP for the quantity of the shoes in that style that had been imported.

CBP has provided an answer in ruling no. H088115 (Apr. 19, 2010). There, CBP relied on an earlier ruling issued to another importer, Reebok, ruling no. W563531 (Oct. 27, 2006). It is worth quoting at length:

> As in Reebok, here the price paid by American Honda to HdM includes a charge for tooling and molds amortized over an estimated production quantity. The amortization quantity varies by part number and is based on market forecasts. In addition, *American Honda and HdM agree that HdM will invoice American Honda for any under-amortized tooling costs, and credit American Honda for any over-amortized tooling costs.*
>
> Subsequent to Chrysler, Customs has looked to the intent of the parties and the evidence presented and found the apportionment of such costs acceptable if it is reasonable, in accordance with Generally Accepted Accounting Principles, and not in violation of other provisions of the Customs laws. See HRL 548196, dated December 13, 2002; HRL 546771, dated March 27, 1998; and HRL 545500, dated March 24, 1995. Similarly, based on the intent of the parties and the evidence presented, we find that the tooling payments in the instant case were properly apportioned over the total number of products that the parties anticipated to be produced. We note that *American Honda's purchase price from HdM includes a charge for certain tooling and molds that is amortized over the anticipated production quantity. The amortization quantity represents American Honda's anticipated need based on market forecasts.*
>
> Upon examination of the facts in this case and the documentary evidence submitted, we find American Honda's method of allocation to be reasonable and consistent with the court's decision in Chrysler and Customs' decision in Reebok. *Therefore, the price actually paid or payable already includes these allocated tooling*

401. Ruling no. 543806 (March 12, 1987) as cited in ruling no. 545500 (March 24, 1995). *See also* ruling no. 544694 (June 23, 1993) (after liquidation importer not permitted to change expected production run resulting in twenty-fold change in per-unit assist calculation).

402. *See also* ruling no. H235895 (8/22/14) ("If the entire anticipated production using the assist is for exportation to the United States, the total value may be apportioned over (i) the first shipment, if the importer wishes to pay duty on the entire value at once, (ii) the number of units produced up to the time of the first shipment, or (iii) *the entire anticipated production*" (emphasis added)).

payments, and no further adjustments are needed on the basis of the under-amortized tooling costs (emphasis added).

The instruction is clear: Separate payments made for under-amortized tooling are not dutiable.

That leads to the question of over-amortized tooling. This term refers to the fact that production of a given product may continue after the anticipated production run has been reached. In that case, once the original production target has already been met and surpassed, the factory will have been fully paid for the tooling. After that point has been reached, the factory will remove the tooling charge from the sales price, but there may be a delay, perhaps, say, a two-three month gap, before the factory is able to do so. Typically, the parties would have agreed in advance and unconditionally to the lowering of the price going forward and to the refund of the tooling charges paid during the gap period. With that advance agreement, the issue of a post-import reduction in price or rebate, which would have to be disregarded, is avoided.[403]

This is the rationale of ruling no. H235895 (August 22, 2014), which articulated that:

> the purpose of these amortization schedules is to ensure that Keen [the importer] does not overpay for tooling. A tooling element was included in the price the factory charged for the footwear so that the factory could recover the cost of the tooling over a given quantity of footwear. Once the designated quantity of footwear was produced and sold, the tooling element was removed, and the price of the footwear was reduced.

CBP rulings show a high degree of flexibility in accepting various other individually crafted or "bespoke" apportionment methodologies.[404] Additionally, one must recognize that there must be a connection between the apportionment method and the imported goods.[405] Moreover, one must be mindful that CBP has placed a high value on the practical necessity of administering and reviewing the required calculations in a relatively straightforward manner. Methods that are too complex and unwieldy will not be acceptable.[406] The primary guiding principles in these analyses is that the apportionment must be reasonable and consistent. The former is a subjective standard, of course, and a judgment on what is reasonable will depend on the circumstances. Thus, CBP has held that a tooling factor apportionment method was not reasonable where

403. In the US, 19 USC § 1401a(b)(4)(B) and 19 CFR § 152.103(a)(4); Canada Customs Act, paragraph 48(5)(c); EU, Implementing Act, Article 130.3 (discounts arising from amendments to the contract subsequent to the time of acceptance of the customs declaration shall not be taken into account).

404. *See* ruling no. H015975 (September 13, 2007) (importer may apportion its assist costs as requested, i.e., in a monthly declaration such that all assists will be declared on the first entry of the month following the incurrence of such costs provided that such apportionment is in accordance with generally accepted accounting principles). *See also* ruling nos. H190269 (February 20, 2014) (first shipment apportionment after close of quarter; almost all goods in same two subheading and thus duty free) and H044163 (January 13, 2009) (flexible approach to valuing and apportioning dutiable assist in the form of used machinery and equipment).

405. *See* ruling no. 545031 (June 30, 1993) (IRS-approved depreciation method rejected).

406. *See* ruling no. 544874 (October 22, 1993).

there were 233 different subheadings and forty-two separate countries of origin, but there had been no attempt made to more discretely apportion the assists.[407]

Some oft-encountered issues include the following.

Only some articles are imported. A common planning challenge arises if only some of the articles produced with the assist will be imported into the country of importation. In such a case, in the US, the importer may apportion the costs of the assists in accordance with GAAP.[408]

Transport Charges. It is well for the importer to pay close attention to the transportation costs associated with making a dutiable assist available at the place of production. We have seen that such costs must be included in the valuation of the assist on imports into the US and Canada, and if the full costs are understated, you might expect that the customs authority will require an addition for the shortfall. In fact, even if the element that is potentially a dutiable assist escapes that status because there is no showing that it has been provided free or at reduced cost, the subsidized transportation of the element will itself tip the issue into a dutiable assist status. That was the lesson of a 2012 CBP ruling,[409] over what appears to be strenuous objections by the importer's counsel. CBP Headquarters found that where the foreign seller paid for fabric but did not pay the full amount for the transport of fabric shipped via airfreight, the fabric was being provided to the dressmaker in Vietnam at a reduced cost. In other words, the "take away" lesson is that it is always necessary to examine the fully loaded, goods-cost-cum-transport-charges-cost of getting the article into the hands of the producer or seller of the merchandise before concluding whether the circumstances of a given good denote a dutiable assist. In that effort, it is well to realize that transport costs will include incidental or ancillary charges.[410] What is an open question is whether customs duties or brokerage charges would be included in a broad interpretation of "transportation charges."

The status of wastage or scrap. For example, 10 yards of cloth are provided to the seller. The cloth bolt is cut into dress patterns. As a result of the cutting, only 8 yards are used in the dresses and 2 yards are discarded. What is the assist—the full 10 yards or only the 8 yards that are included in the finished dresses? CBP changed its position on the status of wastage or scrap. Formerly, only that portion of material which is incorporated into the final imported article constitutes an assist.[411] The current position dates to 1995—even waste or scrap which winds up on the cutting room floor instead

407. Ruling no. H311213 (February 10, 2021).
408. Ruling no. 544337 (April 9, 1990).
409. Ruling no. H135296 (May 29, 2012) (airfreight payments to a third party constitute a dutiable assist).
410. Ruling no. 544323 (March 8, 1990) (importer's New York-based shipping department arranges for the transportation of the materials to the related party seller's factory. These activities are incidental to the transportation of the materials and the costs associated with arranging the shipment of the materials are included in the value of the assists).
411. Ruling nos. 544758 (February 21, 1992) and 543924 (May 29, 1987) and others have been revoked or modified.

of the finished product, if it results from production, may be considered an assist as it is material consumed in the production process.[412]

Testing and Inspection Charges. The general rule here, at least as expounded by CBP, is consistent with its focus on production versus nonproduction equipment or personnel costs. Fees paid to third parties for testing that is done pre- or post-production will be nondutiable.[413] Very much in the same vein, a 2021 ruling provides helpful guidance.[414] There, Bureau Veritas' "social compliance testing" did not implicate design or production as it merely ensured that the manufacturer actually used fabrics that comply with US regulations, as specified by the end US customer. In this time of forced labor enforcement regimes, heightened scrutiny by government agencies and increased reputational risks, fees to ensure social compliance, e.g., no forced labor or child labor in the supply chain, will become routine.

[4] Royalties and License Fees (RLFs)

RLFs which are paid by the importer and which are related to the goods being valued[415] and which the importer must pay as a condition of sale of the goods being valued are dutiable.[416]

A preliminary observation is in order. The Valuation Agreement does not precisely define RLFs, nor does the implementing legislation in the US. Canada[417] and, previously, the EU have used more descriptive texts.[418] For its part, the Commission's current administrative guidance points us to the OECD definition:

> payments of any kind received as a consideration for the use of, or the right to use, any copyright of literary, artistic or scientific work including cinematograph films, any patent, trade mark, design or model, plan, secret formula or process, or for information concerning industrial, commercial or scientific experience.[419]

---

412. General Notice of Modification or Revocation of Customs Rulings Letters Relating to Assists. 29 Cust. Bull. & Dec. No. 51 (December 20, 1995). *See*, e.g., ruling no. 547018 (September 10, 1999). The CBP position was validated in *Salant Corp. v. United States*, 24 CIT 24 (2000). For a discussion on this "consumed in" criterion, *see* ruling no. 548557 (October 20, 2004) (defective watches are merely repaired and thus are not "consumed in the production of the imported merchandise").
413. *See*, e.g., ruling nos. H316932 (August 5, 2021) and H253767 (March 30, 2015) (quality control service does not constitute an assist, unless it involves production-related design and intimate involvement in the nature of the goods sold).
414. Ruling no. H316932 (August 5, 2021).
415. In Canada, "in respect of the goods." Canada Customs Act, subparagraph 48(5)(a)(iv).
416. Valuation Agreement, Article 8 .1 (c); 19 USC § 1401a(b)(1)(D); Canada Customs Act, subparagraph 48(5)(a)(iv); EU, UCC, Article 71.1(c).
417. The Canadian statute looks to, "royalties and licence fees, including payments for patents, trademarks and copyrights ... ." Canada Customs Act, subparagraph 48(5)(a)(iv).
418. The EU had formerly provided more specificity in the CCC, Article 157, with separate provisions for rights associated with manufacture, sale or use or resale of the imported goods.
419. Quoted in the EU Commission Compendium 2022, Commentary No. 13, Guidance on Articles 128 and 136 UCC IA, 70, point 3.2 Scope, paragraph 1. Note that RLFs had been the subject of a separate Commentary No. 3 in the 2008 and 2018 editions of the Compendium. Personally, I believe that this definition does not add much to the Interpretative Note to Article 8, Paragraph

Starting with the three-decade-old Hasbro ruling in the US,[420] and with developments in Canada and later in the EU, one of the more vexing customs valuation details facing professional advisors in the US and elsewhere has to be the treatment of RLFs. This is due in large measure to the increasingly prevalent transfer of IPRs among related entities, or the fact that some companies have outsourced the manufacture of products altogether. The result is that, often, RLF payments are no longer embedded in the price of the goods but, rather, are separately charged and collected. In fact, the manufacture and sale of goods are frequently divorced—or so the importer would have it—from the licensing of the IPRs. Payments for the grant of separate IPRs have also been a controversial transfer pricing concern.[421]

The Hasbro I ruling was remarkable in that it upset a long-standing CBP practice. In the years immediately following the 1979 adoption of the new customs valuation law, if the royalty or fee in question were not dutiable as a royalty, CBP had concluded that it had no authority to include it as dutiable under another provision, i.e., the proceeds of a subsequent resale. In 1982, Customs Headquarters had revealed that:

> [T]his office concurs with the opinion expressed by counsel for the importer on this point. The existence of two separate categories, one specifically relating to royalty and license fees and the other to the proceeds of subsequent resale, use or disposal of the imported merchandise, clearly indicates to us that the two categories were not intended to cover the same set of circumstances. Thus, when a royalty or license fee is found not to be part of transaction value under category (D), no authority exists for including the fee in transaction value as [proceeds of subsequent sale].[422]

In that ruling request, the importer had pointed to the legislative history for Congressional intent not to:

> divide royalty payments into dutiable and non-dutiable categories only to negate that division by returning most royalty payments found to be not dutiable under (D)[royalty] to a dutiable status under (E)[subsequent proceeds].[423]

Thus, royalty/license fee payments were to be evaluated for their dutiable status only under the statutory provision for such payments, and not under the separate subsequent proceeds standard. With Hasbro I, CBP discarded this position. CBP decided that, even if an RLF were not a condition of the import transaction and, thus, not dutiable as a royalty, the payment could be dutiable as a share of subsequent proceeds if accruing to the benefit of the seller.[424] With its Hasbro I ruling, CBP swept aside the criticisms of commentators who had earlier written approvingly of TAA 56.[425]

1(c). Note: The customs authorities themselves and the trade community would have been better served if the Compendium discussions on RLFs had not been divided into four separate Commentaries: 3, 13, 16 and 17.

420. Ruling no. 544436 (February 4, 1991) (Hasbro I).

421. *See* Part II on the intersection of customs valuation and transfer pricing.

422. Ruling no. 542900 (December 9, 1982) (TAA 56).

423. *Ibid.*

424. *See* discussion below.

425. Sherman and Glashoff, no. 425 at 155.

In one learned treatise, our old reliable commentators saw a clear distinction between the royalty and proceeds categories, declaring that:

> The first and most important thing to be said about this "proceeds" provision is what it does *not* mean. It surely cannot have been intended—following as it does immediately after the intricate special provision on royalties and licence fees which we have just analyzed at such great length—to mean that any royalty which is expressed as a percentage of resale proceeds is automatically added to customs value under Article 8.1 (d), even if it has successfully withstood the test of Article 8.1 (c). Article 8.1 (d) is intended to deal with situations where the payment is for the goods and not for a related intangible right. If there are fictitious royalties or licence fees, i.e., payments for no other economic reason than the purchase of the imported goods, then the provisions on proceeds of resale can be applied (emphasis in original).[426]

These experts believed that the RLF and subsequent proceeds categories are mutually exclusive but can be easily reconciled. The royalties under category (D) relate to intangibles, while the subsequent proceeds under category (E) relate to sales or use of tangible property. Mindful of this dichotomy, some feel that the two can be distinctly different but can be read *in pari materia*. I would agree that the two subsections actually spring from a common source. The tangible/intangible dichotomy may be left aside for a moment. As we have already noted, the rationale of both, indeed of all of the defined Article 8 adjustments, is that the Agreement tells us that these adjustments have been recognized to be composed of elements that by their very nature should be subsumed within the PAPP but that they may have been "unbundled" by an artifice or, in the case of RLFs, at the least by a now common distinct business model of separate payments, resulting in any event in an artificially lowered PAPP regardless of the motivation of the parties. The purpose of Article 8 is to restore the value of these missing goods, services or the fruits of resale or use if not to their proper place within the PAPP but at least added to the PAPP.

I would disagree with Messrs. Sherman and Glashoff in one respect only. If RLF payments are entirely fictitious, then they should certainly be examined for dutiable implications, but as integral elements to be added to the PAPP and not under a subsequent proceed rubric or any other Article 8 lens. Given the timing of the *Mattel* decision (2001) and the 2015 CBSA "D Memo"[427] which calls for payment steams by the buyer to be examined as potential adjustments under a subsequent proceeds analysis, one might surmise that CBSA widened its review beyond putative RLFs, as in *Mattel*, to include management fees and other services provided to the buyer.

As for the controversial back door into dutiable status as a subsequent proceed after dutiability as an RLF has been precluded, in now superseded guidance, the EU

426. *Ibid.*, 424 at 155. This authority was cited by the Supreme Court of Canada in *Mattel* (paragraphs 75-76) and on the strength of it the court declined to examine subsequent proceed status after dutiability as an RLF had been discarded.
427. CBSA, Memorandum D13-4-13, *Post-importation Payments or Fees (Subsequent Proceeds)* (March 31, 2015), originally issued on July 8, 2009, is discussed in §3.01[I][5] and in Part II at §10.08.

Commission followed the Sherman and Glashoff lead in a commentary on the predecessor CCC:

> The provisions of Article 31(1)(a)(e) of the Code, which concern additions to the price actually paid or payable for the imported goods, each have their own scope. Thus payments which fall within the definition of royalties or license fee are to be examined in the light of Article 31(1)(c) of the Code. When the requirements of that provision are not met, such payments are not to be considered under Article 31(1)(d).[428]

This guidance has not been retained in the current Compendium, but there is no reason to imagine that the EU has disavowed this interpretation.

We must be mindful, however, that an RLF paid to acquire an element that is a dutiable assist might be considered to constitute part of the value of the assist even if that payment did not merit an adjustment as a dutiable royalty or license fee.[429]

CBP was not impassive in the face of the controversy that its fundamental shift generated and, to its credit, CBP solicited comments beginning in June 1991, indicating that they would be reviewing the entire subject. After considering the comments received, it published a General Notice to the trade in February 1993, concluding that they had gotten it right in Hasbro I after all.[430]

In the event, the post-Hasbro I backdoor route to dutiability via the subsequent proceeds provision has evolved over the years since the 1993 Hasbro II ruling. As a preliminary matter, CBP typically reviews dutiability of the RLF payments in their capacity as royalties or license fees. The IPR payments are not typically tested as subsequent proceeds unless that initial review leads to a negative conclusion.

Since Hasbro II, CBP has applied a three-factor test to RLF payments, asking the following questions:

(1) Was the imported merchandise manufactured under patent?[431]
(2) Was the royalty involved in the production or sale of the merchandise?
(3) Could the importer buy the product without paying the fee?

A "no" to the first two questions, which are based on the royalty being related to the imported merchandise, and a "yes" to the third question, which is grounded in the royalty being a condition of the import sales transaction, point to nondutiability.

---

428. EU Commission Compendium 2008, Commentary No. 3 on the Incidence of Royalties and License Fees in Customs Value, 22, point 20.
429. *See*, e.g., Case C-116/89, *BayWa AG v. Hautpzollamt Weiden*, 7.3.1991, ECLI:EU:C:1991:104.
430. 27 Cust. Bull. & Dec. No. 6 at 1 (2/10/93) (commonly known as Hasbro II). This was followed by a Notice in which CBP advised importers that any ruling request regarding the dutiability of royalties and license fees must be accompanied by both the license agreement and the purchased/supply agreement. 29 Cust. Bull. & Dec. No. 36 (September 6, 1995).
431. I believe that this question should not be narrowly applied only to patents. In later rulings, CBP has drawn a broader distinction between marketing-related IPR such as trademarks versus production-related IPR such as patents and trade secrets. *See*, e.g., ruling no. 546748 (February 11, 1998) at 6.

As explained immediately below, the "condition of sale" test is generally the most important, indeed it is usually the decisive, factor in an inquiry into the dutiable status of RLF payments. But it would be a mistake to overlook a close analysis of the earlier "related to the goods" threshold factor, grounded in the fact that there are importations of goods and there are in fact RLF payments being made. If the payment can be shown to be unrelated to the imported goods, i.e., not involved in their production or sale, then the inquiry stops at that point without ever getting to the "condition of sale" test.

An importer was able to convince CBP on that point in a 2013 ruling.[432] The question arose from an Internal Advice request from the port in the course of an audit. The point about that administrative posture is that the importer was unable to convince Regulatory Audit locally, and the issue had to be referred to Headquarters for resolution. In this case, we learn:

> [t]he royalty provisions in the agreements indicate that the payments are for the right to use various patents in the production of Contract Batteries in the United States, but are not for the imported merchandise itself. The royalties are payable annually and not tied to each importation. Moreover, we note that although the royalty provisions are included in the same agreements that control the sale of production lines previously imported by [the importer], those production lines are not the imported merchandise in the instant case. Standard machinery parts are imported. Thus, we find that the purchase of the imported merchandise and the payment of the royalties are not inextricably intertwined.[433]

The obvious lesson is that importers must be mindful of these and all other customs valuation law nuances and must "layer" their legal arguments accordingly.

There is an emerging challenge to a consensus on customs valuation questions that centers on this "related to the goods" criterion. This is the issue of apportionment.

[a] "Related to the Goods" and Apportionment

The EU has long held specific views on when and how the goods may be related to the RLF, and we learn that:

> Article 136(1) UCC IA states that royalties or licence fees are related to the imported goods where, in particular, the rights transferred under the licence or royalties agreement are embodied in the goods.[434]

432. Ruling no. H186056 (March 26, 2013) (CBP proceeded to address the "condition of sale" and "subsequent proceeds" questions, but decided the issue of dutiability on the basis of this "related to the goods" test).
433. As explained below in the discussion on condition of sale, CBP takes the view that if provisions in two separate legal agreements can be connected, then a provision for the payment of a royalty in a license agreement can be virtually incorporated into a sales agreement for the imported goods, with the effect of the payment and the purchase being "inextricably intertwined" that the royalty payment is at the same time related to and a condition of the sale of the goods despite the fact that the sales agreement is silent on the payment.
434. EU Commission Compendium 2022, Commentary No. 13, Guidance on Articles 128 and 136 UCC IA, 71, point 3.4, Related to the goods being valued, paragraph 1.

The customs authority will want to see if there is a direct link, with the Commission advising:

> A direct link to the imported goods is particularly clear where the imported goods are themselves the subject of the licence agreement (i.e. if the imported goods incorporate the trade mark for which the licence fee is paid, this must be considered as related to the imported goods). The same link may also exist where the licensed goods are ingredients or components of the imported goods.[435]

It is hard to dispute either of those statements.

Note that the Agreement and implementing statutory texts simply posit that the payment is "related to the goods being valued." The question is whether that criterion implicitly carries a qualifier, i.e., whether the RLF for the purposes of Article 8.1(c) is *only* or *solely* related to the imported goods.

Some maintain that it is so qualified. For others, analyzing whether an RLF is related to the imported articles could involve an apportionment. The issue of an "apportionment" or allocation would arise in the context of an RLF which is related partly to the imported goods and partly to other ingredients or component parts added to the goods after their importation or to the services being provided, such as post-importation manufacturing.

Before proceeding further, it is important to remember the proper role of "apportionment" as that term is employed in the Agreement. The Interpretative Note to the provision for dutiable assists, which we have seen does allow for apportionment, makes it clear that there is a vital distinction between the valuation of the assist and apportionment of that value to individual entries.

The EU is claiming to engage in an apportionment, not in the ultimate per-entry assessment phase, which is the context of the term's use in the Agreement, but in the preliminary "related to the goods" phase. In that latter context, the effort is unlike the apportionment of an assist with a settled value by examining the use of tooling on an expected per-unit value over the expected production run. Clearly, using an apportionment to satisfy the requirements of Article 8.1(c) is a very different endeavor from using apportionment in the only use approved by the Agreement, i.e., in properly affixing a portion of the value of the dutiable assist to a given entry.

While the Agreement specifically provides, Article 8.1(b), for an apportionment of dutiable assists, it does not similarly allow for an apportionment of RLFs. Most canons of statutory or treaty construction would preclude extending any authority under the Agreement to apportion payments to RLFs. These canons include, among others, the notion that if a provision is expressly made for apportionment in one context (here, assists) then, in a similar fashion, an express grant of apportionment for RLFs could have/would have been made by the drafters if that had been their intention. Further, if there is an implied authority to make an apportionment for RLFs, and presumably for all other adjustment categories, and such authority is not limited to the

435. *Ibid.*, paragraph 2.

provision expressly made for dutiable assists, such a reading would render a superfluity the Agreement's express grant of apportionment of assists. Such an interpretation would fall of its own weight.

The fact that apportionment might not—ultimately, indeed, would not—be available to all adjustments under Article 8 can be traced back to the then-ongoing Tokyo Round of Multilateral Trade Negotiations in 1978 that led ultimately to the Agreement, where we find the following remark:

> 8.3 Additions to the price paid or payable shall be made in pursuance of this Article only when they can be made on the basis of objective and quantifiable data. If such data is not available such additions shall not be made (P.M. The question of pro-rating should be dealt with separately).[436]

This shows us that even at this very early stage, the notion of "objective and quantifiable data" was to apply to all of what became Article 8 adjustments, but that apportionment, here, "pro-rating," was to be dealt with separately, i.e., presumably would not necessarily apply to all subsections of Article 8 but perhaps be limited to a smaller subset of adjustments. We know that, as adopted, apportionment was indeed dealt with separately and was indeed limited to dutiable assists. This limitation is reflected in the Interpretative Notes, where we find apportionment is treated in the Notes for Article 8.1(b)(ii) and Article 8.1(b)(iv) but is absent altogether from the Interpretative Notes for Article 8.1(c).

Here, we might also turn to the example given in the Interpretative Note to Article 8, paragraph 3 of the Agreement. That Interpretative Note and the underlying text in subsection Article 8.3 are intended to elucidate concerns over the need for "objective and quantifiable data" on which to make additions to the PAPP. That commendable admonition in the Interpretative Note is made an integral part of the Agreement[437] and thus directly applies to any attempt to make an apportionment of an RLF.

Of importance for this discussion, we see that the Interpretative Note directs us to *not* make an addition for a royalty when it is only partially based on the imported goods. The example given in the Note is of imported goods being mixed with domestic ingredients, and the imported goods are no longer separately identifiable:

> Where objective and quantifiable data do not exist with regard to the additions required to be made under the provisions of Article 8.3 the TV cannot be determined under the provisions of Article 1. As an illustration of this, a royalty is paid on the basis of the price in a sale in the importing country of a litre of a particular product that was imported by the kilogram and made up into a solution after importation. If the royalty is based partially on the imported goods and partially on other factors which have nothing to do with the imported goods (such as when the imported goods are mixed with domestic ingredients and are no longer separately identifiable, or when the royalty cannot be distinguished from

436. GATT, Group "Non-Tariff Measures," Sub-Group "Customs Matters" Customs Valuation, Revision MTN/NTM/W/175/Rev. 1 (6 November 1978) at 13.
437. Per Article 14 of the Agreement.

special financial arrangements between the buyer and the seller), it would be inappropriate to attempt to make an addition for the royalty. However, if the amount of this royalty is based only on the imported goods and can be readily quantified, an addition to the price actually paid or payable can be made.

One reaction to those texts—what would the "special financial arrangements" that could not be distinguished from RLFs?

This Interpretative Note direction to generally proceed on the basis only of "objective and quantifiable data" should not be stretched so as to connote a broad license to embark on an attempt to discern if the imported goods are "separately identifiable" and to ultimately make an estimate on possible dutiable impact under the cover of available "objective and quantifiable data." Instead, the precondition for any examination whether a royalty amount is "readily quantifiable" is the fact that the royalty is based "only on the imported goods," i.e., is related to the goods.

For another thing, the text does not bridge the gap and does not extend so far as to countenance an apportionment of RLFs. The Interpretative Note to Article 8, paragraph 3 cannot be read in any way as to effect a change in the Article 8.1 text of the provision for RLFs such that the dutiable RLF may be related "in whole or in part" to the goods being valued. In other words, whether one ascertains that the data is objective and quantifiable for the purpose of apportionment is irrelevant because RLF apportionment is not authorized in Article 8.1 in order to meet the "related to the goods" test by any fair, *in pari materia*, reading of the terms.[438] If we were to be more formal, we might cite the negotiation history and the actual drafting of the text from the perspective of Articles 31 and 32 of the Vienna Convention.[439]

For another, any such analysis would require an exercise of extensive fact-finding which most customs authorities would reflexively abhor as not consistent with their task of finding the customs value on an entry.[440] Finally, such an effort conflicts with the Agreement's stated purpose to make use of "simple and equitable criteria consistent with commercial practices."

Notwithstanding the foregoing, the EU is one of the participants which have advanced the view that RLFs can be apportioned.

438. We also bring attention to another novel use by the EU of text in the Valuation Agreement Interpretative Note to Article 8, Paragraph 3 in the Implementing Regulations (UCC IA) on the valuation of assists. The UCC IA, in Article 135.2, without a citation, invokes "other objective and quantifiable data" as the basis for valuing assists where purchase price or production costs cannot be determined. The Agreement says nothing about this third or fallback basis for valuing assists, and this novel approach departs from and is not supported by the UCC Article 71.2 reference to objective and quantifiable data which latter usage is otherwise consistent with the Interpretative Note to Article 8, paragraph 3.

439. Vienna Convention on the Law of Treaties (1969).

440. On this point, *see Generra Sportswear Co. v. United States*, 905 F.2d 377, 380 (Fed. Cir. 1990). On this issue of burden, *see also* Case C-187/21, *Fawkes Kft*, 6.9.2022, ECLI:EU:C:2022:458 (*Fawkes*) (customs authority not obligated to consult EU databases other than the national databases).

[i] Prior EU Position on Apportionment

The current EU legislation and regulations arising under its post-May 1, 2016 UCC regime mark a departure from the previous CCC and the implementing regulation, the CCC IR, Regulation No 2454/93,[441] dating to 1992 and 1993, respectively.

Prior to the "UCC legal package," the CCC IR, in Annex 23 to Regulation No 2454/93, and its predecessor instruments dating to 1980,[442] had provided, with regard to Article 32(2) [expressing the need for objective and quantifiable data] of that Customs Code, that:

> Where objective and quantifiable data do not exist with regard to the additions required to be made under the provisions of Article 32, the transaction value cannot be determined under the provisions of Article 29. As an illustration of this, a royalty is paid on the basis of the price in a sale in the importing country of a litre of a particular product that was imported by the kilogram and made up into a solution after importation. *If the royalty is based partially on the imported goods and partially on other factors which have nothing to do with the imported goods (such as when the imported goods are mixed with domestic ingredients and are no longer separately identifiable, or when the royalty cannot be distinguished from special financial arrangements between the buyer and the seller), it would be inappropriate to attempt to make an addition for the royalty. However, if the amount of this royalty is based only on the imported goods and can be readily quantified,* an addition to the price actually paid or payable can be made (emphasis added).

This Annex text, which you will have seen tracks the above-cited Interpretative Note, was tied to Article 158 of the CCC IR, which sanctioned an "appropriate adjustment" for an RLF only in narrow circumstances:

> Article 158
>
> 1. When the imported goods are only an ingredient or component of goods manufactured in the Community, an adjustment to the price actually paid or payable for the imported goods shall only be made when the royalty or licence fee relates to those goods.
> 2. Where goods are imported in an unassembled state or only have to undergo minor processing before resale, such as diluting or packing, this shall not

441. CCC: Council Regulation (EEC) No. 2913/92 of 12 October 1992 establishing the Community Customs Code (OJ L 302, 19.10.1992). CCC IR: Commission Regulation (EEC) No. 2454/93 of 2 July 1993 laying down provisions for the implementation of Council Regulation (EEC) No. 2913/92 establishing the Community Customs Code (OJ L 253, 11.10.1993).
442. The predecessor 1983 and 1980 pronouncements were to the same effect. Commission Regulation (EEC) No. 1494/80 of 11 June 1980 on interpretative notes and generally accepted accounting principles for the purposes of customs value, OJ L 154, 21.6.1980. This Commission Regulation presented the Agreement's Interpretative Notes in excerpted format; it followed upon the promulgation of the implementing measure, Council Regulation (EEC) No. 1224/80 of 28 May 1980 on the valuation of goods for customs purposes, OJ L 134/1, 31.5.1980 and Commission Regulation (EEC) No. 3158/83 of 9 November 1983 on the cadence of royalty and licence fees in customs value, OJ L 309/19, 10/11/1983 incorporated by reference (in paragraph 2.3) the Annex strictures of Reg No. 1494/80.

prevent a royalty or licence fee from being considered related to the imported goods.

3. If royalties or licence fees relate partly to the imported goods and partly to other ingredients or component parts added to the goods after their importation, or to post-importation activities or services, an appropriate apportionment shall be made only on the basis of objective and quantifiable data, in accordance with the interpretative note to Article 32 (2) of the Code in Annex 23.

You will have noticed that Article 158.1 and Annex 23 are in harmony with the Interpretative Note closing text with its two combined conditions: the amount of this royalty: (1) is based only on the imported goods and (2) can be readily quantified. The text in Article 158.3 appears to be not aligned and to actually collide with the other authorities—"relate partly" is not the same as "based only" or "relates to the imported goods."

There is a conflict between these provisions. Article 158.1 and Annex 23 are drafted in such a way that an apportionment is not allowed, and an addition for the RLF is allowed when the right conditions are met, notably the presence of objective and quantifiable data AND the RLF is based only on the imported goods.

Article 158.3 is drafted in a way that apportionment and the addition for an apportioned RLF are presumed available as a general rule. Seemingly the only restriction for doing such an apportionment is the availability of objective and quantifiable data. The extreme lengths to which the Commission is prepared to go for apportionment under the UCC will be seen below.

I would maintain that, regardless of the reach of CCC, Article 158 and its predecessor provisions, these earlier Regulations, including the interpretative notes in the successive Annex treatments, curbed an apportionment—if the RLF is only partly related to (is based only partially on) the imported goods, no addition of a royalty should be made. An addition of an RLF should be undertaken only in the case of an RLF that is based only on the imported goods. This apparent limitation imposed by the Annex 23 interpretative note on the range of action under Article 158.3 was apparently "honored in the breach"—ignored—by the Commission and by the Member States customs authorities.

Curiously, the ECJ decision in *Curtis Balkan,*[443] a 2020 case that arose under the earlier CCC, only discussed Article 158.3, ignoring altogether Article 158.1 and Annex 23 but for the narrowly circumscribed allowance for objective and quantifiable data in the latter provision.[444]

443. Case C-76/19, *Direktor na Teritorialna direktsiya Yugozapadna Agentsiya "Mitnitsi," formerly Nachalnik na Mitnitsa Aerogara Sofia v. Curtis Balkan EOOD*, 9.7.2020, ECLI:EU:C:2020:543 (*Curtis Balkan*). To be clear, the decision was concerned with the question of RLFs under the predecessor CCC but, due to the even more expansive remit of the UCC on the question of condition of sale, we could expect the same result under a UCC analysis.

444. Similarly, the Written Observations of the EU Commission cited Annex 23 only in the same narrow context as well as the issue of control as a defining characteristic of a related party, per Article 143.1(e) of the CCC. Translated from the French. Commission Européenne, Ref. Ares (2019)3645195-06/06/2019.

In the event, the ECJ in the *Curtis Balkan* decision detoured around this position on an RLF only partly related to the imported goods. We see that the ECJ dutifully cited apportionment being in accordance Article 158.1 and Article 158.3 taken in tandem (paragraph 29), but we see no reconciliation with the "only related to the goods" criterion of Article 158.1 (paragraph 42). And we also find that Annex 23 was largely absent from the Judgment, having never been cited by the Commission or the Advocate General in this apportionment connection.

In *Curtis Balkan*, the importer purchased from unrelated sellers some imported articles to be used as parts to manufacture finished goods. The importer paid a standard price to its parent company for Curtis kits to be used in the manufacture of fuel supply indicators and high-frequency speed regulators based on its own patented technology. The components incorporated in the finished products were manufactured in accordance with specifications imposed by Curtis USA and were designed specifically for those products. Parenthetically, this direction by the company to only procure parts or components from previously approved vendors is a common business practice. It is one way to manage risks of failure of the finished products.

Curtis Balkan was entitled to produce, using those components, and to sell engine speed regulators and components for electric vehicles. The company paid a fee for the right to use the patent. The importer had a services agreement with its parent company, with agreed monthly fees, as well as a patent use agreement, under which quarterly royalties were paid based on sales of the finished products. These royalty payments were made by Curtis Balkan and other subsidiaries in return for production "know-how" and the right to manufacture products developed by Curtis USA, with the subsidiaries assembling the finished products.

The customs authority was of the view that a portion of the royalty payments for access to the know-how used by the importer to manufacture the finished products was dutiable and should be added to the customs value of the imported semifinished articles purchased from the third-party sellers.

After referring to the above-cited Annex 23, the court in *Curtis Balkan* agreed with the Bulgarian customs authority argument that there was a link between the royalties and the goods being valued, insofar as the latter are components used for the manufacture of licensed products and insofar as those components are certified in connection with the quality requirements of the finished products.

We are supposed to take solace while ignoring the plain language in the Interpretative Note about not proceeding unless the RLF "is based only on the imported goods," from the argument (in paragraph 29) that:

> in so far as the imported goods are merely component parts in the composition of the finished products and the royalties relate, in part, to the imported goods and, in part, to other components added to the goods after their importation, as well as to post-importation activities and services, the Director of Customs at Sofia Airport submits that the royalties were apportioned on a pro rata basis in accordance with Article 158(1) and (3) of Regulation No 2454/93.

And again, from the *Curtis Balkan* court's commentary (in paragraphs 52 and 53):

> It must be added that royalties may be related to the goods being valued, within the meaning of Article 32(1)(c), even if those royalties relate only partly to those goods .... However, as is apparent from Article 32(2) of the Customs Code, additions to the price actually paid or payable are to be made only on the basis of objective and quantifiable data. Citation to GE Healthcare decision omitted.[445]
>
> As regards the referring court's questions concerning the interpretation of Article 158(3) of Regulation No 2454/93, it must be recalled that, under that provision, if RLFs relate partly to the imported goods and partly to other ingredients or component parts added to the goods after their importation, or to post-importation activities or services, an appropriate apportionment is to be made only on the basis of objective and quantifiable data, in accordance with the interpretative note on Article 32(2) of the Customs Code in Annex 23.

To some, this objective and quantifiable data rationale for the action by the Commission and the ECJ is like a driver justifying his driving past a "road closed" sign by saying he had stayed within the speed limit.

Apportionment is expressly provided for in the Agreement only for dutiable assists. Moreover, the Interpretative Note's suggestion that no apportionment should be made where the RLF only partly relates to the imported goods had been previously followed and applied in Annex 23 in the EU's CCC IR.

To be direct: The claim that a customs authority's RLF apportionment estimates are purportedly based "on objective and quantifiable data" does NOT confer the authority to make any RLF apportionment such that some portion of the RLF is related to the goods. The ECJ went in an entirely different, and erroneous, direction (paragraph 58):

> Article 158(3) of Regulation No 2454/93 must be interpreted as applying not only if royalties or licence fees relate partly to the imported goods and partly to other ingredients or component parts added to the goods after their importation, and if royalties or licence fees relate partly to the imported goods and partly to post-importation activities or services, but also if royalties or licence fees relate in part to the imported goods and partly to other ingredients or components which are added to the goods after their importation as well as to post-importation activities or services.

The *Curtis Balkan* court relied on the earlier *GE Healthcare* decision[446] as the justification for an adjustment being permitted for an RLF that was partially related to the imported goods. In the *GE Healthcare* case, the RLF was for trademarks and the use of a tradename (which the court determined were additions to value), and for post-importation services provided to the importer (which are not an addition to value)—this is different from a royalty for a finished product containing some imported components. The court in *GE Healthcare* (in paragraphs 52-53) noted that the customs authority could assign a portion of the RLF to a dutiable status by way of an estimate, albeit one grounded on objective and quantifiable data:

---

445. Case C-173/15, *GE Healthcare GmbH v. Hauptzollamt Düsseldorf*, 9.3.2015, EU:C:2017:195, paragraph 53.

446. *Ibid. see* paragraphs 5-53 of the Judgment. In the Judgment, the court concluded that the RLF can be "related to the imported goods" for these purposes even if it is only partly related to the imported goods. Paragraph 93(2).

> such an adjustment thereby needing to be made on the basis of objective and quantifiable data capable of estimating the amount of the royalties or licence fees related to those goods.
>
> It follows that, under Article 32(1)(c) of the [Community] Customs Code, royalties or licence fees may be "related to the goods being valued," within the meaning of that provision, even if the royalties or licence fees relate only partly to those goods.

The *Curtis Balkan* court also cited the Compendium of Customs Valuation Texts (2008 ed.)[447] prepared by the Customs Code Committee of the EU Commission in paragraph 8 of Commentary No 3 on the incidence of RLFs in the customs value, drawn up by the Commission's Customs Code Committee. The court reasoned that it was necessary to analyze the effect of the payment of RLFs on the customs value not only where the imported goods are themselves the subject of the license agreement but also where the imported goods are only components of the product covered by the license. Although the ECJ having stated in *GE Healthcare*, in paragraph 45, that the Customs Code Committee should be accorded deference,[448] one would have thought that any such administrative commentary that was directly at odds with the Regulation would be ultra vires and discarded.[449]

The ECJ pronounced in its *Curtis Balkan* judgment (in paragraph 51):

> In the present case, it is for the referring court, which alone has jurisdiction to assess the facts of the dispute before it, to determine whether there is a sufficiently close link between the know-how provided under the licence agreement concluded between Curtis Balkan and Curtis USA and the imported goods, and thus to determine whether the royalties paid by the latter to Curtis Balkan USA may be regarded as relating to those goods, in accordance with Article 32(1)(c) of the Customs Code. It is necessary, in that context, to take account of all the relevant factors, in particular the relationships of law and of fact between the persons involved.

The EU Commission impeached the contractual agreements and advanced another argument—perhaps the royalty paid on the sale of the goods produced in Bulgaria might contain some compensation for the design of the imported parts:

> the national court must ascertain whether the components were designed on the basis of the licensor's know-how/intellectual property rights and the extent to

447. https//ec.europa.eu/taxation_customs/sites/taxation/files/customs_valuaton_compendium_2008_en.pdf.
448. "[T]he conclusions of the Customs Code Committee, although they do not have legally binding force, nevertheless constitute an important means of ensuring the uniform application of the Customs Code by the customs authorities of the Member States and as such may be regarded as a valid aid to the interpretation of the Code" (citation omitted).
449. Apart from the RLF analysis, it is apparent from the opinion that an analysis could have been pursued under a dutiable assist inquiry, which would have focused on the question of whether the know-how being furnished was relevant to the production of the imported parts or only for the post-importation production of the finished goods, or both. A dutiable assist could be found if: (i) the licensed know-how was necessary at least in part for the production of the imported parts by third-party suppliers and (ii) that know-how was provided by the licensor, Curtis USA, on a free or reduced cost basis. If that were shown, apportionment of assists is specifically allowed.

which the royalties/licensing fees on the final products relate to the imported components (wholly, in part, or not at all).

If that were the case, it was presumed this might satisfy the initial "related to the goods" criterion and would justify an apportionment. In fact, after the matter was referred back to the court in Bulgaria, Bulgarian court never reached the issue of an apportionment for partial dutiability. Instead, that court skirted the issue altogether, deciding that the royalty was indeed paid for production rights and know-how and not even partly related to the imported goods, as had been suggested by the last sentence in paragraph 50 of the ECJ decision:

> By contrast [to the know-how supplied under the licensing agreement being necessary for the manufacture of the imported goods], the fact that know-how is necessary only for the completion of the licensed goods leads to the conclusion that there is no sufficiently close link.

As a result, the apportionment question raised in the ECJ judgment in paragraphs 52-53 was never reached.

We shall also see below that the EU position on "condition of sale" inquiries has been consistent under both the CCC and the UCC in looking for "implicit" conditions and in granting customs authorities a free hand in their "evaluations."

[ii] EU Position under the UCC

For the first time since 1980, the EU Regulations on RLFs do not incorporate the limiting text from the Interpretative Note to the Agreement.[450] That is one way to avoid an explicit conflict between the administrative practice and the statutory regime.

To be fair, the UCC IA does not expressly address the issue of an "apportionment" of RLFs. The making of an apportionment may nonetheless be implicit to the authority that the EU claims to make an "adjustment" (at UCC IA, Article 136.3):

> If royalties or license fees relate partly to the goods being valued and partly to other ingredients or component parts added to the goods after their importation, or to post-importation activities or services, an *"appropriate" adjustment* shall be made[451] (emphasis added).

In fact, the Commission employs the term "apportionment" in its discussions on RLFs in the 2022 Compendium in Commentary Nos 3 and 17. We may conclude that the terms are being used interchangeably here.

But this begs the question, what is "appropriate"?

We can be expected to conclude that the EU position is that it would be "appropriate" for an apportionment of an RLF to be made. The customs authority will

450. As we have established, the text had appeared as an interpretative note in Annex 23 of the CCC.
451. Article 136.3 of UCC IA. Commission Implementing Regulation (EU) 2015/2447 of 24 November 2015 laying down detailed rules for implementing certain provisions of Regulation (EU) No. 952/2013 of the European Parliament and of the Council laying down the Union Customs Code, OJ L 343, 29.12.2015, p. 558-893; consolidated version: 02015R2447-20200720.

seek to determine what portion of the RLF relates to the imported goods and is thus dutiable and, conversely, what portion is not related to the imported goods and thus is not dutiable. Insight into the current EU perspective on RLF apportionments is gained by a review of the EU Commission Compendium 2022.[452]

As a first observation, as stated, this is a misuse of apportionment as the term has been used in Article 8 of the Agreement.

Second, it would make greater sense if the four separate Commentaries on RLFs—3, 13 (section 3), 16 and 17—had not been scattered.

The Commission introduced a novel view on adjustment/apportionment in Commentary No 3, with the result that the entire RLF was dutiable, even if its payment is only partly related to the imported goods. We learn:

> In many cases examination of licence agreements and contracts of sale will reveal that a part only of the royalty payment will be seen to be potentially dutiable. Where under a licence agreement the benefits conferred are a mixture of potentially dutiable and non-dutiable elements but the licensee does not in fact avail himself of the non-dutiable elements, it may nevertheless be appropriate to regard the whole of the royalty or licence fee as eligible for inclusion in the customs value.[453]

Eliminating any nondutiable elements in that fashion is one way to eliminate the need to make an apportionment—the entire RLF is made out to be related solely to the imported goods.[454]

We find the clearest expression of the Commission's orthodoxy on this question of apportionment in Commentary No 17.[455] The facts present a classic case of imported parts or materials which were not themselves trademarked or made with a patented process but which were used to manufacture finished products in the country of importation. The main and key component of the finished product is the imported goods. A license fee, set at 5% of the total sales of the finished product during the reference period defined in the agreement, was due to the seller/licensor for the right to use a patent in the production process.

The license agreement provides that the importer is obliged to pay the license fee to purchase the imported goods.

According to the Commission, the correct approach, as set forth in a "Formula 1," is to examine the portion of the total production costs (600) represented by the price of the imported goods before the addition for license fees (450), giving what we might term a dutiability factor of 75%. That 75% factor is then applied to the amount of

---

452. *See* Commentary No. 3: Incidence of royalties and licence fees in the customs value, 30 and Commentary No. 17: Apportionment of licence fees under Article 136(3) UCC IA, 95.
453. EU Commission Compendium 2022, Commentary No. 3: Incidence of royalties and licence fees in the customs value, 31, paragraph 7.
454. In a way this is similar to the treatment of quotas allocated on a gratis basis in *Thierschmidt*. In both instances, the prevailing analysis is to ascertain the actual purpose of the payment. If the payment cannot be attributed to something other than the goods themselves or the dutiable elements of an RLF, in other words, there is no separate basis for the payment, the entire payment will be dutiable.
455. EU Commission Compendium 2022, Commentary No. 17: Apportionment of licence fees under Article 136(3) of UCC IA, 95.

license fee paid (50), leading to the conclusion that 37.5 of the license fee was dutiable. A second and third "Formula" were rejected.

In the "Formula 2" rendering, we find a dutiable license fee of 42.5, arrived at by taking the sum of the price paid for the subject goods before the addition for license fees (450) plus the total sales margin (400) and dividing that 850 by the total sales (1,000), giving a factor of 85% which is then multiplied by the license fees (50).

In Formula 3, the price paid for the imported goods before the addition for license fees (450) is divided by the total sales of the finished products (1,000), giving a factor of 45% which when applied to the license fees paid (50) results in a dutiable portion of the license fee of 22.5.

According to the Commission, we must presume that the foregoing arithmetic exercises are compatible with the Interpretative Note to Article 8, paragraph 3. Those computations and the associated cost accounting analyses requiring a "tracing" of the imported goods would be complicated beyond measure if the imported goods are one of a much larger assemblage of parts or components and if the production processes were multiphased.

The Commission was silent on how this obvious "deep dive" into the cost accounting of the importer/producer of the finished goods measures up to or is to be reconciled with the oft-stated antagonism whenever the need for EU customs authorities to engage in lengthy investigations might arise.

Its Additional Remarks introduce two noteworthy statements in paragraph 9. These are:

(1) "besides the requirements for data to be objective and quantifiable, its usage shall take into account concepts that are comparable and homogenous." My reaction is what is meant by "comparable" and by "homogenous" here?
(2) [Citing Commentary No. 3] "The relationship between the licence fees and the goods to be valued can also be determined by considering 'what in fact the licensee receives in return for the payment.'" Exactly, the importer/licensee receives the right to use the patent in post-import manufacturing, and the fee is due on sales of the finished products. Presumably, the importer/licensee could both buy and import the goods but not thereafter use the patent in the production process. Because no license fee is due and owing in that circumstance, is the license fee truly related to and a condition of sale (to be discussed below) of the imported goods?

As a final observation: many would be interested in a Commission effort to reconcile the approach taken in its Commentary No 17, where the patent applied only to the production of the finished products, with the court's statement in *Curtis Balkan* in paragraph 50.

I conclude that there appears to be no authority other than the EU's *ipse dixit* for any adjustment/apportionment of RLFs, regardless whether GAAP rules are observed and/or whether "objective and quantifiable data" are claimed to be available.

[iii] US Position

Each of these Commission interpretations under the new UCC IA regulations, and especially Commentary No 17, conflicts with the long-standing US rule following the *Rieter* ruling[456] on the nondutiable status of a royalty based on the sale of a product produced in the US that: (i) included both imported and local ingredients or components and (ii) whose sale price included the post-import production costs.

In the case of the Rieter company, a royalty was imposed on the sale in the US by a US subsidiary of a Swiss company of textile machinery which had been manufactured in the US using both imported and domestically produced parts and components. Although CBP Headquarters did not cite the regulation, it still concluded that the royalty was nondutiable because the royalty was paid, in substantial part, on parts/components that were not imported.[457]

CBP issued another ruling on similar facts to the effect that the royalty paid was nondutiable.[458] The importer, Pfizer Pharmaceutical, paid a royalty to Bayer for the right to use Bayer's patented process, but not for the right to purchase or resell the patented imported product. The royalty payments were based on the sale of products that included a substantial percentage of US ingredients and, like those royalty payments in the Rieter ruling, were deemed nondutiable.

The US position is aligned with Interpretative Note to Article 8, paragraph 3 of the Agreement and is based upon a third outcome for an RLF that is partly related to the imported goods; i.e., the entire RLF is not dutiable. In a 2006 ruling,[459] CBP found there was no linkage between the payment of the royalties and the production and sale for exportation of the imported chemicals. Instead, it appeared that the royalties paid by the importer were for the know-how, trademarks and patents that enabled the importer to further process the raw materials it sourced from foreign and domestic vendors so as to create new finished products. The answer to the question—was the payment of the royalty related to the imported products—was in the negative.[460]

While CBP opined that the case would be even more clear and nondutiable status more firmly established if the royalty was based on an amount that had netted out the costs represented by the imported articles, CBP concluded that the royalties paid by the importer are for the know-how, trademarks and patents that enable the importer to further process the raw materials it sources from foreign and domestic vendors so as to create new finished products. In short, the payment of the royalty was not related to the imported goods and was not dutiable.

---

456. Ruling no. 544656 (June 19, 1991) (CSD 92-12).
457. *Ibid.*
458. CSD 93-26, ruling no. 545114 (September 30, 1993). *See also* ruling nos. H024566 (October 15, 2008), 544761 (March 14, 2002) and 546626 (November 9, 2001). Note that some rulings will analyze RLFs associated with the sale of the finished goods produced in the US under a condition of sale criterion. *See*, e.g., ruling no. 545307 (February 3, 1995).
459. Ruling no. W548649 (September 5, 2006).
460. The three-part test employed by CBP includes the question, "was the royalty involved in the production or sale of the imported merchandise?."

To be sure, there is some *dicta* in one CBP ruling which suggests, without elaboration, that apportionment of RLFs could be appropriate if a portion of the royalty payment does not relate to the imported product.[461] Other rulings deal with apportionment of RLFs but not in the sense of apportioning between dutiable and nondutiable portions of the RLF.[462] A 2003 ruling[463] presents a muddled "outlier," where we are instructed that a royalty paid for the use of specialized apparatus and equipment for use in oil and gas drilling operations after importation was to be included in transaction value either as part of the PAPP or as an addition thereto under the sections for royalty or subsequent proceeds. The ruling observes that:

> Assuming that the agreement remains in force, and the equipment is used throughout its useful life, then the amount of the future royalty payments can reasonably be determined taking into account the life of the equipment and the length of the contract.

Returning to a point we had made above, any allocation of the royalty payments appears to be actually focused on qualifying the goods as being related to the imported goods as opposed to a per-entry apportionment of the royalty, which latter usage is the only usage contemplated by the Agreement and then only for dutiable assists.

It would be remiss if we did not mention instruments published by the WCO.

[iv] TCCV Instruments

Two instruments published nearly forty years ago by the TCCV present readily distinguishable facts. In Advisory Opinion 4.4,[464] an imported concentrate was purchased from the patent holder/seller and was simply diluted with water after importation. The royalty was held dutiable and it would be hard to deny that the "related to the goods under review" test was met on those facts. You will note the alignment with the example shown in Article 158.2 of the CCC IR. In a companion instrument, Advisory Opinion 4.6,[465] with similar, simple-dilution facts, in one scenario, the finished product was resold without a trademark and with no payment of an RLF. In another scenario, the finished product bore the seller/trademark owner's trademark, and a fee was required to be paid to the seller/trademark owner. No addition was appropriate for scenario 1—in fact, an addition to the PAPP was never confronted—but

---

461. Ruling no. 545710 (October 30, 1998).
462. Ruling no. H078555 (December 18, 2009). The term "apportionment" here appears to refer to accounting treatment of the royalties—how they should be "booked." GAAP consistency was important. Ruling no. 548373 (November 24, 2003) (in determining the value of the royalty stream, the payments should be apportioned to the subject entries in a reasonable manner). Ruling nos. H3123455 (October 28, 2020) and 545279 (Mov. 30, 1994) (cost of acquisition of dutiable assists was license fees; the fees could be apportioned under the dutiable assist provisions).
463. Ruling no. 548373 (November 24, 2003).
464. TCCV, AO 4.4, Royalties and Licence Fees Under Article 8.1(c) of the Agreement (March 1983).
465. TCCV, AO 4.6, Royalties and Licence Fees Under Article 8.1(c) of the Agreement (March 1983).

the fee paid under scenario 2 was dutiable because the payment was a condition of sale of the imported concentrate.

It would be helpful if there were a technical question raised at the TCCV which addressed this issue of apportionment, and specifically the extent of the Interpretative Note, but I believe that a consensus on the question may be unattainable.

[v] Divisible Payment

The "relatedness" question raised by the importation of articles that will be combined with other materials to make a finished product can lead to an attempt at apportionment so as to isolate an RLF amount that is tied to or related to the imported article.

This fact pattern is readily distinguishable from other fact patterns that could be seen as leading to what might be seen as an apportionment. There can be a single, combined payment (say, an aggregate amount that corresponds to 10% of net resales)—as for Treasury convenience, or to avoid double fees for currency remittances, or to manage separate foreign exchange authorizations, etc.—for two separate royalties of 5%, each of which is readily identifiable and itemized. In this latter case, it could be shown easily that only one of the royalties is dutiable (say, a classic trademark royalty of 5%), while the other is not dutiable (such as a payment for management expertise, not directly engaged in production or for design work undertaken in the country of importation). In such a case, we are not really engaged in "apportionment" per se but simply using objective and quantifiable data to apply a dutiable status to the TM royalty of 5% from the combined, but actually divisible, royalty *payment* of 10% in the aggregate. The customs authority should not be prevented from collecting a duty on the 5% due under the trademark license while leaving the 5% that has been itemized as being paid for the management services or the design work undisturbed.[466]

What should be remembered, however, is that oftentimes the common commercial practice is that there is no itemization as negotiators will want the freedom to bundle all of the elements into a single, comprehensive payment without a separate itemization or "breakdown." Such a "lumping together" would frustrate a divisibility analysis.

In the EU Commission Compendium 2022 in Commentary No. 3, paragraph 12 in the first scenario, the Commission took the same view, although it is defined there as an apportionment:

> 12. The basis for apportionment of the total payment into dutiable and non-dutiable elements can sometimes be found in the licence agreement itself, when for example a 7% total royalty may be specified as representing 3% for patent rights, 2% for marketing know-how and 2% for trademark usage.
>
> The para. 12 discussion then proceeds to lay the foundation for its "evaluative" apportionment,

466. This is doubly so because the dutiable status of the payment for the design work should be examined as a potential dutiable assist and not as an RLF.

> More often than not however the basis for apportionment cannot be so found. The respective values of rights and know-how can at times be established by evaluating the extent to which know-how is transferred or availed of and deducting that sum from the total royalty paid or payable.

What the EU Commission has in mind for its evaluation—focused on the license and not on the sales agreement—is presented in paragraph 14:

> 14. Further, inspection of correspondence between licensor and licensee, inter office reports of negotiations which preceded the drawing up of the licence agreement or discussion with one of the negotiators of the licence agreement will frequently provide the bases for apportionment when at first sight apportionment would not seem possible.

Given that the commercial practice may have been to bundle the payments together without an itemization, this seems an especially ill-begotten enterprise. It is also important to recall what could develop into daunting accounting reviews when applying the apportionment exercises set out in Commentary No 17 which we already discussed.

This nice distinction of: (i) a single payment for two distinct royalties arising from separate grants of IPRs from (ii) a single royalty payment based upon two grants of IPRs that have not been assigned a separate value, e.g., a 10% royalty for both trademark rights and local-origin design work, should be clear. The payment in the first context is divisible, with dutiable/nondutiable status assessed separately for each element of the RLF, and in the second it is not divisible, and the entire payment will be dutiable or not, with no apportionment available.[467]

To be sure, if it has been established that there is an adjustment to be made but the data is not objective and quantifiable, then TV will be lost. That is the mandate of the first sentence of the Interpretative Note. In the case of RLFs, one way to apply the Interpretative Note is to assume that before the quality of the data is assessed, that the twin criteria for dutiable status, the payment is solely related to the goods and is a condition of sale, have already been satisfied. This bifurcated or two-step analysis is suggested in the last sentence of the Note, "... if the amount of this royalty is based only on the imported goods and can be readily quantified ... ." This refers to the case where there is an RLF, but the actual amount cannot be properly ascertained (as in, "we know there is a dutiable RLF but we don't know how much ..."). Thus, only in the case of an RLF that is solely based on/related to the imported goods will a failure to meet this underlying third criterion of objective and quantifiable data in establishing the value of that RLF prove fatal to transaction value.

Apart from this inquiry into the RLF being related to the imported goods or not, the other major focus will be on the question whether the payment of the RLF is a condition of sale.

467. Sherman and Glashoff, no. 376 at 143, missed the possibility of the distinction although to their credit they challenged the EEC approach dating to 1983 on "appropriate apportionment" and "objective and quantifiable" data.

[b] *Condition of Sale*

[i] Negotiating History and GATT Discussions

The archival files on the Agreement in the GATT repository and especially on the issue of RLFs and the other "up-lifts," as the adjustments were originally termed, are sparse. Indeed, we find that despite the long run-up to the 1979 acceptance of the Agreement, RLFs only made an appearance in 1977. Transcripts of discussions, minutes of meetings and other documents do not exist, except perhaps unofficially in the participant countries' archives. There is no support in the body of GATT/WTO documents which supports any reading of Article 8.1(c) other than it being grounded in—and limited to—the condition being a feature of the sales agreement between buyer and seller. Indeed, in what may be the earliest specific reference to royalties at the GATT in the context of the Multilateral Trade Negotiations on the Agreement,[468] we see Brazil first assigned dutiable status to the value of the right to use patent, trade mark, design and copyright, to the extent such right is not included in the PAPP. Brazil then suggested nondutiable status for:

> royalties or licence fees paid by the importer to a third party which the manufacturer would otherwise have to pay in order to produce or sell the imported merchandise.

Of course, dutiable status on these grounds makes perfect sense because it shows that the RLF is being paid to relieve the manufacturer/seller of the cost burden that it would otherwise owe to a licensor. There is a common thread to all of the Article 8.1 (a)-(c) adjustments, and that is that each of the provisions is grounded in a rebuff to the attempt to artificially lower what should be the full PAPP for the imported goods by relieving the seller of a cost burden. In the context of this discussion, in very much the same fashion as a buyer separately paying for packing or providing a dutiable assist, a seller might separately invoice the buyer for an RLF or obligate the buyer to pay an RLF to the intellectual property licensor. This would be in lieu of the recoupment of the seller's own costs either in developing the property right itself or in securing license rights from the property owner or IPR holder by means of having the RLF built into the PAPP. In the event, any such separately billed RLF—whether paid to the seller or to the licensor on behalf of the seller—will be added to the declared PAPP to make a customs value.[469]

---

468. GATT, Group "Non-Tariff Measures," Sub-Group "Customs Matters," MTN/NTM/W/167, 7 July 1978, at 8-9. This was slightly revised in a 12 July 1978 version. For Brazil, the RLFs were said to be an exception to the general rule that adjustments should be made to the PAPP for the value of any additional consideration which the buyer is directly or indirectly required to discharge as a condition of the sale. Unless there is a nice distinction between the right to use and the right to produce or sell, the distinction of this formulation is difficult to perceive.

469. We find a compatible analysis in Sherman & Glashoff, Customs Valuation: Commentary on the GATT Customs Valuation Code (1988), no. 299 at 125 (if the royalty pays for costs of the exporter-seller which he must cover any such royalty will be a proper part of customs value)

When we look at Article 8.1(c) of the Valuation Agreement in this light we can also see the efficacy of including an RLF paid to a third-party licensor when the seller would otherwise have been in the position of having to pay the RLF to the licensor. Thus, the RLF is dutiable if and when it is a cost burden that would otherwise have been borne by the seller. The Agreement will assign Article 8.1(c) status to both of the following third-party RLF schemes:

(1) the seller is a licensee and, as a condition of sale, requires that the buyer pay the RLF to the third-party licensor—this would also be a payment that would be an integral part of the PAPP as a payment of the seller's debt (Interpretative Note to Article 1.1); and
(2) the seller is not a licensee but, as a condition of sale, requires the buyer to pay an RLF, implicitly the seller here requiring the buyer to enter into a license agreement in the first instance.

It bears repetition that we are dealing with a sale for exportation and that if we are contending with a condition of sale it must be imposed by the seller. To focus on the license agreement, which is emerging as the principal frame of reference for the EU and others, is to take us to the rights and responsibilities accruing under the license agreement. Those are exercisable by or imposed upon only the parties to those agreements—the licensor and licensee—and not the seller or buyer of the merchandise, who may be and often are strangers to those agreements.

As another aside, from the perspective of the seller being relieved of a cost burden, it seems especially questionable to postulate that the licensee's payment of an RLF to a third-party licensor for rights granted to sell the trademarked article—when the article is a finished product manufactured by the buyer with the imported parts and other components—in a given territory is a seller-imposed condition of the sale. Parenthetically, this very early reference by Brazil to a third-party royalty will come as a surprise to many, as the prevailing view of many customs authorities is that third-party RLFs, at least as a general matter, are a recent business trend. Instead, this was a common enough practice almost fifty years ago.

Despite the fact that there is much daylight between that Brazil suggestion and the final Agreement, not the least of which is that Brazil would have made the RLF payment nondutiable, it is noteworthy in that it shows the logical underpinning for RLF dutiability under the Agreement lying in the seller insisting on its costs being relieved by obliging the buyer to make the RLF payment. The finally agreed later iteration of a "condition of sale" is thus a lineal descendent of and fully consistent with this narrow focus.

and at nos. 409-410, p. 151 (fixed fee RLF paid by buyer to an inventor or owner as a condition of purchase imposed by seller, who had used the patent and is thus a cost of the manufacturer/seller).

You may find the following reported exchange dating to a 1983 meeting of the WTO's Committee on Customs Valuation enlightening.[470] Australia was being questioned about its legislation implementing the Agreement:

> 24. The representative of the European Communities asked why the phrase "in accordance with the contract" had been used instead of the term "as a condition of sale" which appeared in the Agreement in several places. The representative of Australia said that legal advice obtained during the drafting of the legislation had been that the terms were in fact the same. *Australia had chosen the words "in accordance with the contract" on the grounds that a condition of sale had to be a legally enforceable condition, and to be such had to be embodied in the contract of sale.* In practical effect there was no difference between the two terms (emphasis added).

Importantly, there was no "push back" to this statement, suggesting that the Australian legislation was aligned with the CCV consensus in 1983, soon after the Agreement was adopted.[471]

[ii] US Practice

Current administrative practice in the US often points to this factor as defining dutiable status. CBP has taken the view that, even if the royalty payments are related to the

470. GATT, Minutes of the [CCV] Meeting Held 10-11 November 1983, VAL/M/8, 18 January 1984, at 6. Division 2 of Part VIII (sections 154 to 161L) of the Customs Act 1901 contains the legal rules for arriving at the valuation of imported goods. Sections 154 and 157 are concerned with royalties.
471. Section 154 (e) of the current Customs Act 1901 continues to define dutiable royalties by reference to the sales agreement, "all royalties or licence fees paid or payable, directly or indirectly, by or on behalf of the purchaser to the vendor or to another person under the import sales transaction, not being royalties or licence fee." However, this is deceiving. What is meant by the term "import sales transaction" is a broadly defined term and it introduces the notion that a third-party license agreement can be integrated with the sales agreement in forming a single commercial transaction ("any other contract, agreement or arrangement relating to the [contract of sale] ... that a Collector determines is so closely connected with that contract and to the goods the subject of that contract that together they form a single transaction") and "read as one with the contract of sale" as the Australian Border Force puts it. Under this regime, dating in its present form to the two-stage adoption of the Customs (Valuation) Amendment Act 1987 and the Customs and Excise Legislation Amendment Act 1989, the license agreement condition of payment of the RLF becomes a condition of the sale agreement, to relate back to the Agreement, via a deemed merger of the two agreements in a single "import sales transaction." The then-new legislation was reported to the GATT (GATT/VAL/1/Add. Suppl. 2*, 7 September 1988 and GATT, VAL/1/Add. 14/Suppl.3*, 24 August 1989 and GATT. VAL/1/Add.14/Suppl. 4*, 6 November 1990), but the degree of alignment with the Agreement on this perhaps-too-subtle point was apparently never questioned by the CCV although it is worth noting that the legislation was indeed controversial. *See*, Minutes of the [CCV] Meeting Held 11 October 1988, GATT, VAL/M/23, 2 March 1989, at 5-8; Minutes of the [CCV] Meeting Held 21 March 1989, GATT, VAL/M/24, 30 June 1989, at 8-11; Minutes of the [CCV] Meeting Held 10 October 1989, GATT, VAL/M/25, 5 March 1990, at 6-7; Minutes of the [CCV] Meeting Held 20 March 1990, GATT, VAL/M/26, 13 November 1990, at 4-5; Minutes of the [CCV] Meeting Held 7 February 1991, GATT, VAL/M/27, 9 April 1991, at 8; GATT, Minutes of the [CCV] Meeting Held 13 November 1991, VAL/M/28 (5 February 1992), at 9.

imported goods, they will not be dutiable unless their payment is a condition of the import sales transaction.

A 2003 ruling[472] presented the case of a buyer of imported merchandise who had paid a royalty to a third party for right to use trademarks on goods manufactured by unrelated factories. The licensor reserved a number of rights to itself. The licensor needed to approve the production schedule, the factories had to be approved by the licensor, licensor had access to information to all production and storage places, and required the use of specific labels and hang tags for the apparel. CBP concluded that the licensed trademarks were involved in the production of the imported merchandise. Notwithstanding that the royalty was therefore related to the imported merchandise, CBP determined that the royalty was nondutiable because it was not a condition of the sale.

In addition to the Hasbro II factors, as derived from the 1981 Statement of Administrative Action, CBP will often raise the following points:

(i) type of IPR at issue (patents covering processes to manufacture will generally be dutiable);
(ii) to whom the royalty is paid (payments to a seller or a party related to the seller are more likely dutiable than are payments to an unrelated third party);[473]
(iii) whether the purchase of the imported merchandise and the payment of the royalties are inextricably intertwined (e.g., provisions in the same agreement covering both payment of royalty and purchase of the imported articles, license agreements which refer to sale of the imported merchandise, termination of either agreement upon termination of the other, termination of the purchase agreement due to failure to pay the royalties);
(iv) payment of the royalties on each and every importation.[474]

The US customs regulations establish a broad rule of thumb that fees and royalties for patents covering processes to manufacture the imported merchandise will generally be dutiable, whereas payments to third parties for the use of trademarks or copyrights in the US will be nondutiable selling expenses of the buyer.[475] In this

472. Ruling no. 548368 (December 24, 2003).
473. If payment goes to the seller or to a related entity, CBP is very likely to see it as being related to the imported merchandise. CBP will likely override both form and substance in such cases by eliminating any distinction between seller and related licensor, and view payments to a licensor related to the seller as tantamount to a payment to the seller and, typically, without any rationale expressed therefor. *See*, e.g., ruling no. 547622 (September 28, 2002).
474. *See* ruling no. 548552 (August 19, 2004) at 3-4. If it can be shown that the fee or royalty must be paid regardless of the number of articles imported, if any, then CBP might conclude that the payments are not a condition of the import transaction and are, thus, nondutiable. Ruling no. 542360 (June 10, 1981). The Statement of Administrative Action was presented to the US Congress when the 1979 implementing legislation was under review. It plays a principal role in the 1979 law's legislative history.
475. 19 CFR § 152.103(f); *see* ruling no. 544727 (December 4, 1991).

post-Hasbro II environment, importers seeking to structure nondutiable royalty arrangements may also rely on the growing body of rulings which establish broad patterns.

Importers and their advisors will try to take great care in strictly segregating manufacturing and licensing activities and in ensuring that the seller of the goods and the licensor are separate parties.

The relevant agreements must be strictly separated as well to ensure that a royalty payment to a third party is not imposed as a condition of the import transaction by the seller. In the case of "inextricable linkage" between the two agreements, the royalty will be dutiable. In other words, mere payment to a third party is not enough to impart nondutiability in the face of the payment being related to, and a condition of, the import sales transaction.[476]

In one ruling, CBP concluded that a patent license fee paid to a third party was a condition of sale of the imported merchandise because the license agreement specifically conditioned manufacture, sale and importation of the goods on the payment of royalties.[477] In another ruling, the sales agreements for automobiles were subject to the terms of the royalty agreement, and the right to purchase was conditioned on the payment of the royalty. As a result of the "inextricable linkage," the importer could not buy the imported goods without the payment of the royalty, and the all-important third question was answered in the negative.[478] In a third ruling, CBP's logic progressed along the track that a license agreement between an importer's indirect parent company with a third-party patent licensor was a practical requirement to make the goods—that without the license the goods would never have been manufactured—and, thus, would never have been sold.[479] In this factual context, the importer purchased television sets made by related vendors located in Mexico and in the Philippines. The importer reimbursed the parent company for the royalty payments that the parent had remitted to the third-party licensors. Thus, the importer was not directly paying the royalty, nor paying either the licensor or the foreign vendor, pursuant to the license agreement in which the foreign parent had agreed to pay the royalty to the licensor or "cause its affiliates" to pay the royalty. In this analysis, the royalty payment made via the parent company was seen as a "condition of sale." The fact that this was a patent license should not be overlooked.

The US customs regulations provide,[480]as an example of a license fee not imposed as a condition of the sale, the case of further-manufactured imported goods where the buyer imports parts or components and uses them, along with US-origin materials, to produce the finished goods in the US, the selling price for which was the basis of license fee. In that case, the fee is not dutiable. As we have already seen, this scenario might be analyzed under the "related to the imported goods" criterion.

476. Ruling no. 543070 (July 28, 1983) (CSD 84-25).
477. Ruling no. W548692 (March 2, 2007).
478. Ruling no. 544978 (April 27, 1995) at 3-4.
479. Ruling no. 545071 (June 28, 1995).
480. 19 CFR § 152.103(f).

An inquiry into TCCV instruments and an emerging EU policy position reveals a departure from previously settled orthodoxies. It is helpful to examine each of these developments in its turn.

[iii] Guidance from TCCV

A regrettable source of the presumed authority to take an expansive view of a "condition of sale" inquiry is Commentary 25.1, issued by the TCCV in 2011,[481] whose authority has been effectively nullified in the US by the *Trimil* decision[482] and in Canada by the *Mattel* decision. Two of the factors that the instrument serves up as germane to a condition of sale determination refer to provisions in the license agreement even where such a condition is otherwise missing from the sales transaction deserve comment. These license agreement provisions are: (1) the notion that if the royalty or license fee is not paid, then the manufacturer (who would not ordinarily be a party to the license agreement) is forbidden to sell to the importer and (2) if the royalty or license fee contains terms that permit the licensor to manage the production or sale between the manufacturer and importer go beyond QC.[483]

Two comments: First, these features are tied to an agreement—but it is the license agreement, not the sales agreement for the imported goods. If they impose an enforceable condition arising from a legal agreement, they are a condition of the grant of the license and not of the sale of the imported product. In the face of silence in the latter sales agreement, a condition of sale cannot be inferred. Second, the notion that a customs authority is qualified to determine whether specific measures "go beyond QC" is a trifle far-fetched. In this connection, we point out that what are deemed to be prudent measures of brand protection and commercial reputation in RLF agreements are the subject of constantly evolving commercial practice standards and are considerably removed from the province of customs authority expertise.[484]

To pose a salient question, how many such RLF agreements would have regularly included forced labor or child labor restrictions twenty or twenty-five years ago? Nowadays, such measures to manage risks to the reputation of the licensor are quite routinely included with license agreements to the point that they are *de rigeur*. Do these restrictions go beyond QC considerations and thus suggest a "condition of sale"? Is a customs authority qualified to answer that question?

---

481. TCCV, Com. 25.1, Third Party Royalties and Licence Fees—General Commentary (April 2011).
482. *Trimil S.A. v. United States*, 419 F. Supp. 3d 1307 (CIT 2019). For another discussion of this decision, *see* Neville, "Customs Valuation Status of Royalties and Advertising Fees," 31 J. Int'l Tax'n (July 2020) at 27. For a ruling on the dutiability of RLFs issued by CBP in the wake of *Trimil, see* ruling no. H307034 (September 29, 2020).
483. The EU Commission Compendium 2008 had contained Commentary No. 11, on the application of Article 32(1)(c) CCC in relation to royalties and licence fees paid to a third party according to Article 160 of Reg. (EEC) no. 2454/93, paragraph 1, which applied this second principle of Com. 25.1 in reviewing third-party RLFs. The 2022 edition of the Compendium deleted this Commentary.
484. The EU Commission Compendium 2008 had contained Commentary No. 11, which applied the same logic as Com.25.1 in reviewing third-party RLFs.

The adoption of Commentary 25.1 was followed closely by the adoption of Advisory Opinion 4.15 in 2013.[485] There, the TCCV announced that a licensor's separate authorization to a party to manufacture the goods was a key to the dutiability of a royalty payment made by an importer/licensee to a licensor. This was a "third party" royalty scenario; i.e., there were two separate agreements, a license agreement between the importer and licensor and a supply agreement between the licensor and a manufacturer (M), who was not related to the licensor. The supply agreement authorizes the manufacturer to make the goods bearing the trademark and to sell the goods to the importer or other designated companies and to follow quality, design and technical specifications. There was also a sales agreement between the manufacturer and the importer. Even though the latter agreement makes no reference to the license agreement in general or to the effect of the nonpayment of the royalty specifically, the TCCV held that the royalty payment was a "condition of sale." The reasoning was that if the royalty was not paid to the licensor by the importer, then the manufacturer's authorization to make the goods would be rescinded ("[importer] would not be able to buy them if it failed to make that payment to [licensor]. Non-payment of the royalty ... would cause not only the termination of the license agreement but also the withdrawal of the authorization given to M to manufacture and sell to [importer] the goods bearing such trademark").

Not to put too fine a point on it, even if there were some basis for this logic, and there is not, the consequence of a nonpayment of an RLF could only be a failure to produce or to sell product in the future. The nonpayment would be a condition for future or continued sales and not of the sale presented with the entry.

Neither Commentary 25.1 nor Advisory Opinion 4.15 can be reconciled with earlier TCCV instruments which had paid attention to the sale for export. In Advisory Opinion 4.2,[486] we are confronted with a royalty that was to be paid on the resale of the imported phonograph records. As a result, the RLF was not dutiable as it was not a condition of sale of the imported goods—there was no legal obligation on the importer arising from the sales transaction. Instead, the obligation to pay the royalty was a condition of the resale of those goods. In the same way, another 1982 instrument, Advisory Opinion 4.3,[487] disposed of a royalty payment for the right to use a patented process as nondutiable. The process was used to manufacture certain products in the country of importation, which incidentally would be produced using an imported machine. The royalty for the process was not dutiable because it was not part of the customs value since its payment was not a condition of sale of the machine for export.

Note that under the "but for the RLF payment ..." theory, if the royalty were not paid then: (i) the process would not be available and (ii) if the process were not available then the machine would not be bought or imported and (iii) on that basis the machine would not be sold and thus (iv) the royalty payment would be a condition of sale of the machine. That line of thinking was not pursued in that Advisory Opinion. In 1982, when these instruments were adopted by the TCCV, there was no conjecture

485. TCCV, AO 4.15, Royalties and Licence Fees Under Article 8.1 (c) of the Agreement (April 2013).
486. TCCV, AO 4.2, Royalties and Licence Fees Under Article 8.1 (c) of the Agreement (March 1982).
487. TCCV, AO 4.3, Royalties and Licence Fees Under Article 8.1 (c) of the Agreement (March 1983).

such as whether the royalty might nevertheless be a condition of sale because a failure to pay the royalty would cut off the possibility of future sales.

In the same vein, the instrument adopted in October 1993 as Advisory Opinion 4.8[488] made it clear that there was no "condition of sale" imposed where a buyer/importer purchased and imported shoes which had been produced by a manufacturer who had been supplied with a trademark under a trademark license from a third-party licensor. The TCCV noted that the goods were purchased from the supplier under a contract other than the license agreement, and the payment of royalty is not a condition of sale of these goods. With apparent ease, the TCCV concluded that the royalty was not to be added to the PAPP. Again, there was no search for a missing connection between the two contracts.

Based upon a review of these early TCCV instruments, as much as an understanding of the parties during the negotiations and the early days under the Agreement, we find that the TCCV has strayed away from the plain text of the Agreement and its intended effects. It is the post-*Trimil* position in the US that is realigned with a proper understanding of this "condition of sale" criterion.[489]

[iv] Condition of Sale Is a Matter of Enforceability of the Sales Agreement

As the *Trimil* court decided, and just as the *Mattel* court in Canada had earlier decided (in paragraph 71), just because the nonpayment of the royalty might lead to a halt in production does *not* make the royalty payment a condition of the sale of the imported goods. On this point, I have previously argued that the parties to the sale—the buyer and the seller—cannot rely on the payment or nonpayment of a royalty in either forcing performance or as an excuse from performing under the sale agreement. If the buyer wanted to walk away from its obligation to buy the goods, it cannot cite nonpayment of the royalty to a third-party licensor as an excuse for its nonperformance. In the case of the seller seeking to walk away from its obligation to make and sell the goods to the buyer, the seller cannot excuse its nonperformance by pointing to the buyer's nonpayment of the royalty to a third-party licensor. Simply put, in the absence of the sales agreement mandating that RLF payment status will exert such a dispositive effect on the sale and purchase of the imported goods, the payment of the RLF cannot be said to be a condition of the sale.

The *Trimil* court held that an RLF was not and could not be a condition of sale unless payment was a legally enforceable right of the seller. In other words, the

488. TCCV, AO 4.2, Royalties and Licence Fees Under Article 8.1 (c) of the Agreement (October 1993).

489. As was noted in the article cited at n. 490, the *Trimil* decision aligns the US jurisprudence with that of Canada. *See Mattel* and also *Reebok Canada v. Canada (Deputy Minister of National Revenue)*, 2002 FCA 133, 2002 Fed. Ct. Appeal LEXIS 90 (Canada Federal Court of Appeal 2002).

presence of a legally enforceable condition could not be inferred where an express condition was absent from the sales contract.[490]

The terms used are significant. The text here prescribes that the buyer must pay the RLF not as a prerequisite or an obligation or as a requirement but as a "condition of sale." Any interpretation must be founded on its use in the world of commerce, given the consistent focus on "commercial realities" during the Tokyo Round negotiations and on the Agreement's pledged consistency to "commercial practices."[491]

That takes us to the reliance on the law of contracts, for it is the law of contracts and specifically the law of sales that govern traders' dealings generally and the definition of sales specifically.[492] A full review of the concept of "condition" within those legal disciplines would take us into a study of contracts and sales in various jurisdictions, in both the common law and civil law systems, with a comparative law analysis and perhaps a conflicts of law illustration or two. Suffice it to say that a "condition," when used in a sale context, as is the case here, refers to: (i) an event, not certain to occur (payment of the RLF) (ii) which must occur (iii) before the seller's performance (making the sale) becomes due. Or, as would be stated in a legal pleading, the obligor's (here, the buyers') failure to meet the condition will suspend or discharge the obligee's (here, the seller's) duty to perform.

What we find in Advisory Opinion 4.15 is a very different perspective altogether. There are also reports that some customs authorities find that there is a condition of sale (presumably implied) for payment of the RLF even in the face of the parties to the sales agreement expressly stating that the written contract is fully integrated, that it

490. CBP had previously followed this narrower interpretation. *See*, e.g., ruling no. 548368 (December 24, 2003). CBP later moved away from this interpretation. *See* ruling no. H233376 (September 19, 2016).

491. Of course, any formal interpretation of the terms of the Agreement would be conducted under the United Nations, Vienna Convention on the Law of Treaties, May 23, 1969, 1155 U.N.T.S 331, Articles 31 and 32 (Vienna Convention), available at: https://www.refworld.org/docid/3ae6b3a10.html. Interestingly, the United States signed the treaty on April 24, 1970, but the US Senate has not given its advice and consent to the treaty. While not a party to the Convention, the United States considers many of the provisions of the Vienna Convention to constitute customary international law on the law of treaties.

492. As has emerged in the preceding discussions, there is a regrettable want of precision and clarity in the Agreement as well as in the body of TCCV instruments. The TCCV adopted AO 1.1, The Concept of "Sale" on the Agreement (October 1981) (the title is telling), observing (in introductory paragraph (a)) that there is no definition of "sale" in the Agreement before proceeding to make the hortatory remark that transaction value should be used to the greatest extent possible, and that can be achieved only with the definition of "sale" in the "widest sense." Its examples showing no sales (consignment, lease, etc.) are not helpful. As we have already observed, we do have examples of individual Member countries confronting the legal requisites for a sale. In the US, CBP continues its reliance on the pre-Agreement decision in *J.L. Wood v. United States*, 62 CCPA 25, 33; C.A.D. 1139 (1974) (a sale consists of passage of title and risk of loss for a consideration); *see also VWP of Am., Inc. v. United States*, 175 F.3d 1327 (Fed. Cir. 1999) which cited *JL Wood*. The Canadian International Trade Tribunal in *Cherry Stix Ltd. v. President of the Canada Border Services Agency*, Appeal No. AP-2008-028 (May 10, 2010) is also relevant. The court rejected the CBSA argument that "commercial realities" showed there was a sale and instead applied the relevant law of sales. *See* Neville, "Back to Basics: An Intention to Buy or Sell is Not a Sale," 21 J. Int'l Tax'n (August 2010) at 25. The law of contracts which governs the sale transaction will also need to be consulted on the crucial issue of whether there is a condition obligating the payment of the RLF.

embodies the entire agreement of the parties and that nonperformance of either the seller or the buyer of an obligation arising under any other agreement will not excuse performance under the sales agreement; i.e., the sale will go through even if the RLF is not paid. To be more clear, some sales agreements will affirmatively state that payment of an RLF is NOT a condition of sale, but apparently some customs authorities will disregard that.

All interpretations which deviate from a proper contract law analysis focused squarely on the buyer's agreement with the seller and are, instead, founded on a "commercial realities," "practical effect" or "real world" perspective on performance under the sales agreement are misguided and a departure from rules governing the commercial practices on which the Agreement is founded.

I submit that the notion of "commercial realities" is not in the eye of the beholder, and certainly not if the beholder is a customs authority.

To illustrate the potential for a collision with actual commercial practices, consider a third-party royalty where the buyer has not paid the RLF. The sales agreement between buyer and seller makes no reference to the underlying license agreement nor the payment of the RLF, let alone make it a condition of sale. Indeed, that condition might have been discussed between the parties but was dropped in negotiations. Nevertheless, the buyer refuses to buy the goods, and posits its nonpayment of the RLF as a defense, looking to be excused from performance, i.e., its obligation to buy the goods proffered for sale. The parties' dispute will be resolved on these facts in a court or arbitral panel in favor of the seller, with the forum specifically holding that the payment of the RLF was not a condition of sale and that the buyer was not excused from its performance.[493] That is the commercial reality—grounded in the rights and responsibilities arising under the legally binding sale agreement—of and for the buyer and seller.

Was the Agreement intended to permit the customs authority to ignore or override that legal resolution and, instead, to substitute its own judgment founded on its own perception of what is meant by a condition of sale? That is the direction toward which the EU appears to be headed.

[v] EU Perspectives on Condition of Sale

In yet another point of divergence, the ECJ approved the EU customs authorities' very expansive interpretation of the condition of sale criterion for dutiable status for an RLF. The decision in *Curtis Balkan* came shortly after *Trimil* was published in the US.

Perhaps it is more correct to state that it was the CIT decision which marked a divergence since the CBP position had been sometimes more aligned with that of the TCCV and the EU.[494]

But before we address *Curtis Balkan*, let us lay the groundwork.

493. Whether the remedy for the seller would be specific performance under the contract or money damages is a tangential discussion—worthy of a digression at another opportunity.
494. *See*, e.g., ruling no. H233376 (September 19, 2016).

EU Texts Under the Community Customs Code and the Union Customs Code

In identical text, the CCC (in Article 32.1(c)) and the UCC (in Article 71.1 (c)) provide for the addition of:

> (c) royalties and licence fees related to the goods being valued that the buyer must pay, either directly or indirectly, as a condition of sale of the goods being valued, to the extent that such royalties and fees are not included in the price actually paid or payable.

This text tracks the Valuation Agreement, and there is surely nothing objectionable there, but we find, under the implementing regulations, that the scope has been expanded, subtly but expanded nonetheless.

Under the previous customs program, the CCC IR (in Article 160) provided for the condition of sale test that:

> When the buyer pays royalties or licence fees to a third party, the conditions provided for in Article 157 (2) shall not be considered as met unless the seller or a person related to him requires the buyer to make that payment.

Under the quaintly termed "UCC package," the UCC IA, in Article 136.4 prescribes:

> Royalties and licence fees are considered to be paid as a condition of sale for the imported goods when any of the following conditions is met:
>
> (a) the seller or a person related to the seller requires the buyer to make this payment;
> (b) the payment by the buyer is made to satisfy an obligation of the seller, in accordance with contractual obligations;
> (c) the goods cannot be sold to, or purchased by, the buyer without payment of the royalties or license fees to a licensor.

Each of these three alternative criteria prompts comment.

First, we should acknowledge that Commentary No. 3 of the EU Commission Compendium 2008, while the CCC was in effect, addressed "condition of sale" as well as the issue of apportionment.

It is interesting to note the EU practice under the CCC that payments of royalties or license fees where all of the parties (seller, buyer/licensee, licensor) were related were deemed to be paid as a condition of sale. This was the holding in *GE Healthcare* (paragraph 71):

> Having regard to the foregoing, the answer to the third question is that Article 32(1)(c) of the Customs Code and Article 160 of Regulation No 2454/93 must be interpreted as meaning that royalties or licence fees are a "condition of sale" of the goods being valued where, within a single group of undertakings, those royalties or licence fees are required to be paid by an undertaking related to both the seller and the buyer and were paid to that same undertaking.

The court had cited (paragraph 70) the Commission's position:

> In addition, paragraph 13 of Commentary No 3 (Customs Valuation Section) on the incidence of royalties and licence fees in customs value, drawn up by the Customs Code Committee, states that "when goods are purchased from one person and a royalty or licence fee is paid to another person, the payment may nevertheless be regarded as a condition of sale of the goods ... The seller, or a person related to him, may be regarded as requiring the buyer to make that payment when, for example, in a multinational group goods are bought from one member of the group and the royalty is required to be paid to another member of the same group. Likewise, the same would apply when the seller is a licensee of the recipient of the royalty and the latter controls the conditions of the sale."

That reasoning equates an RLF payment to a licensor who is related to the seller as having been made under a condition of sale imposed by the seller. That is itself remarkable.

Rather than a focus on the seller/buyer relationship, as embodied in the sale agreement, we find in *GE Healthcare* a focus on the seller OR the buyer. This gives equal status to an inquiry into the buyer's responsibilities and, to be clear, not to those responsibilities arising from its role as a buyer qua buyer. Instead, we see in the Implementing Act in Article 136.4 the door opening on a review of the buyer's responsibilities as a licensee arising from its agreement with a licensor:

Royalties and licence fees are considered to be paid as a condition of sale for the imported goods when any of the following conditions is met:

(a) the seller or a person related to the seller requires the buyer to make this payment;
(b) the payment by the buyer is made to satisfy an obligation of the seller, in accordance with contractual obligations;
(c) the goods cannot be sold to, or purchased by, the buyer without payment of the royalties or license fees to a licensor.

But here, we detect a widening of the text not authorized by the UCC.

First, the underlying text in the UCC Article 71.1(c) refers to payments made directly or indirectly. The text there says nothing about payments being required by a person related to the seller, nor for that matter, does the Valuation Agreement, Article 8.1(c), refer to conditions imposed by persons related to the seller. Here is where we see bootstrapping at work: If we transform a third-party licensor into a person related to the seller by virtue of a theory of licensor control over the seller, then we can use the expanded text in those regulations to meet the condition of sale criterion.[495] This approach was embedded in Commentary No 11 of the 2008 Compendium in the CCC, but there is no indication that it is not being applied *mutatis mutandis* under the UCC.[496]

495. The UCC IA text was not original, since Article 160 of the CCC IR was to the same effect.
496. As we have observed above, the EU Commission Compendium of Customs Valuation texts 2008 had contained Commentary No. 11, on the application of Article 32(1)(c) CCC in relation to royalties and licence fees paid to a third party. The 2022 edition of the Compendium deleted this Commentary.

You may recognize that all of this turns on the definition of a related person, and we return to this feature below.

In subsection (b), the imprecision may be deliberate. The "contractual obligations" is mysterious. This last subsection (c) is where still other mischief lurks. What is the distinction between these first and third standards? Can there be a situation where there is no requirement imposed on the buyer, as in subsection (a), and yet it would be a situation under which, notwithstanding that fact, the goods cannot be sold to or purchased by the buyer? This is far afield from the meaning of a "condition of sale" under the Agreement, the UCC and the previous Customs Code and its Regulations.

What is so difficult to comprehend about a condition of sale being imposed as a requirement by the seller of the imported goods? That is a straightforward concept, and it happens to be aligned with the actual text of the Valuation Agreement. We can only surmise that the present EU position on the "condition of sale" inquiry for RLFs appears firmly rooted in a "commercial circumstances" analysis, one that goes beyond a review of the applicable contract, which is the sales contract, and that would allow an expanded search for an "implicit" or "real world" condition of sale.

The Commission's revised (from September 2020) Customs Valuation Guidance on the UCC IA[497] charted a new course. In the context of third-party royalties, we find the following (at 3.7.2 and 3):

> 2. A third party may be the owner or licensor of the relevant rights. In such cases, the relevance (and therefore the application) of the "condition of sale" may not be directly applicable, because the commercial circumstances are outside of the circumstances that are governed by the "condition of sale" rule in the first place.
> 3. However, it is advisable to apply the same basic approach and that is what we set out in the UCC IA.

I am not sure how to parse that.

As for what should be decisive, the EU answer to the question "Does the sale agreement set forth payment of the RLF as a condition of sale?" suggests that we may find that the contract may not actually mean what it says it means. Instead, we found (at point 3.7.10) that the contract means what EU customs authorities think it means:

> Customs will examine all commercial contracts or reach conclusions on contractual intentions or obligations, where necessary.

497. European Commission, Guidance, Customs Valuation, Implementing Act, Articles 128 and 136 UCC IA, Article 347 UCC IA, Approved in the 8th CEG-VAL, 17 July 2020, TAXUD/ 2623395rev2/20, CEG-VAL/20/8/3.4, 17 September 2020. The EU advises: *These guidance documents are of an explanatory and illustrative nature. Customs legislation takes precedence over the content of these documents and should always be consulted. The authentic texts of the EU legal acts are those published in the Official Journal of the European Union. There may also be national instructions.* The 2020 Guidance was superseded by the EU Commission Compendium 2022 with many of its provisions adopted in that 2022 publication. This RLF advice was not among them.

That disjunctive device in the middle of that text tells us that the customs authority may either examine the commercial contracts themselves OR (possibly even to the point of not examining the contracts) reach its own conclusions regarding the intentions or obligations of the parties, as it deems necessary.

Even first-year law students recognize that this type of excursion violates the "Four Corners Rule"—that is, the meaning of a legal contract or other written instrument should be found within the textual content of the "four corners" of the document itself and not beyond its borders.[498]

And now we may turn to *Curtis Balkan*.

Curtis Balkan Judgment

The fact pattern presented in *Curtis Balkan* was different from *GE Healthcare*, where all the parties were related by means of ownership (CCC IR Article 143.1(d)) and the court held that:

> royalties or licence fees are a "condition of sale" of the goods being valued where, within a single group of undertakings, those royalties or licence fees are required to be paid by an undertaking related to both the seller and the buyer and were paid to that same undertaking.

In *Curtis Balkan*, the relationship turned on meeting the test of control under CCC IR Article 143.1(e)—one of them directly or indirectly controls the other.

It is frustrating not to have access to the importer briefs filed with the *Curtis Balkan* court, as it would be interesting to see what arguments were made and what arguments were overlooked. But we do have access to the interpretations advanced by the EU Commission.[499] We find that the Commission urged the court (paragraphs 55-56) to find that there could be an implied condition of sale if the buyer was unable to purchase the goods from the seller without paying the royalty to the licensee and the seller was not prepared to sell the goods to the buyer in those circumstances. The Commission cited its own Commentary 11 from the 2008 Compendium of Customs Valuation texts as the authority for that proposition. That Commentary was also cited (paragraph 58) for the notion of control establishing a relationship and we find there a recitation of licensor-imposed restrictions that is remarkably similar to the list that came to be included with the TCCV's Commentary 25.1 in 2011. That compilation does not arise to the level of management control that was cited by the TCCV in EN 4.1, and, in any event, the brand protection measures that supposedly denote "control" are quite commonly demanded by savvy rights holders. In any event, all of this proceeds from the alchemical notion that an RLF that is paid to a third-party licensor as a condition of a license is made into a dutiable RLF because the licensor and the seller are deemed to be related parties by virtue of standard licensing terms and the RLF is thus transmuted

498. To be sure, evidence can always be adduced to determine whether the parties' conduct conformed to the agreement or whether the parties ignored some or all of the agreement terms, rendering the agreement a "dead letter."
499. Written Observations of Commission in *Curtis Balkan* (6 June 2019).

into a condition of the sale of the imported goods. This is the backdrop to the statement in the Written Observations (in paragraph 59) that:

> The relationship between the buyer and the licensor is not essential for the determination of the customs value and Article 160 of Regulation (EEC) No 2454/93. The issue that seems to be important is the relationship between the seller and the licensor.

The rejoinder to that statement is that, while that text may flow from Article 160 of the CCC IR (now Article 136.4 of the UCC IA), the cited provision departs from the terms of the Agreement and is susceptible to challenge at the DSB of the WTO.

Additional Commission Views

Some further insight into the Commission's approach can be derived from a review of the 2020 Guidance even though this text was not included in the EU Commission Compendium 2022. In Case 1 of the practical examples of point 3.9 on condition of sale, for example, we find the following illustration, which is worthwhile to quote verbatim:

> Facts
>
> The license agreement obliges the licensee to conclude a manufacturing agreement with the manufacturer of the licensed products to deliver them exclusively to the licensee. The manufacturer is not related to the licensor in the meaning of Article 127 UCC IA. The license agreement requires the licensee to use a template for such manufacturing agreement or to instruct manufacturers of the licensed products to produce these goods only for the licensee and supply them only to him. In the cases in question the products are neither created nor developed by the licensor.
>
> The rationale of such approach may be to ensure that the licensed goods are only supplied to the licensee, so that he can benefit from the exclusive trade mark rights within a given territory. This protects, on the one hand, the trade mark and, on the other hand, it is ensured that the licensor receives the royalty or license fee from the licensee after the resale of the products.
>
> In some cases, the licensor does not explicitly indicate or influence the choice of the manufacturer. The manufacturer is therefore chosen by the licensee and signs the manufacturing agreement, which may contain the clause that the manufacturer only produces for the licensee. There are no further links or interdependencies between the license agreement and the sale contract.
>
> The question is whether in such cases the payments for the license fees are to be considered as made as a condition of sale, in the meaning of Article 136(4)(c) of UCC IA, and therefore included in the customs value of the imported goods.
>
> Analysis and conclusion
>
> In the cases described above, the seller is obliged by virtue of a manufacturing agreement to sell the goods only to licensees—*who in turn have to pay royalties or license fees to the licensor pursuant to the license agreement* (emphasis added).

As a consequence, therefore, the goods covered by the license agreement may be sold by the manufacturer/seller only to licensees designated by the licensor.

Moreover, the obligation to conclude a manufacturing agreement (or the obligation for the exclusive delivery to the licensees) is set up by the licensor, who is therefore guaranteed to receive RLFs for all the goods supplied by the manufacturer.

The licensee/buyer cannot purchase the goods in question without payment of the royalties or license fees to the licensor. It seems appropriate to conclude that, for the case described, the payment for the license fees/royalty is made as a condition of sale in accordance with Article 136 (4)(c) UCC IA and must therefore be included in the customs value in accordance with Article 71 of the Code.

Some comments:

(1) The obligation of the licensee to pay the RLF presumably is a function of the license agreement only—despite the text in bold suggesting otherwise—as there is nothing to suggest from the description of the manufacturing agreement that there is even a collateral reference there to the licensee's obligations let alone a direct reference to any such obligation.
(2) The seller's obligation under the manufacturing agreement would presumably refer to a sale only to the licensee as a potential buyer and not in its capacity as a licensee—in most cases, the licensee would not even be characterized or identified as such in a "manufacturing agreement."
(3) If the licensee/buyer does purchase the goods without payment of the RLF, the buyer will presumably be in breach of the license agreement but that would not prevent the sale to the buyer under the manufacturing agreement, which is the only proper focus of inquiry.
(4) There is nothing in the description of the manufacturing agreement, which we are told obligates the manufacturer to produce these goods only for the licensee and supply them only to him, which dictates that a nonpayment of the license fee will cut off sales to the buyer/licensee. The argument that "As a consequence, therefore, the goods covered by the license agreement may be sold by the manufacturer/seller only to licensees designated by the licensor" is not supported by the text. Of course, other contractual obligations assumed by the buyer and seller may require a different result.
(5) It would be interesting to see a discussion of a fact pattern where the buyer is the licensee and has been given the authority to sublicense production to a foreign manufacturer.
(6) If this case demonstrates a condition of sale, it would be interesting to get the Commission's view on a case where that RLF criterion is not met.

[vi] Whither Shall We Go?

The foregoing analysis points to the TCCV and the EU having taken positions that mark a widening gap between those recent positions and the Agreement and earlier instruments adopted by the TCCV and the judicial interpretations of the US and Canada.[500] It is also worthwhile to point to the gap between the UCC text (Article 32.1(c))—which is both congruent with the Agreement and should control customs

500. At the same time we should recall the discussion above on the novel interpretation of dutiable assists as including "intangible assets" which emerged in the *BMW* case.

valuation analyses and determinations within the EU—and the UCC IA and the Commission's administrative positions which deviate from the UCC text.

One would hope for an independent judicial review, with specific subject matter expertise, such as we find in the US or Canada, and one that does not pay undue deference to administrative interpretations.

On the subject of "condition of sale," we must be prepared to identify and then apply first principles. This requires a focus on the seller and whether there is a condition imposed by that seller on the RLF payment by the buyer, thereby relieving a cost burden that the seller would otherwise have had to shoulder. Here the TCCV and its Commentary 25.1 and Advisory Opinion 4.15 also come in for a candid and far-reaching review. They effectively overturned TCCV instruments that had been in place for decades, which would have significance under the Vienna Convention.[501]

We can benefit from a quotation from an early expression of the principles underlying the Article 8 adjustments by the Commission of the European Communities in 1977:

> In Article 7 [present Art. 8] we have laid down the various elements of cost which we would expect to see reflected in the invoice price and made a provision for their addition to the invoice price if they are not included. As I have already indicated, this provides a certain security against a situation where a buyer and seller may agree on an artificially low price for customs purposes but recover the additional amounts through some other kind of arrangement.[502]

Words to live by. The purpose of Article 8 was to thwart certain strategies to artificially lower the PAPP to the seller and thereby improperly lower the customs value. It is critical to return to this "sales price" focus and, by doing so, to ensure that the "condition of sale" test is limited to such schemes.

There is a divergence of views on RLFs, and there is no uniform interpretation on these vital questions, yet there is a need for a therapeutic intervention. Short of an entirely new Agreement—surely a most herculean task—what can be done?

There are some possible corrective steps. I believe the WTO's CCV, at its first session, adopted the same rules as well as the various instruments promulgated by the Tokyo Round Technical Committee. There is a pre-WTO precedent under the GATT for the Customs Valuation Committee at the WTO to send back instruments adopted by the TCCV on an after-the-fact basis for a further review by the TCCV. In essence, this would be a rejection of Commentary 25.1 and Advisory Opinion 4.15, which cannot be reconciled to the earlier instruments. In any event, views on RLF apportionment cannot be reconciled with the text of the Agreement and, assuming that there would be

501. Article 31.3 of the Convention cites: (a) any subsequent agreement between the parties regarding the interpretation of the treaty or the application of its provisions; (b) any subsequent practice in the application of the treaty which establishes the agreement of the parties regarding its interpretation; (c) any relevant rules of international law applicable in the relations between the parties. An argument could be made that the earlier TCCV instruments, having been accepted by the CVC, were in the nature of such subsequent agreements or practices under subsection (a) or (b).

502. GATT, Statement Made By The Commission of the European Communities at the Meeting of the Sub-group of 15 November 1977, MTN/NTM/W/126 (21 November 1977), in paragraph 17.

consensus, any adopted TCCV instrument that holds to the contrary would be suspect. Caveats? Any such action at the CCV would depend on one of the members at the CCV to raise and pursue the issue. Volunteers?

We should be mindful of the timing, as well—the delay in raising the objection to the 2011 and 2013 instruments would be an issue, but that should not prevent this remand to the TCCV. Alternatively, the CCV might consider issuing a Decision, as was done for interest charges (3.1) and carrier media-bearing software (4.1). Contemporary documents show that these were done in lieu of amending the Agreement. Of course, there is always the possibility that a complaint could be brought to the DSB at the WTO, and the issue of the proper treaty interpretation would be presented for resolution in that forum.

[c] Exclusivity Fees

There is one species of payment that might be considered as a RLF, even if it enters the discussion through the back door—and in disguise. That is a payment for an exclusivity right, as in a distributorship agreement. Distribution rights are normally established by written agreement between the parties and they may be either exclusive—the distributor has been granted the exclusive right to distribute the product in the territory—or nonexclusive, in which latter case the seller retains the right to distribute, or it has granted third parties the right to distribute as well.

A valid first reaction to such an inquiry is one of bewilderment, as in, "How does a payment for such a right qualify as one of the intellectual property rights which one normally assumes are the province of royalty and license fee payments?" The answer lies in the Interpretative Note 2 to paragraph 8.1(c) of the Valuation Agreement, which states (in paragraph 2) that:

> Payments made by the buyer for the right to distribute or resell the imported goods shall not be added to the price actually paid or payable for the imported goods if such payments are not a condition of the sale for export to the country of importation of the goods.

This precept allows the customs authorities to analyze exclusivity fees as an exotic species of royalty or license fee and/or, in the US, as a vehicle for the payment of subsequent proceeds to the seller as well. The proper approach to a review of such a fee would be to ascertain if the fee is for a separate property right. After all, such an exclusive right is worth something to the distributor—it eliminates competition and guarantees a monopoly in the market. If the agreement calls for the payment of the fees independent of import volumes, or even whether there are any imports at all, there should be no problem in attaining nondutiable status. The importer will have established the independent nature of the fee.[503] This would allow the importer to avoid the

503. That is the case in the US ruling no. H242894 (December 4, 2013) (exclusivity fee not dutiable).

fate of the importer in a 2000 CIT case[504] where the exclusivity fee was pegged at 5% of its retail sales of the imported goods.

In the EU, the 2020 ECJ decision on exclusivity fees in *5th AVENUE Products*[505] held that the fees were dutiable as a part of the PAPP. Regrettable contract drafting created weak facts—there was no hard and fast schism between the payments for the exclusivity right and the purchase price of the goods and no showing that the exclusivity fee was for a separate property right.

From the Judgment, we find that the arguments advanced by the importer (cited in paragraph 14) were weak:

> According to the applicant, first, the payment of that compensation is not of such importance that the seller would have refused to sell if that compensation had not been paid. That compensation was to be paid only in return for the exclusive right to distribute in Austria and only for the period corresponding to the first four years. Secondly, the exclusive distribution right goes beyond the right to dispose of the goods for resale and does not influence the value of the goods on importation. The sale of the goods would not be precluded by law if the exclusive distribution right had not been granted.

In paragraph 15, the court noted that there was no evidence that goods would continue to be sold without payment of royalty—this was fatal. The further court statement in paragraph 15 that the request for "territorial protection" did not start with the buyer elicits a demurrer—the definition of the applicable territory normally starts with either the seller or the buyer, and there may be negotiation on the extent of the territory and/or the duration of the contractual relationship. As far as exclusivity is concerned, that right may be sought by the seller, or by the buyer or by both and this point should be quite irrelevant. The only conceivable role as to which party had proposed exclusivity would be if the court or customs authority were trying to see if there was a benefit to the seller. That in itself would be quite irrelevant. As a commercial reality, an exclusivity right would ordinarily be a benefit to both parties; otherwise, the parties would not have agreed to it.[506]

In paragraph 29, the court observed the EU Commission's position on RLFs being limited to IP rights grants. That turning of a blind eye to the Interpretative Note triggered the court's pivot to a PAPP (Article 1) analysis in the immediately ensuing paragraphs in which the court felt constrained to explore whether the payment of the exclusivity fee was a condition of sale of the imported goods. That was an irrelevant task since the PAPP is defined as being a payment for the goods, as I have demonstrated at length.

---

504. *Tikal Distrib. Co. v. United States*, 24 CIT 149 (2000). With ruling no. H242894, it appears that CBP has moved to the possibility of there being an independent basis for such a fee. As a result, this 2000 decision might be distinguishable, and, thus, its continued vitality as a broad expression of CBP's position is open to question.

505. Case C-775/19, 5th *AVENUE Products Trading GmbH*, 19.11.2020, ECLI:EU:C:2020:948.

506. For more background, *see* TCCV, EN 4.1, Consideration of Relationship Under Article 15.5, Read in Conjunction with Article 15.4 (October 1985), especially paragraphs 5-8. You will recognize that the "sole distributor" of that instrument is the exclusive distributor of this discussion.

The Court set forth its interpretation (in paragraph 38) of the PAPP when it broadly stated that:

> a payment made by the buyer to the seller must be included in the transaction value of the goods concerned where that payment forms part of the "conditions of sale" of that product ... .

In summary, apart from the unsound findings of law on the question of the PAPP, exceedingly poor contract drafting failed to establish the independent status of the exclusivity fee and it was inextricably tied to the imported goods. I agree with the result—that exclusivity fee in *5th AVENUE* should have been dutiable, but as an addition to the PAPP because it is a species of RLF and not as an integral part of the PAPP, per Interpretative Note 2 to paragraph 8.1(c) of the Valuation Agreement, I would hope that this decision might be distinguished and limited to its facts. A proper agreement establishing an exclusivity fee as compensation for the grant of a separate property right to the distributor, one: (i) with compensation not based upon turnover or on levels of import purchases and (ii) where nonpayment would result solely in loss of exclusivity but that the sales will continue, as was the case in the cited 2013 US ruling, would/should achieve nondutiable status, even in this legal environment.

The subject of exclusivity fees has been a topic of much discussion at the TCCV, but, to this point, there has not been any consensus on the status of this species of payment. Consensus was reached in the May 2017 Session of the TCCV, however, on the status of a franchise fee paid by an importer.

[d] Franchise Fees

That 2017 consensus led to the issuance of an Advisory Opinion on the status of a fee paid by a franchisee.[507] The TCCV reviewed the franchise fee question through a royalty/license fee lens and was convinced that the payment was not related to the imported goods, none of which incorporated any of the franchisor's brands or other intellectual property, but was related to the use of the brands and the system of the franchisor in the manufacture and sale of products post-importation.

Fees paid by a franchisee are similar to a distributor's exclusivity fee. In fact, the term often applied to the ongoing business of a distributor of product in a given territory is that the business is its "franchise." Also, both the distributor and the franchisee would be the parties making the payments for rights associated with, indeed arising from, their operative agreements.

But we should be clear that in the typical franchise agreement the franchisor will be making available its full panoply of rights associated with the branded business. This will ordinarily include tradename and trademark rights, know-how and access to proprietary software and other business processes, as well as assistance of a more general nature such as being placed in connection with vendors and service providers

507. Consensus was reached at the 44th Session of the TCCV in May 2017 and AO 4.17, Royalties and License Fees Under Article 8.1 (c) of the Agreement, was formally adopted in July 2017.

across all manner of sectors. The franchisee will pay fees to the franchisor for access to these rights and for this support.

It is where the franchisee needs to buy various inputs that we may be entering into the customs valuation field. That is because the franchisee may need to be importing some of those inputs (e.g., buns or meat for hamburgers, flour for baked goods) and, further, the franchisee may need to purchase some of those imported inputs from the franchisor or from a party related to the franchisor. If that is the case, then we may confront the same issues that arise when the distributor pays for exclusivity. Specifically, the question becomes, do the franchise fees become part of the customs value of any imported product, such as the imported buns or meat or flour?

With Advisory Opinion 4.17, the TCCV concluded an instrument that determined that certain royalties paid by a franchisee were not dutiable. The franchisee purchased a number of ingredients for use in making baked goods and selling them from a franchised location. That location shared the typical presentation, i.e., licensed tradename and trademarks and trade dress, associated with the franchise.

The TCCV determined that the payments were not an integral part of the PAPP, a point not developed in the Opinion, nor were they dutiable as royalties or license fees. This latter point was the focus of the discussion and this conclusion was sustained for several reasons.

First and foremost, the payments were not related to the imported ingredients in any direct way but, instead, were for use of the brands and the systems that were central to the operation of the stores displaying the brands of the franchisor.

Second, many of the ingredients (e.g., flour, milk, butter, eggs) were commodity products that would be purchased locally in the country of importation and would not be imported by the franchisee.

Third, none of the imported ingredients bore any of the franchisor's trademarks or were produced with patents or any other form of intellectual property. Even though all of the ingredients were required to be sourced from the franchisor or from a third party authorized by the franchisor, that was not enough to overcome the first and third points. As an aside, this restriction on sourcing is quite typical as a brand protection requirement in order to ensure uniform quality in franchise agreements or in those instances where a license to manufacture a product bearing a licensed trademark has been conferred. The franchisor or the trademark licensor wants to ensure uniformity in the "look and feel" of products that are associated with the business, and the last development that will be tolerated is a franchisee or a licensee resorting to shoddy ingredients or materials that will deviate from quality standards. As another example of this attention to quality, contract manufacturers of garments are typically required to purchase all inputs, ranging from fabrics, fittings and accessories, hang tags, hangers, in fact all the way to specifically designated plastic bags and cardboard boxes, only from approved vendors.

The EU Commission has applied the lesson of AO 4.17 in the 2022 edition of its Compendium, where it dealt with the subject of franchise fees in two separate Commentaries. In Commentary 3, while dealing with know-how, the Commission advised that:

> Where ... know-how applies to the imported goods, any royalty or licence fee payment therefore will need to be considered for inclusion in the customs value. Some licence agreements however (for example in the area of "franchising") involve the supply of services such as the training of the licensee's staff in the manufacture of the licensed product or in the use of machinery/plant. Technical assistance in the areas of management, administration, marketing, accounting, etc. may also be involved. In such cases the royalty or licence fee payment for those services would not be eligible for inclusion in the customs value.[508]

[e] Other License Fees

The exclusivity and franchise fees hardly cover the field. There can be fees charged for the grant of potentially innumerable property rights, and it would be impossible to discuss the customs valuation status of all of them, especially because the result will depend on the specific facts presented.

Even so, we can look to three additional species of license fees.

[i] License Key Payment

The first is the license key payment which, as we saw earlier in a 2013 ruling from CBP, may not be a part of the PAPP in CBP's eyes.[509] CBP went further to analyze the status under the RLF rubric:

> If the payments are optional and not inextricably intertwined with the imported merchandise, or are paid solely for the exclusive right to manufacture and sell in a designated area, they do not constitute additions to the price actually paid or payable under 19 U.S.C. §1401a(b)(1)(D). *** In this case, Company A can always purchase the software alterable machines without paying the fees for a license key; therefore, these fees are not paid as a condition of sale for the imported goods. The purchase of the imported machines is not inextricably intertwined to the payment of license fees. Rather, the payment of license fees relates to the installation of additional software, not the sale of the imported software alterable machines.

We are still awaiting guidance from other authorities on these types of payments.

[ii] Community Development Premiums

Still another interesting issue with customs valuation implications arises in the case of fees paid to nongovernmental organizations (NGOs) or other organizations with a social agenda. The first ruling issued by CBP that touched on these issues dealt with

508. Commentary No. 3: Incidence of royalties and licence fees in the customs value, 31, paragraph 6. *See also* Commentary No. 11: Guidance on Articles 128 and 136 UCC IA, point 3.5 Existing Guidance, 71, paragraph 3.
509. Ruling no. H239671 (June 7, 2013).

fees paid for the right to affix the "Fair Trade" logo on imported merchandise. A similar issue would arise in the case of an "Organic" designation applied to food or beverages or, conceivably, to certain animal rights groups to display "dolphin safe" or similar slogans.

In the case of the "Fair Trade" logo, we learn from Wikipedia that there is a World Fair Trade Organization and, further, that:

> Fair Trade is a trading partnership, based on dialogue, transparency and respect, that seeks greater equity in international trade. It contributes to sustainable development by offering better trading conditions to, and securing the rights of, marginalized producers and workers—especially in the South.

Patagonia requested a binding ruling from CBP on the dutiable status of two separate payments: (1) certain community development premiums paid by Patagonia for the benefit of a Fair Trade account, controlled by factory workers who use the funds for socioeconomic development; as well as (2) a license fee paid by Patagonia to Fair Trade USA, an unrelated third-party licensor. In a well-crafted ruling that applied its typical *Hasbro* metrics,[510] CBP responded that:

> the community development premiums, paid by Patagonia are not part of the price actually paid or payable for the imported merchandise and should not be included in the transaction value of the imported merchandise as proceeds of subsequent resale under 19 U.S.C. §1401a(b)(1)(E). Additionally, we determine that the base license fee paid by Patagonia to Fair Trade USA, an unrelated third-party licensor, should not be included in the transaction value of the imported merchandise as royalties.

The community development fees were not part of the PAPP despite the fact that they were paid to the seller. Obviously, the fees were not interpreted as payments for the imported goods. The monies paid to the seller went directly to the Fair Trade Committee account, and the invoicing arrangement was followed only because the Fair Trade Committee was not registered as a charity and could not issue its own invoices. Likewise, the subsequent proceeds addition was inapplicable as the premiums paid had nothing to do with the subsequent resale or disposition of the imported goods. As for the status of the license fees, on the all-important third *Hasbro* question, there was no question but that the license fee was nondutiable, CBP remarking that:

> the answer to the third question is yes; Patagonia could still buy the product without paying the fee. In this case, Patagonia is free to opt out of the Fair Trade Certification program and cease the payments at any time. Doing so would result in the loss of the right to certify covered goods as Fair Trade Certified and to display the certification marks. However, Patagonia would still be able to purchase, and [the seller] would be obligated to sell, the sportswear in question, as agreed by the parties in their purchase and sale contract.

To sum up in general terms, for the US importer, royalty payments where the licensor and the seller are the same person, or where they are related, are most likely

510. Ruling no. H26285 (March 23, 2015).

dutiable. Where the licensor and the seller are unrelated and there is no linkage between the two, there is a chance that the royalty payments will be nondutiable. A prudent planner would want to closely examine the extensive body of rulings on the dutiability of royalty payments, or file his own ruling request, before proceeding.

[iii] Reproduction Rights

A distinction may be drawn between payments for the right to reproduce imported goods and royalty payments. The Valuation Agreement states that:

> The charges for the right to reproduce the imported goods in the country of importation shall not be added to the price actually paid or payable for the imported goods in determining the customs value.[511]

While valuable, the payments for such reproduction rights are nondutiable.

The US customs regulations limit the nondutiable right to reproduce only to the following four classes of merchandise:

- originals or copies of artistic or scientific works;
- originals or copies of models and industrial drawings;
- model machines and prototypes; and
- plant and animal species.[512]

Both Canada[513] and the EU[514] exclude, without limitation, charges for the right to reproduce imported goods from consideration as an adjustment to the PAPP.

As for the TCCV, there is one instrument concerned with reproduction rights. In 1994, the TCCV issued a Commentary that suggests that a wide meaning be attached to the exceptional status of reproduction rights.[515] The TCCV referred not only to a physical reproduction of the imported goods themselves but also to the right to reproduce an invention, creation, thought or idea incorporated in the imported goods. Examples provided of the latter rights included the etching of an imported schematic diagram onto circuit boards (seen as the reproducing an invention), the making of a reduced-size version of an imported sculpture by a museum (reproducing a creation) and the reproduction of an imported transparency of a cartoon character onto greeting cards (reproduced thought or idea). The TCCV concluded by suggesting that customs authorities should inquire whether there is a separate agreement conferring a right of reproduction and should review these matters on a case-by-case basis.

---

511. Interpretative Note to Article 8, Paragraph 1(c), point 1.
512. 19 CFR § 152.103(h).
513. Canada Customs Act, subparagraph 48(5)(a)(iv).
514. UCC, Article 72(d).
515. TCCV, Com. 19.1, Meaning of the Expression "Right to Reproduce the Imported Goods" Within the Meaning of the Interpretative Note to Article 8.1(c) (October 1994).

[5] *Proceeds of Subsequent Resale*

Aside from a possible application in the US under a Hasbro analysis to royalty payments which are not dutiable under Article 8.1(c),[516] this category of additions under Article 8.1(d) will normally arise from an agreement with a foreign seller in which the importing buyer has undertaken directly to make a further payment from its resales of the imported goods.[517] Payments under such a profit-sharing arrangement are dutiable.

If we keep in mind the notion that the buyer and seller could easily manipulate the sale price, as in "instead of paying me 100 currency units, pay me 95 currency units and you can then pay me a percentage of your profit on the resale," we see the purpose behind the adjustment.

The TCCV has wrestled with this issue for some time. While recent discussions suggest an attempt by some delegations to interpret this provision quite broadly, an earlier instrument that was adopted in 1983, Case Study 2.1, is actually quite conservative. The instrument illustrates a classic profit-sharing model (buyer remits 40% of the net profit realized on the resale of the imported product) and is replete with arithmetic calculations to arrive at the correct amount of net profit.[518] The direct connection of the payment to the post-importation resale should be a key consideration here.

Case Study 2.2[519] followed, and it effectively analyzed the various payments on the three hypothetical situations as proceeds. It left an ambiguity in Situation 2, however, as the importer agreed to pay 1% of its gross profit to Service Company A. The TCCV concluded that because Service Company A was related to the seller, it could be considered as an indirect payment to the seller. It then proceeded to note that the payment was for low interest loans to the importer and for other financial services provided by Service Company A. According to the TCCV, that meant that the payment could not fall within the ambit of Article 8.1(d) as a proceed of a subsequent sale. Certainly, that showing of the true purpose of the payment would have ruled out a participation in the PAPP, as well. This last point—a payment can be a part of the PAPP only if it is for the imported goods—has already been established.

In the US, CBP has been willing to accept TV as the basis for appraisement if imported goods were entered at a provisional price with an additional payment made to the seller if the resale were made within a reasonable time. Transaction value is not disqualified merely because the value of the subsequent proceeds is not quantifiable until sometime after importation.[520] A timely resale means that there will be "sufficient information" for CBP to make an appropriate adjustment. A long hiatus between

516. Sherman and Glashoff, nos. 423-425, at 155, opine that such a position is not appropriate, Article 8.1(c) being meant to cover payments for intangible rights, while Article 8.1(d) is meant to cover payments for the goods. Their discussion of the BDV origins of Article 8.1(d) is helpful. *Ibid.*, at 156.
517. Ruling no. 554999 (January 5, 1989).
518. TCCV, CS 2.1, Application of Article 8.1(d) of the Agreement (March 1983).
519. TCCV, CS 2.2, Treatment of Proceeds Under Article 8.1(d) (March 1985).
520. Ruling no. 542701 (April 28, 1982) (TAA 47).

importation and resale, however, will lead to a disqualification of transaction value on the grounds that CBP has insufficient information on which to make a transaction value appraisement.[521] You will recall that an inability to value the shared profit from the proceed is a disqualifying factor for TV appraisement.[522]

The practical case is that CBP is unwilling to withhold liquidation of entries indefinitely. As a practical solution, the US importer may be able to enter the imported goods under the reconciliation program,[523] which will allow the importer to hold the valuation of the goods open for up to twenty-one months after entry and to later "reconcile" with the price information once it has become available.

Apart from the Hasbro gambit by CBP, another significant application of the customs valuation law to subsequent proceeds was the 2009 Canadian administrative "D Memo," Customs Memorandum, D13-4-13, *Post-Importation Payments or Fees (Subsequent Proceeds)*, July 8, 2009.[524]

Proceeds of subsequent resale, which are dutiable additions to the price paid or payable constituting transaction value, must be distinguished from consignment sales which, as noted above, will preclude a transaction value appraisement. In this regard, one observation is that the customs authority or the importer should always consider whether post-importation payments to the seller or to a party related to the seller are amenable to dutiable status under two alternative analyses. First, the stronger case may be that the payment is a missing constituent of the PAPP itself, as in, "is this actually a disguised payment for the imported goods?"[525] The answer to that question will depend on the importer's relative ability to show that the payment is indeed for something else of value that has been received by the importer. If the importer cannot demonstrate that the payment is for a separate service which it has received, then I would submit that it is dutiable as a part of the PAPP except in the case where the payment can be linked directly to a subsequent resale, distribution or use. In such a latter case, it might be a subsequent proceed to be added to the PAPP in order to form the customs value.

This is the direct lesson of a 2002 ruling by CBP that held that technical service fees were dutiable under both statutory schemes.[526] In fact, in most cases, the customs authority and the importer should examine whether a payment is dutiable variously as an element of the PAPP, as a royalty or license fee, as an element of value for a dutiable assist[527] or as a subsequent proceed.[528]

---

521. Ruling no. 543281 (August 9, 1984).
522. Valuation Agreement, Article 1.1(c). Sherman and Glashoff, nos. 542-544 at 183-184.
523. First rolled out in 1998, information about the program is available at https://www.cbp.gov/trade/programs-administration/entry-summary/reconciliation.
524. *See* Part II at §10.9. This D Memo was reissued on March 31, 2015, with some revisions.
525. We find that Sherman and Glashoff, nos. 430-431 at 156-157, reached the same conclusion.
526. Ruling no. W548014 (September 13, 2002). *See also* ruling no. H242894 (December 4, 2013).
527. *See*, e.g., Case C-116/89, *BayWa AG v. Hautpzollamt Weiden*, 7 March 1991, ECLI:EU:C:1991:104. This is one of the relatively rare instances where the Advocate General Opinion was not followed.
528. *See* ruling no. H239671 (June 7, 2013) (fee paid to unlock application software was examined under all three possible categories; the fee was accorded nondutiable status even though the payment was to the seller of the software-alterable imported machine).

[J] Article 8.2 Costs Included in Customs Value: International Transportation, Insurance and Loading/Unloading Expenses

As has been discussed, the negotiations during the Tokyo Round failed to resolve the dilemma surrounding the status of these charges. The adoption of Article 8.2 resulted, with the effect of a split of authorized opinions, in some countries not including these charges in the customs value[529] and others—in fact the vast majority of countries—treating them as dutiable. For the larger subgroup, we might refer to these as "CIF countries" because that sales term embraces the price of the goods plus the insurance and the international freight. In those latter countries, if the PAPP does not include such charges—as would be the case in an EXW or an FOB sale—the charges will be treated as an additional adjustment.

The US, Australia and Canada are in the smaller group of countries where the costs of international freight and insurance charges are nondutiable charges (NDCs).[530] As such, transaction value under their valuation statutes equates to an FOB or similar appraisement,[531] so that if the parties have agreed to sales terms with a later passage of title, such as "C&F" or "delivered duty paid" ("DDP"), the affected costs are stripped out of the inclusive price and a dutiable value is established. It is noted that almost all other countries' customs laws provide for a CIF transaction value basis which had been the rule under the BDV. This is authorized by the Valuation Agreement, which left the treatment of international freight and insurance costs to the discretion of the Contracting Parties (now the Member States of the WTO) precisely because consensus could not be reached.[532] Note that the Valuation Agreement uniformly excludes post-importation transportation costs from dutiable value.[533]

From time to time, CBP has chosen to concentrate on amounts claimed to be nondutiable international freight and insurance charges. The position of CBP is that only actual costs rather than estimated costs can be reckoned in accounting for transportation and other NDCs. In an important distinction, the deduction applies to the amounts actually paid to the transportation or insurance provider rather than the amount paid by the importer for such services.[534] Consider the following circumstances: if an importer prepays for freight, i.e., has the foreign seller arrange for ocean

529. Most notably, Australia, Canada and the US. For them, these charges are nondutiable by statute. Mexico changed to a "CIF" approach when it first implemented the Agreement.
530. The US customs valuation law defines the PAPP as excluding "costs, charges, or expenses incurred for transportation, insurance and related services incident to the international shipment of the merchandise form the country of exportation to the place of importation in the United States." 19 USC § 1401a(b)(4)(A).
531. As discussed above, the term "FOB" is shorthand for "Free on Board" which is one of the international trade terms promulgated by the International Chamber of Commerce (Incoterms) in common use in international commerce. Note that, strictly speaking, the Incoterms do not dictate passage of title, as they do assumption of risk, but this is a little-known fact and most commerce is organized on the prevailing, but mistaken, assumption that title and risk are always shifted at one and the same time.
532. Valuation Agreement, Article 8, paragraph 2.
533. Valuation Agreement, Interpretative Notes, Note to Article 1.
534. *See*, e.g., ruling no. 546226 (March 25, 1996). At the international level, there is support for this position. TCCV, Com. 21.1, Cost of Transportation: Free-on-Board System of Valuation

freight and insurance for the importer's account, the seller might invoice the importer an amount reflecting the standard cost while negotiating for itself a reduced price. Thus, the importer might remit payment on an invoice for USD 100 to the seller for such services, while the seller pays USD 90 to the shipping company, getting a USD 10 volume discount or rebate from the shipping line or insurance company. CBP's view is that the importer is not entitled to a USD 100 exclusion, even though that is the amount the importer actually paid. In most instances, the importer might not even be aware of any discrepancy between the amount it paid and the amount actually remitted by the seller to the shipping line or insurance company. Nonetheless, CBP would still regard the USD 10 in this example as an additional amount accruing indirectly to the seller and, therefore, constituting an amount that should be added to the invoice price.[535]

In the past, CBP has chosen to focus enforcement activities related to transportation NDCs on imported steel shipments, a product sector where, at least historically, it has proven difficult for importers to identify actual costs of freight.

In the US, loading, unloading and handling charges will be accorded NDC status if they are seen as charges incidental to the international movement of the goods.[536] This treatment is discussed below as an exclusion from the PAPP.

Finally, in order to be nondutiable, any payments for insurance must be for costs incurred in connection with the physical movement of the goods, i.e., the cost of transport to the place of importation and such related charges as loading, unloading and handling charges.[537] Payments made for service before that international transport will not be accorded NDC status.[538]

Let us next turn to the EU, which is one of the CIF "countries" where, if the sales price does not include such costs, the adjustments to the customs value may include additions for the transport, insurance and associated loading and unloading costs incident to bringing the imported goods to the place where they are brought into the customs territory.[539]

In the EU, the question of what costs should be included within international transportation charges arose in litigation. At issue was whether the costs of transport

---

(October 1998), paragraph 3 (the actual costs would be those amounts ultimately paid to, for example, the international carrier or freight forwarder for the movement of the goods subject to the transaction). Of course, in those jurisdictions where dutiable value is set on a CIF platform, the costs under discussion would be dutiable and, thus, there would be as much incentive for their customs authorities to focus on a strict actual cost basis.

535. Note that this issue of the amount actually paid for ocean freight is of interest also to the Federal Maritime Commission ("FMC"), and CBP and the FMC have collaborated in developing information on payments which diverge from published tariffs for freight charges.

536. *See*, e.g., ruling no. 547146 (May 14, 1999) (terminal handling charges were incurred for loading and similar services incident to the international shipment of the merchandise. As such, they are excluded from the price actually paid or payable as costs incident to the international shipment of the merchandise).

537. *See* TCCV, Advisory Opinion 13.1, Scope of the Word "Insurance" Under Article 8.2 (c) of the Agreement (September 1983).

538. Ruling no. 543501 (May 2, 1985) (charges for storage and insurance paid to the seller before the international shipment commenced were not found to constitute costs for international shipment).

539. UCC, Article 71.1(e). Under the CCC, this provision was found in Article 32.1(e).

only comprised the charges paid to the transport provider or should also include a forwarding agent's supplemental fee in arranging for the transportation. The ECJ determined in *The Shirtmakers BV* that the forwarding agent's charges should also be included.[540] In another case, *Unifert Handels*,[541] the ECJ was tasked with determining the status of demurrage charges, i.e., if these charges should be included in the customs value as elements of the international transport charges. The ECJ concluded that demurrage charges fell within the category of dutiable transport charges.[542]

The UCC Implementing Act[543] takes into account the fact that the goods may be delivered to a buyer located in the interior of the EU customs territory. In that case, only the costs to bring the goods to the point of entry to the customs territory being dutiable, the dutiable transport costs shall be assessed in proportion to the distance to the place where the goods are brought into the customs territory of the Union in accordance with Article 137, unless evidence is produced to the customs authorities to show the costs that would have been incurred under a standard schedule of freight rates for the carriage of the goods to the place where goods are brought into the customs territory of the Union.

With the EU, there is an anomaly as it pertains to transport costs being provided by the buyer. In those cases, as well as those cases where the goods are provided at no charge to the buyer, the transport costs to be included in the customs value of the goods shall be calculated in accordance with the schedule of freight rates normally applied for the same modes of transport.[544]

The EU also has a special rule for calculating air transport costs, including air express transport costs.[545] These are based on a table organized by continents and third countries with departure airports assigned to zones within those countries. Thus, as an example, for Canada, 70% of the air transport costs for a flight from Montreal, which is within Zone A, to the EU would be counted toward customs valuation, while a flight from Vancouver, which is within Zone B, would see 78% of its air transport costs included within customs value in the EU.

On the subject of transport costs, in 2013, there was a disappointing failure to reach a consensus at the TCCV on a draft hypothetical case study. This resulted in the

540. Case C-ECJ 11 May 2017, *The Shirtmakers BV*, ECLI:EU:C:2017:362 (the supplement charged by the forwarding agent to The Shirtmakers corresponds to costs incurred by that agent in organizing the transport of goods to the customs territory of the European Union as well as its profit margin; that supplement must be regarded as being connected with the movement of those goods to the customs territory of the European Union. Those costs therefore constitute costs of transport for the purposes of Article 32(1)(e)(i) of the Customs Code). Note: CBP takes the same view, with the expected different result: freight forwarder fees should be considered to be an element of international transportation costs. Ruling no. 547074 (September 17, 1999).
541. Case C-11/89, *Unifert Handels GmbH v. Hauptzollamt Münster*, 6.6.1990, ECLI:EU:C:1990:237 (*Unifert Handels*).
542. The US follows the same approach but with a different impact on valuation—the demurrage charges falling within the category of nondutiable international freight charges. *See* ruling no. 546868 (August 19, 1998).
543. UCC IA, Article 138.1.
544. UCC IA, Article 138.3.
545. UCC IA, Article 138.2; Annex 23-01. The predecessor provision under the Implementing Regulation, 2454/93, for the Community Customs Code was Annex 25.

question of accounting for transport and insurance charges in a CIF-based jurisdiction being placed in the limbo of Part III of the WCO Compendium's Conspectus.

A recent European Court of Justice (ECJ) decision, *Lifosa*,[546] reintroduced the topic. As is typical of ECJ opinions, only a very brief glimpse of the facts is provided. We are told that the sales term for a 2016 purchase of sulfuric acid by a Lithuanian buyer, a fertilizer producer, from a Belarus vendor was the 2000 INCOTERM Delivered at Frontier (DAF).[547] Under a DAF sale, the costs of transporting the imported goods are borne by the producer up to the agreed place of delivery at the border.

The importer declared the invoice price for the goods as the customs value and paid that amount. So far, so good.

On audit, however, the Lithuanian customs authority discovered that the cost of the transport alone was greater than the declared DAF price of the goods, which would have included the cost of the transport plus the underlying cost of the goods. The customs authority sought to add the costs of the transport to the declared customs value, which was the goods' invoice price. The importer sought judicial review, and that review resulted in the matter being referred to the ECJ.

Here is where the lack of detail impairs our ability to fully assess the decision. We are told only that the total DAF price was less than the transport costs (Judgment, paragraphs 13, 18). The customs authority position (paragraph 19) was that if the adjustment to the transaction value was not allowed then the customs value would be missing an element of economic value and, it was implied, the goods would be undervalued. I agree with that logic in general, but would pare back the authority to account for a missing element of value and not to a broader writ to review "real economic value."

The importer maintained (paragraph 20) that the sale price reflected the real value of the goods because the producer was unable to process and store them and also because recycling them would be very costly and uneconomical. It follows that the price was still justified even though it did not cover all of its costs because the alternative to the sale would have carried greater costs in Belarus for the producer.

The ECJ framed the question as whether the actual costs of transport incurred by the producer (seller) should be added to the transaction value of the goods when, according to the delivery terms, the obligation to cover those costs lies with the producer, those costs exceed the price actually paid by the importer and the price corresponds to the "real economic value of the goods."

546. Case C-75/20, *"UAB Lifosa" v. Muitinės departamentas prie Lietuvos Respublikos finansų ministerijos*, 22.4.2021, ECLI:EU:C:2021:320. The following discussion is excerpted from my earlier article, Neville, "The ECJ Wrestles with Transport Charges … and Loses," 32 J. Int'l Tax'n (July 2021) at 32.

547. In 2010, the International Chamber of Commerce removed the term "delivered at frontier (DAF)" from their glossary. Effective 2011, Incoterms replaced delivery at frontier with the terms "delivered at terminal (DAT)" and "delivered at place (DAP)." These terms superseded DAF. Note that DAT was also replaced in the 2020 edition by the term "delivered at place unloaded (DPU)."

The notion that the customs authority can look past the PAPP to "the real economic value of the goods" should be troubling.[548] Apparently, the EU has embarked on these forays under an expansion of the judgment in *Stretinskis*, a 2016 ECJ decision.

The noteworthy point here is that *Stretinskis* was a related party case—in paragraph 23 observing:

> the customs value of imported goods is, in principle, to be made up of their transaction value, Article 29(1)(d) and (2) have the objective of ensuring that the customs value reflects the real economic value of imported goods and is not determined arbitrarily or fictitiously (see, to that effect, judgments in *Mitsui & Co. Deutschland*, C-256/07, EU:C:2009:167, paragraph 20, and *Christodoulou and Others*, C-116/12, EU:C:2013:825, paragraphs 39 and 40). To that end, customs authorities are entitled to examine the price indicated by the person making the declaration and to reject it if they consider that the latter has been influenced by the relationships which exist between the parties to the transaction (judgment in *Carboni e derivati*, C-263/06, EU:C:2008:128, paragraph 37).

Obviously, there is nothing objectionable to such a program in that related party context. But there should be some sound, demonstrable basis, the relationship of the parties or a missing element of value or some outward evidence of fraud, which justifies the customs authority having to search for the "real economic value" and not recognizing the declared price.

Beyond that point, in *Lifosa*, we had a DAF sale where it was revealed that the sale price did not include the full transport cost—indeed, the full transport cost was greater than the DAF price.

The ECJ applied a narrow reading of Article 138, paragraph 3 of the UCC IA, Implementing Act (EU) 2015/2447.[549]

In that reading, only if the transport is free of charge or is provided by the importer can the transport charge be calculated by the customs authority. For this purpose, the schedule of freight rates normally applied for the same modes of transport will be used.

This narrow grant of authority was cited in the Judgment in paragraphs 6 and 9 and later in paragraph 29 the ECJ concluded that "the transport costs [are] to be added to the transaction value [sic] of the imported goods only where transport is either free of charge or provided by the importer." The ECJ proceeded to conclude that neither of those factual predicates had been established (paragraph 31). After stating that "a different interpretation of those provisions"—presumably discarding the two conditions for the customs authority to calculate transport costs—the ECJ concluded (in paragraph 32) that such a calculation would lead to a double payment of transport costs. The ECJ warned that this would also establish a principle that, where imports are subject to conditions of sale providing for such costs to be included in the sale price of

548. Case C-430/14, *Valsts ieņēmumu dienests v. Artūrs Stretinskis*, 21.1.2016, ECLI:EU:C:2016:43, paragraphs 22ff.

549. Identical authority was conferred under the Community Customs Code regime by Article 164 (c) of Commission Regulation (EEC) No. 2454/93 of 2 July 1993.

those goods [such as a DAF or DAP sale], the transaction value should automatically be corrected.

The obvious rejoinder is that neither of those results would necessarily obtain. Further, having to pay increased duty and VAT on a previously missing portion of transport cost hardly qualifies as a double payment of the costs themselves. The rhetorical question "Would that same rationale apply to a payment of duty on a missing portion of a sale commission or a royalty?" shows the court's rationale to be on shaky ground.

We might record the *Lifosa* decision principle to be:

> In a DAF or another destination sale term, such as CIF, a declared PAPP which contains what is discovered to be only a partial amount of the transport cost, is not a candidate for a supplement to that PAPP to account for any missing transport cost … .

This is mystifying and fraught with the potential for fraud, in equal measures.

Hopefully, the ECJ will be called upon to revisit the issue in another case. International guidance for "CIF countries" is also wanting and we can only hope that the TCCV might consider another technical question.

[K] Exclusions from the Customs Value

[1] Post-importation Charges, Duty and Taxes

The customs valuation law provides that any cost or charge that is incurred for the following is nondutiable:

- the construction, erection, assembly, or maintenance of, or the technical assistance undertaken after importation on imported goods such as industrial plant, machinery or equipment;
- the cost of transport after importation;
- duties and taxes of the country of importation.[550]

The first two charges must be separately identified on the invoice and, in the US, are explicitly required to be reasonable.[551] As an example, a service agreement between the buyer and seller covered the four-phase development of production technology and methods to be employed in the assembly of automobiles in a foreign trade zone (FTZ). CBP reviewed the facts and concluded that the phase IV payments related only to post-importation activities and these were determined to be nondutiable.[552]

We have already seen that, in the US, charges for transportation incurred after importation will be as nondutiable as those transportation charges incurred for the

550. Valuation Agreement, Interpretative Notes, Note to Article 1, Price Actually Paid or Payable, point 3 3; 19 USC §§ 1401(a)(b)(3)(A)(i) and (ii); 19 CFR § 152.103; Canada Customs Act, paragraph 48(5)(b); UCC, Article 72.
551. Ruling no. 544693 (September 10, 1991).
552. Ruling no. 546697 (August 26, 1999).

international movement of the imported goods.[553] But it is important that the importer be able to provide detailed evidence of the charges to justify backing them out or deducting them from an inclusive payment. If sufficient evidence cannot be provided to CBP to make the adjustment, then CBP will not make any adjustment to the PAPP.[554]

It is also important to note that fees paid to arrange for post-importation transportation, while they may be related to transportation, may be dutiable. This was the lesson of a 1990 ruling, in which an importer had paid a handling charge to the subsidiary of the seller. The handling charge was for processing purchase orders, selecting a customs broker, arranging for the unloading of the vessel and delivery, preparing delivery instructions and processing insurance claims. All of these actions were related to post-importation transportation, but were not themselves transportation services. In fact, the handling fee was in recompense for the support services rendered and, because they were made to a party related to the seller, were dutiable.[555]

State sales taxes imposed as a result of post-importation services are deductible and nondutiable.[556] Some importers will want to take advantage of this opportunity to lower dutiable value by breaking out, or unbundling, the charges for these services. Otherwise, an all-inclusive invoice price, including an amount for these categories of potentially nondutiable costs, will be dutiable in its entirety. One *caveat* however: that foreign seller which would otherwise avoid tax nexus problems by merely selling merchandise to a US importer might cross the "trade or business" or bilateral tax treaty "permanent establishment" lines by breaking out charges for these services and separately providing such services in the US.

[2] Foreign Inland Freight on US Imports

As befits an appraisement on an FOB basis, ordinarily, dutiable value in the US will be comprised of the price of the goods plus the cost of moving the goods, normally via truck or rail but occasionally barge, to the foreign point of exportation, i.e., the airport or seaport. While their nondutiability is not grounded in the statute, the US customs regulations provide the authority and specify the conditions required for an exception: excluding the charges incurred for foreign inland freight from dutiable value.

The importer must show that either (i) the sale is an ex-factory sale or when it is not an EXW sale, (ii) those freight charges are separately identified and (iii) the parties use a through bill of lading.[557] The customs courts confirmed CBP's administrative strictures. To be nondutiable, the freight charges must be incurred *after* the subject merchandise has been sold for exportation to the US.[558] The CIT has gone on record as

553. Ruling no. 543267 (March 16, 1984).
554. Ruling no. 544501 (October 18, 1991).
555. Ruling no. 544332 (November 19, 1990).
556. Ruling no. 542451 (June 4, 1981) (TAA 27).
557. 19 CFR § 152.103(a)(5). *See also* TD 84-235 (November 29, 1984). *See* ruling no. H249096 (March 17, 2015).
558. *All Channel Products v. United States*, 16 CIT 169, 787 F. Supp. 1457, *aff'd* 982 F.2d 513 (Fed Cir. 1992). *See also* ruling no. H189076 (June 26, 2013).

permitting the deduction of foreign inland freight charges in a CIF or other non-ex-factory sale as incident to international shipment of the merchandise only in cases where the merchandise was placed with one freight forwarder or carrier for through shipment from the factory to the US documented by a through bill of lading (or other satisfactory documentation establishing through shipment).[559]

Moving the goods from the factory to the port for staging prior to sale will disqualify the exclusion. The obvious point here is that a little logistics planning can go a long way.

[3] Additional Exclusions from Price Paid or Payable

Still other costs that may be associated with the transaction are never a part of TV. These exclusions are often collectively referred to as nondutiable charges ("NDCs").

The first category embraces charges incidental to the international shipment of the imported merchandise.

[a] Incidental Charges on US Imports

In the US, the term PAPP is defined as:

> [T]he total payment (whether direct or indirect, and exclusive of any costs, charges, or expenses incurred for transportation, insurance, and related services incident to the international shipment of the merchandise from the country of exportation to the place of importation in the United States) made, or to be made, for imported merchandise by the buyer to, or for the benefit of, the seller.[560]

As a result, costs that are "incident to the international shipment" should not be included in the PAPP, with the result that they are not dutiable.

In "TD" 00-20, CBP reiterated its long-standing position that with regard to freight, insurance and other costs incident to international shipment, including foreign inland freight, the IOR must deduct the actual costs for these charges from the PAPP in determining transaction value, if these costs are included in the PAPP. The notice advised that CBP considers actual costs to constitute those amounts ultimately paid to the international carrier, freight forwarder, insurance company or other appropriate provider of such services.

CBP has issued perhaps a dozen or more rulings issued on the subject of the dutiable value status of "incidental charges" incurred in the country of export prior to shipment. These include ruling no. H237182 (April 16, 2013) in which the customs valuation law status of a wide variety of such charges was reviewed.[561] Headquarters

559. *Ibid.*, 16 CIT at 173, 787 F. Supp. at 1460.
560. 19 USC § 1401a(b)(4)(A).
561. Fee charged by the carrier's booking agent for booking services; bill of lading charge by the carrier for issuing the bill of lading; container freight station fee for receiving, unloading, storing and packing cargo into containers; foreign customs clearance fee; container yard monitoring fee; foreign inland freight costs in the country of export; fee charged by the carrier

attached significance to the fact that the freight forwarder's invoice to the seller itemized the various charges. CBP further concluded that the fact that the seller's invoice to the importer did not similarly itemize the charges was not a reason to disallow their deduction because the "FOB" sales term signifies that all costs associated with or relating to the goods until they are loaded on the vessel—necessarily including the charges in question—are included in the FOB sale price.

CBP allowed a deduction for those charges that were specifically named in the freight invoice to the vendor. CBP also noted that certain other charges might conceivably be deducted as well, providing that there was documentary proof that the charges had been paid by the seller. Here, Headquarters was following the lead of ruling no. H092560 (April 7, 2010), in which CBP had noted:

> Commercial documents to and from the service provider such as an invoice or written contract separately listing freight/insurance costs, a freight/insurance bill, a through bill of lading or proof of payment of the freight/insurance charges (i.e., letters of credit, checks, bank statements) are examples of some documents which typically serve as proof of such actual costs. Other types of evidence may be acceptable.

In other words, even though all of the costs for services might be charged in any given transaction, a deduction will be allowed only to the extent it can be shown that such charges were, in fact, charged by the freight forwarder or other service provider to the vendor and are therefore embedded or subsumed within the vendor's FOB sale price. We note that ruling no. H237182 also dealt with other issues, including foreign inland freight charges, whose status is discussed below.

By their nature, these charges are normally associated with the transportation of cargo. In fact, each of the five specified charges is of types which, among many others, CBP has assigned a nondutiable status when found to have been incident to international shipment and embedded within the invoice price:

(1) Terminal handling charge (e.g., ruling nos. H235776, April 16, 2013; H219516, July 30, 2012; H092560, April 7, 2010).
(2) Seal fee (e.g., ruling nos. H249096, March 17, 2015; H237182, April 16, 2013, and H219516, July 30, 2012).
(3) Booking fee (e.g., ruling nos. H249096, March 17, 2015, and H237182, April 16, 2013).
(4) Handling charges (for handling the cargo and processing the shipment or for the freight forwarder to process the shipment) (e.g., ruling no. H237182, April 16, 2013, and H092560, April 7, 2010).

---

for equipment management; fee for handling Less than Container Load ("LCL") cargo; port construction fee; port security charge; supply chain security fee; wharfage charge; 10 + 2 filing fee; terminal fee charged by the carrier for entering the terminal; handling charges by the freight forwarder to process the shipment; documentation fee for issuing the bill of lading and/or the Freight Cargo Receipt; container seal fee charged by the freight forwarder for issuing a container seal.

(5) Documentation charges (e.g., ruling nos. H237182, April 16, 2013, and H092560, April 7, 2010).

Following these rulings' authority, an importer into the US might declare an entered value on the basis of the deduction of these and other specified "incidental charges" from the FOB commercial invoice price, where there is satisfactory written documentation.

Quite apart from those charges declared by statute or the regulations to be NDCs, it is important to realize that transaction value will also *not* include certain amounts if separately stated.

[4] Interest Charges

The status of interest charges arising from a delayed payment is not directly treated in the Valuation Agreement or the US legislation, but CBP and the WTO's CCV filled the gap in coverage soon after that Agreement was promulgated in 1979.[562]

In the US, these first pronouncements came in a series of rulings issued in the period 1981-1983.[563] The rulings establish in broad terms that a separate payment for interest as part of an overall financing arrangement is nondutiable. These preceded the CCV decision in April, 1984 to ascribe nondutiable status to interest payments if certain conditions were met.[564] In Decision 3.1, TREATMENT OF INTEREST CHARGES IN

562. This discussion is derived from an earlier treatment in Neville, "Customs Valuation Status of Interest Charges," 31 J. Int'l Tax'n (April 2020) at 24. *See also* the earlier discussion at Neville, "Discounting your way to lower duties," 18 J. Int'l Tax'n (April 2007) at 16.

563. Three of these rulings are nos. 543023 (March 17, 1983), 542703 (August 25, 1982) and 542775 (June 11, 1981).

564. Decision 3.1 on interest charges on deferred payment was adopted by the CVC in April, 1984. GATT, Committee on Customs Valuation, Minutes of the Meeting Held on 26 April 1984, VAL/M/9 (13 July 1984), paragraph 38. The Decision is contained in document VAL/6, 4 May 1984. Interestingly, after an inability to reach consensus at the TCCV on the issue, the EEC had first proposed an amendment to the Agreement to deal with interest charges in May, 1982 (GATT, Committee on Customs Valuation, Possible Amendments to the Agreement, Treatment of Interest Charges in the Customs Value of Imported Goods, Proposal by the European Economic Community, VAL/W/8 (4 May 1982)). Almost simultaneously, the US had proposed an amendment to the Agreement to address the valuation of computer software, also to be added to the Interpretative Note to Article 1 on exclusions from the PAPP. GATT, Committee on Customs Valuation, Possible Amendments to the Agreement, Communication from the United States Concerning the Valuation of Computer Software, VAL/W/7 (23 April 1982). Status as CCV Decisions, and not amendments to the Agreement, was the alternative procedural route which was ultimately adopted. *See* discussions in GATT, Committee on Customs Valuation Treatment of Interest Charges in the Customs Value of Imported Goods, VAL/W/13 (26 October 1982); GATT, Committee on Customs Valuation, Valuation of Computer Software, VAL/W/14 (4 November 1982). Parenthetically, Decision 4.1 on computer software was adopted by the CCV in September 1984. GATT, Committee on Customs Valuation, Minutes of the Meeting Held on 24 September 1984, VAL/M/10 (5 November 1984), paragraph 7. The Decision is embodied in VAL/8. 10 October 1984. It is clear that assuming that a Decision would be universally accepted and that would lead to clarity and to uniformity of treatment (*see*, e.g., VAL/W/13 in paragraph 5) may have been a major miscalculation. At one point in the discussions, the GATT Secretariat had advised that there was little practical difference between an amendment to the Agreement itself and a Decision. GATT, Committee on Customs

THE CUSTOMS VALUE OF IMPORTED GOODS, the WTO body set forth the following three conditions for nondutiable status:

Charges for interest under a financing arrangement entered into by the buyer and relating to the purchase of the imported goods shall not be regarded as part of the Customs value provided that:

(1) the charges are distinguished from the PAPP,
(2) the financing arrangement was made in writing, and
(3) where required, the buyer can demonstrate that:
   - such goods are actually sold at the price declared as the PAPP; and
   - the claimed rate of interest does not exceed the level for such transactions prevailing in the country where and at the time when the financing was provided.

The status of the CCV Decision is not binding. Instead, we find only that "Each Party shall notify the Committee of the date from which it will apply the Decision." Indeed, there are some countries which have never applied the Decision.

Importantly, the WTO provided that its Decision should apply regardless whether the financing is provided by the seller, a bank or another natural or legal person.[565]

This Decision was adopted virtually word-for-word by the US with the CBP promulgation of TD 85-111 (July 17, 1985), with a required showing that the interest charges are "identified separately" from the PAPP. From that point forward, if the importer into the US can satisfy the criteria of TD 85-111, then the interest charge is eligible for nondutiable status. Eligibility can apply equally whether the financing can be part of an overall or general financing scheme or relate to the purchase of specific goods.

The US Court of Appeals for the Federal Circuit has ruled that interest paid on the imported goods is excludable from dutiable value if it is separately stated, paid pursuant to agreement and not excessive.[566] In this last regard, the interest rate must not exceed the prevailing interest rate in the country where the financing was provided.

Valuation Treatment of Interest for Deferred Payment: Valuation of Computer Software, Note by the Secretariat, VAL/W/16 (16 February 1983), paragraphs 8 ("Decisions in the GATT are normally taken by consensus and usually enter into force immediately for all Parties unless otherwise set out in the decision") and 9 (these governments [which accede to the Valuation Agreement after the Decisions have been adopted] would also be expected to abide by decisions previously taken by the Committee). In the event, the Decisions were not adopted on a binding-upon-all basis. There was and is no such uniformity, with WTO Members permanently split into two camps on each of these issues which persists to the present day. It is likely that, even at this very early stage in the life of the Valuation Agreement, these issues were intractable.

565. Currently available in the Compendium on Customs Valuation. Note that the TCCV has not published any later instruments that deal with the question of the dutiable status of interest payments.

566. *Luigi Bormioli v. United States*, 304 F.3d 1362 (Fed. Cir. 2002); T.D. 85-111; ruling nos. 548332 (October 31, 2003), 546030 (June 13, 1995) and 543765 (August 8, 1986).

Likewise, Canada recognizes the nondutiable status of interest charges, and administrative guidance is provided by the CBSA in a D Memo.[567] In contrast to the US and Canadian approach, the EU provides for the exclusion of interest charges in its customs valuation statute.[568] The ECJ issued the *Kyocera* decision[569] with a liberal interpretation on the manner in which excludable interest charges might be presented:

> payments of interest are distinguished from the price of the goods even if, at the time when the customs declaration is accepted, the customs authorities are in possession only of the invoice for the net price of the goods and neither that invoice nor the declaration of customs value reveal expressly or by implication that the buyer paid or must pay interest to the seller in the context of the import transaction in question.

[a] *In the US, Some Financing Arrangements Are Outside TD 85-111*

In spite of the seeming broad reach of the WTO Decision, which purports to govern all financing arrangements regardless of the lender (whether seller, a bank or another natural or legal person), there is a latent point of departure by CBP that lies in TD 85-111. A close reading reveals that the last WTO prescription, about the person providing the financing, is missing from TD 85-111.

Harkening back to an earlier policy position,[570] but without citing that precedent, there is a line of CBP rulings which have held that financing arrangements with parties other than the seller do not give rise to a TD 85-111 inquiry. Such payments for financing are presumptively nondutiable.

In a 2006 ruling,[571] CBP considered interest and finance service fees payable by the importer to its parent company pursuant to a "Financing Agreement." The service charge, assessed on a monthly basis for each month's activities, was the greater of USD 75 or 1% of the aggregate face amount of accounts receivable in which the parent company obtains a security interest. CBP determined that:

> It is the determination of this office that recourse to T.D. 85-111 is not warranted. Since ABC [buyer/importer] and XYZ [parent company] do not have the relationship of buyer and seller, and neither the interest payments or service fees will inure directly or indirectly to the benefit of the unrelated, foreign seller-manufactures [sic], a review of the guidance provided in T.D. 85-111 is not appropriate. The interest payments and finance service charges paid to a lender that is not also the seller should not be included in the price actually paid or payable to determine the transaction value of the relevant entries.

---

567. Customs Memorandum D13-3-13, *Customs Valuation: Interest Charges for Deferred Payment for Imported Goods*, January 7, 2014.
568. UCC, Article 72(c).
569. Case C-152/01, *Kyocera Electronics Europe GmbH v. Hauptzollamt Krefeld*, 20.11.2003, ECLI:EU:C:2003:623, paragraph 43.
570. In ruling no. 542775 (June 11, 1981) (TAA 31), CBP had held that interest payments to a party other than the seller or a party related to the seller and which did not accrue to the benefit of the seller were not dutiable.
571. Ruling no. W548547 (March 7, 2006).

CBP did not explicitly posit the payment-to-seller exception, but its implicit broad exception is discernible. One could argue, as this importer did, that only interest payments to the seller or to a party related to the seller, which have the potential of being part of the overall PAPP, raise dutiability questions. Payments to third parties cannot possibly be considered as part of the PAPP. This rationale was followed in a 2010 ruling[572] in which the buyer and the lender were related, with CBP determining:

> We agree with counsel's assertion that HRL W548547 is directly applicable to this case. Even though Company A and Company B are related, the companies do not have a relationship of buyer and seller. Pursuant to the Financing Agreement between these parties, the finance fees will not inure, directly or indirectly, to the benefit of the unrelated sellers/manufacturers. The manufacturers are not parties to the Financing Agreement. Additionally, neither Company A nor Company B are related to any of the manufacturers/sellers. Therefore, a review of the guidance provided in T.D. 85-111 is not necessary, and the finance fees, paid to a lender that is not also the seller, need not be included in the price actually paid or payable to determine the transaction value of the imported merchandise.

These two rulings establish that an importer might avoid a TD 85-111 inquiry altogether if the financing charge is being paid to a party that is not the seller nor related to the seller—even if that financing party were related to the buyer. As noted, these payments would be presumed to fall outside the PAPP. This is probably the correct result, although one could argue that CBP's policy did not go far enough and is still wrong since there is no authority to broadly hold that payments to a party related to the seller are inevitably part of the PAPP, despite CBP's long-held contrary view on this key point.[573]

To the extent that there is an inquiry under TD 85-111, however, the importer will need to establish that the amount paid is a bona fide interest payment.

[b] Bona Fide Interest Charges

CBP has taken the view that only bona fide interest payments will be accorded nondutiable status. This was expressed in a limiting clarification issued in 1989. On July 17, 1989, CBP published a Statement of Clarification regarding T.D. 85-111 (54 Fed Reg 29973)[574] in which it was stated that for the purposes of T.D. 85-111, the term "interest encompasses only bona fide interest charges, not simply the notion of interest arising out of delayed payment." CBP added that "bona fide interest charges are those

572. Ruling no. H099255 (May 24, 2010).
573. This somewhat strict construction of the PAPP was jettisoned by CBP along the way in favor of an expansive reading of what constitutes the PAPP and dutiable royalty payments. These two rulings stand in stark contrast to CBP's customs valuation interpretations as they evolved, at least until that administration was checked by the CIT decision in *Trimil S.A. v. United States*, 419 F. Supp. 3d 1307 (CIT 2019). A reading of that opinion, especially on the narrow notion of how the phrase "for the benefit of the seller" should be interpreted, will show that it is aligned with the spirit and holdings of these two rulings and will also show how far astray CBP had gone.
574. General Notice, 23 Cust. B. & Dec., No. 30 (July 26, 1989), cited at ruling no. H235895 (August 22, 2014).

payments that are carried on the importer's books as interest expenses in conformance with generally accepted accounting principles." This clarification became effective on October 16, 1989. This means that, to qualify for nondutiable status, the interest payments must be carried in the importer/buyer's books as interest payments in conformity with GAPP.[575] If the importer's own books do not list the payments as interest but rather as part of the CIF cost of the goods, the putative interest charges will be dutiable.[576]

As a practical matter, the US importer may be called upon to show that the goods were actually sold at the price declared as the PAPP, perhaps by showing that there had been an opportunity to buy the imported goods or identical or similar goods without a financing arrangement at a price that closely approximates the ex-financing charge price paid for the goods.[577] It is a certainty that an importer into the EU will be obligated to prove this point.[578]

An important final consideration is the rate of interest being paid. What if the rate of interest is excessive? Will that disqualify the entire payment? No. In TD 85-111 Customs announced that "... only that amount which is consistent shall be allowed as non-dutiable, the excess being disallowed."

[c] Written Evidence

The need for the financing arrangement to be in writing is interpreted rather narrowly by CBP. One might assume that a separate invoice line for an interest charge would be acceptable proof of a financing arrangement, especially if the interest rate was in line with Treasury Department acceptable limits. While such a separate line would satisfy the need to separately identify the financing charge, it would not suffice as evidence of the financing arrangement. The ordinary rule is that the importer would have to actually present the written financing agreement.[579] That has been the case for a number of years, but it was recently confirmed in CBP ruling no. H299343 (February 12, 2019). There, citing ruling no. H235895, CBP pointed out that:

> The commercial invoice lists the merchandise, model number, quantity, unit price, and the total price. There is a separate line showing an amount in dollars for the interest charge. As such, the vendor's invoice denotes a separate interest charge from the price actually paid or payable for the goods. However, the requirement that the financing agreement must be in writing has not been satisfied. The memo ... merely indicates that a sales contract would be made with [the buyer] for the sale of automotive batteries from the Republic of Korea ... .The letter further indicates that [the seller] would invoice [the buyer] on the product cost of the battery plus an interest charge, which is a surcharge for extending the payment terms to 120 days from shipment on board date. The memo states that the interest charge is a percentage of the product cost. As of the date of the memo, the rate

575. *See* ruling no. 544580 (March 1, 1991).
576. Ruling no. 546349 (August 23, 1996).
577. Ruling no. 544334 (June 27, 1989).
578. UCC, Article 72(c)(i).
579. Ruling no. 546056 (March 22, 1996), modified by ruling no. 546399 (March 20, 1997).

> would be 2.6% of the product cost and would be varied by the LIBOR. While the memo signed by [the seller] outlines the terms, conditions and rate of interest alleged to constitute the financing understanding, there is no written confirmation indicating that [the buyer] agreed to the proposed financing terms. Since we have not been provided a valid written financing agreement between the parties, we find that the interest charges should be included in the appraised value of the imported merchandise.

There is a certain degree of leniency that was introduced in 1997, and the importer may be able to prevail in the absence of a formal financing agreement. As is sometimes the case, especially where the parties are not proceeding with the benefit of advice of counsel, the buyer and seller may not have a written agreement, but they may have writings that constitute enough of a body of writings that would meet the "made in writing" evidentiary requirement. With ruling no. 546399 (March 20, 1997) CBP took the view that back-and-forth correspondence amounted to the needed "writing."

[d] Conduct of Parties

Now let us examine what happens if the parties have a written agreement, which would satisfy the need to show that financing arrangement was made in writing. Would that end the inquiry? Here we find the answer and, as is the case with so many inquiries by CBP, it is in the negative. CBP will look for a written buying agency agreement and will then inquire whether the parties have applied and followed the terms of their agreement. In like fashion, an importer may have a written import compliance program, and CBP will react by saying that is a good start, and then will explore whether the compliance program has been followed. Here, CBP will review the financing agreement and then will immediately inquire whether its terms have been followed. If the course of the parties' conduct has not followed those terms, then CBP will deny nondutiable status even if the interest payments actually made would have been nondutiable if they had been made pursuant to a written agreement. This was the conclusion reached in a 2015 ruling[580] in which CBP determined that the terms of a 1985 agreement calling for interest to be computed on a 120-day basis were not followed:

> [The importer] began to compute the interest on a 75 day basis, which is an average of the 60 and 90 day payment dates. Therefore, now the invoices include a charge of 75 days of interest, not 120 days. Our reading of the 1985 agreement shows that the agreement provides for an interest calculation on the basis of a 120-day term, and not the interest computations based on averages. In other words, the 120-day payment term is the point of reference to calculate the applicable interest. Accordingly, since [the importer] never provided documentation or evidence of any modification to their 1985 interest agreement to reflect the new terms, we agree with Regulatory Audit's determination that [the importer]

580. Ruling no. H259861 (January 28, 2015).

> failed to follow the terms of the written agreement. To find otherwise would not allow CBP to verify the proper interest to deduct from the price actually paid or payable. Therefore, we find that the interest payments made by [the importer] to its parent company pursuant to a written interest agreement are dutiable since these charges constitute a part of the price actually paid or payable for the imported merchandise.

Apparently, the parties changed their conduct along the way. As a strict matter of contract law, that new course of conduct could be recognized and given effect as an amendment to the contract, but CBP is looking for a writing. If we were to apply the holding of ruling no. 546399, with its measure of lenience, so long as there is some written evidence, an importer might profitably argue that correspondence memorializing the changed terms would suffice to constitute evidence of a written financing arrangement. Naturally, we would be happier if the amended terms were captured in a formal amendment to the underlying 1985 agreement, but we could argue in its absence that the requirement does not call for a formal agreement but for a writing, which could be in the form of correspondence.

[e] Practical Considerations

The ability to take advantage of the exemption created for interest payments does not mean that the parties will invariably want to do so. The first obvious point us that the exemption may not be available in the country of importation because that country has not adopted Decision 3.1. For another thing, there could be the matter of a withholding tax on the interest on a trade payable. If there is a tax treaty in place, however, that obstacle might be cleared and planning opportunities created for extended payment terms. As a third point, interest charges are associated with deferred payments—say, 90 or 120 days or longer. If the payment terms in the sales agreement call for payment within 30 or 60 days, then the ability to claim a separate interest payment is limited. For one thing, the interest paid for such a short-term delay will be relatively modest. Then there is the fact that many sellers are not in a position to offer products with an extended financing option. In fact, far from the seller offering financing, many undercapitalized vendors will seek payment in advance or will rely on the buyer furnishing dutiable assists or financing packages to the vendor.

Beyond these practical considerations, there are the ever-present transfer pricing (TP) considerations when the buyer and seller are related parties. The tax authority may look for an adjustment for an imputed interest on the trade payable if there is no interest imposed or if the rate used is deemed inappropriate.[581]

Still, if the facts and circumstances are right, the smart importer will want to explore whether to take advantage of this carve-out from dutiable status. Just

581. For example, when imputing an interest expense in the course of applying the Comparable Profits Method, the IRS suggests looking to the interest rate for short-term debt. IRS Regulations 1.482-5(e), Examples 5 and 6.

remember to "break out" the interest from the PAPP and get the agreement of buyer and seller in writing.

[5] Additional Excludable Charges

[a] Payments to a Third Party

Payments to a third party for services connected with the purchase, such as testing[582] or for providing bonds and safeguarding fabric and raw materials[583] which will not accrue to the benefit of the seller, may be nondutiable. This takes us back to the "to or for the benefit of the seller" criterion of the PAPP.

[b] Activities Undertaken by the Buyer on the Buyer's Own Account

The Interpretative Notes to Article 1 establish the principle of nondutiable status for payments for activities undertaken by the buyer in the buyer's own account. Unless there is an express adjustment to the PAPP dictated by Article 8—the statutory additions discussed at length above—such payments:

> are not to be considered to be an indirect payment to the seller, even though they might be regarded as of benefit to the seller. The costs of such activities *shall not*, therefore, be added to the price actually paid or payable in determining the customs value (emphasis added).[584]

That appears straightforward. A further gloss is added by paragraph 1(b) of the Interpretative Note to Article 1 which specifically discusses marketing expenses:

> if the buyer undertakes on the buyer's own account, even though by agreement with the seller, activities relating to the marketing of the imported goods, the value of these activities is not part of the customs value nor shall such activities result in the rejection of transaction value.

Again, the text is plain.

Nevertheless, some commentary is warranted.

First, current commercial practice is to more expansively refer to advertising, marketing and promotional activities—AMP. There would seem to be no valid reason to narrowly apply this nondutiable treatment only to the AMP subset of marketing expenses.

Second, even though the second clarifying excerpt specifically refers to both marketing activities and to a contractual arrangement between buyer and seller, there

582. Ruling nos. W564380 (June 9, 2006); 542946 (January 27, 1983).
583. Ruling no. 544423 (June 3, 1991).
584. Interpretative Note to Article 1, Price Actually Paid or Payable, paragraph 2. Cf. US customs regulations, 19 CFR § 152.103(a)(2). *See also* ruling nos. 544638 (July 1, 1991) and 544482 (August 30, 1990).

have been some musings that the key phrase "on the buyer's own account" is a limitation which would not cloak all such marketing expenditures of the buyer. Instead, in this telling, the phrase connotes only a payment that has been instigated by or has been made at the initiative of the buyer. That betrays a profound lack of knowledge of the legal meaning of the phrase at issue. The term "on his own account" or "for his own account" refers to a payment for which the buyer is ultimately responsible, one which is not being made on behalf of another and for which he cannot seek reimbursement from the seller. In the case where the payment is made by the buyer for the account of the seller, that payment would be made "on the seller's account."

Moreover, in light of the reference to the agreement of the parties, any placing of the burden on the buyer to show that, even though the parties agreed, the arrangement was at the initiation of the buyer is onerous in the extreme and is contrary to commercial practice. Seen in the light of the full discussion of the PAPP, with its focus upon the price agreed by the parties, any search for the initiating party would be unique and without precedent.

In the EU, there was an early ECJ review into the interpretation to be given to the phrase.[585] In the *van Houten* decision, the focus was not on the question which party initiated the payment for weighing charges for a delivery of cocoa beans. Instead, the issue was whether the buyer's payment might be seen as an indirect payment to the seller because it was an activity carried out by the buyer "to satisfy an obligation of the seller" within the meaning of that provision. The court rejected that unless the contract at issue provides for such an obligation. Prompted by the preceding sentence, a further comment is in order. The judgment recites that the Commission had taken the position that trade practice had been displaced under the then-relatively new customs valuation scheme. But that overlooks the continuing role of trade practice that might be embedded in the agreement of the parties or be applicable through a course of dealing. It overlooks, too, the assignment of obligations on the parties by the INCOTERMS or other sales terms.

While there is a 1990 TCCV instrument on this topic generally,[586] it does not address this narrower question of the meaning of "on the buyer's own account." I would suggest that might be a candidate for a separate instrument.

585. Case No C-65/85, Hauptzollamt [Principal Customs Office] Hamburg-Ericus vs. Van Houten International GmbH, 2.4.1986, ECLI:EU:C:1986:53.

586. TCCV, Com. 16.1, Activities Undertaken by the Buyer on His Own Account After Purchase of the Goods But Before Importation (October 1990). Note that the above-cited Interpretative Notes place no restriction on the timing of the buyer's payments for marketing efforts. In regard to the timing of installation, erection, etc., it is true that such costs are referred to as being post-importation. In the earlier TCCV Com. 9.1, Treatment of Costs of Activities Taking Place in the Country of Importation (October 1984), paragraph 6, the TCCV opined that the phrase "undertaken after importation" in Interpretative Note to Article 1, Price Actually Paid or Payable, in point 3(a), should be interpreted flexibly to refer to activity taking place in the country of importation even if it took place prior to importation.

[c] Cancellation Payments

Cancellation payments, as in a contract termination fee, have been held to be nondutiable in the US.[587] As cited in a 1988 ruling,[588] CBP's determination in a 1987 ruling is instructive:

> In Headquarters Ruling No. 543943 dated December 8, 1987, an importer agreed to reimburse a foreign seller for lost sales and profits due to a cancellation of a six month purchase requirement in the original contract. Subsequent to the payment of the termination fee, the importer neither purchased nor imported the product from the manufacturer in question. In that case, we ruled that the "price actually paid or payable" for merchandise imported prior to the payment of the termination fee does not include the amount representing the termination fee. If charges are incurred for termination of a contract, and merchandise is not imported to the US as a result of the terminated contract, then payments made to the seller are not to be included in the "price actually paid or payable."

Delay payments in the nature of liquidated damages have also been held nondutiable.[589] But, as with almost all aspects of customs valuation law, the question of the dutiability of cancellation fees can only be answered on the basis of the operative facts. Thus, a minimum quantity cancellation charge may be regarded as a dutiable indirect payment to the seller.[590]

If transaction value should not be available as a basis for appraisement, the valuation law prescribes the transaction value of "identical merchandise" or "similar merchandise."

[d] Certain Warranty Charges

The general rule is that charges for warranty are dutiable. That is the lesson of several rulings in the US. In ruling no. 545153 (December 21, 1993), the payment for an extended warranty was considered dutiable as a part of the PAPP for the imported merchandise. There, CBP noted that the warranty costs attach to, and are an integral part of, the merchandise upon its importation. CBP observed that it follows that the consideration paid for the merchandise, i.e., the PAPP, must include all charges paid for any warranty which is a guarantee that the merchandise will be free from defects. Because the involved warranty under consideration there attached to and was an integral part of the imported merchandise, CBP determined that the payment made for the warranty was part of the consideration paid for the merchandise. Because the commercial invoice attached to the entry summary indicated that the warranty payment was included in the total price for the protested merchandise, the warranty

587. Ruling no. 544121 (June 24, 1988). *But see* ruling no. 544516 (January 9, 1991) (payment dutiable because importer failed to provide satisfactory proof of nature of payment), *aff'd* ruling no. 544689 (September 26, 1991).
588. Ruling no. 544031 (January 19, 1988). *See also* ruling no. 544615 (September 11, 1991) and earlier rulings cited therein.
589. Ruling no. 543812 (April 20, 1987).
590. Ruling nos. 544340 (September 11, 1990) and 543445 (October 23, 1985).

costs in question formed an integral part of the merchandise upon importation. CBP held that the cost of the warranty was part of the PAPP and was dutiable under transaction value. This inclusion of a cost element for the warranty coverage made the decision an easy one for CBP, whose doctrine is that no unbundling of a PAPP will be allowed. We shall see if the same result would obtain where the amount for warranty coverage was not subsumed within a PAPP.

In a pair of 2002 rulings,[591] CBP dealt with the issue of warranty support payments in imports from Japan. These were separately itemized charges, and the importer sought to lower the customs value to reflect refunds made by the seller. The recitation of facts stated that:

> the commercial invoice for each imported product will show a deduction in price for the applicable warranty support payment. Thus, if the invoice price of a piano is $1000 and if the specified percentage for warranty support for pianos is 10%, the invoice price would reflect a $100 deduction and would be shown as $900. However, the price paid to Yamaha Japan would still be $1000. The $100 warranty support amount would be paid by Yamaha Japan to Yamaha America after importation in accordance with Section 4 of the Agreement.

CBP rejected the argument that the warranty payments by the seller should lower the PAPP. CBP viewed the payments made after importation as rebates made or otherwise effected between the buyer and seller after the date of importation of the merchandise, and thus should be disregarded. Likewise, CBP rejected the claim that the parties had agreed to a formula for determining the price which was established prior to importation. CBP's analysis of the sales agreement showed that there was nothing which established a formula for determining the price of the products based on warranty support rebates. CBP also noted that, although over the years there had been various price changes, none reflected a reduction to the price based on warranty support payments.

The heading "warranty costs" might refer to the costs associated with repairs to defective merchandise. In a 1990 ruling,[592] CBP held that such costs would not lower the customs value:

> The importer sells the merchandise to U.S. consumers and guarantees the quality of the merchandise by means of a warranty which lasts for a period ranging from ninety days to one year from the date of purchase. The warranty covers latent defects in material and workmanship under normal conditions. Initial returns of latently defective merchandise are repaired by the importer and resold as second quality merchandise at a discounted price. The importer also contracts with unrelated service centers to repair latently defective merchandise in use. These service centers invoice the importer for the total cost of repair, including parts and labor. The importer maintains records showing the amount of repair costs incurred and the losses on resale of second quality merchandise.

591. Ruling no. 548184 (November 5, 2002) aff'g ruling no. 548093 (April 26, 2002).
592. Ruling no. 544394 (October 9, 1990).

CBP rejected the importer's novel argument that the warranty costs are in the nature of post-importation maintenance costs, which would be excluded from transaction value under the US analogue to the Agreement at the Interpretative Note to Article 1, PAPP, paragraph 3 (a). CBP noted that there is no statutory authority to make adjustments to transaction value for post-importation repairs for latent production defects.

A different result was reached in 2012,[593] where CBP allowed for the deductions of a warranty discount and a competitive discount which had been agreed prior to the shipment of the goods. Headquarters also found that the discounts were unconditional to be important factors:

> we find that both warranty and competitive discounts are unconditional because there are no specified purchasing obligations placed on the importer in order to receive these discounts. The competitive discount is provided to the importer so that the importer can keep old customers and encourage new customers. The warranty discount, agreed to by the parties prior to the importation, is provided in case there are defective products for which [the seller] would credit its customers. The warranty discount is a fixed percentage, and the importer receives it regardless of whether it has actual defective merchandise or not.

In a 2014 ruling,[594] CBP again reached the conclusion that a separate warranty charge was nondutiable. CBP noted that:

> the documents presented indicate that there were two separate transactions, one involving the sale of the imported gear boxes and a second subsequent separate transaction involving the purchase of an extended warranty. The purchase order for the merchandise indicates that following an order on September 29, 2011, from a U.S. customer, VTI entered into an agreement to purchase the imported gear boxes on November 11, 2011 from Voith Turbo in Germany. The CBP Form (CF) 7501 indicates that the entry for the imported merchandise was made on January 2, 2012. In a second transaction, VTI issued a purchase order for an extended warranty from Voith Turbo, the seller of the gear boxes on June 18, 2012. Hence, the extended warranty was purchased from the seller after the merchandise had already been imported into the U.S. and delivered to VTI's customer. Therefore, we find that the payment for the extended warranty was not part of the price actually paid or payable for the imported merchandise, and would not be dutiable.

In other words, CBP concluded that, on those facts, the payment for the warranty was for something else—it was not for the imported goods.

The TCCV has issued two instruments on warranty charges,[595] and I believe that they are both unsound as presently configured and ripe for modification, either at the instigation of the CCV or on its own initiative.

In Case Study 6.1, the TCCV considered two payments for insurance against warranty costs for two years which were made a condition of sale by the seller of

---

593. Ruling no. H218255 (June 7, 2012). Strictly speaking, this ruling might be studied as an example of allowable, i.e., nondutiable, discounts.
594. Ruling no. H253493 (September 4, 2014).
595. TCCV, CS 6.1, Insurance Premiums for Warranty (October 1990), TCCV, Com. 20.1, Warranty Charges (October 1998).

automobiles. The first-year costs (presumably the insurance premium) were included within the price. I would agree that there is no authority to unbundle those first-year costs from the PAPP. It is noteworthy that the claims and compensation during the first year are settled directly between the manufacturer and the importer/buyer. Note that the text is imprecise and does not inform us whether the manufacturer is the seller. That imprecision on these important facts alone is grounds for a modification.

The premium for the second-year coverage is separately calculated on a per-car basis and is billed separately by the seller to the buyer after shipment. We are told only that the seller negotiates a contract with an insurance company—we do not know if the seller is a party to that contract; thus, we do not know if the seller is directly obligated by contract to the insurance company to pay the premium or if the party that is obligated to pay the premium is the buyer. As for the second-year costs, any claims or compensation are settled directly between the insurance company and the buyer, the insurance company having received the premium from the seller. Because the facts are imprecise, we do not know if the payment by the seller is in order to discharge the buyer's obligation or the seller's obligation.

I see the premium for the second-year coverage, which is separately calculated and separately charged and presumably separately paid, as possibly nondutiable. That is because, as we have seen, the fact that the payment is a condition of sale is not dispositive. Nor would the fact that the payment was related to the imported goods be dispositive. Even if the payment is to the seller or for the benefit of the seller, it must still be shown to be for the imported goods. Here, the warranty costs would not be dutiable if they were for something else—a warranty coverage of an independent nature—and were not to be properly included within the consideration for the imported cars.

In Commentary 20.1, the TCCV saw all payments to the seller for warranty charges that are imposed by the seller, even if invoiced separately, as dutiable (paragraph 7). The TCCV then drew a distinction (in paragraph 8) between payments to a third party for warranty cover that are required by the seller (dutiable) and payments incurred by the buyer where the buyer decides to bear the cost of warranty on his own account (nondutiable) (paragraph 9).

Here, too, it would be helpful to modify the text. The warranty charges are either dutiable or not, depending on whether the charges are deemed to be part of the PAPP. That depends on whether they payments are for the imported goods, i.e., whether they are to be considered part of the consideration for the goods.

The recital of facts in this Commentary is overly simplistic and liable to be misinterpreted. For example, the seller may have signed an agreement with a third-party insurance provider who will make available to buyers insurance coverage for an optional extended warranty plan. The buyer is free to take advantage of that availability by signing up with the insurance carrier or not, at its discretion. If the buyer opts to take advantage of that opportunity, and pays the insurance provider, we can imagine that some would apply the text from paragraph 8:

> If the seller contracts with a third party to transfer warranty risk to a third party it may appear that the transaction has been split. That the seller has entered into a

> contract with the third party indicates that any warranty risk undertaken by the third party is at the behest of the seller and therefore to his benefit. The price actually paid or payable is defined in the Note to Article 1 as the total payment made or to be made by the buyer to or for the benefit of the seller for the imported goods.

That text is an oversimplification which misses the nuances of the real commercial world in which transactions occur. If strictly applied, it would lead to an erroneous conclusion that payments for an optional warranty plan form part of the PAPP solely because of the seller's involvement. Cf. ruling no. H253493 (September 4, 2014).

CHAPTER 4

Methods Based on Comparable Sales

§4.01 TRANSACTION VALUE OF IDENTICAL OR SIMILAR MERCHANDISE (ARTICLES 2 AND 3)

Not surprisingly, the definitions of TV of identical or similar merchandise at the international level are provided for in the Valuation Agreement in terms which are mirrored in the domestic statutes in the US and in the other WTO Members.[1] The customs law definition of identical merchandise is that which is identical in all respects to the merchandise being appraised and produced in the same country and ideally by the same person.[2] Similar merchandise is defined as being like that merchandise in characteristics and component material and is commercially interchangeable and is ideally, but not necessarily, produced by the same person.[3]

[A] Time Factor

To be clear, the transaction value of the identical or similar merchandise must have been previously accepted by the customs authority.[4] That precludes the importer from organizing an after-the-fact entry for comparison.

There is a further potential chronological barrier in place, as the comparable sales transaction must be based on identical or similar merchandise which was exported "at or about the same time" that the subject entry was exported. In Canada, the goods in the comparison sale must have been exported "at the same or substantially the same

1. Valuation Agreement, Articles 2 and 3, 15.2.
2. 19 USC § 1401a(h)(2); Canada Customs Act, section 49; UCC IA, Article 141.
3. 19 USC § 1401a(h)(4); Canada Customs Act, section 50; UCC IA, Article 141.
4. Valuation Agreement, Interpretative Note to Article 2, point 4. *See also* TCCV, Comm. 10.1, Adjustments for Differences in Commercial Level and in Quantity Under Article 1.2 (B) and in Articles 2 and 3 of the Agreement (October 1984) in paragraph 4. The US practice is in accord. *See* ruling no. 543628 (November 4, 1985).

time."[5] The US and the EU follow the Valuation Agreement text, and the exports must be "at or about the same time." Note the focus is on dates of export, *not* dates of import or dates of sale.

This is obviously a loosely woven text, and the CIT has approved CBP's interpretation in a case of imported fresh produce (asparagus) that the "about the same time" element was a period extending from one week before to one week after the entry.[6] The CIT was impressed by the specialized experience of CBP officials in valuing merchandise, the thoroughness of CBP's reasoning, the rank of the official who issued the ruling letter and CBP's serious consideration of the importer's position. All of that notwithstanding, it is the considered opinion of many customs and trade professionals that CBP expertise often pales in contrast with that of veterans from the business community.

That commentary on the degree of commercial expertise of the customs officers leads us to observe that, as we have shown, the Valuation Agreement and its interpretations by the TCCV have placed great and continuing emphasis on commercial practices. That recurring theme is specifically invoked by the TCCV in a very early instrument which addressed these time elements:

> "at or about the same time" should be taken to cover a period of time, as close to the date of exportation as possible, within which the commercial practices and market conditions which affect prices remain the same. In the final analysis, the question must be decided on a case by case basis within the overall context of the application of Articles 2 and 3.[7]

The same instrument reminds us that the time elements cannot override the strict hierarchical course. Thus, an export in a sale of similar goods whose date of export is closer to that of the goods being appraised cannot be chosen over a comparison sale of identical goods.[8]

[B] Differences Between the Identical and Similar Goods Standards

A further gloss is available through a TCCV instrument[9] which succinctly draws the distinction between the two standards:

Identical goods—these are the same in all respects, including:

- Physical characteristics.
- Quality.

---

5. CBSA interprets this phrase: "Generally, the expression 'at the same or substantially the same time' will be taken to mean a period extending 30 days prior to and 30 days following the exportation of the goods being appraised," but if the market or manufacturing conditions dictate, longer or shorter time periods may be used. Customs Memorandum D13-5-1, *Application of Sections 49 and 50 of the Customs Act*, paragraphs 5 and 6, February 25, 2014.
6. *Four Seasons Produce v. United States*, 24 ITRD 1022 (CIT 2001).
7. TCCV, EN 1.1, Time Element in Relation to Articles 1, 2 and 3 of the Agreement, paragraph 12 (October 1981).
8. *Ibid.*, in paragraph 13.
9. TCCV, Com. 1.1, Identical or Similar Goods for the Purpose of the Agreement (March 1982).

- Reputation.

Minor differences in appearance do not preclude otherwise conforming goods from being classed as identical.

Similar merchandise—although not alike in all respects, present:

- Like characteristics. and
- Like components.

These traits enable them to perform the same function and be commercially interchangeable.

When determining whether goods are similar, consideration is to be given, among other factors, to the quality of the goods, their reputation and the existence of a trademark.[10]

The presence of a trademark plays an important role in such an inquiry. If only one product bears a trademark, and that trademark is well recognized in the market, it is unlikely that the two goods will be similar. If both of the goods bear trademarks, the goods can be similar if the trademarks are of equal strength in the marketplace.[11] It is more likely, however, that products bearing different trademarks will command different prices in the marketplace and will not be qualified as similar. To be clear, the presence of a trademark on an otherwise identical product will preclude standing as an identical product.

The definitional section of the Valuation Agreement, Article 15, notes that the goods must be from the same country and, preferably, by the same person as the producer of the goods under review.[12]

One disqualifying factor is that the goods in the comparison sale cannot have been produced with the benefit of any of the services that are described in subsection (b)(iv)—engineering, design work, etc.—which were performed in the country of importation and which are thus exempt from dutiable assist status.

[C] Lowest Price

If there is identical or similar merchandise being entered at two or more prices, importers "get a break" as the customs authority must apply the lowest price.[13] Note

10. The ECJ engaged in a detailed explanation of the various factors to be considered in a "similar merchandise" inquiry. Case C-1/18, *Oribalt Rīga SIA v. Valsts ieņēmumu dienests*, 20.6.2019, ECLI:EU:C:2019:519 (*Oribalt Riga*) (its mistaken reference to the method employed under Article 30.2(b) of the CCC as the deductive method, *see* paragraphs 20 and 29, is disconcerting).
11. In Com. 1, Example No. 5 showed that the similar products, despite bearing different trademarks, were made to the same standard, are of the same quality, enjoy equivalent reputations and are used by the same users in the country of importation.
12. Valuation Agreement, Articles 15.4.2(d) and (e).
13. Valuation Agreement, Article 2, paragraph 3 and Article 3, paragraph 3; 19 USC § 1401a(c)(2); 19 CFR § 152.104(d); *see* ruling nos. 545755 (May 18, 1995) and 545638 (February 13, 1995); Canada Customs Act, subsections 49(5) and 50(5); UCC IA, Article 141.3.

also that suitable adjustments must be made so as to account for any differences in commercial level of sales or quantities of sale.[14]

[D] Transport Costs

One distinction among the US, Canada and the EU legal provisions is that the US does not also allow for adjustments based on differences in significant differences between the costs and expenses that are based on differences in distances and modes of transport.[15] The authority for an adjustment for transport charges is in Article 1.2 (b) and in Articles 2.2 and 3.2, which state that:

> Where the costs and charges referred to in paragraph 2 of Article 8 (transport, insurance and related charges) are included in the transaction value, an adjustment shall be made to take account of significant differences in such costs and charges between the imported goods and the identical [or similar] goods in question arising from differences in distances and modes or transport.

The need to account for transport cost differences is most obvious in CIF countries but, as Sherman and Glashoff observed, even in FOB countries, there can be customs valuation consequences, as in the effect of an EXW versus an FCA or FOB sales term.[16] Nevertheless, the US does not overtly recognize that possibility arising in the context of a related party "test value" comparison[17] although the statute does refer generally to adjustment for "costs incurred by the seller in sales in which he and the buyer are not related that are not incurred by the seller in sales in which he and the buyer are related."[18] That basket category could capture differences in transport and related charges. The US does not provide, however, in such an open-ended manner, for transport charge adjustments in the TV of identical or similar merchandise, adjustments being limited to commercial level and quantity.

[E] Adjustments for Differences in Commercial Levels or Quantities

The adjustments to be taken in respect of these commercial level and/or quantity differences was the subject of yet another early TCCV instrument.[19] The first point to make is that a difference in commercial level and/or quantity need not require an adjustment. Only if such a difference results in a difference in price will there be a need

14. 19 USC § 1401a(c)(2); Canada Customs Act, subsections 49(3) and 50(2); ICC IA, Articles 141.1 and 141.2.
15. CBSA has made clear that adjustments are to be made only for differences in distance and mode of transportation. No adjustments can be made for differences in transportation costs for other reasons, for example differences in the quantities shipped. Customs Memorandum D13-5-1, *Application of Sections 49 and 50 of the Customs Act*, February 25, 2014, paragraph 10.
16. Nos. 656-657 at 207.
17. *See* 19 USC §§ 1401a(b)(2)(B) and (C).
18. 19 USC § 1401a(b)(2)(C)(iv).
19. Parenthetically, this early flurry of instruments speaks to a focus by the TCCV on the challenges to applying Articles 2 and 3.

for an adjustment. And the need for a price difference must be demonstrated by evidence which is reasonable and accurate.[20]

Moreover, there is no authority to adjust the transaction value of similar merchandise in a manner that accounts for differences other than commercial levels or quantities.[21] This is a failing of the Valuation Agreement which should have profound implications for customs valuation.

Let us consider, there could easily arise a situation where two products were sold, and the comparison factors noted above revealed that the goods were either identical or similar, and let us further assume that the commercial levels and quantities were the same on both sales. The sales prices were wildly different, however, due to one sale being a single, all-in bundled price which included post-importation erection or maintenance charges. Or let us suppose that one sale price included an Article 8 adjustment for a selling commission or another of the Article 8 adjustments? Or let us suppose that one sale price shows a discounted price, but the other shows a higher price as the post-importation rebate in that second sale was disregarded? Should the presence of these price-distortions in one of the sales be simply ignored or should these price-distortions be taken into account and transaction value of identical or similar merchandise be precluded? A blinkered perspective would overlook the price-distortion, for which no adjustment is possible, but that is contrary to the spirit of the Agreement and, in fact, would violate the Valuation Agreement commitment to a system that is fair.[22] I would argue that the effect of such a price-distortion should be that transaction value of identical or similar merchandise is not available.

A growing practice has developed over the past two decades in which customs authorities reject a transaction value appraisement in favor of an Article 2 or Article 3 identical or similar goods method. The trend is so widespread, and at the same time so underreported formally, that it poses a risk to the international system. The risk lies in the misuse of customs valuation databases.

With that in mind, let us briefly examine recent developments in the EU—the ECJ Judgment and the Attorney General opinion in *Baltic Master UAB*[23] and the Judgment in the *Fawkes* case.[24]

[F] *Baltic Master* and *Fawkes* Judgments

The customs authority which seeks to move away from a transaction value appraisement and, instead, move to Article 2 or 3 or an Article 7 flexible application of Article 2 or 3 and, in that process, to make use of a customs valuation database, should ordinarily be stopped in its tracks if it has not actively conducted an examination of the COS.

20. TCCV, Com. 10.1, Adjustments for Differences in Commercial Level and in Quantity Under Article 1.2(b) and in Articles 2 and 3 of the Agreement (October 1984).
21. *See* ruling no. 545999 (December 12, 1995).
22. Valuation Agreement, Preamble, fourth clause.
23. Case C-599/20, *Baltic Master UAB*, 9.6.2022, ECLI:EU:C:2022:457 (*Baltic Master*).
24. Case C-187/21, *Fawkes Kft*, 9.6.2022, ECLI:EU:C:2022:458 (*Fawkes*).

Valencia's Professor Santiago Ibanez Marsilla reminds us that this is the requirement imposed on the customs authority under Article 1.2 (a) of the Valuation Agreement.[25] While their examination might not be exhaustive,[26] it surely imposes an obligation on customs officials to undertake a substantive review that goes beyond a mere recitation that they have an undefined or unsupported "doubt" before proceeding to an alternative basis for appraisement.

As for the fact that Article 1.2 applies only to related party transactions, the *Baltic Master* court (in paragraph 34) referred to the Commission position that:

> the customs authorities [are permitted] to disregard the transaction value for the purposes of determining the customs value where those authorities take the view that the declared value does not reflect the *real economic value* of the imported goods, regardless of whether there is a relationship between Baltic Master and the seller (emphasis added).

The Court simply stated (in paragraph 1 of its ruling) as a matter of legal principle that:

> the buyer and the seller may be deemed to be related on account of a direct or indirect relationship of de facto control in a situation in which the circumstances surrounding the conclusion of the transactions at issue, substantiated by objective elements, may be regarded as demonstrating not only that there is a close relationship of trust between that buyer and that seller, but that one of them is in a position to exercise constraint or direction over the other or that a third party is in a position to exercise such constraint or direction over them.

What can one say to that other than "And ... "? Parsing the imprecise text, we find that the key criterion of a relationship based upon the de facto exercise of management control has been ignored.

Coming to the use of databases, the customs authority should not be permitted to look to an appraisement founded on Article 2 or 3 if it cannot meet all of the requirements imposed by those latter or to an Article 7 flexible application of Article 2 or 3 if doing so would disregard the essential adjustments which are dictated by those Articles As the ICC has noted on the use of databases, for customs purposes, "a rose is not necessarily a rose." Or to refer to a different example, a used bicycle ridden by Eddy Merckx in a Tour de France may be classified for tariff purposes in the same HTS subheading, but it will hardly be identical or similar to other bicycles for customs valuation purposes. That is because the Merckx bicycle is unique and is not commercially interchangeable with other used bicycles. An HTS database reference will contain no such discrete, differentiating information. One of the salient features of the *Oribalt Riga* judgment is that it imposes a significant task upon the customs authority:

---

25. He directs our attention to the decision in the Thailand Cigarettes case decided by the DSB, DS371, Thailand—Customs and Fiscal Measures on Cigarettes from the Philippines. There the Panel noted that an active investigation was called for. The customs authority is required to carefully consider, inquire and investigate. Paragraph 7.159.
26. *See* TCCV, CS 10.1, Application of Article 1.2 (October 1996), paragraph 12 and TCCV, Comm. 14.1, Application of Article 1, paragraph 2 (November 1989), paragraphs 8 and 14.

> when the customs value of goods ... is calculated by applying the [transaction value of similar goods] method ..., the competent national customs authority must, in order to identify "similar goods," take into consideration any relevant factor, such as the composition of those goods, their substitutability in the light of their effects and their commercial interchangeability, thus conducting a factual assessment which takes into account any factor that may have an impact on the real economic value of those goods, including the market position of the imported goods and of their manufacturer.[27]

Beyond this is the contemporaneity standard required—the comparison sales must have been exported "at or about the same time" as the subject sales. Would a database meet this second requirement?

The Advocate General in the *Baltic Master* case[28] had advanced a conclusion that was even more tenuous than that expressed in the Judgment. In his Opinion, the conclusion admitted (in paragraphs 67 and 77) that the goods were not identical or similar, but noted (in paragraphs 77 and 84):

> Although the shipment used as reference did not necessarily concern "identical goods" or "similar goods," within the meaning of Article 30(2)(a) and (b) of Regulation No 2913/92, the fact that both shipments concerned goods classified under the same TARIC code is indicative of a reasonable degree of commonality between those goods. In my view, such commonality may well be sufficient when some goods are valuated under Article 31 of Regulation No 2913/92, if no other characteristics of the products in question are known. In practice, the authorities applied the method of determination of the customs value on the basis of the transaction value of similar goods, interpreting the concept of "similar goods" in a flexible manner (footnote omitted).
>
> * * *
>
> Article 31(1) of Regulation No 2913/92 does not preclude the determination of the customs value on the basis of information contained in a national database relating to a customs value of goods which have the same origin and which, although not identical or similar, are ascribed to the same TARIC heading.[29]

This is much broader than—indeed ignores altogether—the limiting criteria set forth in the EU Commission's Written Observations (Article 66.2):

> Article 31(1) of Regulation (EEC) No 2913/92 must be interpreted as meaning that it does not preclude the customs value from being determined on the basis of the information contained in the national database relating to a single customs value of goods of the same origin and under the same TARIC heading. However, *these goods must have similar characteristics, be made of similar materials, perform the same functions and be commercially interchangeable* (emphasis added).[30]

The Advocate General's argument was specious when it noted (paragraph 79) that customs valuation is primarily based on information furnished by the importer at the same time that the resort to the TARIC information, uniquely held by the customs

27. *Oribalt Riga*, paragraph 29.
28. Opinion of AG Nicholas Emiliou in Case C-599/20, *Baltic Master UAB*, 20.1.2022, ECLI: EU:C:2022:46.
29. The TARIC (the Integrated Tariff of the European Union) is the EU's HTS program.
30. Translated from the French. Commission Européenne, Ref. Ares (2021)2179759-29/03/2021.

authority, was validated. Perhaps that access to the TARIC data allowed the customs authority from having to engage in "time consuming tasks." The ECJ judgment acknowledged that the goods that were embodied in the TARIC database were not similar goods—and the Opinion had admitted (paragraph 79) that the relevant TARIC code was "residual and generic."

The Opinion relied (paragraph 80, n. 41) on a 2008 ECJ antidumping case arising under the Customs Code. In that case, *Carboni e Derivati*,[31] the court wrestled with the intersection of the First Sale rule (it was permissible at that time) and the antidumping regime before concluding (in paragraph 64):

> If the customs authorities have reasonable doubts as to the accuracy of the declared value and their doubts are confirmed after they have asked for additional information or documents and have provided the person concerned with a reasonable opportunity to respond to the grounds for those doubts, without it being possible to determine the price actually paid or payable, they may, in accordance with Article 31 of the Community Customs Code, calculate the customs value for the purpose of applying the anti-dumping duty established by Decision No 67/94 by reference to the price agreed for the goods in question in the most recent sale prior to that on the basis of which the customs declaration was made and in regard to which the customs authorities have no objective reason to doubt its accuracy.

I fail to grasp the precedential authority of the *Carboni e drivati* decision for the *Baltic Master* customs valuation question. There appears to be no valid basis in *Baltic Master* for what can only be described as a jump to a "last resort" (the Advocate General used the term "extrema ratio" in the Opinion, paragraph 71) appraisement under Article 31.1 of the CCC[32] (now UCC, Article 74.3). But here we note a continuation under the 1992 CCC and its successor, the UCC. Under the current Implementing Act, UCC IA, Article 144.1, what we understand as the traditional fallback method—the reasonable, flexible application of the stated methods—must first be attempted before we get to the last resort of Article 144.2.[33] This is the case in the US, where CBP has advised[34] about the limited manner in which its last resort—beyond fallback—approach may be used.

This is under section 500 of the Tariff Act of 1930, as amended,[35] which, as we noted very early in this book, constitutes CBP's general appraisement authority. The appraising officer may:

> fix the final appraisement of merchandise by ascertaining or estimating the value thereof, under section 1401a of this title, by all reasonable ways and means in his power, any statement of cost or costs of production in any invoice, affidavit, declaration, other document to the contrary notwithstanding … .

31. Judgment of 28 February 2008, *Carboni e derivati* (C-263/06, ECLI:EU:C:2008:128).
32. Community Customs Code – Regulation (EEC) No. 2913/92.
33. This sequencing is discussed below in the fallback/residual method discussion.
34. Ruling no. H008101 (October 9, 2012).
35. 19 USC § 1500.

The Statement of Administrative Action (SAA), which forms part of the legislative history of the TAA, provides in pertinent part:

> Section 500 is the general authority for Customs to appraise merchandise. It is not a separate basis of appraisement and cannot be used as such. Section 500 allows Customs to consider the best evidence available in appraising merchandise. It allows Customs to consider the contract between the buyer and seller, if available, when the information contained in the invoice is either deficient or is known to contain inaccurate figures or calculations ... . Section 500 authorize [sic] the appraising officer to weigh the nature of the evidence before him in appraising the imported merchandise. This could be the invoice, the contract between the parties, or even the recordkeeping of either of the parties to the contract.
>
> In those transactions where no accurate invoice or other documentation is available, and the importer is unable, or refuses, to provide such information, then reasonable ways and means will be used to determine the appropriate value, using whatever evidence is available, again within the constraints of section 402.[36]

The important point here is that this speaks of a last resort—when even the fallback method is not available—but even then, the prohibited methods are out of bounds.

Coming back to the EU, the provision in the first sentence in Article 144.1:

> When determining the customs value under Article 74(3) of the Code, reasonable flexibility may be used in the application of the methods provided for in Articles 70 and 74(2) of the Code.

is found in the 1993 CCC IR.[37] To that extent, the UCC and its predecessor CCC have been aligned with the Valuation Agreement, which directs us:

> The methods of valuation to be employed under Article 7 should be those laid down in Articles 1 through 6 but a reasonable flexibility in the application of such methods would be in conformity with the aims and provisions of Article 7[38]

In *Baltic Master*, while there was a contention that the use of the database was reasonable, that rationale may be a slender reed. There was no showing how and why this database approach of looking at statistical values derived from a national database does not result in an arbitrary or fictitious value—think Eddy Merckx's competition bicycle—in contravention of Article 31.2(g) of the CCC (now found in the UCC IA, Article 144.2 (g)).

Beyond that vital factor, the ECJ judgment is further flawed. It never directly establishes the specific method by which the customs valuation exercise is to be conducted. Instead, it merely comments vaguely (paragraph 52) that a reasonably flexible application of both transaction value and the transaction value of identical or similar goods is permitted:

36. Statement of Administrative Action, H.R. Doc. No. 153, 96 Cong., 1st Sess., pt 2 ("SAA") reprinted in, Department of the Treasury, Customs Valuation under the Trade Agreements Act of 1979 (October 1981), at 67.
37. Regulation (EEC) No. 2454/93, Annex 23, Interpretative Note to Article 31(1) CCC, in paragraph 2.
38. Valuation Agreement, Interpretative Note to Article 7, point 2.

> the valuation methods to be used under Article 31 of that code should be those defined in Articles 29 and 30(2) thereof, that point of the note states that those methods must be applied with reasonable flexibility, in particular as regards the assessment of the term "similar goods."

With a resort to a fallback appraisement, the Valuation Agreement's strict prohibition against the use of the higher of two alternative values[39] becomes a potential issue. The judgment never addressed that issue, either.

Published the same day as *Baltic Master*, the ECJ released its judgment in the *Fawkes* case, another case which had turned on the use of databases. What was at stake there was the customs valuation of apparel imported into Hungary from China. The customs authority suspected that the value was understated and made an appraisement using the TV of similar merchandise as the appropriate method:

> That authority then adopted the contested decision in which the customs value was determined in accordance with Article 30(2)(b) of the [Community] Customs Code. To that end, it used information from a national database covering a period of 90 days, including 45 days before and 45 days after customs clearance. That authority did not take account of other customs clearances granted to the applicant in the main proceedings.[40]

The importer challenged, asserting variously that it was impermissible to not make use of its own imports' data, that other databases in the EU should have been consulted and that the ninety-day time frame was too short. Apparently, the importer did not directly challenge the use of databases as a source for the customs valuation exercise.

The *Fawkes* court decided (paragraphs 33-57) that there was no obligation for a national customs authority to go beyond its own database, assuming that it was sufficient for that purpose. Despite the reminder by the court (paragraphs 52, 56) that the customs authority was supposed to provide the importer with details which formed the basis for the adverse decision and the observation (paragraphs 49-50) that the databases could not themselves provide precise information allowing the customs value to be determined in accordance with Articles 30(2)(a) and (b) of the CCC, the decision is deeply troubling. We are witnessing the normalization of the use of databases as a source for customs valuation—here, explicitly to be conducted under the auspices of the TV of identical or similar goods. What was not addressed was how a violation of UCC IA, Article 142.3 (prohibition against not using the lowest transaction value of identical or similar goods) could be avoided when resorting to a database, nor how proper adjustments could be made to account for differences in commercial levels of sale or in quantities. Similarly avoided with silence was the stricture of UCC IA, Article 134.4, which dictates that, in the case of related party transactions, the test values are to be used at the request of the importers AND that they shall not substitute for the declared transaction value.

---

39. Valuation Agreement, Article 7.2(b).
40. *Fawkes*, paragraph 27.

As for the importer's own imports of identical or similar goods, the decision held (paragraph 65) that the Customs Code must be interpreted as meaning that the customs authority of a Member State may exclude, under certain circumstances, when determining the customs value, transaction values relating to other transactions performed by the applicant for customs clearance, even if those values have not been challenged either by that customs authority or by the customs authorities of other Member States. We emphasize that there was no explicit showing that the importer's data were suspect.

In another nod at the flexibility to be accorded to customs authorities, the *Fawkes* court held (paragraphs 72-73) that a ninety-day window would be appropriate provided there were sufficient comparable importations in that time period. Otherwise, a slightly longer time period would be appropriate, but not too far removed from the date of export of the goods being valued, provided that, during that longer period, the commercial practices and market conditions affecting the prices of the goods being valued have remained substantially the same.

The *Baltic Master* and *Fawkes* cases have introduced us to customs valuation databases. We should explore those resources in more depth.

[G] Customs Valuation Databases

Many countries make extensive use of "customs valuation databases," ordinarily organized on a tariff classification basis. When properly used, this means that there is a set value or a range of values that is associated with a given tariff provision. The problem arises when a value is assigned to a given tariff provision. We saw this latter *modus operandi* come up in the *Baltic Maste*r and *Fawkes* decisions, so we should realize that this is a widespread trend not limited to developing countries.

Some customs authorities will refer to a valuation database, an external source that the customs authorities themselves will have prepared and which is normally not accessible to the importer, in appraising the imported goods, whether or not there is a related party transaction at issue. Of course, transaction value is established on the basis of the PAPP, and third-party pricing is presumptively valid—or it should be presumptively valid.

We should be clear: valuation databases are meant to be used only in a very narrow application. The WCO Guidelines, which were promulgated at the commission of the CCV, provide that:

> [A]pplication of an appropriate *risk assessment* and management procedure enables Customs to exercise this right in a pragmatic manner. Such procedures may use, inter alia, a valuation database[41] (emphasis added).

41. WCO, Guidelines on the Development and Use of a National Valuation Database as a Risk Assessment Tool (2005), paragraph 6.

The intended use is as a risk indicator in examining import declarations for customs fraud. The anecdotal evidence, however, suggests that several dozen countries are using these databases in other ways that violate the Valuation Agreement. In fact, there is a body of evidence that developing countries, which had been lobbying for the database guidelines, had long chafed under the constraints imposed by the Valuation Agreement. Almost from the outset, there has been an effort to attain greater "flexibility," which some critics might translate as simply license to disregard the Valuation Agreement. The databases are an example of the greater freedom which they had long sought.

One prominent advocate of reference prices was the World Bank. The Minutes of a 2000 WTO General Council meeting record the endorsement by the delegate for India of a World Bank recommendation for reference prices:

> At least for basic goods, a valuation system based on observed world prices might offer a better opportunity to introduce transparency, objectivity and accountability into the system. At periodic reviews of these "reference prices" both import users and import-competing interests might be given "standing" and could be offered the opportunity to submit evidence in support of revisions. It might also be possible to establish a collective system of reference prices, over which no one government had control. Schedules of reference prices might be determined by an intergovernmental group, their preparation and circulation might be contracted to an independent agency."[42]

To be sure, the Indian delegate stopped short of advancing databases as a substitute valuation method in its own right:

> The Agreement did not explicitly provide for adoption of reference values as a method of valuation. However, there might be no objections to using such values for price comparison purposes to test the truth and accuracy of declared values and for rejection of the transaction value method.[43]

This, then, appears to be the starting point to the effort that resulted in the TCCV adoption of the Guidelines in 2005, with the WCO playing an active and supportive role in that effort. India may have failed in its concerted effort to force changes to the Valuation Agreement in 2000-2003,[44] but, to my dismay, it ultimately succeeded with this database gambit.

Notwithstanding the limited role claimed for valuation databases, the anecdotal evidence suggests that if a customs authority rejects a declared value and thus moves away from a TV appraisement, the databases are playing one of two roles. Normally, the stage is set by asserting that the customs authority has reasons to doubt the truth

42. Cited in WTO, G/VAL/W/97, Compilation of Discussions in Various WTO Bodies on Implementation-related Issues Concerning Customs Valuation (26 March 2002), Minutes of General Council Sessions, Meeting of 22 June and 3 July 2000 in paras 149-150, p. 8.
43. *Ibid.*, in paragraph 150.
44. India's skepticism about transaction value has already been noted. It is one reason for the inclusion of Article 17 and Annex III, paragraph 6 and the adoption of Decision 6.1. Tokyo Round documents reveal that India's persistent efforts to permit a move away from a transaction value appraisement began at the very outset. *See* text at n. 53 below.

or accuracy of the entry documents. This will be prompted by CCV Decision 6.1. Then, in the first role, the databases will masquerade as the basis for a TV of identical or similar merchandise. That is why I raise it in this section. The objection is that this appraisement is being done without the need to respect any of the limitations or conditions set down by the Valuation Agreement in Articles 2 and 3.

We might have discussed valuation databases later in this presentation, as there is often a second role for them—they have made an appearance as the basis for a fallback appraisement. This was the direction taken in *Baltic Master*. What's the objection? The databases are the source of "reference" or "indicative" prices which are actually prohibited substitute or minimum prices, and the importer usually has little or no opportunity to challenge the validity of these prices.

These indiscriminate and across-the-board misuses of valuation databases to furnish an alternative to a declared value ignore the restrictions and conditions that must be met in these secondary valuation methods. Both the comparability factors that preclude the use of these precisely crafted earlier methods and the enumerated methods that preclude a fallback appraisement are disregarded with a wholesale use of databases.

To be clear, I am not saying that customs authorities must automatically accept any customs value declared by any importer at any time.[45] I am saying that importers and customs authorities alike must adhere to the Valuation Agreement. Working together, they should form a community of interest, committed to a faithful application of and adherence to that Agreement.

I am mindful that the Valuation Agreement allows Members to satisfy themselves as to the truth and accuracy of any statement, document or declaration presented for customs valuation purposes.[46] Coupled with that authority, when customs authorities have "reasonable doubts" as to the accuracy of declared values, they can ask for more information and, ultimately, reject transaction value if the doubts are not resolved or "dispelled" to use the EU's turn of phrase.[47] It is that authority which opens the door to many an abuse of databases. Beyond the example of the *Baltic Master* case, we are seeing another misuse of databases, in this instance arising in Belgium. There is anecdotal evidence that the Belgian customs authorities follow the playbook:

- Express doubts about the declared value, under the authority of Article 140 of the UCC IA.
- The burden has now shifted to the importer to provide information, often quite voluminous and with tight deadlines.
- The customs authority refers to the customs valuation database—formerly called the Market Access Database (MADB), now Access2Markets[48]—for a

45. Customs authorities have every right, indeed an obligation, to install adequate systems of customs controls, empowering them, *inter alia*, to verify the accuracy of declared customs values. E.g., *see* UCC, Article 46.
46. Valuation Agreement, Article 17.
47. Implementing Act, Article 140.
48. This open-source base does not provide access to values for the public.

"statistical value" assigned to the HTS—that statistical value is an average value for that HTS—it is not shared with the importer.

- Often the doubts persist and the customs authority will reject transaction value and apply a secondary method, usually the transaction value of similar goods, with a value pegged at the difference between the declared value and the statistical value.
- The customs authorities rely on a 2016 ECJ decision arising under the CCC[49] for the authority to reject a transaction value where there were "reasonable doubts" and the price was "unreasonably low."

The notion that, in the absence of fraud or another factor such as a price having been influenced by the relationship of the parties or undeclared Article 8 adjustments, the customs authorities have the authority to ascertain whether a price is unreasonably low is suspect. You will recall from the earlier discussion of the PAPP that the TCCV has issued various instruments which undergird a bedrock principle that dismisses this rejection of a transaction value appraisement merely because the price is low or appears to be too low.[50] Instead, the EU is applying an arrogated right to look for the "real" or "true" economic value of the imported merchandise.[51]

Beyond that, this playbook relies on an impermissible expansion of the *Euro 2004* decision. In *Euro 2004*, the recitation of facts informs us that Hungarian customs authorities conducted a post-clearance examination, and the importer had not provided any additional information when requested by the customs authority. The importer "merely stated that it had paid the amount stated on the invoice to its Chinese partner." The customs authority "still had doubts as to whether that value was correct, using statistical data, it analysed the unit price at which the types of goods at issue were sold to Hungarian importers and determined their customs value in accordance with the 'transaction value of similar goods' referred to in Article 30(2)(b) of the [Community] Customs Code." In reply, the importer argued that the customs authority did not accept the customs value declared for the goods at issue only because it had been able to purchase the goods at a lower price, thanks solely to its good business relations, which cannot serve as a basis to call that value into question. For its part, the customs authority maintained the line of argument on which its decision was based, arguing that the importer had not explained why the price of the goods at issue was unreasonably low in relation to the comparable statistical values in the database.[52] The court's further observations, meant to assist the referring court, were interesting—these were that the 50% disparity between the declared price and the

49. Case C-291/15, *Euro 2004. Hungary kft v. Nemzeti Ado*, 16.6.2016, ECLI:EU:C:2016:455 (*Euro 2004*).
50. TCCV, AO 2.1, Acceptability of a Price Below Prevailing Market Prices for Identical Goods (October 1981), Com. 3.1, Goods Sold at Dumping Prices (March 1982); CS 12.1, Application of Article 1 of the Valuation Agreement for Goods Sold for Export at Prices Below Their Cost of Production (November 2000); TCCV, AO 23.1, Valuation of Imported Goods Purchased in "Flash Sales" (May 2019).
51. In this connection, *see*, e.g., the EU Commission written observations in the *BMW Decision*, in paragraph 14.
52. *Euro 2004*, paragraphs 14-17.

statistical value justified the customs authority doubts (paragraphs 38-39); that the authenticity of the invoice was not central to the question of customs valuation (paragraphs 40-41); that the importer had been given a reasonable opportunity to respond the customs authority doubts (paragraph 42), but the company did not present new evidence and declared that it had paid to the other contracting party the value shown on the invoice (paragraph 43).

This is a seriously flawed decision. The facts do not support the statement made throughout the judgment that the importer had not provided any information other than the statement that it had paid the price shown on the invoice. Applying my own experience to the task of substantiating the PAPP, I would turn to the importer's payment records, wire transfer or other bank statements and its internal accounting records—all to show that the amounts declared were indeed the full amounts paid for the imported goods. And we find in paragraph 13 of the *Euro 2004* judgment that the importer had apparently done exactly that: the customs authority compared the commercial invoice which had been submitted to it with the importer's accounting records and proofs of payment and with the bank certificate produced and found that the amount indicated in those documents corresponded to the content of the customs declaration. When pressed beyond that, the importer had not thereafter provided additional information.

But surely there should be some weight to the qualifying term "reasonable" when the UCC IA allows the customs authority to question the importer's declared price on the basis of "reasonable doubts." In paragraph 44 of the *Euro 2004* judgment, we find the only other reference to the other documentary evidence which had been provided by the importer:

> the customs value of the imported goods [may be] determined on the basis of the transaction value of similar goods, the method appearing at Article 30 of the Customs Code, where the declared transaction value is considered to be unreasonably low in comparison with the statistical average of the purchase prices verified in the context of the importation of similar goods and despite the fact that the customs authority does not refute or call into question the authenticity of the invoice or the bank transfer certificate produced in order to establish the price actually paid for the imported goods, without the importer having submitted, in response to a request to that effect from the customs authority, additional evidence to demonstrate the accuracy of the declared transaction value of those goods.

The judgment reveals no other basis for customs authority doubts than the comparison with the reference prices shown in the statistical database. Remember Eddy Merckx's bicycle! Even assuming that the resort to the transaction value of similar merchandise was proper, there was no showing that suitable adjustments were even considered to account for differences in quantity or commercial levels as would be required under Article 142 of the UCC IA.

When we examine the negotiation history of the Agreement, we find that India had proposed in 1979 an addition to Article 1 which aligns with the EU approach in *Euro 2004* decision:

> In cases where there is any marked variation in the transaction value of a particular importation as compared with other importation of identical or similar goods, at the same level and substantially similar quantities, at or about the same time, and no satisfactory explanation is forthcoming, value shall be determined by proceeding sequentially through the following Articles to the first of the Articles which can be applied.[53]

This proposal was rejected, but it has found its way back *sub silentio*.

Surely, the customs authority, which acknowledged the veracity of the additional documentary proof, should be put to the task of explaining how or why it still harbors doubts despite the presence of this documentary evidence. The fact that a statistical database shows a difference in pricing may be enough to raise a question or to create a doubt in the first place, but such a difference should not by itself invalidate documentary proof that has been furnished by the importer in response to the customs authority inquiries and has been acknowledged by the customs authority itself to be valid. At the very least, the customs authority should be obligated to disclose what are the grounds for considering that transaction value is not acceptable.[54]

This is the mirror image of the expected treatment of fraudulent documents. In one of its early instruments, the TCCV declared that "an administration cannot be required to rely on fraudulent documentation."[55] The grants of Article 17 and Annex III, paragraph 6 of the Valuation Agreement notwithstanding,[56] it would be worthwhile for the TCCV to consider whether a customs administration can be required to rely on valid documentation, i.e., in those cases where there is no evidence of fraud or misrepresentation, in fixing the PAPP for the imported goods. That is the foundational principle of the Valuation Agreement. In this connection, we might turn to a 1985 GATT document to quote from the US delegate to the TCCV:

> the United States believe that the rights conferred under Article 17 and the Protocol are not unlimited. Customs administrations may not use these rights in an arbitrary or capricious manner, or in a wholesale effort to avoid valuation under Article 1. Rather, it must be recognized that commercial reality dictates that some individuals will be able to purchase goods at prices lower than others (e.g., due to volume of purchase, seasonal discounts, purchases of discontinued or "grey-market" goods, to satisfy a seller's desire to penetrate a market, etc.) and that the

---

53. GATT, Multilateral Trade Negotiations Group, "Non-Tariff Measures," Sub-Group "Customs Matters," Customs Valuation, MTN/NTM/W/215 (10 January 1979).
54. The TCCV issued Com. 14.1, Application of Article 1, paragraph 2 (November 1989). In Questions 4 and 5, the TCCV invoked paragraph 6 of Annex III and Article 7 to the effect that a customs authority did not need to explain the reason for its "doubts," but the customs authority did need to communicate the reasons for its conclusions. While this instrument was issued in the context of related party pricing, it applies to all transactions since the cited authorities are not limited to related party transactions.
55. TCCV, AO 10.1, Treatment of Fraudulent Documents (September 1983).
56. Article 17 of the Valuation Agreement allows the customs authority to satisfy itself as to the truth or accuracy of any statement, document or declaration presented for customs valuation purposes.

primary method of valuation under the Code was specifically designed to recognize the use of the free-market trading system.[57]

Faced with a *Euro 2004* situation, in which the customs authorities keep pressing for documents that may not exist (note: in some circumstances, the traders will not sign formal agreements—there could be simply orders and invoices or even "handshake" or telephone "deals"),[58] we might expect that many traders will shift their import activities to avoid dealings with those customs authorities. We would be witnessing the impact of the trade-distorting effects of a Member State's customs regime, presumably anathema to the EU's Single Market first commandment.

In contrast to this misuse, the EU does offer us a sterling example of the proper use of customs valuation databases as a measure for risk management/risk assessment tool to curb fraud. The workings of the program were discussed at length in a 2022 ECJ decision, in a case in which the UK was accused of not doing enough to prevent massive fraud, resulting in the loss of duty and VAT "own resources" revenues for the EU.[59]

The EU had been confronted with staggering levels of organized criminally fraudulent undervaluation of textiles and clothing from China. In response, the EU devised a customs valuation database for Chapters 61-64 of the Harmonized Tariff System in order to establish a baseline for evaluation.[60]

This limited use was entirely permissible, indeed unobjectionable, in all respects,[61] but I am just as mindful that such limiting authority will not justify misuse. Recognizing that the misuse of customs valuation databases was a pressing issue, the CCV sponsored an Informal Workshop on Valuation Databases and Reference Pricing held in conjunction with its regular session in October 2014.

57. GATT, Committee on Customs Valuation, Report By the Technical Committee on Customs Valuation Concerning the Effects of False Invoicing on Customs Valuation, VAL/W/32, 7 November 1985, paragraph 17.
58. There is a pending case at the ECJ filed by Bulgaria, Case No. C-770/291, *OGL-Food Trade Lebensmittelvertrieb GmbH v. Direktor na Teritorialna direktsia "Mitnitsa Plovdiv" pri Agentsia "Mitnitsi,"* OJ C138/10 ("OGL") which raises similar questions on documentary proof but within the narrow context of the customs valuation program for fresh fruits and vegetables.
59. Case C-213/19, *European Commission v. United Kingdom*, 8.3.2022, ECLI:EU:C:2022:167. *See* paragraphs 51-84.
60. Perhaps the EU, with its OLAF anti-fraud database regime, is seeking a low budget alternative to a more robust enforcement regime, as applied by the US or Canada, which also boast the extensive use of post-entry audits and investigative staff tasked to prevent fraud and to ensure higher levels of customs compliance.
61. The US makes extensive use of a statistical review of entry documentation to ensure the integrity of the statistical information, a joint responsibility of CBP, the International Trade Commission and the Census Bureau (19 USC § 1484). One of the parameters set is for the valuation of goods, with an error message flashed where the declared value falls outside the upper or lower limits of the statistical range for that 10-digit tariff line item. That error message triggers an inquiry by CBP not a resort to a further use of statistical data in any way. The CBP Directive on CENSUS INTERFACE-PROCESSING PROCEDURES is available at https://www.cbp.gov/sites/default/files/assets/documents/2017-Nov/3560-001A.PDF.

For its part, the ICC felt so strongly about the subject that it issued a comprehensive Policy Statement on the misuse of customs valuation databases in 2015.[62]

Unfortunately, there is little to suggest that the risks of misuse have abated in the intervening years. The use of valuation databases to establish reference or minimum pricing—regardless of the typical "window dressing" that would state that they are being used only for risk assessment purposes or upon the supposition that their use allows for a permissible application of one of the secondary methods—is based upon a gross oversimplification, on the false assumption that "a rose is a rose is a rose" for valuation purposes as well as for tariff classification. Simple, easy ... and wrong.

There is ample evidence to show that valuation databases are being used, not as a valid customs control measure as was the case with the cited use in the EU fraud investigation, but to promote reference pricing, i.e., valuation based upon substitute or minimum pricing. That usage marks a return to the "normal value" concept of the BDV, which is a notional value, and violates the "positive" basis of the PAPP which is the core principle of Transaction Value under the Valuation Agreement. In short, when used to provide an alternative customs value, the valuation database is neither more nor less than a tool to violate the Valuation Agreement.[63]

For a fuller understanding, you should also know that reference pricing has been the subject of three WTO Dispute Settlement cases and of numerous discussions at the WTO's CCV meetings.

If there is no suitable sale or not sufficient information on which to appraise at this level, then the customs authority must proceed to another methodology. Article 4 of the Valuation Agreement allows the importer to flip the order of the next method to be applied.

62. ICC Policy Statement on the Misuse of Customs Valuation Databases, available online at https://iccwbo.org/publication/icc-policy-statement-on-the-misuse-of-customs-valuation-databases/.

63. These include Colombia, WT/DS366R (2009), Romania, WT/DS198R (2001) and Mexico, WT/DS298R (2005). The first two resulted in losses for the jurisdictions with reference pricing and the third was settled with the withdrawal of the challenged program.

CHAPTER 5

Importer's Option

§5.01 ARTICLE 4: COMPUTED VALUE PRECEDENCE OVER DEDUCTIVE VALUE

The Valuation Agreement[1] allows the importer to reverse the normal ordering and to proceed with a computed value method, which is set out in Article 6, instead of an Article 5 deductive value method. At the insistence of the developing country bloc, however, Annex III, paragraph 3 allows developing countries to make a reservation, negating the importer's option.

Both of these methods are intended to get the importer back to something approaching a qualifying price for the imported goods, which you should recognize as the basis for TV. In the quest to end up at the same place as TV, deductive value takes a route similar to a "resale minus" or "build-down" analysis, backing out of the sale price in the country of importation amounts for:

- profit and general expenses;
- Transport and insurance;
- duties and taxes.

In the case of computed value, similar on a macro level to a "cost-plus" or "build-up" approach, the importer must build up to what would be a valid sale price by adding together:

- cost or value of materials and standard cost of fabrication;
- profit and general expenses;
- any dutiable assists;
- packing costs.

1. Article 4; in the US, 19 USC § 1401a(a)(2); Canada Customs Act, subsection 47(3); EU, UCC, Article 74.1.

As will be seen, both of these methods pose challenges for the importer.

Assuming that there is no reversing of the normal hierarchy, the next method to be tried would be deductive value.

CHAPTER 6

Method Based on Deductions from the Resale Price

§6.01 DEDUCTIVE VALUE

As established by the customs valuation rubric,[1] deductive value is often viewed as the customs law equivalent of the Resale Price Method (RPM) as defined in the US under the section 482 transfer pricing regulations.[2] It is also possible that deductive value might find a closer analogue in the Transactional Net Margin Method (TNMM) with its reliance on a measure of operating margin rather than gross profit. You should be aware that, for its part, the statute does not specify whether the profit being factored into the calculation is gross or net, but the Interpretative Notes to the Valuation Agreement define general expenses for the purpose of fixing deductive value as including direct and indirect costs of marketing the goods, which expenses are typically used to arrive at an operating margin.[3]

[A] Role of Identical or Similar Goods

The first point to make is one that is easily—and, in practice, I would wager is often—overlooked. The focus of appraisal under this approach is broader than the sale

1. Valuation Agreement, Article 5, paragraphs 1 and 2; 19 USC § 1401a(d). The US customs regulations track the relevant Interpretative Notes. E.g., cf. 19 CFR § 152.105(i) and Interpretative Note to Article 5, points 11 and 12. In Canada, Customs Act, section 51; EU, UCC Article 74.2 (c), Implementing Act, Article 142. Interestingly, the EU provides for a separate regime for perishable goods, Implementing Act, Article 142.6. This calls to mind the fact that CBP has issued several rulings on deductive value for perishable vegetable imports from Mexico.
2. IRS Reg. § 1.482-3(c)(1).
3. Valuation Agreement, Interpretative Notes, Article 5, point 7. Likewise, the Interpretative Note to computed value reference to "general expenses" refers to those incurred in producing and selling the goods. Valuation Agreement, Interpretative Notes, Article 6, point 7.

of the imported goods themselves. To be sure, Article 5 and the implementing statutes look to the sale of the imported goods but as well as to the sales of identical or similar goods.[4]

I believe that this has the potential of a serious flaw—establishing that goods are commercially interchangeable may establish them as similar merchandise for deductive value purposes,[5] but the inquiry should not stop there. The statute is silent on the question of adjustments to the prices of identical or similar merchandise, however, and we have noted that Articles 2 and 3 each address adjustments for commercial level and quantity in the limiting context of "applying this Article," i.e., Article 2 or Article 3 only. Beyond that, neither Article 2 or 3 nor their Interpretative Notes refer to the potential connection with Article 5. This setting of the benchmark goods without any possibility for an adjustment to correct for the impact of differences even in commercial level or quantity, notwithstanding commercial interchangeability, is flawed and the Valuation Agreement should be amended.

A central role in this method is the unit price.

[B] Unit Price in Greatest Aggregate Quantity

The starting point for fixing a deductive value is the unit price, i.e., the resale price in the country of importation at which the goods are sold in the condition as imported in the single greatest aggregate quantity at or about the time of importation or within a longer period.

The Valuation Agreement Articles 5.1(a) and (b) definitions of unit price are the functional source for a deductive value appraisement and they are expressed in terms of the greatest aggregated quantity of resales.

Timing aspects of the deductive method are discussed below but there is a timing element at play in determining the operative unit price. The ninety-day window for resales contemplated by Article 5.1 (b) inserts another time element, the "earliest date" after the date of importation. That term is itself explained in the Interpretative Notes[6] to refer to:

> the date by which sales of the imported goods or of identical or similar goods are made in sufficient quantity to establish unit price.

If you are following along closely, you will have now come to the important question, what is meant by "sufficient quantity"? The Valuation Agreement itself

4. For ease of use, the US statute uses the term "merchandise concerned" to refer to all three referents. 19 USC § 1401a(d)(1). In fact, CBP sees a parity among the three types of merchandise. Ruling no. W563483 (December 28, 2006) ("all three types of merchandise may be utilized for appraisement but one type does not take priority over the other. Hence, from a practical standpoint, while Customs generally concerns itself with the sale of the goods being valued, it is not precluded, based on the information available at or about the date of importation, from utilizing on-going sales of identical or similar goods for appraisement"). Canada Customs Act, subsection 51(2); UCC, Article 74.2(c).
5. *See*, e.g., ruling no. 544784 (August 10, 1992).
6. Interpretative Note to Article 5, paragraph 10.

provides no insight, but we should turn to the implementing statutes and administrative regimes.

In the US, the SAA informs us:[7]

> No definite quantity can be stated. If all of the imported merchandise concerned is not sold, it must be determined, on a case-by-case basis, if the quantity sold is sufficient to be representative of the shipment as a whole, in a commercial sense. Sufficient quantity may vary greatly depending on the type of merchandise, the time sold, and the commercial level at which sold.

In the Canadian experience, CBSA has furnished some valuable administrative guidance:[8]

11. The number of sales that constitutes a sufficient number will depend on the circumstances and the marketing practices surrounding an importation and the sales in Canada of the imported goods.
12. For example, if only a small percentage of the imported goods are sold within the time limits established in subsection 51(2), these sales may be acceptable for the purposes of establishing a price per unit if the price at which they are sold is consistent with the usual selling price of the goods. This usual price may be indicated by a "bona fide" price list supported by commercial invoices or, where a price list is not used, by examining the recent trading history of the importer.
13. The price per unit at which the greatest number of goods is sold would not be acceptable if the number of goods sold is only a small percentage of the total sales of those goods.
14. However, there will be situations in which a single sale may be a sufficient number to permit determination of a price per unit. For example:
    (a) a single unit is imported and the nature of the goods is such that no identical or similar imported goods have been imported, or are likely to be imported, within the time limits established in subsection 51(2). In this case, only one sale can occur on which to base a price per unit and such a sale will be deemed to constitute a sufficient number of sales;
    (b) 1000 units of a particular item are imported and only one sale, consisting of the whole 1000 units, is made in Canada within the time limits established in subsection 51(2). In this case, only one sale has occurred but since this sale constitutes the total amount imported, and no other sales are possible, it will be considered to be a sufficient number of sales.
15. A price per unit determined on a single sale of previously imported goods, as in examples *(a)* and *(b)* in paragraph 14, will normally not be acceptable in valuing any future importations of identical or similar goods. The circumstances pertaining to any future importations would have to be reviewed to ensure that the sales in Canada did not significantly differ with respect to the quantities and prices at which the goods were previously sold. However, if the imported goods are only sold to one trade level and at one price on an ongoing basis, and that price is substantiated by evidence such as a "bona fide" price list supported by commercial invoices or several previous sales reflecting the

7. SAA, at 91.
8. Customs Memorandum D13-7-1, *Deductive Value Method—Determination of the Price Per Unit*, August 9, 2013, in paragraphs 11-15.

usual commercial practices of the importer, the single sale of previously imported goods may be acceptable in determining the price per unit.

In the EU, we find that the Implementing Act[9] does not provide much clarity, merely observing that, "sales in quantities which are not sufficient to allow the unit price to be determined are to be disregarded."

The Interpretative Notes of the Valuation Agreement and the US and Canadian administrative regimes[10] provide examples of accounting for qualifying quantities and they should be consulted.

We reach a final question in regard to fixing a unit price starting point for allowable deductions: can a discounted price be used? This was a question raised in *Oribalt Riga*, with the ECJ holding that discounted prices could not be so used. This may have been an error—I wrote "may" here because the statement of facts is vague (*see* Judgment paragraphs 13-14).

We have established that the definition of unit price is based on the price at which the imported goods or identical or similar imported goods are sold within the country of importation in the greatest aggregate quantity to persons not related to the sellers. That sale price may be a discounted price. If so, the discount has been built into the unit price. That should be a perfectly acceptable unit price if it meets the greatest aggregate quantity requirement.

It is only if there is a discount that is applied to the resale customers on an after-the-sale basis which raises the question, can that discount be taken as an allowable deduction? The AG Opinion[11] is especially unsound. In fact, it appears to take the position, broadly, that no discounts "of a commercial nature" will be allowed (paragraph 71). The AG seeks to admit that a discount is acceptable under a TV appraisement but that allowing discounts under the other methods would adversely affect the approximation of the real economic value of the imported goods (paragraphs 65-66). The AG appears ill at ease with the deductive method (*see* paragraph 67) and, as far as foreseeing the need to reduce the margin of error (paragraph 68), in Article 30.2(c) of the CCC, the EU was simply implementing a provision of the Valuation Agreement which, by the way, the predecessor body of the present EU had itself drafted.

Even if setting a base resale price has been established—and we have just outlined some of those challenges—the project is far from over. Allowable deductions from that price must then be established.

As discussed in greater detail below, various deductions are then taken from that unit price:

- any commission usually paid or an amount for profit and general expenses that is usual for sales of the same class or kind of imported goods;
- actual costs and associated costs of international transportation and insurance;

9. Article 142.4(d).
10. For the latter, *see* 19 CFR § 152.105(h), Customs Memorandum D13-7-1 in paragraph 9.
11. Opinion of AG Nils Wahl in Case C-1/18, *Oribalt Rga SIA v. Valsts ieņēmumu dienests*, 24.1.2019, ECLI:EU:C:2019:64.

- usual costs associated with post-importation freight to the place of delivery in the country of importation;
- customs duties and national taxes.

[C] Further Processed Goods

If neither the imported goods nor identical or similar goods are sold in the same condition as imported—if they have been subjected to further processing—the Valuation Agreement allows, at the importer's request, that: (i) deductive value might be based upon the imported goods[12] which have been further processed (ii) with due allowance for the value added to the imported merchandise by such further processing.[13] The Interpretative Note states that deductive value would not normally be available if the goods have lost their identity.[14] This means, of course, that deductive value would be available in some cases of a loss of identity. In fact, the Interpretative Note proceeds to observe that if the "value added by the processing can be determined accurately without unreasonable difficulty" then deductive value will be allowed. On the other hand, if the imported goods maintain their identity but form such a minor element in the goods sold in the country of importation, deductive value would be precluded.[15]

In the US, the term used to refer to the method based upon sales of further processed imported products, which is available at the importer's option, is "superdeductive value." The statute provides that a deduction will be allowed for:

> the value of any post-importation processing if the goods are processed prior to their resale, based on sufficient information.[16]

You may note that the statute refers to goods not sold in the condition as imported and not resold before the close of the 90th day after the date of importation. In that case, the superdeductive value will be based on resales made within 180 days of importation. Query, what happens to the goods that are further processed and are resold before the 90th day after the date of importation? The Statement of Administrative Action, at 92, explains that a waiting period is necessary before applying a superdeductive value, to ensure that there are no sales of goods in the same condition within that first 90-day period. That serves to open up a 90-day window of sales of further processed imported goods.

12. But apparently not identical or similar goods which have been further processed.
13. Article 5.2.
14. Interpretative Note to Article 5, point 12.
15. *Ibid.*
16. 19 USC §§ 1401a(d)(2)(A)(iii) and (3)(a)(iv). You may note that the statute refers to goods not sold in the condition as imported and not resold before the close of the 90th day after the date of importation. In that case, the superdeductive value will be based on resales made within 180 days of importation. Query, what happens to the goods that are further processed and are resold before the 90th day after the date of importation? The Statement of Administrative Action, at 92, explains that a waiting period is necessary before applying a superdeductive value, to ensure that there are no sales of goods in the same condition within that first 90-day period. That serves to open up a 90-day window of sales of further processed imported goods.

Canada's customs valuation law anticipates post-importation processing and, as is the US position, specifically provides for deductions of the costs associated with those operations.[17] The EU follows suit:

> In the absence of a unit price [of goods sold in the condition as imported], at the request of the declarant the unit price at which the imported goods are sold in the customs territory of the Union after further working or processing shall be used, due allowance being made for the value added by such working or processing.[18]

Unlike the US and Canadian regime, there is no time limit applied to the sales of further processed imported goods.

In the case of developing countries, the Agreement provides special treatment for the manner in which further processed goods will be treated. Annex III, paragraph 4, allows developing countries to make a reservation on the applicability of Article 5.2, to value further processed imported goods on a deductive value basis whether or not the importer so requests that. This is powerful. Coupled with a reservation to Article 4, as authorized by Annex III, paragraph 3, a developing country may insist on a deductive value appraisement for further processed goods even if the importer would prefer to proceed to a computed value method.

[D] Time Element

The statute has a distinct chronological ordering, starting with post-import sales taking place at or about the time of importation, proceeding to sales occurring up to 90 days after importation and, finally, in the case of the further processed imported goods in the US and Canada, sales occurring up to 180 days after importation.

The imported goods or identical or similar goods can be sold in their imported condition at or about the time of import[19] but, failing that, a sale within 90 days after importation will be acceptable.[20] In the US, the phrase "at or about the time of importation" is given an open-ended meaning—before, on or after the date of importation.[21] The program for further processed goods is more relaxed—if the goods are not sold in the same condition but the goods as further processed are sold within 180 days from the date of importation then the deductive value method may be used.

The time elements imposed by statute can be an insurmountable hurdle to the use of this method.[22] If the statutory criteria cannot be matched, as for example there

17. Canada Customs Act, paragraphs 51(2)(c) (assembly, packaging or further processing in Canada) and 51(4)(e).
18. UCC IA, Article 142.3.
19. Valuation Agreement, Article 5.1(a).
20. Valuation Agreement, Article 5.1(b).
21. Statement of Administrative Action, at 91.
22. The ECJ ruled in *Oribalt Riga* that the ninety-day time limit must be strictly applied, paragraphs 33-39.

is no guarantee that the goods will be sold with ninety days after importation, then CBP may appraise on a modified deductive value basis under the fallback method.[23]

[E] Related Parties

For deductive value purposes, a relationship between the foreign seller and the importer is irrelevant because the customs authority is looking to the later sale, the post-importation sale of the imported goods. In fact, the reason why the customs authority may be looking to appraise on a deductive value basis in the first place is that it has moved past a discredited related party price.

The possible relationship between the importer and the post-importation buyer is another matter. The Valuation Agreement calls for sales to related purchasers to be disregarded.[24] A further disqualification due to a commercial relationship is offered by the Valuation Agreement and the implementing statutes, which hold that a post-importation sale to a person who supplied a dutiable assist to the foreign seller will be disregarded.[25]

[F] Commercial Level

There is a further element that demands close attention. That is the level of sale in the post-importation sale.

In the ordinary course, a common progression has been the time-honored model of an importer/distributor exclusively pursuing this course: importing in bulk and placing goods into inventory, importer/distributor selling to wholesalers, the wholesalers selling to retail customers, the retailers selling to individual customers. In that case, the post-importation sales would be at the wholesale level. If that is the case, all sales being at the same commercial level, then it is a simple matter of applying the criteria.

But what if there are different commercial levels? What then?

The Interpretative Note devotes much attention to the question of sales at different quantity levels. While there is a focus on the "greatest aggregate quantity," the Valuation Agreement ignores the possible skewing effect of sales at different commercial levels.

Is this an issue something that should worry us? First, let us put this in perspective.

Let us not forget that the Valuation Agreement was drafted in the 1970s. One of the developments that will exert a profound impact on the task of finding a deductive

23. 19 USC § 1401a(f). *See* ruling no. 546312 (January 17, 1997), cited in ruling no. H304125 (August 2, 2019).
24. Valuation Agreement, Article 5.1 (a). In the US, 19 USC § 1401a(d)(2)(B); *see* ruling nos. 544469 (August 16, 1990) and 542267 (April 3, 1981) (TAA 22); Canada Customs Act, paragraph 51(3)(a); EU Implementing Act, Article 142.4(b).
25. Valuation Agreement, Interpretative Note, Article 5, point 5; 19 USC § 1401a(d)(D); Canada Customs Act, paragraph 51(3)(b); EU Implementing Act, Article 142.4(c).

value is the proliferation of sales channels. That importer may be selling to wholesalers and also selling directly to individual customers in a business-to-customers (B2C) channel. The rise of the internet has spawned the "ecommerce" phenomenon, in which individual customers "browse" the net—a modern day form of "shopping" and one that avoids having to physically visit the stores at the Mall, itself a modern phenomenon of centralizing Main Street or High Street shops. In the US, Canada and other countries that permit nonresident importers of record, there is a further scrambling of the traditional model. All these and myriad other iterations of both business-to business (B2B) and (B2C programs which have "disintermediated" sales channels present the possibility that the scrambled sales channels and their commercial levels are multivarious.

The Valuation Agreement[26] refers to commercial levels in its discussion of unit price, which is defined as:

> the price at which the greatest number of units is sold in sales to persons who are not related to the persons from which they buy such goods at the first commercial level after importation at which such sales take place.

The Agreement does not address the question of an adjustment. As a result, given the possibility of two more commercial levels in the resale pathways, the pending question of worry cannot be avoided. The US statute and regulation omit any discussion. In Canada, the statute demands[27] that:

> the price per unit, in respect of goods being appraised, identical goods or similar goods, shall be determined by ascertaining the unit price, in respect of sales of the goods at the first trade level after importation thereof.

The question being begged is "what is the first trade level?" Administrative guidance from the CBSA[28] tells us that there are to be no distinctions made:

> The first level of trade ... means the level at which the first domestic sale concluded after importation has occurred, and includes sales to a purchaser at any commercial level (for example, a wholesaler, a distributor, a retailer). In determining the price per unit, no account is to be taken of the trade level of the purchaser.

Presumably the EU takes the same approach: there is no discussion of commercial levels, but the Implementing Act directs: sales of goods at a commercial level other than the first after importation are to be disregarded.

As a result, the commercial levels in the sale of the imported goods and the resales of the imported goods or identical or similar goods may differ and there is no provision for any adjustments as there is under Articles 2 and 3. On the question of quantities, that other Article 2 or 3 basis for adjustments, we find another cause for concern.

---

26. Interpretative Note to Article 5, paragraph 1.
27. Canada Customs Act, subsection 51(3).
28. Customs Memorandum D13-7-1, *Deductive Value Method—Determination of the Price Per Unit*, August 9, 2013, in paragraph 7.

[G] Allowable Deductions from Resale Price

As its name implies, the major focus here is on the allowable deductions from the resale price. Another general observation—by its insistence that the commissions, profits and general expenses must be "usual" it should be obvious that the Valuation Agreement reinstates a market value concept. In the same fashion, the deduction for amounts representing post-importation transport, insurance and associated costs must be shown to be "usual." The deductions for post-import processing and for customs duties and national taxes are based on the actual expenses incurred by the importer, however, so the setting of the deduction should be less problematic.

[1] Usual Commission or Usual Profit and General Expenses

The Interpretative Notes advise that profit and general expenses "should be taken as a whole."[29] Presumably, this means that the profit and general expenses can be tracked and accounted for on an allocated basis. That may pose a burden for the importer.

Note that there is no subcategory of expenses that is to be excluded from the broad category of general expenses,[30] instead, we are directed that the category is to include the direct and indirect costs of marketing the goods.[31]

The customs law follows accounting practice in addressing "profit and general expenses" that are "usually made."[32] The US statute will not permit CBP to disallow information on the basis of the accounting method employed if that method is in accordance with GAAP.[33] In Canada, section 5 of the Valuation for Duty Regulations states that the amount for profit and general expenses is to be determined on the basis of information prepared in a manner consistent with GAPP. The Interpretative Notes to the Valuation Agreement make it clear that the GAAP in question is that of the country which is appropriate for the Article in question, i.e., the country of importation in a deductive value inquiry.[34] On this, or any other question where the GAAP might play a role, the importer will be well served with an expert opinion on GAAP conformity.

The deductions for profits and general expenses will be the importer's own profits and general expenses unless they are inconsistent with those reflected in sales of the class or kind of imported merchandise in the country of importation.[35] If an importing

29. Interpretative Note, Article 5, point 6.
30. In ruling no. 546120 (March 26, 1996), CBP stated that if an expense is incurred by the importer after the merchandise is released from CBP, it is likely to be a general expense.
31. Interpretative Note, Article 5, point 7.
32. Customs Memorandum, D13-7-1 at point 3.
33. 19 USC § 1401a(g)(3).
34. Interpretative Notes, General Note, Use of generally accepted accounting principles, point 2.
35. Valuation Agreement, Interpretative Note, Article 5, point 6; 19 USC § 1401a (d) (3) (B) (i); Customs Memorandum D13-7-1 (the information, in the first instance, is to be supplied by or on behalf of the importer. Normally, this information need only relate to sales in Canada made by the importer. If these figures are themselves based on sufficient information prepared in accordance with generally accepted accounting principles and are consistent with figures obtained from sales in Canada of imported goods of the same class or kind, they will be considered acceptable); N.B. The EU is silent on this issue.

taxpayer has a transfer pricing study prepared for income tax purposes, and the importer is the tested party, that company might employ that study to satisfy CBP of the bona fides of its profit/general expenses, i.e., that they are "usual," for these purposes.

As for commissions paid, CBP will likewise scrutinize whether the amount paid is "usual" for sales of that class or kind of imported merchandise in the US.[36]

For these purposes, the "class or kind" category is broader than the qualifying standard laid down for "identical" and "similar" goods in Articles 2 and 3 and 15.2 (d), where the goods will have to be manufactured in the same country as the goods being valued. For deductive value purposes, class or kind is defined to include goods imported from the same country as the goods being valued as well as goods imported from other countries.[37] On this point, lest there be any doubt, the US customs regulations specifically refer to "... sales in the United States of imported merchandise of the same class or kind from all countries ..."[38]

"Class or kind of merchandise" is a hoary term in the US customs laws, with the tariff classification in "chief use" provisions controlled by the principal use in the US of goods comprising the same "class or kind" of merchandise as the imported merchandise.[39] The tariff classification jurisprudence on this point is helpful here, as the criteria to establish "class or kind" have been clearly stated:

- General physical characteristics of the merchandise.
- Expectation of the ultimate purchasers.
- The channels, class, or kind of trade in which the merchandise moves.
- The environment of the sale.
- The use, if any, in the same manner as merchandise that defines the class.
- Economic practicality of so using the import.
- Recognition in the trade of this use.

These are often referred to as the "*Carborundum* factors" or "*Carborundum* criteria."[40] On the issue of "class or kind," the US customs valuation regulations comment:

> Sales for export to the United States of the narrowest group or range of imported merchandise, including the merchandise being appraised, will be examined to determine the usual profit and general expenses. For the purpose of computed

36. Ruling nos. 544086 (August 10, 1992) and 544365 (May 24, 1991).
37. Interpretative Note to Article 5, paragraph 9—assuming we were to take country of import to connote country of manufacture for these purposes. But the Statement of Administrative Action, at 90, reminds us that the definitions of identical and similar merchandise are as set forth in the statute—and presumably the Valuation Agreement and other implementing statutes. Those definitions require the same country of product as the merchandise being appraised.
38. 19 CFR § 152.105(e)(1).
39. *See* Part I. In the current HTSUS, this standard is enunciated in Additional U.S. Rule of Interpretation 1(a). *See also* such rulings as nos. N027262 (May 20, 2008) and 952878 (February 11, 1993).
40. The case that established these criteria is *United States v. Carborundum Co.*, 63 CCPA 98, 102, 536 F2d 373, CAD 1172, cert. den., 429 US 979 (1976). For a tariff classification ruling in which the *Carborundum* factors played a vital role, *see*, e.g., ruling no. H312459 (October 25, 2020).

value, merchandise of the same class or kind must be from the same country as the merchandise being appraised.[41]

It is clear that the burden of establishing that the importer's own financial experience makes for an allowable deduction for commission or for profit and general expenses is placed on the importer. Presumably, that burden is met by a showing that the importer's experience is consistent with the levels "usually" seen in the relevant class or kind. We have no further elaboration to guide us on what should be the standard, however, not even the "closely approximates" standard for related party pricing.[42] As the legislative history in the US notes, there is no hard and fast rule for what is a consistent profit or general expense. Each case must stand on its own.[43] In this application of a class or kind category, we see some guidance, insofar as the narrowest group or range of imported goods of the same class or kind should be examined.[44] But that begs the question, what is the class or kind of imported goods?

The essence of the problem is that there is at play an across-the-board character to the profit and general expenses standard. The unit price for the resale of the imported product is established with some clarity. The deduction for profit and general expenses presupposes that: (i) there are single levels of each that (ii) apply to a single relevant class or kind of imported goods. For the former question, there can be a limitless variety of business models (e.g., brick and mortar versus ecommerce site versus multilevel marketing structure) or commercial circumstances (e.g., new market entrant, closeout goods, ongoing sales for an established enterprise) which result in a limitless number of possible "usual" level of profits and general expenses. For the latter question, there is the chance of a similarly diverse range of product groupings, especially when "class or kind" here does not pertain to nor allow for any country-by-country origin differentiation, which might have value consequences. Further, there is no ability to account for disparities arising from enhanced or compromised efficiency or innovative developments.

The deduction here would require sufficient information. To my mind, the importer would generally not have access to this market information unless, perhaps, the importer has available transfer pricing or other market analysis study. The income tax authority in the country of importation might have this information but I would doubt that the customs authority would have that information readily available.[45]

---

41. 19 CFR § 152.106(e).
42. Valuation Agreement, Article 1.2 (b).
43. Statement of Administrative Action at 93.
44. Interpretative Note, Article 5, point 9. In the US, 19 CFR § 152.105(e)(2); Customs Memorandum D13-7-1 in paragraph 4; compare the Implementing Act, Article 142.5 (sales in the customs territory of the Union of imported goods of the same class or kind which are goods that fall within a group or range of goods produced by a particular industrial sector).
45. The Valuation Agreement allows the amount for profit and general expenses might be derived from relevant information other than that supplied by or on behalf of the importer. Interpretative Note, Article 5, point 6.

[2] *Transport, Insurance and Associated Costs*

As previously discussed, Article 8.2 of the Valuation Agreement recognizes the split on international transport and freight charges between FOB and CIF countries after import. We come to the need to take account of that split in the deductive value provision. Article 5.1 (a) (iii) allows for a deduction of those international charges "where appropriate." This means that, exceptionally, in those FOB countries there is a deduction for some actual charges that are incurred before importation. Because the theory for both deductive vale and computed value is that one should arrive at a value that is roughly equivalent to a valid TV, this deduction makes perfect sense.

The deduction is not limited to such international costs, as Article 5.1 (a)(ii) provides for the deduction of the usual costs of transport and insurance and associated costs incurred within the country of importation. Note the reappearance of the "usual" costs usage here.

Sherman and Glashoff ventured[46] that this might be an "averaged" amount. That hardly helps, as we encounter another challenge, as in, realistically how can the "usual" transport cost be determined given the potential for a multiplicity of different modes of transport and distances involved. Likewise, finding the usual level for the associated costs such as storage and handling would be a challenge. In all but the most simplistic, or Lilliputian, of circumstances, this task would appear to be a squaring-of-the-circle exercise. Beyond that, we also note that, although there is no explicit grounding in the class or kind of goods, we might infer such a limitation. Without that implicit limitation, the deduction would appear to be entirely open-ended—cutting across all product sectors. This would pose a challenge even for the insurance costs deduction, which might appear at a glance to be more readily ascertainable.

[3] *Duties and Taxes on Import or Sale of the Goods*

Duties and national taxes, such as excise taxes or Value Added Tax, that are included within the price in the sale after importation, meaning that they have not already been refunded, are to be deducted, assuming that they have not already been included within the general expenses deduction.[47] A question that may arise is the status of antidumping or countervailing duties. There appears to be a split of authority. In the US, the legislative history shows that these trade enforcement duties are not to be deducted as "customs duties": only the ordinary customs duties as established in the Tarff Schedules would be deducted.[48] This is consistent with their status in a TV appraisement, where they would be excluded from dutiable value.[49] The statutory references to customs duties in the transaction value and deductive value methods are

46. Sherman and Glashoff, no. 734 at 222.
47. Interpretative Note, Article 5, point 8.
48. Statement of Administrative Action at 94.
49. 19 USC § 1401a(b)(3)(B) excludes from transaction value, in addition to federal excise taxes, "the customs duties and other Federal taxes currently payable in the imported merchandise by reason if its importation." *See* ruling no. 545304 (January 4, 1994) (antidumping duties

identical.[50] At the international level, the TCCV has opined that antidumping or countervailing duties are to be deducted from unit price.[51]

[H] Deductive Value at Work: Ruling No. H281093

A 2018 ruling issued by CBP may serve as a useful illustration of the deductive value method in practice and as a cautionary tale. In ruling no. H281093 (May 17, 2018) CBP validated the deductive value method as the basis for ascertaining the customs value for imported automobiles.[52] The episode illustrates how daunting can be the effort required.

In the course of ruling no. H281093, CBP analyzed the importer's general expenses and found that they were typical for the imported motor vehicle industry and in line with GAAP. They included

Holdback:

The importer pays a "holdback" amount to dealers as an effective deduction to the dealer invoice price.

[Unnamed price reduction]:

During FY 2011, the importer also provided a reduction in the dealer invoice price.

Marketing Allowance:

The importer provides a marketing allowance to the automobile dealers.

Floor Plan Allowance:

The importer provides a "Floor Plan Allowance" ("FPA") to dealers to assist them in purchasing products, with this allowance operating as another effective discount to the dealer invoice price.

Sales Discounts and Incentives:

The importer offers a variety of sales discounts and incentives, that is, payments to dealers based upon the reporting of the dealer's retail sales of eligible vehicles during a program period that are not reflected in the importer's invoices to the dealers.

Full Tank of Fuel Credit:

The full tank of fuel ("FTF") credit is a fixed amount that the protestant pays to the dealers to provide retail purchasers with a full tank of fuel upon their purchase of a vehicle.

Pre-Delivery Inspection Credit:

---

constitute "customs and other Federal taxes" such that they would not be included in transaction value, provided the amount of such duties are identified separately from the PAPP for the imported merchandise).

50. Cf. 19 USC § 1401a(b)(3)(B) and 19 CFR § 1401a(d)(3)(A)(iv).
51. TCCV, AO 9.1, Treatment of Anti-dumping and Countervailing Duties When Applying the Deductive Method (September 1982).
52. The importer was in a deductive value appraisement mode because it had failed to meet the "all costs plus a profit" COS test in its related party transaction. With the adequate support of an economics study of the industry pricing practices, the importer might have been better off if it had sought to justify its price as having been set in line with the normal pricing practices of the industry. These issues are discussed in Part II.

The importer reimburses dealers for their pre-delivery inspection ("PDI") services before a new vehicle [X] is delivered to the retail purchasers. The Dealer Pricing Guides thus refer to a "pre-delivery payment" that is "credited to the dealer's open account when specified Pre-Delivery Service is completed and the importer receives notification."

Ocean Freight and Marine Insurance:

The importer calculated the amounts for ocean freight and marine insurance as further deductions from the price. The ocean freight charges are based on the volume (cubic meters) included in each shipment of vehicles. The importer has information on the volume in cubic meters of each model code imported from the seller.

The marine insurance charges reflected are based upon the value of the shipment. Accordingly, the marine insurance amounts in the individual shipments covered by the FY 2011 period were allocated to individual models based upon their proportionate value, and weighted average marine insurance amounts by model number were calculated from this data.

US Duty, HMF and MPF:

The amounts for the models imported from the seller include US customs duty, the harbor maintenance fee (HMF), and the merchandise processing fee (MPF). Accordingly, the importer calculated the amount for duty, HMF and MPF amounts by model code for the imports from the seller for the FY 2011 period. Specifically, these amounts were calculated by totaling these amounts for imports of each model code from the seller during the period and dividing by the units imported to arrive at a per-unit amount.

US Inland Freight:

The importer calculated the costs related to transportation of the vehicles imported from the seller from the US port to the dealer for the FY 2011 period. These calculations were based upon the monthly Logistics Expense Reports.

General Expenses and Profit: Advertising

The importer calculated results for various categories of general expenses and profit on a fiscal year basis. The first of these is the advertising amount. The protestant has advertising expenses relating to specific automobile models, as well as general advertising that is not specific to a particular model. Accordingly, the advertising expenses recorded in the protestant's accounting records can be divided into model-specific and nonspecific advertising expenses, using product codes associated with the advertising expenditures. This information was used to calculate both: (1) per-unit-model-specific advertising expense for each model imported from the seller and (2) per-unit-nonspecific advertising expense applicable to certain models generally. The total advertising expense for each model was calculated as the sum of these two amounts.

General Expenses and Profit: Selling, General & Administrative Expense

The importer incurs other SG&A expenses on its sale of imported and other automobiles, including costs for sales operations, business operations, and service and technology. Accordingly, after adjusting for the advertising expenses and other non-allocable SG&A expenses not applicable to imports from the seller, the importer calculated the other SG&A expenses based upon the account detail reflected in the importer's reports. The resulting amounts were allocated among individual models based on relative sales values, and per-unit amounts were calculated from the sales units.

The adjustments made for Non-Allocable Expenses include: (1) the Advertising expenses that were already reflected in the calculation of the Advertising expense, (2) the Royalty Expense that relates to automobile production in and not to imports from the seller, (3) certain Non-Allocable Cost Centers such as those for that are not subject to the deductive value calculations, (4) Depreciation on Leased Property, (5) Depreciation on Leased Cars, and (6) SG&A. There are also additions for Revenue Programs that offset SG&A expenses.

General Expenses and Profit: Nonoperating Income/Expense

The importer's operations include a variety of nonoperating items associated with revenues or expenses to the company. Nonoperating income and expense items for FY 2011 were analyzed to determine which categories were allocable to imports of automobiles from the seller. The resulting amounts were allocated among individual models based on relative sales, and unit sales were used to calculate per-unit amounts.

You can appreciate the cost accounting expertise which was at the heart of this exercise.

The extremes to which the importer will be pushed to meet the deductive value method and, as will be seen, the computed value method as well, should be obvious at this point. What is equally obvious is that the prudent importer will want to avoid that ordeal at any and all costs and, instead, will want to satisfy the customs authority that transaction value is appropriate.

CHAPTER 7

Method Based on "Cost Plus"

§7.01 COMPUTED VALUE

The customs valuation law requires that the appraising officer look to a computed value basis of appraisement if there is no deductive value. Parenthetically, computed value is the customs law equivalent of the cost-plus method under the transfer pricing regulations, section 482 in the US.[1]

Computed value is arrived at by adding together the following elements:

(1) cost or value of materials and cost of fabrication and other processing employed in producing the imported goods;
(2) profit and general expenses usual for producers in sales of the same class or kind of merchandise in the country of exportation for export to the country of importation;[2]
(3) international transport, insurance and associated costs (in those countries which include them in customs value per Article 8.2);
(4) any assists (if not included in no. 1);
(5) packing costs (if not included in no. 1).[3]

1. IRC Reg. §1.482-3(d)(1).
2. The definition of "merchandise of the same class or kind" is narrower than the standard in deductive value. Here, the class or kind refers only to the narrowest group or range of imported merchandise, including the merchandise being appraised, for which information will be available. That merchandise must be from the same country as the merchandise being appraised. Interpretative Note to Article 6, paragraph 8. For the US, *see* 19 CFR 152.106(e). In Canada, Customs Memorandum D13-8-1, *Computed Value Method*, February 4, 2014, paragraph 15. In the EU, there is no further definition.
3. Valuation Agreement, Article 6 and accompanying Interpretative Note; 19 USC § 1401a(e)(1); Canada Customs Act, section 52; EU, UCC Article 74.2(d). Interestingly, the EU includes the cost of international transport, insurance and loading/unloading charges per UCC, Article 71(e) as they are specifically incorporated by reference in the Agreement in Article 6.1(c). The UCC does

As a prefatory note, as in the case of deductive value, the producer's own profits and expenses will be used unless they are inconsistent with those of producers in sales of the same class or kind or merchandise for export to the country of importation.[4]

But even a first glance at the criteria should reveal the strain caused by computed value.

Deductive value derives from the importer's own experience in its sales activities in the customs territory as well as accounting for usual levels of profit and general expenses and usual costs arising in the country of importation. In contrast, computed value prefers to look away to the foreign producer/exporter's books and records, in light of the "usual" profits and general expenses in that country for a producer/exporter. The GAAP standard is that of the foreign country, not the country of importation.[5] It is fair to say that familiarity with or expertise in that foreign country GAAP standard may be a challenge for both the importer and the customs authority alike.

Premised on the availability of foreign production costs and general expenses of the imported goods, computed value presupposes the cooperation of the foreign producer. On this point, the text of the Valuation Agreement posits that:

> No Party may require or compel any person not resident in its own territory to produce for examination, or to allow access to, any account or other record for the purposes of determining a computed value.[6]

Further guidance is available from the WTO signatories themselves, who had recognized in an Interpretative Note to the Valuation Agreement that:

> As a general rule, customs value is determined under this Agreement on the basis of information readily available in the country of exportation. In order to determine a computed value, however, it may be necessary to examine the costs of producing the goods being valued and other information which has to be obtained from outside the country of importation.***The use of the computed value method will generally be limited to those cases where the buyer and seller are related, and the producer will be prepared to supply to the authorities of the country of importation the necessary costings and to provide facilities for any subsequent verification which may be necessary.[7]

Some further comments on the elements are appropriate.

not specifically refer to assists or packing costs in this computed value context. Those latter costs are identified in the Agreement's Interpretative Note and are dealt with by the EU in the UCC IA, Article 142.2.

4. Valuation Agreement, Interpretative Note, Article 6, point 1; 19 USC § 1401a(e)(2)(B).
5. Valuation Agreement, Interpretative Notes, General Note, Use of generally accepted accounting principles, point 2.
6. Article 6, paragraph 2.
7. Interpretative Note, Article 6, point 1.

[A] Cost or Value of Materials and Fabrication

Not surprisingly, these costs are the actual costs of the foreign producer. The US statute mandates that the cost of materials may not include VAT or any other taxes which would be remitted upon export.[8]

Amounts recorded as general expenses or profits in the importer's books, by contrast, are to be disregarded and normally would not be added to the producer's book amounts.[9] On this subject, customs law commentators observe that:

> the computed value provisions say little as to what is or is not included in general expenses. The concept is apparently (and wisely) left to be defined mainly by GAAP and the accounting methods used by the manufacturer.[10]

Allocated costs of production machinery and equipment are a part of the cost of fabrication. If such machinery/equipment are given free or at reduced price to the manufacturer, then an assist will have been conferred and the dutiable value will be increased accordingly. If nonproduction machinery and equipment are provided, there will not be a dutiable assist, but their value might be included in the cost of fabrication and general expenses.[11] Ordinarily, the foreign manufacturer's own accounting decisions will prevail. In short, if the seller is provided with production machinery/equipment, then it might be a dutiable assist, which must be included as an element in computed value; if the machinery/equipment is nonproduction, then it will not be an assist, but its value might be dutiable as a cost of fabrication or GE under the foreign GAAP.

To further illustrate the primacy of the manufacturer's own accounting decisions, it is noted that post-production costs are not normally counted as fabrication costs. But, if the manufacturer itself books costs—such as insurance and transport costs to move the goods from the factory to the point of exportation—as general expenses, CBP will include them, too.

This was the case in *Campbell Soup*.[12]

In *Campbell Soup*, the US importer had purchased tomato paste from a Mexican subsidiary, which product was appraised based on computed value. Campbell sought to have CBP take into account certain deductions that would have lowered the computed value.

Campbell Soup submitted a cost submission to CBP that showed that it was deducting rebated internal taxes from its general expenses, while the subsidiary producer had recorded the tax rebates as miscellaneous profit. In addition, the cost of internal freight was included within the cost of materials. CBP auditors disallowed the rebated taxes and also concluded that the transportation charges should have been

8. 19 USC § 1401a(e)(2).
9. Ruling no. 545088 (February 14, 1995). *But see* ruling no. 547094 (June 3, 1999).
10. Sherman and Glashoff, no. 776 at 230.
11. Ruling nos. 544083 (August 16, 1988) (C.S.D. 88-20) (storage tanks, conveyor system, air compressors); 543576 (March 3, 1986).
12. *Campbell Soup Co. v. United States*, 107 F3d 1556 (Fed. Cir. 1997), aff'g in part, rev'g in part, 853 F. Supp. 1443 (CIT 1994).

treated as selling expenses and were not deductible. Campbell protested the CBP determinations, asserting that the rebated internal taxes should have been deducted from material costs and that the freight costs that, consistent with Mexican GAAP, had been carried on the producer's books as production costs should also have been deducted. The matter went up for judicial review after the protest denial by CBP.

The CIT granted summary judgment for the government. On appeal, the Federal Circuit reversed in part, noting that the trial court had too hastily dismissed the deduction of the rebated internal taxes. The CIT had dismissed the importer's argument as "misplaced," observing that there was no authority to deduct the rebated taxes from general expenses, as had been the importer's position with the cost submission. The trial court overlooked the point that Campbell corrected itself on the protest, arguing accurately that the rebated taxes should be accounted for and deducted from the cost of materials. So far, so good, but the partial reversal and the importer's ensuing victory was short-lived, as the appellate court's opinion went on to snatch away the "win."

In essence, the appellate court's reasoning was tantamount to stating that the importer had scored an "own goal" because the producer had included the rebated taxes as profits. The importer was not required to adjust the producer's own figures for profit and general expenses, unless the importer could show that the accounting treatment was inconsistent with other Mexican producers. The producer's own books and records trumped the statute's clear call for rebated internal taxes to be eliminated from material costs and the importer's timely placed argument before CBP and the courts. The appellate decision on internal taxes was issued over a strong dissenting opinion, which argued that the rebated tax could not correctly be characterized as a profit and also picked up the importer's argument that to include this tax was violative of GATT obligations. The appellate court affirmed the inclusion of the internal transport charges because they, too, had been included by the producer in its financial accounting as general expenses, and because this treatment was consistent with Mexican GAAP.

Perhaps Campbell's misfortune can serve as a lesson for other importers. First, Campbell might have been better served at the outset if its Mexican subsidiary's accounting books had been prepared with these customs valuation principles in mind.[13] Second, even if accounting records had been prepared that showed higher producer's expenses, and a correspondingly greater computed value, it still might have been possible to prevail if the importer could have impeached the producer's financials as inconsistent with the applicable GAAP.

In spite of the deference accorded to the manufacturer's own accounting decisions, issues have arisen in accounting for the cost of fabrication used by the manufacturer. Booking these costs as production-related will result in their being included in determining computed value. When these costs are excluded, the issue arises as to whether that accounting decision is consistent with the foreign GAAP.

---

13. Given the presumption that all, or nearly all, of the subsidiary's production was for exportation to the United States this should not have been as far-fetched as the suggestion would be in other circumstances.

[B] Profit and General Expenses

As is the case with deductive value, a single aggregated mount will be taken for profit and general expenses. General expenses are all those direct and indirect costs of producing and selling the goods for export which are not already included as direct production costs.[14] The element of "profit" is arrived at after netting out all expenses from receipts of sales for export to the country of importation. In a sharp contrast to the deductive value method, there is an understanding in the Interpretative Note to Article 6, in paragraph 5, that the "usual" profit level might be a very low profit or even a loss.

This could be the case with a new product being introduced into the country of importation, where the producer accepts either no profit or a low profit to offset the high general expenses required to introduce the product into this market. If the producer can demonstrate that there is a low profit on sales of the imported merchandise because of "peculiar commercial circumstances,"[15] those actual profit figures will be accepted provided the producer has valid commercial reasons to justify them and his pricing policy reflects the usual pricing policies in the industry. It could also be that producers have been forced to lower prices temporarily because of an unforeseeable drop in demand, or they sell merchandise to complement a range of merchandise being produced in the country of importation and accept a low profit to maintain competitiveness.[16]

The next point to make is that this amount need not be those of the actual producer. Normally, the producer's own profits and expenses, as carried in its books, will be relied upon[17] but only if they are consistent with those usually reflected in sales of merchandise of the same class or kind as the merchandise being valued which are produced in the country of exportation for export to the country of importation. Otherwise, the amount for profit and general expenses will be based upon relevant or reliable and quantifiable information other than that supplied by or on behalf of the producer of the merchandise.[18]

---

14. Interpretative Note, Article 6, point 7. This is reproduced in the Canadian legislation, Canada Customs Act, subsection 52(4).
15. This is the phrase employed in the US regulations, 19 CFR § 152.106(c)(1). It is "particular commercial circumstances" in the Interpretative Note. Canada recognizes that "There may be valid commercial reasons" for the producer's low level of profit. Customs Memorandum D13-8-1, *Computed Value Method*, February 4, 2014, paragraph 14.
16. This acknowledgment of the dynamics of a competitive marketplace, marked by traders' responses to competitive conditions, is welcome. It exposes a lack of balance in the Valuation Agreement, however. In very much the same fashion as laid out in this valuation method, I would argue that there could be "peculiar commercial circumstances" which similarly exert an influence on the profit and general expense level and in fact constitute the usual experience in the country of importation in a deductive value analysis.
17. 19 USC § 1401a(e)(2)(B); ruling no. 543076 (September 6, 1983).
18. The Valuation Agreement uses the term "relevant," the US regulations use the phrase "reliable or quantifiable." Valuation Agreement, Interpretative Note, Article 6, point 5, 19 CFR § 152.106(c), interpretative note 2. The approach by Canada is noteworthy. Customs Memorandum D13-8-1, paragraph 15 suggests a valuation database reference (the amount added for profit and general expenses will be based on information drawn from an examination of sales for export to Canada. The sales examined would be of the narrowest group or range of goods of the same class or kind as the goods being appraised made by producers in the country of export,

Unlike the deductive value method, which looked as a starting point to the importer's resale price or to the resale price of identical or similar imported goods, in computed value we find that computed value looks only to the producer's own costs of production. When we get to profit and general expenses, however, we find that the "usual" standard is set by producers who export goods of that class or kind to the country of importation. Because it may be supposed that the initial focus would be on the experience of the actual producer of the imported goods, I used the term "producer/exporter" above. But that presupposes that the producer is an actual exporter, i.e., that the producer has entered into "sales of the same class or kind of merchandise in the country of exportation for export to the country of importation," to quite from the Valuation Agreement.

Computed value appears to assume that the seller of the imported goods is the producer of those goods. As we have already seen in the forty-five years since the text was first proposed, however, there has been a proliferation of other business models. The foreign seller may not be the producer but a trading company, a buyer/reseller of the goods, or a related party which had relied on a contract manufacturer to produce the goods.

In the absence of any export sales by the producer, as would be the case where the foreign producer acts as a contract manufacturer and/or only sells on a domestic sale basis to other intermediate parties, such as buyer/reseller trading companies, or only sells to other foreign markets, there can be no reliance exclusively on the producer's own experience. At the same time, assuming that the buyer/reseller exporter does not also function as a producer and has no qualifying export sales of its own—it is only an exporter—the exporter's profit and general expenses must be ignored.

In the absence of the producer having qualifying sales for export, there can be no qualifying profit and general expenses of the producer to serve as a benchmark.

What then? Sherman and Glashoff argue[19] that the producer's profit and general expenses must be accepted through a liberal interpretation of a "sale for export" criterion; otherwise, computed value could not be applied at all.

After reading my extensive discussions on sale for export and First Sale above, you will not be surprised that I do not entirely agree. Sherman and Glashoff refer to a case in which a sale from producer P to vendor V, both of whom are in country X, providing for a "drop shipment" directly to V's customer C in country I, might be recognized as a sale for export to country I. In such a case, producer P is also deemed to be the exporter. Beyond that scenario, First Sale treatment might apply and a sale from producer P to the vendor V would qualify as a sale for export. That would allow an application of producer P's profit and general expense data.

In the absence of such circumstances then I would agree that computed value may not be applied, but only as a practical matter. The importer might still be able to

including the goods being appraised, from which sufficient information can be obtained). One would hope that a narrowed comparison would be applied but one would still be confronted with profit and general expense amounts being inferred from declared prices.

19. Sherman and Glashoff, no. 784 at 232.

look beyond producer P and cobble together the needed information from other producer/exporters to sustain a computed value appraisement. Assuming that the importer will have access to: (i) the producer's own production costs and also to (ii) the amount for usual profit and general expenses of producers generally in the country of export who have made sales of the same class or kind of goods for export to the country of importation, computed value may yet be available.

The Valuation Agreement is clear and direct on the authority of the customs authority to look beyond the information supplied on or behalf of the producer.[20] In doing so, the customs authority is instructed to provide the importer with the provenance of that other information:

> the authorities of the importing country shall inform the importer, if the latter so requests, of the source of such information, the data used and the calculations based upon such data, subject to the provisions of Article 10 [business confidential information].[21]

Another issue plaguing the test value comparison is the requirement that the customs authority must be satisfied with the accuracy of the financial records. Of course, it must be expected that CBP and other customs authorities have at times taken pains to avoid accepting the accounting at face value and to discredit an importer's efforts to substantiate an appraisement when the financial records are not "verifiable."

This is one of the lessons of the 1998 CIT decision in *La Perla Fashions*,[22] where the trial court rejected the importer's computed value and deductive value calculations because they were deemed unreliable.

In *La Perla*, CBP had determined that there was no bona fide sale of imported merchandise, women's swimwear, and instead fixed the dutiable value on the resale price in the US less certain elements of cost (international freight, insurance, duties, and incidental charges) but, importantly, leaving intact an amount for the importer's profit or commission. The importer admitted that the relationship had affected the price paid for the imported goods but sought to validate the transfer price paid to the related party seller in Italy on the ground that the price closely approximated test values (i.e., in this case, values derived from both computed value and deductive value analyses). La Perla provided witnesses who testified that the computed value was calculated in accordance with the valuation statute directly from the accounting records of the Italian seller, and that the accounting records were kept in accordance with Italian law and Italian GAAP. The importer argued that the computed value could not be rejected merely because the government might have chosen different allocation methods and that the court need not exclude the evidence from consideration merely because it was not created exactly as CBP would have liked. So, too, with deductive value; the importer argued that that calculation had been prepared in accordance with GAAP.

20. Interpretative Note, Article 6, point 5.
21. Interpretative Note, Article 6, point 6.
22. *La Perla Fashions, Inc. v. United States*, 9 F. Supp. 2d 698, 22 CIT 393 (1998) (Musgrave, J.), aff'd per curiam w/o op., 185 F3d 885 (Fed. Cir. 1999).

The trial court agreed with CBP on an important legal point. CBP argued that the evidence advanced by the importer on the computed and deductive value methods, for use in comparison with the PAPP by the importer, was not admissible. CBP asserted that the importer's calculations were not admissible because they represented summaries or summaries of summaries that were not verifiable by a CBP auditor.

The court summarized the CBP position:

> [CBP auditors] [c]ould not verify the bases for virtually all of the critical factual information relating to [La Perla's] proposed CV comparisons, and unequivocally testified that in his experience there have been occasions where information submitted based upon a companies [sic] summaries of business records and financial statements were erroneous and understatements of value, even though the basic documents were audited business records of the company.[23]

The court apparently accepted this argument in its entirety, substituting its own review as the basis for appraising the imported merchandise:

> The Court finds that its examination of the transactions in the trial record provide the objective, market-based price of the subject merchandise upon which this opinion is based. The computed and deductive values submitted by La Perla exposed the dangers of utilizing unverified deductive and computed values to value merchandise . ... La Perla's use of cost information derived from audited records does not provide the Court with inherently accurate information. The purpose behind Customs' verification procedures is to ensure that an accurate computed and deductive value calculation is formulated. The Court agrees with Customs that La Perla's failure to provide the records that laid the foundation for the summaries presented at trial prevents a verification of La Perla's computed and deductive value calculations. Without a verifiable record, Customs was correct in rejecting La Perla's computed and deductive value formulations. The Court rejects La Perla's computed and deductive value calculations because of their lack of reliability, not their form.[24]

In a daring feat of rewriting the customs valuation law, the *La Perla* court slipped badly, but inexplicably the appellate court failed to reverse. The *La Perla* court wrote that CBP should not have looked in vain for unrelated sales from the exporter to other importers, and then proceeded to write that CBP should have looked to unrelated sales from the exporter to other importers:

> Customs should have instead focused its scrutiny on the comparison of the price charged by GLP [the Italian parent/seller] to its direct US customers with the price between GLP and La Perla. It is this comparison that the Court finds provides the requisite market-based price upon which the correct valuation is based. ... For the foregoing reasons, the Court finds that the subject entries of garments were correctly valued on the price between La Perla and its customers in the United States.

23. *La Perla Fashions, Inc. v. United States*, 9 F. Supp. 2d 698, 704, 22 CIT 393 (1998).
24. *La Perla Fashions, Inc. v. United States*, 9 F. Supp. 2d 698, 705, 22 CIT 393 (1998).

Quite beyond this self-contradiction, a broader review of the opinion shows that the trial court was lost in what for him appears to be the vastness of the customs valuation law without a map or compass. The affirmation by the Federal Circuit of this decision, without an opinion to be sure, is a complete mystery. The decision is unsound and should be discredited.

Some further comments on the trial court decision. First, the importer had complained that CBP had not examined the third-party sales between exporter GLP and US customers. Those sales should have formed the basis for a comparison with the sales under review, as they would have made for a test value comparison based on the TV of identical or similar merchandise. In this connection, as noted above, the customs valuation law specifically requires that any such comparison take due account of commercial levels of sales, quantities, and other costs.[25] To proceed otherwise without adjustments makes for an apples-to-oranges comparison. In fact, this is exactly what happened to *La Perla*. The court found that the sales prices from the foreign seller to unrelated buyers in the US were within 2% of the price on resales from La Perla to its US customers. Further, the court noted that the price paid by La Perla to the related party seller was typically 35% less than the price paid to the foreign seller by the unrelated direct buyers. The court concluded darkly that "the importer was receiving the benefit of the lower price paid to GLP."[26] The court would have been better served had it applied the customs valuation law as it is written and used as a basis for comparison either: (1) the TV of identical or similar merchandise with suitable adjustments[27] or (2) computed or deductive value comparisons, which would have backed out profit and general expenses from the calculation.

Second, the reference to a "market-based price" is entirely out of place under the present customs valuation law and is reminiscent of a 1997 opinion by the same CIT judge, discredited for having applied an "export value" analysis.[28] Third, the court reached the legal conclusion that because the importer had stipulated that the price had been influenced by the relationship, the importer had thereby negated a sales relationship and admitted to an agency relationship with its parent company.[29] Fourth, the court drew a negative inference from the importer's failure to provide verifiable accounting work papers:

---

25. 19 USC § 1401a(b)(2)(C). The regulations are clear: valuation based on the TV of identical or similar merchandise must be based on sales at the same commercial level and in substantially the same quantity. If there are no such sales, i.e., if the commercial level or quantities differ, adjustments must be made to the test values to take account of that difference. 19 CFR §§ 152.104(d), 152.104(e).
26. *La Perla Fashions, Inc. v. United States*, 9 F. Supp. 2d 698, 703, 22 CIT 393 (1998).
27. This calls to mind the lack of merit in the *Fawkes* and *Euro 2004* decisions by the ECJ discussed in Part I where a database source would similarly not allow for adjustments.
28. *VWP of Am., Inc. v. United States*, 21 CIT 1109 (CIT 1997), *vacated by* 175 F3d 1327 (Fed. Cir. 1999), 259 F. Supp. 2d 1289 (CIT 2003), *aff'd in part, vacated and remanded*, 117 Fed. Appx. 113 (Fed. Cir. 2004), *reh'g denied*, 2005 US App. LEXIS 2291 (Fed. Cir. 2005). The cases were ultimately settled at appraised value less 17%, probably equating to a deductive value appraisement whose 17% post-importation markup is deducted from the resale price. *See*, e.g., CIT, Slip Op. 06-87 (June 7, 2006) and Slip Op.06-144 (September 26, 2006).
29. *La Perla Fashions, Inc. v. United States*, 9 F. Supp. 2d 698, 702, 22 CIT 393 (1998).

> [A]s a practical matter, La Perla's failure to provide the supporting information raises the specter that they are withholding information. It is clear from the record that Customs persistently requested the underlying records that were used to compile the computed and deductive values prepared by La Perla. The reluctance of La Perla to provide this information casts doubt as to what that record contained. If there were no discrepancies in the underlying records, it would seem that La Perla would have been more forthcoming in furnishing them to Customs and the Court.[30]

However, access to such foreign records was recognized from the outset of the promulgation of the Valuation Agreement as problematic, especially for computed value, where the importer is forced to rely on the cooperation of a separate legal entity located in a foreign jurisdiction. For that very reason, computed value is availed of relatively rarely.[31]

We can derive another lesson from a 1994 US ruling which concerned pre-production costs.[32] It seems that certain excess start-up and pre-production costs that had been carried on the producer's books were part of general expenses. The issue was whether or not the inclusion of such expenses was inconsistent with that which is usually reflected in sales of merchandise of the same class or kind. The importer itself argued that the accounting for the expenses was inconsistent with usual practice because they should be amortized over a period of five years. They had not been amortized on the producer's books, so the importer was impeaching the status of the producer's accounting practice.

In CBP's analysis, they reasoned that where expenses are carried on the producer's books, but are not amortized therein, the appraised value of the merchandise must be based on the non-amortized costs as reflected on those books. As the importer did not show that the inclusion of such expenses was inconsistent with other sales for export from that country, CBP held that the non-amortized excess start-up and pre-production costs were general expenses for the purposes of computed value appraisement.

CBP confronted the issue of "billed back" costs in ruling no. W547548.[33] The costs at issue were certain start-up costs for a new production facility in Mexico. The costs were in the nature of: (i) training (limited to salaries and benefits paid to new workers before they were assigned to a production department) and (ii) excess overhead costs (comprise utilities, supplies (not including materials incorporated into

30. *La Perla Fashions, Inc. v. United States*, 9 F. Supp. 2d 698, 705, 22 CIT 393 (1998).
31. *See* Valuation Agreement, Interpretative Note, Article 6, point 1.
32. Ruling no. 544863 (September 22, 1994).
33. Ruling no. W547548 (September 26, 2001) ("[The importer] has made no showing that these expenses are inconsistent with expenses related to the sales of men's shirts of the same class or kind, they appear to be typical of new factory start-ups, and not unusual or extraordinary. In this regard, they are similar to the non-production-related general expenses at issue in [earlier rulings] ... .Therefore, the non-production salary and training expenses currently at issue are general expenses, includable in the calculation of the amount to be added for profit and general expenses for the determination of the computed value of the imported merchandise").

garments), management and supervisory personnel and equipment amortization) in order to establish the Mexican production facility.

The importer contended that these expenses were carried exclusively on its books in the US, were reimbursed to the Mexican producer on a monthly basis and should not be counted as a general expense. CBP countered that an invoice from the producer to the importer for reimbursement of the costs was itself proof that the costs had been carried in the producer's own books.

CBP has held that salary and other employee compensation, as well as other costs not directly related to processing, were part of general expenses for the purposes of computed value appraisement. The general expenses of a foreign manufacturer will include various payments to its employees in the nature of training expenses, language classes, general development and a matching savings plan.[34] In a 1984 ruling, CBP concluded that salaries for producer's employees' time spent in training classes relating to the development of general skills, and reimbursements for voluntary job-related training in English, accounting, etc., were general expenses includable in the computed value of the imported merchandise.[35] At times CBP has studied the salaries and related expenses of an importer's personnel seconded to a foreign manufacturer. CBP has held that the salaries of engineers who were detailed to the foreign assembler were not dutiable either as costs of fabrication or as assists.[36] The importer had stressed that the salaries were not carried on the assembler's books and were not reflected in the standard cost estimates.[37]

For the costs associated with severance pay for discharged employees, CBP ruled that these expenses are to be included in the general expenses of the foreign manufacturer. This holding was over the objections of the importer who argued, in the ruling request, that such expenses were, almost by definition, not "general" but extraordinary, nonrecurring charges. CBP's reasoning was that the severance payments were made pursuant to a legal obligation that resulted from the producer's decision to terminate its employees. On that basis, they determined that they were not extraordinary, but were within the category of general expenses usually reflected in sales of merchandise of the same class or kind.[38]

Finally, we can see in yet another ruling that an attempt to limit an inclusion as a general expense was unsuccessful. The interest paid by the Mexican assembler to acquire fixed assets of the assembly plant is 100% dutiable. The importer had sought a pro rata dutiability only, limited to the plant capacity utilization.[39]

---

34. Ruling no. 543031 (April 12, 1983).
35. Ruling no. 543166 (January 6, 1984).
36. In ruling no. 544481 (May 8, 1991) (citing three earlier rulings).
37. *But see* ruling no. 543502 (June 11, 1985), in which CBP held that the expenses for a plant manager traveling back and forth to Mexico, his entertainment expenses, travel expenses to the United States for a Mexican engineer for training, membership fees and dues for the plant manager are not includable under computed value as either cost of fabrication or GE.
38. Ruling no. 544616 (April 15, 1991).
39. Ruling no. 543159 (May 7, 1984).

[C] Assists

To the extent that the value of assist is not already included in fabrication or general expenses,[40] dutiable assists must also be accounted for.

The Interpretative Note[41] limits the inclusion of dutiable assists in category (b)(iv) which are comprised of engineering, design and development activities undertaken in the country of importation—which you will recognize as being excluded from assist status—only to the charges which are imposed on the producer. Accordingly, if the producer benefits from such services provided on a free basis, the costs are not treated as assists and they are not to be included in a computed value buildup.[42] This is an anomaly unless the theory is that there should be symmetry with the treatment accorded to transaction value, where an Article 8 adjustment would not be made for such excluded services.

[D] Packing Costs

It would be unlikely that packing costs would not already be included within the category of materials or fabrication costs, but if that is the case then packing costs as a separate category would be included in the computed value buildup.

[E] Parting Words on Computed Value

There are two hurdles to the use of computed value that may be insurmountable, both for the importer and the customs authority. First, access to the producer's financial information—material and fabrication costs, profit and general expenses—may be totally out of reach for the importer—and for the customs administration as well. No party can be compelled to provide such information.[43] If that is the case, there can be no further discussion.

Second, even if the producer's information were available, there can be another problem in having reliable access to the standard for "usual" profits and general expenses for producers of that class or kind of merchandise in the country of production. The reference in the US regulations to "reliable and quantifiable information other than that supplied by or on behalf of the producer of the merchandise" may prove hollow. Finally, finding demonstrated expertise in the foreign country GAAP may be a challenge.

---

40. Presumably, this would refer only to those dutiable assists provided at reduced costs, because if they had been provided for free, it is not likely that any cost would have been recorded in the producer's financial records.
41. Interpretative Note, Article 6, point 3.
42. The US applies this limitation in its regulations. 19 CFR § 152.106(d). Likewise, Canada, Customs Act, paragraph 52(3)(c); EU, UCC IA, Art 142.2.
43. That is explicit in the Valuation Agreement, Article 6.2, and in the UCC IA, Article 143.1. It is implied in the US regulations, 19 CFR § 152.106(f)(ii).

For all of these reasons, most importers and customs authorities find little to favor in the computed value method.

If there is no computed value, as will certainly be the case if the foreign producer fails to cooperate and provide the needed information, then the customs authority must go to the "fall back" basis for appraisement.

CHAPTER 8

Last Resort Method

§8.01 VALUE IF OTHER VALUES CANNOT BE DETERMINED (FALLBACK)

The Agreement and the implementing customs valuation statutes look to a "fallback" method where the previous stops along the hierarchy have been unfruitful.[1] With this approach, which is the customs law analog of a transfer pricing "unspecified method," the customs authority is empowered to use reasonable means based on the preceding methodologies, as suitably adjusted.

There are subtle differences in the implementing legislation in the US, Canada and the EU. In the case of Canada, the statute specifically requires its "residual method" to be based upon information available in Canada. The EU's UCC specifically requires that the customs authority use reasonable means consistent with the principles and general provisions of the Valuation Agreement, Article VII of the GATT and section 3, Chapter 3 of the UCC. As noted earlier in the context of the *UAB Baltic Master* observations, in its Implementing Act, the EU more specifically directs that:

> reasonable flexibility may be used in the application of the methods provided for in Articles 70 and 74(2) of the Code. The value so determined shall, to the greatest extent possible, be based on previously determined customs values. The value so determined shall, to the greatest extent possible, be based on previously determined customs values.[2]

Taken together, those EU directions convey the same specific instruction to first attempt to reasonably adjust the earlier methods as is expressed in the Valuation Agreement and in the US and Canadian statutes.

1. 19 USC § 1401a(f); Customs Act, section 53 (termed the "residual method"), UCC, Article 74.3; *see* Valuation Agreement, Article 7, paragraph 1.
2. EU, UCC IA, Article 144.1.

As we saw in the opening pages of this book, the customs authority is mandated to find a customs value. When it comes to an appraisement under the fallback method, it is probably well to consider that there is—or should be—a two-tier methodology in play. In the first instance, the customs authority will seek to "reasonably adjust" one of the earlier specific methods. Only when that first-tier effort is unavailing, as the EU directs, the customs authority looks to employ a reasonable approach that is consistent with the broad principles of the Valuation Agreement, Article VII of the GATT and implementing statutes. In the US, that second tier "last resort" appraisement will be under section 500. We discussed section 500 in our *Baltic Master* review above. But it is well to return to this two-step process with a quotation from another CBP ruling.[3] After first observing that none of the specific methods were available, CBP cited the SAA, noting that:

> Section 500 allows Customs to consider the best evidence available in appraising merchandise ... [It] authorize (sic) the appraising officer to weigh the nature of the evidence before him in appraising the imported merchandise. This could be the invoice, the contract between the parties, or even the recordkeeping of either of the parties to the contract.
>
> Accordingly, if the value of imported merchandise cannot be determined on the basis of a method derived from 19 U.S.C. § 1401a(b)-(e), we find that the value of the imported merchandise may be determined under the fallback method provided for in 19 U.S.C. § 1401a(f), using all reasonable ways and means, so long as the method is not specifically precluded under 19 U.S.C. § 1401a(f)(2) (citation omitted).

In other words, when there really is no other option, this allows for a flexible application of the fallback method, which is itself a flexible application. While the customs authorities justifiably have great latitude in applying this methodology, and especially in light of their broad charge to appraise goods,[4] in no event are they permitted to use certain prohibited values as set forth in the customs valuation statute.[5] These include appraisements based on the sales price in the country of importation or prices in foreign countries or arbitrary or fictitious values.[6] Also, CBP Headquarters has warned about the excessive use of the fallback method, cautioning port officials and importers to first look to higher-ranked alternative bases of appraisement.[7]

In practice, the fallback method often shows up when the strict standards of the other methods cannot be met in all respects, e.g., when there are no contemporary sales of the imported goods within the statutory time frame for deductive value.[8] In

3. Ruling no. H262963 (March 3, 2016).
4. In the US, 19 USC § 1500.
5. USC § 1401a(f)(2). This reflects the Valuation Code prohibition in Article 7, paragraph 2.
6. 19 USC § 1401a(f)(2)(A), (C) or (E) and (G); Customs Memorandum D13-9-1, *Residual Basis of Appraisal Method,* November 19, 2013, paragraph 7; EU, Implementing Act, Article 144.2.
7. Ruling no. H165361 (November 1, 2011) (flowers imported under consignment at Miami). But for a careful analysis of the hierarchy of methods which resulted in a fallback appraisement, *see* ruling no. H301482 (March 15, 2019).
8. In ruling no. H012409 (June 10, 2011), for instance, a modified computed value was applied because not all of the relevant production data was available. The Reconciliation Entry program was noted as an option.

those instances, the fallback method may be the formal means of appraisement, but it will actually be recognizable as the earlier deductive value method in all respects save the appropriate time frame. One commercial context where this fallback method is often applied is in "vendor managed (or owned) inventory" (VMI or VOI), in which the foreign seller retains title to imported goods that are warehoused after importation, usually under the control of the importer and does not conclude the sale to the buyer until some point after importation, often at the withdrawal from inventory. Because the time in inventory is normally indeterminate, a deductive value appraisement is often ruled out.[9] To clarify: deductive value is unavailable whenever it is not certain that the goods will be resold within the statutory ninety-day period, not limited to the context of a VMI model which does not meet this time frame.[10]

A 2009 ruling issued by CBP shows the nimble approach that can characterize the customs valuation process.[11] At issue was the customs valuation of artworks imported for auction. Some of the works would be sold within the ninety-day window set by the deductive value method. Other imported products would be sold after that period. Still, other works would remain unsold.

How to proceed? In ruling no. H085036, CBP held that there were three separate approaches:

> The items imported for sale at auction may be appraised under the deductive value method when sold within 90 days of importation. Articles sold more than 90 days after importation may be appraised under the fallback method using a modified deductive value. Those items imported for sale at auction, but which are ultimately not sold, may be appraised under the fallback method using the mean value proposed by [the importer].

The "mean or average value" value of the auction estimates ("mean estimate") was also the value that the importer used to insure property being offered at auction. The importer felt that the mean estimate constitutes a more accurate and proper method of valuation than the auction reserve price [this is the confidential threshold price below which the consignor will not sell], and was always higher than the reserve price. If a client's property is damaged or lost while in Sotheby's custody or control before it is offered at auction, the importer was contractually liable to the client at the mean estimate for the property. Accordingly, the importer used the mean estimate as the declared value for insurance purposes.

The company believed that the mean auction estimate more accurately reflected what the property was likely to earn at auction and thus will result in less discrepancy between the import value and subsequent sale price. CBP agreed, and the resulting published ruling shows an admirable responsiveness to the differing circumstances surrounding the post-importation sales status of the imported artworks.

9. For good examples of the appraisement of VOI, *see* ruling nos. H021399 (April 29, 2011) (practice termed "supplier managed inventory"), H131663 (April 14, 2011), and H125115 (April 6, 2011) and earlier rulings cited therein.
10. *See*, e.g., ruling no. H144042 (October 30, 2013) (modified deductive value applied).
11. Ruling no. H085036 (December 18, 2009).

The "adjustment" factor is often seen at work in the non-sales importation of leased goods,[12] goods imported for repairs,[13] scrap materials for recycling[14] or used merchandise.[15] The administrative practice allows valuation for used merchandise to be based on depreciated book values, but only if these values approximate the market value for the goods.[16]

It is important to recognize that CBP will not completely jettison all customs valuation rules when resorting to the fallback method. As an example, if the importer of goods imported on consignment should seek to use a modified transaction value, CBP may still require that the importer demonstrate that the pricing meets the COS test if it is a related party transaction.[17]

For an illustration of how much of a modification may be involved in a fallback method appraisement, there is no better place to start than a 2019 CBP ruling. In ruling no. H301860,[18] the importer conceded that the relationship between the parties influenced the price, which precluded a transaction value appraisement. Computed value[19] was not available because the importer claimed that it did not have access to profit data for the related party seller or for other companies in the country of exportation. In applying a modified computed value, CBP accepted the profit data for the US parent company/buyer. CBP noted that it looks to parent company data under one of the transfer pricing COS exemplars ("CBP may consider whether the supplier is earning a profit equal to or greater than the profit the parent company receives in sales of goods of the same class or kind") and concluded that the modified computed value model that was suggested—using the seller's costs but the buyer's profit—was acceptable. This may be taking flexibility and modification beyond the stretching point.

A cautionary note is in order. As noted above, CBP Headquarters has warned against an overreliance on the fallback method. Before we jump to this last method and get to questions of adjustments to or modifications of the prior methods, we must first establish that none of those earlier methods can be met. In a recent ruling, CBP reminded us of that burden. CBP rejected an importer's suggestion of a fallback method

12. *See*, e.g., ruling no. 546020 (April 17, 1996).
13. *See*, e.g., ruling no. 563407 (April 13, 2006).
14. *See*, e.g., ruling no. H251593 (October 9, 2014) (imported scrap materials shall be appraised under the fallback method based on the price of the precious metal contained in the imported scrap material as determined on the New York Mercantile Metal Exchange on the day of entry minus the cost of the processing fee paid by to recover the precious metals from the scrap materials. If the value of the precious metal obtained is less than the cost of the processing fee, the imported scrap material should be appraised based on the cost of the fees the recycler charged to do the processing).
15. *See*, e.g., ruling no. H251594 (September 22, 2014).
16. Ruling nos. 548211 (July 2, 2003), 543970 (March 13, 1989), 543265 (July 2, 1985).
17. Ruling no. 246651 (February 5, 2014) (importer should be prepared to substantiate its values by maintaining and providing accounting records from its books and/or financial statements if requested by CBP).
18. Ruling no. H301860 (April 10, 2019).
19. *See* §7.01 above.

valuation for goods imported under consignment because the post-import sales were all made within the ninety-day period established by the deductive method.[20]

In closing, perhaps the CBSA's advice may be a helpful *aide-mémoire* for all customs authorities:

> In flexibly applying the provisions of [the earlier methods], the CBSA will be guided, to the greatest extent possible, by the principles and spirit of the (WTO's) International Agreement on Customs Valuation. These principles state that values should be fair, reasonable, uniform, neutral, and reflect commercial reality. Thus, deriving a value under the [fallback provision] will, in many cases, require close consultation and cooperation between importers and the CBSA to ensure adherence to the principles inherent in the Agreement.[21]

20. Ruling no. H308722 (April 17, 2020) (the goods will remain in inventory for an average of thirty-five days and no longer than ninety days before they are sold and delivered to the ultimate purchaser. Based on this information, the items are sold within ninety days of importation and should be appraised under the deductive value appraisement method).
21. Customs Memorandum D13-9-1, *Residual Basis of Appraisal Method*, November 19, 2013, paragraph 2.

CHAPTER 9

The Special Case of Related Party Sales

§9.01 TRANSFER PRICING CONSIDERATIONS

Because there is so great an interaction between transfer pricing and customs valuation, we present in the immediately following Part II a separate, lengthy discussion of their intersection. That treatment should be read against the general framework of this Part I discussion.

Conclusion

For many, customs valuation has proven to be a more intimidating study than tariff classification or other substantive areas of customs and trade law. Many see it as the stuff of hieratic scrolls accessible to and understood only by a cadre of ardent votaries.

But there is no cause to be faint of heart. Instead, long experience has taught that one should approach open customs valuation questions from the proper perspective and within the proper framework. If one then budgets sufficient time to trace the current state of the law, the definitive and correct answer to nearly all customs valuation questions will readily emerge. Some mastery will follow. Hopefully, I have succeeded in presenting that perspective and in sketching that frame here.

For those questions that linger and do not admit of a clear-cut answer, an application of the principles we have presented will usually allow for sufficient clarity to reach a position that is consistent with an importer's due diligence and reasonable care obligations or that is sufficient for a customs authority to fulfill its mandate. In those jurisdictions where advance rulings are available, a well-informed application which sets forth both the reasons for one's position and the reasons why another or contrary result is not warranted is the only prudent course to pursue. I trust that this guide will support any such endeavor.

As a final point, we should bear in mind that: (i) it took over thirty years for the adoption of the initial Valuation Agreement in 1979, (ii) it has been in force for close to another forty-five years and (iii) the flaws inherent in the Agreement and the growing number of disputed interpretations suggest that an amendatory reconstruction or replacement of the Agreement is a matter of the highest consequence. Perhaps this study may point the way toward some such future effort.

Part II Intersection of Customs Valuation with Transfer Pricing

CHAPTER 10

The Roles, Rules and Reach of the Two Disciplines

Introduction

Two Sets of Rules

Transfer pricing can be an elusive subject because there are actually two sets of rules, one governing customs valuation and the other controlling liability under the income tax laws. The question is whether the two versions merely coexist or intersect, with some degree of overlap and influence on one another.

Transfer pricing is well known and understood by income tax professionals and the taxpayers whom they advise and the income tax authorities who are seeking to collect income tax. In the most common application of this revenue collection effort, transfer pricing is the process whereby income arising from sales transactions between related parties—or "controlled parties" in the language of the US income tax regulations or "associated enterprises" in the language of the OECD[1]—is to be allocated among the parties.[2]

Under the second version, transfer pricing will often not answer when called by that name. The revenue effort in this second connection is by customs administrators who are tasked with collecting duties and associated indirect taxes and fees based on the "dutiable" value of imported merchandise. As we have seen in Part I, the customs valuation law is grounded, first and foremost, in the pricing of import transactions, including those between "related persons." Importers, customs advisors, and customs administrations are all concerned with the validity of related party pricing. Specifically, the customs law version of transfer pricing is an effort to determine whether the price

1. *See below* §10.02[A][1].
2. For example, the congressional purpose behind section 482 of the Internal Revenue Code, the transfer pricing centerpiece of the US Internal Revenue Code, is as follows: "Congress intended to ensure that the division of income between related parties reasonably reflects the economic activities that each undertakes." HR Rep. No. 841, 99th Cong., 2d Sess., pt. 2, at II-637 (1986).

in a specific import transaction has been influenced by the relationship of the parties or by "nonmarket considerations."

Conflicting Goals

Taken together, tax and customs administrators, exporters/taxpayers and importers/taxpayers[3] are all stakeholders, and all are concerned with transfer pricing. The revenue agencies want to be satisfied that the price has not been manipulated. The income tax authorities in both the country of exportation and of importation have a stake in the outcome. An inflated transfer price will lead to more income, and a correspondingly higher income tax, in the country of exportation and less income in the country of importation. A deflated price will have the opposite effect. For customs duties, except in the unusual case of a levy on exports by some jurisdictions, there is a concern only in the country of importation. A higher price on the import transaction will necessarily result in a higher duty assessment, presuming that duties are assessed on an ad valorem basis, and a greater levy of indirect taxes, such as the value added tax (VAT) or Goods and Services Tax (GST).[4] A lower price declared at import will result in a smaller duty/indirect tax exposure for the importer/taxpayer—and less revenue for the customs authority. Another concern specific to the income tax authorities in the country of importation could be that the importer/taxpayer might "whipsaw" the government by declaring a low value at importation and then restating the tax basis of the imported merchandise in inventory. This would lower both the duty and the income tax exposure.

At the close of this part, we explore some of the varying results on a total tax basis when income tax rates and customs duty rates are examined in conjunction. Admittedly, one motivation is to demonstrate to skeptical or suspicious customs authorities that importers/taxpayers will not always be motivated to artificially lower their declared customs values. Depending on a complex matrix of facts and circumstances, even if importers/taxpayers and their related party sellers could: (1) first ascertain their total tax liability on a combined basis on different pricing models and (2) thereupon deviate from the market forces that drive their internal transfer pricing policies in setting prices, on a "total tax" basis they might be better off paying more duties.

For their part, the importers/taxpayers will be worried that the customs and tax administrations in the country of importation may whipsaw them. And rightly so. This could arise when, on a transfer pricing review, the income tax collection agency might lower the transfer price, thereby increasing the income tax liability, but the customs collectors might not permit the dutiable value to be lowered or otherwise allow a refund of the duty collected on the originally declared higher price.

3. Unless the context dictates otherwise, the combined term "importer/taxpayer" is used, as befits the dual role of, and the twin demands placed on, a buyer in a related party import transaction.
4. In most countries with a VAT or a GST, the tax base for such tax collected at the border will be the dutiable value of the imported articles plus the duty. Thus, an artificially lower—or higher—dutiable value will exert a doubly direct relationship with VAT/GST collections.

Importers/taxpayers will want to be able to affirmatively use transfer pricing documentation prepared for review, or approved, by income tax authorities to prove that the PAPP for the imported merchandise was not influenced by the relationship.

§10.01 TRANSFER PRICING DOCUMENTATION

There are two primary vehicles for the taxpayer to manage its income tax exposure. The first is the Advance Pricing Agreement or the Advance Pricing Arrangement (APA) program and the second is through transfer pricing studies.

[A] APA

An APA is an arrangement reached by a taxpayer and its related party and one or more income tax authorities that prospectively, and for a defined term, determines the appropriate transfer price for the related party transactions. In essence, the APA is an alternative dispute resolution mechanism to resolve what might develop as lengthy transfer pricing disputes. APAs are in wide use in many developing countries as well as the more developed countries.

In its Transfer Pricing Guidelines, the OECD uses the term "Advance Pricing Arrangement."[5] I believe that the term "Arrangement" here is regrettable. It is misleading because it misses the true, binding nature of the APA—it is an agreement to which the taxpayer is a party. That binding nature cannot be overlooked. We discuss that important characteristic below.

In the case of the US, the APA has been adopted by the US since 1991, with the process now governed by Rev. Proc. 2006-9, 2006-2 IRB 278. The US income tax authority, the IRS, gives this working definition of an APA:

> An APA is an agreement between a taxpayer and the [Internal Revenue] Service in which the parties set forth, in advance of controlled transactions, the best transfer pricing method ("TPM") within the meaning of § 482 of the Code and the regulations. The agreement specifies the controlled transactions or transfers ("covered transactions"), TPM, APA term, operational and compliance provisions, appropriate adjustments, critical assumptions regarding future events, required APA records, and annual reporting responsibilities.[6]

A further working description was provided by the IRS in its prior series of Annual Reports:

> The APA Program is designed to resolve actual or potential transfer pricing disputes in a principled, cooperative manner, as an alternative to the traditional examination process. *An APA is a binding contract between the IRS and a taxpayer*

5. OECD (2022), *OECD Transfer Pricing Guidelines for Multinational Enterprises and Tax Administrations 2022*, OECD Publishing, Paris https://doi.org/10.1787/0e655865-en (hereinafter "OECD Guidelines"). The OECD Guidelines devote considerable attention in Chapter IV to the APA program, paragraphs 4.134-4.176.
6. Rev. Proc. 2006-9, in section 2.04, available at https://www.irs.gov/pub/irs-drop/rp-06-9.pdf.

> by which the IRS agrees not to seek a transfer pricing adjustment under IRC § 482 for a covered transaction if the taxpayer files its tax return for a covered year consistent with the agreed transfer pricing method (TPM) (emphasis added).[7]

[B] Transfer Pricing Studies (TP Studies)

Turning from APAs to TP Studies, we should be aware that income tax authorities will regularly review cross-border transactions between related parties to the same, or greater, extent as do customs authorities. The prices in these transactions are Transfer Prices, and the close scrutiny is not limited to the prices paid for goods. Transactions in services, IPRs and other intangibles also come in for review.

In the US and many other jurisdictions, in the absence of an APA, the taxpayer is expected to have contemporaneous documentation that serves the purpose of showing that the TP was justified, i.e., that it was at arm's length.[8] That contemporaneous documentation showing due diligence and "reasonable care," to borrow CBP's customs term, usually takes the form of TP Studies. A TP Study offers reasonable cause or reliance in a tax audit or other review and the taxpayer is expected to have it ready when sought by the income tax authority.

That other customs path is marked by interactions between the customs authority in pursuit of its revenue collection efforts and the importer/taxpayer.

Customs Focus on TP/Related Party Transactions

The importer will be called upon to demonstrate that its related party price has not been influenced by that relationship.

§10.02 INTERSECTING OR PARALLEL PATHS?

In response to the initial question—intersecting or parallel paths for the two regimes?—some professionals have been aware for decades that the statutory standards and administrative practices that govern the income tax concept of transfer pricing and the customs valuation law concept of related party pricing are layered and intersecting more than simply coexisting side-by-side. But many other professionals

7. E.g., IRS, 2010 Announcement and Report Concerning Advance Pricing Agreements at 1, available at https://www.irs.gov/pub/irs-utl/2010statutoryreport.pdf.
8. In the US, the operative statute is section 6662 of the Internal Revenue Code. In that US context, a contemporaneous TP Study is intended to provide a substantial portion of items (1) through (8) of the "principal documents" that Treasury Regulations § 1.6662-6(d)(2)(iii)(B) indicates are needed when the tax return is filed. Taxpayers must also maintain principal documentation relating to subparts (9) and (10) of Treasury Regulation § 1.6662-6(d)(2)(iii)(B) plus any necessary background documentation. Note: In the US, the Treasury Regulations are in Title 26 of the Code of Federal Regulations. In Canada, this is section 247(4) of the Income Tax Act. In the UK, post-BEPS OECD-standard documentation based upon OECD protocols is recommended as a best practice, particularly for larger groups. From April 1, 2023, groups with a Country-by-Country Reporting (CbCR) obligation (broadly those with a consolidated global turnover of at least EUR 750 million) and UK operations must maintain a Master File and a UK Local File. BEPS is discussed in depth at §10.07 below.

from each discipline are only recently becoming aware of the other field. Cross-discipline dialogue is an important development.

[A] Participants in the International Dialogue

One of the recently emerging trends has been the discourse between the Paris-based OECD[9] and the Brussels-based WCO on that intersection. More precisely, the issue that has been framed in the dialogue between the two agencies is whether there is, or should be, "convergence" between the two disciplines. These two international bodies, with their respective focus on economic development and taxation and on customs issues, have a common ancestry, curiously one tied to international trade and not tax.

They trace their origins to 1947, when thirteen European governments represented in the Committee for European Economic Cooperation, which administered Marshall Fund monies, agreed to set up a study group. This group examined the possibility of establishing one or more inter-European customs unions based on the principles of the GATT. In 1948, the study group set up two committees—an economic committee and a customs committee.

[1] OECD

The economic committee was the predecessor of the OECD. The OECD is a multinational, quasi-governmental body located in Paris and dates from 1961. It comprises thirty-eight signatory countries at the present time but it is a resource for some seventy developing countries and emerging economies, some of which are in the process of gaining membership. Its mission has been to help its member countries achieve sustainable economic growth and employment and raise the standard of living in member countries while maintaining financial stability to contribute to the development of the world economy.

In the context of transfer pricing, the OECD has been a prime mover, alongside the IRS, in the development of an international consensus on transfer pricing policies and methodologies since its 1979 report, "Transfer Pricing and Multinational Enterprises." Most relevant for this analysis, the OECD Guidelines has served as a model for the administration of transfer pricing rules for numerous income tax administrations, the US being a prominent exception.

As the OECD itself describes them:

> The *OECD Transfer Pricing Guidelines* provide guidance on the application of the "arm's length principle," which represents the international consensus on the valuation, for income tax purposes, of cross-border transactions between associated enterprises. In today's economy where multinational enterprises play an increasingly prominent role, transfer pricing continues to be high on the agenda of tax administrations and taxpayers alike. Governments need to ensure that the taxable profits of MNEs are not artificially shifted out of their jurisdiction and that

9. Further information is available at www.oecd.org.

> the tax base reported by MNEs in their country reflects the economic activity undertaken therein and taxpayers need clear guidance on the proper application of the arm's length principle.[10]

Originally published in 1995, the OECD Guidelines have been revised numerous times, most recently in January 2022.[11]

Use of the OECD Guidelines is widespread:

- Competent Authorities use them to solve transfer pricing disputes and eliminate double taxation where they are bound by a bilateral tax treaty that includes language similar to that of Article 9 of the OECD Model Tax Convention; in this respect, the US generally abides by the OECD Guidelines in its Competent Authority discussions with treaty partners.
- Governments use the Guidelines to develop domestic transfer pricing legislation. In this respect, some OECD countries have domestic legislation that is closer to the Guidelines than others; doubtlessly, there are differences between the US domestic regulations and the OECD Guidelines.
- Increasingly, non-OECD member countries also use them, as recommended in the Commentary on Article 9 of the OECD Model Tax Convention.[12]

[2] WCO

The very first meeting of the WTO's CCV in 1981 was the occasion for inquiries into practices concerning related party transactions.[13] There were occasional references to related party pricing and transfer pricing at the WCO in the ensuing years but the first extended discussion of transfer pricing by the WCO dates only from the April 2005 twentieth session of its TCCV.[14] Since the theme meeting on that occasion, a focus group has been formed and the topic has been included, and presentations by the OECD and private sector experts have been introduced, at virtually every subsequent semiannual session of the TCCV. Moreover, there were two conferences jointly sponsored by the two bodies in May 2006 and May 2007. As stated, much of this discussion has been focused on the "convergence" of the two disciplines.

The WCO efforts to treat the interface of related party customs valuation and transfer pricing found expression in its long-awaited Guide to Customs Valuation and Transfer Pricing, released in 2015 for inclusion in the Revenue Package. Included in its

10. Website reference, available at https://www.oecd.org/tax/beps/oecd-releases-latest-edition-of-the-transfer-pricing-guidelines-for-multinational-enterprises-and-tax-administrations.htm.
11. With the January 2022 edition, the OECD consolidated into a single publication the changes to the 2017 edition of the OECD Guidelines.
12. Recommendation of the OECD Council C(95)126/FINAL, as amended.
13. *See* GATT, Committee on Customs Valuation, Information on Implementation and Administration of the Agreement, VAL/2 (19 February 1981). *See also* GATT, Minutes of the Meeting Held on 5 May 1981, VAL/M/2 (17 June 1981), paragraphs 20-30.
14. The TCCV was established pursuant to Annex II of the Valuation Agreement with a view to ensuring uniformity in interpretation and application of the customs valuation rules at the technical level.

excellent and comprehensive discussion is the ICC Policy Statement that was reissued in 2015.

[3] ICC

The International Chamber of Commerce is the self-styled "world business organization," the leading international organization representing the private sector. The ICC issued a revised version of its policy statement on Transfer Pricing and Customs Valuation—2015. Importantly, the policy statement recites that its proposals are intended to:

- Secure harmonized tax and customs valuation of transactions between related parties in an international context.
- Clarify rules for both companies and administrations.
- Suppress or at least reduce financial impact linked to divergent valuations.
- Simplify regulations.

The ultimate goals of the policy statement proposals are to:

- Reduce compliance costs to companies.
- Eliminate the risk of penalties resulting from disputes arising from divergent views taken by customs and tax authorities.
- Streamline intercompany operations and facilitate international business.

These are words we can live by.

[B] Internal Discussions in the United States

The international agency dialogue between the OECD and the WCO, as well as internal discussions of the WCO multilateral constituency, is mirrored in the domestic discussions in the US, to a point.

[1] Separate Revenue Agencies

Let us begin at the beginning—there are two separate revenue agencies.

Prior to 2003, the IRS and the Customs Service were sister agencies within the US Department of the Treasury. Dating from 1789, for well over 125 years, Customs effectively was the Treasury Department, and its revenue collection efforts accounted for the vast majority of federal revenue. That began to change with the enactment of legislation implementing the collection of an income tax in 1913. While today's customs duty and associated fee collections typically account for some USD 34.5 billion annually, this is a small fraction of the USD 1.6 trillion in income taxes collected annually by the IRS.

With the passage of the Homeland Security Act in 2002[15] in the wake of the events of September 11, 2001, the Customs Service was separated from Treasury and placed within the Department of Homeland Security,[16] where it was linked with the Immigration and Naturalization Service and with the Border Patrol. With effect from March 1, 2003, the Customs Service was renamed the Bureau of Customs and Border Protection and, later still, simply US Customs and Border Protection (in short, CBP).[17]

There have been some contacts between CBP and the IRS,[18] and how CBP itself has spoken to the topic is discussed below. The most recent major pronouncement by CBP was the April 2007 issuance of its Informed Compliance Publication, "What Every Member of the Trade Community Should Know About: Determining the Acceptability of Transaction Value for Related Party Transactions" (ICP: Related Party Transactions).[19] The publication did not mark any departure from existing administrative practice, but rather memorialized and punctuated its evolved practice. This discussion cites, and comments on, that publication extensively, and examines that practice in depth within the wider context of the customs valuation law and its counterparts in income tax law at both the US domestic and international levels.

Since the focus here is on the customs valuation of related party pricing, perhaps the most appropriate starting point for a review of the customs practice would be CBP's own summary statement on how it views APAs and transfer studies:

> [T]he mere fact that an importer provides CBP with an APA[20] or transfer pricing study is not sufficient to establish that a related party transaction value is acceptable. The importer must provide information and evidence regarding the circumstances of sale and/or test values. If the importer believes that information in an APA or transfer pricing study and/or in the supporting documentation is relevant to the application of the circumstances of sale test, the importer should identify that information, explain why it is relevant, and submit the relevant documentation to CBP.[21]

15. Pub. L. No. 107-296, 116 Stat. 2135 et seq. (2002).
16. 6 USC § 211.
17. The note to 6 USC § 211 says that the name change was effectuated by Reorganization Plan Modification of the Department of Homeland Security, effective March 1, 2003. HR Doc. No. 32, 108th Cong., 1st Sess. Effective March 31, 2007, the name was shortened to US Customs and Border Protection. *See* announcement at 72 Fed. Reg. 20,131 (April 23, 2007). The US customs regulations usually continue to refer to the agency as "Customs."
18. A formal IRS-Customs Policy Board was chartered in late 1992. *See* Government Accountability Office, "IRS' Administration of Tax-Customs Valuation Rules in Tax Code Section 1059A," (February 4, 1994), GAO/GGD-94-61, at 13 (GAO Rep.). In 1994, the IRS and CBP entered into a Working Arrangement for Mutual Assistance and Exchange of Information, whereby customs entry forms (CF 7501s) were shared with the IRS for section 482 reviews by the latter. 94 TNT 184-68 (September 19, 1994). *See* comments of Treasury Assistant Chief Counsel (International) in FSA 0983, FSA 1992-0213-1 (CCH).
19. The Informed Compliance Publications are a series of topical discussions promulgated by CBP so as to state CBP's position on the issues and to assist importers in meeting their "reasonable care" compliance burdens. These are mandated by 19 USC § 1484.
20. *See* definition at §10.01[A] above.
21. ICP: Related Party Transactions, at 16.

Clearly, the CBP perspective is that:

- CBP is a separate agency with responsibilities for deciding transfer pricing questions on products imported into the US customs territory.
- CBP might, or might not, accept as helpful a transfer pricing study prepared, or an APA entered into, by a taxpayer for income tax purposes.

Understanding the proper role of the revenue collection agencies regarding transfer pricing questions is critical for understanding whether the reach of an APA, or for that matter a transfer pricing study that may have been accepted by the IRS or other national income tax authority, extends to acceptance by CBP or the customs authority in another jurisdiction in its administration of the customs valuation law. So far so good, but this statement actually begs the question, and assumes that agencies other than the IRS or the other income tax authority (i.e., those without an income tax focus) are also concerned with transfer pricing and have a say on transfer pricing matters.

Many traditionalists from the ranks of international tax advisors are not prepared to make that assumption. Many who have dealt with the IRS or crossed swords with foreign tax authorities in transfer pricing disputes think that this issue is within the exclusive province of those direct tax agencies. In other, more vernacular words, they generally see the IRS and the income tax inquiry more generally as the only transfer pricing "game" in town.

Those tax advisors are wrong, because transfer pricing is also within the province of a taxing jurisdiction's customs authorities. In the US, transfer pricing has been a major customs law concern since at least the Customs Simplification Act of 1956.

For those other international tax advisors who know that transfer pricing is also a major focus of the tax authorities with responsibilities for such indirect taxes as customs duty and ad valorem VAT, there is a belief—or perhaps an earnest hope—that securing the approval of the income tax authorities will serve a dual purpose, obviating the need to undertake additional measures to separately satisfy the customs/VAT authorities. Those tax advisors are also wrong to assume that governments have organized their revenue collections rationally (i.e., in any relevant jurisdiction the income tax and customs/VAT authorities are either integrated within a single superior agency or, if they have independent status, coordinated to the extent that satisfying one tax agency will satisfy the other). In fact, a unity of these tax agencies is a state of affairs that exists in a minority of tax jurisdictions.[22] As discussed below, the contrary situation of the US, with entirely separate federal revenue agencies pursuing entirely

22. These include Argentina, the United Kingdom, and Belgium. There is a growing trend to unify tax and customs administrations. For further information on the organizational aspects of revenue collection, *see* an earlier OECD report of its analysis of forty-three countries, "Tax Administration in OECD and Selected Non-OECD Countries: Comparative Information Series" (CIS) (2008), www.oecd.org/dataoecd/57/23/42012907.pdf.

disparate goals through entirely separate processes,[23] is the norm in many jurisdictions. And to complete the picture, there may be little dialogue between the agencies.[24]

The lessons stressed in this discussion are threefold:

(1) Tax and customs duty collections are often the responsibilities of completely separate administrative agencies.
(2) Each of these tax authorities will have its own, independent functional concern with transfer pricing.
(3) Satisfying either one of the taxing authorities on transfer pricing (e.g., the IRS through an APA) may not adequately satisfy the tests applied by the other agency, even when the agencies' rules are sometimes nearly identical.

These points are neatly summarized in the following observation drawn from a ruling issued by CBP Headquarters in response to an importer's counsel stating that the prices for its imports purchased from a related party seller would be designed to conform to all IRS regulations on international transactions:

> As you are aware, a sale between a related buyer and seller must be at arm's length for the merchandise to be appraised under transaction value. To prove the arm's length nature of the transaction, an importer has to satisfy one of two tests, otherwise known as the "circumstances of sale test" or "test values." Although IRS approval of a transfer price will satisfy that agency's tax requirements, such approval does not automatically translate into an acceptable price for customs purposes. The importer is still required to demonstrate that the pricing structure meets one of CBP's two tests (citations omitted).[25]

Because transfer pricing might be mistakenly construed as the only touchpoint between customs and income tax collection, Part I gives examples where income tax planning and customs planning can trigger unintended consequences where the structures established under one tax discipline trigger disadvantageous results within the other.[26]

---

23. To be sure, prior to the 2003 reorganization in which the Customs Service was split off from the Department of the Treasury, renamed as Customs and Border Protection and placed within the Department of Homeland Security, the Customs Service and the IRS had been sister agencies within Treasury.
24. To be sure, there has been an MOU between the two agencies dating to the early 1990s. Pursuant to the MOU, CBP has access to the submissions to the IRS if the importer/taxpayer waives its confidential status.
25. Ruling no. W563545 (January 9, 2007). Unless otherwise stated, all rulings are issued by CBP. The two customs valuation tests—circumstances of sale and "test values"—are discussed at length below.
26. E.g., a "stripped down" or "limited risk" distributor whose functions are strictly curbed for tax planning purposes runs the risk of being characterized by customs authorities as a selling agent, whose markup thus becomes dutiable. The degree of similarity in functions and in the ensuing comparability in gross profit margins for agents and limited risk buy/sell distributors has been recognized by the IRS in its temporary regulations on the transfer pricing of intangibles, including services. *See*, e.g., discussion on the gross services margin method (GSMM), Temp. Reg. § 1.482-9T(d)(3)(ii)(D) and Temp. Reg. § 1.482-9T(d)(4), Ex. 2. This may be a distinction without a difference for income tax purposes, but there is a profound difference in treatment and results under the customs law.

The overarching point in all of this "compare and contrast" discussion is the recognition that the two tax disciplines, while separated, are very related and it is a foolish importer/taxpayer who does not attempt to integrate planning simultaneously rather than dealing with them on a seriatim, albeit coordinated basis.

Lest one conclude that this organizational separation was tantamount to a surgical procedure to separate conjoined twins, and that the agencies had theretofore been thoroughly integrated and had collaborated on transfer pricing or other matters, three incidents betray the reality that the two agencies were disconnected.

These are the 1986 enactment of Internal Revenue Code section 1059A and its subsequent administration by the IRS, the lack of familiarity on the part of both CBP and the IRS with the other agency's mandate, and the publication of a customs ruling in 2000 that concerned the intersection of customs valuation and transfer pricing.

[2] Section 1059A

In the US, the Tax Reform Act of 1986 (the 1986 Tax Act)[27] ushered in section 1059A, whose purpose was to prevent whipsawing of the government by an importer/taxpayer. In the government's view, a taxpayer who imported an article would try to attain the lowest possible valuation for customs duty purposes, because duties are normally assessed on an ad valorem basis. That same taxpayer would then want to subsequently carry the imported articles on its books for a higher value, so as to increase its COGS and thereby lower its income tax exposure on the later disposition of the article. Precisely because of the perceived disconnect between the customs and income tax collection functions, and because it felt that taxpayers might exploit that dysfunction, Congress enacted section 1059A.

Case law prior to the 1986 Tax Act provided some guidance, but was generally silent on the differences between the tax and customs approaches to transfer pricing. One exception was the US Tax Court's 1973 decision in *Ross Glove*, which stated that the methods of CBP and the IRS in making pricing determinations were "quite similar" and that the markups used by CBP were the "best available evidence as to the amounts that a seller would receive to cover overhead and profit in an arm's length sale."[28] The *Ross Glove* court rejected the IRS' arguments that customs valuations are basically unreliable and cannot form the basis for a determination of an arm's-length price for tax purposes.

---

27. Pub. L. No. 99-514, 100 Stat. 2085 (1986). A substantive assessment of section 1059A is discussed below.
28. *Ross Glove Co. v. Comm'r*, 60 TC 569, 584-585, 604-606 (1973). CBP had appraised the importations based on an alternative valuation method, constructed value, which stands in the same place under the "old" value law relative to export value appraisement as computed value is related to transaction value in the current customs valuation law. *See* Part I. The Tax Court, while validating the CBP methodology, presumed to discover that CBP had not always applied the customs valuation formula correctly and proceeded to make an adjustment of a reduction of 3.5% of costs to determine the arm's-length price under section 482.

By the time of the 1976 Tax Court decision in *Brittingham*,[29] however, the IRS had learned to appreciate customs valuation, or at least understand its potential role, as it sought to apply the customs value to establish an arm's-length price for tax purposes. The IRS determined that a US importer paid more than an arm's-length price for the purchase of ceramic tile imported from a company owned by family members in Mexico. The purchase price for the ceramic tile was substantially higher than the value reported for customs duty purposes. The importer/taxpayer in *Brittingham* had used customs valuation law aggressively to deviate from the invoice price, and appraisement was initially based on the price of similar tile sold by a Mexican competitor of the taxpayer's related party Mexican supplier.[30] This price was lower than the invoice price; hence, the IRS wanted to use it as the basis for computing the taxpayer's tax liability.

The Tax Court in *Brittingham* held that the customs determinations were not determinative of an arm's-length price, since they were based on certain erroneous factual assumptions as to the relative market values of the subject tile and the referent tile. This rejection by the court in *Brittingham* was made more interesting because the taxpayer had won a previous dispute with CBP on the same issues. The Tax Court stated that its findings and holdings were made without having to decide whether some of the factual assertions made by the taxpayers to CBP were reconcilable with their testimony before the court.[31]

The practical result of *Brittingham* was that many multinational companies could employ one value for customs purposes and another for income tax. Congress was well aware of this potential for abuse because of the "disconnect" between the two disciplines.

The legislative history stated that, under the then-present law, importers may claim a transfer price for customs purposes that is too low to be consistent with the transfer price they claim for income tax purposes, specifically citing *Brittingham*. The congressional conferees expected Treasury to provide rules for coordinating customs and tax valuation principles.[32]

Section 1059A established, for property imported into the US in a transaction between related persons, that the dutiable value will serve as the ceiling for inventory cost or tax basis for income tax purposes, subject to some adjustments to account for certain elements of price that would be nondutiable (e.g., international transportation and insurance, post-importation installation, or erection charges). Nevertheless, the section was not intended to give the value declared for customs purposes definitive status in establishing a value for income tax purposes. In its General Explanation of the Tax Reform Act of 1986, the staff of the Joint Committee on Taxation observed that the section fashioned customs value as:

29. *Robert M. Brittingham v. IRS*, 66 TC 373, 387-390, 401-403 (1976), *aff'd*, 598 F2d 1375 (5th Cir. 1979).
30. Subsequently, customs valuation of this importer's entries was based on constructed value (in 1962) and later still (in 1970) CBP shifted to appraisement based on export value, which was grounded in the invoice price.
31. *Robert M. Brittingham* et al. *v. IRS*, 66 TC 373, 402 (1976).
32. HR Rep. No. 841, 99th Cong., 2d Sess., paragraph E.8 (1986).

- "[A] ceiling on transfer price valuation for income tax purposes, [but] it does not provide a floor on that valuation."
- "In no event does a customs declaration or valuation constrain the ability of the Commissioner to adjust transfer prices under section 482."[33]

The implementing regulations are likewise quite clear on this limited role of section 1059A:

> This section imposes no limitation on a claimed basis or inventory cost or property which is less than the value used to compute the customs duty with respect to the same property.
>
> ***
>
> *Relationship of section 1059A to section 482.* Neither this section nor section 1059A limits in any way the authority of the Commissioner to increase or decrease the claimed basis or inventory cost under section 482 or any other appropriate provision of law. Neither does this section or section 1059A permit a taxpayer to adjust upward its cost basis or inventory cost for property appropriately determined under section 482 because such basis or inventory cost is less than the customs value with respect to such property.[34]

Congress foresaw a quite limited, indeed a *de minimis*, revenue effect for the section, less than USD 5 million annually.[35] Perhaps this was a result of an inability of Congress at that time to predict the future expansion of international trade by related parties, now estimated to characterize roughly one-half of the 60% of global trade that is carried on by multinational enterprises.[36]

Section 1059A bridges what Congress perceived to be the functional and structural gap between the two agencies, as it specifically refers to both section 482 and to customs value:

> (a) In general. If any property is imported into the United States in a transaction (directly or indirectly) between related persons (within the meaning of section 482), the amount of any costs—
> 1) which are taken into account in computing the basis or inventory cost of such property by the purchaser, and
> 2) which are also taken into account in computing the customs value of such property,
>
> shall not, for purposes of computing such basis or inventory cost for purposes of this chapter, be greater than the amount of such costs taken into account in computing such customs value.[37]

33. Staff of Joint Comm. on Tax'n, 100th Cong., 1st Sess., General Explanation of the Tax Reform Act of 1986, at 1061, 1062 (JCS-10-87) (1987). *See also* Neville, "Customs Planning May Avoid Conflict with IRS Transfer Pricing Rules," 4 J. Int'l Tax'n (February 1993) at 70.
34. Treas. Reg. §§ 1.1059A-1(c)(1), 1.1059A-1(c)(7).
35. Staff of Joint Comm. on Tax'n, 100th Cong., 1st Sess., General Explanation of the Tax Reform Act of 1986, at 1061, 1062 (JCS-10-87) (1987). Cost basis or inventory cost is the focus of 26 § USC 263A and Treas. Reg. § 1.471-11.
36. Ping & Silberztein, "Transfer Pricing, Customs Duties and VAT Rules: Can We Bridge the Gap?," 1(1) World Com. Rev. (2007) at 1.
37. 26 USC § 1059A(a).

A technical analysis of section 1059A is discussed in detail below.

Turning aside from that provision, international tax practitioners could cite other points of contact between the IRS and CBP. One is another mandated reference to the customs valuation of imported goods—IRS Form 5472, the information return required for certain 25% foreign-owned US corporations or foreign corporations engaged in a US trade or business.[38] Part VI of the form directly asks the taxpayer if it imports goods from a foreign related party and, if so, whether the basis or inventory cost of the goods is valued greater than the customs value of the imported goods and, if it is, to explain the reasons for the difference.

Beyond that, restrictions on disclosure of tax return information by the IRS to CBP were eased with the 1993 amendment that allowed the disclosure of this information, but only in the context of customs audits or CBP enforcement proceedings.[39] The implementing regulations do not allow the disclosure to CBP of information relating to an APA or whose disclosure would violate a tax treaty obligation, however.[40]

[3] Mutual Lack of Understanding by CBP and the IRS

Even though the IRS had referred to a formal working agreement between the two agencies, as well as the formation of an IRS-Customs Policy Board, as long ago as August 1993,[41] most observers feel that there is little common understanding between them. For example, on a panel discussion on the interplay of the two agencies on transfer pricing matters that was hosted by the American Association of Exporters and Importers in New York in 1997, a senior CBP official with customs valuation responsibilities confessed privately that he did not know what an "APA" stood for! To be sure, there is a greater awareness today but, clearly there was little, if any, dialogue between IRS transfer pricing authorities and their confreres in the Customs Service charged with the same responsibilities.

In this same vein, the agencies have generally used different terms to refer to the same phenomenon. As may have been inferred, the IRS and tax practitioners refer to "transfer pricing," the term that we have employed generally. CBP officials and customs valuation law experts generally identify this issue as "related party" or "related person" pricing. To our knowledge, the first recorded instance in which CBP

38. *See* Treas. Reg. § 1.6038A-2(b)(5).
39. Treas. Reg. § 301.6103(l)(14)-1. This prohibition on the routine transfer of IRS information was acknowledged by CBP in the course of announcing a reconciliation test for section 482 adjustments in response to a comment that the IRS might routinely provide CBP with copies of Form 5472. 60 Fed. Reg. 46,141, 46,144 (September 5, 1995).
40. Treas. Reg. § 301.6103(l)(14)-1(d) reads: "The following return information may not be requested or disclosed pursuant to section 6103(l)(14) of the Internal Revenue Code: any Advance Pricing Agreement or information submitted to or generated by the IRS as part of the negotiation process for an Advance Pricing Agreement, or any information to the extent its disclosure would be inconsistent with a tax treaty or executive agreement with respect to which the United States is a party."
41. Letter from IRS Commissioner Richardson to GAO, Appendix XII to GAO Rep., at 65-67 (August 6, 1993).

used the term "transfer pricing" did not occur until 1993.[42] Thereafter, transfer pricing has remained a seldom-used term within CBP, at least in any formal context. This chapter uses the terms interchangeably, but the usage of "related party" or "related person" will generally connote a customs inquiry.

Finally, the statements of the IRS, both as recorded in the Government Accountability Office (GAO) Report[43] and as promulgated in Field Service Advice 200036015,[44] show an agency entirely at ease with going its own way.

[4] CBP 2000 Ruling

A third point is CBP's issuance of a customs valuation ruling in 2000 in which it not only referred to, but expressed reliance on, information derived from a bilateral APA. This access to, and use of, the data filed with the IRS was so ground-breaking that its release gave rise to a lengthy commentary entitled "The Customs and IRS Intersection on Transfer Pricing."[45] The ruling, no. 546979 (August 30, 2000), was hailed as an important first step in bridging the perceived divide between the agencies, which at the time were both housed within Treasury. The hope of future joint action by the agencies on transfer pricing was loudly if not widely (because of the limited awareness of the issue) cheered.

Some especially wistful souls even dared to hope for future concerted action by the agencies with a single, dual-purpose submission seeking an APA and a binding ruling concurrently filed with the IRS and CBP.[46] Whether that promise of concerted agency action has been fulfilled is examined below.

With the benefit of these prefatory remarks, this is the ultimate question:

> Given the very brief recitation that comprises the entire text and commentary on related-party pricing in customs valuation law, can importers/taxpayers or customs authorities use transfer pricing methods used in allocating income for income tax purposes, and the documentation based on those methods, to help determine dutiable value for customs purposes?

42. General Announcement, 27 Cust. Bull. & Dec. No. 4, at 4 (January 27, 1993).
43. *See* discussion below § 10.05[A][3][b].
44. *See* below § 10.05[A][4].
45. Neville & Harris, "The Customs/IRS Intersection on Transfer Pricing," 12 J. Int'l Tax'n (September 2001) at 28. That discussion is still timely, as later customs pronouncements on transfer pricing have not departed from the positions established in the ruling. *See also* Wrappe, Pike & Chung, "Joint APA Effort Signals New Level of IRS-Customs Coordination," 9 Transfer Pricing 551 (November 29, 2000); Meyer & Outman, "U.S. Tax and Customs Consequences of Dealing With a Related Foreign Supplier (Part 2)," 13 J. Int'l Tax'n 16 (January 2002). For an earlier treatment of the intersection of these disciplines, *see* Sheldrick, Lowell & Briger, "The Relationship of U.S. Customs Law and International Transfer Pricing," Tax Mgmt. Transfer Pricing Rep., Special Rep. No. 21 (April 24, 1996).
46. One of the obstacles to a single filing is the restriction on the release of tax return information to CBP, which specifically precludes the sharing of APA information. The importer/taxpayer in ruling no. 546979 had executed a waiver to allow the sharing of the APA information with CBP.

But before proceeding to a discussion of a cross-discipline approach to transfer pricing, it is essential to understand the basics of the distinct transfer pricing methods separately embedded within the customs and income tax laws.

[C] Internal Discussions in Other Countries

There have been similar policy statements made by other countries, such as Canada with its very informative "D Memos"[47] issued by the CBSA[48] and the equally informative statement of the income tax authorities, Canada Revenue Agency, Information Circular IC 06-1 (October 5, 2006).

Australian Customs and Border Protection Service (ACBPS) has also issued a statement that is important to the field, Valuation-Transfer Pricing Policy Practice Statement B_IND 08 (April 12, 2013).[49] This replaced a 2009 Practice Statement, PS 2009/21, and is intended to have a three-year life. In Australia, customs valuation rulings, which are termed Valuation Advices (VAs), are to be sought from the ACBPS, while APAs may be sought separately from the Australian Tax Office (ATO). Interestingly, in contrast to the US where binding rulings have an indefinite lifespan unless, of course, material facts have changed or where CBP changes its position and goes through a public modification or revocation process,[50] in Australia the VAs have only a five-year term of validity. Importantly, if there is a transfer pricing study, it should be included in the VA application. Moreover, if the importer has obtained an APA, the importer must provide a copy of the APA as well as any supporting documentation to ACBPS in support of its VA request. Compensating adjustments[51] are implicitly recognized if they are based on actual transfers of funds rather than merely notional adjustments. As another observation, the Practice Statement does a good job of setting forth the documentation requirements.

Perhaps the fullest expression of the convergence of customs valuation and transfer pricing is the legislation in Chile, Ley No. 203630, D.O. 27/09/2012, which specifies that in the case of imported goods, an Advance Pricing Agreement must be jointly executed by the income tax and the customs authorities.

---

47. Customs Memorandum D13-4-5, *Transaction value method for related persons*, December 6, 2021. The earlier Customs Memorandum D13-3-6, *Income Tax Transfer Pricing and Customs Valuation*, October 18, 2006 was superseded.
48. Accessible at http://www.cbsa-asfc.gc.ca/publications/dm-md/d13/d13-3-6-eng.html.
49. Accessible at http://www.border.gov.au/Importingandbuyinggoodsfromoverseas/Documents/B_IND08Valuation-TransferPricingPolicy.pdf#search = Transfer%20Pricing%20Practice%20Statement.
50. *See* Neville, "Some Thoughts on Ruling Requests," 33 J. Int'l Tax'n 27 (March 2022).
51. A "compensating adjustment" is a transfer pricing term of art referring to the report by a taxpayer of a transfer price for tax purposes that is, in the taxpayer's opinion, an arm's-length price for a controlled transaction even though this price differs from the amount actually charged between the associated enterprises. OECD Guidelines Glossary definition and paragraph 4.38. In the United States, the Treasury regulations anticipate that this self-initiated adjustment needs to "true up" the pricing to the arm's-length standard to be made with the tax return. Treas. Reg. § 1.482-1(a)(3). Other OECD members do not recognize compensating adjustments that they term as "notional," so care must be taken to avoid double taxation.

In Italy, an administrative guideline, 16/D/2015 (November 6, 2015) notes the relevance of OECD transfer pricing methodologies for customs valuation.

Finally, in Korea, on January 13, 2009, the Korean Ministry of Strategy and Finance entered into a Memorandum of Understanding (MOU) with its constituent agencies, the National Tax Service and the Korea Customs Service, to provide for joint transfer pricing audits by the two agencies. The MOU also provides for exchanges of information and cross-training. This move was in large measure a response to complaints by the American and EU Chambers of Commerce of inconsistencies in treatment by the two agencies.

For the position of the WCO Technical Committee on the use of transfer pricing studies in customs valuation, *see* Commentary 23.1, issued in 2010, and discussed in §10.06 below. You will discover that it is aligned with the US position.

§10.03 CUSTOMS VALUATION LAW TESTS OF TRANSFER PRICING

[A] In General

As explained in Part I, the customs valuation law is based on a hierarchy of methods employed by CBP, with the preferred method being the transaction value (TV) of the imported merchandise, defined as the "price actually paid or payable when sold for exportation to the country of importation."[52] Only if appraisal on a TV basis is not possible, are alternative methods applied in a strict descending order from within the statutory hierarchy.[53]

[1] "Related Person" Defined

To be sure, the customs valuation law permits a TV appraisal of imported merchandise where the buyer and seller are related persons. The customs law definition of "related persons" in the US is both narrowly defined and open-ended:

> [T]he persons specified in any of the following subparagraphs shall be treated as persons who are related:

52. In the US, this is set forth at 19 USC § 1401a(b)(1); Valuation Agreement, Article 1.1. Parallel citations are generally provided to the US customs valuation statute and regulations and their international counterparts, the Valuation Agreement and its Interpretative Notes. This is not a market value-based concept, as had been the case in the pre-1979 valuation statute with its use of "export value," defined as "the price ... at which such or similar merchandise is freely sold, or in the absence of sales, offered for sale in the principal markets of the country of exportation, in the usual wholesale quantities and in the ordinary course of trade." 19 USC § 1401(b) (repealed). In such a context, the law contemplated a single price for the same merchandise at the same time in the market. *See*, e.g., *Luckytex, Ltd. v. United States*, 56 Cust. Ct. 575, 581, RD 11119 (1965).
53. The statute sets forth these alternatives as TV of identical or similar merchandise, deductive value, computed value, and the "fallback" method. 19 USC §§ 1401a(a)(1)(B)-1401a(a)(1)(F); Valuation Agreement, Articles 2-7. This scheme is discussed extensively in Part I.

(A) Members of the same family, including brothers and sisters (whether by whole or half blood), spouse, ancestors, and lineal descendants.
(B) Any officer or director of an organization and such organization.
(C) An officer or director of an organization and an officer or director of another organization, if each such individual is also an officer or director in the other organization.
(D) [in the Valuation Agreement: Legally recognized] Partners.
(E) Employer and employee.
(F) Any person directly or indirectly owning, controlling, or holding with power to vote, 5 percent or more of the outstanding voting stock or shares of any organization and such organization.
(G) Two or more persons directly or indirectly controlling, controlled by, or under common control with, any person.[54]

To state the obvious, the customs law imposes a very low threshold for "related person" status. Apart from the obvious common ownership or control, a mere 5% stock ownership will trigger the status.[55] This is in marked contrast from the shareholding standard for controlled persons in the income tax law, which in the case of the US is typically the 25% interest noted in relation to Form 5472.[56]

While the application of different financial and tax accounting treatments may lead to divergent results, financial accounting standards and developments therein could have an impact and provide guidance for use in transfer pricing and other income tax issues.

In this connection, because of the movement toward the adoption of a single international accounting standard, in 2009, with effect from January 1, 2011, the IASB revised the definition of "related party" for the purposes of International Accounting Standard (IAS) 24 on related party disclosures. The IAS 24 standard places no reliance on share ownership at any stated threshold level. Instead, the standard dropped its former reference to "significant voting power" and now relies on defined notions of "control," "joint control," and "significant influence," the latter term acknowledging a role for share ownership.[57]

54. 19 USC § 1401a(g)(1); 19 CFR § 152.102(g); Valuation Agreement, Articles 15.4 and its Interpretative Note, 15.5. You will recognize that the implementing legislation will vary slightly from one jurisdiction to another, with the US definition being the most specific. CF Canada Customs Act, subsection 45(3); UCC IA, Article 127.
55. 19 USC § 1401a(g)(1)(F); Valuation Agreement, Article 15.4(d).
56. The US Treasury Regulations (at 1.482-1 (i)) define these terms:

> (4) Controlled includes any kind of control, direct or indirect, whether legally enforceable or not, and however exercisable or exercised, including control resulting from the actions of two or more taxpayers acting in concert or with a common goal or purpose. It is the reality of the control that is decisive, not its form or the mode of its exercise. A presumption of control arises if income or deductions have been arbitrarily shifted.
> (5) Controlled taxpayer means any one of two or more taxpayers owned or controlled directly or indirectly by the same interests, and includes the taxpayer that owns or controls the other taxpayers. Uncontrolled taxpayer means any one of two or more taxpayers not owned or controlled directly or indirectly by the same interests.

57. "Control" is defined as the power to govern the financial and operating policies of an entity so as to obtain benefits from its activities. "Joint control" is the contractually agreed sharing of

[a] *The Role of Control*

Not surprisingly, the customs valuation law provides for a related party status based on the notion of de facto control.[58] At the international level, this concept of "control" was refined through the Interpretative Note to Article 15, paragraph 4 (e), on the ground that control by one person over another person is present only when the former is legally or operationally in a position to exercise restraint or direction over the latter.[59] As a further refinement, the TCCV has issued an Explanatory Note[60] on this issue, observing that control must relate to the management of activities of the other person and that this issue raises questions of fact and degree that must be based on the particulars of each individual situation.

This EN with its "management of activities" standard appears consistent with the principle that establishing a related party status will follow upon one party's exercise of restraint or direction over another party. In addition, the TCCV has published a case study,[61] again noting that the essential features of control that create a "related party" status for customs valuation purposes must extend to management of the firm, such as the power to decide on management personnel, ownership or voting control, or location of places of business.[62]

[b] Baltic Master *Judgment*

As we explore this issue we discover that the EU appears to be pursuing the same troubling pattern of expansive interpretations that was made evident in the discussions in Part I. This is revealed in the submission of the Advocate General filed with the ECJ

control over an economic activity. "Significant influence" is defined as the power to participate in the financial and operating policy decisions of an entity, but not control over those policies. Significant influence may be gained by share ownership, statute, or agreement.

58. 19 USC § 1401a(g)(1)(G); Valuation Agreement, Articles 15.4(e), 15.4(f), 15.4(g).
59. Valuation Agreement, Interpretative Note to Article 15, paragraph 4(e). This explanation was not adopted in the US customs regulations. As noted in Part I, the Interpretative Notes are fully integrated into the Valuation Agreement per Article 14 of that Agreement.
60. TCCV, EN 4.1, Consideration of Relationship Under Article 15.5, Read in Conjunction with Article 15.4 (October 1985). Only one published CBP ruling discusses the notion of "control." Ruling no. 545481 (September 14, 1994). That ruling does not discuss management control and appears to deviate from EN 4.1, paragraph 14.
61. TCCV, CS 11.1, Application of Article 15.4 (e) Related Party Transactions (April 1999).
62. This standard is also reflected in IAS 24, which specifically denies "related party" status to a customer, franchisor, distributor, or general agent with whom an entity transacts a significant volume of business, simply by virtue of the resulting economic dependence. IAS 24, paragraph 11 (d). This narrowed definition will not be well received by those customs officials who are seeking to depart from the existing standard that looks to "control" as a concept based on management power. These officials would invoke a broad definition of "control" in which economic dependence alone could confer "related party" status. In the US context, the Financial Standards Accounting Board (FASB) Statement No. 57, Related Party Disclosures, defines "control" as, "[t]he possession, direct or indirect, of the power to direct or cause the direction of the management and policies of an enterprise through ownership, by contract, or otherwise."

in *Baltic Master* judgment.[63] There, the issue surrounded the tariff classification as well as customs valuation of certain air conditioning parts upon import into Lithuania. For our purposes,[64] the issue that concerns us is the notion of de facto control between two business entities. The Advocate General did not definitively reject the reasoning of the customs authority and the referring Lithuanian court in perceiving that the buyer and seller were related persons.

Let us allow the Advocate General to state the question (in paragraph 26 of his Opinion), quoting from the referring court:

> the referring court asks whether ... the buyer and the seller are deemed to be "related persons" where, despite the absence of evidence proving business partnership or control, the circumstances surrounding the conclusion of transactions are not indicative of the performance of economic activities under normal conditions, but of *particularly close business relations* or of de facto control between those persons (emphasis added).

As an initial observation, there is no authority cited in the AG Opinion for the referring court's "particularly close business relations" criterion. That is not surprising as there is no such standard.

The views of the referring court are set out in the Judgment, and we learn:

> 35. the referring court indicates that a number of/factual /elements provide grounds for taking the view that the seller and the buyer enjoy a particularly close connection, as a result of which the transactions between those persons were concluded and executed under conditions that are not characteristic of the ordinary course of business. In the referring court's view, there does not appear to be any objective conditions capable of justifying the economic logic of such transactions.
>
> 36. In that regard, the referring court points to the following facts: (i) the seller and the applicant are linked by a long-term commercial relationship; (ii) the goods were supplied without the conclusion of any contracts of sale that would provide for the delivery, payment or return of the goods and other conditions specific to such transactions; (iii) the fact that goods were delivered without any advance payment and despite the fact that the applicant owed significant amounts to the seller in respect of previous supplies; (iv) no provision was made for enforcement or risk-mitigation measures (advance payments, sureties, guarantees, default interest, and so forth) that are normal in the ordinary course of business, notwithstanding the particularly high value of the disputed transactions; (v) there was no evidence to suggest that the seller in general exercised any control over payment and other obligations; (vi) cases were identified in which persons working for the applicant's company acted on behalf of the seller under an authorisation and used its corporate stamp.
>
> 37. The referring court adds that, in its view, patterns of conduct of economic entities similar to those mentioned are generally typical in cases where one party to the transaction controls the other or both are controlled by a third

63. Opinion of AG Nicholas Emiliou in Case C599/20, *UAB "Baltic Master" v. Muitinės departamentas prie Lietuvos Respublikos finansų ministerijos*, 20.1.2022, ECLI:EU:C:2022:46. Judgment: Case C-599/20, *Baltic Master UAB*, 9.6.2022, ECLI:EU:C:2022:457 (*Baltic Master*).
64. We should note that the case also raised the issue of the reliance on customs valuation databases—this issue was discussed in Part I.

> party. Therefore, although there is no evidence as to the /de jure/ existence of such control, the referring court is of the opinion that the circumstances of the case at issue may possibly justify the seller and the applicant being regarded as de facto related.

There we have it—in the Lithuanian court's view, the conduct of the parties, i.e., the activities set forth in paragraph 36 above, is generally typical of one party controlling another. With respect, there is as little experience or expertise to inform such an opinion as there would be for a court or a customs authority opining on what licensor measures go beyond QC in RLF inquiries.[65]

After setting the standard for what one might term an "on the basis of all of the facts and circumstances" review, to which we would not raise any objection, and after raising doubts as to any of the business practices connoted an element of control (paragraphs 48, 55) the Advocate General never rendered an opinion whether there was a de facto control in play. Instead, the standard was enunciated (paragraphs 66 and 84): the buyer and the seller are deemed to be "related persons" where, despite the absence of elements proving business partnership or control, on the basis of the circumstances surrounding the conclusion of transactions, it can be reasonably inferred that, de facto, one person controls the other or that both persons are controlled by a third person. This tautology really does not add anything to our understanding and it certainly does not specifically render an opinion on the status of the parties before the court. If the effect of the opinion is merely to send the matter back to the Lithuanian court and for the latter to apply the rationale then its effect is limited.

With the judgment in *Baltic Master*, the ECJ followed the lead of the Attorney General and we find ourselves with a statement of principle (in paragraph 42) that begs for further elucidation:

> the buyer and the seller may be deemed to be related on account of a direct or indirect relationship of de facto control in a situation in which the circumstances surrounding the conclusion of the transactions at issue, substantiated by objective elements, may be regarded as demonstrating not only that there is a close relationship of trust between that buyer and that seller, but that one of them is in a position to exercise constraint or direction over the other or that a third party is in a position to exercise such constraint or direction over them.

Management or operational control is the key standard here and that remains an open question after *Baltic Master*. The answer to the ultimate question is not about the nature and/or extent of relaxed business dealings between parties with long-term relationships but, more narrowly, whether those dealings signify the requisite management or operational control that can be identified as "sufficient constraint or direction" to connote a relationship for these purposes.

We find that the implementing regulations provide little assistance. In amended form, the UCC IA follows (in paragraph 127) the lead of the earlier Community Customs Code IA. In Annex 23 of the Community Customs Code IA we found a gloss

---

65. *See* TCCV, Com. 25.1, Third Party Royalties and License Fees-General Commentary (April 2011), paragraph 9 (e).

on Article 143.1 (e), in that control by one person over another is shown when the former is legally or operationally in a position to exercise restraint or direction over the latter.[66] Under the UCC IA, the "restraint" test was dropped. This obviously begs the question, "what is meant by direction"? Presumably any seller—or any buyer—with leverage over the other party in a sales transaction could dictate price or other terms. Would that be regarded as direction for these purposes?

To be sure, the *Baltic Master* decision explored the de jure versus de facto status of control. It also examined whether a legally recognized partnership could be ascertained on the basis of a de facto review. The court decided (in paragraph 35) that the very wording of Article 143.1 (b) of the Community Code IA[67] excludes any de facto business relationship. In this connection, the TCCV issued an instrument in 1996 which directs that a determination of a partnership status should be grounded in the national law on partnership in the jurisdiction.[68] The TCCV concluded that it would not be appropriate for a Member to devise a different definition of partnership specifically for customs valuation purposes.

[B] Effect of Related Party Status

What is the effect of the buyer and seller being "related parties" on customs valuation? The obvious answer is that the importer may be put to the task of justifying the declared customs value,[69] which means proving that the price was not influenced by the relationship of the parties. To be clear, the Valuation Agreement plainly ordains that the customs authority cannot disregard a transaction value solely because the buyer and seller are related.[70] By the same token, doubts may arise in the importation of goods even where there is no relationship between buyer and seller.[71] In this last connection, the ECJ has been confronted with an effective expansion of this area of inquiry:

> Even if the parties are not shown to be related under the UCC definition ("categorised as 'legally recognised partners in business' or as related persons"), is

66. You will recognize that this is the text of the Interpretative Note to Article 15.4 (e).
67. Now Article 127.1(b) of the UCC IA.
68. TCCV, AO 21.1, Interpretation of the Expression "Partners in Business" in Article 15.4(b) (March 1996).
69. Valuation Agreement, Article 1.1(d). In the US, the importer is required to declare at Box 32 on the face of the entry summary, CBP Form 7501, whether the buyer and seller are related. This is intended to enable CBP to determine which entries it should more closely scrutinize. In Canada, the importer in a related party transaction is instructed by CBSA as follows, "The importer who believes that the price is not influenced and uses a transfer price as the basis for establishing the value for duty under the transaction value method must retain on file the information justifying their conclusion and the calculation of the transfer price. This information may be examined by the CBSA at any time … ." Canada Memorandum D13-4-5, *Transaction value method for related persons*, December 6, 2021, paragraph 5.
70. Valuation Agreement, Article 1.2(a), in the US, *see* 19 CFR § 152.103(l).
71. *See* the discussion in Part I on *Euro 2004*. *See also* Article 17 of the Valuation Agreement on the authority of the customs administration to further examine documentation and representations made in customs entries. It is notable that UCC IA Article 140.1 is not limited to related party importations.

> the customs authority obliged to inquire whether the relationship between the traders influenced the determination of the higher price of the product subject to the specific importation, in order to counteract the evasion of customs duties and the loss of tax revenue to the EU budget?[72]

To be sure, that question in *OGL* arises in the specific context of the imported fruit and vegetable sector which relies on am entry price system based on product-specific average representative prices.[73] Nevertheless, the question itself suggests an expansion beyond the permitted borders, e.g., although management control is not evident, which should close down a related party review, is it still possible to see if the "relationship" influenced the price? If the answer is in the affirmative, that blurring or erasure of the standard does not bode well.

[1] Validation or Not?

Beyond the principle that a related party transaction will not preclude a TV appraisement of the imported goods, the US regulations continue on this positive note:

> There will be related person transactions in which validation of the transaction value, using the [verification] procedures contained in 152.103(j)(2), may not be necessary.[74]

The Interpretative Notes to the Valuation Agreement go even further:

> It is not intended that there should be an examination of the circumstances in all cases where the buyer and the seller are related.[75]

The importer/taxpayer's first argument should be that no further examination or validation is necessary in its case. The US regulations provide an example where no validation is required:

> Customs may have previously examined the relationship or may already have sufficient detailed information concerning the buyer and seller to be satisfied that the relationship did not influence the price actually paid or payable. In such case, if Customs has no doubts about the acceptability of the price, the price will be accepted without requesting further information from the importer.[76]

---

72. Case No C-770/291, *OGL-Food Trade Lebensmittelvertrieb GmbH v. Direktor na Teritorialna direktsia "Mitnitsa Plovdiv" pri Agentsia "Mitnitsi,"* OJ C138/10 ("*OGL*").
73. Commission Delegated Regulation (EU) 2017/891 of 13 March 2017 supplementing Regulation (EU) No. 1308/2013 of the European Parliament and of the Council with regard to the fruit and vegetables and processed fruit and vegetables sectors and supplementing Regulation (EU) No. 1306/2013 of the European Parliament and of the Council with regard to penalties to be applied in those sectors and amending Commission Implementing Regulation (EU) No. 543/2011 (OJ 2017 L 138, p. 4).
74. 19 CFR § 152.103(l); *see* Valuation Agreement, Article 1.2(a) and Interpretative Note to Article 1, Paragraph 2, point 2.
75. Interpretative Note, Article 1, Paragraph 2, point 2.
76. 19 CFR § 152.103(l)(1)(i). The parallel reference at the international level is Valuation Agreement, Interpretative Note, Article 1, Paragraph 2, point 2.

What if CBP is examining the relationship for the first time or otherwise has doubts? Again, the regulations are clear:

> If Customs does have doubts about the acceptability of the price and is unable to accept the transaction value without further inquiry, the importer will be given an opportunity to supply such further detailed information as may be necessary to enable Customs to examine the circumstances of the sale. In this context, Customs will examine relevant aspects of the transaction, *including* the way in which the buyer and seller organize their commercial relations and the way in which the price in question was arrived at in order to determine whether the relationship influenced the price[77] (emphasis added).

Assuming that an argument that no validation is necessary proves unavailing, the regulations instruct CBP to examine the COS, the first of the validation procedures that are in the valuation statute and regulations. The point of a COS inquiry by the customs authorities, as established by the last sentence in the above quotation, is a general and undefined review of "relevant aspects" of the transaction, with two broad examples of these aspects, "*including* the way in which the buyer and seller organize their commercial relations and the way in which the price in question was arrived at" (Emphasis added).

It is beyond cavil that the regulations and the Interpretative Notes are open-textured. These last two criteria are mere examples. They suggest that there are other ways in which the importer/taxpayer may show that the relationship between the parties did not influence the price. An importer can be successful in proving that the relationship did not influence the price in meeting this broad test based on the totality (all relevant aspects) of the circumstances without having to meet any of the more specific examples.[78]

If the customs authority has doubts, the importer is "on to the validation."

[C] Validation Methods: COS and "Test Values"

[1] In General

The customs valuation law establishes a bifurcated route to validation of a transfer price. First, as noted, the importer/taxpayer has the option of satisfying a doubting customs officer that its transfer price is acceptable for customs purposes by the COS test. Second, the importer/taxpayer can opt to show that the subject price "closely approximates" one of the "test values":

77. 19 CFR § 152.103(l)(1)(i). The WCO's TCCV has opined that a customs authority is under no obligation to explain why it has doubts when seeking information, but it must communicate its reasons for believing that the parties' relationship has influenced the price. Cf. paragraphs 12 and 14, Com. 14.1, Application of Article 1, paragraph 2 (November 1989). *See* Thailand—Customs and Fiscal Measures on Cigarettes from the Philippines, WT/DS 371, Panel Report (November 15, 2010), Appellate Body Report (June 17, 2011).
78. Ruling no. H029658 (December 8, 2009), discussed below in §10.03[D][1].

> The transaction value between a related buyer and seller is acceptable for the purposes of this subsection if an examination of the circumstances of sale of the imported merchandise indicates that the relationship did not influence the price actually paid or payable [the COS] or if the transaction value of the imported merchandise closely approximates [one of the test values] (i) the transaction value of identical merchandise, or of similar merchandise, in sales to unrelated buyers in the US;[79] or (ii) the deductive value or computed value for identical merchandise or similar merchandise.[80]

The level of precision in the two alternative proofs is very different. On the one hand, the notion of "circumstances" itself is loosely stitched. The US text comprising the COS test at the statutory level is quite meager. The text has been quoted in its entirety: the circumstances of the sale should be examined to discern whether the relationship influenced the price. The discussion in the regulations, or in the Interpretative Notes at the international level, is similarly quite abrupt, totaling but a handful of sentences, including references to the two broad examples noted and descriptions of three more specific exemplar proofs.[81] These sentences are replete with references to such vague sources as "relevant aspects" and "such further detailed information as may be necessary." There are no bright lines or tight definitions in these standards.[82]

By contrast, the "test values" criteria are quite specific, with precise instruction on the appropriate adjustments to be made, although the notion when one value "closely approximates" another value cannot be based on a uniform standard.[83]

[2] Importer/Taxpayer's Choice

Some importers have been pressured by CBP or other customs authorities to meet a specific validation test—COS or one or more test values—or to meet one or more of the

---

79. "Identical merchandise" is defined alternatively as: (1) merchandise that is identical in all respects to, and was produced in the same country and by the same person as, the merchandise being appraised or, generally, absent such goods; as (2) merchandise that is identical in all respects to, and was produced in the same country as, but not produced by the same person, as the merchandise being appraised. "Similar merchandise" is defined alternatively as: (1) merchandise that was produced in the same country and by the same person as the merchandise being appraised, is like the merchandise in characteristics and component material, and is commercially interchangeable with the merchandise being appraised or, generally, absent such goods; as (2) merchandise that is produced by another person but is otherwise described above. Valuation Agreement, Article 15.2; 19 USC §§ 1401(h)(2), 1401(h)(4).
80. 19 USC § 1401a(b)(2)(B). At the international level, leaving the Interpretative Notes aside, the Valuation Agreement text on the circumstances of sale consists of one sentence. Article 1.2(a).
81. The relevant source in the customs regulations is 19 CFR § 152.103(j)(2). The relevant Interpretative Note is Note 3 to Article 1, paragraph 2.
82. Compounding the problem is that there is apparently no documentation either at the WTO or the WCO that would constitute "legislative history" in the common law sense for the Valuation Agreement, and the legislative history of the implementing legislation in the United States is almost totally silent on these issues.
83. It will be seen that, in contrast to both, the transfer pricing methods (TPMs) applied in income tax reviews are far more detailed.

COS validation exemplars, but this pressure is to be resisted.[84] It is the importer's choice, and not CBP's or another customs authority's, which test is selected for validation.[85] The importer may elect to meet one or more of the specific exemplar COS proofs or, instead, decide to meet the COS standard based only on the more free form, overarching standard, simply to show that the relationship has not influenced the price, or perhaps by means of the two broad examples, the way in which the buyer and seller have organized their business or the manner in which the price was arrived at, or by other means.

It can be surmised that, just as TV is the preferred methodology for setting the dutiable value of imported merchandise under the customs valuation law, the regulations, which lead off with the importer given the opportunity to develop facts to enable a COS validation, set up that validation route as the preferred approach.

[D] COS Tests

As discussed, the regulations contain both broadly worded standards as well as slightly more specific tests.

[1] Broad Standard COS Proofs

Until the issuance of a 2009 ruling, CBP held an importer/taxpayer to a strict application of the somewhat specific exemplars of the regulations, discussed immediately below. An importer/taxpayer who could not meet one of these tests faced a sure denial of its transfer price. With its December 2009 ruling,[86] however, CBP reaffirmed that it was willing to accept a related party price as a basis for TV when the importer/taxpayer met the broad standard proofs of the regulations.

Tracking, and citing, the prescriptive language of the regulations, in allowing a TV appraisement to proceed based on the related party transaction, CBP examined "all relevant aspects of the transaction, including the way in which the buyer and seller organize their commercial relations and the way in which the price in question was arrived at."

This is notable in that it marks a return to an earlier precedent, as the importer who had been unable to satisfy any of the more specific exemplars nonetheless prevailed. If CBP's more then-more recent practice had been followed, the importer/taxpayer would have failed. CBP had determined in 2003[87] that an importer had demonstrated that the price had not been influenced by the relationship of the

---

84. *See* 19 CFR § 152.103(l)(2)(iii). "If one of the test values ... has been found to be appropriate, the port director shall not seek to determine if the relationship between the buyer and seller influenced the price."
85. Valuation Agreement, Article 1.2(c), states that the test values are to be used at the initiative of the importer. Accord, UCC IA, paragraph 134.4.
86. Ruling no. H029658 (December 9, 2009). *See also* ruling no. H310087 (March 18, 2022).
87. Ruling no. 548233 (November 7, 2003).

parties, even if no more specific exemplar test had been met, and the 2009 ruling was a return to this position.

The underlying premise of the 2009 ruling is sound and admirable, and should be studied and similarly applied by other customs authorities. The principal notion is that the COS standard is extremely loosely worded and amenable to any variety of proofs that the relationship did not influence the price. Even the concepts—the way in which the parties have organized their commercial relations or the way in which the price was arrived at—are merely examples. There is no strict rhyme scheme or convention here. In other words, the proofs are and should be protean and not procrustean, a theme which we revisit below.

[2] More Specific COS Proofs

Beyond these broader examples, the regulations set forth three examples of favorable COS proofs, demonstrating that the relationship has not influenced the price:

- If the buyer and seller buy from and sell to each other as if they were not related.
- If the price has been settled in a manner that is consistent with the normal pricing practices of the industry in question.
- If the price has been settled in a manner that is consistent with the way the seller settles prices for sales to buyers who are not related to him.[88]

Although the relevant texts specifically state that these are only "examples," CBP and other customs authorities have perceived them as more in the nature of dispositive "tests" instead of the simple examples that they are. Too often, CBP and other customs authorities have overlooked the salient fact of their true, limited nature and role. They are meant to be illustrative and helpful in the context of an overly spare legal standard and not mandatory, exclusive, or exhaustive of the proofs. By virtue of being simply examples, the assumption should be that the importer/taxpayer may be free to proffer other proofs of the COS that demonstrate that the price has not been influenced by the relationship between the buyer and seller.

[3] Buy and Sell as if Not Related

The first example calls for a review of the process, perhaps the course of dealings, between the buyer and seller. In its defense of a related party price, the importer/taxpayer must be prepared to meet CBP's scrutiny with adequate documentation proving, for example, that the seller used a common price list for sales to related

88. Valuation Agreement, Interpretative Note, Article 1, Paragraph 2, point 3. Cf. 19 CFR §§ 152.103(l)(1)(i)-(iii).

and unrelated buyers.[89] Mere references to pricing policies will not suffice.[90] Obviously, if the foreign vendor only sells to related buyers, there will be no ground for comparison.

[4] Pricing Is Consistent with the Industry Norm

The Interpretative Note and the US regulations advance the second point and its "industry in question" context as an example of the arm's-length standard that is implicit in the first point. As for the second exemplar, at first glance, this exercise in comparison between the price and an external industry referent invokes whiffs of the "functional equivalency" studies undertaken for many transfer pricing studies. But CBP administrative practice requires that an importer furnish objective evidence both on what constitutes the "normal pricing practices of the industry," as well as that the transfer price in question was settled consistent with that standard.[91]

For CBP, the definition of "industry" in the COS context is further defined to mean the industry that produces goods of the "same class or kind" as the imported merchandise.[92] Class or kind determinations necessarily relate to the specific type of goods at issue, and CBP has stated:

> CBP does not consider the industry in question to consist of other functionally equivalent companies if those companies do not sell goods of the same class or kind.[93]

The customs valuation statute and regulations define "class or kind":

> Merchandise (including, but not limited to, identical merchandise and similar merchandise) within a group or range of merchandise produced by a particular industry or industry sector.[94]

Some observers have commented that an even narrower construction of the industry may be needed and that "class or kind" is not an appropriate context in a COS analysis. This perspective is based on the concept that the test values extend only to identical or similar goods and that there should be symmetry between the two test protocols.

---

89. *See* ruling nos. 547019 (March 31, 2000) (identical price discounts given to related and unrelated buyers) and 546285 (June 7, 1996) (related buyer's discount of 20% from published price list not dissimilar from unrelated distributor's 10% discount once volume discount is factored).
90. *See* ruling no. 563400 (March 29, 2006), in which a COS justification was not accepted by CBP, in contrast with a ruling cited therein, no. 547019 (March 31, 2000), in which the importer had furnished actual copies of a price list and pricing formula and other detailed information.
91. ICP: Related Party Transactions, at 7-8, citing ruling no. 542261 (March 11, 1981). *See also* ruling no. 548095 (September 19, 2002).
92. ICP: Related Party Transactions, at 7-8.
93. *Ibid.*, at 8. *See also* ruling no. H029658 (December 8, 2009).
94. 19 USC § 1401a(g)(2); 19 CFR § 152.102(h). This definition tracks the Valuation Agreement, Article 15.4. The notion of class or kind of merchandise also has an application in tariff classification by principal use. *See*, e.g., ruling no. 967408 (February 9, 2005), and authorities cited therein. "Class or kind" in connection with computed value is discussed below.

The practical result of this narrow focus and insistence on a "same class or kind" outer perimeter is that many of the "comparables" that are typically cited in transfer pricing studies will be rejected by CBP. As an example, an economic consulting group may have prepared a benchmarking study or a full economic analysis of contract manufacturers in the electronics industry as functionally equivalent companies to a contract manufacturer/vendor or "toll packer" of food products. Alternatively, the economic analysis may be of limited risk distributors regardless of the specific products being purchased and resold. Although the economic analyses may suffice for the purpose of measuring the economic activity of the parties under section 482 or a similar income tax statute, such a comparative analysis has been, and presumably will continue to be, rejected out of hand by CBP.[95]

For all of this additional detail, a close reading of the text may yet result in a heightened level of uncertainty. That is because, unlike the text in either deductive or computed value,[96] "industry" is not defined geographically. Take the hypothetical case of wearing apparel imported into the US from Italy. Would the relevant industry be that composed of the Italian manufacturers/sellers of apparel? The apparel importers or buyers in the US? Or, even more narrowly, only US buyers of imported Italian wearing apparel? Should one measure be seen as equivalent to the other, or should one be inherently superior/inferior to the other? If a customs authority ordinarily prefers one definition, for example, with a focus on foreign sellers,[97] absent such evidence, should that customs authority accept evidence of the alternative (e.g., that of the importers' industry)? This last question is quite significant, as data and other relevant information from foreign markets may not be accessible to a customs authority—or to an importer.

In any event, CBP will insist on: (1) objective evidence of the normal pricing practices of the industry in question and (2) evidence that the transfer price was settled in accordance with this industry's pricing practices.[98]

---

95. In ruling no. 548482 (July 23, 2004) CBP observed (at 8) that the consultant in preparing a transfer pricing study had selected companies deemed to be "broadly comparable ... based on functions performed, markets served and risks borne." CBP's review led it to conclude that the comparable companies were not engaged in the "same class of kind" of merchandise. In addition, CBP noted that no independent verification was performed to confirm functional comparability. In a 2011 ruling issued to an importer/distributor of parts for cigarette-making machines, CBP rejected a transfer pricing study in which the comparable companies were in diverse industry sectors, such as the automotive, appliance, aerospace, construction, and transportation industries. Ruling no. H138203 (October 11, 2011).

    Likewise, in a 2015 ruling the importer failed to meet the rubric of this method because its transfer pricing study was focused on functional comparability and was not limited to the companies dealing with the same class or kind of goods. Ruling no. H254700 (November 25, 2015) ("The comparable companies, none of which are in the crop protection industry, sell a variety of pharmaceutical and medical products. Accordingly, in line with previous rulings, we find that [the importer] has failed to show that the prices will be settled in a manner consistent with the normal pricing practices of the crop protection industry").

96. *See* below §10.03[E][2][b] and [c].

97. This is the situation in Japan, where the focus is on the "sale," with the result that the industry is that which includes foreign sellers.

98. *See* ruling no. W563467 (June 22, 2009) (importer of automobiles from the United Kingdom presented concept of "market driven" pricing (aka "target-based pricing")). *But see* ruling no. H029658 (December 8, 2009) ("market driven MSRP" is the standard pricing practice in the automobile industry).

A study of the many rulings that CBP has issued on related party/transfer pricing reveals that importers should be prepared for an in-depth review of the documentation submitted and a comparison between the contractual provisions and the actual course of the parties' conduct. A 2019 ruling[99] in which CBP rejected the importer's industry norm validation of the transfer price can serve as a minicourse.

CBP noted the significant ambiguities and discrepancies within the documentation as to the role of the parties and the lack of substance in the importer, and determined that there was no valid sale for export from the related party Canadian seller to the US entity, IWC.[100] Beyond that, even if there had been a qualifying sale for export, CBP concluded that there was no showing that the pricing was consistent with the industry norm. The excerpted discussion can serve as a model for future application of this test:

> counsel encourages CBP to accept that the relationship did not influence the prices because the related parties set their prices based on the TNMM methodology stated in the transfer pricing analysis performed for tax purposes. This argument is contrary to CBP's longstanding position that the mere fact that an importer provides CBP with an Advance Pricing Agreement ("APA") or transfer pricing study is not sufficient to establish that a related party transaction value is acceptable. Additionally, CBP has repeatedly ruled that the mere fact the importer/buyer allegedly earned an operating profit comparable to other functionally equivalent companies is not sufficient to establish compliance with the normal pricing practices of the industry, or that the related party price was settled in a manner consistent with the normal pricing practices of the industry in question. See HQ 548482, dated July 23, 2004; HQ 548095, dated September 19, 2002; HQ H029658, dated December 8, 2009; HQ H037375, dated December 11, 2009; HQ H138203, dated October 11, 2011; and, HQ H260036, dated February 24, 2015. We also note that the pricing practices must relate to the industry in question, which generally includes the industry that produces goods of the same class or kind as the imported merchandise. See HQ 546998, dated January 19, 2000; see also HQ 548095, dated September 19, 2002.
>
> In this case, the prices are set pursuant to the TNMM methodology (specified in the Distribution Agreement). Counsel claims that the price determined by the TNMM is estimated using budgeted sales prices, sales volumes, and operating expenses and that the parties consult with each other to determine that arm's length price. There is no evidence presented to support any negotiations between the parties. Furthermore, in this instance, a set of functionally comparable companies was used to determine a target margin range. However, our review of the [***] comparable companies identified in [***] analysis for the fiscal year 2013, indicates that these companies were chosen based on their functional comparability with IWC. The comparable companies, none of which is in a coated woven products market, sell a variety of lumber and other construction materials, industrial supplies, and non-durable goods. On the other hand, IWC operates in a coated woven products market, distributing extrusion coated woven and diverse multi-layer laminated plastic substrates for packaging purposes. Accordingly, in line with previous rulings, we find that IWC has failed to show that the prices were

99. Ruling no. H263045 (March 15, 2019).
100. To this extent, the ruling is a useful additional study for a sale for export analysis as discussed in Part I.

settled in a manner consistent with the normal pricing practices of the coated woven industry.

Obviously, functional comparability alone will not suffice for CBP under this industry pricing COS exemplar.

[5] Manner of Settling Prices

The attention in the third exemplar—the seller settles the price in a manner consistent with its sales to unrelated buyers—is on the seller, so the ambiguity of the "industry" referent is avoided. From this perspective, the customs officer will be looking for a consistency in courses of dealing as proof of the acceptability of the transfer price. CBP offers the following illustrations of this concept:

> [I]f the importer establishes that the price paid by unrelated and related buyers to the seller is the same or that the price was determined based on an arm's length negotiation, this would be an indication that the relationship between the parties did not influence the price. Or, if the seller uses a specified formula for determining the price (for example, based on the quantity purchased or other specified criteria) and applies the same formula in both sales to related and unrelated buyers.[101]

It is well to realize that CBP will closely scrutinize all submissions by an importer seeking to validate the transfer price, and none more so than those which are purported to meet the COS tests. An example of a failed attempt by an importer to meet this "manner of settling prices" reveals that an unrelated distributor enjoyed a net discount of 68% while a related party received a discount of 77%.[102] Not surprisingly, CBP noted that this was preferential pricing to its wholly owned subsidiary, and concluded that the importer's price was not "settled in a manner consistent with the way the seller settles prices for sales to buyers who are not related to it."

CBP prefers comparison sales to buyers in the US but will accept sales to third-party buyers in other jurisdictions if they are relevant.[103]

[6] All Costs Plus a Profit

Proceeding beyond these three exemplars, the COS test foresees that the importer/taxpayer can also show that the relationship has not influenced the price by means of a profit comparison:

> If it is shown that the price is adequate to ensure recovery of all costs plus a profit which is equivalent to the firm's overall profit realized over a representative period of time (e.g., on an annual basis), in sales of merchandise of the same class or kind,

101. ICP: Related Party Transactions, at 8-9.
102. Ruling no. H256779 (January 20, 2016).
103. *Ibid.* This makes for an interesting point since sales to buyers in third countries is prohibited under Article 7 of the Valuation Agreement. Article 7.2(e). *See* 19 USC § 1401a(f)(2)(E); UCC IA, Article 144.2(e).

this would demonstrate that the price has not been influenced by the relationship.[104]

An early question that arises is, Whose costs and profit? This "all costs plus a profit" postulate does not refer to either a buyer or a seller when it uses the more general term "firm," but it can be deduced that the profit compared is the seller's profit because it is profits arising from "sales" rather than from "purchases" or "resales" which would reflect on the buyer's profit experience.[105]

In its scores of rulings on a COS analysis, CBP has not always trod a consistent path. In some instances, CBP has referred to the foreign seller's costs and profit.[106] CBP has also measured the acceptability of pricing based on the buyer's costs and overall profit.[107] In some rulings, CBP has expressed the criterion in terms of the exporter's costs and profit.[108] There is even a ruling in which CBP has referred to the manufacturer's costs and profit.[109]

Based on its citation in the 2007 ICP and subsequent rulings, however, the prevailing CBP interpretation of the "all costs plus a profit" example is that the text looks neither to the buyer nor the seller but to the parent company of the seller as the benchmark. This arose in a First Sale inquiry,[110] where all three of the parties (manufacturer, middleman, and importer/buyer) were related. The manufacturer/seller was a subsidiary of the parent company, and the qualifying PAPP for the merchandise had to be adequate to ensure recovery of all the seller's costs plus a profit that is equivalent to the parent company/buyer's overall profit.[111]

104. 19 CFR § 152.103(l)(1)(iii).

105. In Canada, the focus is on the related vendor's cost and profit experience. *See* Customs Memorandum D13-4-5, *Transaction value method for related persons*, December 6, 2021, paragraph 9(c).

106. *See*, e.g., rulings nos. H017761 (September 27, 2007), 545800 (June 28, 1996), 546166 (April 5, 1966), 546052 (October 27, 1995), 545960 (August 16, 1995), 545349 (March 24, 1995). CBP has mischaracterized the text of this example in its effort to focus on the seller. Ruling no. H138203, at 8 (October 11, 2011) ("The focus of interpretive note 3 is the seller's cost and profit").

107. *See*, e.g., ruling nos. H029658 (December 8, 2009), 563400 (March 29, 2006), 548291 (May 28, 2003), 546072 (May 21, 1998), 546211 (June 10, 1996), 545669 (November 17, 1994).

108. *See*, e.g., ruling nos. H003845 (August 17, 2007), W547982 (May 20, 2002).

109. Ruling no. 548239 (June 5, 2003).

110. *See* Part I.

111. Ruling no. 546998 (January 19, 2000), cited in ICP: Related Party Transactions, at 9. In many ruling treatments, CBP analyzes this criterion by reference to "the firm's" profit without discussion or further identification. *See*, e.g., ruling no. 546865 (August 6, 1999). In ruling no. H065015 (April 14, 2011), CBP again cited ruling no. H546998 (in applying the all costs-plus-profit test, CBP normally considers the "firm's" overall profit to be the profit of the parent company. Thus, if the seller of the imported goods is a subsidiary of the parent company, the price must be adequate to ensure recovery of all the seller's costs plus a profit that is equivalent to the parent company's overall profit). *See* also ruling no. H204424 at 6 (July 31, 2013) ("there is no identifiable parent in this case for purposes of comparison of profit in sales of merchandise of the same class or kind, i.e., the overall profit of the parent comparison"). *See* 19 CFR § 152.103 (1)(iii). In a later ruling CBP has again confirmed this approach—where the seller is a subsidiary company, the seller's profit must be compared with the parent company's profit as the benchmark. Ruling no. H194998 (July 24, 2014), citing the 2000 ruling. *See also* ruling no.

To this point, CBP has never provided any explanation or shared any rational basis for this interpretation. Nor had there been any judicial approval of this CBP interpretation until the 2021 Court of International Trade decision in *Meyer Corporation US*.[112] There, the trial court judge merely adopted as the findings of the court the government's recital of facts which included its exposition of the "parent's costs" standard.[113] At the present time, despite the issuance of four separate opinions, the true nature of this COS test remains an open question and we must await a definitive judgment of the CBP interpretation.[114]

At the WCO, the TCCV has issued a helpful instrument on the all costs plus a profit test. This is Case Study 10.1.[115] Unfortunately for these purposes, however, the facts as recited there suggest that the seller (XCO) was itself the ultimate parent company, so the CBP interpretation was never tested.

The hypothetical case introduced the notion that two ingredients were sold by XCO to its related party buyer, ICO. One of the ingredients was sold to third parties as well as to ICO, and the prices to ICO were set lower than in those comparable (same quantities, same commercial level) third-party sales. As a result of the price difference, transaction value was disallowed.

For the second ingredient, there were no comparable sales by XCO to unrelated buyers. Transaction value was allowed for those sales based upon an analysis showing that the price from XCO to ICO was adequate to ensure recovery of all XCO's costs plus a profit that "was representative" of XCO's overall profit for goods of the same class or kind.

Parenthetically, most importers had formerly held back from advancing an FSFE claim where the foreign factory and the middleman were related. That was because it is so difficult to establish that the foreign transaction was at arm's length (i.e., freed of the influence of the relationship).[116] We are beginning to see more rulings in which transfer pricing COS analyses or transfer pricing studies are relied on to validate that first sale between those foreign parties and not the sale in which the importer/taxpayer was a party.[117]

H258447 (January 19, 2016) (citing three earlier rulings, "the firm's overall profit" is determined by the parent company's profits over a representative period of time (e.g., annually) in sales of merchandise of the same class or kind).

112. *Meyer Corporation, US v. United States*, Slip Op. 21-26, 2021 WL 777788 *(CIT 2021) (Meyer II)*. *See* earlier discussion in §3.01[D][1][a].
113. *Ibid.*, Slip Op. 21-26 at 112, 115-116.
114. A review of the trial transcript in *Meyer II* shows very little challenge by the importer to the testimony of the CBP official on this point. Hopefully any later examination will be conducted more vigorously and the court will be presented with the necessity to opine on a carefully framed question.
115. TCCV, CS 10.1, Application of Article 1.2 (October 1996).
116. *See*, e.g., ruling no. 546672 (May 21, 2002) (FSFE is not available because the importer was not able to establish an arm's-length first sale and because information on the statutory additions was missing).
117. *See*, e.g., ruling nos. W563542 (July 24, 2009), H016585 (December 30, 2008) (transfer pricing study furnished), 547332 (January 22, 2002), 546998 (January 19, 2000); Neville, "First Sale Meets Transfer Pricing," 21 J. Int'l Tax'n (February 2010) at 16.

Based on the loose texture of the text and the variegated patterns that make up the administrative practice, it may be that the importer/taxpayer will be able to advance his case based on an analysis of any of the parties, depending on the availability and reliability of the supporting documentation. In this fashion, in selecting the party whose costs and profit are measured, there may be the same degree of flexibility as is embodied in the notion of "tested parties" in transfer pricing studies.[118]

CBP has held that unless audited financial statements and internal management accounts are accessible, they may not be persuaded.[119] A statement by importer's counsel that a profit of a stated percentage "is not unreasonable" will not suffice, and neither will a statement that the price "represents the cost of production plus a fair profit as gauged against sales between unrelated firms.[120] Again, there is a focus on sales of merchandise of the same class or kind.

You will have noticed that the statute does not specify the level of profit that should be examined—gross profit or operating profit? CBP prefers to analyze operating profit but will accept a gross profit review if operating profit is not available.[121]

For its part, the WCO advises on the use of the operating profit:

> The [all costs plus a profit] example does not define whether "profit" is "gross" or "operating" profit, but this gives Customs the flexibility to review both kinds of profit, depending in what is considered to be useful. Normally, operating profit is a better measure of real profitability because it shows what is earned after all expenses have been paid. Also, it is the measure for which information concerning independent parties will most often be available. Operating profit is also the most common Profit Level Indicator when the transactional net margin method is used.[122]

I would venture that few customs authorities will want to review both gross and operating profit comparisons.

CBP has issued a ruling in which the profit tested was net profit, which goes beyond an operating profit to reflect after-tax results. In ruling no. H284014 (July 27, 2018) CBP explained:

> CBP Regulations do not define what profit we are to consider. However, CBP is of the view that the operating profit margin is a more accurate measure of a company's real profitability because it reveals what the company actually earns on its sales once all associated expenses have been paid ... .
>
> In this particular case, the importer relies upon a comparison of the net profit margin to show that the manufacturer's sales of products to the importer resulted in a profit equivalent to, or greater than, the manufacturer's sales of products worldwide. The net profit margin equals the net profits after taxes divided by sales. According to Investopedia.com:
>
> Net profit margins are those generated from all phases of a business, including taxes. In other words, this ratio compares net income with sales.

118. *See* below §10.04[B][2][a].
119. Ruling no. 546267 (December 14, 1998).
120. Ruling nos. 547790 (September 10, 2001) and 544666, IA 81/90 (April 5, 1993), respectively.
121. *See* ruling no. H194998 (July 24, 2014). *But see* ruling no. H258447 (January 19, 2016). *See also* ruling no. H292026 (February 1, 2018).
122. WCO Guide to Customs Valuation and Transfer Pricing, 65.

> The reason provided for using the net profit margin for comparison purposes is that the net profit margin is a financial ratio which minimizes inconsistencies in accounting principles related to the classification of direct and indirect expenses and returns for companies. For this reason, the importer indicated that the net profit margin is the most reliable profit level indicator for comparison purposes. The net profit margin differs from the operating profit margin, which is normally considered by CBP in the context of the all costs plus a profit test, in that the net profit margin calculation utilizes profit after taxes, and the operating profit margin calculation utilizes profit before deductions for interest and taxes paid. However, in this case, as the manufacturer/seller is the parent and extensive documentation has been submitted to explain the derivation of the submitted figures, we agree that the use of the net profit margin is acceptable (citations omitted).

Readers are cautioned to bear in mind that CBP employs rigorous standards for this costs-plus-profit test and that most importers fail the test.

CBP has apparently interpreted this test as requiring a full equivalency in the profits being compared, and has rejected importers' arguments in several instances where there were discrepancies between the profit levels.[123] The text seemingly requires this full equivalency, but this comes at the cost of a more nuanced approach that is common to the income tax transfer pricing inquiries into arm's-length pricing. To be more direct, such an approach ignores any analysis, as discussed *infra*, which relies on the respective comparability factors—assets employed, risks undertaken, and functions performed by the parties.

There is a built-in COS obstacle for the importer here arising from the design of the business model for a limited risk contract manufacturer. Thus, for example, it may be perfectly acceptable for income tax purposes for a contract manufacturer/seller to post an operating profit of 1.5% while the entrepreneur parent company buyer/reseller earns an operating profit of 8.0%. Parenthetically, we may put it the other way around—if the profits are equivalent when the comparability factors (assets, risks, and functions) are out of balance, income tax authorities will surely pose objections. But for CBP—and potentially other customs authorities if they were to follow suit—it makes perfect sense to disallow a transaction value where a manufacturing entity makes 6% profit which is less than the corporate parent company's 10% profit level.[124]

Likewise, if the "all costs plus a profit" test continues to be applied with this rigorous interpretation of "equivalency," where there is a limited risk contract manufacturer as the foreign seller, importers will want to steer well clear of its shoals in all but those exceedingly rare instances where there will be such equivalency.

Indeed, an informal survey reveals that importers in the US who have attempted to meet the COS test by relying on this "all costs plus a profit" method have failed in roughly 80% of the cases making up the body of relevant Headquarters rulings. This statistic should serve as a further cautionary note.

123. *Ibid.* and rulings cited therein.
124. Ruling no. H303474 (January 4, 2022).

[7] Substantiation

CBP has put US importers on notice that it expects adequate records and documentation to substantiate the claim, and has emphasized that:

> [t]he importer should be prepared to provide a thorough explanation of the circumstances surrounding the sale, supporting evidence, and an explanation of why the importer believes that such circumstances establish that the relationship did not influence the price.
>
> CBP often rejects circumstances of sale claims because the allegations are conclusory and not supported by evidence.[125]

The regulations supply an example to this last note, which makes the point that the seller's profit experience on unrelated sales need not be mirrored in related party sales if the relationship has not affected the price. In a somewhat circular fashion, the regulations posit that a price found by CBP to have been unaffected by the relationship will remain valid even if sales of similar merchandise, presumably within the same class or kind of merchandise, generate higher profits for the seller:

> Example. A foreign seller sells merchandise to a related US importer. The foreign seller does not sell identical merchandise to any unrelated parties. The transaction between the foreign seller and the US importer is determined by Customs to be unaffected by the relationship.
>
> How should the merchandise be appraised?
>
> [Answer] Transaction value based on the price actually paid or payable. A transaction value between a related buyer and seller is acceptable if the relationship did not affect the price actually paid or payable. This is so even if similar merchandise is sold at a higher price, which includes a higher percentage for profit and general expenses.[126]

The example is meant to stand for the proposition that a price determined to have been unaffected by the relationship on other grounds will not, or at least should not, thereafter be "trumped" and determined to be invalid if the seller's profits on the subject sales are less than those generated in other sales, whether related or unrelated.

In Canada, CBSA has similarly put importers on notice:

> The importer who believes that the price is not influenced and uses a transfer price as the basis for establishing the value for duty under the transaction value method must retain on file the information justifying their conclusion and the calculation of the transfer price. This information may be examined by the CBSA at any time … .[127]

125. ICP: Related Party Transactions, at 10.
126. 19 CFR § 152.103(l)(1). Of course, coming immediately after the discussion of a profit comparability demonstrating that the relationship did not influence the price, one is left to guess the basis on which CBP had determined in this hypothetical that the price had been unaffected by the relationship.
127. Canada Memorandum D13-4-5, *Transaction value method for related persons*, December 6, 2021, paragraph 5.

The elastic "circumstances of sale" term and the guidance provided by the regulations make for a wide compass in arguing that the relationship of the parties has not affected the price. This is the proper background for the question whether, in validating the TV based on related party pricing, an importer might draw on the proofs and methodologies that were adduced to show that its transfer pricing is at arm's length for income tax purposes.

[E] Test Values

[1] General Considerations

It is helpful to note that the "test values" have a dual life. On the one hand, as discussed below, they are a reference point and provide the means of validating a transaction value appraisement. On the other hand, if the related party price is rejected and a transaction value appraisement is not available, these test values are at the heart of the alternative methods of appraisement to which CBP or other customs authorities will turn in the same hierarchical order enumerated above.[128] Theoretically, a deductive or computed value appraisement should render a result similar to a TV appraisement.

As just noted, the statute and regulations organize the test values as an alternative path for the importer to validate his transfer price. To be clear, the COS route is for the purpose of showing that the relationship has not influenced the price. If the importer is unable to prove this in the affirmative or if there is proof to the contrary that the relationship has influenced the price, the importer may still be able to validate the transfer price through the test values. In this effort, the importer may not need to show further proof if CBP already has sufficient information that one of the test values has been met.[129]

If the importer is put to the task of comparing the transfer price to one of the test values, those are as follows:

- Transaction value of identical or similar merchandise in sales to unrelated buyers in the country of importation.
- Deductive value for identical merchandise or similar merchandise.
- Computed value for identical merchandise or similar merchandise.

128. As discussed in detail in Part I, the customs law gives the importer the choice to use a computed value appraisement before deductive value. Valuation Agreement, Article 1.2(c) ("[t]he tests set forth … are to be used at the initiative of the importer and only for comparison purposes"); 19 USC § 1401a(a)(2); UCC IA, Article 134.4 (also noting that the test values shall not substitute for the declared transaction value). Given their dual roles, I chose to include a brief discussion here of the test values/alternative methods in Part II, to save the reader from having to constantly interrupt a review in order to scroll up or turn back the pages for a treatment.

129. 19 CFR § 152.103(l)(2)(iii). "If the port director already has sufficient information to be satisfied, without further detailed inquiries, that one of the test values is appropriate, he shall not require the importer to demonstrate that the test value is appropriate." Of course, it is up to CBP to determine if the available information is sufficient. Accord, Valuation Agreement, Interpretative Note, Article 1, Paragraph 2, point 2.

You should know that there was an additional test value that had been initially adopted and was dropped only in October 1979 with the Protocol.[130] This would have sanctioned the comparison to prices of identical or similar merchandise coming from other countries, provided that the sellers in any two compared transactions were not related.

[a] Contemporaneous Transactions

The tested values must apply to merchandise that was exported to the country of importation at or about the same time as the imported merchandise.[131] CBP has issued rulings on the time constraints imposed by the statute, expressing the view that the statute sets a hierarchy in which export sales "at" the time of the transaction, i.e., on the exact date of the subject importation, should be examined before looking to sales "about" the same time.[132]

[b] Safeguard Against Potential Skewing

Another important requirement for the test value comparison is that it be conducted with due account taken of any differences in or the effects of:

- Commercial levels.
- Quantity levels.
- Assists.
- Costs incurred by the seller in sales in which he and the buyer are not related that are not incurred by the seller in sales in which he and the buyer are related.[133]

This admonition has been overlooked by CBP and the court. Albeit not in a related party context, recall the failure in *Euro 2004* to consider that skewing effects had been considered and adjusted for when looking to statistical average values for "comparable goods" in the valuation databases.

130. The Protocol was discussed at length in Part I. GATT, Multilateral Trade Negotiations Group, "Non-Tariff Measures," Sub-Group Customs Matters, Customs Valuation Agreement on Implementation of Article VII of the General Agreement on Tariffs and Trade, Addendum, MTN/NTM/W/229/REV. 1/Add 1 (22 October 1979).
131. Valuation Agreement, Article 2.1; 19 USC § 1401a(b)(2)(B); 19 CFR § 152.103(j)(2)(i); Canada Customs Act subsections 49(1), 50(1) and 51(2); UCC, Article 74.2(a) and (b).
132. Ruling nos. 546217 (April 8, 1998) (for perishable commodities, "about" is construed to mean a total of fourteen days, one week before and one week after the export of the imported merchandise under scrutiny) and 546999 (April 12, 1999).
133. 19 USC § 1401a(b)(2)(C); 19 CFR § 152.103(j)(2)(ii). UCC IA, Article 134.3. This requirement of symmetry in commercial level and quantity is repeated in the customs valuation law's first alternative method of appraisement, the TV of identical or similar merchandise. 19 USC § 1401a(c)(2). *See* ruling no. H254164 (March 19, 2018).

[c] Test Value Comparisons Restricted to Actual Use in Other Transactions

The "test value" methodology is profoundly burdensome and usually inapplicable for most transfer pricing validations owing to customs authority insistence that the test values must have been actually applied to a contemporaneous, actual entry of merchandise.[134] This requirement may not pose an obstacle where the importer can rely on a contemporaneous entry arising from a sale by the related party seller to an unrelated buyer/importer, assuming that a TV appraisement would not be available as the basis of appraisement for that other sale. The transaction value of identical or similar merchandise would apply to the other transaction, further assuming that the related party foreign seller can prevail on the unrelated importer to make the documentation available to its related party buyer for this purpose.[135] But for the remaining test values, the importer cannot simply resort to the detailed calculations necessary to show a computed value or deductive value comparison with the transfer price under scrutiny. CBP has announced:

> It continues to be [CBP's] position that in determining whether a test value closely approximates an instant transaction value, that the test value reflect a value previously accepted as a customs value. We have no legal authority to utilize values for the same entries of merchandise, based on different valuation methods, as evidence as to whether a test value closely approximates the instant transaction value.[136]
>
> There is authority at the international level for this interpretation, which rejects a "notional" use of a test value, as the Interpretative Notes to the Valuation Agreement state that the importer may be permitted "to demonstrate that the transaction value closely approximates to a "test" value *previously accepted* by the customs administration"[137] (emphasis added).

A close reading of the Valuation Agreement and the implementing statutes shows us that alternative test values either: (i) the transaction value of identical or similar merchandise or (ii) the deductive or computed value for identical or similar merchandise only.[138] This qualification necessarily means that the test values in play: (1) must have been derived only from other transactions involving identical or similar merchandise and (2) preclude a reference to computed or deductive value calculations of the very merchandise undergoing appraisement.

But assume that the importer is seeking to validate his transfer price with either a computed or deductive test value and does the calculation to establish the alternative methodology for the subject transaction only to discover that the customs authority will not accept it because it is not a calculation that had, in fact, been used for the

134. *See*, e.g., ruling nos. 545878 (July 31, 1966), 543568 (May 30, 1986).
135. This burden would be avoided only in those other importations where the related party seller is the importer of record. While the commercial invoice might be available, the other entry documents would have been prepared by or for the buyers in those other transactions.
136. Ruling no. 544455 (March 14, 1995); ICP: Related Party Transactions, at 11. *See* recitation of authorities cited in ruling no. H254164 (March 19, 2018).
137. Valuation Agreement, Interpretative Note, Article 1, Paragraph 2, point 4.
138. Valuation Agreement, Article 1.2 (b); 19 USC § 1401a(b)(2)(B); Canada Customs Act subsection 48(3); UCC IA, Article 134.2.

valuation of a different transaction. In such an event, the customs authority may reject the transaction value and proceed to appraise the merchandise on an alternative basis. Those alternative bases include computed value and deductive value analyses of the merchandise appraised. The upshot of the exercise is that the customs authority may well use the very calculations that would have been disallowed in the validation analysis.

Another twist is that the disallowed computed value or deductive value calculations might find life in the context of a COS validation. There is nothing in the statutes or regulations that would preclude such an application. Moreover, as one of the ways to meet the COS is to show that the transfer price was enough to cover all costs plus ensure a profit, computed value and deductive value both require cost and profit analyses. But those analyses can raise significant legal and factual issues about these crucial elements.

[d] Profit and General Expenses

For deductive value, the amount for usual commissions or profit and general expenses will be the importer's, provided that the profit and general expenses are consistent with those reflected in sales in the country of importation of imported merchandise (regardless of origin) of the same class or kind.[139] In this regard, state and local sales taxes imposed on the resale are to be treated as a general expense.[140]

For computed value, the amount for profit and general expenses will be the producer's, unless this amount is inconsistent with that of producers in the country of exportation on sales of that class or kind of merchandise.[141]

[e] Producer's or Importer's Own Records

As discussed separately at greater length below in the contexts of both computed value and deductive value, the use of the producer's own accounting records will create both an opportunity and a challenge for the importer on a subsequent computed value calculation, as will the need to use an importer's own profit and general expense records in a deductive value calculation. The opportunity is for the importer to use economic analyses, similar to those that underlie a transfer pricing study, as a shield in support of the producer's or importer's amounts for profit and general expenses as consistent with the industry. A challenge may arise if the importer must use the economic analyses as a sword in discrediting the actual financial data of the producer or itself as inconsistent with industry standards.

Because the actual data are derived directly from the actual accounts and are locked in and cannot be restated, absent a showing that they had been inconsistent with those of relevant other producers' or other importers' accounting practices, the

139. Valuation Agreement, Interpretative Note, Article 5, point 6; 19 USC § 1401a(d)(3)(B).
140. 19 USC § 1401a(e)(2)(B).
141. 19 USC § 1401a(d)(3)(B)(ii); 19 CFR § 152.105(e).

importer may have been boxed into a disadvantageous position by the foreign producer's accounting treatment. This was the harsh lesson meted out by the courts to *Campbell Soup*.[142]

Another harsh lesson was dealt in the 1998 CIT decision in *La Perla Fashions*,[143] where the trial court rejected the importer's computed value and deductive value calculations because they were deemed unreliable.

Quite apart from the negative inferences that might be drawn from a lack of documentation, there is a statutory basis for CBP's estimation of duties if the importer is unable to verify its submissions.

[f] Inadequate Records: Estimated Basis for Appraisal

In the face of inadequate records or supporting information, CBP might seek to appraise the imported merchandise by emulating the IRS, which can estimate taxes. In fact, CBP has already asserted this authority in a judicial review of a customs valuation dispute.

The importer, Heng Ngai Jewelry, sought to challenge CBP's denial of a TV appraisement and the alternative appraisement of its goods based on computed value.[144] Among other key facts in the administrative record, the importer had not responded to requests for information during the administrative review and only presented certain information to the CIT. CBP claimed that the importer had failed to provide detailed verifiable records and, in response, CBP was prevented from substantiating TV or calculating computed value properly. As a result, CBP invoked its statutory authority to appraise the imported merchandise based on an estimate.[145]

Beyond this, CBP argued before the CIT that the importer should be estopped from presenting new evidence to the court that was not presented to CBP in the administrative review process. It contended that its estimation of duties was analogous to the estimation of taxes by the IRS when presented with insufficient income

---

142. *See* Part I, §7.01[A].
143. *See* Part I, §7.01[B].
144. *Heng Ngai Jewelry, Inc. v. United States*, 318 F. Supp. 2d 1291 (CIT 2004) (cross-motions for summary judgment denied). On the question of additional information not being provided, this case may remind one of the *Euro 2004* judgment.
145. Under 19 USC § 1500:

> The Customs Service shall, under rules and regulations prescribed by the Secretary (a) fix the final appraisement of merchandise by ascertaining or estimating the value thereof, under section 1401a of this title, by all reasonable ways and means in his power, any statement of cost or costs of production in any invoice, affidavit, declaration, other document to the contrary notwithstanding.

You will recognize that the customs authorities in the EU have a similar mandate to find customs values and similar latitude. Formerly, Community Customs Code IA, Art. 181a; at present, UCC IA Art. 140. My criticism of the *Baltic Master* judgment is twofold: there was no showing that (1) the customs authority had engaged in the active examination of the circumstances of sale that is mandated by Art. 134.1 of the UCC IA and (ii) an application or a reasonably flexible application of the test values was not available before the "last" "Hail Mary" resort turn was made to the data base, given the likelihood of abuse.

records.[146] But the de novo standard of judicial review in the CIT for CBP decisions permits the CIT to consider any new grounds raised by an importer for the first time in court, as long as the grounds relate to the same administrative decision and the merchandise encompassed by the administrative protest.[147] The court rejected[148] the CBP argument that civil penalties are an insufficient remedy for violations of an importer's obligation to exercise "reasonable care" when importing merchandise.[149]

Regardless which test value comparison is applied, the importer must deal with the question, how closely must the two values match up? Following the Valuation Agreement,[150] the statute applies a fluid "closely approximates" standard.

[g] "Closely Approximates"

The importer must show that the transfer price "closely approximates" one of the test values, and this standard will vary, depending on:

A. The nature of the imported merchandise and the industry.
B. The season in which the merchandise is imported.
C. Whether the difference in value is commercially significant.
D. Whether the difference in value is attributable to internal transport costs in the country of exportation.[151]

The US regulations observe that, because these factors may vary, CBP will not be able to apply a uniform standard, such as a fixed percentage, in all cases.[152] A small difference in value in a situation involving one type of imported merchandise may be unacceptable, although a large difference in a situation involving another type may be acceptable. In this context, Canada's administrative guidance is helpful:

> 13. The decision as to whether a difference between the transaction value of the goods being appraised and the test value is commercially significant will be made after all other relevant factors and differences, including those set out in section 3 of the Regulations, have been taken into account. An assessment of the commercial significance of a difference in values would take into account that market conditions and pricing practices may vary from industry to industry.

---

146. The statutory authority for the IRS to estimate taxes is section 446(b) of the Internal Revenue Code.
147. 28 USC § 2638.
148. *Heng Ngai Jewelry, Inc. v. United States*, 318 F. Supp. 2d at 1304. The CIT had earlier rejected a similar argument for evidentiary estoppel by the CBP in *E.I. DuPont de Nemours & Co. v. United States*, 123 F. Supp. 2d 637, 24 CIT 1301 (2000).
149. 19 USC § 1484.
150. Interpretative Note, Article 1, Paragraph 2(b).
151. 19 CFR § 152.103(l)(2)(i); Interpretative Note, Article 1, Paragraph 2(b); UCC Article 134.3.
152. 19 CFR § 152.103(l)(2)(ii). The same position was expressed in the Community Customs Code in Annex. 23.

14. A minor difference in value need not preclude the acceptance of a transaction value provided the importer can demonstrate that such a difference is not commercially significant.[153]

After establishing the situational nature of the test value validation exercise, the regulations make the point that CBP will be consistent in over/under comparisons in determining if one value "closely approximates" another value. The same approach will be taken if CBP considers a TV that is higher than any of the enumerated test values as will be taken if the TV is lower than any of the test values.[154] The example in the regulations is that if 95 does not closely approximate 100, a TV of 105 will also be rejected, while if a TV of 103 were found to closely approximate 100, a TV of 97 will likewise be acceptable. In actual practice, CBP has rejected a related party price that differed by as narrow a difference as 4% from a computed value serving as a test value.[155]

[2] Specific Test Values

[a] Transaction Value of Identical or Similar Merchandise

The first of the test values, the TV of either identical or similar merchandise, finds its analogue in transfer pricing in the Comparable Uncontrolled Price (CUP) method.[156]

In considering the applicability of an appraisal of imported merchandise based on the TV of identical or similar merchandise, the importer must first look to the definitions. The factors used in ascertaining comparability make for a useful contrast between "identical" and "similar" merchandise.

As we saw in Part I, "identical merchandise" is merchandise identical in all respects to, and that was produced in the same country and by the same person as, the merchandise being appraised, *or* alternatively, merchandise that is identical in all respects to, and that was produced in the same country as, but not produced by the same person as, the merchandise being appraised. The term does not cover merchandise that incorporates engineering, development, artwork, and the like that was furnished free or at reduced cost in connection with the foreign production.[157]

153. Canada, Memorandum D13-4-5, *Transaction value method for related persons*, December 6, 2021 in paragraphs 13-14.
154. 19 CFR § 152.103(l)(2)(ii).
155. Ruling no. 543546 (June 7, 1985). For a useful analysis that amply demonstrates the difficulty of ascertaining whether a TV closely approximates a test value, *see VWP of Am., Inc. v. United States*, 259 F. Supp. 2d 1289 (CIT 2003) (16% difference between USD 4.00 TV and USD 4.70 test value was rejected by CBP because it was "significant") and related decisions.
156. Treas. Reg. § 1.482-3(b)(1).
157. 19 USC § 1401a(h)(2). When the TV of identical merchandise is used as a test value, as opposed to its use in its own right as a basis for appraisement, the importer need not first show that merchandise from the same producer cannot be found before resorting to merchandise produced by another person.

"Similar merchandise" is merchandise produced in the same country and by the same person as the merchandise being appraised, is like the merchandise being appraised in characteristics and component material, and is commercially interchangeable with the merchandise being appraised, *or* merchandise produced in the same country as, but not produced by the same person as, the merchandise being appraised and is like the merchandise being appraised in characteristics and component material, and is commercially interchangeable with the merchandise being appraised. As with identical merchandise, the term does not cover merchandise that incorporates engineering, development, artwork, and the like that was furnished free or at reduced cost in connection with the foreign production.[158]

The regulations note that minor differences in appearance will not preclude otherwise conforming merchandise from being considered "identical."[159] Quality, reputation, and the existence of a trademark are all factors considered to determine whether merchandise is "similar."[160]

The statute and regulations anticipate that there could be differences in commercial levels and quantities of the sales under comparison, and that these differences could affect prices. As noted, adjustments should be made to take into account any such differences.[161] Any such adjustment must be based on "sufficient information," which is defined as "information that establishes the accuracy of such amount, difference or adjustment."[162] The regulations refer to valid price lists containing prices referring to different levels or quantities as an example of "sufficient information."[163]

The law and regulations also anticipate that a review of other transactions could result in two or more transaction value matches being found. In such a situation, the lower or lowest of these values will be used as the TV of identical or similar merchandise.[164]

[b] Deductive Value Calculation

Deductive value is the customs valuation law analogue to the RPM under transfer pricing rules. In its simplest form, deductive value is derived as follows:

- The resale price of goods sold in the country of importation.

158. 19 USC § 1401a(h)(4). When the TV of similar merchandise is used as a test value, as opposed to its use in its own right as a basis for appraisement, the importer need not first show that merchandise from the same producer cannot be found before resorting to merchandise produced by another person.
159. 19 CFR § 152.104(b).
160. 19 CFR § 152.104(c).
161. 19 CFR § 152.104(d).
162. 19 USC § 1401a(h)(5).
163. 19 CFR § 152.104(e).
164. Valuation Agreement, Articles 2.3, 3.3; 19 USC § 1401a(c)(2); 19 CFR § 152.104(d); UCC IA, Article 141.3.

Less:

- The usual commission or profit and general expenses associated with sales in the country of importation of imported goods of the same class or kind of merchandise, regardless of the country of exportation.
- The actual costs of international transportation and insurance.
- The usual costs of transportation and associated costs from port to the place of delivery in the country of importation.
- The customs duties and taxes levied on the imported goods at entry.

Plus:

- The costs of any value added by post-importation processing.[165]

Four more points are in order. First, the resale price that is the starting point for the calculation must be the unit price at which the merchandise is sold in the greatest aggregate quantity in the relevant period, at or about the time of the sale or, alternatively, within ninety days of importation. In addition, that resale price must be to an unrelated person.[166] Deductive value is not limited to any first sale after importation. If the first resale in the US is to a related party, that sale will be disqualified as a basis for reckoning deductive value and, instead, deductive value will be applied to a later third-party sale.[167] In another limitation, the qualifying post-importation sale may not be to a person who has provided a dutiable assist to the foreign producer.[168]

Second, as discussed, the deductions from the resale price for profit and general expenses, as was the case with computed value, are from the importer's actual books and records unless they are inconsistent with the profit and general expenses reflected in sales of the same class or kind of merchandise in the relevant market. In the latter regard, resort will be made to the "usual profit and general expenses of such importers in such sales, as determined from sufficient information."[169] In examining profit and general expenses, the statute sets forth a GAAP acceptability standard.[170] As in *Campbell Soup* and *La Perla*, the GAAP that are to be applied are those pertaining to the country appropriate to the appraisement methodology. In a computed value determination, that would be the GAAP of the country of production; in a deductive value appraisement, it would be the GAAP of the US or other country of importation.

165. Valuation Agreement, Article 4; 19 USC § 1401a(d).
166. 19 USC § 1401a(d)(2)(b); ruling no. 544469 (August 16, 1990).
167. Ruling no. 545481 (September 14, 1994).
168. Valuation Agreement, Interpretative Note, Article 5, point 5; 19 USC § 1401a(d)(3)(D); 19 CFR § 152.105(g).
169. 19 USC § 1401a(d)(3)(B)(i). The definition of "sufficient information" is somewhat circular, as such information is simply that which "establishes the accuracy" of the amount in question. 19 USC § 1401a(h)(5).
170. 19 USC § 1401a(g)(3); 19 CFR §§ 152.102(c)(1)-152.102(c)(3); Valuation Agreement, Interpretative Notes, General Note, Use of Generally Accepted Accounting Principles.

Third, any processing to which the goods might be subjected after importation means that the goods will not be resold in their condition as imported. In such a situation, appraisement is done on a "superdeductive" method basis, backing out the value added by the post-importation processing.[171] In support, the importer must present objective and quantifiable data relating to the work performed. Accepted industry formulas, recipes, methods of construction, and other industry practices would form the basis for the deduction. CBP will also take into account spoilage, waste, or scrap deriving from the processing.[172] Still more difficulties arise in the context of imported goods that lose their identity as a result of the post-importation processing, with the Interpretative Notes to the Valuation Agreement observing:

> It is recognized that the [deductive] method of valuation ... would normally not be applicable when, as a result of the further processing, the imported goods lose their identity. However, there can be instances where, although the identity of the imported goods is lost, the value added by the processing can be determined accurately without unreasonable difficulty. On the other hand, there can also be instances where the imported goods maintain their identity but form such a minor element in the goods sold in the country of importation that the use of this valuation method would be unjustified. In view of the above, each situation of this type must be considered on a case-by-case basis.[173]

Fourth, an importer could face an issue in determining the amount to be deducted for customs duties on imported merchandise that benefits from a partial duty exemption, such as outward processing relief or American goods returned.[174] Should the statutory deduction for "customs duties and other federal taxes currently payable on the merchandise concerned by reason of its importation" equate to the duties that would apply to the imported merchandise without the benefit of the partial duty exemption or, instead, should they be the lower duties to be actually assessed on the imported merchandise (i.e., factoring in the full or partial exemption)? In a 1989 decision, the CIT decided that it was the latter measure,[175] with the result that, in such a case, the deductive value will always be higher than would otherwise have been the case.

171. As an example, CBP issued a ruling on the superdeductive method as the valuation methodology for defective goods that were to be repaired and resold after importation. Ruling no. 543123 (December 20, 1983). *See also* ruling no. 548688 (October 20, 2005).
172. 19 CFR § 152.105(i)(1).
173. Valuation Agreement, Interpretative Note, Article 5, point 12. The customs regulations closely track this note, 19 CFR § 152.105(i)(2).
174. The HTSUS (Harmonized Tariff Schedule of the United States) contains a number of preferential provisions that serve to eliminate duties or confer partial exemptions on imported articles with full or partial US origin. Examples include item numbers 9801.00.10 (US goods returned after having been exported, without having been advanced in value) and 9802.00.80 (articles assembled abroad from US fabricated components).
175. *Figure Flattery, Inc. v. United States*, 907 F2d 141 (Fed. Cir. 1990), aff'g 720 F. Supp. 1008, 13 CIT 726 (1989).

[c] *Computed Value Calculation*

The computed value[176] alternative basis for appraisement is the customs law analogue of the familiar cost-plus transfer pricing methodology. "Computed value" is defined as the sum of:

- Cost or value of materials and of fabrication.
- An amount for profit and general expenses equal to that usually reflected in sales of merchandise of the same class or kind as the imported merchandise that are made by producers in the country of exportation for export to the US.
- Any "dutiable assist."
- Packing costs.

The computed value that functions as a "test value" for a related party price is that derived for identical or similar merchandise.[177] Owing to the sensitive nature of the information, most importers are not able to establish a computed value basis and its use has been limited almost exclusively to related party transactions.[178]

Important terms are defined by the customs valuation statute and regulations. For starters, "cost or value of materials" does not include internal taxes levied by the country of exportation that are remitted or refunded on exportation of the finished goods.[179] This is a reference to such indirect taxes as VAT.[180]

"Class or kind of merchandise" is a hoary term in the customs laws, with the tariff classification in "chief use" provisions controlled by the principal use in the US of goods comprising the same "class or kind" of merchandise as the imported

176. 19 USC § 1401a(e); Valuation Agreement, Article 6.
177. As discussed, the test values are based on prior import transactions that, of necessity, will have been based on identical or similar merchandise.
178. Valuation Agreement, Interpretative Note, Article 6, point 1, states:

> As a general rule, customs value is determined under this Agreement on the basis of information readily available in the country of importation. In order to determine a computed value, however, it may be necessary to examine the costs of producing the goods being valued and other information which has to be obtained from outside the country of importation. Furthermore, in most cases the producer of the goods will be outside the jurisdiction of the authorities of the country of importation. The use of the computed value method will generally be limited to those cases where the buyer and seller are related, and the producer is prepared to supply to the authorities of the country of importation the necessary costings and to provide facilities for any subsequent verification which may be necessary.

See CCC IR, Note in Annex 23.

179. 19 USC § 1401a(e)(2)(A).
180. You will recall that this issue was central to *Campbell Soup*. For the role of refunded/remitted VAT in a TV appraisement, *see Caterpillar, Inc. v. United States*, 941 F. Supp. 1241, 20 CIT 1169 (1996) (refunded VAT not includable in TV of imported merchandise).

merchandise.[181] The tariff classification jurisprudence on this point is helpful here, as the criteria to establish "class or kind" have been clearly stated:

- General physical characteristics of the merchandise.
- Expectation of the ultimate purchasers.
- The channels, class, or kind of trade in which the merchandise moves.
- The environment of the sale.
- The use, if any, in the same manner as merchandise that defines the class.
- Economic practicality of so using the import.
- Recognition in the trade of this use.

These are often referred to as the "Carborundum criteria."[182] On the issue of "class or kind," the US customs valuation regulations comment:

> Sales for export to the United States of the narrowest group or range of imported merchandise, including the merchandise being appraised, will be examined to determine the usual profit and general expenses. For the purpose of computed value, merchandise of the same class or kind must be from the same country as the merchandise being appraised.[183]

There is an important nuance to the inclusion of "dutiable assists" in a computed value calculation. The customs valuation law prescribes that, in a transaction value appraisement, certain pricing elements that are not reflected in the commercial invoice for the imported goods must be added to the invoice value for the goods (i.e., the "price actually paid or payable" to the foreign manufacturer) to make dutiable value, if they are not already reflected in the invoice price.[184] Often, these are collectively referred to in the US parlance as the five "statutory additions."[185] They include packing costs, selling commissions, dutiable assists, royalty and license fees, and subsequent proceeds inuring to the benefit of the seller. One of these factors, "dutiable assists," is comprised of the value of goods or services that are provided free or at reduced cost to the foreign manufacturer. These include tooling, dies, molds, components and materials used in production, production equipment,[186] and certain production-related services, and are often overlooked by importers. Their omission, which understates the true value of the imported goods, is a common cause of importers' noncompliance. But there is an important exception carved out of the general definition of assists. To the extent that certain service or work (engineering, development, artwork, design work,

181. *See* Part I. In the current HTSUS, this standard is enunciated in Additional U.S. Rule of Interpretation 1(a). *See also* such rulings as nos. 952878 (February 11, 1993) and N027262 (May 20, 2008). In the EU, the CCC IR addressed the topic of class or kind in a Note in Annex 23.
182. The leading case that established these is *United States v. Carborundum Co.*, 63 CCPA 98, 102, 536 F2d 373, CAD 1172, cert. den., 429 US 979 (1976).
183. 19 CFR § 152.106(e).
184. 19 USC §§ 1401a(b)(1)(A)-1401a(b)(1)(E); 19 CFR § 152.103(c).
185. The statutory additions are discussed more fully in Part I.
186. *Texas Apparel Co. v. United States*, 12 CIT 1002 (1988) (sewing machines likened to tools and dies; machinery that was used directly in production of the imported merchandise is a dutiable assist to be included in a computed value calculation).

and plans and sketches that are essential for the production of the imported merchandise) is performed or developed in the US or other country of importation, or if in a foreign country, by an individual domiciled in the US or other country of importation, who is an employee or agent of the buyer, and the service or work is incidental to other work undertaken in the US or other country of importation, the service or work is not an assist.[187]

Although technically not an assist in a TV appraisement, such country of origin-centric service or work does represent an element of cost that ordinarily should be fully included within a computed value calculation if the calculation is to accurately comprise the full costs of production. Surprisingly, the regulations for computed value take a middle ground position on their inclusion, as the excepted, Article 8.1(b)(iv) design and other designated costs are included, but only to the extent that they have been charged to the producer.[188] Thus, such service or work provided gratis to the producer or, if chargeable to the producer to some extent, that portion of their value that has not been charged, will be omitted from the computed value calculation. This will yield an obviously skewed result, and should predetermine that a TV appraisement (from which these payments will be excluded altogether under the statutory exception) and a computed value appraisement (in which chargeable payments will be included) will never match.

Parallel to deductive value appraisements, the statutory obligation to include amounts for profit and general expenses is keyed to the producer's own profit and expense records unless they are inconsistent with those usually reflected in the country of manufacture in sales of merchandise of the same class or kind as the imported merchandise for export to the US.[189] The customs regulations provide Interpretative Notes to the effect that even a producer's low-profit level or no-profit level coupled with high-expense levels will be accepted if there are valid commercial reasons and they are consistent with the foreign industry pricing experience. The regulations posit that such might be the case with a new product launch or an unforeseeable drop in demand.[190]

The obvious point is that if reference must be made to an industry profit or general expense study in the foreign country of production, economic studies and cost accounting projects undertaken for the purposes of analysis under section 482 or similar transfer pricing inquiries could play a significant role. Transfer pricing professionals will be thoroughly familiar and entirely comfortable with these notions, which depend on price and profit comparisons.

---

187. 19 USC § 1401a(h)(1)(B); *see also* 19 CFR § 152.103(d)(2), Ex. 1; Customs Act, subparagraph 48(5)(iii)(D); UCC, Article 71(b)(iv). This exception is sanctioned by the Valuation Agreement, which looks to an adjustment for such work being done "elsewhere than in the country of importation." Article 8.1(b)(iv).
188. Interpretative Note, Article 6, point 3; 19 CFR § 152.106(d); UCC IA, Article 143.2.
189. 19 USC § 1401a(e)(2)(B).
190. 19 CFR §§ 152.106(c)(1) and (2). These interpretative notes are based on those in Valuation Agreement, Interpretative Note, Article 6, points 4, 5.

§10.04 VALIDATION OF TRANSFER PRICING UNDER THE INCOME TAX RULES

[A] General Considerations

The first point to establish is that the definition of "related party" for the purposes of section 482 and its analogue statutes in other jurisdictions is not coextensive with the standards in the customs valuation law, with shareholdings set in the latter at a mere 5%, enough to trigger related party status in customs valuation. Section 482 grants the IRS the power to reallocate income among taxpayers (i.e., organizations, trades, or businesses owned or controlled directly or indirectly by the same interests) whenever it is necessary to prevent evasion of taxes or to more clearly reflect the income of any of the organizations, trades, or businesses. Rather than explicitly defining the relationships or conditions that establish this notion of relationship, which is expressed as one of control, the Treasury regulations define "controlled taxpayers" broadly:

> Controlled taxpayer means any one or more taxpayers owned or controlled directly or indirectly by the same interests, and includes the taxpayer that owns or controls the other taxpayers.[191]

[1] Arm's-Length Standard

The constant goal for income tax authorities in the US or in those jurisdictions that apply the OECD Guidelines in a given transfer pricing inquiry is to allocate the taxpayer's income under the arm's-length standard, or arm's-length principle as it is denoted in the OECD:

> In determining the true taxable income of a controlled taxpayer, the standard to be applied in every case is that of a taxpayer dealing at arm's length with an uncontrolled taxpayer. A controlled transaction meets the arm's length standard if the results of the transaction are consistent with the results that would have been realized if uncontrolled taxpayers had engaged in the same transaction under the same circumstances (arm's length result).[192]
>
> Despite the concerted efforts of the United States and the OECD to advocate the arm's-length standard, some local taxing jurisdictions have advanced an

---

191. Treas. Reg. § 1.482-1(i)(5).
192. Treas. Reg. § 1.482-1(b). The OECD Guidelines (Glossary and Article 1.6) define the "arm's-length principle" as the international standard that OECD member countries have agreed should be used for determining transfer pricing for tax purposes. It is drawn from Article 9 of the OECD Model Tax Convention:

> [Where] conditions are made or imposed between the two [associated] enterprises in their commercial or financial relations which differ from those which would be made between independent enterprises, then any profits which would, but for those conditions, have accrued to one of the enterprises, but, by reason of those conditions, have not so accrued, may be included in the profits of that enterprise and taxed accordingly.

alternative—a "global formulary apportionment method,"[193] and some pundits advocated its use by national tax authorities.[194] This approach would allocate the global profits of a multinational enterprise on a consolidated basis through the mechanistic application of a predetermined formula. The OECD takes direct aim at this alternative, stating that it is not acceptable in theory, implementation, or practice and publishing an extensive critique.[195]

[2] Principles

There are three generally applicable principles applied to a transfer pricing evaluation—the best-method rule, comparability analysis, and the arm's-length range.

[a] Best-Method Rule

One major departure from customs valuation practice is that there is no strict hierarchy of methods to be applied by the importer/taxpayer or the IRS. Instead, the best-method rule requires that the taxpayer apply that method that:

> under the facts and circumstances, provides the most reliable measure of an arm's length result. Thus, there is no strict priority of methods and no method will invariably be considered to be more reliable than others.[196]

The OECD had formerly expressed a strong preference for the three traditional transaction methods[197] in Chapter II of the OECD Guidelines over the transactional profit methods which were separately covered in Chapter III of the OECD Guidelines.

The early iterations of the OECD Guidelines viewed the traditional transaction methods as inherently more reliable.[198] The transactional profit methods were relegated to:

193. As its name implies, global formulary apportionment would allocate the profits of a multinational group on a consolidated basis among the associated enterprises in different jurisdictions on the basis of a predetermined and mechanistic formula. OECD Guidelines, paragraph 1.17.
194. *See* discussion in Cockfield, "Formulary Taxation Versus the Arm's Length Principle: The Battle Among Purists, Doubting Thomases and Pragmatists," 52 Canadian Tax J./Revue Fiscale Canadienne No. 1, at 114 (2004).
195. OECD Guidelines, paragraphs 1.16-1.32.
196. Treas. Reg. § 1.482-1(c). The regulations offer examples of the best-method rule in play. Treas. Reg. § 1.482-8.
197. These methods are: comparable uncontrolled price (CUP), resale price (RPM), and cost plus, discussed below, §10.04[B][1].
198. 2009 OECD Guidelines stated that these "methods are the most direct means of establishing whether [the related-party transactions] are arm's length ... [and] are, therefore, preferable to other methods." Paragraph 2.49; *see also* paragraph 3.49 ("Traditional transaction methods are to be preferred over transactional profit methods as a means of establishing whether a transfer price is at arm's length ...").

> last resort status ... to be used only in the exceptional cases where there are no or insufficient data available to rely solely or at all on the traditional transaction methods.[199]

However, in September 2009, the OECD proposed revisions to Chapters I-III of the OECD Guidelines which were thereafter adopted in the 2009 edition and which survive in great part in the 2022 version. The perspective on the hierarchy of methods shifted, and the transactional profit methods were placed in a more favorable light. As expressed in that 2009 OECD Proposed Revision, the OECD views on its "most appropriate method" appear closer to the "best-method rule" familiar to US practitioners:

> Based on the experience acquired in applying transactional profit methods since 1995, the OECD proposes removing exceptionality and replacing it with a standard whereby the selected transfer pricing method should be the "most appropriate method to the circumstances of the case." ... In order to reflect this evolution, it is proposed to address all transfer pricing methods in a single chapter, Chapter II (Part II for traditional transaction methods, Part III or transactional profit methods).[200]

In the event, the separate chapter treatments were retained in 2022. To be sure, as revised, the OECD 2022 Guidelines still express a "soft" preference for traditional transaction methods over transactional profit methods as the most direct means of establishing whether or not controlled transactions had been at arm's length.[201] The OECD was quick to add, however, that the transactional profit methods might be more appropriate.[202]

In fact, the 2022 Guidelines establish that the method employed should be that which is "the most appropriate given the circumstances of the case."[203] Moreover, the OECD advocates that a working arrangement (a "reasonable accommodation") should be reached between the taxpayer and the tax authority, noting, *inter alia*:

> It should not be the case that useful information, such as might be drawn from uncontrolled transactions that are not identical to the controlled transactions, should be dismissed simply because some rigid standard of comparability is not fully met.[204]

In any event, in another prudent note, the OECD observes that the use of more than one method may be appropriate in "difficult cases, where no one approach is conclusive."[205]

---

199. Proposed Revision of Chapters I-III of OECD Transfer Pricing Guidelines (OECD Committee on Fiscal Affairs, September 9, 2009) (OECD 2009 Proposed Revision), at 2.
200. OECD 2009 Proposed Revision, at 2.
201. OECD (2022), *OECD Transfer Pricing Guidelines for Multinational Enterprises and Tax Administrations 2022*, OECD Publishing, Paris https://doi.org/10.1787/0e655865-en (hereinafter "OECD Guidelines"), paragraph 2.3.
202. OECD Guidelines, paragraph 2.4.
203. OECD Guidelines, paragraphs 2.1-2.11.
204. OECD Guidelines, paragraph 2.11.
205. OECD Guidelines, paragraph 2.12.

Finally, the OECD counsels an approach that is grounded in flexibility and good judgment on the part of the taxpayer and the tax authority.[206]

[b] Comparability

In turn, the reliability of the underlying comparison inherent in a given method is measured through comparability analysis. US Treasury regulations define this criterion:

> Whether a controlled transaction produces an arm's length result is generally evaluated by comparing the results of that transaction to results realized by uncontrolled taxpayers engaged in comparable transactions. For this purpose, the comparability of transactions and circumstances must be evaluated considering all factors that could affect prices or profits in arm's length dealings (comparability factors) ... . Such factors include the following—
>
> Functions;
> Contractual terms;
> Risks;
> Economic conditions; and
> Property or services.[207]

The Treasury regulations establish that comparability need not mean that the transactions are identical, but simply sufficiently similar enough for a reliable measure of an arm's-length result. Adjustments may be made to account for material differences with a measurable effect on prices or profits.[208]

[c] Arm's-Length Range

Finally, the arm's-length range is a principle stemming from a recognition that application of a pricing method may give a single result, but in most instances a pricing method will yield a number of results from which a range of reliable results may be derived. A taxpayer will not be subject to adjustments if his results fall within that range.[209] Typically a taxpayer will strive to show that his price falls within the "interquartile range" (i.e., from the twenty-fifth to the seventy-fifth percentile of the results derived from the uncontrolled comparables).

206. OECD Guidelines, paragraphs 1.13, 2.74.
207. Treas. Reg. § 1.482-1(d). The analogous comparability factors are discussed in OECD 2022 Guidelines, paragraphs 1.33-1.138. The five factors that the OECD will consider in a comparability analysis will be the contractual terms, functions, characteristics of property or services, economic circumstances, and business strategies. Paragraph 1.36.
208. Treas. Reg. § 1.482-1(d). One example of a required adjustment to factor in the effect of the potential imposition of antidumping duties in an application of the comparable profits method (*see* below) is FSA 199945011 (November 12, 1999).
209. Treas. Reg. § 1.482-1(e). The OECD Guidelines analogue on the arm's-length range discussion is in Chapter III at point A.7 in paragraphs 3.55-3.66.

[B] Transfer Pricing Methods

The OECD has developed five transfer pricing methods (TPMs) to validate a transfer price for income tax purposes.[210] The first three TPMs comprise the "traditional transaction" methods. The remaining two methods are "transactional profit" methods. In the US, there is a sixth unspecified method.

[1] Traditional Transaction Methods

[a] CUP

With this method, the object is to evaluate whether the amount charged in a controlled transaction is at arm's length by reference to the amount charged ("the price") in a comparable uncontrolled transaction.[211]

Although all of the comparability factors must play a role in determining the reliability of the CUP method, similarity of the products will have the greatest effect on comparability. Moreover, the Treasury Regulations take note of the role that could be played by even minor differences in contractual terms or economic conditions. The IRS says that reliability will be greatest where there are either no differences with an effect on price or, if there are minor differences, their effect on price is reasonably ascertainable and appropriate adjustment can be made.[212] The regulations provide an example of a circumstance where CUP will not lie. A taxpayer affixes its trademark to a product sold in its controlled transactions but does not affix its trademark to the products sold in the uncontrolled transactions. If the effect on the price of the trademark is material but cannot be reasonably estimated, precluding adjustment, CUP would be unreliable.[213]

For its part, the OECD states that, for the purposes of an application of the CUP, an uncontrolled transaction is comparable to a controlled transaction when one of two conditions is met:

(1) none of the differences, if any, between the transactions being compared, or the enterprises undertaking those transactions, could materially affect the price in the open market; or
(2) reasonably accurate adjustments can be made to eliminate the material effects of such differences.

210. A discussion of the comparable uncontrolled transaction (CUT) and the other transfer pricing methods for determining taxable income in connection with the transfer of intangible property under Treas. Reg. § 1.482-4 and OECD Guidelines Chapter VI is outside the scope of this treatment, as is any discussion of cost sharing (or "cost contribution" arrangements). *See* Treas. Reg. § 1.482-7; OECD 2022 Guidelines, Ch. VIII.
211. Treas. Reg. § 1.482-3(b); OECD Guidelines, paragraphs 2.14-2.26.
212. Treas. Reg. § 1.482-3(b)(2)(ii)(A).
213. Treas. Reg. § 1.482-3(b)(4), Ex. 2.

As the OECD has observed the CUP will give the most direct and reliable way to test the arm's-length principle.[214] The problem is that companies that are dealing exclusively in related party transactions will not have any comparable uncontrolled transactions as a basis for comparison. Such an importer/taxpayer might be tempted to arrange to purchase minimal quantities of goods from an unrelated supplier, or the foreign supplier might want to consummate token sales to an unrelated importer. The goal will be to establish these extraordinary sales as comparable uncontrolled transactions to validate the controlled transactions.

The Treasury Regulations anticipate this turn, however, and disqualify these extraordinary transactions as "comparables" if they are not made in the ordinary course of business or if one of the principal purposes was to serve as an arm's-length standard for the controlled transactions.[215]

The CUP is a rough analogue to two of the test values—the transaction value of identical or of similar merchandise—under the customs valuation law.[216]

[b] Resale Price Method (RPM)

The RPM[217] evaluates whether the amount charged in a controlled transaction is at arm's length by reference to the gross profit margin realized in comparable uncontrolled transactions. This method measures the value of functions performed and is typically used where the controlled party reseller of tangible property has not added substantial value to the tangible property by physically altering the goods[218] before resale or by use of intangible property (i.e., trademarks).[219] Thus, the reseller would normally be filling a distributorship function or, as the OECD terms it, a "marketing function."

The arm's-length price is measured by subtracting the "appropriate" gross profit margin from the "applicable resale price" for the property involved in the controlled transaction under review. The applicable resale price is equal to either the resale price of the particular item or the price in contemporaneous resales of the same property. The appropriate gross profit is computed by multiplying the applicable resale price by the gross profit margin (expressed as a percentage of total revenue derived from sales) earned in comparable uncontrolled transactions.

The comparison resale price margins are either those earned by the reseller itself in sales to unrelated buyers (internal comparables) or those of independent enterprises in comparable uncontrolled transactions (external comparables).[220]

Because a reseller's gross profit provides compensation for resale functions, including a return for invested capital and risks assumed, the reliability of the RPM is

214. OECD Guidelines paragraph 2.15.
215. Treas. Reg. § 1.482-1(d)(4)(iii)(A).
216. 19 USC § 1401a(c); Valuation Agreement, Articles 2, 3.
217. Provided for at OECD Guidelines paragraphs 2.27-2.44.
218. "Physical alteration" goes beyond packaging, repackaging, labeling, or minor assembly. Treas. Reg. § 1.482-3(c)(1).
219. Treas. Reg. § 1.482-3(c)(1); OECD Guidelines, paragraphs 2.21-2.38.
220. OECD Guidelines paragraph 2.28.

especially dependent on the similarity of functions performed, risks borne, and contractual terms. One example of a probably skewed result under RPM would arise from the widely diverging functions and risks borne by an importer/reseller in a Multilevel Marketing (MLM) program versus the costs borne by a traditional retailer importer/reseller. The gross profit of the typical MLM reseller would not bear any relation to a traditional retailer's and an RPM based on a comparison of the gross profits of an MLM importer and those of a traditional retailer importer would likely reflect those material differences and, thus, would be fatally flawed. In this connection, the Treasury regulations note that differences in functions performed and risks assumed may show up especially in the levels of related operating expenses, singling out, *inter alia*, sales, marketing, advertising programs, and services, and the level of the market. These factors are considered especially relevant for RPM because of the possibility of significant differences in these "below the [gross profit] line" expenses,[221] as would be the case when comparing an MLM with a traditional retailer. Thus, a measurement that stopped at a gross profit analysis would produce a skewed result. As a result, adjustments to the gross profit margin in the uncontrolled transaction would be required.[222]

If possible, RPM should be based on internal comparables (i.e., comparable uncontrolled purchases and resales of the reseller involved in the controlled sale). While comparability under RPM is less dependent on close physical similarity than it is with CUP, the IRS has come to expect comparisons within the same general type of goods. The OECD also observes that closer product comparability will produce a better result.[223]

The Treasury Regulations also acknowledge the possible material effect on the value of distributed goods of trademarks and of other factors, such as cost structures, age of plant and equipment, business experience, and management efficiency.[224] Differences in accounting practices may require appropriate adjustments.[225]

Another significant feature of the OECD promulgation of the RPM is its acknowledgement of the effect of an exclusive grant of a distribution right may exert on the resale price margin. The distributor having a monopoly to buy and resell the goods.[226] The OECD sees the value of ascertaining the effect of such a grant on the reseller's profit experience.

RPM is the rough analogue of one of the test values under the customs valuation law—deductive value, which also looks to an analysis of the importer/reseller's profits and general expenses.[227]

221. Operating expenses that will typically be composed of selling, general, and administrative (SG&A) costs are "below the [gross profit] line."
222. Treas. Reg. § 1.482-3(c)(3)(ii)(C).
223. OECD Guidelines, paragraph 2.31.
224. Treas. Reg. § 1.482-3(c)(3)(ii)(B). *See* OECD Guidelines, paragraph 2.33.
225. OECD Guidelines, paragraph 2.41.
226. OECD Guidelines, paragraph 2.40.
227. Valuation Agreement, Article 5; 19 USC § 1401a(d); Canada Customs Act, section 51; UCC, Article 74.2(c). As is the case with deductive value, the OECD instructs that the RPM is more accurate if it is realized within a short period of time of the reseller's purchase of the goods. OECD Guidelines, paragraph 2.36.

The OECD clearly sees such a grant as a separate property right. As such, beyond the impact on the RPM or deductive value, another customs valuation issue arises for the customs valuation of all imports under a distribution model with an exclusivity grant—regardless of whether this is a related party transaction or not. That is the question, whether a fee paid for exclusivity will potentially be included in the PAPP of the imported goods in a transaction value appraisement. As discussed in Part I, the potentially nondutiable status of such an exclusivity fee has already been recognized by CBP but may be questioned by other customs authorities. Any further discussion should include this OECD discussion.

[c] Cost-Plus Method

The cost-plus method evaluates whether the amount charged in a controlled transaction is at arm's length by reference to the gross profit markup realized in the controlled transaction versus that realized in comparable uncontrolled transactions. For the IRS, this method is ordinarily used in cases involving the manufacture, assembly, or other production of goods that are sold to related parties. For the OECD, in the context of tangible goods, this method is most suitable for sales of semifinished goods between associated enterprises, where associated parties have concluded joint facility agreements or long-term buy-or-supply agreements.[228]

The preference is for "internal comparables," comparable uncontrolled transactions of the taxpayer producer involved in the controlled sale (i.e., sales to third parties), because similar characteristics are more likely to be found among sales of property by the same producer than among uncontrolled sales by other producers ("external comparables").[229] In comparison with the CUP method, comparability is less dependent on close physical similarity between the products transferred. Nonetheless, the IRS expects that the transactions would take place within the same product categories and also that significant differences in "value" due to the value of a trademark be accounted for.[230]

Cost plus is arrived at by subtracting the cost of producing or acquiring the goods sold COGS, itself composed of both direct and indirect expenses, from sales. COGS is thus accounted for "above the [gross profit] line."

The OECD has divided the producer's costs into three categories. These are:

(1) Direct costs of producing the product, such as raw materials.
(2) Indirect production costs, such as costs of a repair department which services equipment across all product lines.
(3) Operating expenses of the enterprise as a whole, such as supervisory, general and administrative costs.[231]

228. Treas. Reg. § 1.482-3(d); OECD Guidelines, paragraphs 2.45-2.61, 2.45.
229. Treas. Reg. § 1.482-3(d)(3)(ii)(A); OECD Guidelines, paragraph 2. 46.
230. Treas. Reg. § 1.482-3(d)(3)(ii)(B).
231. OECD Guidelines, paragraph 2.53.

After observing the difficulties in ensuring any greater exactitude in the comparability of the costs treatment, the OECD proceeded to note that what was needed was consistency in treatment of costs for controlled and uncontrolled transactions and consistency over time.

The cost-plus method is a comparison of gross profits (i.e., before operating expenses are deducted to arrive at net operating margin). Accordingly, the comparability under the cost-plus method demands consistency in the accounting treatment of costs in the controlled and the comparable uncontrolled transactions.[232] One way to frame the issue is whether costs will be characterized as part of the COGS (above the line) or as operating expenses (below the line).[233]

Another point of comparison that must be taken into account is the treatment of inventory in the controlled transaction and the comparable uncontrolled transaction. For instance, if the manufacturer in a controlled transaction bears the expense of sourcing its own inventory of raw materials, while the manufacturer in a comparable uncontrolled transaction did not carry such an inventory, that would most likely be a significant difference with a material effect on the gross profit markups.[234] If the effect cannot be measured and reliably adjusted for, the cost-plus method would be unreliable.

The cost-plus method is the rough analogue to computed value, one of the test values under the customs valuation law.[235]

[2] Transactional Profit Methods

[a] Comparable Profits Method (CPM)/Transactional Net Margin Method (TNMM)

These are essentially the same method, with CPM being the name assigned in the US and the TNMM being promulgated by the OECD.[236]

The US does not apply the TNMM, but it is the featured transactional profit method in the OECD Guidelines[237] and is recognized by the forty-eight other OECD

232. Treas. Reg. § 1.482-3(d)(3)(iii)(B). The OECD concern is registered at OECD Guidelines, paragraphs 2.52-2.53, 2.58.
233. *See* OECD Guidelines, paragraphs 2.54-2.57, with its focus upon accounting for costs.
234. Treas. Reg. § 1.482-3(d)(4), Ex. 3.
235. *See* above §10.03[E][2][c].
236. The WCO Guide to Customs Valuation and Transfer Pricing notes (at 37, n. 21) that the major difference is that the CPM provides for a comparison of the profit of the controlled entity with the results of uncontrolled entities while the TNMM compares the profits of controlled transactions with those uncontrolled transactions.
237. OECD Guidelines, paragraphs 2.64-2.113. The OECD Guidelines recognize the transactional net margin method (TNMM) and the transactional profit split as the two acceptable "transactional profit methods." OECD Guidelines, paragraph 2.63.

countries, such as Canada, Australia, and the Western European countries which apply the Guidelines.[238]

Because CPM and TNMM measure operating profit, there is great emphasis on resources employed and risks assumed, but less emphasis on functional comparability than is required for RPM or cost-plus analyses. This is because the latter tests measure gross profit levels, and functional differences reflected in operating expenses can lead to disparate results if the analysis stops at the gross profit level. Similarly, because operating profit is typically less sensitive to product differences than gross profit, there is greater latitude in product similarity than with RPM or cost plus.[239] The OECD has noted that product differences may result in differences in price and that differences in function may result in differences in gross margin.[240]

The OECD considers that the TNMM is unlikely to be reliable if each party makes unique and valuable contributions—in such a case, a transactional profit split method is more appropriate.[241]

The TNMM is based on a comparison of the net profit margin (i.e., at the operating profit level) of a controlled taxpayer with the net profit margin of an uncontrolled taxpayer in similar transactions. The TNMM generally provides a more reliable result when there is a high degree of comparability between transactions, including the comparability of intangible assets. The OECD comments that the lack of significant intangibles does not automatically imply that TNMM is the most appropriate method.[242]

The OECD Guidelines assess TNMM's strengths and weaknesses in terms quite close to the commentary in the US Treasury regulations on the CPM:

Strengths:

- Net profit indicators (e.g., return on assets, operating income to sales, and possibly other measures of net profit) are less affected by transactional differences than is the case with price, as used in the CUP method. Net profit indicators also may be more tolerant to some functional differences between the controlled and uncontrolled transactions than gross profit margins. Differences in the functions performed between enterprises are often reflected in variations in operating expenses. Consequently, this may lead to a wide range of gross profit margins but still broadly similar levels of net operating profit indicators.
- As with any one-sided method, it is necessary to examine a financial indicator for only one of the associated enterprises (the "tested party"). Similarly, it is often not necessary to state the books and records of all participants in the business activity on a common basis or to allocate costs for all participants as

238. It is possible that a US taxpayer might rely on the TNMM in the context of an unspecified method, especially if the taxpayer were applying for an APA or had already prepared TNMM analyses for presentation to foreign tax authorities.
239. Treas. Reg. §§ 1.482-5(c)(2)(ii) and (iii).
240. OECD Guidelines, paragraph 2.75.
241. OECD Guidelines, paragraph 2.62.
242. OECD Guidelines, paragraph 2.61.

is the case with the transactional profit split method. This can be practically advantageous when one of the parties to the transaction is complex and has many interrelated activities or when it is difficult to obtain reliable information about one of the parties.[243]

Weaknesses:

- The net profit indicator of a taxpayer can be influenced by some factors that would either not have an effect, or have a less substantial or direct effect, on price or gross margins between independent parties. These aspects may make accurate and reliable determinations of arm's-length net profit indicators difficult. Thus, it is important to provide some detailed guidance on establishing comparability for the TNMM.
- Required information on uncontrolled transactions may not be available at the time of the controlled transactions. In addition, taxpayers may not have access to enough specific information on the profits attributable to comparable uncontrolled transactions to make a valid application of the method. It also may be difficult to ascertain revenue and operating expenses related to the controlled transactions to establish the net profit indicator used as the profit measure for the transactions. Tax administrators may have more information available to them from examinations of other taxpayers that may not be disclosed to the taxpayer (i.e., the "secret comparables" problem).
- Like the resale price and cost-plus methods, the TNMM is applied to only one of the associated enterprises. The fact that many factors unrelated to transfer prices may affect net profits, in conjunction with the one-sided nature of the analysis under this method, can affect the overall reliability of the TNMM if an insufficient standard of comparability is applied.
- There may also be difficulties in determining an appropriate corresponding adjustment when applying the TNMM, particularly where it is not possible to work back to a transfer price. This could be the case, for example, where the taxpayer deals with associated enterprises on both the buying and the selling sides of the controlled transaction. In such a case, if the TNMM indicates that the taxpayer's profit should be adjusted upwards, there may be some uncertainty about which of the associated enterprises' profits should be reduced.[244]

In recognition of the sensitivity of gross and net profit indicators in the TNMM, the OECD Guidelines have an Annex discussion which specifically treats the effects of functional differences models.[245]

Briefly stated, under the CPM/TNMM method, a taxpayer's pretax profit margin is compared to a range of results from a selected group of uncontrolled taxpayers. If the

243. OECD Guidelines, paragraphs 2.62-2.63.
244. OECD Guidelines, paragraphs 2.64-2.67.
245. Annex I to Chapter II. Separate examples cover extent and complexity of distributor marketing functions, distributor risks and manufacturer capacity utilization.

taxpayer's results fall within the arm's-length range derived from the comparable companies, then it is considered to be an arm's-length result.

CPM

For its part, despite the similarities of the CPM and the TNMM, the OECD has expressed antagonism to the CPM. Along with the "modified cost-plus/resale price method," CPM is acceptable only to the extent that it is consistent with the Guidelines.[246]

The IRS has summarized the CPM:

> Under the comparable profits method, the determination of an arm's length result is based on the amount of operating profit that the tested party would have earned on related party transactions if its profit level indicator were equal to that of an uncontrolled comparable (comparable operating profit).[247]

As for determining the arm's-length result through an application of the CPM, the Treasury Regulations advise that:

> Under the comparable profits method, the determination of an arm's length result is based on the amount of operating profit that the tested party would have earned on related party transactions if its profit level indicator were equal to that of an uncontrolled comparable (comparable operating profit). Comparable operating profit is calculated by determining a profit level indicator for an uncontrolled comparable, and applying the profit level indicator to the financial data related to the tested party's most narrowly identifiable business activity for which data incorporating the controlled transaction is available (relevant business activity). To the extent possible, profit level indicators should be applied solely to the tested party's financial data that is related to controlled transactions. The tested party's reported operating profit is compared to the comparable operating profits derived from the profit level indicators of uncontrolled comparables to determine whether the reported operating profit represents an arm's length result.[248]

As a general rule, the Comparable Profits Method (CPM)[249] evaluates whether the amount charged in a controlled transaction is at arm's length based on objective measures of profitability, profit-level indicators (PLIs), derived from the data of uncontrolled taxpayers that engaged in similar business activities under similar circumstances. The profit is measured at the operating margin level by applying a PLI derived from uncontrolled comparables and applying it to the tested party's most narrowly identifiable business activity for which data incorporating the controlled transaction is available.[250] The information on the comparable companies is derived from publicly available data sources, and finding a sufficient number of comparable companies is often the major challenge in applying the CPM or TNMM.[251]

You will note the US uses the term "PLIs." The US regulations state that:

246. OECD Guidelines, paragraph 2.62.
247. Treas. Reg. § 1.482-5(a).
248. Treas. Reg. § 1.482-5(b)(1).
249. Treas. Reg. § 1.482-5.
250. Treas. Reg. § 1.482-5(b).
251. *See* OECD Guidelines, paragraph 2.74.

> Profit level indicators are ratios that measure relationships between profits and costs incurred or resources employed. A variety of profit level indicators can be calculated in any given case. Whether use of a particular profit level indicator is appropriate depends upon a number of factors, including the nature of the activities of the tested party, the reliability of the available data with respect to uncontrolled comparables, and the extent to which the profit level indicator is likely to produce a reliable measure of the income that the tested party would have earned had it dealt with controlled taxpayers at arm's length, taking into account all of the facts and circumstances. The profit level indicators should be derived from a sufficient number of years of data to reasonably measure returns that accrue to uncontrolled comparables. Generally, such a period should encompass at least the taxable year under review and the preceding two taxable years.[252]

The Treasury Regulations list several varieties of PLIs that may prove a reliable basis for a comparison of operating profits, including:

(1) rate of return on capital employed;
(2) financial ratios, such as the ratio of operating profit to sales and the ratio of gross profit to operating expenses (the so-called Berry Ratio);
(3) others, as appropriate.[253]

TNMM

With the TNMM, the OECD makes use of Net Profit Indicators (NPIs), which are not a defined term but each NPI is said to be the ratio of the net profit to various economic bases—principally sales, assets or costs—serving as the denominator.[254] The OECD devotes considerable attention to choosing the specific NPI—factors include such considerations as the strength and weaknesses of the NPIs, availability of reliable information and the degree of comparability. In making the choice for the denominator, the OECD emphasizes the need for a base that is capable of being measured in a reliable and consistent manner at the level of the taxpayer's controlled transactions.[255]

The actual functioning of the TNMM is a comparison of the NPI for the controlled transaction with the NPI for uncontrolled transactions.

That begs the question, what is the comparability standard to be applied in selecting the uncontrolled transactions? The OECD lays spells out the comparability standards, including the necessity of making adjustments where necessary.[256]

---

252. Treas. Reg. § 1.482-5(b)(4).
253. Treas. Reg. §§ 1.482-5(b)(4)(i)-(iii). One of the financial ratios is the "Berry Ratio," which measures the ratio of gross profit to operating expenses. Treas. Reg. § 1.482-5(b)(4)(ii)(B). OECD Guidelines, paragraphs 2.100-2.102. One of the financial ratios is the "Berry Ratio," which measures the ratio of gross profit to operating expenses. Treas. Reg. § 1.482-5(b)(4)(ii)(B). OECD Guidelines, paragraphs 2.100-2.102.
254. While it has been the subject of much criticism, centered on its vulnerability to abuse and to its use of gross profit, the OECD includes the Berry Ratio as a possible financial indicator. OECD Guidelines, paragraphs 2.106-2.108.
255. OECD Guidelines, paragraph 2.95.
256. OECD Guidelines, paragraphs 2.74-2.81.

An early observation is that the CPM and the TNMM are similar to the "all costs plus a profit" COS exemplar contained in the Valuation Agreement, Interpretative Note to Article 1, Paragraph 2, point 3.

As has been shown, the "tested party" in the CPM or the TNMM is the participant in a controlled transaction whose operating profit from the controlled transactions can be most easily and reliably verified and for which reliable data on uncontrolled comparables can be located.[257] This typically results in the tested party being the least complex of the controlled parties, without the contribution of intangible property or unique assets that might distinguish it from potential uncontrolled comparable enterprises. As an example, this would normally result in a distributor with limited functions beyond a buy/resell activity being the tested party. That would simplify matters greatly, eliminating the need to access books and records of the foreign seller which are usually located outside the country of importation.[258]

[b] Profit Split Method

The profit split method is the second of the transactional profit methods after the CPM or TNMM.

In its opening sentence in the presentation of the profit split method, the OECD advises that:

> The transactional profit split method seeks to establish arm's length outcomes or test reported outcomes for controlled transactions in order to approximate the results that would have been achieved between independent enterprises engaging in a comparable transaction or transactions.[259]

Its aim is to evaluate whether the allocation of the combined operating profit or loss[260] attributed to one or more controlled transactions is at arm's length by reference to the relative value of each controlled taxpayer's contribution to the combined operating profit or loss. The combined operating profit or loss must be derived from the most narrowly identifiable business activity of the controlled taxpayers for which data is available that includes the controlled transactions (relevant business activity).[261]

257. Treas. Reg. § 1.482-5(b)(2); OECD Guidelines, paragraph 3.18.
258. This could have implications for customs valuation. While it is contained in an Interpretative Note to Article 6 of the Valuation Agreement (computed value), the text there states a rule of general applicability ("As a general rule, customs value is determined under this Agreement on the basis of information readily available in the country of importation"). Notwithstanding, the US and EU regulations implicitly limit this availability of information restriction to computed value, 19 CFR 152.106(f), UCC IA, Article 143. Canada deals with this issue obliquely as its statute requires a "sufficiency of information." Canada Customs Act, subsections 45(1), 48(6) and Memorandum D13-2-1, *Responsibility of Importers and/or Authorized Agents With Respect to Valuation*, November 21, 2013.
259. OECD Guidelines, paragraph 2.114. *See* Treas. Reg. §§ 1.482-6 et seq.
260. To be sure, the OECD observes that reference here to "profit" must be applied equally to losses. OECD Guidelines, paragraph 2.115. This is reminiscent with the treatment of "profit and general expenses" in computed value under the Valuation Agreement. Interpretative Note to Article 6, paragraph 5.
261. Treas. Reg. § 1.482-6; OECD Guidelines, paragraphs 2.114-2.183.

In apportioning (or "splitting the overall profit" up the individual taxpayers) the appropriate share of the profits and losses to each controlled taxpayer (i.e., in making the profit split), the tax authority seeks to reflect the functions performed, risks assumed, and resources employed by each participant, consistent with the standard comparability factors.[262] This allocation should correspond to the division of profits and losses that would result from an arrangement between uncontrolled taxpayers if each were performing functions similar to those of the controlled taxpayers engaged in the relevant business activity.

The US Treasury regulations establish two separate profit split methods: the comparable profit split and the residual profit split methods.

Comparable Profit Split

A comparable profit split is derived from the combined operating profit of uncontrolled taxpayers whose transactions and activities are similar to those of the controlled taxpayers in the relevant business activity.[263]

The combined operating profit is then divided among the controlled taxpayers in a split that must be shown to be similar to a division of the operating profits among uncontrolled taxpayers, i.e., if the taxpayer entities were not related, how much profit would have been earned by each.[264] Needless to say, comparability is at a premium.

Residual Profit Split

The residual profit split method also seeks to allocate operating profits among controlled taxpayers.[265] In contrast to the comparable profit split method, however, the residual profit split method uses a two-step process.

The first step is to allocate income to routine contributions, which are contributions of the same or a similar kind to those made by uncontrolled taxpayers involved in similar business activities for which it is possible to identify market returns. Routine contributions ordinarily include contributions of tangible property, services and intangible property that are generally owned by un controlled taxpayers engaged in similar activities. A functional analysis is required to identify these contributions according to the functions performed, risks assumed, and resources employed by each of the controlled taxpayers.[266]

The second step is to take into account and allocate among the controlled taxpayers the unallocated "residual" profit that is a function of the taxpayers' nonroutine contributions, which may take the form of valuable intangible property. These contributions would not be reflected in the taxpayers' routine contributions. The relative value of intangible property may be measured by external market benchmarks,

262. Treas. Reg. § 1.482-1(d)(3).
263. Treas. Reg. § 1.482-6(c)(2).
264. Treas. Reg. § 1.482-6(c)(2).
265. Treas. Reg. § 1.482-6(c)(3).
266. Treas. Reg. § 1.482-6(c)(3)(i) (A).

estimated by the capitalized costs of developing, improving, and updating the intangibles or, in certain circumstances, estimated based on the actual intangible development expenditures of the parties.[267]

The OECD has furnished some cogent commentary on the profit split methods, which are "two-sided" or "multi-sided" in the sense that there is not a review of only one tested party. First, the OECD Guidelines note some real advantages to the transactional profit split method:

- The main strength of the transactional profit split method is that it is the most appropriate method in cases where both parties to a transaction make unique and valuable contributions (e.g., contribute unique intangibles) to the transaction.[268]
- Another strength of the transactional profit split method is that it can offer a solution for highly integrated operations for which a one-sided method would not be appropriate.[269]
- Another strength of the transactional profit split method is that it offers flexibility by taking into account specific, possibly unique, facts and circumstances of the associated enterprises that are not present in independent enterprises while still constituting an arm's-length approach to the extent that it reflects what independent enterprises reasonably would have done if faced with the same circumstances.
- A final strength is the fact that all relevant parties to the transaction are evaluated as part of the review of the pricing, i.e., the contributions of all parties are identified and measured.[270]

For the OECD, there are perceived weaknesses to the profit split method as well:

- A weakness of the transactional profit split method relates to difficulties in its application. On the first review, the transactional profit split method may appear readily accessible to both taxpayers and tax administrations because it tends to rely less on information about independent enterprises. However, associated enterprises and tax administrations alike may have difficulty accessing information from foreign affiliates.
- It may be difficult to measure combined revenue and costs for all the associated enterprises participating in the controlled transactions, which would require stating books and records on a common basis and making adjustments in accounting practices and currencies.
- It may be difficult to identify the appropriate profit splitting factors.[271]

267. Treas. Reg. § 1.482-6(c)(3) (i) (B).
268. *See* OECD Guidelines, paragraphs 2.130-2.132.
269. *See* OECD Guidelines, paragraphs 2.133-2.138.
270. OECD Guidelines, paragraphs 2.119-2.222. Earlier versions had included the notion that it is less likely that no one controlled party will be left with an extreme or improbable profit since all parties are evaluated.
271. There are different categories of profit splitting factors such as asset-based, capital-based or cost-based. OECD Guidelines, paragraphs 2.169-2.173 and 2.179-2.183.

- It may be difficult to measure the revenue and costs for each relevant entity.
- When the method us applied to operating profit, it may be difficult to identify the appropriate operating expenses associated with the transactions and to allocate costs between the transactions and the associated enterprises' other activities.[272]

Staying with the OECD program, we find an approach similar to that of the US, with two separate profit split approaches: (i) a "contribution analysis" of the relative contributions of each party, based on comparables where available or, if not, by the relative contributions of each party; (ii) a residual analysis where at least one party has not made unique—or has made less complex—contributions which are capable of being benchmarked by reference to comparable, uncontrolled transactions.[273] The OECD observes that it divides the profits into two categories. The first category is comprised of profits which can be reliably benchmarked. These are typically less complex contributions for which reliable comparables can be found. Ordinarily this first amount will be determined by applying a traditional transaction method or the TNMM. For the second, or residual, profit, the allocation will be on the basis of the relative value of the second category of contributions of the parties in the same manner as the contribution analysis mentioned above.[274]

Where comparable uncontrolled transactions of sufficient reliability are lacking, the OECD sanctions the use of the taxpayer's own information (internal data). The OECD goes further, acknowledging that internal data will be essential to assess the values of the respective contributions of the parties to the controlled transaction.[275]

In this last regard, we see an echo of the Valuation Agreement and its primary focus on the importer/taxpayer's own transactional documents and other data.

[3] Unspecified or Other Methods

Just as the customs valuation law provides a fallback method of appraisement when no specifically defined method in the hierarchy applies,[276] so too does the transfer pricing law in the US have a distinct fallback method. The unspecified method[277] allows for hybrid methodologies or for methods derived from the specified methods. The Treasury regulations insist on the notion that the compared uncontrolled transaction should be a "realistic alternative" to the controlled transaction.

Consistent with the best-method rule, an unspecified method will not be applied unless it provides the most reliable measure of an arm's-length result. The example in the regulations is of a bona fide offer to purchase from an unrelated buyer. Since the offer had not been accepted, there was no transaction and, therefore, no possibility of

272. OECD Guidelines, paragraph 2.123.
273. *See* OECD Guidelines, paragraphs 2.174-2.178.
274. OECD Guidelines, paragraph 2.152.
275. OECD Guidelines, paragraphs 2.149-2.153.
276. 19 USC § 1401a(f); Valuation Agreement, Article 7.
277. Treas. Reg. § 1.482-3(e).

a CUP. Nevertheless, the similarity of the circumstances between the controlled transaction and the offer permits the use of the unspecified method.[278]

As previously noted, a taxpayer might make use of a TNMM study as an unspecified method in its dealings with the IRS. The receptivity of the IRS to the TNMM is demonstrated by the fact that the IRS refers to the methods jointly as the "CPM/TNMM."[279]

While the OECD Guidelines do not present a "fallback" or "unspecified" method under a separate heading, they effectively establish such a regime in their reference to an "other method" in paragraph 2.9 that a member of a multinational group or enterprise (MNE) might employ. Then, too, the repeated references such as "reasonable accommodations," "flexibility," a method being "agreeable" to the taxpayers and the tax authority and "pragmatic solutions" as well as the use of more than one method, speak to "work-around solutions" to what the OECD views as the "imprecision" of the methods.[280] Thus, unlike the Valuation Agreement's Article 7 and the US "unspecified method," an entirely separate fallback method is eschewed but we arrive at the same point via inherently flexible applications of the methods because, as the OECD phrases it, "transfer pricing is not an exact science."[281]

Even a cursory glance at the extant transfer pricing authorities in the context of the OECD, the US and other national jurisdictions—statutes, guidelines, regulations, rulings, treatises, commentaries and case law—reveals the wealth of authoritative income tax sources for guidance and interpretation that is in very stark contrast to the meager body of customs law sources.

One final observation about the OECD Guidelines is in order. Reading through them after having attended years' of TCCV sessions where the OECD had been an active participant, warmly greeted by the Members and the WCO Secretariat and had made many contributions on the customs valuation and transfer pricing interchange, I was taken aback by the near-silence on customs valuation. Chapter IV is devoted to Administrative Approaches, with much discussion on safe harbors, arbitration, simultaneous tax examinations, APAs and other topics. There was no discussion of the customs and income tax administrations coming together and certainly no discussion on joint or dual-purpose filings by importer/taxpayers with both agencies.

Another thought was triggered when reviewing the discussion on tax authority-initiated adjustments: whether (i) a *primary adjustment* made by the tax authority in one jurisdiction to increase or decrease the taxable income of one associated enterprise, i.e., related party, in accordance with the arm's-length principle or (ii) a *secondary adjustment*,[282] which arises from imposing taxes on "secondary transactions," which are constructive (or "deemed") in order to make the actual allocation of profits is

278. Treas. Reg. § 1.482-3(e)(2).
279. *See* the IRS Annual Report on APA for 2018, Announcement and Report Concerning Advance Pricing Agreements March 22, 2019, 9, available at https://www.irs.gov/pub/irs-apa/announcement_2019-03_apa_report.pdf.
280. *See*, e.g., OECD Guidelines, paragraphs 2.11, 2.12, 2.146, 3.81, 3.83.
281. OECD Guidelines, paragraph 3.55.
282. OECD Guidelines, paragraphs 4.68-4.78. Parenthetically, the WCO Guide acknowledges the use of secondary adjustments, at 45-46.

consistent with the primary adjustment. The secondary adjustments take the form of constructive dividends, equity contributions or loans. You will recognize that they would be a means to ensure that transfer pricing targets are met by means other than post-import, retroactive price adjustments. In such a case, there would be no changes to the PAPP.

There is a further category of adjustment taken by tax authorities—the *corresponding adjustment* made by the tax authority in another jurisdiction to the tax liability of another associated enterprise so as to ensure consistency in the allocation of profits between the associated enterprises and to avoid double taxation. Again, there would be no changes to the PAPP.

The changes are made to a taxpayer's tax liability and not to the prices paid for imported goods or services. The OECD advises that a corresponding adjustment initiated by the tax authority in foreign country 2 might be avoided after the tax authority in country 1 has issued a primary adjustment, through "repatriation," i.e., a payment from the taxpayer in country 1 to the associated enterprise in country 2 or vice versa when the taxpayer in country 1 is due a refund[283] Only two of the repatriation techniques—payments or refunds of the transfer price—would change the PAPP. The other techniques—setting up an account receivable or reclassifying other transactions such as dividend transfers between parent and subsidiary—exert no customs valuation.

The lesson is that it would be an error to assume that any and all transfer pricing adjustments will have customs valuation implications. In fact, staying with imported tangible goods, if there are no changes to the PAPP, then there should be no customs valuation issues. In point of fact, we should acknowledge that there are many economic factors beyond price that affect profit at either the gross margin or operating margin level. Interpretative Note to Article 1, in paragraph 4, reminds us that the flow of dividends or other payments from buyer to the seller that do not relate to the imported goods are not part of the customs value.

This issue of primary, secondary and corresponding adjustments—made without a price change and not on a discrete, product-specific, entry-specific basis—would be a fit topic for inclusion in a TCCV/OECD dialogue and/or a TCCV technical question on transfer pricing and compensating adjustments.

§10.05 BRIDGING THE TRANSFER PRICING GAP: RECONCILING THE TWO TAX REGIMES

The importer/taxpayer will often find itself dealing anew with one of the two revenue agencies after having concluded matters with the other agency. For instance, the US importer/taxpayer will need to come to closure with the IRS under the auspices of section 1059A on the basis of a customs valuation previously established with CBP. Or the importer/taxpayer that has already participated in an APA, or that has withstood a transfer pricing audit by the income tax authority or has gathered contemporaneous

283. OECD Guidelines, paragraph 4.74.

documentation to substantiate its transfer price may want to make use of that income tax-driven material to convince the customs authority that its transfer price is acceptable for customs valuation purposes.

At this point it should be clear that related party importer/taxpayers must be prepared to satisfy both taxing authorities, each of them with separate mandates and separate statutory/regulatory rubrics. To borrow a phrase from the London underground system, the importer/taxpayer must "mind the gap." This section explores how importers/taxpayers might proceed.

[A] An Interdisciplinary Discourse: Tax and Customs Standards in Section 1059A

For the US importer/taxpayer, the demands of section 1059A cannot be ignored. This is the nexus between the two disciplines when starting from a fixed customs valuation point.

[1] Scope

It is essential to understand the exact borders of section 1059A. A full exposition of the provision is beyond the scope of this treatment, but some observations are surely warranted.

First, it applies only to "related party" transactions within the meaning of section 482. Second, because Congress foresaw the possibility of related parties inserting an intermediary in the sales and physical movement of the goods, the section will also apply in "indirect" transactions, which are defined in the Treasury regulations:

> *Indirectly*. For purposes of this section, *indirectly* refers to a transaction between a controlled taxpayer and another member of the controlled group whereby property is imported through a person acting as an agent of, or otherwise on behalf of, either or both related persons, or as a middleman or conduit for transfer of the property between a controlled taxpayer and another member of the controlled group. In the case of the importation of property indirectly, an adjustment shall be permitted under paragraph (c)(2) of this section for a commission or markup paid to the person acting as agent, middleman, or conduit, only to the extent that the commission or markup: is otherwise properly included in cost basis or inventory cost; was actually incurred by the taxpayer and not remitted, directly or indirectly, to the taxpayer or related party; and there is a substantial business reason for the use of a middleman, agent, or conduit.[284]

The Treasury regulations will not apply if there has been an intervening sale from the foreign related party to an intermediary acting on its own behalf and not cast in the role of an agent for either or both of the related parties. If the intermediary is an agent,

284. Treas. Reg. § 1.1059A-1(b)(2).

the importer/taxpayer is permitted to upwardly adjust the customs value by including an amount that represents the buying agent's commission.[285]

The third important element of scope is that of customs value, which is defined in the statute:

> The term "customs value" means the value taken into account for purposes of determining the amount of any customs duties or any other duties which may be imposed on the importation of any property.[286]

By its terms, the statute applies only to those importations where the duty is assessed on an ad valorem basis. Duties assessed on imports on a specific basis or by means of compound duties will not be subject to section 1059A. Likewise, imports of duty-free merchandise or those imports subject only to the merchandise processing fee of 19 USC § 58(c) or the harbor maintenance tax of IRC section 4461, are outside the scope of the section.[287] For articles that are imported with benefit of one of the "American goods returned" tariff provisions,[288] the section will not apply to the value of the US-origin portion of the article.

There is a provision for "averaged customs values" that is curiously opaque.[289] It is aimed at those situations in which an appropriate transfer price for tax purposes is determined by reference to post-importation events. The Treasury regulation recites that entry will have been made on an estimated value basis, with some entries showing values higher and other entries showing values "lower than the actual transaction value." With a novel application of a US customs practice, the entries are said to "have been liquidated upon importation."[290] The regulations continue to restrict this averaging provision:

> exclusively to cases of property imported in transactions that are open for tax purposes in which the actual transaction value cannot be determined and the entry has been liquidated for customs purposes on the basis of a value estimated at the time of importation in accordance with customs regulations; in these cases, the property is appropriately valued for tax purposes by reference to a formula, in existence at the time of importation, based on subsequent events and valued for customs purposes by a different formula.[291]

The example given is a consignment sale. Apart from the Treasury regulation seeming to conflate the separate notions of formula-based pricing and the need to go to alternative methodologies absent a bona fide sale for export (i.e., the consignment case), it is hard to envisage a customs appraisal ever proceeding to liquidation based on "estimated values" rather than deferring liquidation, which is the chronology in the

285. There is no need to adjust for a selling agent's commission, as it should already have been included in dutiable value.
286. IRC § 1059A(b)(1).
287. Treas. Reg. § 1.1059A-1(c)(1).
288. These are contained, along with other exceptional tariff provisions, in Chapter 98 of the HTSUS and are the US versions of "outward processing relief."
289. Treas. Reg. § 1.1059A-1(c)(9).
290. Liquidation of entries is discussed in Part I and below.
291. Treas. Reg. § 1.1059A-1(c)(9).

given example. Importers/taxpayers and their experienced customs or income tax advisors would benefit from a Rosetta Stone to decipher this provision, which sets up a dichotomy between something termed a "[f]inally-determined customs value" and "transaction value."

Fourth, the section applies only to entries for consumption,[292] and should not apply, for example, to imported articles that are: (1) admitted under bond into a foreign trade zone or entered into a customs bonded warehouse (CBW) and subsequently withdrawn for exportation or (2) entered under the Temporary Import Under Bond (TIB) program.[293] Importers/taxpayers will be able to physically receive goods under these bonded programs in the US for storage or for manipulation or manufacturing and directly reexport the goods without any contact with section 1059A, which will apply only if the goods are entered for consumption.

As a fifth observation, the importer/taxpayer has an alternative means of demonstrating compliance. In lieu of calculating all adjustments and offsets, an importer/taxpayer can demonstrate compliance by a side-by-side comparison of costs used in arriving at customs value and in arriving at its basis or inventory cost for income tax purposes. If the same costs are used and if the inventory cost is equal to or lesser than the customs value, the importer/taxpayer is deemed to have met section 1059A requirements.[294]

[2] Customs Value

Liquidation has a starring role in customs value for the purposes of section 1059A because the "finality" of customs value is defined in the income tax regulations[295] as attaching at the liquidation of the entry. In turn, the customs regulations define "liquidation" as the final computation or ascertainment of duties or drawback accruing on an entry[296] and, by administrative practice since 1997, it typically occurs 314 days after entry.[297]

---

292. Section 1059A defines "import" thusly:

> Except as provided in regulations, the term "import" means the entering, or withdrawal from warehouse, for consumption.

293. For many goods that will be in the United States temporarily before they are reexported, duties can be eliminated. The importer must take care to observe all of the required procedural steps, including the posting of a bond whose purpose is to back up the promise to reexport or destroy the product. As is the case of all obligations that are backed up by a bond, the bond is enforced through a liquidated damages assessment when the bond is not properly canceled, in this case through exportation or destruction. Not surprisingly, then, the program is called Temporary Importation Under Bond, which is universally shortened to "TIB." The TIB program is composed of various provisions in subchapter XIII to Chapter 98 of the HTSUS.
294. Treas. Reg. § 1.1059A-1(c)(6).
295. Treas. Reg. § 1.1059A-1(d).
296. 19 CFR § 159.1.
297. The customs law provides that an entry is deemed liquidated by operation of law one year from the date of entry unless a delay beyond that point is authorized or required by law. 19 USC § 1504(a). The general rule is that all liquidations, including erroneous liquidations, must be protested to avoid a bar of administrative or judicial review. *But see United States v. Cherry Hill*

In fact, liquidation does not itself become final but remains open for: (1) CBP for a ninety-day period, within which time CBP can voluntarily reliquidate the entry[298] and (2) the importer, who has 180 days within which period the importer can file a protest, *inter alia*, to change the declared value.[299] If a protest were to be filed, the finality of the liquidation is "tolled,"[300] and finality is reached only after the protest has been ruled on and all judicial review, if any, has been concluded.

In the instance where a protest has been granted, the entry will be reliquidated with a refund.[301] If a protest is denied, the original liquidation stands and will become final as of the date of the determination on the protest unless the importer seeks judicial review in the CIT by filing a summons within the 180-day period prescribed by statute.[302]

Changes to the dutiable value occurring: (1) after entry but before liquidation should be distinguished from (2) those occurring after liquidation. For the former changes, a protest will not lie. In lieu of a protest, the importer must file a PSC,[303] theoretically at any time in the period between the entry date and liquidation. The PSC can accommodate requests for refunds as well as tenders to the government, so an importer/taxpayer will be able to make an upward or downward adjustment to the dutiable value declared at entry. Because of the time involved in making the requested changes so that they will be embodied in the liquidation, a PSC may be filed up to 270 days from the date of entry and must be filed no later than twenty working days before the scheduled liquidation date. If the PSC is accepted, the liquidation of the original entry will be "unset" and liquidation will be based on the importer/taxpayer's revision. Accordingly, PSCs, which are pre-liquidation submissions, raise no section 1059A implications. For a PSC that is not granted, however, CBP may still voluntarily reliquidate or the importer/taxpayer will be able to file a protest.[304]

Textiles, Inc., 112 F3d 1550 (Fed. Cir. 1997) (a purported liquidation occurring after a deemed liquidation need not be protested). *See also United States v. Utex Int'l, Inc.*, 6 Fed. Cir. 166, 857 F2d 1408 (1988).

298. 19 CFR § 173.3.
299. 19 USC § 1514; 19 CFR §§ 174.0 et seq.
300. *See* ruling no. 221017 (November 19, 1990).
301. 19 CFR § 159.6(b)(1); Protest/Petition Processing Handbook, HB 3500-08A, at 25 December 2007.
302. 28 USC § 2636.
303. The PSC is the 2011 successor to the Post Entry Amendment (PEA) as the primary vehicle for dealing with post-entry, pre-liquidation amendments and corrections. The PSC, a full entry summary replacement, is filed through the secure Automated Commercial Environment (ACE) portal. While there is a lack of guidance on the point presumably the importer will continue to have the right to protest against liquidations where the PSC was not fully accepted. The PEA itself had been the successor to the Supplemental Information Letter (SIL) process that CBP originally announced in 1997 but discontinued in 2007. *See* ABI Administrative Message No. 97-0727 (August 4, 1997) and 72 Fed. Reg. 46,654 (August 21, 2007). What is noteworthy is that the procedures for the SIL, the PEA, and the PSC have remained in a "test" mode and are not yet provided for in the customs regulations. Additional information can be obtained from the User Guide at the CBP website https://www.cbp.gov/sites/default/files/assets/documents/2017-Jun/ACE%20Post%20Summary%20Corrections%20User%20Guide.pdf.
304. This was the case with the predecessor PEA. *See* notice to the effect that an earlier CBP administrative position, that an unsuccessful PEA would be treated as a protest, was being revised. 73 Fed. Reg. 19,865 (April 11, 2008) ("where the entry summaries covered by the PEAs

The section 1059A regulations here, as at other points,[305] need to be revised, as they speak to a ninety-day post-liquidation period for protests and because they still refer to both petitions for clerical errors or mistakes of fact that were formerly available under now-repealed 19 USC § 1520(c),[306] which would be recognized with the effect of allowing an adjustment to the customs value and to increased duty payments under 19 USC § 1521, which was repealed in 1993, as being disregarded. Moreover, they make no reference to the collection of additional duties that is now available under 19 USC § 1592(d) if the importer has violated 19 USC § 1592.[307] Presumably, these 19 USC § 1592(d) collections would be disregarded today, as they have effectively superseded 19 USC § 1521.[308]

Apart from the silence and lack of guidance regarding 19 USC § 1592(d), the regulations carry embedded within them an inherent anomaly facing the taxpayer/importer, who may face increased duties because a domestic competitor has been successful in challenging his customs valuation under 19 USC § 1516.[309] The importer will not be able to correspondingly adjust his customs value for the purposes of section 1059A.

To be sure, the Treasury Regulations state[310] that the taxpayer/importer is bound by the "finally determined customs value." An often overlooked but crucial element is that the section 1059A Regulations are faithful to, and consistent with, customs law and practice on the point that "all U.S. Customs Service determinations are considered final, when liquidation of the entry becomes final."

Section 1514(a) of the Tariff Act of 1930 states:

> [D]ecisions of the Customs Service, including the legality of all orders and findings entering into the same, as to—.
> (1) the appraised value of the merchandise;
> * * *
> shall be final and conclusive upon all persons (*including the United States and any officer thereof*) unless a protest is filed in accordance with this section, or unless a civil action contesting the denial of a protest, in whole or in part, is commenced in the United States Court of International Trade[311] (emphasis added).

were liquidated without consideration of the requested amendment, ... CBP may reliquidate the entry summaries under 19 USC § 1501 based on the PEAs or the importer may file a protest in accordance with 19 USC § 1514. CBP will not treat single PEAs filed before liquidation as protests").

305. For instance, the regulations in subsection (c)(1) refer to Tariff Schedules of the United States (TSUS) provisions that have been inapplicable since January 1, 1989.
306. 19 USC § 1520(c) was repealed in 2004. Pub. L. No. 108-429, § 2105.
307. 19 USC § 1592. With effect from December 8, 1993, section 1592(d) effectively expanded and replaced 19 USC § 1521, as it prescribes the collection of duties if the importer had been negligent or grossly negligent in addition to the fraud level of culpability that had solely occupied 19 USC § 1521 before its repeal.
308. *See* ruling no. 228125 (January 11, 1999), and authority cited therein.
309. 19 USC § 1516. *See*, e.g., Notice, Receipt of Domestic Interested Party Petition Concerning the Tariff Classification of Wickless Wax Objects, 75 Fed. Reg. 420 (January 5, 2010).
310. Treas. Reg. § 1.1059A-1(d).
311. 19 USC § 1514(a).

With the filing of a protest, the liquidation is tolled or put into a suspended status. Because a liquidation that has been protested is not final, the section 1059A Regulations must be read as permitting an adjustment to be made in the face of a customs value embodied in a protested, and thus not-yet-final, liquidation or voluntary reliquidation by CBP[312] which, under customs law, is a new and superseding liquidation.

Stated otherwise, an importer/taxpayer will be able to freely adjust an otherwise final customs value at any time up to any of the following:

- The date of the decision on a protest where the importer has reopened the liquidation by filing a protest and the importer stands by and does not contest the decision on the protest.
- The date when the judgment on the CIT decision is final where the importer has sought judicial review of the decision on a protest.
- The date of reliquidation where CBP has voluntarily reliquidated the entry.

A likely scenario is that the importer will be caught between a hammer and anvil fashioned by Congress, faced with a final value for customs purposes once liquidation has become final, but that is then rendered immovable for tax purposes. This risk of anomalous treatment is evident in any discussion on adjustments of customs value that are cognizable under section 1059A.

[3] Adjustments

Since 1994, the US transfer pricing regulations have permitted a controlled taxpayer to voluntarily make an adjustment on its tax return to prices actually paid if necessary to reach an arm's-length result.[313] But section 1059A will intervene if the timing is not right (i.e., the customs value has gone to final liquidation), and the taxpayer will be precluded from making an upward adjustment under this "self-initiated" provision.[314] As seen, such an adjustment made by the taxpayer is not one of the qualifying events in the regulation permitting a taxpayer to upwardly adjust a final customs value.

Both CBP and the IRS apparently noticed this dilemma soon after the July 1994 promulgation of the regulations, but a proposed 1995 pilot program to make use of reconciliation in the limited context of controlled taxpayers' upward section 482 adjustments never became operational.[315] The intention was to use the proposed pilot

312. Pursuant to 19 USC § 1501.
313. Treas. Reg. § 1.482-1(a)(3).
314. Rev. Proc. 99-32, 1999-2 CB 296, marks a clear distinction between self-initiated adjustments that result in a lower transfer price (one resulting in "an increase in taxable income") that can be made by the taxpayer at any time and those adjustments that result in a higher transfer price (one resulting in "a decrease in taxable income") that can only be reported in a timely return and then only "after appropriate accounting for section 1059A of the Code."
315. 60 Fed. Reg. 46,141 (September 5, 1995). Parenthetically, CBP conducted a second limited reconciliation test with a very limited number of participants for entries exposed to antidumping and countervailing duties, as proposed in 61 Fed. Reg. 21,534 (May 10, 1996). A third test, with reconciliation focused on valuation issues, was announced in February 1997 in 62 Fed.

to gather data to help the agencies decide whether and to what extent the section 1059A Regulations should be amended or whether the reconciliation procedure could provide a "work around" solution.

[a] Nondutiable charges

Apart from self-initiated adjustments springing from the section 482 Regulations, importers might seek to adjust for payments that are excluded from dutiable value due to the contours of the customs valuation law. Because of the underlying differences in the customs valuation law and the income tax law, one of the key elements arising under section 1059A is the opportunity for the taxpayer to make adjustments to the customs value to take into account those cost or price elements that are nondutiable charges (NDCs) but that should play a role in the acquisition cost of the imported goods.

The section 1059A Regulations specifically provide for the adjustment of customs value for income tax purposes to take into account such NDCs as freight, insurance, post-importation construction or erection charges.[316] For buying commissions, the regulations do not specifically provide for adjustments but, by virtue of the reference in the discussion of indirect transactions to such an adjustment in subsection (c)(2), they must fit within the basket provision of the section 1059A Regulations:

> *Any other amounts* which are not taken into account in determining the customs value, *which are not properly includible in customs value,* and which are appropriately included in the cost basis or inventory cost for income tax purposes[317] (emphasis added).

The corollary is that a customs value for which the liquidation is final may not be adjusted to account for costs that are dutiable (i.e., properly includable in customs value).

The disadvantage is especially acute for the importer who follows prescribed customs law principles and makes a voluntary tender to CBP of additional duties after the liquidation of the entry has become final, perhaps but not necessarily, in the context of a prior disclosure.[318] The importer/taxpayer cannot upwardly adjust the

---

Reg. 5673 (February 6, 1997), but was later replaced by a test expanded to cover four issues, in the context of the automated commercial system (ACS), 62 Fed. Reg. 51,181 (September 30, 1997), as enhanced by 63 Fed. Reg. 6257 (February 6, 1998), in parallel with a test under the National Customs Automation Prototype (NCAP/P), at 62 Fed. Reg. 14,731 (March 27, 1997). This broad-based reconciliation program, not limited specifically to a single open issue, began as a two-year prototype on October 1, 1998, and is discussed below.

316. Treas. Reg. §§ 1.1059A-1(c)(2)(i)-(iii).
317. Treas. Reg. § 1.1059A-1(c)(2)(iv).
318. As is the case with some other countries, the US has a voluntary disclosure program with a built-in incentive. A perfected disclosure will lower penalty exposure. The US version, entitled prior disclosure, is set forth at 19 USC § 1592 and 19 CFR § 162.74. For Canada's program, *see* Canada, Customs Memorandum D11-6-4, *Relief of Interest and/or Penalties Including Voluntary Disclosure,* November 25, 2015. In the EU, there is no EU-level voluntary disclosure regime; it is limited to those Member States which offer it. For example, in France there is no official statutory program, though in practice a voluntary disclosure will often result in a

customs value for *section 1059A* purposes because such voluntary tenders do not and cannot alter the dutiable value inherent in a final liquidation. The liquidation remains unaffected and the tenders serve only the more limited purpose of eliminating a potential exposure to civil penalties for underpayment of duty.[319]

A US importer/taxpayer may need to decide whether to eliminate civil penalty risk under the customs laws by paying additional duty to CBP or to ignore the customs law compliance risk because such a voluntary payment is essentially non-tax deductible, as section 1059A will not allow him to upwardly adjust his tax basis above the customs value.[320] With a statute of limitations under 19 USC §§ 1592 and 1621 of five years, the importer/taxpayer must be especially careful in weighing his options.[321]

The areas of importer/taxpayer payments that have already caused significant problems for the IRS have fallen within the two categories of "statutory additions" under the customs valuation law. These are dutiable assists and royalties.

[b] Dutiable Assists

For dutiable assists, the section 1059A Regulations attempt to bridge the divide between tax basis and declared customs value that arises from the ability of an importer/taxpayer to account for dutiable assists on either a single entry or a periodic basis.[322] These regulations specifically allow for adjustments to the customs value to account for dutiable assists that have been apportioned over entries on a periodic basis, but only if the adjustment meets the arm's-length standard of section 482.[323]

The GAO issued a notable report on the lack of symmetry between the customs law and Sections 482 and 1059A.[324] The GAO Report was issued in response to a House

mitigated penalty amount. As for amending a customs declaration, UCC Article 173 allows for amendment within three years of the acceptance of the declaration—it is available only prior to release of the goods. For October 2021 Guidance on the UK voluntary disclosure program, *see* https://www.gov.uk/guidance/civil-penalties-for-contraventions-of-customs-law-customs-notice-301. For a 2013 WCO study of such programs, *see* http://www.wcoomd.org/en/topics/facilitation/resources/~/~/media/4C64301A393745989A29EAF535AE8D08.ashx.

319. *See*, e.g., FSA 200036015 (May 31, 2000).
320. In this connection, under the present regulatory scheme, post-final liquidation payments of duty and civil penalties are most likely nondeductible in all instances, whether under the auspices of a prior disclosure, a penalty assessed under 19 USC § 1592, or a simple tender outside the customs compliance context.
321. 19 USC §§ 1592, 1621 (suits or actions to recover any duties under 19 USC § 1592 must be filed within five years of the date of the alleged violation).
322. 19 CFR § 152.103(e).
323. Treas. Reg. § 1.1059A-1(c)(2) explicitly requires conformity with the standard of Treas. Reg. § 1.482-1(d)(3).
324. Government Accountability Office, "IRS' Administration of Tax-Customs Valuation Rules in Tax Code Section 1059A," (February 4, 1994), GAO/GGD-94-61 (GAO Report), available at https://www.govinfo.gov/content/pkg/GAOREPORTS-GGD-94-61/html/GAOREPORTS-GGD-94-61.htm. Given the *de minimis* potential revenue effect of section 1059A as foreseen by Congress, the GAO concern over potential revenue loss is curious.

oversight request that was prompted by the issuance of a Technical Advice Memorandum (TAM) in July 1992.[325] The TAM had concluded that a taxpayer was not precluded by section 1059A from claiming a deduction for payments of a supplier's overhead expenses that were nondutiable.

In the course of issuing the GAO Report, the GAO observed that only nine IRS audits had raised section 1059A issues and, of those, seven had arisen in the context of imports from Mexico where the goods had been assembled by contract or toll manufacturers under the maquila regime. The related party supplier had charged the taxpayer on a cost-plus basis for the imported goods, which were appraised by CBP on a computed value basis.[326] As previously established in the foregoing discussion of computed value as one of the "test values," computed value may be roughly summarized as the sum of direct manufacturing costs, including labor and materials, plus an amount for profit and dutiable assists. The dilemma for the IRS arose because the taxpayer had paid, on behalf of the related Mexican assembler, almost twenty categories of general, administrative, and overhead expenses, such as legal fees, janitorial services, office equipment rental fees, trash removal, and consulting fees. The customs valuation law on computed value appraisements requires that for expenses to be included within dutiable value they must have been incurred by the producer unless they are dutiable assists. CBP interprets the customs law on assists to require that the putative assist be directly related to production. For those costs associated with US-origin engineering, design, and artwork, which would have been a dutiable assist if the services had not been performed in the US, the customs regulations will include these costs within computed value only to the extent that their value has been charged to the producer.[327]

The TAM held that the importer/taxpayer was entitled to the deduction (i.e., was entitled to upwardly adjust customs value by the amount of the payments it had made) even though the payments were not dutiable assists. On review of the issue, the IRS furnished letters to the GAO which, along with letters from CBP, are reprinted in Appendixes to the GAO Report. The IRS believed that the loss of revenue, which it freely characterized as "an evasion of customs duties," was due to a problem in customs valuation, indeed was a "loophole," a flaw in the customs law. The GAO had raised the notion that perhaps section 1059A might be amended or, alternatively, the customs valuation law might be amended. CBP and the US Trade Representative both observed in formal letters to the GAO that it was not feasible to amend the customs valuation law, as it would violate the GATT, or to renegotiate the multilateral agreement on which it is based. The IRS felt that section 1059A should not be amended because it was "inappropriate to solve a customs problem through a change in the Internal Revenue Code."

325. TAM styled as Priv. Ltr. Rul. 9301002 (July 10, 1992).
326. Computed value, 19 USC § 1401a(e), and the other customs appraisement methods are discussed in detail in both Part I and earlier in this Part.
327. 19 USC § 1401a(h)(1)(B); 19 CFR §§ 152.102(a)(2), 152.106(d).

The lack of symmetry between the two disciplines is the obvious explanation for the lack of understanding by the IRS of the subtleties of the customs valuation law[328] or the place of domestic customs law in the GATT/WTO context[329] and its characterization of the customs valuation law as flawed.

[c] *Royalty and License Fees (RLFs)*

For RLF payments, another of the statutory additions of the customs valuation law, there is a similar and equally strong possibility that the importer/taxpayer might make a payment that is not dutiable under the customs law but that should serve as the basis for an upward adjustment under the section 1059A Regulations, assuming, of course, that the timing of the adjustment is no bar.

The simple fact is that not all royalty payments are dutiable, nor are all payments for the benefit of foreign manufacturers dutiable assists. Some of the characterizations on dutiability will turn on fine points of customs law honed by thirty years of judicial and administrative law precedents. As we explored in Part I, for dutiable status, the customs valuation law holds that a royalty or license fee must be both related to the import transaction and paid as a condition of the import transaction.[330]

Thus, an importer might make a royalty payment to a licensor, unrelated to the seller of the imported merchandise (the vendor), for the right to use a trademark on goods to be manufactured in the country of importation. Such a royalty payment might well be "related to" the imported goods because it was involved in the production of the imported goods, but such a payment might not be a condition of the sale underlying the import transaction. The customs jurisprudence on royalty and license fees, represented by dozens of CBP rulings and published documents, as well as further opinions and commentaries promulgated by the WCO, should hold such a royalty to be nondutiable.[331]

[d] *Offset Reductions of Adjustments*

The Treasury regulations provide for an offsetting reduction to an upward adjustment to customs value to reflect that certain amounts might properly reduce the cost basis for income tax purposes but are not taken into account in determining customs value.[332]

---

328. Query, how would the IRS respond to 19 USC §§ 1401a(h)(1)(A) and (B), the organic customs valuation law concerning dutiable assists, with its carved-out exception for engineering and development work undertaken in the United States? This service or work might be directly tied to, indeed possibly essential for, production, but would nonetheless be nondutiable in a transaction value appraisement as a matter of law.
329. "We think it unfortunate, however, if GATT has caused customs law to be frozen in the state it was on the date that GATT entered into effect." Letter from Chief Counsel, IRS, Appendix VIII to GAO Rep., at 51-54.
330. 19 USC § 1401a(b)(1)(D).
331. *See*, e.g., ruling no. 548368 (December 24, 2003).
332. Treas. Reg. § 1.1059A-1(c)(3).

The regulation cites the example of post-importation rebates or other price reductions that would be ignored by CBP.

This application of an offset is consistent with the view that the section does not act as a floor and assuredly the IRS is not restricted to an offset-of-adjustments context within which to lower customs value as a result of rebates or other price reductions. This outcome perfectly illustrates the point that many practitioners have long argued—section 1059A actually whipsaws the importer/taxpayer, who is generally not allowed by CBP to reduce its dutiable value once it has become final to take into account retroactive price decreases, but who must reduce his cost basis for section 482 purposes. Section 1059A can be a trap for the unwary and, as seen, the importer/taxpayer can spring the trap on himself with adjustments based on post-importation rebates or other price-altering changes.

[4] IRS Administration of Section 1059A

Does the IRS have the capacity to both properly understand and apply customs law, a body of law in equal measures precise and abstruse?[333] Such a question is neither rhetorical nor idle musing, because the IRS has already determined in Field Service Advice 200036015 (September 8, 2000) the dutiable status of a license fee. The IRS did not merely gauge the effect of a dutiable royalty on the taxpayer's income tax liability, but went further. The IRS itself, indeed IRS field auditors, made the determination of dutiability. There is no indication that the IRS, either at the field level or at the Headquarters Branch level, obtained or even sought CBP advice in the matter.

The facts underlying Field Service Advice 200036015 are that the IRS determined on audit that the license fees paid by the importer/taxpayer should have been taken into account in the dutiable value of the imported merchandise. The IRS examination by field agents led to the issuance of an IDR advising the importer/taxpayer that the payments might be dutiable and, if so, section 1059A might preclude an adjustment for the omitted dutiable charges. The importer/taxpayer was US corporation A, whose shares were owned jointly by a US individual and foreign corporation B. Corporations A and B had entered into a license agreement, only briefly summarized in the Field Service Advice, whereby A was granted a license by B for the right to sell and service products bearing a trademark owned by B. A license fee was due to B on sales by A.

A purchased products from C, a wholly owned foreign subsidiary of B, and thus a party related to A. The trademark had presumably been placed on those products. A imported those products into the US. The dutiable value of the imported products that had been purchased from C had not included the trademark license fees paid to B. Some of the imported products were used to produce goods in the US, which finished goods were then resold by A. Other imported products were resold by A in the same condition as at the time of import.

333. The IRS has continued to apply section 1059A despite the GAO Report statement that IRS implementation of section 1059A in those situations that involve direct payments by importers/taxpayers effectively ceased following the 1992 TAM. GAO Report, at 2.

The factual recitation in the Field Service Advice suggests that the license fees were based on total sales of both further-manufactured and same-condition goods.

The reaction of the importer/taxpayer to the IDR and its pronouncement on the status of the license fees was apparently to promptly file a prior disclosure (PD) of a customs law violation with CBP as a means of limiting exposure to civil penalties under 19 USC § 1592. In so doing, the importer/taxpayer would have been admitting to a violation of the customs valuation law. This proved a fatal error in the contest with the IRS. With its PD filing, the importer had acknowledged to CBP that the license fee was dutiable, and ascribing the failure to declare them as founded on inexperience and an oversight rather than the result of any intentional act. The importer/taxpayer then sought to argue with the IRS that the payments were for marketing rights and were based on its total sales of products, including goods manufactured in the Unites States and goods with no connection to the imported merchandise. These positions have a sound basis in customs law for nondutiable status. Nevertheless, the IRS was unwilling to give any credence to any of the later arguments from the importer for nondutiability.

The Field Service Advice primarily drew on customs jurisprudence on what constitutes the PAPP in a transaction value appraisement instead of the more relevant body of customs law based on the dutiable status of royalty and license fees as an addition to the PAPP. One possible explanation for this is that there was a failure to appreciate this subtle and nice distinction. Another is that most of the latter corpus, while quite robust, is largely grounded in administrative precedents, less accessible to a research effort by a lawyer less familiar with customs law than the judicial decisions actually cited by the IRS.

The IRS ascribed dutiable status to the license fees paid to *C* as an indirect payment under a PAPP and as a subsequent proceed that inured to the benefit of the seller, B. The indirect payment analysis in connection with the payment of a royalty is extraordinary. In so finding, the IRS misstated the law on the finality of liquidation, omitting timely filed protests in its recitation of post-liquidation events that, as discussed above, support a change in customs value. While the Field Service Advice is undoubtedly correct in its statement that a "voluntary tender" will not disturb the final status of customs value for customs purposes and, consequently, for the purposes of section 1059A as well, the analysis is troubling. In a different case, one in which the importer/taxpayer took a different path by, for example, requesting from CBP Headquarters advice on the dutiability of the license fee payments, or where the licensee was not related to either the seller or the importer/taxpayer, how would the IRS proceed? Would the IRS defer to a CBP determination that a royalty or license fee was nondutiable because, for example, it was based on a finding that the payment was not a condition of sale, as in the above-cited ruling no. 548368?

The IRS had been clearly frustrated by the CBP determination that the payments to the Mexican producer were not dutiable assists in the circumstances leading up to the issuance of the 1994 GAO Report. But the IRS did defer to CBP. The question is, would the IRS, apparently comfortable with reaching customs valuation law decisions through its unconventional and, frankly, suspect analysis in the Field Service Advice, continue to so defer? One might speculate that the IRS believes that it can avoid having to defer to a CBP determination of nondutiability by not seeking CBP's input. More importantly, did Congress intend that it would be the IRS that would have the last word on dutiability, rather than simply on the income tax effect of dutiable payments? Or did Congress intend the two agencies to "stay inside their own lanes"?

This crucial point of the administrative mandate to the IRS in the marches between customs and tax law has not heretofore been discussed at any length.[334]

[B] Price Changes

Query, what should an importer/taxpayer do if there is an unresolved question about the price for the goods or if there is the possibility that the price might be changed after the importation to realign the price in line with the obligations imposed internally by a transfer pricing policy or externally by an APA or transfer pricing study that has been approved by the tax authority? It is appropriate to explore some options that begin and end with the customs law as it assigns dutiable value to an entry. Specifically, what is the effect of price changes, both upward and downward.

We might start with the general rule for price increases.

[1] General Rule: Price Increases Are Dutiable and Reportable

The general rule is that all price increases are dutiable, and many advisors will express the view that, in any and all circumstances, the importer is obliged to advise the customs authority of any retroactive price increase since it would constitute a revised PAPP, and tender any duty due on the increased amount in a higher price.

[2] Status of One-Time, Post-entry Price Increases

In the US, and potentially in other jurisdictions as well, there may be a little recognized exception to the general rule. For a price increase that was not in the contemplation of the parties at the time of the exportation, the price declared at the time of entry is final, and a retroactive price increase is not dutiable and, thus, is not reportable.

In a 1999 ruling, CBP followed a 1982 ruling in which:

> Customs [had] determined that retroactive price adjustments between related parties agreed to after the merchandise was imported did not affect the transaction value of the imported merchandise. Customs found that, at the time the goods

334. Before ultimately receding, the IRS independently determined in a section 1059A matter that a taxpayer's buying commission payments should be disallowed because, in the IRS view, the payments were dutiable. This determination flew in the face of a CBP ruling on nondutiability. *See* "IRS Concedes § 1059A Issue in Limited," 4 Transfer Pricing 68 (June 7, 1995). In contrast, with 1997 WL 33314783 (IRS FSA) (January 31, 1997), the IRS conferred with CBP on the dutiable status of tooling costs paid by the importer/taxpayer. In another 1997 Field Service Advice, the IRS likewise sought CBP views on the consequences under section 1059A of an exchange rate variation between the amount declared as the customs value and the amount claimed as a tax basis. 1997 FSA Lexis 45 (July 9, 1997).

> were sold for exportation, *the price between the parties was firm and the parties did not intend the price to be subject to an adjustment.* However, due to unforeseen circumstances, i.e., currency fluctuations, the parties agreed to an increase in price. Thus, the price of previous shipped merchandise was retroactively increased. [Ruling no. 542797 (May 19, 1982)] determined that the additional payments represented retroactive adjustments to the agreed price and were not part of the price actually paid or payable[335] (emphasis added).

The key is whether the intention of the parties at the time of the sale was that the sale price be final. That would rule out the situation of an importer who has a transfer pricing policy in place, or an APA, pursuant to which pricing will be reviewed and adjusted as necessary. Such a price is arguably not final at the time of exportation. So, too, would a sales agreement with a price review clause give rise to the potential for a later price adjustment.[336]

But a one-time, stand-alone retroactive price increase, not in the parties' contemplation at the time of the sale, will not be dutiable and might not be reported to CBP and/ potentially, to other customs authorities.[337]

For price decreases, the customs valuation law is onerous, with an importer/taxpayer generally unable to lower the value declared at the time of entry.

[3] Downward Price Adjustments

[a] In General

Curiously, the Valuation Agreement does not directly address the issue of retroactive downward price adjustments.[338] With the notable exception of the previously discussed allowances for price adjustments for defective or out-of-specification goods,[339] the customs valuation law as implemented by the US, and others take the general view that all price decreases after importation are to be disregarded:

> Any rebate of, or other decrease in, the price actually paid or payable that is made or otherwise effected between the buyer and seller after the date of the importation of the merchandise into the United States shall be disregarded in determining the transaction value.[340]

335. Ruling no. 547273 (April 22, 1999).
336. The TCCV was emphatic that a price review clause should not preclude valuation under the transaction value method. TCCV, Com. 4.1, Price Review Clauses (March 1982).
337. Of course, such a price increase might be forced on the parties by a tax examiner. Accordingly, in the US, section 1059A should not be an obstacle to such an upward adjustment.
338. Presumably, the argument could be made that transaction value is based on the PAPP "when sold for export." A retroactive price decrease would be ignored because it had not been agreed at that time. In its various instruments on cash and quantity discounts the TCCV treatments are consistent with that interpretation.
339. *See* Part I, §3.01[H][4].
340. 19 USC § 1401a(b)(4)(B). The legislative history suggests that Congress was concerned with renegotiated, deferred quantity discounts or rebates. HR Rep. No. 317, 96th Cong., 1st Sess. 81 (1979). Accord, Canada and the EU. *See* Customs Memorandum D13-4-3, *Customs Valuation: Price Paid or Payable,* January 7, 2014 (paragraph 18) ("... in accordance with paragraph 48(5)(c) of the [Canada Customs] Act, any rebate or decrease in the price paid or payable

[b] US Practice: Is There a Formula?

The restriction on post-entry price decreases does not depend on liquidation but begins with the date of importation. There is one major exception to the disregard of post-entry price decreases, that of pricing in accordance with a formula:

> In determining transaction value, the price actually paid or payable will be considered without regard to its derivation. It may be the result of discounts, increases, or negotiations, or may be arrived at by the application of a formula, such as the price in effect on the date of export in the London Commodity Market.[341]

For decades, CBP's administrative practice has been to require that the formula be in existence prior to the date of exportation and be based on a future event over which the parties have no control.[342]

With this background, I had long advocated that one solution to the section 1059A adjustment dilemma could be to style a price adjustment mandated by a transfer pricing study as having been the result of a pricing formula. Certainly, there is even greater authority if the adjustments are made by application of an APA. For an APA, whether unilateral or bilateral, the importer/taxpayer has obligated itself—after all, it is a binding contract[343]—to make adjustments for the purpose of aligning its profits so as to meet its income tax responsibilities—section 482 in the US. As a result, and regardless that the original motivation would lie in transfer pricing, the pricing formula: (1) will have been in place prior to exportation, (2) is not subject to revision by the importer/taxpayer, and (3) and cannot be ignored or gainsaid by the importer/taxpayer.[344]

In short, an executed APA is outside the importer/taxpayer's control unless it is felt that the constraints of the transfer pricing methodology or APA protocols can be casually disregarded. A transaction value appraisement might then be set based on the declared value as suitably adjusted pursuant to, and in accordance with, the APA.

The underlying reason why a related party price might be suspect is that it is subject to manipulation—"nonmarket influence"—might be present. That same suspicion is what motivates customs authorities to insist that formula-based pricing be beyond the control of the parties. If a PAPP is based on a valid formula, one that is outside the parties' ability to control, such a PAPP should be acceptable to customs

occurring after importation must be disregarded") and Customs Memorandum D13-4-10, *Price Reductions*, paragraph 4 and Customs Memorandum D13-4-7, *Adjustments to the Price Paid or Payable*, August 29, 2013, paragraph 20; UCC IA, paragraph 130.1 (discounts arising from amendments to the contract subsequent to the time of acceptance of the customs declaration shall not be taken into account).

341. 19 CFR § 152.103(a)(1).

342. *See*, e.g., ruling nos. H012424 (February 3, 2009), 545622 (April 28, 1994) and 543352 (March 30, 1984).

343. *See* above at §10.1[A].

344. CBP requires that a formula be in place prior to the importation, and any future events that are recited in the formula are outside the control of the parties. *See*, e.g., ruling nos. H023813 (December 1, 2008), and rulings cited therein and 545242 (April 16, 1996).

authorities. In COS terms, the parties have treated each other as if they are not related. But CBP did not agree in 2009, still insisting that the normal related party price justification models be applied even if the formula is acceptable.[345] There is no reason, however, why the validity of a PAPP derived from a valid formula, and thus beyond the reach of the parties to manipulate, should not be acceptable. In other words, there is no reason why the importer/taxpayer in such a transaction, whose validity issues from the formula, should be put to the additional task of meeting any other tests.

In fact, with a ruling published in 2012,[346] CBP significantly revised its approach to post-importation price adjustments by following this lead. When certain conditions are met, CBP will take the view that price adjustments taken pursuant to a transfer pricing policy or APA have been made pursuant to an objective formula. CBP has set forth the specific conditions[347] under which the price adjustments might be recognized in a transaction value appraisement.

In order to claim the post-importation adjustments (upward and downward), all of the following five factors must be met:

(1) A written transfer pricing policy in place prior to importation and the policy is prepared taking Internal Revenue Code section 482 into account.
(2) The US taxpayer uses its transfer pricing policy in filing its income tax return, and any adjustments resulting from the transfer pricing policy are reported or used by the taxpayer in filing its income tax return.
(3) The company's transfer pricing policy specifies how the transfer price and any adjustments are determined with respect to all products covered by the transfer pricing policy for which the value is to be adjusted.
(4) The company maintains and provides accounting details from its books and/or financial statements to support the claimed adjustments in the US.
(5) No other conditions exist that may affect the acceptance of the transfer price by CBP.

To be quite clear, CBP has stated:

> if the Importer meets the above referenced factors, CBP will accept the adjusted values, because the prices would be established pursuant to a "formula," even though the prices were not fixed at the time of the importation.

345. Ruling no. W563467 (June 22, 2009) (importer is not correct in its assertion that transaction value must apply if CBP considers the intercompany pricing program to be a formula, absent satisfaction of the COS test or test values tests). The cited authorities did not discuss formula-based pricing, however.
346. Ruling no. W548314 (May 16, 2012) (revoking ruling no. 547654, November 8, 2001). The first published ruling to apply this new policy was ruling no. H219515 (October 11, 2012). This was followed by ruling no. H024857 (January 7, 2014). For a discussion of this then-pending policy change proposal, *see* Neville, "Customs Treatment of Price Reductions Prompted by Transfer Pricing Policies: New Approach Proposed," 22 J. Int'l Tax'n (December 2011) at 17.
347. Ruling no. W548314, at 12-13. For an earlier ruling which had disallowed a price decrease even though it was acknowledged that CBP was considering the "formula" issue, *see* ruling no. H022287 (December 30, 2010).

For those transactions that do not meet all of those precise criteria, CBP may be expected to take the view that the entry is disqualified from a transaction value appraisement because the price might be subject to a condition or consideration for which a value cannot be determined.[348] In such a case, CBP might hold that an alternative basis for appraisement is required and, in so doing, continue to apply the rationale of the 2001 ruling, no. 547654,[349] which has been otherwise revoked by ruling no. W548314. In that 2001 ruling, CBP concluded that the lack of an actual formula for the adjustments precluded pricing formula treatment and ultimately resulted in a "fallback" appraisement based on a modified transaction value. We may conclude that, when formula treatment will be precluded, as when any of the enumerated factors has not been satisfied, the rationale of ruling no. 547654 still has some vitality.

[c] Other Countries

Canada has published a notice[350] that establishes that they, too, will recognize a downward post-importation price adjustment. To be clear, this administrative action was not grounded in a "pricing formula" analysis. It was motivated by a need to recognize the decision in a 2014 Canadian International Trade Tribunal decision, *Hudson's Bay Co. v. President of Canada Border Services Agency* [CBSA], which allowed for such price decreases if there had been an agreement in place between the parties at the time of the importation. To be sure, the *Hudson's Bay* case dealt with agreed-upon price discounts and was not a transfer pricing case with a compensating adjustment. However, the breadth of the decision was such that any agreement between the parties with a pricing effect that was in effect at the time of entry of the goods should be respected by the CBSA. That the Customs Notice specifically recognized price changes arising from transfer pricing agreements between the parties was both entirely consistent with the *Hudson's Bay* case and possibly motivated by an opportunity to go on the record in reference to transfer pricing, on the understanding that such administrative guidance was needed for the proper treatment of compensating adjustments. On the other hand, it could be the case that the CBSA concluded that the *Hudson's Bay* decision left them with no viable way to distinguish price changes arising from transfer pricing agreements.

The UK has also followed the approach of recognizing post-importation price movements, including a statement of its position on "retrospective price adjustments"

348. 19 USC § 1401a(b)(2)(A)(ii).
349. Ruling no. 547654 (November 8, 2001). *See also* ruling no. 563407 (April 13, 2006) (fallback appraisement based on pricing formula). *But see* ruling no. H304841 (April 23, 2021) where transaction value was retained as the basis for customs valuation although CBP denied a sought-after downward adjustment to the PAPP (because the transfer pricing policy was not based on an objective formula, we find no basis upon which to grant the Protestant's request to reconcile the transaction value initially declared).
350. Customs Notice 15-001, accessible at http://www.cbsa-asfc.gc.ca/publications/cn-ad/cn15-001-eng.html.

in a general notice to importers.[351] This method does not follow the "formula-based" US approach, but the following excerpt will show the utility of its "provisional pricing" construct:

> Where, at the time of entry, there are contractual arrangements in place between you and the seller indicating the possibility of retrospective price adjustments, the invoice price for the goods concerned would, in effect, be provisional.
>
> This means that you cannot arrive at a final value for Customs Duty at the time of entry. Therefore you should make security arrangements (see paragraph 2.5). Alternatively you can ask us to agree to an arrangement whereby you can pay customs duty outright at the time of entry. Such an arrangement would involve you giving an undertaking to notify us of any price adjustments. Then we would both adjust the Customs Duty payable upwards or downwards as appropriate, according to any agreed price adjustments subsequently notified.
>
> Where there has been a retrospective price increase, we will treat this as part of the total payment made by you to the seller for the imported goods. The fact that you agree to pay such a price increase is regarded as confirmation that the contractual arrangements implied or there was an implicit understanding between you and the seller that such an adjustment may occur, when the goods were ordered or purchased. Thus we will issue a demand (form C18) to you for the arrears of Customs Duty.
>
> Where there has been a retrospective price decrease you may submit a claim for a refund of duty. Your claim must be accompanied by appropriate evidence including full details of the contractual arrangements as well as rebates received from and credits notes issued by the seller.
>
> The key item of evidence is the contract between you and the seller.
>
> * * *

Australia's issuance in 2013 of its Practice Statement had the effect of promulgating a three-year program under which ACBPS was to treat retroactive price adjustments equally, such that price increases must give rise to additional duty payments and price decreases may support a refund of duties.[352]

In the case of Mexico, the practice is to permit aggregate reporting for upward adjustments, but entry-by-entry reporting is required for downward adjustments. Finally, in the case of the EU, Italy allows the use of provisional pricing with advance approval and many countries allow for informal understandings with the customs authorities whereby provisional pricing at entry is permitted, but we are left to wonder if these will survive a roll out of the new Union Customs Code.

In a startling move, the European Court of Justice issued a decision in December 2017 that had the effect of precluding a transaction value appraisement where there

351. This is at point 30.3 of HMRC, General Notice 252 (July 1, 2013), available at https://www.gov.uk/government/publications/notice-252-valuation-of-imported-goods-for-customs-purposes-vat-and-trade-statistics.

352. Paragraphs 1.6.1 and 1.6.2, respectively, of Valuation-Transfer Pricing Policy Practice Statement B_IND 08 (April 12, 2013), accessible at http://www.border.gov.au/Importingandbuyinggoodsfromoverseas/Documents/B_IND08Valuation-TransferPricingPolicy.pdf#search=Transfer%20Pricing%20Practice%20Statement. *See also* n. 10 above.

was a transfer pricing review and potential for a retroactive pricing adjustment.[353] In the *Hamamatsu* case, the First Chamber of the ECJ held that, as a matter of law, for a price declared at importation that is subject to review and adjustment through application of an Advance Pricing Agreement (APA) (and, by extension, to any transfer pricing policy), a transaction value appraisement is not available.

This marks a radical departure from the trend that is reflected in the other jurisdictions just noted. It stands as the only expression of the notion that the possibility of TP adjustments would throw the customs valuation process out of transaction value, save the 1994 and 1995 expressions from the US customs authorities, cited in note 314, which were outliers that were never followed.

But regardless whether the adjustment is mandated by a transfer pricing methodology or a formalized APA, and regardless whether the adjustment is accommodated within a transaction value appraisement or a fallback appraisement based on transaction value or deductive value, the practical result should be the same. The adjustment should be taken into account and not disregarded. Another perspective is that, for importers/taxpayers who are applying a transfer pricing policy or are subject to an APA, prices declared at entry are in all instances provisional only, as they are subject to review and possible later adjustment.

A particularly vexing problem arises in some developing country jurisdictions which treat compensating adjustments as violations of the customs law. In those jurisdictions, the importer is seen as having declared a customs value that was false or misleading. The fact that this flies in the face of there having been almost two decades of discussions at the TCCV on the interplay of related party pricing and transfer pricing, with ample focus upon the need for and the role of compensating adjustments, is especially galling. Thankfully such a benighted view is absent from many jurisdictions.

In the US, given the effect of liquidation, it is difficult to imagine that a US importer/taxpayer faced with the prospect of a certain transfer pricing review and possible compensating adjustment[354] would consciously allow a dutiable value declared at entry to proceed to liquidation. Liquidation makes it far more difficult to make the compensating adjustments, for both customs and section 1059A purposes. For that reason, delaying liquidation is the optimum vehicle to allow for compensating adjustments to be made based on a "formula."

Alternatively, permitting the customs value to be reopened may be a good backup strategy.

353. Case C-529/16, *Hamamatsu Photonics Deutschland GmbH v. Hauptzollamt Munchen*, 20.12.2017, ECLI:EU:C:2017:984. A further analysis of the decision and its potential impact is found at Neville, "European Court: Transfer Pricing Adjustments Derail Transaction Value," 29 J. Int'l Tax'n (March 2018) at 25.

354. A "compensating adjustment" is a transfer pricing term of art referring to the report by a taxpayer of a transfer price for tax purposes that is, in the taxpayer's opinion, an arm's-length price for a controlled transaction even though this price differs from the amount actually charged between the associated enterprises. OECD Guidelines Glossary definition and paragraph 4.38. In the United States, the Treasury regulations anticipate that this self-initiated adjustment needs to "true up" the pricing to the arm's-length standard to be made with the tax return. Treas. Reg. § 1.482-1(a)(3). Other OECD members do not recognize compensating adjustments that they term as "notional," so care must be taken to avoid double taxation.

[4] *Strategies to Change Declared Customs Value in the US*

The customs law proceeds on the basis of importers filing their entry documents and tendering estimated customs within ten working days of entry,[355] but, as discussed, the entry and its constituent elements, such as dutiable value, are not final until "liquidation." Since 1997 the CBP administrative practice has been to liquidate 314 days after entry. With the additional 180-day post-liquidation protest period, the importer/taxpayer, in theory, has approximately sixteen and one-half months after entry of the goods within which to revise its dutiable value upward. After that point, with no other event, such as a protest, the importer is "stuck" with a final customs value for the purposes of section 1059A.

[a] *Delay of Liquidation*

The importer/taxpayer can delay liquidation by means of reconciliation or the withholding of liquidation.

Reconciliation. A dilemma for the importer might arise at the very outset of the administrative process, when he is called on to enter a declared value with the final price for the goods still unresolved. First promulgated by Congress in 1993, reconciliation is an administrative program that allows an importer to file a custom entry while some key elements might be unresolved.[356] As a result, liquidation of the entry as to those open issues is pushed back beyond the normal date range. In short, the customs reconciliation program allows an importer to make entry while some key elements might be unresolved. The four elements that are eligible for reconciliation are classification, valuation, eligibility under the USMCA and several other FTAs that are covered in 19 USC § 1520(d), and assembly abroad.[357] The remainder of the entry will become liquidated on schedule but, except for the USMCA and other FTA issues, the "flagged" elements will remain open for a period extending up to twenty-one months[358] after the flagging at entry.

Reconciliation was not a response by Congress to any concern from CBP or the trade community about transfer pricing adjustments. Instead, there had been an administrative practice along the Southern border called "block liquidation." The practice grew in the days before NAFTA as a result of large numbers of entries for which dutiable value at the time of customs entry was not yet settled. This was because

355. 19 CFR § 142.12(b), unless the importer has opted for filing on a monthly payment basis under the Automated Clearing House (ACH) protocol under 19 CFR §§ 24.3 and 24.25.

356. *See* CBP, Reconciliation External Guidance, ver. 2.0, Pub. No. 1197-0820 (August 2020), available at https://www.cbp.gov/sites/default/files/assets/documents/2020-Aug/RECONCILIATION%20EXTERNAL%20GUIDANCE-updated.pdf.

357. "Assembly abroad" refers to the partial duty exemption available for the foreign assembly of goods with some or all US fabricated components. Normally this is covered in subheading 9802.00.80, HTSUS. This would be considered an "outward processing" program. In fact, the reconciliation program embraces three distinct item numbers—9802.00.60 (further processing of metal articles), 9802.00.80 (general assembly abroad provision) and 9802.00.91 (assembly of textiles and apparel in Mexico), HTSUS.

358. Formerly fifteen months, amended in 2004 to apply to entries made after February 9, 2005.

many of the entries were of goods that had been manufactured in Mexican maquiladoras on a "production cost plus a markup" basis, and the final production costs could not be ascertained until the close of the accounting period, which usually occurred post-importation.[359] In this situation, where there were multiple entries over the course of the year, the common practice was for all but a few entries to be liquidated as entered, say at an estimated value of USD 5.00 per unit, with the importer catching up to the final "true up" or reconciliation to account for the aggregated duties owed on the few open entries, for example, at a declared value of USD 100.00 per unit. The importers and most CBP officials at the border were quite content with the block liquidation program, as the proper duties were ultimately paid in full measure, but CBP Headquarters saw it as wildly skewing the system and convinced Congress to amend the law by providing for reconciliation in the Customs Modernization Act in 1993.[360]

Knowing that the customs value is subject to review and possible revisions, the importer can tender an estimated duty but leave the appraisement in an open or "pending" status for up to twenty-one months. CBP will also liquidate the reconciled entries but the typical 314-day cycle will not apply.[361] Depending on port practice and administrative work load, CBP will typically liquidate from anywhere between a few weeks to seven or eight months.

CBP has acknowledged that reconciliation entries are identical to consumption entries for legal purposes.[362] Accordingly, liquidation may be withheld or extended for up to an additional three years.[363] After liquidation, the standard 180-day period before the liquidation becomes final will apply. In the aggregate, assuming three months to liquidation, the liquidation of a reconciled entry will not become final for a total period of some thirty months before section 1059A attaches to a final customs value. If the time for liquidation is extended, a final customs value would be at a full sixty-three months (twenty-one months to reconciliation plus thirty-six months to liquidation, plus six months for the liquidation to become final) from entry.

As noted, prior to this 1998 reconciliation program, in 1995, CBP first proposed a reconciliation that was limited to self-initiated transfer pricing adjustments.[364] Given the legislative history of reconciliation, which was not focused on transfer pricing, one

359. This was the factual circumstance that gave rise to the computed value appraisements that figured in the import transactions under review in the GAO Report on section 1059A.
360. 19 USC § 1484(b) added by Customs Modernization Act, Pub. L. No. 103-182, tit. VI, § 637(a), 107 Stat. 2200 (1993). The customs regulations do not yet include procedures for reconciliation. Useful information is available at CBP's website www.cbp.gov/xp/cgov/trade/trade[low bar]programs/reconciliation/participate.xml.
361. Current administrative practice at CBP has been for a "one touch" approach which shortens this 314-day period. Thus, if CBP issues a CF 28 Request for Information, CBP will liquidate the entry as soon as the response is filed rather than awaiting the 314-day liquidation cycle to run its course.
362. Ruling no. H078555 (December 18, 2009).
363. A reconciliation entry will liquidate by operation of law on the fourth anniversary of the reconciliation filing. 19 USC § 1504(b); 19 CFR §§ 159.12(e) and (f). Note that if not extended, the reconciled entry will be deemed liquidated after one year from filing. 19 USC § 1504(a)(1)(D); *see also Ford Motor Co. v. United States*, Slip Op. 10-80 (CIT 2010) in 44 Cust. Bull. & Dec. No. 32, at 29 (August 11, 2010).
364. 60 Fed. Reg. 35,105 (July 5, 1995).

can surmise that the 1995 proposal was based on the twin 1994 events already discussed—the GAO Report and the addition of self-initiated adjustments to the transfer pricing regulations. Apparently, there were no applicants for the program.[365] There were two troublesome aspects of the proposal. First, it was limited to upward adjustments only, which would be faithful to its limited purpose of accommodating income tax transfer pricing adjustments in a section 1059A context, but that deviated from congressional intent in leaving valuation open and fluid for both upward and downward adjustment through reconciliation. The second problem was that CBP viewed an importer's upward adjustment as evidence that the relationship had influenced the PAPP. This would require a disallowance of a transaction value appraisement, although the "fallback" method of appraisement would be tantamount to the after-adjustment price.[366] In its 2007 ICP: Related Party Transactions, CBP carefully skirted this issue:

> This ICP does not address the applicability of transaction value when the related party price is subject to adjustment after importation or the proper treatment of post-importation adjustments in the determination of transaction value.[367]

Of course, there is no reason why an importer/taxpayer would not be able to avail itself of reconciliation, holding liquidation of the dutiable value in abeyance while the adjustments to price are calculated and applied.

[b] Withholding of Liquidation

The US customs law provides for a second means of delaying liquidation. As an alternative to reconciliation, which remains a voluntary program, the importer/taxpayer has the option of requesting that the time for liquidation be extended for one-year periods.[368] The importer/taxpayer will need to show good cause, which criterion is met if the importer satisfies the port director that more time is needed to present to CBP information that will affect pending action, or if there is a similar question under review by CBP. It is also possible that the importer/taxpayer might argue that information needed by CBP for appraisement is not available. As has been

365. *See* Offerman, "The Effect of Customs Reconciliation on Taxable Income," 25 Brook. J. Int'l L. 693, 718 & n. 219 (1999). The initial lack of participation is attributable in large measure to the September 5, 1995, announcement that participants were required to enroll before October 2, 1995—a scant three weeks. Subsequently, CBP reopened the enrollment up to May 1, 1996. 60 Fed. Reg. 64,470 (December 15, 1995).
366. 60 Fed. Reg. 35,105-35,106 (July 5, 1995). There had been an earlier ruling, no. 545481 (September 14, 1994), which described how a "special fund" was set up by the parties to implement price adjustments in order to adjust ABC's profit and thereby satisfy concerns raised by the Internal Revenue Service (IRS) under section 482 of the Internal Revenue. The importer did not demonstrate that this is the manner in which the related party seller settles prices with unrelated buyers, nor that this method of setting prices is consistent with the normal pricing practices of the industry. Transaction value was disallowed. The use of a "special fund" speaks to the early time frame for this transfer pricing program.
367. ICP: Related Party Transactions, at n. 1.
368. 19 USC § 1504(b); 19 CFR § 159.12.

noted, up to three one-year extensions may be granted.[369] Depending on when the initial request has been made, this leaves open the possibility that the importer/taxpayer may have close to four years before liquidation occurs.

[c] Reopening or Revising Customs Value

Once an entry is liquidated, the importer/taxpayer may yet be able to revise the customs value regardless of, or perhaps fully consonant with, any strictures of section 1059A.

Protests. While it is preferable to resolve these valuation issues prior to liquidation attaching, the customs law permits an importer/taxpayer to protest a final administrative decision by CBP (i.e., one that has ripened to liquidation status). A timely protest prevents a liquidated customs value from becoming finalized.[370]

The first strategy open to the importer/taxpayer saddled with a liquidated entry may be to file a protest. In the case of a retroactive upward price adjustment, the importer would be looking to make a payment to CBP. Absent any further factors, this alone should be no occasion to file a Prior Disclosure as there would have been no violation to disclose because the importer would be merely "doing the right thing" to report the correct value information and paying the correct duty. The importer might simply reveal the underlying facts and make a voluntary tender of the additional duty owed but that would not revise the customs value.

Rather than simply making a voluntary tender, however, the US importer/taxpayer might seek to avoid being whipsawed by section 1059A—saddled with a COGS based upon the original price after having increased that price with the tender. In that case, the importer might try to file a protest. There is a statutory basis precluding such a protest, however, with the text of section 1514 referring to a final CBP determination that was "adverse to the importer." CBP's administrative practice, following the statue, prevents the filing of a protest from increasing dutiable value as the liquidated value and the duties owed amount were lower than those sought by the importer/protestant and, therefore, CBP's determination at liquidation was not adverse to the importer.[371]

That practice is based on questionable authority, and the practice has never been tested in court. The earliest such ruling[372] applies dictum from a Federal Circuit decision to the effect that Congress had not provided for a refund mechanism to redress errors in the government's favor analogous to the importer's since-repealed 19 USC

369. This four-year mark corresponds to the customs statute that entries are deemed liquidated by operation of law four years after the date of entry. 19 USC § 1504(b); 19 CFR § 159.12(f).
370. 19 USC § 1514(a). Likewise, Post Summary Corrections (PSCs) serve as pre-liquidation amendments to the customs entry and allow the declared value to be increased or decreased.
371. *See*, e.g., ruling nos. 228838 (September 27, 2002), 228570 (December 10, 2001). CBP has also determined that an importer could not file a petition under 19 USC § 1520(c) for a price increase because the importer had suffered no injury or damage under the customs laws even when the importer sought to avoid adverse income tax liability. Ruling no. 222981 (July 1, 1991).
372. Ruling no. 220678 (August 23, 1989).

§ 1520(c).[373] While it is true that the government can revise a liquidation only by means of either a timely reliquidation or under 19 USC § 1592(d), that curb on the government's right to take action should not be applied to the importer's right to file a timely protest.

As seen, CBP practice is to allow PSCs to increase dutiable value. It might be argued that liquidation should not close off that right to amend the entry in the government's favor. It might also be argued that the term "adverse to the importer" should be read broadly enough to embrace a protest filed to ensure that the correct, as adjusted final PAPP and the corresponding increased duty payment were properly submitted to CBP to avoid exposure to civil penalties under section 1592 or other enforcement measures. To be sure, a prior disclosure could be filed and a tender of the proper duties submitted, but that route is based upon an acknowledged violation. As noted above, there is no evidence of any such qualifying violation save the failure to report the price change.

If an importer were to file a protest, the protest might allege that the declared customs value was based on a simple clerical error in the entry. Because section 1520(c), the procedural route to correct clerical errors and mistakes of fact, was repealed in 2004,[374] importers are left with the option to: (i) file PSCs in the case of entries that have not yet been set for liquidation or have not yet liquidated or (ii) file protests when those entries have liquidated.[375] Therefore, any such filing, and especially that of a protest for further review by Headquarters, will be closely scrutinized. One importer was unsuccessful in lodging its protest, which was based on an alleged clerical error in transcribing the correct transfer prices, because CBP determined that it had failed to provide sufficient information.[376] The importer had produced documents to indicate that there was a change in the calculated transfer price, but no explanation was provided as to how the unit price changed, what the original and correct values were, or why the adjusted transfer pricing value was preferable.

Of course, in addition to protests to increase dutiable value—if that were deemed allowable—the importer/taxpayer might want to protest a CBP determination on dutiable value that included an amount that the importer/taxpayer will argue is nondutiable. For instance, the dutiable value at liquidation might have included an amount that the importer/taxpayer contends is not a dutiable royalty or assist or dutiable under any other customs valuation principle. The importer/taxpayer will argue, of course, that he should be allowed to downwardly adjust his dutiable value for customs purposes and seek a refund by the filing of a timely protest and also be able to sustain his "customs value" for the purposes of section 1059A at an adjusted value that is based on the lowered customs value plus an upward adjustment of the nondutiable payment.

---

373. *Omni U.S.A., Inc. v. United States*, 840 F2d 912, 914 (Fed. Cir. 1988).
374. 19 USC § 1520(c), repealed by Pub. L. No. 108-429, Title II, § 2105, Act of December 3, 2004.
375. Because PSCs must be filed on an entry-by-entry basis, while protests can be filed against multiple entries at the same port or at the Center of Excellence and Expertise (CEE), some importers and their advisors will prefer to await liquidation of the entries to file a many-to-one protest.
376. Ruling no. H287403 (January 18, 2018).

Once a protest is filed, customs law generally gives CBP up to two years to decide a protest.[377] Because of the chronology inherent in the customs law procedures, it is entirely possible that an importer/taxpayer will have the ability to make an adjustment to customs value because that customs value is not yet "final," within the following timetable:

- Date of Entry.
- Liquidation: 314 days later.
- Protest: 180 days later.
- Decision on protest: Up to two years or more later.

This adds up to over forty months from the date of the original entry. Moreover, if the protest is denied, customs law grants the importer/taxpayer six months after the date of the denial of the protest within which to file a summons for judicial review by the CIT.[378]

During all of this time—including the additional time before the CIT—the liquidation of the entry is held in abeyance and is not final. Section 1059A and its imposed stop-action effect will thus not apply. The importer/taxpayer can adjust the customs value freely at any point from the date of entry to the point of closure (i.e., the date of the decision on the protest) or, if the dutiable value is under review in the CIT, the date on which finality attaches to any judgment of the CIT (i.e., appeal to the Federal Circuit is not sought within sixty days after the CIT decision).[379]

Apart from section 1059A, is there any other role for customs valuation in an income tax transfer price determination?

§10.06 GENERAL ROLE OF INCOME TAX TRANSFER PRICING STUDIES IN CUSTOMS VALUATION

At this time, section 1059A appears to be unique. There is no other income tax legislation at the national level with the same effect (i.e., setting the role of a value, previously declared for customs purposes in a related party transaction, in allocating income for the purposes of levying an income tax). Neither section 482 nor the implementing regulations specifically assign a role to customs valuation in the context of a transfer pricing method.

At the international level, the OECD Guidelines do make specific reference to customs valuation within the presentation of the arm's-length principle.[380] The OECD observes, *inter alia*, that:

377. 19 USC § 1515(a).
378. 28 USC § 2636. The customs law also creates an opportunity for an importer/taxpayer to request that a protest denial be voided where the protest was denied contrary to instructions (e.g., when action on the protest should have been suspended). 19 USC § 1515(d).
379. 28 USC § 2107.
380. OECD Guidelines, paragraphs 1.157-1.158.

> Valuation methods for customs purposes ... may not be aligned with the OECD's recognised transfer pricing methods. That being said, customs valuations may be useful to tax administrations in evaluating the arm's length character of a controlled transaction transfer price and vice versa. In particular, customs officials may have contemporaneous documentation regarding the transaction that could be relevant for transfer pricing purposes, especially if prepared by the taxpayer, while tax authorities may have transfer pricing documentation which provides detailed information on the circumstances of the transaction.
>
> * * *
>
> Cooperation between income tax and customs administrations within a country in evaluating transfer prices is becoming more common and this should help to reduce the number of cases where customs valuations are found unacceptable for tax purposes or vice versa.[381]

At the WCO's TCCV, the issue of the use of a transfer pricing study for customs valuation in related party transactions was the subject of a 2010 instrument, Commentary 23.1,[382] which noted that such a study might be "a good source of information," with the exhortation (in paragraph 9) that transfer pricing studies as a means of examining the COS of an import transaction should be examined on a case-by-case basis. The TCCV has considered two hypothetical studies as illustrations of this principle.

The first was a hypothetical case in which the facts recited that the customs authorities made use of a TP study based on the TNMM method in examining customs value in a related party context. After much deliberation and careful shepherding by the Chair, the TCCV adopted an instrument, Case Study 14.1, at its April 2016 session which serves as the practical example of the principle that had been set out in Commentary 23.1.[383] A transfer pricing study as well as additional information on operating expenses was analyzed, and the conclusion was that the relationship between the parties did not influence the price.

The second instrument, Case Study 14.2, was adopted in 2017. It concerns the use of a TP study that was based on the resale price method.[384] The facts presented were quite extraordinary, in that the importer's TP policy called for compensating adjustments to be made when the importer/buyer showed profit levels that were outside the targeted interquartile range of gross margins, but those adjustments were not made. The facts stated were silent, but perhaps the only reason why the price adjustments would not have been made, after having been specifically provided for, is because the authorities in the county of importation would not permit them to be made, perhaps for restrictions on capital outflows. The issue for determination which we might paraphrase as "could the TP Report provide information for the customs authority to conclude whether the PAPP was influenced by the relationship?" was

381. *Ibid.*
382. TCCV, Com. 23.1, Examination of the Expression "Circumstances of Sale" Under Article 1.2(A) in Relation to the Use of Transfer Pricing Studies (October 2010).
383. TCCV, CS 14.1, Use of Transfer Pricing Documentation When Examining Related Party Transactions Under Article 1.2(A) of the Agreement (April 2016).
384. TCCV, CS 14.2, Use of Transfer Pricing Documentation When Examining Related Party Transactions Under Article 1.2 (a) of the Agreement (October 2017).

implicitly answered affirmatively. The conclusion stated that the customs authority had concluded that the declared import price was not settled in a manner consistent with the normal pricing practices of the industry and thus had been influenced by the parties' relationship. One comment is that the factual recitation did not establish that there was a manner for settling prices in a particular manner within that industry. This is a preliminary matter that CBP will focus on if the importer seeks to validate its declared PAPP on the basis of this COS exemplar.[385]

We still await a TCCV instrument which illustrates the opposite result, i.e., a TP Report effectuating a TP policy or an APA providing support for the customs authority to conclude that the price had not been influenced by the parties' relationship and the declared PAPP was acceptable when there had been a compensating adjustment.

WCO Guide

Under the auspices of its Revenue Package,[386] the WCO published a Guide to Customs Valuation and Transfer Pricing (2018 ed.).

ICC Policy Statement

It is also important to note that the International Chamber of Commerce has issued a 2015 revised Policy Statement[387] on the use of transfer pricing studies in customs valuation. It is fitting that the Policy Statement was prepared jointly by the Commission on Taxation and the Commission on Customs and Trade Facilitation. The ICC calls for greater alignment between the two disciplines and makes several concrete proposals to harmonize the processes.

The ICC made six proposals:

1. Recognition by the customs administration that businesses which establish prices between related parties in accordance with the arm's-length principle (as per Article 9 of the OECD Model Tax Convention) have *generally* demonstrated that the relationship of the parties has not influenced the price paid or payable under the transaction value basis of appraisement, and consequently the prices establish the basis for customs value (emphasis added).
2. Recognition by the customs administration of post-transaction transfer pricing adjustments (upward or downward). This recognition should be applicable for adjustments made either as a result of a voluntary compensating adjustment—as agreed upon by the two related parties—or as a result of a tax audit.
3. It is recommended that in the event of post-transaction transfer pricing adjustments (upward or downward), customs administrations accede to review the customs value according to either of the two following methods as

385. *See*, e.g., ruling no. H260036 (February 24, 2015) (the Importer/Buyer must have objective evidence of the normal pricing practices of the industry in question and present evidence that the transfer price is settled in accordance with these industry pricing practices).
386. The Revenue Package was initiated by the WCO as a response to Members' concerns over declining revenue returns in the face of the global economic downturn, following the WCO Council's Resolution in June 2009.
387. Transfer Pricing and Customs Valuation—2015. The Policy Statement is reproduced as Annex VI to the WCO Guide.

selected by the importer: application of a weighted average duty rate, or an allocation according to specific codes of the customs tariff nomenclature.

4. It is recommended that in the case of post-transaction transfer pricing adjustment (upward or downward), companies be relieved from:
   a) The obligation to submit an amended declaration for each initial customs declaration.
   b) The payment of penalties, as variations of the transfer price.
5. It is recommended that customs administrations recognize that functions and risks undertaken by the parties as documented in a transfer pricing study following an OECD transfer pricing methodology are crucial to the economic assessment of the circumstances of the sale.
6. Recognition of the acceptability of relevant transfer pricing documentation by the customs administration as evidence that the price paid for imported goods was not influenced by the relationship of the parties.

You will have noted that Proposal 1 stops short of positing that a TP that has been set in line with the OECD Guidelines must be accepted as having met the customs valuation test, i.e., establishing that the relationship of the parties has not influenced the PAPP. In fact, Proposal 6 is in perfect harmony with the less decisive position advanced by Commentary 23.1.

You will also have noted the aspirational nature of some of these proposals; *see* especially Proposal 3.

The ICC Policy Statement is due for an updating—it will be interesting to see what will be forthcoming.

[A] Use of Transfer Pricing Materials in Validating a Dutiable Value

[1] In General

Like the prevailing CBP administrative position on the customs law validation tests and the CBP expectations of what documentation will be expected, discussed above,[388] CBP has expressed its views on the relevance of APAs and transfer pricing studies for customs valuation.

As noted, the section 1059A regulations establish that a customs value is not binding on the IRS.[389] For its part, CBP is equally adamant that IRS approval of a transfer pricing study will not close out CBP's inquiry into transfer pricing for customs valuation. Merely because an importer has entered into an APA or has undertaken a transfer pricing study will not obviate the need for the importer to secure CBP's own validation of the transfer price.

As discussed, CBP's position on the acceptability of APAs and transfer pricing studies is as follows:

> [T]he mere fact that an importer provides CBP with an APA or transfer pricing study is not sufficient to establish that a related party transaction value is

388. *See* above §10.03; *see also* ICP: Related Party Transactions, at 9-10 and ruling nos. H238027 (February 19, 2015) and H228298 (June 13, 2014) and H029658 (December 8, 2009).
389. Treas. Reg. § 1.1059A-1(c)(7).

> acceptable. The importer must provide information and evidence regarding the circumstances of sale and/or test values. If the importer believes that information in an APA or transfer pricing study and/or in the supporting documentation is relevant to the application of the circumstances of sale test, the importer should identify that information, explain why it is relevant, and submit the relevant documentation to CBP.[390]

There is at least one seemingly isolated incident of a ruling in which CBP has set an even more limited role for section 482 documentation—that it must have been used to set the related party price.[391] In yet another ruling,[392] the fact that the TP Study had not been reviewed by the IRS was a negative factor in CBP determining that the importer did not satisfy the "normal pricing practices of the industry" test.

CBP notes that while the broad goals of both the relevant provisions of the customs and tax laws are the same—to ensure that related party transactions are at arm's length—there are substantial differences in the legal requirements. CBP contrasts the customs law need to determine a value for each imported article and to determine the acceptability of transaction value on a product-specific basis with the section 482 allocation of income, which does not necessarily require a valuation of each transaction.[393]

But while it is true that section 482 is primarily concerned with income allocation, the income tax regulations are clear that the transfer pricing methods are generally stated in terms of individual transactions. Those regulations recognize that it would simply be impractical to analyze every individual transaction and, as a result, it is permissible to evaluate the arm's-length result by applying the appropriate methods to the overall results for product lines or other groupings. Sampling and other valid statistical techniques may also be employed to evaluate the arm's-length results of all related party transactions.[394] CBP also reserves the right to base its findings of dutiable value on estimates.

CBP also notes that there are differences in the transfer pricing methods. While recognizing that there are similarities between the traditional transaction methods (CUP, RPM, and cost plus, which are not specifically identified as such by CBP) and the customs methods, CBP states summarily that they are not the same. Next, without any comparative analysis of the transaction methods, CBP observes that CPM has little similarity to the customs methods, as it is typically based on a functional analysis only, without a hard application of a product similarity stricture. CBP emphasizes that product similarity ("class or kind of merchandise," the product factor in the "industry in question," and identical or similar merchandise standards of the test value) is required for the customs methods. CBP has based its view that an importer/taxpayer's

390. ICP: Related Party Transactions, at 16. It bears repetition that the congruence of Com. 23.1 (*see especially* paragraph 8) and the ICP is readily apparent.
391. Ruling no. H016585 (December 30, 2008) ("we caution that documentation in support of the arm's length nature of a transaction should be contemporaneous with the transaction and that an analysis on an Internal Revenue Code ('IRC') method is only valid where it is used to set the price").
392. Ruling no. H314296 (August 12, 2021).
393. ICP: Related Party Transactions, at 14.
394. Treas. Reg. § 1.482-1(f)(2)(iv).

transfer pricing for tax purposes is not determinative on the basis of these distinctions.[395]

Indeed, in a further application of these precepts, CBP, in a 2009 ruling, rejected a CPM transfer pricing study that was based on a set of twenty-one functionally equivalent companies.[396] The importer was an exclusive distributor of motor vehicles, and the functionally equivalent companies were wholesalers of durable goods. Because of the failure to meet the "class or kind" criterion, neither of the COS tests of pricing in line with industry standards, nor "all cost plus a profit," discussed above, was satisfied. Nonetheless, and this is the especially important lesson, even though the specific COS tests were not met, CBP considered that the information presented gave insight into how the automobile industry determines the price. The buyer's overall profit experience was one of the factors that may be considered to indicate that the relationship between the buyer and the seller did not influence the price. CBP actually accepted the aggregated profitability data inherent in a CPM in the particular circumstances presented in that ruling request. There was no need to further break down the profitability into product line details. CBP felt that the information submitted to the IRS was important, as was the fact that the information was subject to scrutiny in the context of a bilateral APA process. The foreign tax authority review that characterizes the bilateral APA process was a significant factor, as was the rigorous negotiations between the buyer and seller and a background paper that had been prepared by an accounting firm that described the industry pricing practices. These other factors were also helpful in leading CBP to determine, based on a "review and examination of all relevant aspects of the transaction," that the price had not been influenced by the relationship for the purposes of the COS test. By examining the way in which the buyer and seller organized their commercial relations and the way in which the price in question was arrived at, in actuality, CBP was applying the general COS test. The overall facts in that general test analysis outweighed the importer's inability to meet the specific COS exemplars.

CBP followed the important precedent of ruling no. H029658, allowing that the COS test was met despite the fact that no specific exemplar was satisfied, in a 2012 ruling, H219515.[397] In this ruling, the importer was able to rely upon transfer pricing studies using a CPM method in its successful showing that the price had not been influenced by the relationship.

This result is consistent with the CBP acknowledgment that in some cases the underlying facts and conclusions in an APA or a transfer pricing study may contain some relevant information about the COS. CBP has stated that the weight accorded to APA or transfer pricing studies will depend on the circumstances and method. CBP has signaled that the CUP has the most relevance for customs valuation purposes and, despite the result of ruling no. H029658, CPM's overall profit comparison has the least

395. ICP: Related Party Transactions, at 15.
396. Ruling no. H029658 (December 9, 2009). *See also* a more recent ruling, no. H310087 (March 18, 2022).
397. Ruling no. H219515 (October 11, 2012). *See also* ruling nos. H238027 (February 19, 2015), H228298 (June 13, 2014) and H029658 (December 8, 2009).

relevance.[398] The CPM is the prevalent transfer pricing method used by US taxpayers. The IRS annual report for 2008 on the APA program reveals that CPM was overwhelmingly used by taxpayers for transfers of tangible and intangible property—in eighty-seven covered transactions, using various PLIs—while CUP was used in six or fewer cases.[399]

Moreover, if an importer/taxpayer wants to make use of an APA or transfer pricing study, it is incumbent on the importer/taxpayer to identify the submitted information, explain why it is relevant, and submit supporting documentation to CBP, as CBP ended by warning that:

> [i]f the importer simply submits a copy of an APA or transfer pricing study without further explanation and documentation, the circumstances of sale claim will be rejected.[400]

In another ruling, CBP approved the use of a transfer pricing study based on the RPM.[401] The importer/taxpayer, Cardinal Health, was a distributor of medical devices. There was no APA and, consequently, no IRS approval and acceptance of the RPM. But the importer/taxpayer's gross margin was tested against those earned on its resales of third-party medical products (internal comparables) and on resales by comparable distributors of medical devices of third-party medical products (external comparables). CBP observed that the set of six comparable companies that was ultimately selected was composed of direct competitors of Cardinal Health and the products fell within the arc of the same "class or kind" criterion.

CBP again noted that the transfer pricing study by itself was not sufficient to show that the price was an acceptable basis for a TV appraisement, but again went on to state that such a study might contain relevant information. The importer/taxpayer presented information in the transfer pricing study that satisfied CBP that the price was settled in a manner consistent with the normal pricing practice of the industry. A comparison of the importer/taxpayer's gross margin was within the interquartile range of the external comparables. The internal comparables' comparison revealed that it earned less gross margin on resales of third-party products, but that was because it bore the burden of additional marketing and distribution activities for the related party sales.

With lines that track the regulations,[402] CBP concluded that it had examined all relevant aspects of the transaction, including the way in which the parties had organized their commercial relations, as well as the way in which the price in question was arrived at by the parties. The importer/taxpayer had demonstrated that the price had not been influenced by the relationship.

With all that it said in the 2007 ICP, CBP did not discuss any of the reasons why the traditional transaction methods are not acceptable, and merely noted in a conclusory fashion that they are "not the same" (i.e., identical to the customs methods). An

398. ICP: Related Party Transactions, at 15-16.
399. IRS, 2008 APA Statutory Rep. (Ann. 2009-28, 2009-15 IRB 760).
400. ICP: Related Party Transactions, at 16.
401. Ruling no. H037375 (December 11, 2009).
402. 19 CFR § 152.103(l)(1)(i). The parallel reference at the international level is Valuation Agreement, Interpretative Note, Article 1, Paragraph 2, points 2 and 3.

importer/taxpayer may want to emphasize their decided similarity and base a validation for customs purposes on a traditional transaction method, suitably adjusted to account for any differences arising from the special demands of the customs valuation law, such as the need to account for dutiable assists or some RLFs.

As for the profit-based methods, there is no reason why they should be discounted out of hand if APAs or transfer pricing studies employing them have been built on sufficient product similarity bases. Clearly, any CBP reluctance to accept the APAs or transfer pricing studies will have far less force if there is a high degree of product similarity. Moreover, it might be possible to use those profit-based transfer pricing methods, such as TNMM, that yield reliable results even absent a high degree of product comparability. Indeed, several of the customs valuation tests to validate transfer pricing require profit analysis. These are the "all costs plus a profit" and both computed and deductive values. In fact, what has been overlooked by those who would disregard the profit methods that are used in satisfying the income tax authorities that a transfer price is acceptable is that the TPMs actually prove more than is necessary to meet the customs valuation tests. For customs valuation law, the importer/taxpayer is merely required to show that the profit from a given import transaction equates to the overall profit of the seller's parent firm[403] under the "all costs plus a profit" analysis. In the deductive test value, the importer/taxpayer's own profit is a necessary element, while the computed value test requires an inclusion of the producer's profit.

The profit-based TPMs should certainly be directly relevant to a customs valuation inquiry if all the TPMs did was establish the relevant profit levels. But the profit-based TPMs actually go an important step further. The customs valuation tests do not proceed to this next level, which is to show that the profit levels, once ascertained, meet external arm's-length standards. But to recognize this is not to discredit the profit-based TPMs. Query, if CBP or another customs administration were to struggle with the validation of a related party price and a profit-based TPM were to be a source of information on the profit of a relevant entity and, beyond that, were to provide some evidence that that profit represented an arm's-length result, why would it make sense to dismiss the profit-based TPM? And, especially, why would it make sense if the profit-based TPM were to wield the weight of authority of an APA or a transfer pricing study that had been accepted by the income tax authority? CBP rulings may point a clear way forward for importers/taxpayers.

[2] The Lessons of Ruling No. 548095

The broad policy statements in its 2007 publication set the standard for CBP's future administration of its transfer pricing rules and the acceptability of APAs and transfer pricing studies. Its cited rulings serve as both a primer of CBP's cumulative practice and a more detailed predictor of future CBP action.

403. In one US interpretation of the exemplar.

In one notable 2002 ruling, ruling no. 548095 (September 19, 2002), CBP stated that information in a transfer pricing study may be relevant to an application of the COS test, but the weight to be given will vary depending on the facts presented.[404] Ruling no. 548095 was issued in response to an importer seeking to gain CBP's acceptance of a transfer pricing study based on CPM.[405] Counsel for the importer had cited the earlier 2000 ruling, no. *546979*, and its use of CPM.[406] CBP cited the following factors to be considered in according weight to a transfer pricing study:

- Has the transfer pricing study been considered and approved by the IRS?
- Are the products covered by the study comparable to the imported products at issue?
- Are the methodologies and specific details provided comparable?[407]

CBP further observed that, under CPM, the IRS reviews profitability on an aggregate basis, and not product by product like CBP. In ruling no. 546979, despite these differences and even though CBP was not a party to the APA and the valuation ruling request did not include the APA submission, CBP still relied extensively on the APA. In its 2002 ruling, no. 548095, CBP cited the special circumstances that had been present in the 2000 ruling:

> The transfer pricing methodology had been approved by the IRS through the APA.
>
> Customs had participated in the APA prefiling conference between the importer and the IRS.
>
> The importer provided a waiver to CBP to enable access to the APA documents.
>
> All of the importer's products were covered by the APA.
>
> The APA was bilateral, in which both taxing authorities (US and Japan) had examined the relevant aspects of the transaction.

For those practitioners seeking to discover what CBP will require of a transfer pricing methodology for application to a COS inquiry, seek no further. CBP went on the record in ruling no. 548095 to characterize these five factors that drove the result in ruling no. 546979:

> *Based on these special circumstances*, Customs determined that the circumstances of sale test had been met (emphasis added).

These factors were replicated in 2009's ruling no. H029658. This five-factor test derived from ruling no. 546979 limiting the use of CPM was also followed in ruling no. H065015.[408]

---

404. This foreshadowed the policy statement of ICP: Related Party Transactions.
405. The CPM is described above in §10.04[B][2][a].
406. In fact, the taxpayer who had sought this customs valuation ruling had entered into an APA in reliance on the CPM, as well as the Japanese profit split (JPS) method, the latter necessary in light of the CPM not being recognized by the National Tax Administration of Japan.
407. Ruling no. 548095.
408. Ruling no. H065015 (April 14, 2011) (transfer pricing study cannot be accepted without further evidence).

The nature of a bilateral APA is a key element because the interests of the foreign income tax authorities and CBP are aligned—both agencies will want to maximize the PAPP for the imported goods to enhance revenues.[409] For the foreign income tax authority, the higher the price, the higher the seller's taxable income on the sale transaction. For CBP, the higher the price, the higher the dutiable value and the greater the revenue collected.[410]

To this point, there has not been a perceived movement in the US toward the fully integrated, single procedure leading to an APA and a customs valuation ruling that many have hoped for. That does not mean it would be impossible to attain. An example of such an integrated procedure is offered by the decision of the Belgian *Collège du SDA* in 2008.[411] An importer/taxpayer had purchased both finished and semifinished products from a related party seller. The seller had acted as a limited risk (contract) manufacturer of the semifinished products, which the importer used in its production of finished goods in Belgium. The importer acted as a limited risk distributor for the finished goods. There was no possibility of a CUP and the *Collège du SDA* approved the transfer price on the strength of a TNMM, with "net cost plus" as the PLI for the semifinished goods purchases and operating margin as the PLI for the finished goods purchases. The purchase prices were considered valid bases for TV appraisement, with adjustments for delivery charges (*frais de livraison*). The decision was valid for five years from January 1, 2007.

Until the hallelujah! moment when there is similar full integration of the process, after weaving all of the factors together, the successful importer/taxpayer in the US and perhaps elsewhere will be one that will have a bilateral APA, preferably based on a transaction method, that covers all of its products and in which CBP has been involved. The importer/taxpayer that is paying attention to CBP's administrative position will want to make maximum use of the participation by CBP in the process that is so obviously a key to CBP approval and, further, will want to ensure that the bilateral APA meets the level of proof that CBP will expect. Most importantly, the bilateral APA will feature a level of product comparability, or put forward an explanation why this product comparability is not essential (i.e., is inherently reliable even without it) that will satisfy CBP.[412]

409. For another ruling in which a bilateral APA figured prominently in the CBP analysis and acceptance of the transfer price, *see* ruling no. 548233 (November 7, 2003) ("more detailed information is unnecessary since the importer operates under a bilateral APA, in which both countries have reviewed the submission and negotiated a fair result for both taxing authorities").

410. *But see* the policy arguments why a unilateral APA should not be discounted or regarded less authoritative than a bilateral APA. Neville & Harris, "The Customs/IRS Intersection on Transfer Pricing," 12 J. Int'l Tax'n (September 2001) at 28, 34-35.

411. Belgium, *Collège du SDA*, Decision 700.473 (January 22, 2008). The *Collège* is a four-person office within the *Service Public Fédéral Finances*. SDA is the acronym for *Service des Décisions Anticipées en matière fiscale*.

412. For the customs implications of an APA covering multiple product lines, *see* Neville & Harris, "The Customs/IRS Intersection on Transfer Pricing," 12 J. Int'l Tax'n (September 2001) at 28, 35-36.

The best use for customs purposes of an APA, or a transfer pricing study that has been presented to and accepted by the IRS, may lie not in setting customs value for the purposes of section 1059A, as discussed above, or in validating the transaction value in the direct sense of proof based on a COS test. Rather, the APA or approved transfer pricing study can and should be interpreted as a pricing formula. The importer/taxpayer is bound by the terms of the APA and by a transfer pricing study approved by the IRS, and any compensating adjustment taken by the importer/taxpayer is mandated by the terms of that agreement. As an importer who voluntarily agrees to a pricing scheme based on the price prevailing on a certain date cannot intervene, so is an importer/taxpayer unable to intervene in the objectively determined price, with relevant adjustments, as determined under an APA or transfer pricing study. If CBP or other customs authorities were to insist on a COS review, in COS terms, the presence of the pricing formula should be tantamount to the buyer and seller dealing with each as though they are not related. This analysis of the APA as an instrument that promulgates a binding pricing formula should be submitted as an additional rationale for the acceptability of a transfer price by CBP.

Finally, it would not be appropriate to close this discussion without debunking one of the prevailing "urban myths"—the importer/taxpayer whose sole focus is on lowering customs duty liability. It should not be necessary to raise the issue, after having spent a considerable time on the duality, and the ensuing push-pull torque, of status as an "importer/taxpayer."

In analyzing the multiple effects of transfer pricing manipulations on the tax liability of the related parties, the income tax liability can be measured on a combined basis for the related parties as well as separately gauged for both the importer/taxpayer and the related party seller, and the customs duty exposure of the importer/taxpayer can also be measured. The effects will vary greatly depending on the variables—high versus low effective income tax rates, zero duty, and low and high ad valorem duty rates.[413]

The results set forth in the Appendix demonstrate that those customs authorities that presume in the most overly simplistic fashion that related parties are motivated in any and all instances to artificially lower those customs valuations so as to lower their customs duty exposure are greatly mistaken.

[3] Access to US Tax Return Information in Customs Audit

In the US, there is an express statutory exemption from the general rule granting tax return and tax return information confidentiality in the case of: (1) audits undertaken by CBP within the authority of section 509 of the Tariff Act of 1930[414] to ascertain the correctness of entries and (2) actions taken pursuant to such an audit to recover any

413. For the effect of varying levels of profitability on transfer pricing for customs valuation purposes, *see* Neville & Harris, "The Customs/IRS Intersection on Transfer Pricing," 12 J. Int'l Tax'n (September 2001) at 28, 35-36.
414. 19 USC § 1509.

loss of revenue, or to collect duties, taxes, and fees, determined to be due and owing pursuant to such audits.[415]

Given that these customs valuation issues often arise in the context of an audit being conducted by CBP's Regulatory Audit, importer/taxpayers should anticipate that they may be forced to deal with an audit team that has been given access to their federal income tax returns.

Obviously, this issue of information-sharing in the course of a customs audit or other review is not limited to the US. In other jurisdictions, too, importer/taxpayers may be faced with questions about accessibility to tax return information and the sharing of information between the tax and customs authorities.

§10.07 IMPACT OF OECD'S BEPS PROJECT

One of the most long-awaited developments in the field of transfer pricing at the international level was the October 2015 release by the OECD/G20 of guidance in the form of recommendations to address Base Erosion and Profit Shifting (BEPS). This came after a two-year project to devise measures designed to curtail what were perceived to be transfer pricing abuses by multinational taxpayers. As the OECD website now proclaims:

> Domestic tax *base erosion and profit shifting (BEPS)* due to multinational enterprises exploiting gaps and mismatches between different countries' tax systems affects all countries. Developing countries' higher reliance on corporate income tax means they suffer from BEPS disproportionately.
>
> Business operates internationally, so governments must act together to tackle BEPS and restore trust in domestic and international tax systems. *BEPS practices cost countries 100-240 billion USD in lost revenue annually,* which is the equivalent to 4-10% of the global corporate income tax revenue.
>
> Working together in the OECD/G20 Inclusive Framework on BEPS, over 135 countries and jurisdictions *are implementing* 15 Actions to tackle tax avoidance, improve the coherence of international tax rules, ensure a more transparent tax environment and address the tax challenges arising from the digitalisation of the economy[416] (emphasis in original).

The principal feature of the BEPS is more rigorous reporting in TP documentation in the form of enhanced transfer pricing documentation in the form of: (1) a master file, (2) local files as needed and (3) country-by-country reporting.[417] This mandated transparency is intended to prevent taxpayers from designing plans to misstate functions, misrepresent economic activities and, ultimately, understate income in one or more tax jurisdictions.

Taken altogether, multinational taxpayers will be forced to prepare and submit information to tax authorities. Depending on the extent to which there is already

415. IRC § 6103(l)(14).
416. http://www.oecd.org/tax/beps/. Note that the current tally of BEPS participants is 141 countries and counting.
417. These transparency measures were built into the documentation requirements of Chapter V and its Annexes to the OECD Guidelines.

information-sharing legislation or there are administrative protocols with the same effect, the importer/taxpayer should expect that this information will be shared with and employed by customs officials. This is a further sign of convergence between the two disciplines, even if there are still gaps between or differences in the tests used by the two tax authorities on TP/related party pricing.

For our purposes, Actions 8-10 concern substantive transfer pricing issues (respectively, intangibles, risks and capital and high-risk transactions) which have been incorporated into the OECD Guidelines.

A major step in the BEPS Project was the development of a "Two Pillar" solution in response to digitalization. In that regard, the tax rules that have governed taxability questions date back hundred years, grounded as they have been in rules in permanent establishment and nexus which principally look to a physical presence. Added to that, the rise of data intangibles skews the validity of the current regime. Today's environment has evolved to the point that the traditional, long-standing approach no longer makes sense.

As described by the OECD, some features of the Two Pillar approach are as follows.[418]

Pillar One

Scope

In-scope companies are the multinational enterprises (MNEs) with global turnover above €20 billion and profitability above 10% (i.e. profit before tax/revenue) with the turnover threshold to be reduced to €10 billion, contingent on successful implementation including of tax certainty on Amount A,[419] with the relevant review beginning seven years after the agreement comes into force, and the review being completed in no more than one year.

Extractives and Regulated Financial Services are excluded.

Nexus

There will be a new special purpose nexus rule permitting allocation of Amount A to a market jurisdiction when the in-scope MNE derives at least €1 million in revenue from that jurisdiction. For smaller jurisdictions with GDP lower than €40 billion, the nexus will be set at €250 000. The special purpose nexus rule applies solely to determine whether a jurisdiction qualifies for the Amount A allocation.

Compliance costs (incl. on tracing small amounts of sales) will be limited to a minimum

* * * * *

418. https://www.oecd.org/tax/beps/statement-on-a-two-pillar-solution-to-address-the-tax-challenges-arising-from-the-digitalisation-of-the-economy-july-2021.pdf.
419. Amount A establishes a new taxing right over a portion of the profit of a group (large, high-revenue enterprises) for jurisdictions in which their goods or services are supplied or consumers are located. Attaching tax liability for a portion of residual (or nonroutine) profits earned from activities in relevant market countries even though they lack sufficient physical presence in that particular country is the principal impact of Pillar One.

Pillar Two

Overall design

Pillar Two consists of:

- two interlocking domestic rules (together the Global anti-Base Erosion Rules (GloBE) rules): (i) an Income Inclusion Rule (IIR), which imposes top-up tax on a parent entity in respect of the low taxed income of a constituent entity; and (ii) an Undertaxed Payment Rule (UTPR), which denies deductions or requires an equivalent adjustment to the extent the low tax income of a constituent entity is not subject to tax under an IIR; and
- a treaty-based rule (the Subject to Tax Rule (STTR)) that allows source jurisdictions to impose limited source taxation on certain related party payments subject to tax below a minimum rate. The STTR will be creditable as a covered tax under the GloBE rules. The GloBE rules will apply to MNEs that meet the 750 EUR million threshold as determined under BEPS Action 13 (country-by-country reporting). Countries are free to apply the IIR to MNEs headquartered in their country even if they do not meet the threshold.

The minimum tax rate used for the purposes of the IIR and UTPR will be at least 15%.

If we were to summarize even further, we might state that

- Pillar One is limited to the largest multinational enterprises—profits of > 10% and global turnover greater than €20 bio—perhaps hundred enterprises—the tax authorities might go beyond the arm's-length standard if necessary. For all other taxpayers, the ordinary transfer pricing rules remain in full force.
- Pillar Two imposes a global minimum tax of 15% on large companies.

* * * * *

Beyond that, the effects of BEPS on all but the largest multinational groups—caught by Pillar One—are to leave intact the arm's-length-based transfer pricing rules of the Guidelines and to heighten reporting requirements through incorporation into Chapter V of the Guidelines.[420] Those master and local files may be shared with the local customs authorities. Some have predicted that the effect of BEPS will be to hobble the effectiveness of international tax planning initiatives such as the use of centralized financial centers and on tax minimization models that assign functions, assets and risks among deployed related entities. In turn, that could lead to what we might term a "rebundled" model, simplifying the overall structure which the overall costs for a given imported good are captured in a single commercial invoice for a sale for export. If that were to be the case, it is easy to predict that the customs valuation will be a straightforward exercise, based on the declared price comprising the PAPP. There would be no additional payments that might be dutiable as elements to be

420. Even though Pillar Two is designed to apply to enterprises with over €750 turnover, smaller enterprises will be caught by the documentation requirements if they must abide by the OECD Guidelines.

added to comprise the PAPP or as adjustments to the PAPP under Article 8 of the Valuation Agreement.

As a final point, the digital economy has imposed challenges in the customs field. To begin with, the ongoing debate on the status of the moratorium on collection of duty on digital downloads points to a lack of consensus on this important question. We can also point to the TCCV instrument on flash sales, which held, *inter alia*, that the actual, highly discounted price arising from a flash sale should be accepted for an Article 1 Transaction Value appraisement.[421]

§10.08 USE OF TRANSFER PRICING MATERIALS IN OTHER CUSTOMS VALUATION CONTEXTS

The focus of this discussion has been on inbound transfer pricing as it pertains to the price paid or payable for tangible property that, by its very nature, raises customs valuation issues at the same time.

Quite apart from a purchase from a related party foreign seller, another possible use of transfer pricing analysis is to justify a first sale from a foreign factory to a related foreign middleman as the basis for an FSFE appraisement.[422]

In an FSFE import, the importer will be required to justify that the "first sale" from the foreign factory to the foreign middleman is free of nonmarket influence. Some importers seeking FSFE treatment will make use of transfer pricing studies that would serve to justify that foreign-to-foreign sale as at arm's length.[423] For a good illustration of this application of transfer pricing principles to an FSFE analysis, *see* ruling no. H088815 (September 28, 2011). Despite its use of transfer pricing studies, the importer was unable to show that the first sale price between a related factory and middleman was at arm's length. Similarly, the importer in ruling no. H097035 (November 15, 2011) was unsuccessful. There, the importer had sought to show that the First Sale price between related parties was not influenced by the relationship. Among its proofs, the importer pointed to a subcontract by the related factory to an unrelated producer at the same price as had been contracted between the related middleman and factory. CBP observed that, in some cases, the factory was actually losing money on the subcontracts and was unconvinced. The request for reconsideration was unsuccessful as well.[424]

Moreover, there may well be a cross-over effect between a CBP determination that parties are or are not related by control and an antidumping law determination on "affiliate" status.[425]

421. TCCV, AO 23.1, Valuation of Imported Goods Purchased in "Flash Sales" (May 2019). The original facts had posited an internet sale from a foreign seller.
422. FSFE is a customs valuation strategy discussed at length in Part I; *see* there the IRS view on section 1059A and FSFE.
423. *See* ruling nos. H023269 (October 27, 2010) and W563542 (September 4, 2007).
424. Ruling no. H215658 (June 11, 2012).
425. *Compare* 19 USC §§ 1520(c), 1677(33)(g) *with* 19 USC § 1401a(g)(1)(G) and ruling no. 545481 (September 14, 1994).

Beyond that, there are other customs valuation law contexts in which an importer/taxpayer may choose to rely on the use of a transfer pricing study or an APA. These potential applications will arise whenever there is any payment by an importing buyer to a related party vendor. The customs valuation law directs that, in addition to the PAPP for the merchandise, the importer will have to account for and add to the PAPP any of the relevant five statutory additions.[426] The customs valuation law mandates that no other amounts may be added to the PAPP. But the prospect that off-invoice payments in the nature of sanctioned "statutory additions" could be added to the PAPP should prompt a review by the importer/taxpayer of any such payments.

This only makes sense as customs authorities could examine the totality of any of the buyer's off-invoice payments to the seller to determine whether any such payments could be dutiable. Certain of the additions will be more likely to trigger such an examination. Making use of a related party buying agent for product sourcing is one such instance. Apart from ascertaining that the agent is acting on behalf of the buyer instead of the seller, because the commission would be an amount paid to a related party, both CBP and the IRS may have questions about the level of commissions paid.

Because the buying agents are related parties, the IRS will be keen to ensure that the commission paid, which would be an ordinary and necessary business expense for the US taxpayer and would thus serve to lower taxable income in the United Sates, is set at an arm's-length rate. Because the agent would be performing a service, the transfer pricing rules for tangible property will not apply. However, the IRS has an extensive body of temporary transfer pricing regulations for services dating to 2006.[427]

As for CBP, there is no safe harbor here; i.e., commission rates below a set percentage are presumptively valid. Instead, there is authority in the body of rulings that the appropriateness of the rate of an agent's commission depends on the level of service provided to the principal.[428] That seems correct because the commission should represent that level of compensation to the agent for the services it is providing and that standard is obviously situational.

Query, if an importer/taxpayer has prepared a transfer pricing study to validate the arm's-length nature of the agency relationship and the commission rate paid to the foreign buying agent, why would the importer/taxpayer not be able to make similar good use of that study in demonstrating to CBP that the agent's commission rate is justified? The importer/taxpayer would still have to meet all of the customs law tests for a valid buying agency relationship, which task may not have arisen in the context of the income tax laws. The point is that transfer pricing studies, with their close attention to detail in functional analysis and comparability factors, may be a fruitful source of data for an importer/taxpayer in other customs valuation law contexts, including buying agency commission rates.

Some would say that the CBSA has thrown down the gauntlet with its promulgation of a controversial rule embodied in one of its "D Memos" on the last of the

426. *See* above §10.04[B][2][a].
427. Temp. Reg. § 1.482-9T.
428. *See*, e.g., ruling no. 547523 (March 28, 2001).

statutory additions, subsequent proceeds inuring to the benefit of the foreign seller.[429] While the focus of the 2009/2015 "D Memo" was not limited to related party payments, the issue may be more likely to arise in a related party context (*see* D Memo at point 10). Certainly, the D Memo devoted considerable attention to related party scenarios—payments such as marketing and promotion, management fees, and cost sharing arrangements were all swept into the sack.[430]

Still, we must recognize that there may be an incentive and opportunity for an importer to disguise a portion of the PAPP as a payment for other services provided, and that customs authorities are fully justified in examining whether that has been the case.

The rubric here goes well beyond the classic understanding of subsequent proceeds, in which the seller is paid a portion of the proceeds earned by an importer on the resale of the imported article. The D Memo's original publication in 2009 had insisted (at point 9) that the subsequent proceed need not be "a condition of sale of the goods" or be "in respect of the goods." Those statements were dropped from the 2015 version, but the D Memo still recites (now at point 10) that "the fact that such payments exist requires that they be added to the price paid or payable," even if CBSA has dropped the qualifying adjective ("the mere fact that").[431]

Even after these revisions, this statement somewhat begs the question. Of course, few would argue that a payment that is shown to be a share of a subsequent proceed is not dutiable. However, the fact that there is a separate payment from the buyer to the seller by itself cannot make the payment dutiable. As we have seen, the payment must either be a disguised payment for the imported goods (and therefore included with the PAPP) or fall within one of the adjustment categories of Article 8.

Much more is needed for dutiable status to apply, and to apply specifically because it is a missing element of the customs value, a "subsequent proceed." The CBSA takes the view that if a payment can be shown to be for some other service being provided—and especially that the payment is commensurate with the level of services received—then it is "justified." If the payment cannot be justified, then the payment may be shown to be a subsequent proceed. There is additional consolation in an admission (at point 36) that dividends and other payments to the seller in the nature of financial transactions that do not relate to the imported goods are not part of PAPP.[432]

In the case of Canada, the theory is that payments for management or other fees might be dutiable pursuant to Article 8.1(d) of the Valuation Agreement as a statutory addition to customs value under the "subsequent proceeds" category, springing from

429. CBSA, Memorandum D13-4-13, *Post-importation Payments or Fees (Subsequent Proceeds)* (March 31, 2015), originally issued July 8, 2009, available at http://www.cbsa-asfc.gc.ca/publications/dm-md/d13/d13-4-13-eng.html.
430. Related party transactions are at the basis of the entire discussion in Appendix B (marketing and promotional fees) and in seven of the eight hypothetical "situations" put forward in Appendix C. This D Memo is also replete with references to Canada's Income Tax Act and income tax filings (e.g., point 37) and to the OECD Guidelines (point 8 of Appendix A).
431. A close side-by-side textual analysis of the 2009 and 2015 versions is recommended.
432. Quoting the text, without full attribution, from Valuation Agreement, Interpretative Note, Article 1, Price Actually Paid Or Payable, point 4.

the resale, disposal, or use "of the imported goods."[433] Nowhere does the D Memo explain its way around, or out from under, the implication in Canada's customs statute or in the Agreement that there must be a direct tie-in between the payment and the subsequent resale, disposal or use of the imported goods.

Apparently, the Canadian viewpoint has been followed by Norwegian customs authorities, who are applying a variation of the D Memo approach just discussed. In Norway, if it cannot be proven that the management fees paid by an importer are for a full measure of management services, then the fees will be seen as comprising part of the PAPP and dutiable under Article 1 of the Valuation Agreement. That is a much more plausible line of reasoning, as the connection between a missing element of the PAPP disguised as a fee for management or other services is generally less attenuated than the putative connection between that same payment and a later resale or disposition of the imported goods.

The Directorate of Customs and Excise in Norway requires proof that the services had actually been rendered, and if there is any question, then the entire management fee is dutiable. This is another example of a customs authority co-opting the authority of the income tax officials who must be presumed to have a parallel interest in management fees paid by a Norwegian taxpayer. The reports are that management fee services were invoiced according to a turnover based norm of distribution according to the OECD guidelines. The Directorate dismissed the guidelines as irrelevant for customs valuation purposes.

The D Memo also takes the view that payments such as management fees will be dutiable if the importer/taxpayer is unable to show that the payment tallies with the value of management service actually rendered. Such simple conventional intercompany financial arrangements as management fees set at a given percentage of net sales may therefore fall into a dutiable category if the degree of "granularity" or level of cost accounting detail were not forthcoming. Of course, in the case of a related party transaction the payment might be closely reviewed by both the income tax authorities of Canada, the Canada Revenue Authority (CRA), and the exporting country. In the case of a third-party transaction, the income tax authority in the country of importation may likewise question the level of compensation as an ordinary and necessary business expense, to use the US terminology.

In a perverse way, the justification for the extraneous payment may be more difficult to prove in the absence of an APA or TP study.

Query, what if CRA or other income tax authority(ies) finds the compensation level for the extraneous payment to be perfectly acceptable? Does that/should that automatically end the debate with the customs authority? Unlike the income tax authority, does the customs authority have the expertise to examine whether the payment in question is appropriate? On the other hand, it may be as simple as showing

433. Valuation Agreement, Articles 1.1(c), 8.1(d); Customs Act, subparagraph 48(5)(a)(v); in the United States, the relevant citations are 19 USC §§ 1401a(b)(1)(E), 1401a(b)(2)(A)(iii). Presumably, the D Memo observation stems from an attempt to distinguish the criteria for a subsequent proceeds analysis from those applying to royalties and license fees.

the CBSA or other customs authority that some services were indeed provided to the buyer.

The timing of such a levy could also raise the chance that the importer/taxpayer could be whipsawed, with an additional customs duty levied but without the opportunity to increase the COGS.

The CBSA interpretation has been challenged directly in court after the D Memo position is applied to an importer in Canada.[434] As we saw in the *Scentsy Canada* decision, the Tribunal accepted the importer's income tax documentation and rejected the notion that an adjustment to the PAPP for various service fee payments was appropriate.[435]

The D Memo application of a subsequent proceeds theory is broad enough to reach the issue of payments for intangible property rights in general and cost sharing arrangements in particular. Even absent the D Memo, however, any such payments to the seller or to a party related to the seller may be of real interest to CBP and other customs authorities in the narrower and arguably more appropriate inquiries into the status of payments for the imported goods or to statutory additions for dutiable assists and royalty and license fee payments. The importer/taxpayer may want to use transfer pricing studies affirmatively to demonstrate that the payments were fully "justified" to borrow the CBSA's phrase or may be required to furnish them to an inquisitive customs authority.

One other touch point with related party pricing that is internal to customs valuation law pertains to royalty and license fees. As discussed in Part I, RLFs paid to third parties unrelated to the seller may be nondutiable. There is a very common commercial situation where there is a license agreement between a licensor and a licensee and a totally separate sales agreement between a foreign manufacturer and the buyer, who may happen to be the licensee in the other agreement. None of the parties to the two separate agreements need be related in any conventional sense. As we have discussed, one definition of a related party centers on the notion of "control," and that control has been defined to refer to restraint or control of the management activities of one party by another.[436] In earlier versions of its Compendium, the EU Customs Code Committee explored the notion that the reservation of a combination of certain rights by a licensor in an intellectual property license, such as the right to inspect samples or to preapprove manufacturers that the licensee wanted to engage, might go beyond purely QC checks by the licensor and thus would demonstrate a degree of control that would result in a "related party" tie between the licensor and the seller under the Community Customs Code.[437] This is a stretch. Does the Commission, or any other customs authority, have the experience or expertise to discern what is a QC level—and

434. In the most recent forty years, there have been many more customs valuation issues litigated in Canada—and the EU, for that matter—than in the United States.
435. *Scentsy Canada Enterprises LLC v. President of the Canada Border Services Agency* (October 4, 2022), AP-2019-021 (CITT) (paragraphs 121-125).
436. *See* above §10.03[A][1][a] and [b].
437. Commentary no. 11 of the Customs Code Committee (customs valuation section) on the application of Community Code Article 32(1)(c) in relation to royalties and license fees paid to

here we must add reputational risk management measures—that would be an acceptable or "normal?" That assumes that the line between normal versus extraordinary measures is an acceptable gauge whether there is a relationship between the parties.

Such a reservation of rights by a licensor, quite unexceptional in itself, would mean that the otherwise completely separate royalty or license fee would be paid by the licensee/buyer to a party related to the seller, with the effect that the payment would become dutiable. And that dutiable effect further relies on the notion that a payment to a party related to the seller must be deemed to be a payment to the seller.[438]

a third party according to Article 160 of Reg. (EEC) no. 2454/93. This has been deleted from the 2022 Compendium as the CCC is no longer in effect but has not been updated for the UCC regime.

438. I show in Part I that there is no cognizable basis in the Valuation Agreement on which to conclude that a payment to a party related to the seller, without more, is to be treated as a payment to the seller.

Conclusion

To restate the question that has driven this discussion:

> Given the very brief recitation that comprises the entire text and commentary on related-party pricing in customs valuation law, can importers/taxpayers or customs authorities make use of transfer pricing methods used in allocating income for income tax purposes, and the documentation based on those methods, to help determine dutiable value for customs purposes?

The weight of authority suggests that importers/taxpayers as well as customs authorities should be able to make use of transfer pricing methods, as expressed in either APAs or in transfer pricing studies, in the course of proving the acceptability of a related party price for customs duty purposes. The presence of APAs and transfer pricing studies should neither close out the dialogue with the customs authorities nor should they be dismissed out of hand. As is so often the situation, the true answer to their utility lies in the middle ground.

Consider the first three lessons of Part II.

Income tax and customs duty collections are often the responsibilities of completely separate administrative agencies.

Each of these tax authorities will have its own, independent functional concern with transfer pricing.

Satisfying either one of the taxing authorities on transfer pricing (e.g., the IRS through an APA) may not adequately satisfy the tests applied by the other agency, even though the agency rules are sometimes nearly identical.

Some of the additional facts ascertained or trends identified in Part II include the following.

The customs valuation standards on transfer pricing are indeed quite terse, providing scant guidance—but unfettered discretion—for a customs administrator seeking to determine the acceptability of a TV appraisement. By contrast to its few dozen lines in the statute and the regulations, and including in the total both the Valuation Agreement and its Interpretative Notes to which they are faithful, the sources of authority for transfer pricing comprise many hundreds of pages in the US and in the OECD Guidelines. Moreover, the customs valuation texts have been largely static since their adoption in 1979 or soon thereafter for developed countries, while the income tax transfer pricing regulations and the OECD Guidelines have been in a state of almost constant revision, reflecting an ever more focused and sophisticated analysis, as the authorities strive to keep pace with the evolving forms of, and the consequent demands on, international related party transactions. This point is demonstrated by the escalation in the use of contract manufacturers and cost sharing arrangements, both of which have had important transfer pricing consequences but are outside the scope of this presentation.

The COS test has an overarching criterion, that the relationship did not influence the price. Following that principle, there are two sets of examples, two broader expressions, and three more specific exemplars. Further, as seen in ruling nos. 548233, H029658, H037375 and H310087, an importer/taxpayer in the US who is unable to meet any of the discrete requirements of the more specific tests may nonetheless prevail based on the more general COS analysis. This is especially the case where, as in the cited rulings, there are so many positive considerations and relevant indicia of arm's-length dealings. Because the standards are, or very nearly are, word-for-word identical between the US customs valuation law and the Valuation Agreement text at the international level as well as other municipal implementations, there is no reason why the sound logic of a US ruling or court decision—or for that matter, a ruling or court decision issued by another jurisdiction—cannot and should not be applied by any other WTO Member State's customs authority or judicial body.

While the transfer pricing precepts in each discipline is similar, they are not identical, and so it is unlikely that any customs authority will accept an APA or a transfer pricing study as determinative *ipso facto*. Instead, most customs authorities should follow the lead of the US and Australia, which acknowledge that the APA or income tax documentation might well be relevant but require that the importer/taxpayer demonstrate how and why the APA or transfer pricing study is relevant and persuasive. In consequence, the trade community should tone down assertions that an APA or a transfer pricing study should be given dispositive effect, full stop.

Importers/taxpayers who rely on APAs or transfer pricing studies that focus on functional comparability without a corresponding emphasis on comparability of product lines will struggle to gain traction in dealings with CBP and possibly other customs authorities. Nonetheless, it may be possible for an importer/taxpayer to successfully argue that functional comparability trumps a lack of product comparability in a given situation, such as the case of the direct marketer or MLM company, where profitability patterns are arguably comparable regardless of product line.

In the US, section 1059A and its regulations are sorely in need of revision.

While conventional analysis would have it that section 1059A poses a serious risk of the importer/taxpayer being whipsawed, available strategies, such as reconciliation, requests for the withholding of liquidation, PSCs and protests (at least in the case of downward price adjustments) might eliminate or seriously curtail these risks.

There is still much evidence that the IRS and CBP are not aligned on transfer pricing matters. This is especially true of the IRS, where its boldness in determining points of customs valuation law on its own counsel is matched only by its lack of sophistication in reaching those determinations.

One of the most fundamental features of this discussion has been the notion that an importer is not simply an importer, nor is that entity simply a taxpayer. Instead, the entity has two roles—at one and the same time both an importer and a taxpayer, charged with the payment of both customs duty and, later, income tax. Hence, the dual title "importer/taxpayer." Once customs authorities think in those terms, though the actual use of the same or an equivalent term is not necessary, they should be more receptive to the use of APAs or transfer pricing studies.

The APA is a contract, notwithstanding the "arrangement" status assigned by the OECD, that legally binds the importer/taxpayer and the tax authority or authorities and sets up a predetermined transfer pricing regime. Importers/taxpayers should exploit the legal status of the APA, and also that of a transfer pricing study that has been vetted and approved by the IRS or a comparable income tax authority, as a valid pricing formula, on the basis of which the transfer price may be justified for customs purposes.

The governments in all jurisdictions should plan to work toward the ultimate goal of a joint program, with a single administrative filing that would serve the dual purpose of an APA or similar undertaking for income tax purposes and a request for a binding ruling for customs valuation purposes. There has been little if any discussion of such a concerted administrative action.

The "brief to the point of vagueness" status of the transfer pricing tests under the COS test should be acknowledged and then rectified. Their status as non-exhaustive exemplars should be explicitly emphasized. Such an amendment of the Valuation Agreement would probably be resisted in some quarters because of the prospect of opening up other aspects of the Valuation Agreement. As an alternative, the TCCV, benefiting as it has from the continuing input of the OECD and the private sector experts on income tax transfer pricing, might be convinced to issue one or more instruments (advisory opinions, commentaries, explanatory notes, case studies, or studies) that would acknowledge that: (1) the customs valuation texts are lacking in substance, (2) the texts proffer some examples but that their listing is by no means exhaustive, and (3) the income tax authorities might be a resource in reaching determinations under Article 1.2 of the Valuation Agreement whether the price has been influenced by the relationship of the parties.

In all of these efforts, the same spirit that animates the application of the methods put forward under OECD Guidelines should be applied to related party evaluations by customs authorities. I refer to the permeation of such suggestions under the OECD Guidelines as reasonable accommodations and working solutions rather than rigid-to-the-point-of-wooden insistence on the scant few lines of the Valuation Agreement. Remember: protean and not procrustean, IVP collaboration and not preemption.

The customs authorities must reassure themselves that, whatever is meant by the term "convergence" when applied to the relationship of income tax and customs valuation, no one is advocating the suppression in municipal law of the Valuation Agreement or its supplanting by the OECD Guidelines or any other income tax authority.

Importers/taxpayers may be able to make effective use of transfer pricing studies in situations beyond the appraisement of imported merchandise that has been sold by a foreign related party. As the Canadian D Memo suggests, transfer pricing studies may have a wide application in the context of "subsequent proceeds," the breadth of which term would theoretically capture any off-invoice payment to the seller. Additionally, transfer pricing studies on IPR may be relevant to customs valuation issues relating to these rights if payments therefor are not embedded in the purchase price for the imported goods. Other situations might include use of a TP Study in: (i) FSFE claims to validate related party "first sales" between foreign factories and foreign middlemen and in (ii) justifying the commission rate paid to a related foreign buying agent.

One final, extended observation and a final recommendation. The problem that an importer/taxpayer encounters when seeking the current state of the law on transfer pricing in income tax and even more so in customs valuation matters, is a pervasive lack of transparency.

The US practice stands virtually alone as an exception to this general shortcoming. The statute, regulations, administrative agency pronouncements, legislative history, and general access to the corpus of administrative rulings and case law, including access to the legal arguments embodied in pleadings, court filings, and briefs, make for a wide open, accessible and, for all of that, fair body of law. Almost everything is "on the record" and freely available in the US legal system. One major shortfall, however, is that, despite the plenitude of administrative guidance, court decisions on customs valuation in the US are rare.

In other municipal legal systems, even if some were to become equally transparent and their legal, administrative, or judicial products accessible individually, for customs valuation law precedents there is no single repository for these legal authorities. The result is that both the public and private sector alike rely on a patched together social network of contacts in other jurisdictions and on secondary sources or anecdotal references to track down foreign interpretations of the customs valuation law.

As a consequence of this regrettable opacity, the WTO community is missing a chance to develop a richer understanding of the Valuation Agreement, as embodied in a growing consensus of interpretations.

The various instruments of the TCCV, while a valuable gloss on the Valuation Agreement, are but one such source and they stand one step removed from the actual administration of the customs valuation law by a foreign customs authority. The determinations rendered by individual customs authorities and the decisions rendered by courts of competent authority in judicial review of those determinations serve as interpretations of the Valuation Agreement.

The private sector trade community, as well as individual members of the WTO and WCO communities and their Secretariats, would all derive enormous benefit if the mystery were gone. Free, unfettered, and across-the-board access to this growing corpus of precedents should be available in a centralized library of these authorities, which are meant to be published and generally available.[1] These broader and deeper

1. Valuation Agreement, Article 12; GATT 1994, Article X.

sources might be maintained by or on behalf of the WCO and would obviously extend well beyond the WCO's abbreviated and out-of-date Index of Rulings and Conclusions in its Customs Valuation Compendium. Naturally, the availability of a body of published binding rulings by customs authorities in jurisdictions outside the US can only enhance the benefits for the private sector and for other customs authorities alike.

Appendix

Examination of Transfer Pricing Variables

The following tables present differing fact patterns applying customs and income tax law principles, from which it may be inferred that it is sometimes in the best economic interest of the importer/taxpayer or of its related party seller to declare dutiable values that are higher than a benchmark "market" value.

There is no simplistic formula by which an importer/taxpayer or its related party seller may reach quick or easy solutions about pricing from a total tax planning perspective. The effect of pricing on customs duty and income tax liability can be measured, however, and the pricing behavior of importer/taxpayer predicted, only after careful consideration. Applicable duty and tax rates, the availability of foreign tax credits, net operating losses, and other factors, such as exchange rate variables, must be taken into account, but are outside the scope of this discussion.

Table 1 Effect of Customs Valuation on Duty and Income Tax Liability

Number	Category	Market Value			Lower Declared Value			Higher Declared Value		
1	Unit Price		20			10			30	
2	Quantity		100			100			1,000	
3	Total Value		2,000			1,000			3,000	
4	Resale Price		5,000			5,000			5,000	
5	Acquisition Cost		2,000			1,000			3,000	
6	Duty Rate	Free	2.5%	25%	Free	2.5%	25%	Free	2.5%	25%
7	Duty	0	50	500	0	25	250	0	75	750
8	Total COGS	2,000	2,050	2,500	1,000	1,025	1,250	3,000	3,075	3,750
9	Taxable Profit (Earnings Before Tax (EBT))	3,000	2,950	2,500	4,000	3,975	3,750	2,000	1,925	1,250
10	Income Tax @ 35%	1,050	1,032.50	875	1,400.00	1,391.25	1,312.50	700	673.75	437.50
11	Total Tax (lines 7, 10)	1,050	1,082.50	1,375	1,400	1,416.25	1,562.50	700	748.75	1,187.50

Table 1 presents the data in the simplest case, with a focus solely on the experience of the importer/taxpayer. The data present the base case of a declared customs value that is the correct or "market" value, as contrasted with either a lower or a higher declared value. This separate examination of the effect on the duty, income tax, and total tax liability of the importer/taxpayer demonstrates that:

The duty liability (line 7) will be directly affected by the declared value when the applicable duty is a positive duty rate. Understating or overstating the dutiable value will result in a decrease or an increase in the duty owed (line 7). If the duty rate is free, however, there is no duty effect.

The income tax liability (line 10) will also be affected by the declared value (line 3). If the customs value is lower, the importer/taxpayer has a lower COGS (line 8) and will face an income tax liability that is higher than in the base case (1,400 versus 1,050 for duty-free goods) (line 10). If the customs value is higher than in the base case, the importer/taxpayer will face a lower income tax liability (700 versus 1,050 for duty-free goods) (line 10). The impact on income tax liability of market value fluctuations is even greater when the duty rate is high (25%)—1,312.50 in the low-value case and 437.50 in the high-value case versus 875.00 in the market value case.

On a total tax liability basis (line 11), combining both customs duty and income tax liabilities, with constant duty and income tax rates, the importer/taxpayer who is able to manipulate the market value will want to declare a value higher than the market value to achieve the lowest effective total tax exposure (line 11). Compare the base case total tax exposure when the goods are duty free of 1,400 versus 1,050 for the lower declared value and 700 versus 1,050 for the higher declared value.

The lesson should be clear: contrary to the prevailing view subscribed to by many customs authorities, and measuring only the impact on the importer/taxpayer, assuming that the importer/taxpayer is able to: (1) identify, isolate, measure and then analyze these data on tax and duty liabilities and (2) is then free to set its related party prices based solely on its tax minimization strategies, importer/taxpayers will invariably want to declare a higher customs value because that will gain for them a lower income tax and a lower total tax liability, despite the cost of higher duty assessments.

Table 2 Effect of the Availability of Net Operating Losses (NOLS) on Total Tax Liability of Importer/Taxpayer

Number	*Category*	*Market Value*			*Lower Declared Value*			*Higher Declared Value*		
1	Unit Price		20			10			30	
2	Quantity		100			100			1,000	
3	Total Value		2,000			1,000			3,000	
4	Resale Price		5,000			5,000			5,000	
5	Acquisition Cost		2,000			1,000			3,000	
6	Duty Rate	Free	2.5%	25%	Free	2.5%	25%	Free	2.5%	25%
7	Duty	0	50	500	0	25	250	0	75	750
8	Total COGS	2,000	2,050	2,500	1,000	1,025	1,250	3,000	3,075	3,750
9	Taxable Income	3,000	2,950	2,500	4,000	3,975	3,750	2,000	1,975	1,250
10	NOL	(3,000)	(2,950)	(2,500)	(4,000)	(3,975)	(3,750)	(2,000)	(1,975)	(1,250)
11	Income Tax @ 35%		0	0	0	0	0	0	0	0
12	Total Combined Tax (total lines 7 and 11)	0	50	500	0	25	250	0	75	750

The data in Table 2 are meant to demonstrate that income tax liability (line 11) will be negated by net operating losses (NOLs) in the country of importation (line 10). In turn, this income tax effect will directly affect the total tax liability of the importer/taxpayer (line 12). In other words, by removing income tax liability from consideration, the NOLs will effectively lower the "total combined tax" (line 12) by removing income tax liability and leaving the customs duty (line 7) as the only element making up total combined tax (line 12). As a result, there will be an incentive for the importer/taxpayer to lower the declared customs value in the presence of a positive duty rate. Compare the varying results for goods dutiable at 2.5%. The low-value entry will give rise to a total tax liability of 25 versus market value total tax liability of 50 or a high-value case total tax exposure of 75 (line 12).

The focus of Tables 1 and 2 was on the importer/taxpayer only. With Table 3, we examine the calculus of the total tax expense, and its constituent elements, customs duty and income tax, for the enterprise or multinational group. Because the parties are related, it is possible that they were acting in concert to set prices so as to avoid the payment of customs duties and income tax. The parties might be motivated by: (1) purely income tax considerations in the country of exportation or the country of importation, (2) the purely customs duty considerations of the importer/taxpayer, or (3) some combination of either or both of these considerations for either or both of the members of the group. Again, three variations on the duty rate in the country of importation (free, 2.5%, and 25%) and the base case of an income tax rate in the country of importation of 35% with three variations in the income tax rate in the country of exportation (10%, 35%, and 50%) are presented. The effect of a bilateral tax treaty in the country of exportation to prevent double taxation is also set forth.

Table 3 **Effect of Foreign Tax or Tax Credit in Country of Exportation on a Total Tax Basis for Enterprise**

Number	Category	Market Value			Lower Declared Value			Higher Declared Value		
		A. Case of the Importer/Taxpayer (Subsidiary)								
1	Unit Price		20			10			30	
2	Quantity		100			100			1,000	
3	Total Value		2,000			1,000			3,000	
4	Resale Price		5,000			5,000			5,000	
5	Acquisition Cost		2,000			1,000			3,000	
6	Duty Rate	Free	2.5%	25%	Free	2.5%	25%	Free	2.5%	25%
7	Duty	0	50	500	0	25	250	0	75	750
8	Total COGS	2,000	2,050	2,500	1,000	1,025	1,250	3,000	3,075	3,750
9	Taxable Profit (Income)	3,000	2,950	2,500	4,000	3,975	3,750	2,000	1,925	1,250
10	Income Tax @ 35%	1,050	1,032.50	875	1,400.00	1,391.25	1,312.50	700	673.75	437.50
11	Net Income Dividend to Parent	1,050	1,082.50	1,375	1,400	1,416.25	1,562.50	700	748.75	1,187.50
		B. Case of the Exporter/Parent								
12	Selling Price		2,000			1,000			3,000	
13	Acquisition Cost		500			500			500	

A. Case of the Importer/Taxpayer (Subsidiary)										
Number	*Category*	*Market Value*			*Lower Declared Value*			*Higher Declared Value*		
14	EBT		1,500			500			2,500	
15	Subsidiary Dividend	1,950.00	1,917.50	1,625.00	2,600.00	2,583.75	2,437.50	1,300.00	1,251.25	812.50
16	FTC "Gross-Up"	1,050.00	1,032.50	875.00	1,400.00	1,391.25	1,312.50	700.00	673.75	437.50
17	Total Income (lines 14, 15, 16)	4,500.00	4,450.00	4,000.00	4,500.00	4,475.00	4,250.00	4,500.00	4,425.00	3,750.00
18	FTC Limitation	66.7%	66.2%	62.5%	88.8%	88.8%	88.2%	44.4%	43.5%	33.3%
19	Income Tax @ 35%	1,575.00	1,557.50	1,400.00	1,575.00	1,566.25	1,487.50	1,575.00	1,548.75	1,312.50
20	Foreign Tax Credit	1,050.00	1,032.50	875.00	1,400.00	1,391.25	1,312.50	700.00	673.75	437.50
21	Tax Payable (lines 18 and 19)	525.00	525.00	525.00	175.00	175.00	175.00	875.00	875.00	875.00
22	Total Tax of Both Entities (lines 10 and 21)	1,575.00	1,557.50	1,400.00	1,575.00	1,566.25	1,487.50	1,575.00	1,548.75	1,312.50
23	Income Tax @ 10%	450.00	445.00	400.00	450.00	447.50	425.00	450.00	442.50	375.00
24	Foreign Tax Credit	150.00	295.00	150.00	400.00	397.50	375.00	200.00	192.50	125.00

A. Case of the Importer/Taxpayer (Subsidiary)										
Number	*Category*	*Market Value*			*Lower Declared Value*			*Higher Declared Value*		
25	Tax Payable	300.00	150.00	312.50	50.00	50.00	50.00	250.00	250.00	250.00
26	Total Tax of Both Entities (lines 10 and 24)	1,200.00	1,374.25	1,025.00	1,400.00	1,441.25	1,362.50	950.00	923.75	687.50
27	Income Tax @ 50%	2,250.00	2,225.00	2,000.00	2,250.00	2,237.50	2,125.00	2,250.00	2,212.50	1,875.00
28	Foreign Tax Credit	1,050.00	1,032.50	875.00	1,400.00	1,391.50	1,312.50	700.00	673.75	437.50
29	Tax Payable	1,200.00	1,192.50	1,125.00	850.00	846.25	812.50	1,550.00	1,538.75	1,437.50
30	Total Tax of Both Entities (lines 10 and 29)	2,250.00	2,225.00	2,000.00	2,250.00	2,237.63	2,125.00	2,250.00	2,125.00	1,875.00

Assumption: Net income of importer/taxpayer is remitted as divided to parent company.

In calculating the exporter/parent company's total income (line B17), the effect of a foreign tax credit "gross-up" (line B16) is also incorporated in recognition that the income tax codes of the US, Australia, Canada, the UK, and many other jurisdictions contain such a provision. Their purpose is to deal with the issue of potential double taxation by recognizing foreign tax payments. This system of foreign tax credits allows for the direct credit for foreign taxes paid directly on income as it is received by the parent corporation (direct credit), as well as for the foreign income taxes paid on the income out of which a distribution is made to the parent corporation. The latter is a "deemed paid" or "indirect" credit.

Typically, the deemed credit is made available after first adding to the foreign dividend the foreign income tax paid on the dividend. This "gross-up" of the otherwise ex-tax dividend is, in essence, deemed income to the foreign parents. Provisions for foreign income tax gross-up are central to the direct credit available under section 901 of the Internal Revenue Code and for the indirect credit relating to dividends remitted from foreign subsidiaries under section 78.

The foreign tax credit available to the exporter/parent (lines B20, B24, and B28) is derived by first determining the foreign tax credit limitation, which is a ratio calculated by dividing foreign-source income (lines B15 plus B16) by total income (line B17). This is a much simplified example, following the US practice.[1] Foreign tax credits are, in fact, calculated in a number of different ways. In may tax jurisdictions, the parent company is entitled to a foreign tax credit for direct (withholding taxes) and indirect (underlying corporate tax) income taxes paid by the subsidiary on income included in the parent's taxable income. The foreign tax credit available in a tax year may be limited to the ratio of foreign-source income to total taxable income multiplied by the parent's corporate tax rate. Other tax jurisdictions may have a tax regime that provides for a participation exemption where the parent corporation or holding company owns a minimum percentage of the lower-tier entity. As stated, the goal of both regimes is to minimize double taxation.

In the base, market value case with duty-free treatment in the country of importation, this leads to 3,000 ÷ 4,500, resulting in a foreign tax credit limitation of 0.667 (line B18). The available foreign tax credit (line B20) is thus 1,050 [income tax due, 1,575 (line B19) × the foreign tax credit limitation of 0.667 (line B18)]. Continuing with this base case, the tax payable (line B21) is then determined by subtracting the foreign tax credit (line B20) from the income tax due (line B19). In the market value case, this is 1,575 (line B19) less 1,050 (line B20), leaving an income tax due of 525 (line B21).

The data presented in these hypotheses suggest that on a "total tax on the enterprise" basis, with a foreign tax credit available:

1. For a comprehensive discussion of foreign tax credits, *see* R. Andersen, Foreign Tax Credits (Thomson Reuters/WG&L, 2010) www.checkpoint.thomsonreuters.com.

- When the income tax rates in both jurisdictions are equivalent (35% in this case), there is no effect when the duty rate is free and only a negligible incentive or disincentive to declare a higher or lower transfer price if the duty rate is low (2.5%). For a high duty rate (25%), there is a moderate disincentive to declare a low customs value (total tax of 1,487.50 versus 1,400.00) and an equally moderate incentive to declare a higher value (total tax of 1,312.50 versus 1,400.00) (line B22).
- When the income tax rate in the country of exportation (10%) is lower than the income tax rate in the country of importation (35%), there is a strong disincentive across all duty rate levels to declare a lower transfer price and a correspondingly powerful incentive to declare a higher transfer price across all duty rate levels (line B26).
- When the income tax rate in the country of importation (50%) is higher than in the country of importation (35%), there is a negligible effect on total tax liability in scenarios based on free or low (2.5%) duty rates. When the duty rate is high (25%), there is an incentive to declare a high declared value (1,875 versus 2,000) and a corresponding disincentive to declare a low declared value (2,125 versus 2,000) (line B30).

Table 4 **Effect on a Total Tax Basis for Enterprise of Double Taxation Treaty with Exemption for After-Tax Dividend Remitted to Exporter/Taxpayer**

Number	*Category*	*Market Value*			*Lower Declared Value*			*Higher Declared Value*		
1	Unit Price		20			10			30	
2	Quantity		100			100			1,000	
3	Transaction Value		2,000			1,000			3,000	
4	Resale Price		5,000			5,000			5,000	
5	Acquisition (purchase price)		2,000			1,000			3,000	
		A. Importer/Taxpayer (Subsidiary)								
6	Duty Rate	Free	2.5%	25%	Free	2.5%	25%	Free	2.5%	25%
7	Duty	0	50	500	0	25	250	0	75	750
8	COGS (lines 5 and 7)	2,000	2,050	2,500	1,000	1,025	1,250	3,000	3,075	3,750
9	Taxable Income	3,000	2,950	2,500	4,000	3,975	2,000	1,925	1,250	1,250
10	Tax @ 35%	1,050.00	1,032.50	875.00	1,400.00	1,391.25	1,312.50	700.00	673.75	437.50
11	Income after Tax/Dividend	1,950.00	1,917.50	1,625.00	2,600.00	2,583.75	2,437.50	1,300.00	1,251.25	812.50

Number	*Category*	*Market Value*			*Lower Declared Value*			*Higher Declared Value*		
					B. Exporter/Taxpayer (Parent)					
12	Selling Price		2,000			1,000			3,000	
13	Acquisition Cost		500			500			500	
14	EBT Gross Profit		1,500			500			2,500	
15	[Tax Exempt] Dividend from Sub	1,950.00	1,917.50	1,625.00	2,600.00	2,583.75	2,437.50	1,300.00	1,251.25	812.50
16	Total Income	3,450.00	3,417.50	3,125.00	3,100.00	3,083.75	2,937.50	3,800.00	3,751.25	3,312.50
17	Taxable Income	1,500.00	1,500.00	1,500.00	500.00	500.00	500.00	2,500.00	2,500.00	2,500.00
18	Income Tax @ 35%	525.00	525.00	525.00	175.00	175.00	175.00	875.00	875.00	875.00
19	Total Combined Income Tax (lines 10 and 18)	1,575.00	1,557.50	1,400.00	1,575.00	1,591.25	1,737.50	1,575.00	1,623.75	2,062.50
20	Income Tax @ 10%	150	150	150	50	50	50	250	250	250

Number	*Category*	*Market Value*			*Lower Declared Value*			*Higher Declared Value*		
21	Total Combined Income Tax (lines 10 and 20)	1,200.00	1,232.50	1,525.00	1,450.00	1,466.25	1,612.50	950.00	998.75	1,437.50
22	Income Tax @50%	750	750	750	250	250	250	1,250	1,250	1,250
23	Total Combined Income Tax (lines 10 and 22)	1,800.00	1,832.50	2,125.00	1,650.00	1,666.25	1,812.50	1,950.00	1,998.75	2,437.50

In Table 4, the effect of bilateral treaties to avoid double taxation on total customs duty and income tax liability for the combined related parties' enterprise (lines 19, 21, and 23) is measured. By treaty, the dividend remitted on an after-tax basis by the subsidiary (line 11) is tax-exempt income to the parent in this hypothetical:

- When the income tax rates are equivalent, there is little effect from price manipulation except where the duty rate is high, with a strong disincentive to declare a customs value that is either lower or higher than the market value (line B19).
- When the income tax rate in the country of exportation is lower (10%), regardless of duty rate, there is a strong incentive to avoid a customs value that is lower than market value and an equally strong incentive to declare a higher customs value (line B21).
- In contrast, when the income tax rate in the country of exportation is higher (50%) (again, regardless of the duty rate), there is a strong incentive to declare a lower customs value (e.g., total tax of 1,650 versus 1,800), and an equally strong disincentive to declare a higher customs value (e.g., total tax of 1,950 versus 1,800) (line B23).

ANNEX I

Text of the WTO Valuation Agreement

AGREEMENT ON IMPLEMENTATION OF ARTICLE VII

OF THE GENERAL AGREEMENT ON TARIFFS AND TRADE 1994

GENERAL INTRODUCTORY COMMENTARY

1. The primary basis for customs value under this Agreement is "transaction value" as defined in Article 1. Article 1 is to be read together with Article 8 which provides, *inter alia*, for adjustments to the price actually paid or payable in cases where certain specific elements which are considered to form a part of the value for customs purposes are incurred by the buyer but are not included in the price actually paid or payable for the imported goods. Article 8 also provides for the inclusion in the transaction value of certain considerations which may pass from the buyer to the seller in the form of specified goods or services rather than in the form of money. Articles 2 through 7 provide methods of determining the customs value whenever it cannot be determined under the provisions of Article 1.

2. Where the customs value cannot be determined under the provisions of Article 1 there should normally be a process of consultation between the customs administration and importer with a view to arriving at a basis of value under the provisions of Article 2 or 3. It may occur, for example, that the importer has information about the customs value of identical or similar imported goods which is not immediately available to the customs administration in the port of importation. On the other hand, the customs administration may have information about the customs value of identical or similar imported goods which is not readily available to the importer. A process of consultation between the two parties will enable information to be exchanged, subject to the requirements of commercial confidentiality, with a view to determining a proper basis of value for customs purposes.

3. Articles 5 and 6 provide two bases for determining the customs value where it cannot be determined on the basis of the transaction value of the imported goods or of identical or similar imported goods. Under paragraph 1 of Article 5 the customs value is determined on the basis of the price at which the goods are sold in the condition as imported to an unrelated buyer in the country of importation. The importer also has the right to have goods which are further processed after importation valued under the provisions of Article 5 if the importer so requests. Under Article 6 the customs value is determined on the basis of the computed value. Both these methods present certain difficulties and because of this the importer is given the right, under the provisions of Article 4, to choose the order of application of the two methods.

4. Article 7 sets out how to determine the customs value in cases where it cannot be determined under the provisions of any of the preceding Articles.

Members,

Having regard to the Multilateral Trade Negotiations;

Desiring to further the objectives of GATT 1994 and to secure additional benefits for the international trade of developing countries;

Recognizing the importance of the provisions of Article VII of GATT 1994 and desiring to elaborate rules for their application in order to provide greater uniformity and certainty in their implementation;

Recognizing the need for a fair, uniform and neutral system for the valuation of goods for customs purposes that precludes the use of arbitrary or fictitious customs values;

Recognizing that the basis for valuation of goods for customs purposes should, to the greatest extent possible, be the transaction value of the goods being valued;

Recognizing that customs value should be based on simple and equitable criteria consistent with commercial practices and that valuation procedures should be of general application without distinction between sources of supply;

Recognizing that valuation procedures should not be used to combat dumping;

Hereby *agree* as follows:

PART I

RULES ON CUSTOMS VALUATION

Article 1

1. The customs value of imported goods shall be the transaction value, that is the price actually paid or payable for the goods when sold for export to the country of importation adjusted in accordance with the provisions of Article 8, provided:
   (a) that there are no restrictions as to the disposition or use of the goods by the buyer other than restrictions which:

(i) are imposed or required by law or by the public authorities in the country of importation;
(ii) limit the geographical area in which the goods may be resold; or
(iii) do not substantially affect the value of the goods;

(b) that the sale or price is not subject to some condition or consideration for which a value cannot be determined with respect to the goods being valued;
(c) that no part of the proceeds of any subsequent resale, disposal or use of the goods by the buyer will accrue directly or indirectly to the seller, unless an appropriate adjustment can be made in accordance with the provisions of Article 8; and
(d) that the buyer and seller are not related, or where the buyer and seller are related, that the transaction value is acceptable for customs purposes under the provisions of paragraph 2.

2. (a) In determining whether the transaction value is acceptable for the purposes of paragraph 1, the fact that the buyer and the seller are related within the meaning of Article 15 shall not in itself be grounds for regarding the transaction value as unacceptable. In such case the circumstances surrounding the sale shall be examined and the transaction value shall be accepted provided that the relationship did not influence the price. If, in the light of information provided by the importer or otherwise, the customs administration has grounds for considering that the relationship influenced the price, it shall communicate its grounds to the importer and the importer shall be given a reasonable opportunity to respond. If the importer so requests, the communication of the grounds shall be in writing.

(b) In a sale between related persons, the transaction value shall be accepted and the goods valued in accordance with the provisions of paragraph 1 whenever the importer demonstrates that such value closely approximates to one of the following occurring at or about the same time:
(i) the transaction value in sales to unrelated buyers of identical or similar goods for export to the same country of importation;
(ii) the customs value of identical or similar goods as determined under the provisions of Article 5;
(iii) the customs value of identical or similar goods as determined under the provisions of Article 6;

In applying the foregoing tests, due account shall be taken of demonstrated differences in commercial levels, quantity levels, the elements enumerated in Article 8 and costs incurred by the seller in sales in which the seller and the buyer are not related that are not incurred by the seller in sales in which the seller and the buyer are related.

(c) The tests set forth in paragraph 2(b) are to be used at the initiative of the importer and only for comparison purposes. Substitute values may not be established under the provisions of paragraph 2(b).

Article 2

1. (a) If the customs value of the imported goods cannot be determined under the provisions of Article 1, the customs value shall be the transaction value of identical goods sold for export to the same country of importation and exported at or about the same time as the goods being valued.
   (b) In applying this Article, the transaction value of identical goods in a sale at the same commercial level and in substantially the same quantity as the goods being valued shall be used to determine the customs value. Where no such sale is found, the transaction value of identical goods sold at a different commercial level and/or in different quantities, adjusted to take account of differences attributable to commercial level and/or to quantity, shall be used, provided that such adjustments can be made on the basis of demonstrated evidence which clearly establishes the reasonableness and accuracy of the adjustment, whether the adjustment leads to an increase or a decrease in the value.
2. Where the costs and charges referred to in paragraph 2 of Article 8 are included in the transaction value, an adjustment shall be made to take account of significant differences in such costs and charges between the imported goods and the identical goods in question arising from differences in distances and modes of transport.
3. If, in applying this Article, more than one transaction value of identical goods is found, the lowest such value shall be used to determine the customs value of the imported goods.

Article 3

1. (a) If the customs value of the imported goods cannot be determined under the provisions of Articles 1 and 2, the customs value shall be the transaction value of similar goods sold for export to the same country of importation and exported at or about the same time as the goods being valued.
   (b) In applying this Article, the transaction value of similar goods in a sale at the same commercial level and in substantially the same quantity as the goods being valued shall be used to determine the customs value. Where no such sale is found, the transaction value of similar goods sold at a different commercial level and/or in different quantities, adjusted to take account of differences attributable to commercial level and/or to quantity, shall be used, provided that such adjustments can be made on the basis of demonstrated evidence which clearly establishes the reasonableness and accuracy of the adjustment, whether the adjustment leads to an increase or a decrease in the value.
2. Where the costs and charges referred to in paragraph 2 of Article 8 are included in the transaction value, an adjustment shall be made to take account of

significant differences in such costs and charges between the imported goods and the similar goods in question arising from differences in distances and modes of transport.

3. If, in applying this Article, more than one transaction value of similar goods is found, the lowest such value shall be used to determine the customs value of the imported goods.

Article 4

If the customs value of the imported goods cannot be determined under the provisions of Articles 1, 2 and 3, the customs value shall be determined under the provisions of Article 5 or, when the customs value cannot be determined under that Article, under the provisions of Article 6 except that, at the request of the importer, the order of application of Articles 5 and 6 shall be reversed.

Article 5

1. (a) If the imported goods or identical or similar imported goods are sold in the country of importation in the condition as imported, the customs value of the imported goods under the provisions of this Article shall be based on the unit price at which the imported goods or identical or similar imported goods are so sold in the greatest aggregate quantity, at or about the time of the importation of the goods being valued, to persons who are not related to the persons from whom they buy such goods, subject to deductions for the following:
      (i) either the commissions usually paid or agreed to be paid or the additions usually made for profit and general expenses in connection with sales in such country of imported goods of the same class or kind;
      (ii) the usual costs of transport and insurance and associated costs incurred within the country of importation;
      (iii) where appropriate, the costs and charges referred to in paragraph 2 of Article 8; and
      (iv) the customs duties and other national taxes payable in the country of importation by reason of the importation or sale of the goods.

   (b) If neither the imported goods nor identical nor similar imported goods are sold at or about the time of importation of the goods being valued, the customs value shall, subject otherwise to the provisions of paragraph 1(a), be based on the unit price at which the imported goods or identical or similar imported goods are sold in the country of importation in the condition as imported at the earliest date after the importation of the goods being valued but before the expiration of 90 days after such importation.

2. If neither the imported goods nor identical nor similar imported goods are sold in the country of importation in the condition as imported, then, if the importer so requests, the customs value shall be based on the unit price at which the imported goods, after further processing, are sold in the greatest aggregate quantity to persons in the country of importation who are not related to the persons from whom they buy such goods, due allowance being made for the value added by such processing and the deductions provided for in paragraph 1(a).

Article 6

1. The customs value of imported goods under the provisions of this Article shall be based on a computed value. Computed value shall consist of the sum of:
   (a) the cost or value of materials and fabrication or other processing employed in producing the imported goods;
   (b) an amount for profit and general expenses equal to that usually reflected in sales of goods of the same class or kind as the goods being valued which are made by producers in the country of exportation for export to the country of importation;
   (c) the cost or value of all other expenses necessary to reflect the valuation option chosen by the Member under paragraph 2 of Article 8.
2. No Member may require or compel any person not resident in its own territory to produce for examination, or to allow access to, any account or other record for the purposes of determining a computed value. However, information supplied by the producer of the goods for the purposes of determining the customs value under the provisions of this Article may be verified in another country by the authorities of the country of importation with the agreement of the producer and provided they give sufficient advance notice to the government of the country in question and the latter does not object to the investigation.

Article 7

1. If the customs value of the imported goods cannot be determined under the provisions of Articles 1 through 6, inclusive, the customs value shall be determined using reasonable means consistent with the principles and general provisions of this Agreement and of Article VII of GATT 1994 and on the basis of data available in the country of importation.
2. No customs value shall be determined under the provisions of this Article on the basis of:
   (a) the selling price in the country of importation of goods produced in such country;
   (b) a system which provides for the acceptance for customs purposes of the higher of two alternative values;

(c) the price of goods on the domestic market of the country of exportation;
(d) the cost of production other than computed values which have been determined for identical or similar goods in accordance with the provisions of Article 6;
(e) the price of the goods for export to a country other than the country of importation;
(f) minimum customs values; or
(g) arbitrary or fictitious values.

3. If the importer so requests, the importer shall be informed in writing of the customs value determined under the provisions of this Article and the method used to determine such value.

Article 8

1. In determining the customs value under the provisions of Article 1, there shall be added to the price actually paid or payable for the imported goods:
   (a) the following, to the extent that they are incurred by the buyer but are not included in the price actually paid or payable for the goods:
      (i) commissions and brokerage, except buying commissions;
      (ii) the cost of containers which are treated as being one for customs purposes with the goods in question;
      (iii) the cost of packing whether for labour or materials;
   (b) the value, apportioned as appropriate, of the following goods and services where supplied directly or indirectly by the buyer free of charge or at reduced cost for use in connection with the production and sale for export of the imported goods, to the extent that such value has not been included in the price actually paid or payable:
      (i) materials, components, parts and similar items incorporated in the imported goods;
      (ii) tools, dies, moulds and similar items used in the production of the imported goods;
      (iii) materials consumed in the production of the imported goods;
      (iv) engineering, development, artwork, design work, plans and sketches, undertaken elsewhere than in the country of importation and necessary for the production of the imported goods;[1]
   (c) royalties and licence fees related to the goods being valued that the buyer must pay, either directly or indirectly, as a condition of sale of the goods being valued, to the extent that such royalties and fees are not included in the price actually paid or payable;
   (d) the value of any part of the proceeds of any subsequent resale, disposal or use of the imported goods that accrues directly or indirectly to the seller.

1. Reflects changes introduced as a result of the procès-verbal of rectification of 23 September 2014 (WT/Let/986).

2. In framing its legislation, each Member shall provide for the inclusion in or the exclusion from the customs value, in whole or in part, of the following:
   (a) the cost of transport of the imported goods to the port or place of importation;
   (b) loading, unloading and handling charges associated with the transport of the imported goods to the port or place of importation; and
   (c) the cost of insurance.
3. Additions to the price actually paid or payable shall be made under this Article only on the basis of objective and quantifiable data.
4. No additions shall be made to the price actually paid or payable in determining the customs value except as provided in this Article.

Article 9

1. Where the conversion of currency is necessary for the determination of the customs value, the rate of exchange to be used shall be that duly published by the competent authorities of the country of importation concerned and shall reflect as effectively as possible, in respect of the period covered by each such document of publication, the current value of such currency in commercial transactions in terms of the currency of the country of importation.
2. The conversion rate to be used shall be that in effect at the time of exportation or the time of importation, as provided by each Member.

Article 10

All information which is by nature confidential or which is provided on a confidential basis for the purposes of customs valuation shall be treated as strictly confidential by the authorities concerned who shall not disclose it without the specific permission of the person or government providing such information, except to the extent that it may be required to be disclosed in the context of judicial proceedings.

Article 11

1. The legislation of each Member shall provide in regard to a determination of customs value for the right of appeal, without penalty, by the importer or any other person liable for the payment of the duty.
2. An initial right of appeal without penalty may be to an authority within the customs administration or to an independent body, but the legislation of each Member shall provide for the right of appeal without penalty to a judicial authority.
3. Notice of the decision on appeal shall be given to the appellant and the reasons for such decision shall be provided in writing. The appellant shall also be informed of any rights of further appeal.

Article 12

Laws, regulations, judicial decisions and administrative rulings of general application giving effect to this Agreement shall be published in conformity with Article X of GATT 1994 by the country of importation concerned.

Article 13

If, in the course of determining the customs value of imported goods, it becomes necessary to delay the final determination of such customs value, the importer of the goods shall nevertheless be able to withdraw them from customs if, where so required, the importer provides sufficient guarantee in the form of a surety, a deposit or some other appropriate instrument, covering the ultimate payment of customs duties for which the goods may be liable. The legislation of each Member shall make provisions for such circumstances.

Article 14

The notes at Annex I to this Agreement form an integral part of this Agreement and the Articles of this Agreement are to be read and applied in conjunction with their respective notes. Annexes II and III also form an integral part of this Agreement.

Article 15

1. In this Agreement:
   (a) "customs value of imported goods" means the value of goods for the purposes of levying ad valorem duties of customs on imported goods;
   (b) "country of importation" means country or customs territory of importation; and
   (c) "produced" includes grown, manufactured and mined.
2. In this Agreement:
   (a) "identical goods" means goods which are the same in all respects, including physical characteristics, quality and reputation. Minor differences in appearance would not preclude goods otherwise conforming to the definition from being regarded as identical;
   (b) "similar goods" means goods which, although not alike in all respects, have like characteristics and like component materials which enable them to perform the same functions and to be commercially interchangeable. The quality of the goods, their reputation and the existence of a trademark are among the factors to be considered in determining whether goods are similar;
   (c) the terms "identical goods" and "similar goods" do not include, as the case may be, goods which incorporate or reflect engineering, development, artwork, design work, and plans and sketches for which no

adjustment has been made under paragraph 1(b)(iv) of Article 8 because such elements were undertaken in the country of importation;

(d) goods shall not be regarded as "identical goods" or "similar goods" unless they were produced in the same country as the goods being valued;

(e) goods produced by a different person shall be taken into account only when there are no identical goods or similar goods, as the case may be, produced by the same person as the goods being valued.

3. In this Agreement "goods of the same class or kind" means goods which fall within a group or range of goods produced by a particular industry or industry sector, and includes identical or similar goods.

4. For the purposes of this Agreement, persons shall be deemed to be related only if:

   (a) they are officers or directors of one another's businesses;
   (b) they are legally recognized partners in business;
   (c) they are employer and employee;
   (d) any person directly or indirectly owns, controls or holds 5 per cent or more of the outstanding voting stock or shares of both of them;
   (e) one of them directly or indirectly controls the other;
   (f) both of them are directly or indirectly controlled by a third person;
   (g) together they directly or indirectly control a third person; or
   (h) they are members of the same family.

5. Persons who are associated in business with one another in that one is the sole agent, sole distributor or sole concessionaire, however described, of the other shall be deemed to be related for the purposes of this Agreement if they fall within the criteria of paragraph 4.

Article 16

Upon written request, the importer shall have the right to an explanation in writing from the customs administration of the country of importation as to how the customs value of the importer's goods was determined.

Article 17

Nothing in this Agreement shall be construed as restricting or calling into question the rights of customs administrations to satisfy themselves as to the truth or accuracy of any statement, document or declaration presented for customs valuation purposes.

PART II

ADMINISTRATION, CONSULTATIONS AND DISPUTE SETTLEMENT

Article 18

Institutions

1. There is hereby established a Committee on Customs Valuation (referred to in this Agreement as "the Committee") composed of representatives from each of the Members. The Committee shall elect its own Chairman and shall normally meet once a year, or as is otherwise envisaged by the relevant provisions of this Agreement, for the purpose of affording Members the opportunity to consult on matters relating to the administration of the customs valuation system by any Member as it might affect the operation of this Agreement or the furtherance of its objectives and carrying out such other responsibilities as may be assigned to it by the Members. The WTO Secretariat shall act as the secretariat to the Committee.
2. There shall be established a Technical Committee on Customs Valuation (referred to in this Agreement as "the Technical Committee") under the auspices of the Customs Co-operation Council (referred to in this Agreement as "the CCC"), which shall carry out the responsibilities described in Annex II to this Agreement and shall operate in accordance with the rules of procedure contained therein.

Article 19

Consultations and Dispute Settlement

1. Except as otherwise provided herein, the Dispute Settlement Understanding is applicable to consultations and the settlement of disputes under this Agreement.
2. If any Member considers that any benefit accruing to it, directly or indirectly, under this Agreement is being nullified or impaired, or that the achievement of any objective of this Agreement is being impeded, as a result of the actions of another Member or of other Members, it may, with a view to reaching a mutually satisfactory solution of this matter, request consultations with the Member or Members in question. Each Member shall afford sympathetic consideration to any request from another Member for consultations.
3. The Technical Committee shall provide, upon request, advice and assistance to Members engaged in consultations.
4. At the request of a party to the dispute, or on its own initiative, a panel established to examine a dispute relating to the provisions of this Agreement may request the Technical Committee to carry out an examination of any

questions requiring technical consideration. The panel shall determine the terms of reference of the Technical Committee for the particular dispute and set a time period for receipt of the report of the Technical Committee. The panel shall take into consideration the report of the Technical Committee. In the event that the Technical Committee is unable to reach consensus on a matter referred to it pursuant to this paragraph, the panel should afford the parties to the dispute an opportunity to present their views on the matter to the panel.

5. Confidential information provided to the panel shall not be disclosed without formal authorization from the person, body or authority providing such information. Where such information is requested from the panel but release of such information by the panel is not authorized, a non-confidential summary of this information, authorized by the person, body or authority providing the information, shall be provided.

PART III

SPECIAL AND DIFFERENTIAL TREATMENT

Article 20

1. Developing country Members not party to the Agreement on Implementation of Article VII of the General Agreement on Tariffs and Trade done on 12 April 1979 may delay application of the provisions of this Agreement for a period not exceeding five years from the date of entry into force of the WTO Agreement for such Members. Developing country Members who choose to delay application of this Agreement shall notify the Director-General of the WTO accordingly.
2. In addition to paragraph 1, developing country Members not party to the Agreement on Implementation of Article VII of the General Agreement on Tariffs and Trade done on 12 April 1979 may delay application of paragraph 2(b)(iii) of Article 1 and Article 6 for a period not exceeding three years following their application of all other provisions of this Agreement. Developing country Members that choose to delay application of the provisions specified in this paragraph shall notify the Director-General of the WTO accordingly.
3. Developed country Members shall furnish, on mutually agreed terms, technical assistance to developing country Members that so request. On this basis developed country Members shall draw up programmes of technical assistance which may include, *inter alia,* training of personnel, assistance in preparing implementation measures, access to sources of information regarding customs valuation methodology, and advice on the application of the provisions of this Agreement.

PART IV

FINAL PROVISIONS

Article 21

Reservations

Reservations may not be entered in respect of any of the provisions of this Agreement without the consent of the other Members.

Article 22

National Legislation

1. Each Member shall ensure, not later than the date of application of the provisions of this Agreement for it, the conformity of its laws, regulations and administrative procedures with the provisions of this Agreement.
2. Each Member shall inform the Committee of any changes in its laws and regulations relevant to this Agreement and in the administration of such laws and regulations.

Article 23

Review

The Committee shall review annually the implementation and operation of this Agreement taking into account the objectives thereof. The Committee shall annually inform the Council for Trade in Goods of developments during the period covered by such reviews.

Article 24

Secretariat

This Agreement shall be serviced by the WTO Secretariat except in regard to those responsibilities specifically assigned to the Technical Committee, which will be serviced by the CCC Secretariat.

ANNEX I

INTERPRETATIVE NOTES

General Note

Sequential Application of Valuation Methods

1. Articles 1 through 7 define how the customs value of imported goods is to be determined under the provisions of this Agreement. The methods of valuation are set out in a sequential order of application. The primary method for customs valuation is defined in Article 1 and imported goods are to be valued in accordance with the provisions of this Article whenever the conditions prescribed therein are fulfilled.
2. Where the customs value cannot be determined under the provisions of Article 1, it is to be determined by proceeding sequentially through the succeeding Articles to the first such Article under which the customs value can be determined. Except as provided in Article 4, it is only when the customs value cannot be determined under the provisions of a particular Article that the provisions of the next Article in the sequence can be used.
3. If the importer does not request that the order of Articles 5 and 6 be reversed, the normal order of the sequence is to be followed. If the importer does so request but it then proves impossible to determine the customs value under the provisions of Article 6, the customs value is to be determined under the provisions of Article 5, if it can be so determined.
4. Where the customs value cannot be determined under the provisions of Articles 1 through 6 it is to be determined under the provisions of Article 7.

Use of Generally Accepted Accounting Principles

1. "Generally accepted accounting principles" refers to the recognized consensus or substantial authoritative support within a country at a particular time as to which economic resources and obligations should be recorded as assets and liabilities, which changes in assets and liabilities should be recorded, how the assets and liabilities and changes in them should be measured, what information should be disclosed and how it should be disclosed, and which financial statements should be prepared. These standards may be broad guidelines of general application as well as detailed practices and procedures.
2. For the purposes of this Agreement, the customs administration of each Member shall utilize information prepared in a manner consistent with generally accepted accounting principles in the country which is appropriate for the Article in question. For example, the determination of usual profit and general expenses under the provisions of Article 5 would be carried out utilizing information prepared in a manner consistent with generally accepted

accounting principles of the country of importation. On the other hand, the determination of usual profit and general expenses under the provisions of Article 6 would be carried out utilizing information prepared in a manner consistent with generally accepted accounting principles of the country of production. As a further example, the determination of an element provided for in paragraph 1(b)(ii) of Article 8 undertaken in the country of importation would be carried out utilizing information in a manner consistent with the generally accepted accounting principles of that country.

Note to Article 1

Price Actually Paid or Payable

1. The price actually paid or payable is the total payment made or to be made by the buyer to or for the benefit of the seller for the imported goods. The payment need not necessarily take the form of a transfer of money. Payment may be made by way of letters of credit or negotiable instruments. Payment may be made directly or indirectly. An example of an indirect payment would be the settlement by the buyer, whether in whole or in part, of a debt owed by the seller.
2. Activities undertaken by the buyer on the buyer's own account, other than those for which an adjustment is provided in Article 8, are not considered to be an indirect payment to the seller, even though they might be regarded as of benefit to the seller. The costs of such activities shall not, therefore, be added to the price actually paid or payable in determining the customs value.
3. The customs value shall not include the following charges or costs, provided that they are distinguished from the price actually paid or payable for the imported goods:
   (a) charges for construction, erection, assembly, maintenance or technical assistance, undertaken after importation on imported goods such as industrial plant, machinery or equipment;
   (b) the cost of transport after importation;
   (c) duties and taxes of the country of importation.
4. The price actually paid or payable refers to the price for the imported goods. Thus the flow of dividends or other payments from the buyer to the seller that do not relate to the imported goods are not part of the customs value.

Paragraph 1(a)(iii)

Among restrictions which would not render a price actually paid or payable unacceptable are restrictions which do not substantially affect the value of the goods. An example of such restrictions would be the case where a seller requires a buyer of automobiles not to sell or exhibit them prior to a fixed date which represents the beginning of a model year.

Paragraph 1(b)

1. If the sale or price is subject to some condition or consideration for which a value cannot be determined with respect to the goods being valued, the transaction value shall not be acceptable for customs purposes. Some examples of this include:
   (a) the seller establishes the price of the imported goods on condition that the buyer will also buy other goods in specified quantities;
   (b) the price of the imported goods is dependent upon the price or prices at which the buyer of the imported goods sells other goods to the seller of the imported goods;
   (c) the price is established on the basis of a form of payment extraneous to the imported goods, such as where the imported goods are semi-finished goods which have been provided by the seller on condition that the seller will receive a specified quantity of the finished goods.
2. However, conditions or considerations relating to the production or marketing of the imported goods shall not result in rejection of the transaction value. For example, the fact that the buyer furnishes the seller with engineering and plans undertaken in the country of importation shall not result in rejection of the transaction value for the purposes of Article 1. Likewise, if the buyer undertakes on the buyer's own account, even though by agreement with the seller, activities relating to the marketing of the imported goods, the value of these activities is not part of the customs value nor shall such activities result in rejection of the transaction value.

Paragraph 2

1. Paragraphs 2(a) and 2(b) provide different means of establishing the acceptability of a transaction value.
2. Paragraph 2(a) provides that where the buyer and the seller are related, the circumstances surrounding the sale shall be examined and the transaction value shall be accepted as the customs value provided that the relationship did not influence the price. It is not intended that there should be an examination of the circumstances in all cases where the buyer and the seller are related. Such examination will only be required where there are doubts about the acceptability of the price. Where the customs administration have no doubts about the acceptability of the price, it should be accepted without requesting further information from the importer. For example, the customs administration may have previously examined the relationship, or it may already have detailed information concerning the buyer and the seller, and may already be satisfied from such examination or information that the relationship did not influence the price.
3. Where the customs administration is unable to accept the transaction value without further inquiry, it should give the importer an opportunity to supply

such further detailed information as may be necessary to enable it to examine the circumstances surrounding the sale. In this context, the customs administration should be prepared to examine relevant aspects of the transaction, including the way in which the buyer and seller organize their commercial relations and the way in which the price in question was arrived at, in order to determine whether the relationship influenced the price. Where it can be shown that the buyer and seller, although related under the provisions of Article 15, buy from and sell to each other as if they were not related, this would demonstrate that the price had not been influenced by the relationship. As an example of this, if the price had been settled in a manner consistent with the normal pricing practices of the industry in question or with the way the seller settles prices for sales to buyers who are not related to the seller, this would demonstrate that the price had not been influenced by the relationship. As a further example, where it is shown that the price is adequate to ensure recovery of all costs plus a profit which is representative of the firm's overall profit realized over a representative period of time (e.g. on an annual basis) in sales of goods of the same class or kind, this would demonstrate that the price had not been influenced.

4. Paragraph 2(b) provides an opportunity for the importer to demonstrate that the transaction value closely approximates to a "test" value previously accepted by the customs administration and is therefore acceptable under the provisions of Article 1. Where a test under paragraph 2(b) is met, it is not necessary to examine the question of influence under paragraph 2(a). If the customs administration has already sufficient information to be satisfied, without further detailed inquiries, that one of the tests provided in paragraph 2(b) has been met, there is no reason for it to require the importer to demonstrate that the test can be met. In paragraph 2(b) the term "unrelated buyers" means buyers who are not related to the seller in any particular case.

Paragraph 2(b)

A number of factors must be taken into consideration in determining whether one value "closely approximates" to another value. These factors include the nature of the imported goods, the nature of the industry itself, the season in which the goods are imported, and, whether the difference in values is commercially significant. Since these factors may vary from case to case, it would be impossible to apply a uniform standard such as a fixed percentage, in each case. For example, a small difference in value in a case involving one type of goods could be unacceptable while a large difference in a case involving another type of goods might be acceptable in determining whether the transaction value closely approximates to the "test" values set forth in paragraph 2(b) of Article 1.

Note to Article 2

1. In applying Article 2, the customs administration shall, wherever possible, use a sale of identical goods at the same commercial level and in substantially the same quantities as the goods being valued. Where no such sale is found, a sale of identical goods that takes place under any one of the following three conditions may be used:
   (a) a sale at the same commercial level but in different quantities;
   (b) a sale at a different commercial level but in substantially the same quantities; or
   (c) a sale at a different commercial level and in different quantities.
2. Having found a sale under any one of these three conditions adjustments will then be made, as the case may be, for:
   (a) quantity factors only;
   (b) commercial level factors only; or
   (c) both commercial level and quantity factors.
3. The expression "and/or" allows the flexibility to use the sales and make the necessary adjustments in any one of the three conditions described above.
4. For the purposes of Article 2, the transaction value of identical imported goods means a customs value, adjusted as provided for in paragraphs 1(b) and 2, which has already been accepted under Article 1.
5. A condition for adjustment because of different commercial levels or different quantities is that such adjustment, whether it leads to an increase or a decrease in the value, be made only on the basis of demonstrated evidence that clearly establishes the reasonableness and accuracy of the adjustments, e.g. valid price lists containing prices referring to different levels or different quantities. As an example of this, if the imported goods being valued consist of a shipment of 10 units and the only identical imported goods for which a transaction value exists involved a sale of 500 units, and it is recognized that the seller grants quantity discounts, the required adjustment may be accomplished by resorting to the seller's price list and using that price applicable to a sale of 10 units. This does not require that a sale had to have been made in quantities of 10 as long as the price list has been established as being bona fide through sales at other quantities. In the absence of such an objective measure, however, the determination of a customs value under the provisions of Article 2 is not appropriate.

Note to Article 3

1. In applying Article 3, the customs administration shall, wherever possible, use a sale of similar goods at the same commercial level and in substantially the same quantities as the goods being valued. Where no such sale is found, a sale of similar goods that takes place under any one of the following three conditions may be used:

(a) a sale at the same commercial level but in different quantities;
(b) a sale at a different commercial level but in substantially the same quantities; or
(c) a sale at a different commercial level and in different quantities.

2. Having found a sale under any one of these three conditions adjustments will then be made, as the case may be, for:
   (a) quantity factors only;
   (b) commercial level factors only; or
   (c) both commercial level and quantity factors.
3. The expression "and/or" allows the flexibility to use the sales and make the necessary adjustments in any one of the three conditions described above.
4. For the purpose of Article 3, the transaction value of similar imported goods means a customs value, adjusted as provided for in paragraphs 1(b) and 2, which has already been accepted under Article 1.
5. A condition for adjustment because of different commercial levels or different quantities is that such adjustment, whether it leads to an increase or a decrease in the value, be made only on the basis of demonstrated evidence that clearly establishes the reasonableness and accuracy of the adjustment, e.g. valid price lists containing prices referring to different levels or different quantities. As an example of this, if the imported goods being valued consist of a shipment of 10 units and the only similar imported goods for which a transaction value exists involved a sale of 500 units, and it is recognized that the seller grants quantity discounts, the required adjustment may be accomplished by resorting to the seller's price list and using that price applicable to a sale of 10 units. This does not require that a sale had to have been made in quantities of 10 as long as the price list has been established as being bona fide through sales at other quantities. In the absence of such an objective measure, however, the determination of a customs value under the provisions of Article 3 is not appropriate.

Note to Article 5

1. The term "unit price at which ... goods are sold in the greatest aggregate quantity" means the price at which the greatest number of units is sold in sales to persons who are not related to the persons from whom they buy such goods at the first commercial level after importation at which such sales take place.
2. As an example of this, goods are sold from a price list which grants favourable unit prices for purchases made in larger quantities.

Sale quantity	*Unit price*	*Number of sales*	*Total quantity sold at each price*
1-10 units	100	10 sales of 5 units 5 sales of 3 units	65
11-25 units	95	5 sales of 11 units	55
over 25 units	90	1 sale of 30 units 1 sale of 50 units	80

The greatest number of units sold at a price is 80; therefore, the unit price in the greatest aggregate quantity is 90.

3. As another example of this, two sales occur. In the first sale 500 units are sold at a price of 95 currency units each. In the second sale 400 units are sold at a price of 90 currency units each. In this example, the greatest number of units sold at a particular price is 500; therefore, the unit price in the greatest aggregate quantity is 95.
4. A third example would be the following situation where various quantities are sold at various prices.

(a) Sales	
Sale quantity	*Unit price*
40 units	100
30 units	90
15 units	100
50 units	95
25 units	105
35 units	90
5 units	100
(b) Totals	
Total quantity sold	*Unit price*
65	90
50	95
60	100
25	105

In this example, the greatest number of units sold at a particular price is 65; therefore, the unit price in the greatest aggregate quantity is 90.

5. Any sale in the importing country, as described in paragraph 1 above, to a person who supplies directly or indirectly free of charge or at reduced cost for

use in connection with the production and sale for export of the imported goods any of the elements specified in paragraph 1(b) of Article 8, should not be taken into account in establishing the unit price for the purposes of Article 5.

6. It should be noted that "profit and general expenses" referred to in paragraph 1 of Article 5 should be taken as a whole. The figure for the purposes of this deduction should be determined on the basis of information supplied by or on behalf of the importer unless the importer's figures are inconsistent with those obtained in sales in the country of importation of imported goods of the same class or kind. Where the importer's figures are inconsistent with such figures, the amount for profit and general expenses may be based upon relevant information other than that supplied by or on behalf of the importer.
7. The "general expenses" include the direct and indirect costs of marketing the goods in question.
8. Local taxes payable by reason of the sale of the goods for which a deduction is not made under the provisions of paragraph 1(a)(iv) of Article 5 shall be deducted under the provisions of paragraph 1(a)(i) of Article 5.
9. In determining either the commissions or the usual profits and general expenses under the provisions of paragraph 1 of Article 5, the question whether certain goods are "of the same class or kind" as other goods must be determined on a case-by-case basis by reference to the circumstances involved. Sales in the country of importation of the narrowest group or range of imported goods of the same class or kind, which includes the goods being valued, for which the necessary information can be provided, should be examined. For the purposes of Article 5, "goods of the same class or kind" includes goods imported from the same country as the goods being valued as well as goods imported from other countries.
10. For the purposes of paragraph 1(b) of Article 5, the "earliest date" shall be the date by which sales of the imported goods or of identical or similar imported goods are made in sufficient quantity to establish the unit price.
11. Where the method in paragraph 2 of Article 5 is used, deductions made for the value added by further processing shall be based on objective and quantifiable data relating to the cost of such work. Accepted industry formulas, recipes, methods of construction, and other industry practices would form the basis of the calculations.
12. It is recognized that the method of valuation provided for in paragraph 2 of Article 5 would normally not be applicable when, as a result of the further processing, the imported goods lose their identity. However, there can be instances where, although the identity of the imported goods is lost, the value added by the processing can be determined accurately without unreasonable difficulty. On the other hand, there can also be instances where the imported goods maintain their identity but form such a minor element in the goods sold in the country of importation that the use of this valuation method would be

unjustified. In view of the above, each situation of this type must be considered on a case-by-case basis.

Note to Article 6

1. As a general rule, customs value is determined under this Agreement on the basis of information readily available in the country of importation. In order to determine a computed value, however, it may be necessary to examine the costs of producing the goods being valued and other information which has to be obtained from outside the country of importation. Furthermore, in most cases the producer of the goods will be outside the jurisdiction of the authorities of the country of importation. The use of the computed value method will generally be limited to those cases where the buyer and seller are related, and the producer is prepared to supply to the authorities of the country of importation the necessary costings and to provide facilities for any subsequent verification which may be necessary.
2. The "cost or value" referred to in paragraph 1(a) of Article 6 is to be determined on the basis of information relating to the production of the goods being valued supplied by or on behalf of the producer. It is to be based upon the commercial accounts of the producer, provided that such accounts are consistent with the generally accepted accounting principles applied in the country where the goods are produced.
3. The "cost or value" shall include the cost of elements specified in paragraphs 1(a)(ii) and (iii) of Article 8. It shall also include the value, apportioned as appropriate under the provisions of the relevant note to Article 8, of any element specified in paragraph 1(b) of Article 8 which has been supplied directly or indirectly by the buyer for use in connection with the production of the imported goods. The value of the elements specified in paragraph 1(b)(iv) of Article 8 which are undertaken in the country of importation shall be included only to the extent that such elements are charged to the producer. It is to be understood that no cost or value of the elements referred to in this paragraph shall be counted twice in determining the computed value.
4. The "amount for profit and general expenses" referred to in paragraph 1(b) of Article 6 is to be determined on the basis of information supplied by or on behalf of the producer unless the producer's figures are inconsistent with those usually reflected in sales of goods of the same class or kind as the goods being valued which are made by producers in the country of exportation for export to the country of importation.
5. It should be noted in this context that the "amount for profit and general expenses" has to be taken as a whole. It follows that if, in any particular case, the producer's profit figure is low and the producer's general expenses are high, the producer's profit and general expenses taken together may nevertheless be consistent with that usually reflected in sales of goods of the same class or kind. Such a situation might occur, for example, if a product were

being launched in the country of importation and the producer accepted a nil or low profit to offset high general expenses associated with the launch. Where the producer can demonstrate a low profit on sales of the imported goods because of particular commercial circumstances, the producer's actual profit figures should be taken into account provided that the producer has valid commercial reasons to justify them and the producer's pricing policy reflects usual pricing policies in the branch of industry concerned. Such a situation might occur, for example, where producers have been forced to lower prices temporarily because of an unforeseeable drop in demand, or where they sell goods to complement a range of goods being produced in the country of importation and accept a low profit to maintain competitivity. Where the producer's own figures for profit and general expenses are not consistent with those usually reflected in sales of goods of the same class or kind as the goods being valued which are made by producers in the country of exportation for export to the country of importation, the amount for profit and general expenses may be based upon relevant information other than that supplied by or on behalf of the producer of the goods.

6. Where information other than that supplied by or on behalf of the producer is used for the purposes of determining a computed value, the authorities of the importing country shall inform the importer, if the latter so requests, of the source of such information, the data used and the calculations based upon such data, subject to the provisions of Article 10.
7. The "general expenses" referred to in paragraph 1(b) of Article 6 covers the direct and indirect costs of producing and selling the goods for export which are not included under paragraph 1(a) of Article 6.
8. Whether certain goods are "of the same class or kind" as other goods must be determined on a case-by-case basis with reference to the circumstances involved. In determining the usual profits and general expenses under the provisions of Article 6, sales for export to the country of importation of the narrowest group or range of goods, which includes the goods being valued, for which the necessary information can be provided, should be examined. For the purposes of Article 6, "goods of the same class or kind" must be from the same country as the goods being valued.

Note to Article 7

1. Customs values determined under the provisions of Article 7 should, to the greatest extent possible, be based on previously determined customs values.
2. The methods of valuation to be employed under Article 7 should be those laid down in Articles 1 through 6 but a reasonable flexibility in the application of such methods would be in conformity with the aims and provisions of Article 7.
3. Some examples of reasonable flexibility are as follows:

(a) *Identical goods* - the requirement that the identical goods should be exported at or about the same time as the goods being valued could be flexibly interpreted; identical imported goods produced in a country other than the country of exportation of the goods being valued could be the basis for customs valuation; customs values of identical imported goods already determined under the provisions of Articles 5 and 6 could be used.

(b) *Similar goods* - the requirement that the similar goods should be exported at or about the same time as the goods being valued could be flexibly interpreted; similar imported goods produced in a country other than the country of exportation of the goods being valued could be the basis for customs valuation; customs values of similar imported goods already determined under the provisions of Articles 5 and 6 could be used.

(c) *Deductive method* - the requirement that the goods shall have been sold in the "condition as imported" in paragraph 1(a) of Article 5 could be flexibly interpreted; the "90 days" requirement could be administered flexibly.

Note to Article 8

Paragraph 1(a)(i)

The term "buying commissions" means fees paid by an importer to the importer's agent for the service of representing the importer abroad in the purchase of the goods being valued.

Paragraph 1(b)(ii)

1. There are two factors involved in the apportionment of the elements specified in paragraph 1(b)(ii) of Article 8 to the imported goods - the value of the element itself and the way in which that value is to be apportioned to the imported goods. The apportionment of these elements should be made in a reasonable manner appropriate to the circumstances and in accordance with generally accepted accounting principles.
2. Concerning the value of the element, if the importer acquires the element from a seller not related to the importer at a given cost, the value of the element is that cost. If the element was produced by the importer or by a person related to the importer, its value would be the cost of producing it. If the element had been previously used by the importer, regardless of whether it had been acquired or produced by such importer, the original cost of acquisition or production would have to be adjusted downward to reflect its use in order to arrive at the value of the element.
3. Once a value has been determined for the element, it is necessary to apportion that value to the imported goods. Various possibilities exist. For example, the

value might be apportioned to the first shipment if the importer wishes to pay duty on the entire value at one time. As another example, the importer may request that the value be apportioned over the number of units produced up to the time of the first shipment. As a further example, the importer may request that the value be apportioned over the entire anticipated production where contracts or firm commitments exist for that production. The method of apportionment used will depend upon the documentation provided by the importer.

4. As an illustration of the above, an importer provides the producer with a mould to be used in the production of the imported goods and contracts with the producer to buy 10,000 units. By the time of arrival of the first shipment of 1,000 units, the producer has already produced 4,000 units. The importer may request the customs administration to apportion the value of the mould over 1,000 units, 4,000 units or 10,000 units.

Paragraph 1 (b) (iv)

1. Additions for the elements specified in paragraph 1 (b) (iv) of Article 8 should be based on objective and quantifiable data. In order to minimize the burden for both the importer and customs administration in determining the values to be added, data readily available in the buyer's commercial record system should be used in so far as possible.
2. For those elements supplied by the buyer which were purchased or leased by the buyer, the addition would be the cost of the purchase or the lease. No addition shall be made for those elements available in the public domain, other than the cost of obtaining copies of them.
3. The ease with which it may be possible to calculate the values to be added will depend on a particular firm's structure and management practice, as well as its accounting methods.
4. For example, it is possible that a firm which imports a variety of products from several countries maintains the records of its design centre outside the country of importation in such a way as to show accurately the costs attributable to a given product. In such cases, a direct adjustment may appropriately be made under the provisions of Article 8.
5. In another case, a firm may carry the cost of the design centre outside the country of importation as a general overhead expense without allocation to specific products. In this instance, an appropriate adjustment could be made under the provisions of Article 8 with respect to the imported goods by apportioning total design centre costs over total production benefiting from the design centre and adding such apportioned cost on a unit basis to imports.
6. Variations in the above circumstances will, of course, require different factors to be considered in determining the proper method of allocation.

7. In cases where the production of the element in question involves a number of countries and over a period of time, the adjustment should be limited to the value actually added to that element outside the country of importation.

Paragraph 1(c)

1. The royalties and licence fees referred to in paragraph 1(c) of Article 8 may include, among other things, payments in respect to patents, trade marks and copyrights. However, the charges for the right to reproduce the imported goods in the country of importation shall not be added to the price actually paid or payable for the imported goods in determining the customs value.
2. Payments made by the buyer for the right to distribute or resell the imported goods shall not be added to the price actually paid or payable for the imported goods if such payments are not a condition of the sale for export to the country of importation of the imported goods.

Paragraph 3

Where objective and quantifiable data do not exist with regard to the additions required to be made under the provisions of Article 8, the transaction value cannot be determined under the provisions of Article 1. As an illustration of this, a royalty is paid on the basis of the price in a sale in the importing country of a litre of a particular product that was imported by the kilogram and made up into a solution after importation. If the royalty is based partially on the imported goods and partially on other factors which have nothing to do with the imported goods (such as when the imported goods are mixed with domestic ingredients and are no longer separately identifiable, or when the royalty cannot be distinguished from special financial arrangements between the buyer and the seller), it would be inappropriate to attempt to make an addition for the royalty. However, if the amount of this royalty is based only on the imported goods and can be readily quantified, an addition to the price actually paid or payable can be made.

Note to Article 9

For the purposes of Article 9, "time of importation" may include the time of entry for customs purposes.

Note to Article 11

1. Article 11 provides the importer with the right to appeal against a valuation determination made by the customs administration for the goods being valued. Appeal may first be to a higher level in the customs administration, but the importer shall have the right in the final instance to appeal to the judiciary.

2. "Without penalty" means that the importer shall not be subject to a fine or threat of fine merely because the importer chose to exercise the right of appeal. Payment of normal court costs and lawyers' fees shall not be considered to be a fine.
3. However, nothing in Article 11 shall prevent a Member from requiring full payment of assessed customs duties prior to an appeal.

Note to Article 15

Paragraph 4

For the purposes of Article 15, the term "persons" includes a legal person, where appropriate.

Paragraph 4(e)

For the purposes of this Agreement, one person shall be deemed to control another when the former is legally or operationally in a position to exercise restraint or direction over the latter.

ANNEX II

TECHNICAL COMMITTEE ON CUSTOMS VALUATION

1. In accordance with Article 18 of this Agreement, the Technical Committee shall be established under the auspices of the CCC with a view to ensuring, at the technical level, uniformity in interpretation and application of this Agreement.
2. The responsibilities of the Technical Committee shall include the following:
   (a) to examine specific technical problems arising in the day-to-day administration of the customs valuation system of Members and to give advisory opinions on appropriate solutions based upon the facts presented;
   (b) to study, as requested, valuation laws, procedures and practices as they relate to this Agreement and to prepare reports on the results of such studies;
   (c) to prepare and circulate annual reports on the technical aspects of the operation and status of this Agreement;
   (d) to furnish such information and advice on any matters concerning the valuation of imported goods for customs purposes as may be requested by any Member or the Committee. Such information and advice may take the form of advisory opinions, commentaries or explanatory notes;
   (e) to facilitate, as requested, technical assistance to Members with a view to furthering the international acceptance of this Agreement;

(f) to carry out an examination of a matter referred to it by a panel under Article 19 of this Agreement; and
(g) to exercise such other responsibilities as the Committee may assign to it.

General

3. The Technical Committee shall attempt to conclude its work on specific matters, especially those referred to it by Members, the Committee or a panel, in a reasonably short period of time. As provided in paragraph 4 of Article 19, a panel shall set a specific time period for receipt of a report of the Technical Committee and the Technical Committee shall provide its report within that period.
4. The Technical Committee shall be assisted as appropriate in its activities by the CCC Secretariat.

Representation

5. Each Member shall have the right to be represented on the Technical Committee. Each Member may nominate one delegate and one or more alternates to be its representatives on the Technical Committee. Such a Member so represented on the Technical Committee is referred to in this Annex as a "member of the Technical Committee." Representatives of members of the Technical Committee may be assisted by advisers. The WTO Secretariat may also attend such meetings with observer status.
6. Members of the CCC which are not Members of the WTO may be represented at meetings of the Technical Committee by one delegate and one or more alternates. Such representatives shall attend meetings of the Technical Committee as observers.
7. Subject to the approval of the Chairman of the Technical Committee, the Secretary-General of the CCC (referred to in this Annex as "the Secretary-General") may invite representatives of governments which are neither Members of the WTO nor members of the CCC and representatives of international governmental and trade organizations to attend meetings of the Technical Committee as observers.
8. Nominations of delegates, alternates and advisers to meetings of the Technical Committee shall be made to the Secretary-General.

Technical Committee Meetings

9. The Technical Committee shall meet as necessary but at least two times a year. The date of each meeting shall be fixed by the Technical Committee at its preceding session. The date of the meeting may be varied either at the request of any member of the Technical Committee concurred in by a simple majority of the members of the Technical Committee or, in cases requiring urgent

attention, at the request of the Chairman. Notwithstanding the provisions in sentence 1 of this paragraph, the Technical Committee shall meet as necessary to consider matters referred to it by a panel under the provisions of Article 19 of this Agreement.

10. The meetings of the Technical Committee shall be held at the headquarters of the CCC unless otherwise decided.
11. The Secretary-General shall inform all members of the Technical Committee and those included under paragraphs 6 and 7 at least 30 days in advance, except in urgent cases, of the opening date of each session of the Technical Committee.

Agenda

12. A provisional agenda for each session shall be drawn up by the Secretary-General and circulated to the members of the Technical Committee and to those included under paragraphs 6 and 7 at least 30 days in advance of the session, except in urgent cases. This agenda shall comprise all items whose inclusion has been approved by the Technical Committee during its preceding session, all items included by the Chairman on the Chairman's own initiative, and all items whose inclusion has been requested by the Secretary-General, by the Committee or by any member of the Technical Committee.
13. The Technical Committee shall determine its agenda at the opening of each session. During the session the agenda may be altered at any time by the Technical Committee.

Officers and Conduct of Business

14. The Technical Committee shall elect from among the delegates of its members a Chairman and one or more Vice-Chairmen. The Chairman and Vice-Chairmen shall each hold office for a period of one year. The retiring Chairman and Vice-Chairmen are eligible for re-election. The mandate of a Chairman or Vice-Chairman who no longer represents a member of the Technical Committee shall terminate automatically.
15. If the Chairman is absent from any meeting or part thereof, a Vice-Chairman shall preside. In that event, the latter shall have the same powers and duties as the Chairman.
16. The Chairman of the meeting shall participate in the proceedings of the Technical Committee as such and not as the representative of a member of the Technical Committee.
17. In addition to exercising the other powers conferred upon the Chairman by these rules, the Chairman shall declare the opening and closing of each meeting, direct the discussion, accord the right to speak, and, pursuant to

these rules, have control of the proceedings. The Chairman may also call a speaker to order if the speaker's remarks are not relevant.

18. During discussion of any matter a delegation may raise a point of order. In this event, the Chairman shall immediately state a ruling. If this ruling is challenged, the Chairman shall submit it to the meeting for decision and it shall stand unless overruled.
19. The Secretary-General, or officers of the CCC Secretariat designated by the Secretary-General, shall perform the secretarial work of meetings of the Technical Committee.

Quorum and Voting

20. Representatives of a simple majority of the members of the Technical Committee shall constitute a quorum.
21. Each member of the Technical Committee shall have one vote. A decision of the Technical Committee shall be taken by a majority comprising at least two thirds of the members present. Regardless of the outcome of the vote on a particular matter, the Technical Committee shall be free to make a full report to the Committee and to the CCC on that matter indicating the different views expressed in the relevant discussions. Notwithstanding the above provisions of this paragraph, on matters referred to it by a panel, the Technical Committee shall take decisions by consensus. Where no agreement is reached in the Technical Committee on the question referred to it by a panel, the Technical Committee shall provide a report detailing the facts of the matter and indicating the views of the members.

Languages and Records

22. The official languages of the Technical Committee shall be English, French and Spanish. Speeches or statements made in any of these three languages shall be immediately translated into the other official languages unless all delegations agree to dispense with translation. Speeches or statements made in any other language shall be translated into English, French and Spanish, subject to the same conditions, but in that event the delegation concerned shall provide the translation into English, French or Spanish. Only English, French and Spanish shall be used for the official documents of the Technical Committee. Memoranda and correspondence for the consideration of the Technical Committee must be presented in one of the official languages.
23. The Technical Committee shall draw up a report of all its sessions and, if the Chairman considers it necessary, minutes or summary records of its meetings. The Chairman or a designee of the Chairman shall report on the work of the Technical Committee at each meeting of the Committee and at each meeting of the CCC.

ANNEX III

1. The five-year delay in the application of the provisions of the Agreement by developing country Members provided for in paragraph 1 of Article 20 may, in practice, be insufficient for certain developing country Members. In such cases a developing country Member may request before the end of the period referred to in paragraph 1 of Article 20 an extension of such period, it being understood that the Members will give sympathetic consideration to such a request in cases where the developing country Member in question can show good cause.
2. Developing countries which currently value goods on the basis of officially established minimum values may wish to make a reservation to enable them to retain such values on a limited and transitional basis under such terms and conditions as may be agreed to by the Members.
3. Developing countries which consider that the reversal of the sequential order at the request of the importer provided for in Article 4 of the Agreement may give rise to real difficulties for them may wish to make a reservation to Article 4 in the following terms:

   "The Government of .... reserves the right to provide that the relevant provision of Article 4 of the Agreement shall apply only when the customs authorities agree to the request to reverse the order of Articles 5 and 6."

   If developing countries make such a reservation, the Members shall consent to it under Article 21 of the Agreement.
4. Developing countries may wish to make a reservation with respect to paragraph 2 of Article 5 of the Agreement in the following terms:

   "The Government of .... reserves the right to provide that paragraph 2 of Article 5 of the Agreement shall be applied in accordance with the provisions of the relevant note thereto whether or not the importer so requests."

   If developing countries make such a reservation, the Members shall consent to it under Article 21 of the Agreement.
5. Certain developing countries may have problems in the implementation of Article 1 of the Agreement insofar as it relates to importations into their countries by sole agents, sole distributors and sole concessionaires. If such problems arise in practice in developing country Members applying the Agreement, a study of this question shall be made, at the request of such Members, with a view to finding appropriate solutions.
6. Article 17 recognizes that in applying the Agreement, customs administrations may need to make enquiries concerning the truth or accuracy of any statement, document or declaration presented to them for customs valuation purposes. The Article thus acknowledges that enquiries may be made which are, for example, aimed at verifying that the elements of value declared or

presented to customs in connection with a determination of customs value are complete and correct. Members, subject to their national laws and procedures, have the right to expect the full cooperation of importers in these enquiries.

7. The price actually paid or payable includes all payments actually made or to be made as a condition of sale of the imported goods, by the buyer to the seller, or by the buyer to a third party to satisfy an obligation of the seller.

ANNEX II

Selected Administrative Authorities*

WTO Committee on Customs Valuation

DECISION 3.1**

TREATMENT OF INTEREST CHARGES IN THE CUSTOMS VALUE OF IMPORTED GOODS

During its Ninth Meeting held on 26 April 1984, the Committee on Customs Valuation adopted the following decision:

The Parties to the Agreement on Implementation of Article VII of the GATT agree as follows:

Charges for interest under a financing arrangement entered into by the buyer and relating to the purchase of imported goods shall not be regarded as part of the Customs value provided that:

(a) the charges are distinguished from the price actually paid or payable for the goods;
(b) the financing arrangement was made in writing;
(c) where required, the buyer can demonstrate that:
- such goods are actually sold at the price declared as the price actually paid or payable, and

* The cited administrative and judicial authorities are generally in the public domain and are freely available via the internet. The documents shown here are those which are of such fundamental significance that it was a convenience to include them in this volume. The one exception to availability is the body of instruments of the TCCV. These are available from the WCO for a yearly subscription. On an exceptional basis, the author may provide a copy of selected TCCV instruments upon request.

** This Decision was adopted by the WTO Valuation Committee at its first meeting on 12 May 1995.

- the claimed rate of interest does not exceed the level for such transactions prevailing in the country where, and at the time when the finance was provided.

This Decision shall apply regardless of whether the finance is provided by the seller, a bank or another natural or legal person. It shall also apply, if appropriate, where goods are valued under a method other than the transaction value.

Each Party shall notify the Committee of the date from which it will apply the Decision.

DECISION 6.1***

CASES WHERE CUSTOMS ADMINISTRATIONS HAVE REASONS TO DOUBT THE TRUTH OR ACCURACY OF THE DECLARED VALUE

The Committee on Customs Valuation,

Reaffirming that the transaction value is the primary basis of valuation under the Agreement on Implementation of Article VTI of GATI 1994 (hereinafter referred to as the "Agreement");

Recognizing that the customs administration may have to address cases where it has reason to doubt the truth or accuracy of the particulars or of documents produced by traders in support of a declared value;

Emphasizing that in so doing the customs administration should not prejudice the legitimate commercial interests of traders;

Taking into account Article 17 of the Agreement, paragraph 6 of Annex III to the Agreement, and the relevant decisions of the Technical Committee on Customs Valuation;

Decides as follows:

1. When a declaration has been presented and where the customs administration has reason to doubt the truth or accuracy of the particulars or of documents produced in support of this declaration, the customs administration may ask the importer to provide further explanation, including documents or other evidence, that the declared value represents the total amount actually paid or payable for the imported goods, adjusted in accordance with the provisions of Article 8. If, after receiving further information, or in the absence of a response, the customs administration still has reasonable doubts about the truth or accuracy of the declared value, it may, bearing in mind the provisions of Article 11, be deemed that the customs value of the imported goods cannot be determined under the provisions of Article 1. Before taking a final decision, the customs administration shall communicate to the importer, in writing if requested, its grounds for doubting the truth or accuracy of the particulars or

*** This Decision was adopted by the WTO Valuation Committee at its first meeting on 12 May 1995.

documents produced and the importer shall be given a reasonable opportunity to respond. When a final decision is made, the customs administration shall communicate to the importer in writing its decision and the grounds therefor.

2. It is entirely appropriate in applying the Agreement for one Member to assist another Member on mutually agreed terms.

World Customs Organization

Doc # *04-4290* **Access level** *Public*

WORLD TRADE
ORGANIZATION

G/VAL/54/Suppl.1
13 October 2004
(04-4290)

Committee on Customs Valuation Original: English/ French/ Spanish

TECHNICAL COMMITTEE ON CUSTOMS VALUATION – RESPONSE TO THE

TERMS OF REFERENCE FOR THE WORK OF THE TECHNICAL COMMITTEE

ON CUSTOMS VALUATION IN CONNECTION WITH CONCERNS ON THE ACCURACY OF THE DECLARED VALUE (G/VAL/51)

Supplement

The attached communication, dated 7 October 2004, together with the letter of transmission of the Chairperson of the TCCV below, is being circulated to Members.

Brussels, 27 August 2004

In accordance with the mandate of the Technical Committee on Customs Valuation (TCCV) under paragraph 8.3 of the Doha Decision and further to the response to that mandate which the TCCV communicated to the WTO Committee on Customs Valuation in May 2003, I have the honour to transmit herewith the text of the Guidelines on the Development and Use of a National Valuation Database as a Risk Assessment Tool, as adopted by the TCCV at its 18th session and by the WCO Council during its sessions of June 2004.

Chairperson

Technical Committee on Customs Valuation

WCO **OMD**

GUIDELINES ON THE DEVELOPMENT AND USE OF A NATIONAL VALUATION DATABASE AS A RISK ASSESSMENT TOOL

Table of Contents

Preamble:

1. These Guidelines address various issues pertaining to the development and use of a national valuation database. A national valuation database is a risk assessment tool which may be used by a Customs Administration along with other risk tools to assess potential risk regarding the truth or accuracy of the declared Customs value for imported goods. The information in the database should be recent data reflecting the Customs value and other pertinent information for previously imported goods. The values may not be used to determine the Customs value for imported goods, as a substitute value for imported goods, or as a mechanism to establish minimum values. In addition, recognizing that differences in prices, including substantial declines, are a part of international trade, a difference between the declared value and the database value(s) is not by itself a reliable indicator of potential risk with respect to the truth or accuracy of the declared value, subject to the provisions of Decision 6.1.

2. A Customs Administration that uses a valuation database should establish a monitoring mechanism to ensure that the database is being used as a risk assessment tool and that the information stored in the database is updated on a regular basis.

Introduction

3. The Agreement on Implementation of Article VII of the GATT 1994, more commonly known as the WTO Agreement on Customs Valuation (the Agreement), introduces a fair, uniform and neutral system for the Customs valuation of imported goods, which is consistent with commercial practices and precludes the use of arbitrary or fictitious Customs values.
4. The basis for the valuation of goods under this system is, to the greatest extent possible, the transaction value of the imported goods which is the price actually paid or payable for the goods when sold for export to the country of importation, adjusted in accordance with the provisions of Article 8 of the Agreement.
5. Where the Customs value cannot be determined using the transaction value method, the Agreement provides for five other methods, to be used in turn.
6. Customs has the right to satisfy itself as to the truth or accuracy of the value declared. The application of an appropriate risk assessment and management procedure enables Customs to exercise this right in a pragmatic manner. Such procedures may use, *inter alia*, a valuation database.
7. The data contained in a valuation database should be treated in accordance with the applicable confidentiality provisions.
8. Within the context of Customs controls, Chapter 6 of the Guidelines on the General Annex to the Revised Kyoto Convention *(Customs controls)* includes the following definitions of the concepts of risk assessment and risk management:

   Risk assessment: "The systematic determination of risk management priorities by evaluating and comparing the level of risk against predetermined standards, target risk levels or other criteria."
   Risk management: "The systematic application of management procedures and practices which provide Customs with the necessary information to address movements or consignments which present a risk."

9. In the context of Customs valuation, application of the above concepts requires that risk assessment mechanisms must be selective and targeted. It is not appropriate to apply simple statistical or price indicators to all imports on a comprehensive basis, as a means to measure potential risk with regard to the truth or accuracy of Customs value. The development and use of a valuation database must take account of the above-mentioned risk assessment and management procedures.

Use of a database:

10. A valuation database may be used by a Customs Administration only as a risk assessment tool. It has to be designed specially to assess potential risk regarding the truth or accuracy of the declared value for imported goods.
11. Database management systems will usually enable a Customs Administration to compare the declared value to previously accepted Customs value(s). Recognizing that price variations are a normal part of international trade, the results of any such comparison do not in themselves represent a comprehensive or sufficient indicator of potential risk. Therefore, while an abnormally large difference between the declared value and the databases value(s) for that product could constitute a potential risk factor, any such difference must be considered along with other potential risk factors, such as the lack of supporting documentation, prior problems with the importer, etc., in determining what further action, if any, is appropriate with regard to the declared value.
12. Where the application of appropriate database technology indicates the existence of potential risk in well-defined circumstances, Customs may apply a number of measures. For example, Customs may place the operations of a particular importer under scrutiny and take appropriate monitoring action. In other cases where there are concrete indications that the declared values represent a risk with respect to their truth or accuracy, and after taking into account all the relevant risk factors the Customs Administration has doubts about the truth or accuracy of the declared value, it could follow the procedures set forth in Decision 6.1 of the WTO Committee on Customs Valuation. Such procedures start by asking the importer to provide further evidence to support the declared value. Another example of a measure that can be taken by Customs Administration in cases of potential risk is a post-importation audit of the importer.
13. The Customs Administration cannot reject the declared value based solely on a difference between the declared value and the database value(s). Rather, the value(s) stored in the database should, alongside other indicators applied by Customs, serve only as an indicator of potential risk and represents no more than initial indicative information helping to reinforce or dispel Customs' doubts about the truth or accuracy of the declared value.
14. The database can also be used as a risk assessment tool to perform cross-checks in order to target specific import declarations for examination.
15. Normally, a valuation database should form part of a more extensive database embracing risk assessment linked to other aspects of the import/export operation, such as origin, tariff code number, importer's profile, exporter's profile, etc.
16. Each Customs Administration should determine, with reference to its own needs, which authorized staff will have access to the national valuation database.

17. The use of databases in the risk assessment context may occur at any stage: prior to the lodging of the import declaration, at the time when the declaration is lodged (verification of the data entered in the declaration), throughout the clearance process and/or after the goods have been released.

Caveat regarding the use of a database:

18. A Customs Administration may not:
    - Use a database to determine the Customs value of imported goods, as a substitute value for imported goods or as a mechanism to establish minimum values;
    - Reject the declared value solely on the basis of a difference between the declared value and the database values;
    - Disregard the requirements of article 13 of the WTO Valuation Agreement (concerning release of imported goods upon sufficient guarantee) in order to employ a valuation database; or
    - Use a valuation database as a substitute for other techniques, such as post-importation audit, to assess the truth or accuracy of the declared value.

Data to be included in a database:

19. Within the framework of a risk assessment policy for valuation, the data to be included in a valuation database may vary, depending on the state of development of the risk management policy of the Member concerned and should be based on relevant elements from the WCO Customs Data Model.
20. The usefulness of a valuation database as a risk assessment tool depends on the reliability and relevance of the data for the purposes of determining the truth or accuracy of the declared value. Therefore, the data should include the Customs value for previous importations determined in accordance with the Agreement. The data may also include the applicable method of valuation (for example, transaction value, computed value, etc.) and elements included in the Customs value (for example, assists, royalties, selling commissions, etc.). Other data from the import declaration, such as whether the parties are related, may also be included.
21. The data to be included in the database is generally the data found in the import declarations and supporting documents of previous importations. The database may also include other pertinent and reliable data for risk assessment purposes.
22. In an automated database, virtually all of this data could constitute key-words providing search access. For example, doing a search on "country of origin" should, at least, make it possible to find information about all importations of goods from the country concerned during a specified period; at best, it should

provide a range of information about the type of goods exported from that country, etc.

Validity of the data:

23. In order to properly perform its function as a risk assessment tool, data in the database should be recent and up-to-date. What is considered recent and up-to-date may depend on the commodity involved, the frequency of price fluctuations, and other pertinent factors.

Possibility of cross-checking:

24. The database can also be used as a means of performing cross-checks in order to target those importations which are likely to contain a potential risk and, from that starting-point, select the import declarations concerned for examination.
25. Thus, for example, if it has been established in the past - under the provisions of paragraphs 1 (d) and 2 of Article 1 of the Agreement, and paragraph 4 of Article 15 thereof - that a buyer/importer is related to his supplier/seller, that this relationship has influenced the price, and that this has caused the declared value to be rejected, there could be a function in the system which selects all future declarations concerning transactions between that buyer/importer and that supplier/seller, so that Customs will be in a position to check whether the relationship still exists and, if so, whether it is still producing the same effects.
26. Similarly, if it has been established in the past - under the provisions of paragraph 1 (a) of Article 8 - that commissions (other than buying commissions) have been paid in connection with a transaction between a buyer/importer and a supplier/seller, and the declared value was adjusted as a result, the system should be able to select all future declarations for transactions between that buyer/importer and that supplier/seller, so that Customs can check whether this type of payment is still being made and, where appropriate, adjust the declared value accordingly.
27. The same would apply to several other provisions of the Agreement (conditions of application of Article 1, goods and services supplied by the buyer, royalties, proceeds of resale, etc.).

Monitoring Mechanism:

A Customs Administration that uses a valuation database should establish a monitoring mechanism to ensure that it is being used only for the purpose of risk assessment described in these Guidelines and to ensure that the information in the database is updated on a regular and continual basis.

GLOBAL TRADE LAW SERIES

1. Emmanuel T. Laryea, *Paperless Trade: Opportunities, Challenges and Solutions*, 2002 (ISBN 90-411-9897-0).
2. Xiang Gao, *The Fraud Rule in the Law of Letters of Credit: A Comparative Study*, 2002 (ISBN 90-411-9898-9).
3. Yuwa Wei, *Comparative Corporate Governance: A Chinese Perspective*, 2003 (ISBN 90-411-9908-X).
4. Ross P. Buckley (ed.), *The WTO and the Doha Round: The Changing Face of World Trade*, 2003 (ISBN 90-411-9947-0).
5. Bradley J. Condon, Joyce C. Sadka & Tapen Sinha (eds), *Insurance Regulation in North America: Integrating American, Canadian and Mexican Markets*, 2003 (ISBN 90-411-2301-6).
6. Jan Hoogmartens, *EC Trade Law Following China's Accession to the WTO*, 2004 (ISBN 90-411-2301-6).
7. Yang Guohua, Bryan Mercurio & Li Yongjie, *WTO Dispute Settlement Understanding: A Detailed Interpretation*, 2005 (ISBN 90-411-2361-X).
8. Jan Job de Vries Robbé, Paul U. Ali, *Securitisation of Derivatives and Alternative Asset Classes, Yearbook*, 2005 (ISBN 90-411-2375-X).
9. Markus W. Gehring, Marie-Claire Cordonier Segger, *Sustainable Development in World Trade Law*, 2005 (ISBN 90-411-2366-0).
10. Yann Aubin & Arnaud Idiart, *Export Control Law and Regulations Handbook: A Practical Guide to Military and Dual-Use Goods Trade Restrictions and Compliance*, 2007 (ISBN 90-411-2601-5).
11. Henry Kibet Mutai, *Compliance with International Trade Obligations: The Common Market for Eastern and Southern Africa*, 2007 (ISBN 978-90-411-2664-1).
12. Yong-Shik Lee, *Economic Development through World Trade: A Developing World Perspective*, 2007 (ISBN 978-90-411-2681-8).
13. Yanning Yu, *Circumvention and Anti-Circumvention Measures: The Impact on Anti-Dumping Practice in International Trade*, 2007 (ISBN 978-90-411-2686-3).
14. Ross Buckley, Vai Io Lo & Laurence Boulle, *Challenges to Multilateral Trade: The Impact of Bilateral, Preferential and Regional Agreements*, 2008 (ISBN 978-90-411-2711-2).
15. K.D. Raju, *World Trade Organization Agreement on Anti-dumping: A GATT/ WTO and Indian Jurisprudence*, 2008 (ISBN 978-90-411-2780-8).
16. Xiaochen Wu, *Anti-dumping Law and Practice in China*, 2008 (ISBN 978-90-411-2790-7).
17. Amin Alavi, *Legalization of Development in the WTO: Between Law and Politics*, 2008 (ISBN 978-90-411-2795-2).
18. Henrik Andersen, *EU Dumping Determinations and WTO Law*, 2009 (ISBN 978-90-411-2827-0).

19. Sherzod Shadikhodjaev, *Retaliation in the WTO Dispute Settlement System*, 2009 (ISBN 978-90-411-2811-9).
20. Yi Shin Tang, *The International Trade Policy for Technology Transfers: Legal and Economic Dilemmas on Multilateralism versus Bilateralism*, 2009 (ISBN 978-90-411-2825-6).
21. Reem Anwar Ahmed Raslan, *Antidumping: A Developing Country Perspective*, 2009 (ISBN 978-90-411-3128-7).
22. Pietro Poretti, *The Regulation of Subsidies within the General Agreement on Trade in Services of the WTO: Problems and Prospects*, 2009 (ISBN 978-90-411-3162-1).
23. Esther Lam, *China and the WTO: A Long March towards the Rule of Law*, 2009 (ISBN 978-90-411-3144-7).
24. Jorge Alberto Huerta-Goldman, *Mexico in the WTO and NAFTA: Litigating International Trade Disputes*, 2009 (ISBN 978-90-411-3169-0).
25. Laurence Boulle, *The Law of Globalization: An Introduction*, 2009 (ISBN 978-90-411-2828-7).
26. Daniel Lovric, *Deference to the Legislature in WTO Challenges to Legislation*, 2010 (ISBN 978-90-411-3145-4).
27. Gregory W. Bowman, Nick Covelli, David A. Gantz & Ihn Ho Uhm, *Trade Remedies in North America*, 2010 (ISBN 978-90-411-2840-9).
28. Madalina Diaconu, *International Trade in Gambling Services*, 2010 (ISBN 978-90-411-3248-2).
29. Mohamed Ramadan Hassanien, *United States Bilateral Free Trade Agreements: Consistencies or Conflicts with Norms in the Middle East?*, 2010 (ISBN 978-90-411-3281-9).
30. Marie-Claire Cordonier Segger, Markus W Gehring & Andrew Newcombe, *Sustainable Development in World Investment Law*, 2011 (ISBN 978-90-411-3166-9).
31. Nellie Munin, *Legal Guide to GATS*, 2010 (ISBN 978-90-411-2824-9).
32. Thomas G. Kelch, *Globalization and Animal Law: Comparative Law, International Law and International Trade*, 2011 (ISBN 978-90-411-3338-0).
33. Yann Aubin & Arnaud Idiart (eds), *Export Control Law and Regulations Handbook: A Practical Guide to Military and Dual-Use Goods Trade Restrictions and Compliance*, Third Edition, 2016 (ISBN 978-90-411-5443-9).
34. Yulia Selivanova (ed.), *Regulation of Energy in International Trade Law: WTO, NAFTA and Energy Charter*, 2011 (ISBN 978-90-411-3264-2).
35. Germano Franceschin & Francesco Misuraca, *India: Commercial Law, Customs and Taxation*, 2011 (ISBN 978-90-411-2836-2).
36. Humberto Zúñiga Schroder, *Harmonization, Equivalence and Mutual Recognition of Standards in WTO Law*, 2011 (ISBN 978-90-411-3657-2).
37. Kati Kulovesi, *The WTO Dispute Settlement System: Challenges of the Environment, Legitimacy and Fragmentation*, 2011 (ISBN 978-90-411-3406-6).
38. Martín Molinuevo, *Protecting Investment in Services: Investor-State Arbitration versus WTO Dispute Settlement*, 2012 (ISBN 978-90-411-3827-9).
39. Joachim Åhman, *Trade, Health, and the Burden of Proof in WTO Law*, 2012 (ISBN 978-90-411-3825-5).

40. Umair Hafeez Ghori, *Global Textiles and Clothing Trade: Trade Policy Perspectives*, 2012 (ISBN 978-90-411-3875-0).
41. Yenkong Ngangjoh Hodu, *Theories and Practices of Compliance with WTO Law*, 2012 (ISBN 978-90-411-3228-4).
42. Dan Wei & Fernando M. Furlan, *Brazil in World Trade: Contingent Protection Measures*, 2012 (ISBN 978-90-411-3335-9).
43. Jorge A. Huerta-Goldman, Antoine Romanetti & Franz X. Stirnimann (eds), *WTO Litigation, Investment Arbitration, and Commercial Arbitration*, 2013 (ISBN 978-90-411-4686-1).
44. Gilles Muller, *Liberalization of Trade in Legal Services*, 2013 (ISBN 978-90-411-4853-7).
45. Christian Struck, *Product Regulations and Standards in WTO Law*, 2014 (ISBN 978-90-411-4950-3).
46. Gonzalo Villalta Puig, *Economic Relations between Australia and the European Union: Law and Policy*, 2014 (ISBN 978-90-411-3405-9).
47. Maurizio Gambardella, Davide Rovetta & Simon van Cutsem, *Remission and Repayment of Customs Duties in the EU*, 2014 (ISBN 978-90-411-4764-6).
48. Lisa Spagnolo, *CISG Exclusion and Legal Efficiency*, 2014 (ISBN 978-90-411-5407-1).
49. Dennis Ndonga, *Single Windows and Trade Facilitation: A Tool for Development*, 2015 (ISBN 978-90-411-5834-5).
50. Malebakeng Agnes Forere, *The Relationship of WTO Law and Regional Trade Agreements in Dispute Settlement: From Fragmentation to Coherence*, 2015 (ISBN 978-90-411-6274-8).
51. Julien Chaisse & Jiaxiang Hu (eds), *International Economic Law and the Challenges of the Free Zones*, 2019 (ISBN 978-94-035-0893-1).
52. Boris Praštalo, *Uniformity in the Application of the CISG: Analysis of the Problem and Recommendations for the Future*, 2020 (ISBN 978-94-035-2072-8).
53. Manuel A.J. Teehankee, *Trade and Environment Governance at the World Trade Organization Committee on Trade and Environment*, 2020 (ISBN 978-94-035-2202-9).
54. Marco Tulio Molina Tejeda (ed.), *Practical Aspects of WTO Litigation*, 2020 (ISBN 978-90-411-8596-9).
55. James J. Nedumpara, Satwik Shekhar & Akshaya Venkataraman (eds), *Handbook on Product Standards and International Trade: Navigating the Regulatory Landscape in India*, 2021 (ISBN 978-94-035-3413-8).
56. José Rijo, *Customs Law in the European Union: Legal, Doctrinal and Jurisprudential Framework*, 2022 (ISBN 978-94-035-3811-2).
57. Lauri Railas, *Incoterms® 2020 Handbook: Effecting Deliveries in Challenging Times*, 2023 (ISBN 978-94-035-2076-6).
58. Mark K. Neville, Jr., *The Customs Valuation Agreement: Origin, Standards and Interpretations*, 2023 (ISBN 978-94-035-3096-3).

www.ingramcontent.com/pod-product-compliance
Ingram Content Group UK Ltd.
Pitfield, Milton Keynes, MK11 3LW, UK
UKHW020226290926
15470UKWH00001B/402

9 789403 530963